Through the Prism of Gender and Work

Studies in Global Social History

VOLUME 51

The titles published in this series are listed at *brill.com/sgsh*

Through the Prism of Gender and Work

Women's Labour Struggles in Central and Eastern Europe and Beyond, 19th and 20th Centuries

Edited by

Selin Çağatay, Alexandra Ghiț, Olga Gnydiuk, Veronika Helfert, Ivelina Masheva, Zhanna Popova, Jelena Tešija, Eszter Varsa and Susan Zimmermann

BRILL

LEIDEN | BOSTON

This publication is part of a project that has received funding from the European Research Council (ERC) under the European Union's Horizon 2020 research and innovation programme (Grant agreement No. 833691 - ZARAH).

European Research Council
Established by the European Commission

Cover illustration: Demonstration against rent usury, Budapest, Hungary, 1910. Militant tenants' activism and the activities of the labour movement fueled the Budapest rent-strike movement. Women's labour-related activism often took on gendered characteristics, including a focus on issues related to social reproduction and gendered forms of action. *Tolnai Világlapja*, 14 August 1910. (Magyar Nemzeti Múzeum, Történeti Fényképtár [Hungarian National Museum, Historical Photo Collection], inventory no. 66.2807).

The Library of Congress Cataloging-in-Publication Data is available online at https://catalog.loc.gov
LC record available at https://lccn.loc.gov/2023053033

Typeface for the Latin, Greek, and Cyrillic scripts: "Brill". See and download: brill.com/brill-typeface.

ISSN 1874-6705
ISBN 978-90-04-68246-7 (hardback)
ISBN 978-90-04-68248-1 (e-book)
DOI 10.1163/9789004682481

This book is printed on acid-free paper and produced in a sustainable manner.

Contents

PART 3
Activist Travels through Changing Political Landscapes: The Uses of Life Histories

Figures, Maps and Tables

Figures

Maps

Tables

Abbreviations

AAN	Archive of Modern Record (Archiwum Akt Nowych) (Warsaw)
ACCTU	All-Union Central Council of Trade Unions (Всесоюзный центральный совет профессиональных союзов, ВЦСПС)
AFL	American Federation of Labor
AFL-CIO	American Federation of Labor-Congress of Industrial Organizations
ANM	Archive of the National Museum Prague (Archiv národního muzea Praha)
APW OGM	State Archive in Warsaw, Grodzisk Mazowiecki Branch (Archiwum Państwowe w Warszawie Oddział w Grodzisku Mazowieckim)
APW OM	State Archive in Warsaw, Milanówek Branch (Archiwum Państwowe w Warszawie Oddział w Milanówku)
ARZ	Archive of the Labour Movement (Archiwum Ruchu Zawodowego) (Warsaw)
ASC	American Slav Congress
AWW	Association of Working Women (Vereinigung der arbeitenden Frauen)
AYD	American Youth for Democracy
CCW	Committee of Czechoslovak Women (Výbor československých žen)
CFU	Croatian Fraternal Union
CGIL	Italian General Confederation of Labour (Confederazione Generale Italiana del Lavoro)
CGT	General Confederation of Labour (Confédération générale du travail)
CIO	Congress of Industrial Organizations
CISL	Italian Confederation of Trade Unions (Confederazione Italiana Sindacati Lavoratori)
Comintern	Communist International
COVID-19	Coronavirus disease 2019 (also known as SARS-COV-2)
CPSU	Communist Party of the Soviet Union (Коммунистическая партия Советского Союза, КПСС)
CPUSA	Communist Party of the United States of America
CRC	Civil Rights Congress
CRZZ	Central Council of the Trade Unions (Centralna Rada Związków Zawodowych)
ČSSŽ	Československý svaz žen (Czechoslovak Women's Union) (CWU)
CSW	Commission on the Status of Women (of the United Nations)
CTAL	Confederation of Latin American Workers (Confederación de Trabajadores de América Latina)
CTUF	Ceylon Trade Union Federation
CWM	Communist Women's Movement

CWU	Czechoslovak Women's Union (Československý svaz žen) (ČSSŽ)
CZK	Czech crown (Československá koruna)
ČNB	Archive of the Czech National Bank (Archiv České Národní Banky) (Prague)
DISK	Confederation of Progressive Trade Unions of Turkey (Devrimci İşçi Sendikaları Konfederasyonu)
ECCI	Executive Committee of the Comintern
ECOSOC	Economic and Social Council (of the United Nations)
FA	Feminists' Association (Feministák Egyesülete)
FBI	Federal Bureau of Investigation
GAWA	General Austrian Women's Association (Allgemeiner Österreichischer Frauenverein)
GDR	German Democratic Republic (Deutsche Demokratische Republik)
HAPC	Hungarian Association of Private Clerks (Magyarországi Magántisztviselők Országos Szövetsége)
HOLC	Home Owners' Loan Corporation
IASP	International Association for Social Progress
IAW	International Alliance of Women (earlier IWSA)
ICFTU	International Confederation of Free Trade Unions
IFLWU	International Fur and Leather Workers Union
IFPCW	International Federation of Petroleum and Chemical Workers
IFTU	International Federation of Trade Unions
IISH	International Institute of Social History (Amsterdam)
ILO	International Labour Organization
IRLI	Institute of Russian Literature (Институт русской литературы Российской академии наук, ИРЛИ) (St. Petersburg)
ITS	International Trade Secretariats
ITUCWWP	International Trade Union Committee of Women Workers of the Profintern
IWS	International Women's Secretariat (of the Comintern)
IWSA	International Woman Suffrage Alliance (later IAW)
KC PPR	Central Committee of the Polish Workers' Party (Komitet Centralny Polskiej Partii Robotniczej)
KCZZ	Central Council of Trade Unions (Komisja Centralna Związków Zawodowych)
KM PPR	Town Committee of the Polish Workers' Party (Komitet Miejski Polskiej Partii Robotniczej) (in various cities)
KPÖ	Communist Party of Austria (Kommunistische Partei Österreichs)
KSČ	Communist Party of Czechoslovakia (Komunistická strana Československa)
MJ	*Milwaukee Journal*

MNL OL	National Archives of Hungary (Magyar Nemzeti Levéltár Országos Levéltára) (Budapest)
MP	Member of Parliament
MWIA	Medical Women's International Association
NA	National Archive Czech Republic (Národní archiv České republiky) (Prague)
NAACP	National Association for the Advancement of Colored People
NABC	National Association of Bank Clerks (Pénzintézeti Tisztviselők Országos Egylete)
NARA	National Archives and Records Administration (College Park, Maryland)
NAREB	National Association of Real Estate Boards
NAWOW	National Association of Women Office Workers (Nőtisztviselők Országos Egyesülete)
NFHW	National Federation of Hungarian Women (Magyar Asszonyok Nemzeti Szövetsége)
NYPL	New York Public Library
OD	Personnel department (Osobní oddělení) (of the Trade Bank in Prague)
ODI	Open Door International
ÖVP	Austrian People's Party (Österreichische Volkspartei)
PCI	Italian Communist Party (Partito Comunista Italiano)
Petrol-İş	Petroleum, Chemical and Rubber Industry Workers' Union of Turkey (Türkiye Petrol, Kimya, Lastik İşçileri Sendikası)
PKPS	Polish Committee for Social Help (Polski Komitet Pomocy Społecznej)
PPR	Polish Workers' Party (Polska Partia Robotnicza)
PPS	Polish Socialist Party (Polska Partia Socjalistyczna)
PR	Police Directorate (Policajné Riaditeľstvo)
Profintern	Red International of Labor Unions (RILU) (Профинтерн – Красный Интернационал Профсоюзов)
PZPR	Polish United Workers' Party (Polska Zjednoczona Partia Robotnicza)
RGALI	Russian State Archive of Literature and Arts (Российский государственный архив литературы и искусства, РГАЛИ) (Moscow)
RGASPI	Russian State Archive of Socio-Political History (Российский государственный архив социально-политической истории, РГАСПИ) (Moscow)
RGIA	Russian State Historical Archive (Российский государственный исторический архив, РГИА) (St. Petersburg)
RILU	Red International of Labor Unions (Profintern) (Красный Интернационал Профсоюзов, Профинтерн)
RSP	Rosika Schwimmer Papers

SDAP	Social Democratic Workers' Party (of Austria) (Sozialdemokratische Arbeiterpartei)
SDPH	Social Democratic Party of Hungary (Magyarországi Szociáldemokrata Párt)
SED	Socialist Unity Party of Germany (Sozialistische Einheitspartei Deutschlands)
SNA	Slovak National Archive (Slovenský národný archív) (Bratislava)
SPOC	State Population Commission (Státní populační komise)
SPÖ	Socialist Party of Austria (Sozialistische Partei Österreichs)
ŠA BB	State Archive Banská Bystrica (Štátny archív Banská Bystrica)
ŠA ZAM	State Archive Žilina with the registered office in Bytča – Office Martin (Štátny archív Žilina so sídlom v Bytči – pracovisko Archív Martin)
TEKSIF	Textile, Knitting, and Clothing Workers' Union of Turkey (Türkiye Tekstil, Örme ve Giyim Sanayii İşçileri Sendikası)
TUC	Trades Union Congress
Türk-İş	Confederation of Turkish Trade Unions (Türkiye İşçi Sendikaları Konfederasyonu)
UAW	United Auto Workers
UCSSA	United Committee of South-Slavic Americans
UDI	Union of Italian Women (Unione Donne Italiane)
UN	United Nations
UNESCO	United Nations Educational, Scientific and Cultural Organization
U.S.	United States (of America)
USA	United States of America
USSR	Union of Soviet Socialist Republics (Союз Советских Социалистических Республик, СССР)
UWM	University of Wisconsin-Milwaukee (Archives)
ÚV ČSSŽ	Central Committee of the Czechoslovak Women's Union (Ústřední výbor Československého svazu žen)
ÚV ČSŽ	Central Committee of the Czech Women's Union (Ústřední výbor Českého svazu žen)
VGA	Austrian Labour History Society (Verein für Geschichte der ArbeiterInnenbewegung)
VS	People's Solidarity (Volkssolidarität)
WASMME	Women and Social Movements in Modern Empires (database)
WFTU	World Federation of Trade Unions
WIDF	Women's International Democratic Federation
WILPF	Women's International League for Peace and Freedom

WKW PZPR	Warsaw Regional Committee of the Polish United Workers' Party (Warszawski Komitet Wojewódzki Polskiej Zjednoczonej Partii Robotniczej)
WPA	Works Progress Administration
WPC	Women's Publishing Cooperative (Женская издательская артель) (also known as Women's Translation Artel, Stasova and Trubnikova Publishing House, and The Women's Publishing)
YCL	Young Communist League
ZAODRR	Collection of Personal Files of the Labour Movement Activists (Zespół Akt Osobowych Działaczy Ruchu Robotniczego)
ŽB	Trade Bank (Živnostenská Banka)
Zhenotdel	Women's Department of the Communist Party of the Soviet Union (Женский отдел, Женотдел)

Notes on Contributors

Eloisa Betti

is a junior assistant professor (RTD/A) at the Department of Political Science, Law and International Studies of the University of Padua. In 2014–2015 she was a Visiting Fellow at the School of Advanced Study (University of London), and in 2015–2016 she was awarded the EURIAS Fellowship at the Institute for Human Sciences in Vienna. In 2020, she earned the Italian National Scientific Qualification as Associate Professor of Modern History. Her recent English-language publications include "Unexpected Alliances: Italian Women's Struggles for Equal Pay, 1940s–1960s," in E. Boris, S. Zimmermann, D. Hoehtker (eds.), *Women's ILO. Transnational Networks, Global Labour Standards and Gender Equity, 1919 to Present* (Brill 2018), and *Precarious Workers. History of Debates, Political Mobilization, and Labor Reforms in Italy* (CEU Press 2022).

Masha Bratishcheva

is a historian and current PhD student at the Scuola Normale Superiore in Pisa, Italy. She investigates the problematic of the Russian feminist movement in the nineteenth century. She is particularly interested in the issues of women's underrepresentation in the historical narrative of the Russian Empire and feminist critics of the historical approach to descriptions of the Russian feminist movement. She researches the limits of women's political agency and studies the strategies of women's horizontal organizations.

Jan A. Burek

is a Research and Teaching Fellow at the University of Warsaw and a Postdoctoral Research Fellow within the framework of the project "The Socialist Anthropocene in the Visual Arts" at the University College London. His research interests lie at the intersection of labour and gender history, the history of communism and communist parties in Central Europe, and micro-historical methodologies. His recent publications include "History Seems Different from the Shop Floor. A Micro-Historical Challenge to Established Caesurae in the History of 20th-Century Poland: Transwar Continuities in Żyrardów," in L. George and J. McGlynn (eds.), *Rethinking Period Boundaries. New Approaches to Continuity and Discontinuity in Modern European History and Culture* (De Gruyter 2022).

Selin Çağatay
is a postdoctoral researcher at Central European University in Vienna, Austria. Her research as part of the ZARAH project concerns educational programs developed for urban and rural women in Turkey and transnationally. She earned her PhD degree in Comparative Gender Studies from Central European University in Budapest, Hungary. She recently published a monograph, authored collaboratively with Mia Liinason and Olga Sasunkevich, entitled *Feminist and LGBTI+ Activism in Russia, Scandinavia, and Turkey: Transnationalizing Spaces of Resistance* (Palgrave Macmillan 2022).

Daria Dyakonova
teaches in the Department of International Relations of the International Institute in Geneva, Switzerland and is also Head of research at the same institution. She earned her PhD degree in history at the University of Montreal, Canada. Her thesis examined the transnational ties of young Canadian Communists during the interwar period. In Montreal, she participated in several research projects funded by the Canadian Social Sciences and Humanities Research Council (SSHRC) that investigated left-wing international networks, Soviet foreign policy, and Soviet-Western relations during the interwar period. In 2019–2020, Dr. Dyakonova was a Visiting Fellow at the Graduate Institute of International and Development Studies in Geneva, Switzerland, where she worked on her latest project, which has resulted in the publication, co-edited with Michael Taber, *The Communist Women's Movement, 1920–1922. Proceedings, Resolutions, and Reports* (Brill 2023).

Mátyás Erdélyi
was a postdoctoral researcher at the Masaryk Institute and Archives in Prague and a research fellow at the Institute of History, Research Centre for Humanities of the Eötvös Loránd Research Network in Hungary, and is now a postdoctoral researcher at Central European University in the ZARAH team and at the University of Vienna. Erdélyi specializes in the history of the Habsburg Monarchy in the long nineteenth century; in particular, he has researched and published on the history of private clerks in banking and insurance (PhD in 2019 at Central European University in Budapest), the history of statistical thinking, public administration, professional education in trade and management, and educational mobility in the late Habsburg Monarchy. He is currently preparing a book manuscript on the social history of private clerks in Budapest, Prague, and Vienna between 1880 and 1910.

Dóra Fedeles-Czeferner
is a postdoctoral researcher at the University of Vienna, and a research fellow at the Research Centre for the Humanities, Institute of History, Budapest, Hungary. She earned her PhD degree in 2020. She studies the development of the Austrian and Hungarian bourgeois-liberal, feminist movements, their international connections, and their press activities from the 1890s until the end of the 1940s. Her first book on this topic was published in 2021 (in Hungarian) as *Cultural Mission or Propaganda? Feminist Journals and Their Readers in Vienna and Budapest* (Bölcsészettudományi Kutatóközpont 2021). Most recently, she has been researching the history of the Hungarian Feminists' Association during the interwar period and the life and career of Rosika Schwimmer, especially Schwimmer's work in the women's and peace movements and her international network of contacts.

Eric Fure-Slocum
is a historian of twentieth-century U.S. labour and urban history. He is the author of *Contesting the Postwar City: Working-Class and Growth Politics in 1940s Milwaukee* (Cambridge University Press 2013) and co-editor of both *Civic Labors: Scholar Activism and Working-Class Studies* (University of Illinois Press 2016) and *Contingent Faculty and the Remaking of Higher Education: A Labor History* (University of Illinois Press, forthcoming 2024). His current projects include a book on American egalitarianism in 1944, viewed from the neighborhood, city, and national levels. An associate professor (non-tenure-track) of history at St. Olaf College in Minnesota, he has also taught as a Fulbright Scholar at the University of Oslo, Norway (2003) and West University of Timişoara, Romania (2022). He serves on the executive board of the Organization of American Historians.

Alexandra Ghiț
is a postdoctoral research affiliate at Central European University. As member of the ZARAH team, she researches women's labour activism in the tobacco industry in Romania in the twentieth century. She holds a PhD degree in Comparative Gender Studies from Central European University Budapest (2020). Her publications include "Professionals' and Amateurs' Pasts: A Decolonizing Reading of Post-War Romanian Histories of Gendered Interwar Activism," *European Review of History: Revue européenne d'histoire* 25, no. 1 (2018).

Maren Hachmeister
is a postdoctoral research fellow at the Hannah Arendt Institute for Totalitarianism Studies at TU Dresden. Her research interests include the social

and contemporary history of East Central Europe and East Germany, as well as the postsocialist transformation of that region. Her work focuses on forms of self-organization, volunteering, and social care. Her doctoral thesis, which she completed at Ludwig-Maximilian-University in Munich was published (in German) as *Self-Organization under Socialism. The Red Cross in Poland and Czechoslovakia 1945–1989* (Vandenhoeck & Ruprecht 2019). Her most recent publication in English is "Volunteering and Care in Old Age: Voices from People's Solidarity in East Germany," in *Journal of Contemporary Central and Eastern Europe* 31, no. 1 (2023). She is a member of the COST Action 18119 "Who Cares in Europe."

Veronika Helfert
is a postdoctoral research affiliate at Central European University. As member of the ZARAH team, she studies the entangled history of women's labour activism in Austria and transnationally from 1945 to the 1980s. She holds a PhD degree in history from the University of Vienna. She won several prizes for her dissertation, including the Käthe Leichter Award. Her most recent book (in German) is *"Women, Stand up!" A Women's and Gender History of the Austrian Revolution and Council Movement, 1916–1924* (Unipress 2021).

Natalia Jarska
PhD, is a historian, an Assistant Professor at the Tadeusz Manteuffel Institute of History (Polish Academy of Sciences), and a postdoctoral fellow in "Expert Turn. Expertise in Authoritarian Societies. Human sciences in the Socialist countries of East-Central Europe" (Institute of History, Czech Academy of Sciences). Her research interests include women's and gender history, the history of sexuality, and labour history. Recent publications include the articles "Women's Work and Men: Generational and Class Dimensions of Men's Resistance to Women's Paid Employment in State-Socialist Poland (1956–1980)," *Aspasia. The International Yearbook of Central, Eastern, and Southeastern History*, vol. 15 (2021) and "Female Breadwinners in State Socialism: The Value of Women's Work for Wages in Post-Stalinist Poland" *Contemporary European History* 28, no. 1 (2019).

Marie Láníková
is a PhD candidate in Sociology at Masaryk University in Brno. She studies the socialist women's movement, postwar Czechoslovak women's organizations and their relationship to expertise, their approaches to domestic work, and the problem of the "second shift," as well as women's agency under state socialism. She received a BA in Gender Studies and Social Anthropology and an MA in Sociology from Masaryk University. She has published in *Český*

lid: Etnologický časopis and *Gender a výzkum.* She participated in the project "Expert Turn: Expertise in Authoritarian Societies: Human Sciences in the Socialist Countries of East-Central Europe" led by Kateřina Lišková. She has also received the Aktion Österreich-Tschechien Semesterstipendium, which supported her research at the University of Vienna in the spring of 2022.

Jean-Pierre Liotard-Vogt

obtained a master's degree in Hungarian studies at the Oriental Studies School (INALCO) in Paris. He received an award in 2018 from the Association of Friends of the Hungarian Institute in Paris for his master thesis on the history of Hungarian social democracy in Budapest before 1914. He is currently a doctoral student at the Department of History at the École des hautes études en sciences sociales (EHESS). His dissertation focuses on the political life of the Hungarian social democrat Anna Kéthly (1889–1976). His research interests include the history of Hungarian social democracy in Central and Eastern Europe, women's history, women in labour unions, and transnationalism. He has also published a research paper on Leo Frankel, the French-Hungarian *Communard.*

Ivelina Masheva

is a postdoctoral research affiliate at Central European University and a researcher at the Institute for Historical Studies – Bulgarian Academy of Sciences. As a member of the ZARAH team, she studies women workers and trade unions in Bulgaria and internationally from the 1920s to the 1940s. She holds a PhD degree in History from the University of Sofia (2015). She is a contributor and a co-editor, together with Martin Löhnig, of the recently published book *Commercial Law in Southeastern Europe. Legislation and Jurisdiction from Tanzimat Times until the Eve of the Great War* (Böhlau Verlag 2022).

Denisa Nešťáková

is a Research Associate at Comenius University in Bratislava with her postdoctoral project "Privileged to Be in Hell. Jewish Women in the Sereď Camp," which is supported by the Saul Kagan Fellowship in Advanced Shoah Studies. She was a research associate at the Herder Institute, where she focused on the history of family planning in Slovakia, which resulted in the forthcoming monograph: *Be Fruitful and Multiply: Slovakia's Family Planning under Three Regimes (1918–1965).* Her research interests include Holocaust studies, gender studies, and twentieth-century Central-East European history. She is one of the editors of the volume on gender and the Holocaust entitled *If This Is a Woman. Studies on Women and Gender in the Holocaust* (Academic Studies

Press 2021), and editor of the volume (in Slovakian) *Too much Sex. Sex and Sexuality in the Modern History of Slovakia* (Paradigma Publishing 2021).

Sophia Polek
is working on her dissertation on journalistic reporting in the Imperial Russian mass-circulation press from 1895 to 1912 and also serves as a Research Assistant in the Department of History at the University of Basel. Her research is supported by the Swiss National Science Foundation. She holds an MA in Eastern European History and Slavonic Literary Studies from the University of Basel with exchange studies undertaken at the University of Glasgow and the Higher School of Economics Moscow. Her key interests are the cultural history of journalism in the late nineteenth and early twentieth century in the Russian Empire, the Russian Revolution of 1905, applied narratology, and feminist criticism.

Zhanna Popova
is a postdoctoral researcher at Central European University. As part of the ZARAH team, she works on women's labour activism in the lands of partitioned Poland, interwar Poland, and internationally. Prior to coming to Vienna, she was a doctoral researcher at the International Institute of Social History in Amsterdam and defended her PhD at the University of Amsterdam in 2019. She recently published "Exiles, Convicts and Deportees as Migrants: Northern Eurasia, Nineteenth-Twentieth Centuries," in Marcelo Borges and Madeline Y. Hsu (eds.), *The Cambridge History of Global Migrations*, vol. 2 (Cambridge University Press 2023).

Büșra Satı
has recently earned her PhD degree from the Department of Sociology at Binghamton University. Her dissertation, titled "Feeding the Workers. Food, Corporations, and Welfare in 20th Century America," explores the history of corporate welfare programs and food-related employee provisions in the United States. Her research interests include women's labour history and food studies. She received her BA degree in Sociology at Middle East Technical University and her MA in the MATILDA European Master in Women's and Gender History program at Central European University. Her MA thesis entitled "Gendering Trade Unions. Women in TEKSTIL, 1965–1980" explores the union activism of women textile workers and discusses the changing gender politics of labour organizations in Turkey. She published a related article "Working-Class Women, Gender, and Union Politics in Turkey, 1965–1980," *International Labor and Working-Class History* 100, no. 3 (2021).

Masha Shpolberg
is Assistant Professor of Film and Electronic Arts at Bard College. Her teaching and research explore global documentary, Eastern and Central European cinema, ecocinema, and women's cinema. She is co-editor of *Cinema and the Environment in Eastern Europe. From Communism to Capitalism* (Berghahn Books 2023), and *The New Russian Documentary. Reclaiming Reality in the Age of Authoritarianism* (forthcoming from Edinburgh University Press). She holds a PhD degree in Film and Media Studies and Comparative Literature from Yale University.

Georg Spitaler
is a researcher at the Austrian Labour History Society (Verein für Geschichte der ArbeiterInnenbewegung, VGA) in Vienna. He held a postdoctoral position at the Department of Political Science at the University of Vienna (2008–2014) and is a lecturer at the same place. His publications include books, edited volumes, and articles on labour history, political theory, cultural studies, and the political aspects of sports. He is a co-editor (together with Rob McFarland and Ingo Zechner) of *The Red Vienna Sourcebook* (Camden House 2020) (published also in German as *Das Rote Wien. Schlüsseltexte der Zweiten Wiener Moderne 1919–1934*). He co-curated the exhibition *Das Rote Wien 1919–1934* at Wien Museum MUSA (2019–2020), as well as the exhibition catalogue (in German) *Red Vienna 1919–1934. Ideas, Debates, Practice* (Birkhäuser 2019).

Jelena Tešija
is a doctoral researcher at Central European University. As member of the ZARAH team, she researches women's labour activism within the co-operative movement in and beyond the Yugoslav lands from the late nineteenth century to the 1950s. She holds two master's degrees, one in Journalism from the Faculty of Political Science at the University of Zagreb and one in Gender Studies from Central European University in Budapest. She published "'Millions of Working Housewives:' the International Co-operative Women's Guild and Household Labour in the Interwar Period" *Journal of Contemporary Central and Eastern Europe* 31, no. 3 (2023).

Eszter Varsa
is a postdoctoral researcher at Central European University. As member of the ZARAH team, she studies the history of agrarian socialism in Hungary from a gendered perspective during the period between the 1890s and the 1920s. She holds a PhD degree in Comparative Gender Studies from Central European University in Budapest (2011). Her recently published monograph is entitled

Protected Children, Regulated Mothers. Gender and the "Gypsy Question" in State Care in Postwar Hungary, 1949–1956 (CEU Press 2021). She received the Emma Goldman Award 2023.

Johanna Wolf
is a researcher at the Max Planck Institute for Legal History and Legal Theory in Frankfurt am Main on the project "Non-state Law of the Economy" since 2019. Her dissertation – which she completed in Global Studies at the University of Leipzig and which was awarded with the Walter-Markov-Prize in 2017 – focuses on the global challenges of metal trade unions in the shipbuilding industry and was published (in German) as *Assurances of Friendship. Transnational Pathways of Metal Trade Unionists in the Shipbuilding Industry, 1950–1980* (Vandenhoeck & Ruprecht 2018). From September 2020 to June 2021, she was a Research Fellow at the International Institute of Social History in Amsterdam, where she worked on the mobility of communist trade union actors since 1945. This research was funded by a research grant from the German Research Foundation (DFG).

Susan Zimmermann
is a historian of labour and gender politics and movements in the international context and in Hungary and Austria. Her most recent monograph (in German) is *Women's Politics and Men's Trade Unionism. International Gender Politics, Women IFTU-trade Unionists and the Labour and Women's Movements of the Interwar Period* (Löcker Verlag 2021). Together with Eloisa Betti, Leda Papastefanaki and Marica Tolomelli she co-edited *Women, Work, and Activism. Chapters of an Inclusive History of Labor in the Long Twentieth Century* (CEU Press 2022). She holds the European Research Council Grant "Women's Labour Activism in Eastern Europe and Transnationally, from the Age of Empires to the Late 20th Century" (Acronym: ZARAH, 2020–2025).

CHAPTER 1

Women's Labour Struggles in Central and Eastern Europe and Beyond

Toward a Long-Term, Transregional, Integrative, and Critical Approach

Selin Çağatay, Mátyás Erdélyi, Alexandra Ghiț, Olga Gnydiuk, Veronika Helfert, Ivelina Masheva, Zhanna Popova, Jelena Tešija, Eszter Varsa, and Susan Zimmermann

Abstract

The introductory chapter provides a historiographic and thematic framing for the contributions and, we hope, for future research. The first section discusses the existing historiography of the region, highlighting the long history of writing on women's labour activism in Central and Eastern Europe and its adjacent territories within and across the borders of different types of empires and nation-states, and across vastly diverse political regimes. The second section discusses key contributions of the chapters assembled in the volume to the study of women's (and sometimes men's) quests for the improvement of the lives and working conditions of women, pointing to their interconnections and highlighting their contributions to the development of long-term and transregional approaches to the history of women's labour struggles. The third section expands on the rationale for studying women's labour struggles from a long-term, transregional, integrative, and critical perspective, further discusses insights emerging from the volume and other scholarship, and highlights challenges as well as directions for ongoing and future research in the field of women's labour activism.

Keywords

19th century – 20th century – Austria – Bulgaria – Cold War – communism – Central Europe – Czechoslovakia – Eastern Europe – feminism – gender – historiography – Hungary – integrative and critical approach – internationalism – Italy – labour history – labour movement – long-term perspective – Poland – Romania – Russia – Slovakia – socialism – Soviet Union – state socialism – trade unions – transnational approach – Turkey – women's and gender history – women's internationalism – women's labour struggles – women's movement – Yugoslavia

In recent years, the history of women's labour activism has enjoyed renewed scholarly attention, which has, in turn, generated new intersections between labour history and women's and gender history. The emerging scholarship on women's labour activism expands our knowledge of the types of demands women put forward in relation to their gendered labour interests, the repertoires of action they used to achieve their goals, and the wide range of social and political movements in which they mobilized during the past two centuries.[1] However, both older and newer scholarship on labour history and women's and gender history continues to be characterized by geographical, geopolitical, and thematic imbalances. Internationally visible contributions to the history of women's labour activism focus mainly on Western Europe and North America and, to a lesser degree, on parts of Africa and Asia. Studies on the large Eastern European contact zone between the Russian, Habsburg, and Ottoman empires and their successor states—the region covered by this volume—are still rare. New handbooks and volumes on women's and gender history in Eastern Europe do not yet systematically include the theme of women's labour-related activisms and struggles.[2]

As a contribution dedicated to rectifying these imbalances, the present volume collects new research emerging at the intersection of labour and gender history in the Central and Eastern European context and beyond. The contributions collected here were first presented in October 2021 at the international conference "Women's Labour Activism in Eastern Europe and Beyond, 19th and 20th Centuries"[3] we, the editors, organized and held at the Vienna campus of Central European University. Our interest in women's labour activism is rooted in our dedication to moving working women from the margins of labour, gender, and European histories to the center. As researchers collaborating within the large-scale research project ZARAH, we aim to foster wider scholarly collaboration.[4] In autumn 2020, we circulated a call for researchers from multiple disciplines to share, discuss, and publish their work on the topic of women's

1 Betti et al. 2022; Cobble 2021; Boris 2019; Boris, Hoehtker, and Zimmermann 2018; Cobble 2005.

2 Bluhm et al. 2021; Fábián, Jonhnson, and Lazda 2021; Penn and Massino 2009. For a recent publication that deviates from this trend, although still without putting women's labour struggles center stage, see Artwinska and Mrozik 2020.

3 The conference material including the call for papers and a few photographs can be found under https://zarah-ceu.org/events/.

4 *Women's Labour Activism in Eastern Europe and Transnationally, from the Age of Empires to the Late 20th Century* (ZARAH), https://zarah-ceu.org/. Hosted by Central European University in Austria, the project has received funding from the European Research Council (ERC) under the European Union's Horizon 2020 research and innovation programme (Grant agreement No. 833691—ZARAH).

labour activism. Amid the COVID-19 pandemic, the call highlighted that "many different types of sources can be creatively used to foreground and discuss women's labour activism." We invited colleagues to think about their own scholarly interests and ongoing research projects *through the prism of gender and work* to consider how women's activism relates to "work" in their research. During the intensive three-day conference, the participants, two specialist scholars invited as commentators,[5] and ZARAH team members (as prospective editors of this volume), discussed pre-circulated draft papers. Many of the papers presented later became the chapters of this volume. Inevitably, the volume mirrors the composition of the papers presented at the conference, which is reflected in the fact that some lands belonging to the region being studied are not represented. As editors of this volume, we aim to make a modest contribution to rectifying this state of things by discussing in some detail the existing scholarship on these lands in the introductory chapter.

In what follows, we provide a historiographic and thematic framing for the contributions and, we hope, for future research. We advocate for and aim to advance approaches to the history of women's labour struggles that are *long-term*, *transregional*, *integrative*, and *critical*. The chapter proceeds in three steps.

In the first section, we discuss the existing historiography of the region, foregrounding how it can offer solid starting points for up-to-date approaches to the history of women's labour struggles in Central and Eastern Europe and beyond. Just as the chapters collected in this volume refer to earlier scholarship, this section highlights the long history of writing on women's labour activism in Central and Eastern Europe and its adjacent territories within and across the borders of different types of empires and nation-states, and across vastly diverse political regimes. We show how, since the 1960s, the topic of women's labour struggles has been steadily, if not always centrally, present in the historiographies of labour and gender written and published in the many languages of the region addressed in this volume and in other languages as well. We identify four relevant thematic clusters of the historiography on the region: women's activism in labour and left-wing movements; women's movements in the national and international arenas; social histories of gender and work; and life histories of activist women.

In the second section, we discuss key contributions of the chapters assembled in this volume to the study of women's (and sometimes men's) quests for the improvement of the lives and working conditions of women. Each of

5 We would like to express our gratitude to Krassimira Daskalova and Marcel van der Linden for their valuable comments on the papers discussed at the conference. They contributed greatly to the development of many of the chapters published in this volume.

these chapters is the result of using *work* as prism when studying women's activism, revealing not only a broad spectrum of labour-related activism but also the diverse perspectives of the invited scholars. The chapters tackle under-researched topics and present new interpretations in the history of women's labour struggles in the region and transnationally. Highlighting how they advance an integrative approach to the history of women's labour struggles when read together, the chapters are grouped under three headings: "Women's Struggles and Men-Dominated Trade Union and Labour Movements: Rethinking a Complex Relationship"; "Women's Ways of Action: New Perspectives on Repertoires and Agendas"; and "Activist Travels through Changing Political Landscapes: The Uses of Life Histories." Certainly, this volume does not fully cover all relevant spaces and time periods. Yet, as we discuss the chapters, we point to their interconnections and highlight their contributions to the development of long-term and transregional approaches to the history of women's labour struggles in the region on which this volume focuses.

In the third section, we expand on the rationale for studying women's labour struggles from a long-term, transregional, integrative, and critical perspective. In so doing, we further discuss, from this quadruple perspective, the insights emerging from the volume and other scholarship and highlight challenges as well as directions for ongoing and future research in the field of women's labour activism.

1 Historiography

Exploring women's work and labour activism in Central and Eastern Europe and internationally requires creative, resourceful, and critical engagement with many historiographical traditions and clusters of research. In this section, we present the four research clusters we consider most relevant for a fruitful exploration of the history of women's labour struggles in this region. We point out how explicit accounts of women's labour activism and implicit insights into the topic can be traced in these four strands of research. Namely, we focus on histories of left-wing social and labour movements, histories of women's (non-labour) movements, social histories of women's work, and biographies of women workers and women labour activists. As we revisit earlier scholarship and highlight some of the more recent contributions in these four research clusters, we do not aim to offer a comprehensive overview of the available scholarship. Rather, we critically reflect on the linguistically, conceptually, and methodologically diverse traditions in the scholarship on the region and put them in conversation with each other.

1.1 *Women's Activism in Labour and Left-Wing Movements*

Women's presence in labour and left-wing movements became a topic of scholarly inquiry in the second half of the twentieth century in Eastern and Western Europe alike. In the "West," historians' interest in this field was often indebted to their (past) engagement in labour, left-wing, and (so-called second-wave) women's liberation movements. In Eastern Europe, the interest tended to grow out of both institutionalized labour movement historiography and the dedication of researchers and (former) activists, mostly women, to the subject of women's emancipation. Long-term trends, transnational connections, an expanded notion of what constitutes activism, and initial roadmaps to precious primary sources can be brought to the surface through a critical re-reading of a large body of social movement history.

Research on the history of women's participation in labour and left-wing movement in the region examined in this volume has been shaped by contextual differences between countries, especially in terms of social movements and political regimes. In state-socialist countries, women's activism was a consistently legitimate, if sometimes marginal, subject of history-writing that enjoyed periods of greater interest. In Romania, for example, research on women as workers and labour activists flourished as early as the late 1940s to the early 1950s,[6] and again in 1970s. Articles on women's labour organizing appeared regularly in key Romanian historical journals from the 1960s to the 1980s.[7] In the early 1970s, new research emerged on socialist and communist militants,[8] and two volumes on women's activism and women's labour organizing were published. These volumes used evidence from the labour press to document the worsening living and labour conditions and women's activities in organizations dedicated to childcare, prison support, or material aid for struggling workers.[9] Similarly, in socialist Yugoslavia, significant efforts were made from the 1950s on to document women's labour struggles, often by official women's organizations. Publications included collections of primary documents with explanatory comments, memoirs, short biographies of "people's heroines," and summaries of important events and processes in different republics,[10] followed by more scientific works in the 1970s and

6 Constantinescu-Iaşi 1952; Romanian Workers' Party 1949.

7 Tudoran, 1987, 1986, 1985; Ioniţă 1980; Marian 1965.

8 Homenco and Ioniţă 1975; Ioniţă 1973.

9 Câncea 1976; Georgescu and Georgescu 1975.

10 For example, Musabegović 1977; Veskoviḱ-Vangeli and Jovanoviḱ 1976; Cvetić 1975; Kovačević 1972; Gerk, Križnar, and Ravnikar-Podbevšek 1970; Šoljan 1967; Đurović, Lakić, and Vuković 1960; Šoljan 1955. The lack of historical analysis and unequally developed

1980s.[11] In Bulgaria too, publications on women's labour activism based on primary documents and scholarly research appeared throughout the state-socialist period.[12] In Czechoslovakia, there was occasional research into the early involvement of women in the social democratic movement,[13] while a more comprehensive account of the workers' press and women's movements was produced by non-specialists like Božena Holečková, a journalist and member of the communist party, and Eva Uhrová, also a journalist and editor.[14] In the field of Russian and Soviet studies, from the 1970s onward scholars investigated the role of women in the revolution and in the early Soviet working women's movement.[15]

Research on women's activism in left-wing and labour movements enjoyed similar popularity in non-state-socialist contexts from or connected to our region. In Austria, research on the social democratic women's movement and the lives of working women as well as women trade unionists had been carried out since the 1970s.[16] And in Turkey, women's labour struggles appeared in scholarship starting in the 1980s, notably in the work by feminist researchers.[17]

Despite the differences in social histories and political regimes, similar tendencies can be identified in the social movement historiographies produced in both the state-socialist and non-state-socialist contexts of the region in the 1970s and 1980s. In state-socialist countries, the history of socialist and communist movements and revolutionary figures was a favorite topic, one that generated shared and diverse generic conventions and modes of arguing. Such research helped legitimize state-socialist political programs and the communist or workers' parties that brought them to the fore. Thus, in social movement historiographies from across the region, pre-World War Two left-wing and labour movements were often represented teleologically as the predecessors of state-socialist organizations.[18] Some of these works also focused on the

research in different republics were criticized by historian Mira Kolar-Dimitrijević. Kolar-Dimitrijević 1977.

11 For example, Sklevicky 1984a, 1984b; Kecman 1978.

12 Todorova 1982; Bozeva 1981; Vodenicharova and Popova 1972; Bradinska 1969; Todorova et al. 1960.

13 Bednářová 1984; Wohlgemuthová 1965.

14 Holečková 1978; Uhrová 1984.

15 Hillyar and McDermid 2000; Wood 1997; Stites 1978.

16 For example, Bauer (1988) 2015; Hauch 1986.

17 Urhan 2014; Toksöz and Erdoğdu 1998; Ecevit 1986; Kazgan 1981.

18 On some of these works that discuss women's organizations more specifically, see Bozeva 1981; Vodenicharova and Popova 1972.

partly outlawed movements of the interwar period and on communist participation in resistance movements during World War Two.[19]

Mainstream labour history narratives produced in state-socialist contexts tended to treat women as workers without issues or problems that were distinct from the common problems of workers as a class. Alternatively, such narratives pointed to the supposed deficiencies of women workers' political "consciousness" and activist behavior. Focused on men-dominated trade unions and parties, this genre of history writing produced in state-socialist countries prompted or reproduced a limited understanding of activism as it saw the communist parties and trade unions affiliated with them as the pinnacle of the labour movement. Consequently, even though women's labour struggles formed part of the histories of labour and left-wing movements, overall women's labour activism was only marginally addressed, and women's contributions to these movements were not adequately captured conceptually. For instance, a comprehensive collective study of the labour movement in the Bulgarian textile industry between 1878 and 1944 described unorganized women workers' relationship with the (communist) unions in two ways. On the one hand, it explained that the low unionization rates and strike failures were due to the "backwardness" of the predominantly female workforce. On the other hand, it attributed the success of many "spontaneous" strikes to the union leadership or at least to the influence of communists.[20]

Similar to state-socialist countries, albeit in a different time frame, studies concerning women's labour activism in the labour historiographies of Austria and Turkey have focused on women's presence in organized labour and left-wing movements. These works have addressed women's labour activism in trade unions and the socialist movements in the territories of the Habsburg and Ottoman empires and in the postimperial nation-states before and after World War Two, including its social democratic, socialist, and later communist varieties.[21] Strikes stood out as a form of labour activism frequently addressed

19 See, for example, Próchnik 1948.

20 Vasilev et al. 1970. See also Réti 1980; Friss 1974. Some researchers at the time pursued a more critical approach when discussing the relationship between the men-dominated labour movement and women workers. For example, Zsuzsa Fonó (Fonó 1978, 1975), writing on the history of the Hungarian women workers' organizing in the socialist movement between the late nineteenth century and the 1930s, shifted the focus to problems in the approach of party and trade unions rather than the women. Magda Aranyossi (Aranyossi 1963) points, though in a much more limited manner, to the difficulties women's mobilization faced due to gendered social differentiation, including within the working classes and the men-dominated social democratic party organizations and trade unions.

21 Satı 2021; Akbulut 2016; Pervan 2013; Hauch 2009; Lukasser 2002; Toksöz and Erdoğdu 1998; Hann 1988.

with reference to women. For Cisleithanian and post-1918 Austria, through his long-term analysis of strike movements, Christian Koller has shown that women workers, in contrast to their low rates of membership in trade unions, were a crucial part of strikes in the late nineteenth century up until the interwar period.[22] In the Turkish case, historians such as Birten Çelik, Yavuz Selim Karakışla, and Nicole van Os have focused on women's participation in strikes in the late Ottoman period as the earliest examples of women's labour struggles.[23] Studies on the republican period similarly highlighted women's active role in strikes and working-class public protests at the expense of other forms of labour activism.[24] More recently, Büşra Satı's research on the union organizing of textile workers in 1970s Turkey has shed light on the gendered issues and demands women workers raised.[25]

In Western contexts, from the 1980s onward feminist labour historians have been deconstructing labour historiographies that were androcentric in their design and outcomes. They argued that such historiographies misrepresented women's involvement in labour activism, for example by portraying women workers as difficult to organize.[26] In many places in Central and Eastern Europe and its adjacent territories, such rethinking became widespread only in the 2010s. Yet, relevant new studies already reveal a much more complex relationship between women and labour and left-wing movements than earlier studies had shown.[27]

Despite these recent evolutions, however, a more nuanced and fresh engagement with the older mainstream (i.e., androcentric) labour historiographies from state-socialist and non-state-socialist contexts alike still requires further development. This is especially true for the handling of state-socialist scholarship. Ongoing and future research can benefit from replacing postcommunist "withering skepticism" for older works that have addressed or documented women's labour struggles with forms of "qualified interest" for the contents of these materials.[28] Re-reading older works from the region through the lens of women's labour activism can generate insights that are relevant for new research agendas in several ways.

---

22 Koller 2009.

23 Çelik 2013; Karakışla 2002; Van Os 1997.

24 Gülenç 2022; Aydın 2010; Yici 2010.

25 Satı 2021.

26 See, for example, Rose 1988; Milkman 1985; Briskin and Yanz 1983.

27 See, for example, Helfert 2021; Todorova 2020; Akal 2003.

28 Ghiţ 2018.

What are the specific benefits of revisiting the old historiographies of social movements and their established genres for nuanced, up-to-date research on women's labour activism? What can we learn from the often massive publications on the history of "the labour movement" in specific industrial sectors—especially when considerable portions of the workers employed in these branches were women—and time periods? How can we use the historiography of trade unions and their activities in the decades before 1945? We believe that revisiting such publications provides four key insights into the study of women's labour activism in the region.

First, because of their encyclopedic character and dedication to listing, in minute detail, any work-place related activism, in particular strike activity, these works provide important information on *long-term trends* in women's labour struggles in terms of both "waves" and character. Such a repository was produced by Zdeněk Šolle for the second half of the nineteenth century in the Czech lands, which touched on long-term patterns in industrial strikes, including the number of women involved, workers' demands, and archival sources.[29] Regarding the Hungarian textile industry, for example, strikes involving large numbers of women from 1890 onward have been documented.[30] These strikes mostly focused on wages (e.g., planned wage reductions) and issues related to working hours. For later decades, complex interactions between workers and management related to "rationalization" were also recorded. Read carefully, such publications reveal that the offensive and brutal treatment of one worker often served as a trigger for the strikes, and the demand for respectful treatment regularly formed part of striking workers' agenda.

Second, occasional information can be found in these works on the work- and life-activities sustaining the strikes. This includes, for example, the widespread institution of the "strike camp." In 1903, again in the activist world of Hungarian textile workers, the setting up of one such camp involved complex organizational tasks such as the election of representatives, the collection and administration of material and financial support, and the organization of games, dance, and entertainment programs.[31] Excavating such information allows for the *expansion of the classical notions of what constitutes activism*, including its gendered dimensions.

29 Šolle 1960.

30 The following information comes from one book alone, Réti 1980. A comparable work written in another state-socialist country (Bulgaria) is Vasilev et al. 1970. See also Hadzhinikolov et al. 1960.

31 Réti 1980.

Third, these works can help uncover the *transnational links* between women labour activists from the region. For example, in her 1978 monograph on women in labour and feminist movements in the interwar Kingdom of Yugoslavia, Jovanka Kecman mentions several instances of Yugoslav communist women's transnational engagement and analyzes their connection with networks such as the International Women's Secretariat of the Comintern.[32] In Bulgaria too, several publications addressed communist women's transnational ties and their involvement in the international communist movement.[33] Revisiting such publications can contribute to the emerging research on women's border-crossing, transnational engagement in labour organizing and labour struggles in the region and beyond.[34]

Additionally, earlier works can often serve as detailed guides to otherwise difficult to locate *precious primary source material* including, for instance, large sets of published governmental reports (e.g., police reports, reports on the "state of industry," labour inspectorate reports) or material that is not always readily accessible today (e.g., more or less formalized branch trade union archives or interviews with prominent activists). However, one should always take the accuracy of these sources with a grain of salt. In Hungary, for example, a series of edited volumes published by the Institute of the Hungarian Workers' Movement (Magyar Munkásmozgalmi Intézet), later Party History Institute of the Central Committee of the Hungarian Socialist Workers' Party (A Magyar Szocialista Munkáspárt Központi Bizottságának Párttörténeti Intézete) in the 1950s and 1960s, lists and excerpts a vast number of original documents often excavated from local-level archives.[35] Despite the apparent historical rigor of these source materials, elements in the texts that could have shed negative light on the attitudes of members of the (activist) working classes, such as antisemitism, were systematically edited out. This becomes apparent when one revisits the original archival collections or compares them with document collections from the 1980s that provided a full version of the texts. As this example shows, the specificities of the sources produced and edited under state socialism do not make them unusable but require the researcher have thorough knowledge of the context to properly address the biases and lacunae of the publications and source collections. Unquestionably, this situation is not unique to state

32 Kecman 1978.

33 Marinova 1989; Vodenicharova and Popova 1972; Bradinska 1969; Paskaleva 1953.

34 Zimmermann 2023a; Gnydiuk 2022; Ghodsee 2019, 2012.

35 Magyar Munkásmozgalmi Intézet (from 1956, A Magyar Szocialista Munkáspárt Központi Bizottságának Párttörténeti Intézete), 1951–1960.

socialism; similar biases and silences can also characterize the source material from other contexts.

1.2 *Women's Movements in the National and International Arenas*

From the 1990s onward, scholarly interest in the history of the labour and left-wing movements, including the history of women's labour activism in the pre-1945 period, declined considerably in the former (state-)socialist region.[36] Instead, the history of women as women rather than workers in the state-socialist period began to occupy a central place in the work of researchers with an interest in women's and gender history. In Austria, historical research on women and gender since the 1980s has dealt with various aspects of women's lives until well into the Second Republic, including studies on women as subjects of persecution, accomplices, and perpetrators during the National Socialist period.[37] In Turkey, the 1990s saw a growing interest among feminist researchers in women's and gender history of the late Ottoman/early republic period,[38] whereas the post-1945 period became an object of inquiry only in the 2000s.[39]

Drawing on these multiple contexts, since the 1990s,[40] scholars studying the region have produced a large and inspiring body of scholarship on the history of women's movements and activism.[41] At the same time, especially in the early post-Cold War period, much of this research focused on middle- and upper-class women's activism and foregrounded gender over other categories of social difference and inequality. The topic of women's work and labour activism surfaced in this literature as one among many agendas of the organizations in focus but did not attract particular analytical attention. Lower- and working-class women's labour activism when taking place in informal collectives (rather than formal women's associations) or mixed-gender organizational

36 The trend has been reversed only very recently, and this volume as well as the ZARAH project form part of this recent trend. See, for example, Rajković 2021; Todorova 2020; Kučera 2016; Van Duin 2009.

37 Hauch 2003.

38 Çakır 1994; Demirdirek 1993.

39 Çağatay 2017; Talay Keşoğlu 2007.

40 We do not discuss the scholarship on women's movements published before the 1990s here. Significant examples include Kecman 1978; Taşkıran 1973; Szegvári-Nagy 1969; Celasun 1946.

41 Examples of foundational studies include: Malínska 2013; Daskalova 2012; Bahenská, Heczková, and Musilová 2011; Dudeková et al. 2011; Feinberg 2006; Mihăilescu 2006; Jovanović and Naumović 2004; Zihnioğlu 2003; Żarnowska and Szwarc 2000; Nagy and Sárdi 1997; Mazohl-Wallnig 1995; Çakır 1994; Demirdirek 1993.

frameworks (such as the labour movement of denominational contexts) was seldomly addressed. For example, in the pioneering *Biographical Dictionary of Women's Movements and Feminisms in Central, Eastern, and South Eastern Europe* published in 2006, women labour activists are underrepresented, reflecting the volume's focus on women-only movements and its limited interest in class issues within women's movements.

In addition, the better part of this scholarship has tended either to take the nation(-state) as its primary framework of analysis or to reify the nation-building dimension of women's activism in the region. By contrast, some of the research on women's movements in the region can be considered as pioneering in how it de-naturalized national framings—as sustained by both the protagonists of these movements and their earlier historians—and how it captured the cross-border character of women's activism. These works, while not or only partially engaging with women's labour activism, can greatly inspire the study of women's labour activism. In her *Die Töchter der geschlagenen Helden* (*Daughters of the Battered Heroes*), Natali Stegmann offered a detailed history of the women's movement in the Polish lands between 1863 and 1919, elucidating especially the complex interrelationship between this movement and the Polish movement for independence.[42] Dietlind Hüchtker's *History as Performance* used a focus on three women activists to create an integrative history of different national and political activist networks across and beyond Galicia, and touched on the labour-related agendas and demands promoted by these activists.[43] Krassimira Daskalova's 2012 *Жени, пол и модернизация в България 1878–1944* (*Women, Gender and Modernization in Bulgaria 1878–1944*) addressed the narrative of women's activism in the framework of gender discourses connected to the social processes of modernization and state-building.[44] Yaprak Zihnioğlu's 2003 *Kadınsız İnkılap* (*Revolution without Women*) investigated the formation of early republic feminist activism in Turkey, which was then sidelined by the Kemalist regime for being too much of an independent voice in the newly established nation-state.[45] Finally, Martha Bohachevsky-Chomiak reflected on the "pragmatic or community feminism" of Ukrainian women in the Habsburg and Russian empires, who advanced women-specific goals but did not necessarily identify as feminists.[46]

42 Stegmann 2000.
43 Hüchtker 2021.
44 Daskalova 2012.
45 Zihnioğlu 2003.
46 Bohachevsky-Chomiak 1988.

The approaches of authors who, since the 1990s, have explored the relationship between nation-building, nationalism, and women's emancipation vary greatly. Some have foregrounded the empowering character of nationalist contexts for women's emancipation. In this line of argumentation, women belonging to non-dominant nationalities were able to expand their public roles and visibility in cases where women's emancipation was regarded as part of struggle for the emancipation of the nation or when women managed to make and exploit this argument. Others have discussed these same historical settings more critically, pointing to the limits and trouble spots of opportunities thus generated, including persistent gendered hierarchies within national movements, the ethnocentrism of these movements, and the backlash encountered after the establishment of new nation-states.[47] New scholarship on the Habsburg Empire that has moved beyond the inherited foregrounding of the national question and nationalism in the historiography of the empire must engage with the findings of gender historians if it is to fully engage with the gendered dimensions of political and socio-cultural change in the Habsburg lands. The emerging new historiography of women's labour activism in the region has the great potential to contribute to such innovation.

Historians of women's movements in the region have also made important contributions to the development of transregional approaches to women's activism. Transnational links already were featured in scholarship produced during the state-socialist period. Some earlier histories of women's activism, including working-class and left-wing women, had an openness to transnational dimensions, including non-socialist internationalism, and embraced comparative interpretations. For example, a 1948 study of the history of the Hungarian women's movement by Mrs. Péter Ágoston included references "in a rather self-evident manner to the context of both trade-union and non-socialist internationalism when discussing pre-1914 and interwar socialist demands in relation to women's work."[48] A Hungarian Women's Council publication on the history of the international women's movement and historian Katalin Szegvári-Nagy's 1981 book on Hungarian women's movements between the late nineteenth century and World War Two further illustrate the transnational and comparative dimensions present in this older scholarship.[49]

47 For examples of both approaches, see Saygılıgil 2021; Verginella 2017; Bahenská and Malínská 2014; Malínská 2013; Bilal and Ekmekçioğlu 2006; Heindl, Király, and Millner 2006; Malečková 2004; David 1991.

48 Zimmermann 2014, 127.

49 The first publication, authored by Zsuzsa Ortutay (Ortutay 1960), presents both Hungarian and international socialist and non-socialist women's activisms from the eighteenth century onward and discusses the history of Women's Day in various countries. Szegvári-Nagy

From the 1990s onward, women's and gender historians have demonstrated, in the context of the Habsburg Empire as well as the late Ottoman Empire and the early Republic of Turkey, the rich variety of women's organizations' strategic use of internationalism to advance their agendas. For instance, they examined how women's organizations seized the opportunities provided by international organizing to enhance their visibility in the domestic context.[50] In her volume on the interwar Ukrainian women's movement in Galicia, Myroslava Diadiuk focused both on women activists' local agendas and actions and their efforts to participate in international congresses and forge transnational networks.[51] Several publications and editorial enterprises have aimed directly at bringing and "thinking together" various national and transnational branches of the women's movement. The pioneering *Biographical Dictionary of Women's Movements and Feminisms in Central, Eastern, and South Eastern Europe* referred to above described the lives and work of more than 150 women across the region.[52] Focusing on the territories of the Habsburg Empire, *Writing the Women's Movement: Historiography, Documentation, Positions, Bibliographies* presents the history of the different sections of women's movements.[53] In the Ottoman/Turkish context, Elife Biçer-Deveci has discussed the uneven but continuous relationship between international women's organizations and late Ottoman and early republican feminists.[54] A landmark document collection and introductory overview concerning the period from 1820 to 1918 is provided in the Habsburg Empire cluster of the database *Women and Social Movements in Modern Empires* (WASMME). The editors of the cluster provided over six hundred highly curated primary sources, included selected secondary literature, and authored an overview essay on the historiography and documents made available in the database. They deliberately pursued an inclusive approach, featuring women of highly variegated (class, ethnic, and religious) backgrounds and political persuasions active in mixed- and single-gender organizations; claimed to represent different groups of women; and focused on, among other things, labour-related issues. The "Women and Social Movements in the Habsburg Empire" overview essay approached activism

---

1981 in turn addressed domestic developments in a comparative transnational framework with references to women's movements in England and Germany, as well Russia, and (later) the Soviet Union. See also Zimmermann 2014, 134.

50 Biçer-Deveci 2017; Tutavac and Korotin 2016; Dudeková 2011; Zimmermann 2006, 2005.

51 Diadiuk 2011.

52 De Haan, Daskalova, and Loutfi 2006.

53 Gehmacher and Vittorelli 2009.

54 Biçer-Deveci 2017. On the Turkish context, see also Davaz 2020; Azak and De Smaele 2016.

from an integrative, cross-national, and cross-border perspective and identified the wide array of themes addressed in women's activism.[55]

Especially since the 2010s, the "transnational turn" in gender history has led a growing number of researchers studying state-socialist women's organizations to address transregional and cross-Iron Curtain activism.[56] Some scholars of state-socialist women's organizations and activism have developed strategies for reading sources that go beyond the basic rules of source critique established for the historical profession. These scholars engage in productive "against the grain" readings of primary sources produced under state socialism. Writing about the role of the Women's International Democratic Federation (WIDF) in transnational women's activism in the context of the Cold War, Yulia Gradskova has analyzed such sources from a postcolonial perspective.[57] She carefully differentiated between "selective and manipulative official accounts" in WIDF publications and documents, usually aimed at external readers, and "more reliable," internally circulated materials such as protocols, minutes, and letters. Combining these two reading strategies, she investigated the Soviet archives with an eye toward exposing "the silences and internal contradictions" in materials. As she has pointed out, "even if the Soviet archives do not seem to be a place to look for alternative voices and interpretations of the WIDF's ideology and activism, some of the documents kept there clearly indicate dissent, and reveal the voices of women who did not share a 'communist', 'Soviet' or 'Euro-centric' way of thinking."[58] Similarly, Mária Schadt (re)discovered how formal reports on women functionaries' activities in "the world of work" in 1950s Hungary communicated agreement and disagreement, respectively, via constructing bullet point lists that summarized achievements and problems in highly variable levels of detail—a selective reporting strategy that the 1950s functionaries certainly employed intentionally.[59] Schadt used this insight to

55 The lead essay was written by Susan Zimmermann with Birgitta Bader-Zaar, Ágoston Berecz, Jitka Gelnarová, Alexandra Ghiț, and Michaela Königshofer. See Zimmermann et al. 2018. The scholars mentioned above and Dietlind Hüchtker collected and curated the source material contained in the Habsburg Monarchy cluster of the WASMME database.

56 For example, De Haan 2023; Bracke 2022; Donert 2022; Lóránd 2022; Artwinska and Mrozik 2020; Ghodsee 2019; Grabowska 2017; Jarska 2015; Donert 2013; Nečasová 2013; Bonfiglioli 2012; Fidelis 2010; Popa 2009. See also Sercan Çınar's 2023 study on women's transnational activism, which offers insight into collaboration and solidarity between socialist women in 1970s Turkey and their counterparts in state-socialist countries, and Eloisa Betti's contribution to the present volume.

57 Gradskova 2022, 2021.

58 Gradskova 2021, 6.

59 Schadt 2003.

reveal the disagreements, power struggles, and ensuing policy changes within various Hungarian institutions dealing with women's issues. Such creative readings of sources can greatly contribute to the advancement of a new critical history of women's labour struggles under state socialism. We discuss this point further below, in the third section of this chapter.

1.3 *Social Histories of Gender and Work*

A third historiographic cluster relevant for researching women's labour struggles is the social history of gender and work. Starting from the second half of the 1960s and rooted in the early stages of Western women's and gender history,[60] histories of women's work included an explicit focus on labour activism. This literature, covering both the Eastern and Western European contexts, was inclusive of working-class women's living conditions and specific experiences in areas of industrial wage labour, such as in tobacco manufacturing and various branches of the textile industry, or in domestic service.[61] Studies on women's work in the Russian and Soviet contexts, produced largely by researchers working in North American institutions and shaped (to varying degrees) by early Western women's and gender history, are particularly diverse and sophisticated. Beginning in the 1980s, historians such as Rose Glickman and Wendy Goldman offered insight into the social and political lives of working-class women in the Soviet Union in the 1920s and 1930s.[62] In her 1995 study of printing industry workers in the early Soviet Union, Diane Koenker provided a nuanced analysis of the interactions and conflicts of men and women workers on the shopfloor. Through a critical reading of the official Soviet press and archival documents, she painted a vivid picture of conflictual workplace relations and official and unofficial strategies of organizing and disseminating information. Tracing the process of workplace marginalization and the deskilling of women in the printing industry throughout the 1920s, Koenker highlighted the discrepancies between official policies regarding women workers

60 The concept of "gender" emerged in Western scholarship in the 1970s, while in Eastern Europe, with some early exceptions, it came into use after the fall of state socialism. In the Turkish context, the term appeared simultaneously with its use in the postsocialist context in the 1990s. To denote historical works with a focus on women and using what came to be defined as gendered analyses, we use the term "women's and gender history/historians" when referring to works published both before and after this shift, including the historiography from the state-socialist period.

61 Bauer (1988) 2015; Nacar 2014; Quataert 1991; Gyáni 1989; Augeneder 1987; Ecevit 1986; Pasteur 1986; Appelt 1985; Ehmer 1981a, 1981b; Rigler 1976.

62 Goldman 2002; Glickman 1986. See also Ilic 1999; Buckley 1989; McAuley 1981.

and everyday gendered relations in the print shop.[63] Key conceptual contributions made by historians of women's work in Russia and the Soviet Union have been integrated into the mainstream of the field, as in the 2008 edited volume *A Dream Deferred: New Studies in Russian and Soviet Labour History*, where gender and gendered work form a key dimension of analysis in most of the contributions to this "general labour history" volume.[64]

Before the 2000s, research on women's work in Central and Eastern Europe and its adjacent territories from a social history perspective has been unsystematic but still present. It tackled themes such as agrarian labour history and what could today be termed "care work."[65] In the state-socialist period, works on the social history of agrarian labour and the living conditions of the agrarian population evolved into a significant branch of history writing. These works addressed women's work, including women's unpaid family labour. Nevertheless, they treated the gender division of labour as a given and did not consider women's work "a type of work worth a separate contribution" when publishing, for instance, large-scale edited volumes.[66] As for care work, the 1975 volume *Mişcarea democratică şi revoluţionară a femeilor din România* (*The Democratic and Revolutionary Movement of Women in Romania*) mentioned the Great Depression-era protests by Bucharest women who could no longer support their families, as well as the existence of covertly communist associations enthusiastically run by women activists, who especially helped mothers with young children.[67]

Since the mid-1990s, works that undertook a more explicit and systematic gendered analysis of women's paid and unpaid labour in state-socialist contexts have been published regularly. In their overview of the historical scholarship on women and gender in Central and Eastern Europe, Krassimira Daskalova and Susan Zimmermann highlighted three major themes that had been fundamental for the post-1989 scholarly efforts to gender the history of labour in the region: the labour of women in agriculture and farming; the initial and unevenly paced integration of women into wage labour; and the mass entry of women into the workforce under state socialism.[68] Studies investigating these large themes dealt with subjects as diverse as peasant women's (under)paid casualized work, significant opposition to women's entrance into

63 Koenker 1995.
64 Filtzer et al. 2008.
65 Some of this historiography is discussed in Ghiţ 2018 and Zimmermann 2014.
66 Zimmermann 2018, esp. 84.
67 Georgescu and Georgescu 1975.
68 Daskalova and Zimmermann 2017, 283.

the trades and professions in Bulgaria, Czechoslovakia, and Hungary after World War One, the ambiguous effects of women-specific protective labour legislation applied in the region in waves throughout the twentieth century, and women workers' biographies.[69]

Another important theme in post-1990s scholarship has been "gender and everyday life," whereby scholars examined how women workers experienced the effects of labour policies in state-socialist regimes. For instance, Jill Massino argued that "women's experiences of the labour force were diverse and ambiguous";[70] some of the women she interviewed in Romania enjoyed their employment during state socialism, while others felt overwhelmed by the expectation of having to perform equally well as workers and mothers. Harassment by their male colleagues in workplaces and patriarchal relations at home were (mostly) difficult to avoid and reject. Nevertheless, financial independence and access to consumer goods offset negative experiences for some women workers, as in the case of the Hungarian factory workers researched by Eszter Zsófia Tóth, for example.[71] Carola Sachse's book *Der Hausarbeitstag: Gerechtigkeit und Gleichberechtigung in Ost und West 1939–1994* (*The Domestic Workday: Justice and Equality in East and West 1939–1994*) published in 2002 zooms in on how women in the German Democratic Republic (GDR) reconciled family and employment as a delicate negotiation of gender relations and workplace-related activism.[72] Importantly, and increasingly starting in the 1960s, experts (psychologists, sociologists) were asked to weigh in on issues concerning women's work and, by extension, their status in state-socialist societies. Recent work, including this volume, shows that topics such as "the double burden" or women's equality with men had already become carefully studied research subjects back then.[73]

In the twenty-first century, social histories of gender and work flourished at the intersection of labour history and gender history, drawing on both fields and—sometimes—weaving them together. On the one hand, the rise of a "new global labour history" has brought with it a more inclusive perspective in terms of regional coverage, forms and levels of activism, and types of labour relations.[74] While the field as whole has retained its limited engagement with

69 Bahenská, Heczková, and Musilová 2014; Neudorflová 2010; Sekyrková 2010; Papp 2004; Nazŭrska 2003; Żarnowska and Szwarc 2000; Asztalos Morell 1999; Grandner 1995.

70 Massino 2019, 142.

71 Tóth 2009. See also Massino 2009.

72 Sachse 2002.

73 Hîncu 2022; Massino 2019, 155.

74 For an introduction to discussions on this field, see, for instance, Brown et al. 2012.

gender as an analytical category,[75] when labour historians consider gender and gendered interests in activism and organizing, their conclusions challenged the long-standing assumptions of the field and highlighted overlooked dynamics of labour conflicts. Can Nacar has shown how in Istanbul in 1908, employers offered wage increases only to striking women cigarette makers. However, all strikers continued their protest, shunning employers' gendered strategies to divide workers.[76] H. Şükrü Ilıcak similarly described how in Ottoman Salonica (present-day Thessaloniki) in 1911, women workers' exclusion from the negotiation process between strikers and employers led women to reject a proposed agreement and continue the strike on their own. A newly formed labour organization in the city served as the mediator between men and women workers.[77] These examples from the late Ottoman Empire's tobacco industry contribute to overcoming the stubborn notion in labour history that women, as the more precarious category of employee or the subordinate spouses of employed men, were often less willing to organize or engage in long-term resistance. Still, more careful research and an integrative rethinking of women's labour struggles is necessary. Several contributions in this volume show how, for example, working-class culture was not solely a culture of organized men but included many women and various interactions between women and men.

Contributions informed more by interests entertained in women's and gender (rather than labour) history have also focused on state policies regarding women's work and the complexities of their implementation. Daskalova and Zimmermann pointed out how "complexity and unevenness" characterized state-socialist policies focused on drawing increasing numbers of women into paid labour.[78] Luciana Jinga's 2015 volume on gender and political representation in Romania underscores this unevenness. Jinga emphasizes the prevalence of gendered segregation and discrimination in employment despite the policies (particularly starting in the 1970s) that sought to increase women's power and visibility in workplace governance and political structures.[79] By contrast, Chiara Bonfiglioli has argued that complexity and ambivalence characterized the somewhat less oppressive "working mother gender contract" of Yugoslav self-management. This complex legacy has shaped women's labour activism in Croatia into the twenty-first century.[80] Margolzata Fidelis's 2010 monograph

75 Betti et al. 2022.
76 Nacar 2019, 147–150.
77 Ilıcak 2002, 132.
78 Daskalova and Zimmermann 2017, 288–290.
79 Jinga 2015.
80 Bonfiglioli 2020.

on gender and industrialization in postwar Poland is one of a handful of studies written after the end of state socialism that specifically addresses women's labour struggles in Central and Eastern Europe after World War Two. Focusing on the textile and mining industries to recover women workers' agency, Fidelis found complex strategies of compliance and protest employed by women during the turbulent years of postwar reconstruction in Poland.[81] In the Turkish case, Gülhan Balsoy and Görkem Akgöz investigated the impact of state policies on the working conditions of women as factory workers in the late Ottoman and early republic periods, respectively, and pointed out the discrepancies between legal frameworks and women's lived realities at the level of the shopfloor.[82] Yet, while this new historiography acknowledges the ways in which women's work constituted an important element of the politics pursued by women's organizations with close ties to the state, it often overlooks the role of women's activism in trade unions and state institutions in the making and for the realization of state policies.[83]

1.4 *Life Histories of Activist Women*

A final historiographic strand worth noting for the study of women's labour activism concerns studies and ego-writing that is focused on the life histories of left-wing women in social and labour movements.[84] An established genre of women's and gender history, biography has recently become both more popular and more conceptually sophisticated.[85] Close-up analyses of activists' life stories offer a privileged vantage point for studying women's multiple engagements that might not be visible otherwise. Women identifying with working-class women's interests and agendas repeatedly collaborated with both feminist organizations (i.e., cooperated across class lines) and with labour organizations dominated by men. Activists followed this strategy because men-dominated labour organizations foregrounded class issues and—sometimes—could provide more opportunities to pursue the interests of women as workers. Organizations of the women's movement, which were often led by middle- or upper-class women, also addressed issues relevant for working-class women,

81 Fidelis 2010.
82 Akgöz 2021; Balsoy 2009. See also Makal and Toksöz 2012.
83 Fábián, Johnson, and Lazda 2021; Ghodsee 2012; Fidelis 2010.
84 Popova and Helfert 2021. See also the contributions on several women labour activists from Bulgaria, Romania, Poland, and Austria in the ZARAH blog series II, https://zarah-ceu.org/blog/.
85 For a discussion of problem zones of feminist historical political biography, see Hemmings 2018; Bosch 2009.

and women identifying with working-class women's interests aimed to represent their agendas in these organizations.[86] Furthermore, biographies following an activist's life course transgress historical political ruptures (e.g., 1918, 1945, 1953, 1989) and enable a long-term perspective. The life stories of the Romanian Ana Pauker and the Bulgarian Tsola Dragoicheva exemplify communist women's turbulent fate in the interwar period and during the early years of state-socialist regimes.[87]

Put into a wider perspective, women's and gender historians writing especially in Western Europe and North America saw biographies of extraordinary women as valuable in and of themselves, offering key elements for recovering the histories/herstories of "foremothers."[88] They drew on a tradition of biographical writing on remarkable women that reached back to the nineteenth century. In Central and Eastern Europe and its adjacent territories, biographical works pursued a similar recuperative agenda.

Biographies and life stories of women labour activists produced in Austria since the 1970s emerged at the intersection of this West-centric feminist interest and the growing contemporaneous interest in the history of social democratic and socialist militancy. Book-length biographies of prominent social democratic women politicians active in the period before the Cold War like Anna Boschek, Marie Tusch, and Käthe Leichter were published in the late 1990s and early 2000s.[89] Together with works on radical and communist women in interwar Vienna, such as an article on the feminist peace activist Olga Misař or the edited book-length oral life history of Vienna Communist Party of Austria (Kommunistische Partei Österreichs, KPÖ) member Prive Friedjung,[90] these volumes shed light on how activism on behalf of working women underpinned the broader ideological commitments of these left-wing labour activists. Three recent biographies—on social democratic trade unionist and politician Rosa Jochmann, communist antifascist Tilly Spiegel, and the leader of the Austrian and international social democratic women's movement Adelheid Popp—all published in 2019, testify to growing scholarly and public interest in the lives of women labour activists in twentieth-century Austria.[91] As compared to the older, sometimes celebratory literature, these new works are grounded in,

86 A number of the protagonists presented or mentioned in De Haan, Daskalova, and Loutfi 2006 belong to this group.

87 Daskalova 2016; Levy 2001.

88 Chevigny 1983; see also Caine 1994; Alpern et al. 1992.

89 Jobst 1999; Göhring 1998.

90 Rath 2010; Lichtblau and Jahn 1995.

91 Duma 2019; Markova 2019; Trausmuth 2019.

among other things, (self-)critical conceptual reflection on the genre of the activist biography.[92] In Turkey, oral history research with women involved in labour struggles after World War Two since the 2000s stands out as an important tool to reconstruct the undocumented activism of women whose gendered demands were marginalized in the labour historiography dominated by men. Significant examples in this scholarly genre are Emel Akal's and Muazzez Pervan's research on the Progressive Women's Association (İlerici Kadınlar Derneği) and Gülfer Akkaya's work on the Democratic Women's Association (Demokratik Kadın Derneği).[93] More recently, since the 2010s, researchers mobilized primary sources to offer life stories of women intellectuals and labour activists such as Yaşar Nezihe (1882–1971), Sabiha Sertel (1895–1968), Suat Derviş (1905–1972), and Zehra Kosova (1910–2001).[94] Finally, as a distinct category of publication, autobiographies by women workers constitute a relevant source for historians of women's labour activism. An important example of this in the Turkish context is the interwar tobacco worker Zehra Kosova's valuable autobiography *Ben İşçiyim* (*I am a worker*).[95]

Biographies were a key genre of women's history writing in socialist countries as well. In Hungary, Romania, Yugoslavia, and Bulgaria, historians who focused on socialist women's activism published biographies of labour activists from the nineteenth century and the interwar period. In 1949, the Romanian Workers' Party issued a brochure with several biographies of women activists who died while fighting for the communist movement in the previous decades.[96] In Yugoslavia, biographies of numerous "People's Heroines" and their contributions to the antifascist struggle were published as part of biographical collections.[97] In Romania, historians focusing on activist women's history were marginalized in the late 1950s and rediscovered in the 1970s,[98] whereas in Hungary and Bulgaria,[99] the genre thrived throughout the period. *A cselekvés szerelmese* (*In Love with Action*) is the well-known Hungarian intellectual György Dalos's biography of Ilona Duczynska, which he published in 1984.[100] Many of these volumes, while barely engaging in a critical reading of *all* the twists and turns that characterized the life courses of these

92 See also Hauch 2012.
93 Pervan 2013; Akkaya 2008; Akal 2003.
94 Atay 2021; Saygılıgil 2021; O'Brien and Deris 2019; Kırılmış 2014.
95 Kosova 1996.
96 Romanian Workers' Party 1949.
97 Bjelić et al. 1980; Beoković 1967.
98 Ghiț 2018; Homenco and Ioniță 1975; Ioniță 1973.
99 Iankova 1980; Bogdanova 1969; Paskaleva 1953.
100 Dalos 1984; see also Helfert 2015.

women, contain precious information on activism: they detail workplace circumstances, discuss women's paid and unpaid labour, their gendered involvement in social movement work, and their border-crossing and international engagements.

The same is true for the many activist autobiographies published in the state-socialist world of Eastern Europe and the life-history interviews conducted and deposited in a systematic manner in many places but seldom used for research thus far.[101] The material produced about the Hungarian Magda Aranyossi is a case in point. Aranyossi was forced into exile in the interwar period, became a founding member of the Democratic Alliance of Hungarian Women (Magyar Nők Demokratikus Szövetsége, 1945–1956), and was later a party historian who wrote about women's activism. Aranyossi's *Rendszertelen önéletrajz* (*Disorderly Autobiography*), published in 1978, gives detailed information on the history of the communist and popular front international organizing of women in the 1930s. Aranyossi was responsible for the daily operations of its journal *Femmes* (*dans l'action mondiale*) (*Women* [*in global action*]) in the Paris Secretariat of the Women's World Committee Against War and Fascism, and her autobiography paints a multifaceted and detailed picture of the workings of the Secretariat, the organization, and its leaders.[102]

Since the end of (state-)socialist regimes, biographical works continued to be important sources of information about the contexts and dynamics of women's labour activism.[103] In her recent monograph on Bulgarian socialists, Maria Todorova corrects stereotypes that hold that women became activists because they were married to activists, arguing that sometimes it was the other way around: marrying men activists enabled women to continue their activist work.[104] A compact biography of the textile worker and leading communist trade unionist in interwar Czechoslovakia Karla Pfeiferová, published in 2006, was written by Jiří Pokorný, a historian with an unshakable interest in the history of trade unions and the labour movement.[105] Eva Uhrová also published a collection of biographies of women "that we know and we don't know," among them essays on the social democratic politician-activist, women's right activist,

101 In Hungary, for example, this includes two large collections of memoirs and life history interviews of socialist-communist and trade union activists, including a considerable number of women, (originally) kept in the archival division of the Párttörténeti Intézet (Party History Institute) in Budapest.

102 Aranyossi 1978.

103 Gehmacher and Vittorelli 2009; Livezeanu with Pachuta Farris 2007; Zirin and Worobec 2007; De Haan, Daskalova, and Loutfi 2006; Schindler 1993.

104 Todorova 2020.

105 Pokorný 2006.

and journalist Karla Machová, the women's right activist and national social politician Fráňa Zeminová, and the editor of *Socialistka* (*The Socialist Woman*) Miloslava Hrdličková-Šrámková.[106] A more recent contribution sheds light on the life of Luisa Landová-Štychová, the anarchist member of parliament in the interwar period, revealing the ways Landová-Štychová's personal life story and circumstances intersected with her activist and political career, both advancing it and hampering it at different points.[107]

Such contributions show that biographies are not simply about extraordinary individuals worthy of commemoration and perhaps emulation. In sparse historiographical contexts, as is still the case for women's labour activism in the region covered in this volume, biographies can serve as valuable starting points for further research. Indeed, Kevin Morgan has argued that in research on communist activists (and beyond, we would claim), a biographical treatment "allows a distinct and formative role to individual human agency"; reveals how other influences and movements shaped the experiences of individuals committed to the political cause; and enables a deconstruction of the "proverbial conformism, intrusiveness and monolithicity" of the international communist movement.[108] The well-known Hungarian writer Péter Nádas, who was the nephew of and was raised by Magda Aranyossi, has deeply and critically engaged with the life history of his aunt in his recent publications. Contextualizing her published work through a range of diverse unpublished documents, Nádas has laid the foundation for further critical and productive re-readings of Aranyossi's autobiography.[109] For historians studying women's labour activism, then, biographies can spark research questions about the ways in which women were part of larger networks or broader historical processes and the factors that constrained or enabled their remarkable (or indeed singularly infamous) individual choices.

Historians have reflected on the use and potential of the historical analysis of ego documents produced in state-socialist countries and the world of communist organizing. These include not only biographies and autobiographies,

106 Uhrová 2008.

107 Holubec 2021.

108 Morgan 2012, 461. Comparably, Ghodsee 2019 (esp. 13–15) underscores how the stories of the leaders of state-socialist women's organizations help show the ways these women could shape "the will of the state" in systems that were not as monolithic as commonly assumed.

109 An English-language account of the not unproductive encounter of these diverse "politics of history" concerning Magda Aranyossi can be found in Zimmermann 2022. The volume also includes an English translation of (large parts) of Aranyossi's 1954 study of women's role in the Hungarian Republic of Councils.

often solicited by party and academic institutions, but also cadre files containing self-descriptions and political evaluations, petitions, reports, and denunciations addressed to various authorities, letters written to periodicals and, in the period of high Stalinism, a whole genre of self-criticism and self-reporting. Historian of the Comintern Brigitte Studer has characterized these "institutional ego documents" as a scholarly "stroke of luck" because of their sheer quantity and variety.[110] Studer convincingly argued that these sources can be used in a critical manner to help scholars move beyond the "totalitarian" school in Soviet studies, which has denied their value beyond documenting state and party control over the individual and the "revisionist" social history approach that used them as quantifiable data sets. The critical use of these sources requires careful adaptation of the historical profession's general rules of source criticism to the specific context and a focus on the relationship between text and power, namely the production of subjectivity and the communicative process between the addressees and the subjects producing these documents.

2 Chapters in the Volume

The studies collected in this volume demonstrate how fruitful it can be to think and work across not only the historiographical gaps between labour history and women's and gender history but also across time periods and borders. While some chapters cover the period before World War One, the interwar period, or the decades between 1945 and 1989, several contributors cover time spans that include moments of major political rupture or upheaval. Other chapters transgress the borders of nation-states or Cold War divides, and still others, the borders between different social movements. Engaging with a great variety of primary and secondary sources, which include—in addition to archival material—interviews, letters, journals, meeting protocols, and films, the contributions highlight the multiplicity of actors as well as the arenas and scales of activism mobilized throughout the nineteenth and twentieth centuries to further women's interests at the intersection of gender and labour relations. The volume, with surprising density and variety, showcases both the key role labour struggles played in women's activism and the many articulations of women's struggles for social and economic rights. Below, we highlight the

110 Studer 2008.

scholarly significance of these contributions as we provide a summary of the organization of the volume.

2.1 *Women's Struggles and Men-Dominated Trade Union and Labour Movements: Rethinking a Complex Relationship*

Part 1 of the volume moves to center stage women's agendas, demands, and experiences in men-dominated trade union and labour movements in the national and international context. In the organizations to which they belonged, as well as in the larger labour movement contexts in which they operated, women activists simultaneously strived to shape the discussions, decisions, and policies regarding their gendered social and economic interests and waged struggles against men's domination and men-focused policies. Read together from a long-term perspective and in the context of the existing scholarship, the chapters grouped in Part 1 underline the key role of women who engaged with and in men-dominated policy contexts to advance working women's interests in diverse, complex, and historically shifting ways.

Opening Part 1, Sophia Polek's chapter on typesetters in St. Petersburg in the early twentieth century examines the labour movement in Imperial Russia and analyzes a 1906 debate on the "woman question" in the industry which unfolded in the printer's journal *Printers' Herald* (*Вестник Печатников*). An early example of an open-ended and complex exchange of views on key tropes in the gendered history of trade unionism, the debate included discussions about "unity" versus "separate organizing," the marginalization of women in the trade union movement, and women's gender-specific mistreatment in the workplace not only by superiors but also by their male colleagues. In the pages of *Printers' Herald*, women workers questioned the claims to moral superiority upon which men constructed the foundation for class unity; they criticized the denial of disrespectful behavior toward women; and complained that women workers would be forced to create their own unions, which would effect the unity of the typesetters' union. Despite workers' radicalism, the printers' work culture remained strongly masculinist: women were daunted by the cost of membership; meeting locations like pubs and restaurants were not accessible or safe for women; and evening meetings were more difficult to attend because many women had childcare duties; issues that remain on the agenda of trade union women to this day. Polek's chapter develops a new perspective on the question of the "unity" of the labour movement by analytically foregrounding the voices and experiences (as described in the debate) of those on the margins of the labour movement and in the world of work, i.e., women. Women's experience of what today would be called gender-based discrimination and harassment in the workplace is discussed by Polek from the perspective of discussions on "unity." Polek shows that it is the very marginalization of women's work, interests, and experience that historically has inhibited the "unity" of the labour movement, or, if seen from the other direction, genuine unity must be based on the inclusion and accommodation of the realities of those on the margins.

Mátyás Erdélyi's chapter on the labour activism of women bank clerks in Central Europe from 1900 to 1914 brings to light the struggles of women employees and the evolution of their relationship with men-dominated professional associations in the late Habsburg Monarchy. Analyzing men-dominated and women-only organizations of clerks in the banking sector in the territories of present-day Hungary, Austria, Slovakia, and the Czech Republic, Erdélyi shows how women clerks' demands for better education and training, higher wages, and improved civil and social rights (such as the end of the marriage ban, improved access to pension funds, and other benefits) targeted gender discrimination at the white-collar workplace as well as in organizations representing the interests of the sector's employees. When discussing plans to improve women's working conditions, one of its most easily recognizable cluster of demands were those related to equal pay (alternatively "equal pay for equal work" or "equal pay for work of equal value"). Equal pay broadly defined, i.e., the struggles to close the wage gap and to eliminate gender-based discrimination regarding remuneration, holds a special place in feminist labour history.[111] Erdélyi's chapter is one of several contributions in this volume that capture the complexity of gender wage justice, known popularly as the issue of "equal pay," a topic to which we will return in the third section of this chapter.

In our region of focus and beyond, women's labour activism developed in relation to global and supranational developments. This is partly because activist women had to use creative strategies at both the local and national levels and partly on account of the strong internationalist dimension of the feminist, labour, and social reform currents that underpinned the rise of women's labour activism since the 1860s. Focusing on the struggles of women in the communist international labour movement of the 1920s, Daria Dyakonova's chapter considers more specifically the role of communist women in party structures as compared to trade union structures and the role international changes regarding participation structures played in shaping women's activisms on the ground. Bringing in examples from the Bulgarian and Polish national context, the author shows that the shift toward the Profintern within international communist organizing related to women was accompanied by

111 Betti 2021; Zimmermann 2021, 2020a; Betti 2018; Neunsinger 2018; Kessler-Harris 1990.

the establishment of separate women's structures within the Profintern and a vision of enhancing trade union work among women in all countries.[112] Dyakonova's chapter underscores that over time, dedicated women functionaries, whether engaged in party or trade union structures, played a key role in trying to advance practical, workplace-related, pro-women demands and action. The reports of Bulgarian and Polish activists toward the Profintern discussed in the chapter showcase some of the difficulties of communist women's organizing and activism that stemmed from the parallel engagement with women's issues within party-type and trade union-style organizational structures—a difficulty that would haunt women's politics and work-place related activism in state-socialist Eastern Europe throughout the rest of the twentieth century. Studying the varieties of interaction between local communist women's politics and the international changes outlined in the chapter will greatly advance our understanding of left-wing women's workplace-related activism in Central and Eastern European countries and beyond.[113]

Intimately connected to the struggles of working women has been the issue of reproductive rights and the effects of insufficient means of controlling pregnancies and motherhood on working women's lives. In the region considered in this volume, women's public engagement with this huge issue within the labour movement gained new momentum after World War One. Analyzing communist women's activism on behalf of working-class women in the Slovakian territories of Czechoslovakia, Denisa Nešťáková's chapter offers an example of how ideas about sexuality circulated in Central Europe in the early 1920s. Through an analysis of the Slovakian communist women's paper *Proletárka* (*Proletarian woman*)—which was different from its Czech sister paper *Komunistka* (*Woman Communist*)—Nešťáková discusses the inclusive approach of Slovak women to the problems caused by working women's special burden resulting from their involvement in paid and unpaid labour and exacerbated by the large families for which they cared. Marginalized by the state, the Communist Party, and the non-socialist women's movement, Slovak communist women drew on international communist and noncommunist actions and knowledge to make their case for working-class women's liberation. The

112 The shift toward the Profintern described by Dyakonova happened at the beginning of the "Third Period" of international communism, when the struggle against "reformist," i.e., social democratic "traitors" gained prominence and communist activists aimed to put into practice the "class against class" strategy in many countries. Zimmermann 2021, 212–213, 218–225, has first drawn attention to this shift in the women's politics of international communism in the interwar period. See also Devinatz 2019; Manley 2005.

113 See also Masheva (forthcoming).

authors of *Proletárka* conceived of reproductive rights (e.g., family planning, birth control, sexuality) as a key element of working women's liberation and aimed to include these issues and women's sexual liberation more generally in the official agenda of working-class struggle. The chapter adds an important perspective to understanding women labour activists' efforts to problematize various consequences of the fissures and links between women's paid and unpaid labour. It highlights how these efforts were entangled with questions of nationality and internationalism and curbed by the resistance of communist men during the period when expressing ideas of sexual emancipation became gradually unwelcome in Soviet Russia and in communist parties across Central and Eastern Europe.[114]

Similar to Dyakonova's discussion of the Comintern and Profintern in the 1920s, Johanna Wolf's chapter on the equal pay debates and controversies in the World Federation of Trade Unions (WFTU) in the late 1940s shows the important yet overlooked contributions of Eastern European women activists in the making of the international politics of gender and labour in the postwar period. Discussing the WFTU's role in the Economic and Social Council of the United Nations (ECOSOC), Wolf reveals the important but ignored contributions women activists such as Nina Popova of the Soviet Union made to the WFTU's gender politics. Pointing to the key role of discussions about labour market segregation as well as skill and wage systems in the evolution of the international debate on equal pay, the chapter deepens our understanding of the origins and dynamics of the international campaign for equal pay before the ILO adopted its Convention no. 100 on equal remuneration in 1951. In addition, the study carries further the insight that the research on women's international labour activism must situate all actors and organizations within a large arena of activisms and politics informed by both competition and cooperation between women's, labour, and "official" internationalisms.[115] Only such an approach will enable a careful and accurate evaluation of the trajectory of the international politics of women's work in the twentieth century.

Investigating equal pay cannot be done in isolation as it was intertwined historically with wage and job evaluation systems, skill, gender-based work discrimination, segregated labour markets, access to vocational training, and other career-advancing opportunities, in addition to the fight for (but also against) protective labour legislation. Eloisa Betti's chapter demonstrates this entanglement, giving an account of how, in Italy from the late 1940s to

114 Studer 2015, 50–58.
115 See also Zimmermann 2020b, esp. 115.

the early 1960s, vocational training became a key topic in debates on women's work across political parties against the backdrop of the division between the Eastern and the Western blocs. In the context of the Italian "economic miracle" of the late 1950s and early 1960s, Italian socialist and communist women referred to gendered labour politics in Eastern Europe and the Soviet Union to successfully promote vocational training as part of their campaign for equal pay. Betti's chapter contributes to the historicization of the struggle for vocational training, moving as it does beyond ahistorical juxtapositions of conservative—i.e., restrictive and traditionalist—versus progressive—i.e., more egalitarian—visions of vocational training. At the same time, the chapter exemplifies how, during the Cold War, the appropriation of the language and politics of women's work in state-socialist Eastern Europe sustained women's activism in a Southern European, democratic country. In so doing, the chapter highlights the role of communist-led, Western-dominated international organizations in generating and propelling momentum for change in the struggles over vocational training. Thus, Betti's contribution becomes a springboard for research on activism revolving around vocational training in international organizations as well as in other national contexts. Similar to Wolf's chapter, Betti's study confirms that state-socialist Eastern Europe was far from an isolated and insular space. On the contrary, key elements of the politics of women's work traveled across the Cold War divide, shaped discourses, and sustained women's activism on gender and work in Western and Southern European countries and internationally.

The final chapter of Part 1, Büşra Satı's study uses an innovative approach, which is indebted to the anthropological study of labour, to explore how kinship structures facilitated union organization and shaped communal aspects of workers' mobilization in Turkey in the 1960s. Satı analyzes a 1965 strike at the Berec Battery Factory in Istanbul, where mostly young migrant women from the Balkans (Bulgaria and Yugoslavia) as well as rural areas of Turkey worked, as a starting point to understand the role of gendered "fictive kin" in building labour solidarity. Fictive kinship among strikers enabled women workers to engage in labour activism, while labour activism reconfigured the housework and care work they provided for the benefit of their families. Addressing the culture of solidarity-building through familial metaphors and marriage practices in Petrol-İş, (Türkiye Petrol Kimya Lastik İşçileri Sendikası; the Petroleum, Chemical and Rubber Workers' Union of Turkey), this chapter broadens our understanding of what could be called reproductive labour in trade unionism and strike activities—a field that has been studied in the Western European context since the 1980s[116]—while shedding light on paternalism in a Turkish labour union. In this case, examining women's actions within and against a men-dominated context brings to light the important role of women's gendered strategies in advancing working-class interests.

2.2 *Women's Ways of Action: New Perspectives on Repertoires and Agendas*

One of the crucial objectives of the volume, reflected in many of the contributions, is moving women's agendas and demands related to workplace justice from the margins to the center not only of research but of conceptual and historiographic debate. The volume strives to highlight the complexity and interconnectedness of various clusters of demands, addressing women's social and economic inequality in the world of gainful employment within the context of evolving gender and labour regimes. The existing multilingual historiography on women's work covering our region of focus, although valuable, has only rarely captured the full diversity of strategies women's labour activists mobilized to achieve their goals. It has also only partly revealed the nature of engagement with issues of women's work in many different social movements and organizational contexts.

Addressing these lacunae in the scholarship, the chapters in Part 2 of the volume turn to unusual and less studied contexts in which women's labour struggles unfolded; point to the diversity of agendas around women's work; and highlight—following Büşra Satı's chapter (in Part 1)—the rich variety of repertoires of action that women employed to improve the work and life conditions of themselves and others around them.

The first chapter in Part 2, Masha Bratishcheva's analysis of the Women's Publishing Cooperative (Женская издательская артель) in St. Petersburg in the 1860s and 1870s offers insight into the functioning of an enterprise run by the pioneers of the Russian feminist movement. An early women's organization that embodied women's struggle for employment, the Cooperative was highly visible in the public sphere. Examining the demands and the experimental organizational form of the Cooperative, Bratishcheva argues that while not pursuing an explicit agenda related to the struggle for women's rights, the actions of the activists involved in the Cooperative laid the foundation for later generations of activists. Radical Russian women publishers such as those discussed by Bratishcheva helped galvanize the political imaginations of radical socialist women across the region for several decades after their enterprise

116 See, for example, Moriarty 2002.

folded. Thus, in her 1908 pamphlet discussing Russian women radicals in the 1905 revolution, Romanian socialist and labour activist Ecaterina Arbore mentioned the pioneering examples of radical women working as publishers and translators in late 1800s St. Petersburg.[117] Meanwhile, women-only collectives, cooperatives, and trade unions remained an organizational strategy adopted by many leftist or feminist political and practical projects until the 2000s; such structures challenged women's marginalization and oppression by not only addressing their social and economic rights but also applying alternative working models and knowledge distribution. The Hungarian National Association of Women Office Workers (Nőtisztviselők Országos Egyesülete), established in 1897, featured in the chapter by Mátyás Erdélyi discussed above, and the all-Cisleithanian association of women postal workers founded in 1905[118] constitute only two examples of such organizations. It is worth noting, however, that not every group of women workers had the financial means to deal with gender-based discrimination in the professional sphere by establishing a cooperative, as the case of the women printers discussed by Polek in Part 1 shows.

Next, Dóra Fedeles-Czeferner in her chapter on women's labour activism as pursued by and represented in the Austrian and Hungarian liberal and left-liberal feminist press rethinks the established view that this branch of early twentieth-century feminism was mainly concerned with women's suffrage. Analyzing three journals published between the 1900s and 1910s, namely *Woman and Society* (*A Nő és a Társadalom*), *The Woman. A Feminist Journal* (*A Nő. Feminista Folyóirat*), and *New Women's Life* (*Neues Frauenleben*), Fedeles-Czeferner finds that the subject of work, and in particular the discussion and critique of the situation of working women in industry, agriculture, the civil service, and the wider service sector received a great deal of attention. Authors who wrote in these journals not only provided detailed analyses of the poor working conditions and exploitation of women but also offered illuminating insight into how the women's organizations or collectives that published the journals understood the ways that the distinct Austrian and Hungarian historical context shaped (working) women's circumstances. Exploring how specific alignments and intersections of class, gender, and ideology opened spaces for women's labour activism, Fedeles-Czeferner's contribution demonstrates the fruitfulness of reading known sources with fresh eyes, through the prism of work and gender. Read together with Bratishcheva's chapter (introduced above), Fedeles-Czeferner's comparative analysis reveals intra-, trans-, and

117 Arbore-Ralli 1908, 18.

118 See the chapter "Morsé-Zeichen: Post-Front-Post" ("Morse Characters: Postal Services-Troops-Postal Services") in Hacker 1998, 109–119.

postimperial similarities in middle-class progressive women's labour activism. The women in the editorial collectives discussed by both authors creatively interpreted legal frameworks limiting associational life and women's public involvement in the tsarist and Austro-Hungarian empires. There are similarities also in how these women engaged in labour activism, how they worked together, and in what they published. Both Bratishcheva and Fedeles-Czeferner show how these women, in their publication strategies, promoted progressive changes in their respective linguistic spaces by disseminating information on what they considered good, or comparatively better, practices in Western Europe and North America concerning women's access to professions. Unlike the case of the radical Russian women, the non-socialist brand of progressive labour activism espoused by the Hungarian and Austrian women's journals sometimes provoked skepticism from trade unions and socialist women.

In addition to emphasizing the more diverse and distinctive arenas in which educated women engaged in labour activism, several contributors to this volume illuminate how women workers, reacting to the marginalization of their concerns in men-dominated organizations, developed distinctive forms of engagement with trade unions or engaged in union-critical or non-formalized women's labour activism within (and alongside) labour movements. Jan A. Burek's chapter on gender, generation, and labour struggle in the Polish textile city of Żyrardów before and after World War Two is a case in point. Taking a transwar perspective on women's militant labour activism in the textile factories of Żyrardów, Burek shows how, in their pursuit of workplace interests related to wages and work, women workers developed alternative independent working-class cultures beyond (and sometimes within) trade unions, centering on self-organization and direct negotiations with factory management and local authorities. Burek's transgression of the paradigm of World War Two as a historical rupture enables us to see the seemingly nonstrategic tactics of women textile workers in a different light. Shifting from having to deal with conservative authorities in the 1930s to communist-dominated organs in the 1940s, women workers distrusted and were reluctant to act within trade unions; instead, they tapped into interwar repertoires of action. In the early postwar strikes in Żyrardów, an older generation of spinners with experience in prewar labour activism played an important role. The inherited reliance of women workers on self-organization rather than trade union structures helped these women workers insist on self-defined interests and independent action, which in turn explains some of the resilience of labour militancy in the period.

Women's engagements with the state have formed an important area of research in the history of women's activism. Developing new concepts and approaches such as state feminism, femocracy, and feminist institutionalism,

Western feminist researchers have discussed the many ways women participated in policy-making processes despite their frequent and systematic marginalization in formal political structures. For instance, Bereni and Revillard discuss how post-1968 "women's policy agencies" in France worked in conjunction with feminist movements but also—through bureaucracy-specific methods—pursued goals that were not priorities for the non-governmental women's movement (e.g., vocational training).[119] Within state institutions, various forms of labour activist agendas could be pursued, with varying degrees of success. Adding to this growing area of research, the next two chapters in Part 2, authored by Natalia Jarska and Marie Láníková, respectively, show how state-funded agencies as well as state-tolerated "alternative" research on women's working lives emerged in the late 1950s in different state-socialist countries. In her chapter on the equal pay debate in post-1956 Poland, Jarska examines the activities of the Women's Commission of the Central Council of Trade Unions (Komisja Centralna Związków Zawodowych, KCZZ) and a report by the economist and sociologist Janina Waluk to discuss how trade union activists, women experts, and the broader public considered and questioned gender inequalities in the workplace. Conceptualizing knowledge production as a form of activism, Jarska shows how these actors revealed the persistence of wage inequalities in a system that had officially abolished wage discrimination based on gender and which was committed politically to the principle of "equal pay for equal work." Jarska's contribution resonates with the chapters by Wolf and Betti in Part 1 in that it shows how women activists and professionals developed a sophisticated debate on the ways in which questions of, for instance, skill and vocational training related to the definition of unequal pay, and it situates the Polish case vis-à-vis the broader international discussion about (un)equal pay that unfolded after the adoption of the ILO Convention no. 100 on equal remuneration.[120]

Complementing Jarska's contribution on knowledge production and expertise as a significant form of labour struggle in state-socialist regimes, Láníková's chapter investigates how women functionaries, professionals, and activists participated in shaping the politics of women's work in Czechoslovakia in the late 1960s and 1970s. The chapter examines the work of the Czechoslovak Women's Union (Československý svaz žen) regarding women-specific labour protections, paying special attention to change over time, i.e., the union's political negotiation of the changing political context before, during, and after the

119 Bereni and Revillard 2018; Banaszak and Whitesell 2017; Lovenduski 2005; McBride, Stetson, and Mazur 1995.

120 On the key role of labour market segregation in the evolution of the multiscale debate on equal pay and gendered wage justice, see also Jan A. Burek's chapter in this volume.

Prague Spring in 1968. The chapter thereby develops a novel view on the politics of the union and expands our understanding of the complex relationship between women aiming to shape the politics of women's work, policy-making, and the state. The contribution of the chapter to our understanding of women's engagement with the politics of women's work under state socialism is twofold. Pointing to the parallel and intertwined engagement of women professionals with their more independent roles as experts on issues of women's work and the policies of the union, this chapter challenges prevailing views on the character of women's "mass organizations" in state-socialist contexts. It also shows that the politics and activities of these organizations were not simply orchestrated in a top-down manner by the state or the top-level party leadership. In addition, the chapter broadens our understanding of the politics of scale by highlighting how two local branches of the union, in Třebíč and Gottwaldov (present-day Zlín), pursued various social projects in collaboration and constant negotiation with an array of other, often more powerful local actors. At the same time, to achieve their goals, activists in these branches repeatedly referenced the central union and its experts. Láníková's chapter thus serves as a warning against generalizing blanket approaches to analyzing women's labour activism in given national contexts.[121]

Since the 1970s, feminist scholars and labour historians with an interest in the history of working women in the West have published on the questions of social reproduction and reproductive labour as part of their research on capitalist exploitation of the working class. In this way, they also criticized gaps in existing research on labour movements and the working classes.[122] Criticism of men-oriented historiography and political economy was not restricted to the so-called West. As Chiara Bonfiglioli argues, feminist activists in Yugoslavia and East Germany developed "their own specific language vis-à-vis the socialist state" in problematizing women's double burden and the paid-unpaid work divide.[123] In Bulgaria too, women activists successfully pushed the government to allocate resources to build care infrastructure. Yet, as Zhivka Valiavicharska warns, women's activism carried the mark of its time and was deeply entangled in population-management projects and ethnonationalist visions of nationhood. Moreover, it had uneven effects as it left care work largely feminized, even if partly socialized.[124] Since the 2000s, we have witnessed renewed

121 On this point, see also Burek 2017, which points at the differential political agency of women activists on the local and national level.

122 Arruzza 2016; Bhattacharya 2015; Federici 2012; Boris and Lewis 2006; Kessler-Harris 1990; Bock 1989; Laslett and Brenner 1989; Scott 1987.

123 Bonfiglioli 2018, 251.

124 Valiavicharska 2021, 87–88.

attention to the topic of care in the historiography of capitalist and state-socialist countries.[125] Against this background, Masha Shpolberg's chapter encourages us to think of filmmaking as part of labour activism in late socialist Poland. Scrutinizing the work of two Polish filmmakers, Krystyna Gryczełowska (1930–2009) and Irena Kamieńska (1928–2016), who maintained a strong interest in the everyday lives of women workers in state-socialist Poland, this chapter offers a reading of Gryczełowska's and Kamieńska's films in dialogue with the weavers' strike in Łódź in 1970 and the emerging Solidarność movement in 1980. While film has been a medium used widely before (and in other countries) to showcase the gender-specific hardships experienced by working women, Shpolberg's chapter invites us to include it as an important part of critical knowledge production in the state-socialist context, in this case to discuss the working and living conditions of Polish workers. Indeed, as recent research also shows, it was repeatedly filmmakers in (state-)socialist countries such as Poland or Yugoslavia who put the "double burden" of women workers on screen and explored the costs of performing the "second shift" of caring for oneself and others.[126]

Continuing the theme of women's care work, addressed in a growing body of scholarship as a core issue of current historical and sociological debates about the gendered nature of labour,[127] Maren Hachmeister probes the limits of an integrative conceptualization of women's labour struggles. The chapter is based on archival materials from Poland, Czechoslovakia, and the GDR and interviews conducted with care workers from the People's Solidarity (Volkssolidarität), an important social welfare organization in the GDR that survived the regime change and reunification. Hachmeister's account of women's unorganized or only informally organized voluntary work for the elderly during the transition from state socialism to capitalism brings to mind studies that have discussed women's practical grassroots and community engagement as activism based in an alternative ethics of care (aimed at) spreading the seeds of an alternative society.[128] Inviting us to think in terms of the possible continuities and ruptures between the (state-)socialist and postsocialist periods with regard to activist care work, the chapter contributes to recent discussions concerning the reconsideration of the border between activism and non-activism and the inclusion of seemingly non-political acts by marginalized

125 Daskalova and Zimmermann 2017, 288–290.

126 One example is the film *Od 3 do 22* (*From 3 am to 10 pm*) directed by Krešimir Golik in 1966, analyzed in Bonfiglioli 2017.

127 Fraser 2016; Kofman 2012; Benería 2010.

128 Robinson 2011; Naples 1998; Kaplan 1996.

individuals and groups in our understanding of repertoires of action.[129] Similar to the case of Polish textile workers in Żyrardów highlighted in Burek's chapter, the women who undertook care work in the public and private systems of care during the period when formerly state-socialist societies were undergoing transformation (which had dramatic consequences for social welfare systems) had been involved in voluntary yet systematic mobilization of unpaid care work within social welfare organizations long before the system change. Considering this continuity of women's welfare activism, and thus gendering our thinking about the systemic change, alters our perception of welfare and activism in both the pre- and post-transformation periods.

2.3 *Activist Travels through Changing Political Landscapes: The Uses of Life Histories*

In her study of Emma Goldman's archives, Clare Hemmings reminds us that writing the stories of women activists is bound together with "processes of identification and projection" and is "productive of its own passionate political desires."[130] For scholars of state-socialist women's organizations such as Kristen Ghodsee, biographical writing and the recovery of Bulgarian activists' life stories are essential for overcoming post-Cold War historiographical erasures enacted within the history of global feminism, partly in the hope of helping renew left-feminist political imaginations in the Global North.[131] Writing biographies could thus be a good exercise in self-reflexivity. Why historians decide to write about individuals, how they relate to their subjects, and how they deal with the complexities of writing such histories have remained relevant questions in debates about the genre of historical biography. The increasing interest in works with a distinct biographical focus—as we discussed in the previous section—is reflected in the third and final part of the volume.

Part 3 of this volume is centered on the life and activism of socialist and intellectual women who challenged women's subordination in local and border-crossing contexts. These women sought gender justice through their individual or collective involvement in leftist or feminist political and practical projects. In this section, the three authors whose chapters focus on individuals offer valuable insights into the history of women's labour activism in Central and Eastern Europe through the lens of women activists' lives of struggle.

Jean-Pierre Liotard-Vogt's chapter on Anna Kéthly (1889–1976) brings to the fore the theme of the multiple engagements of women's labour activists.

---

129 See Archer 2022; Arik et al. 2022.

130 Hemmings 2018, 2–3.

131 Ghodsee 2019.

Kéthly was a Hungarian politician and trade unionist and a life-long Marxist social democrat. While remaining committed to the same core agendas, she nevertheless adapted her identity and activist focus to the changing historical and personal circumstances as she went into exile in Belgium as the single-party system was established in post-1945 Hungary. In exile, she engaged with the Western European trade union movement and diasporic anticommunist politics. Liotard-Vogt offers a careful reading of Kéthly's life-path, uncovering how a self-identified socialist transgressed the often narrowly defined class allegiances advocated by many within the labour movement—an ideological and political heterodoxy that can be observed among other socialist-identified women of her generation. Kéthly's fight for equal pay and women workers' rights resonated with the program of not only social democracy but also liberal feminism. The fight for women's social and economic rights was a focal point in her political career and permeated her other diverse political interests. The chapter shows how approaching a woman labour activist's multiple engagements may help us rethink movement divides and write more nuanced gender and labour histories. Liotard-Vogt's chapter also reflects two of the threads running through different parts of the volume that help advance new historicizations and conceptualizations of women's labour activism. First, similar to Fedeles-Czeferner's and Erdélyi's chapters discussed above, Liotard-Vogt's contribution demonstrates the connections and interactions between various social movements and their agendas regarding women's work. Women active in the labour, women's, and left-wing political movements pursued issues of gender and work in a variety of contexts and within a large range of competing yet interconnected institutional and ideological frameworks. Second, similar to Burek's and Hachmeister's contributions, this chapter bridges the historiographical divide between different periods. Showing how the broad-scope, multi-layered, and international character of Kéthly's political engagement was present already in the interwar period, when she simultaneously nurtured multiple relationships with nonsocialist women's organizations, the chapter highlights the continuities and ruptures between the interwar and the Cold War periods from the perspective of activist women.

Taking the reader to a working-class neighborhood in the 1930s and 1940s Milwaukee, Wisconsin, Eric Fure-Slocum's chapter explores the dynamics of migration, class, gender, and race in a U.S. industrial city. In his micro-historical study, Fure-Slocum places the antiracist and antifascist activism of Nada Hudson, née Goldner (1922–2015), born to Croatian parents with a Jewish paternal grandmother, within the context of workplace-related and neighborhood-based social and activist networks that transgressed racial and ethnic divides. His findings expand our understanding of multiethnic labour-left antiracist egalitarianism in the 1930s and 1940s. Fure-Slocum's chapter is one of those in the volume that engages with the transnational circulation of knowledge and practices related to women's work and labour activism, thus addressing a gap in research on women's labour transnationalism with roots in or connections to the region.[132] Emphasizing the interwar circulation of radical political practices between Eastern Europe and North America and their effects on the postwar political engagement of a woman with a migration background, the chapter offers an in-depth analysis and interpretation of historical contexts and various factors including family alignments and transnational connections that influence individual choices and shape activism.

Concluding Part 3 and the volume, Georg Spitaler's chapter offers an emotion-historical and epistemological reading of the letters of the Austrian socialist and resistance fighter Hilde Krones (1910–1948). Examining Krones's relation to the labour movement and dissecting factors that influenced her personal and political choices, Spitaler demonstrates that for Krones, the struggle for gender equality included the private, the political, and the economic spheres as her socialist conception of women's emancipation remained grounded in advocacy for paid labour and financial independence. Joining the chapters by Burek, Hachmeister, and Liotard-Vogt which bridge different historical periods, Spitaler transgresses the political ruptures of 1934, 1938, and 1945 in Austria and provides insight into the activities of socialist women in the interwar period and the immediate aftermath of World War Two. An important contribution of the chapter lies in its presentation of Krones's multiple inner struggles, which help us better understand why historical actors used what appear at first glance to be unusual and ideologically unacceptable language, references, and concepts. Offering a type of analysis that is rarely found in historical writing, the chapter emphasizes the importance of the life history perspective for understanding contemporary leftist political projects and calls for further self-reflexivity in biographical writing.

3 Toward a Long-Term and Transregional, Integrative, and Critical Approach

Taken together, the contributions in this volume and the historiography reviewed in the first section of this introductory chapter bring to light a wide

132 See Dyakonova's, Nešťáková's, Wolf's, and Betti's chapters in the first section, Fedeles-Czeferner's chapter in the second, and Liotard-Vogt's chapter in this section.

spectrum of agendas, organizational forms, strategies, and scales of action working women and women activists and professionals of many political persuasions adopted in their struggles for the improvement of the position of working women and their communities and women's social and economic rights. The scholarship reviewed and this volume demonstrate that we can unearth an amazing array of political, practical, and professional engagement with issues of women's work when we analyze the thinking, writing, and action of women's collectives and organizations, women in men-dominated contexts, and individual women through the prism of gender and work. In dialogue with the existing scholarship, this volume invites us to begin to synthesize our knowledge on the history of women's labour struggles from a *long-term, transregional, integrative*, and *critical* perspective, with a view to capturing its historical variety and transformation within and across different political contexts and systems. The volume opens opportunities to reshape the historiographical topography of women's and workers' movements and put women's multiple labour struggles in and connected to Central and Eastern Europe on the global map of gender and labour history.

3.1 *Long-Term and Transregional*

In this section, we discuss the uses of a long-term and transregional—i.e., cross-border, cross-regional and transnational—approach to the history of women's labour struggles. In our cooperative research project ZARAH, we pursue a transregional perspective by looking at the vast Eastern European contact zone between the Russian, Habsburg, and Ottoman empires and the successor states of these empires. We aim to not isolate this space but to relate it to other world regions and to establish the chronology and cartography of women's labour activism in the region and explore its involvement in transnational social movements and organizations. Viewed through the prism of women's labour activism, some of the established caesuras shaping the historiography of Eastern Europe are recast as rather artificial temporal divisions. Women's labour struggles transgressed historical ruptures, and women engaged with historical contexts and change in a gendered manner. Putting their struggles at the center of the story thus contributes to gendering our knowledge of the long-term history of the region. Chapters in this volume, engagement with earlier scholarship, and insights from our own research help us construct a regionally specific historical arc, starting in the 1860s, when the labour movement crystallized in Europe, and ending in the 1990s, when changes in political and/or economic regimes and the end of the Cold War signaled a new phase of globalization.

The advantage of employing a combined long-term and transregional perspective when studying women's gendered labour struggles is that it allows scholars to trace continuity and change in women's labour activism through and across different empires and nation-states. This helps move the state of the art beyond the conceptual limitations of the study of women's labour activism that result from inward-looking perspectives on the history of singular imperial territories, their "national components," or the succeeding nation-states (e.g., Austria versus Hungary, or the Habsburg versus the Ottoman Empire) as well as from simplifying siloed approaches to political regimes (e.g., democracy versus state socialism). Our motivation in pursuing a long-term and transregional approach comes from our interest in grounding the history of women's labour activism in the lived reality and social history of working women and men, histories which involved migration and population exchanges, as well as transnational influence and collaboration. Several scholars have highlighted the social, political, and epistemic constructedness of regions and explored the changing definitions of "Eastern Europe" through different epochs and the political motivations that informed them.[133] They have pointed out how representations of "Eastern Europe" included, for example, the European parts of the Ottoman Empire or excluded the Russian Empire altogether.[134] Yet, beyond dominant regionalizing constructs, workers and workers' movements are "linked to each other by the world scale division of labour and global political process."[135] Therefore, historical trends in women's labour activism should be seen as playing out on a broad, historically changing global stage. Combining a focus on Central and Eastern Europe with the study of its adjacent, historically connected lands helps capture phenomena which have historically transcended or pertained only to subregions of today's seemingly self-evident Central and Eastern European space. Such an analytical shift can foster research questions and comparisons veiled precisely by the unproblematized adoption of regional constructions.[136]

133 Kraft 2018; Mamadouh and Müller 2017; Schenk 2017.

134 Schenk 2017.

135 Silver 2003, 26.

136 For instance, by including in this volume case studies that deal with Austrian and Turkish postwar women's labour activism and communist-led internationalist activism in Italy alongside papers on activism within state socialism, we seek to foster reflection on change and continuity in women's labour activism in postimperial Europe. Such reflection is also necessary when considering the interconnected development of labour movements in the Russian Empire, the Austro-Hungarian Empire, and the Ottoman Empire in Central and Eastern Europe between the 1860s and the end of World War One and their postimperial repercussions.

What kind of insights, then, can a long-term and transregional approach bring? Compared to the available research on the post-1945 period, up-to-date research on women's labour struggles from the late nineteenth century to World War Two is scant regarding most of the countries covered in this volume. Also, there is comparatively little research on the transnational advocacy of women from this region for better living and working conditions for themselves and their communities. Still, considering the emerging research, including contributions assembled in this volume and our own (ongoing) research,[137] we can share several insights into the history of women's labour struggles across the region.

From the nineteenth century onward, women's labour activism in the region was marked by the circulation of activist practices in the empires dominating the region and across their porous borders. As highlighted in the previous section, political radicalism in the Russian Empire around 1905 as well as suffrage politics and labour organizing around the same time in Austria-Hungary shaped the practices and demands of women workers in Romania and Bulgaria. Across the whole region, including the Ottoman Empire, women workers' demands for better pay and working conditions were supported by anarchist and socialist movements whose transnational ties stretched across imperial Russia and the Balkans. At the same time, women's involvement in social movements in imperial contexts was often deeply entangled with nationalist causes and shaped by divisions along ethno-religious lines.[138] Recent scholarship has stressed the "transnational phenomenon" of protest culture marked by the revolutionary events in Russia and a European strike wave that began in 1905 and stretched well into the aftermath of World War One, a wave that combined labour unrest with socio-economic protest and demands for political sovereignty in the form of suffrage, national independence, and an alternative social order.[139]

Within this cycle of protest, the 1900s and 1910s were a period of upswing in women's labour activism throughout our region. This activism occurred in or was supported by a growing number of workers' associations and local socialist organizations. It took place across a wide range of sectors in which women workers were represented in higher proportions such as the textile and tobacco industries. The strongly agrarian and agro-industrial character of many lands

137 In addition to the individual papers of ZARAH team members under review, cited elsewhere in this introduction, the ZARAH team has recently published a journal special issue; for the introduction see Ghiţ et al. 2023.

138 Yılmaz 2021; Konstantinova 2018; Tunçay and Zürcher 1994; Balkanski 1982.

139 Stibbe et al. 2022, 18.

in the region put a specific stamp on this cycle, and this is necessarily reflected in our thinking about the patterns of labour-related activism. For instance, in Hungary, a country where strongly commodified, large-scale agrarian export production involving masses of landless or nearly landless workers constituted a leading sector of the economy, women's agrarian socialist labour organizing and activism reached back into the early 1890s, as demonstrated in Eszter Varsa's research.[140] Peasant women's labour activism in 1890s Hungary inserts a new periodization and a new geography into the established conceptualization of the European history of women's social movements. Strikes involving large numbers of women workers, for instance in the textile and tobacco industries, were recorded already in the 1890s, but it was between 1903 and 1906 when more stable and formalized urban-based socialist women workers' associations, including one for domestic workers, were established in Hungary. The socialist women workers' movement then became very active and faced many challenges simultaneously, including the intense competition with paternalistic middle-class women's activism regarding domestic servants, tensions with men-dominated trade unionism in the textile industry, and the radicalism of unorganized or newly organized industrial and domestic workers.[141] Alexandra Ghiţ's investigation of a 1911 strike of women workers employed in a state-owned tobacco factory in the Transylvanian city of Kolozsvár (Cluj-Napoca, present-day in Romania) shows how state institutions and the paternalist industrial practices they promoted shaped women's labour activism in the Kingdom of Hungary. During the 1911 Kolozsvár labour conflict, well-organized tobacco women, who were backed by local socialists, presented themselves in the local press as ideal—humble, charitable—employees of a paternalist institution and cast the factory director as a manager who did not live up to his claim of treating workers with fatherly benevolence.[142]

During World War One in our predominantly agrarian region of focus, the degree of women's participation in the industrial "home front" and its impact on labour activism differed across more and less industrialized areas. For example, whereas in the more-industrialized Czech lands, there was an upsurge in women's participation in labour activism during the war,[143] in the less-industrialized Ottoman Empire, the increase in women's participation in industrial production was minimal since only Muslim men were allowed

140 Varsa (under review).

141 Zimmermann 1999, Chapters 2.d and 5.c; Réti 1980, Chapters 2 and 3; Fonó 1975; Aranyossi 1963.

142 Ghiţ (under review, a).

143 See the section "Rationed Manliness: The Politics of Gender" in Kučera 2016, 94–129.

to go to war and non-Muslim men replaced them in industrial jobs.[144] At the same time, in countries like Austria,[145] Russia,[146] Bulgaria,[147] Romania,[148] and Hungary,[149] women took the lead in some elements of wartime protest such as hunger riots. Overall, the impact of the 1917 Bolshevik revolution and the wave of social and political unrest that accompanied the fall of the Central and Eastern European empires set the stage for women's increased political participation in the newly formed states and in many social movements. The revolutionary transformation phase of the late 1910s and early 1920s offered an opportunity for radical and reform-oriented socialist women alike, as showcased by Daria Dyakonova's chapter in this volume.

During the interwar period, women's involvement in social movements was increasingly internationalized but ideologically divided. Central and Eastern European women were active in a number of international arenas such as the Comintern, the Profintern, the International Federation of Trade Unions, the Labour and Socialist International, the International Co-operative Women's Guild, as well as the ILO (particularly its Correspondence Committee on Women's Work). By the mid-1930s, women from Eastern Europe were better and more steadily represented in international labour politics.[150] This development was interrupted by the authoritarian tendencies of the interwar governments and (later) the fascist regimes taking root in these lands, but the developments of the 1930s foreshadowed a long-term trend that fully manifested itself after 1945.

At the same time, the advent of the global economic crisis and the increasing push toward rationalization and mechanization in various industrial sectors marked the beginning of a new cycle of women's labour unrest in the late 1920s and the 1930s. Worldwide, the globalization of mechanized textile production generated intense competitive pressures, resulting in a wave of (women's) labour militancy.[151] The introduction of Taylorist, Fordist, and other models of "scientific management" and labour organization brought issues of increased managerial control, overwork, precarity, and deskilling to the forefront of labour movements' agendas. Optimizing production costs often involved

---

144 Karakışla 2015, 59.
145 Helfert 2021, Chapters 3–5.
146 See, for example, Kaplan 1987.
147 Dimitrova 2018a, 2018b.
148 Ghiț (under review, b).
149 Varsa 2023; Ignácz 2020; Zalai 2017a, 2017b.
150 Ghiț 2021; Zimmermann 2021, esp. 179–181, 206–208, 222–223; Lazitch and Drachkovitch 1986; Popova (under review).
151 Silver 2003, 89–93.

increasing the proportion of (cheaper) women workers in the labour force, making the issue of rationalization a highly gendered one. Organized labour displayed ambivalent attitudes toward rationalization's gendered aspects, including the rhetorical defense of all members of the working class and the simultaneous promotion of the male breadwinner ideal.[152] Communists were among the fiercest opponents of rationalization and in the late 1920s and early 1930s, Comintern and Profintern resolutions explicitly linked the fight against rationalization with organizing work among women workers.[153] In Bulgaria, the issue featured high on official communist women's agenda and was routinely present in agitation materials, periodicals, and in International Women's Day's events starting in the early 1930s.

In hindsight, the 1930s signaled the coming of an altogether different period. In the domestic context, in many lands represented in this volume and studied in framework of the ZARAH project, the increased repression of left-wing social movements changed women's modes of engagement in labour activism. Clandestine activism, the move of women aligned with now-illegal communist parties into trade unions,[154] and, from the middle of the 1930s, Popular Front politics changed both the agendas and repertoires of action as communist women activists joined (bourgeois-liberal) women's organizations, cooperatives, trade unions, and cultural associations and aimed to expand their role in these organizations.[155]

The occupation of large parts of Central and Eastern Europe by the National Socialist Third Reich and the ensuing politics of persecution and extermination had an immediate and profound impact on the lives of labour activists and women workers. Many (but by far not all) of the surviving left-wing women activists became ardent supporters of the newly emerging state-socialist regimes. The state-socialist system, while definitely constituting a sharp political and socio-economic historical rupture, must also be conceived of as both an important phase in the long-term historical development of the Eastern European region and a regional variety of a larger transregional post-1945 trend. During the Cold War period, activists who included working women's problems on their agenda concentrated—to varying degrees—on shaping state politics and state-led policies on women's work. Many (but not all) activists in the region now acted within states, which dramatically expanded their

152 Frader 2008, 139; Masheva (forthcoming).

153 Lozovskii 1930, 215–222.

154 Bujaković 2021.

155 For Popular Front tactics in Bulgaria, see Vodenicharova and Popova 1972, 172–181; for Yugoslavia, see Grubački 2020.

(bureaucratic) capacities and ambitions. Ulf Brunnbauer has argued that the Eastern European state-socialist system with its "developmental state" aiming to facilitate economic catch-up policies was part of "a larger story of etatism in the region." In other words, this was not a state-socialist particularity but an all-European post-1945 trend toward more inclusive social and economic policies facilitated by a strong state. From this perspective, the period of state socialism can be considered "as a kind of climax of the Eastern European state."[156]

The long-term history of women workers' engagement with state-led industrialization and related paternalist politics directed at women workers, as showcased in the 1911 tobacco strike in Kolozsvár mentioned above, deserves more attention in future research. Seen from the perspective of labour struggles, the historical rupture marking the creation of the state-socialist regimes, as well as the prolonged period of transition reaching back to the 1930s, possessed a distinctly gendered character. Mark Pittaway has argued for Hungary and Adrian Grama and Alina Cucu for Romania that in the early state-socialist period, an older generation of skilled men workers, building on their traditions and power on the shop floor, were able to resist as well as accommodate the reorganization of wage systems and production processes by bargaining with lower management and trade union functionaries.[157] Jan A. Burek's case study of a Polish industrial town presented in this volume complements these findings, demonstrating that labour unrest in the late 1940s and early 1950s built on women workers' (not always freely chosen) distance from organized labour inherited from the 1930s. Pittaway and Mária Schadt also show how in Hungary, men workers were not simply hostile toward incoming young women workers; they proactively marginalized them on the shop floor.[158]

The engagement of women trade unionists, activists, and professionals with the state-socialist politics of women's work, documented in this volume in the chapters by Natalia Jarska and Marie Láníková, arose in contrast to these experiences, which characterized the early years of state socialism. These women's action targeted integrating—and accommodating—the growing women labour force into the industrialization drive orchestrated by the state; mitigating gendered discrimination on the shop floor, in wage systems, and in vocational training; and tempering the tensions between women's paid and unpaid labour.[159] The state-oriented labour activism of women who aligned with state-socialist institutions was strongly variegated in terms of level and

156 Brunnbauer 2022. For a discussion on etatism in the Turkish context, see Birtek 1985.
157 Cucu 2019, esp. Chapter 5; Grama 2019; Pittaway 2014, esp. Chapter 3.
158 Schadt 2003.
159 See, for example, Tešija 2014. See also Zimmermann 2023b, 2020a.

degree, but all in all, it was a characteristic feature of the state-socialist politics of women's work. Below we discuss how this activism can be analyzed in a critical manner.

At the same time, from a transregional perspective, the Turkish Kemalist and the Austrian corporatist states of the Cold War period displayed characteristics that are in some ways comparable to developments in the world of Eastern European state socialism. In both countries, we see party, trade union, and activist women concerned with working women's labour issues engaging with the state in a distinct manner. In the Turkish case, different groups of activists collaborated with the state to shape the policies that regulated women's work. As Selin Çağatay's research shows, from the 1950s until the 1980s, Kemalist women's organizations, in their encounters with the state, advocated for women's greater inclusion in formal employment as a mode of emancipation. Women organized in the Republican People's Party (Cumhuriyet Halk Partisi) demanded early retirement for women in recognition of their unpaid work at home, while women in the Confederation of Turkish Trade Unions (Türk-İş—Türkiye İşçi Sendikaları Konfederasyonu) called for vocational training for women in the many meetings organized by or in collaboration with governmental institutions (e.g., ministries), which they attended as representatives of women workers.[160] In Yugoslavia, Turkey, and Austria from the 1970s onward, feminist women disenchanted with state-led women's policies mobilized for women's self-organizing apart from and against the state in order to address, among other things, working women's issues. While these developments were in tune with and formed part of the border-crossing emergence of the "second wave" feminist movement, they had distinctive traits in these countries. Veronika Helfert's research brings to light a specific triangle of activist interaction and entanglement between feminist, (state-oriented) social democratic, and communist women with unmistakable repercussions for the politics of women's work in the period.[161] The history of the involvement of these women in multiple negotiations of gendered socio-economic rights disrupts inherited understandings of post-1945 Austria as a capitalist society and its corporatist state as devoid of large-scale political conflict. It also demonstrates that

---

160 On state-oriented women's activism in Kemalist women's organizations and the Republican People's Party, see Çağatay 2017, esp. 108–149. On parallels between Kemalist and state-socialist women's organizations, see Çağatay 2022; on trade union women's engagement in decision-making processes at the state level, see Çağatay 2023; on Kemalist women's advocacy of working women's rights in the 1950s, see Sarıtaş and Şahin Akıllı 2015.

161 Helfert (under review).

women's combined state-oriented and social movement-based activism contributed to bringing about important changes in the gendered politics of work from the late 1960s until the 1980s.

As for the pronounced role of women from the region in international labour politics and the role of women active in the world of communist(-led) and state-socialist activism and policy-making, recent research, including chapters published in the present volume, has begun to show the relevance of the demand for "equal pay" in shaping these engagements. In the long view, the transformation of the demand for "equal pay" for women into a multifarious "full equality" issue[162] is exemplary for women's engagement in labour activism.

Starting in the late nineteenth century, women activists successfully transformed the demand for equal pay from a shrewd slogan into a genuine wage justice issue.[163] Determination and strategic thinking were needed to bring about this transformation. Initially, "equal pay" was often a demand used to curtail the influx of cheap women workers into occupations dominated by men. Mátyás Erdélyi's contribution shows that in early-twentieth-century Central Europe, (men-dominated) organizations that represented the interests of white-collar workers advocated for equal pay or at least a predetermined pay scale for both sexes (somewhat) pro-actively to counteract the "undercutting" of wages. At the same time, they left proactive engagement in politics of promoting women clerks' professional education to associations of women clerks and openly neglected the specific issues of women clerks such as the marriage ban and gender discrimination in company and pension benefits. This implies that their interest in the full equality of women clerks, i.e., in promoting a degendered labour market for women and men clerks, was limited at best.

In interwar Bulgaria, as Ivelina Masheva's research shows, organized labour displayed a wide range of competing and often ambivalent visions of gendered wage justice. Corporatist state-backed unions of the late 1930s were the most conservative, upholding gender-segregated labour markets and (wider) gendered pay gaps in collective bargaining. On the one hand, these unions, resembling fascist and national-socialist trade union models, entertained the idea of equal pay only as a tool to curb the influx of cheap women's labour; yet, they also fought to bring the lowest wage tiers (where women were disproportionally represented) up to par with the increasing cost of living. Communists, on the other hand, displayed a more ambivalent attitude that is best understood

162 Cobble 2021.

163 For a discussion of the extant research on Western and Central European countries, see Zimmermann 2021, 34–49.

by taking into account the different scales of action (local, national, and international). The official gender politics of international communism included demands for equal pay, paid maternity leave, and better working conditions that were far-reaching when compared to the demands advanced by other actors at the time. However, these progressive policies sometimes stood in stark contrast to the conservative attitudes of rank-and-file men activists fighting for a breadwinner family wage and against women's access to skilled and better-remunerated positions.[164]

During the Cold War period, the ambiguity of engagement with the equal pay issue took a back seat in the debates about and policies addressing this key demand of women labour activists. The demand had already gained traction in (women's circles within) the international socialist[165] and communist labour movements—as documented in Daria Dyakonova's chapter—in the 1920s. It was only in the immediate post-World War Two period that practical, overarching, and international action gained momentum, particularly with the adoption of the landmark ILO Convention on equal remuneration no. 100 in 1951. The role of the labour movement and women's activism in this important step forward in the struggle for gendered wage justice and its aftermath have been studied so far with a focus on the "free" trade unions and activists of the West and Global South; but there have been only a few efforts to integrate Eastern European and state-socialist perspectives into the history of this struggle.[166] The chapters in the present volume authored by Eloisa Betti, Natalia Jarska, and Johanna Wolf point to the growing and increasingly professionalized engagement of activist women involved in communist-led organizations with the politics of equal pay in several national contexts and internationally. Their contributions add to our knowledge of the important role of the international encounters and contributions of women identifying with communist politics in bringing about the transformation of "equal pay" from a slogan into a genuine demand for wage justice.

3.2 *Integrative and Critical*

Some of the novelty and significance of this volume is due to its integrative framing of working women's struggles. By an integrative approach we mean, and develop further below, an expansive approach to women's labour activism, the issues women tackled in this activism (for example, not only wage work but

164 Laskova 1974; Masheva (forthcoming).

165 Zimmermann 2021, Chapter 4.

166 Neunsinger 2018; for the latter (i.e., exceptions), see Cobble 2021; Boris, Hoehtker, and Zimmermann 2018, 94–120.

also unpaid work or sexual violence), and the social movements and spaces in which it took place (for example, neighborhoods or state-backed women's organizations). An integrative approach also means making women's labour activism a core part of the history of social movements rather than a side issue that deviates from "standard" activism dominated by men or women's activism dominated by middle-classs women. To this end, many chapters in this volume mobilize new historical sources, while others offer innovative re-readings of previously known and analyzed materials. Taken as a whole, these contributions draw our attention to the full spectrum of women's work and labour activism from the second half of the nineteenth century until after the Cold War. They expand what we know about women's labour struggles within and beyond the region, invite new questions, and contribute to the ongoing and steadily growing scholarly debate.

We argue that, conceptually speaking, an integrative approach is necessary to capture the full variety of women's labour struggles. First, this is because women's labour struggles always involved class and gender issues simultaneously—and often addressed other elements of socio-cultural difference and conflict. It is for this reason that we find women's labour struggles in highly diverse social movement contexts. To capture this variety, we need historical writing that does not prioritize class over gender or gender over class issues but integrates the study of various social movement contexts. Second, as this volume amply demonstrates, women's labour struggles often involved gendered modes of action. To have a comprehensive view of these modes of action, we need to overcome masculinist modes of defining the political and expand the very concept of what constitutes activism in the first place.

We can develop such an integrative conceptualization of women's labour struggles with the help of three distinct levels of scholarly engagement. First, we must reconsider, i.e., integrate, sources that might not seem directly related to or relevant for women's labour activism at first glance. When we mentioned that different types of sources from very diverse contexts could be creatively used to discuss women's labour activism to our colleagues who attended the "Women's Labour Activism in Eastern Europe and Beyond" conference, this was an invitation to "re-work" some of the sources available (despite the closure of many archives and libraries during the COVID-19 pandemic) so as to bring about new insights and enable us to "think together" different contexts to integrate them into a cohesive whole. Second, we need to look at "all" kinds of women's social action that sought to improve the position of working women and their communities and advance women's social and economic rights, with a view to establish how they—and how many—engaged with issues related to gender and work in a way that was hitherto underestimated and understudied in different scholarly traditions. Third, we need to make use of and, again, "think together" (as discussed in the first section of this chapter) a large variety of literatures. We should engage with such scholarship even when some of it has reproduced rather than questioned both the historical divides between different social movements and masculinist concepts of what constitutes the political. The contributions to this volume as well as our own research indeed demonstrate that women pursued their struggles not only in a wide variety of social movement organizations but also in various non-formalized settings. To achieve their goals, they expanded the inherited spaces and repertoires of action available to them. For instance, they acted as self-organized entrepreneurs or public commentators calling for action on working women's issues (Bratishcheva and Fedeles-Czeferner in this volume) or attached new social meanings to seemingly trivial types of activities (Hachmeister in this volume). They also engaged with the state from within, through organizations that were—more or less closely—aligned with states (Jarska and Láníková in this volume) and through international authorities.

When conceptualizing women's labour struggles in an integrative manner, it is important to bear in mind the risks of indiscriminately considering "everything" as constitutive of women's labour activism. It is also important to be aware of the dangers of uncritically approaching the various trends in and types of women's labour struggles. In this volume, we deliberately aimed to bring together contributions that would analyze women's labour struggles in all their historical diversity, to go beyond modes of analysis that have left this diversity under-researched—much like a woman scientist aiming to draw new conclusions would diffract light through a prism to analyze the beam's full spectrum. The contributions, while united by a large common theme, are heterogenous in terms of why and how they discuss the various threads and instances of women's (and sometimes men's) engagement with women's work as a form of struggle or activism. We are convinced that open-ended collaborative efforts resulting in a volume such as this one are an important means of moving the field forward and promoting its integration and visibility in the larger realms of labour and gender history.[167]

167 We have also generated, and continue to develop, the database ZARAH DB, a collection of research data and reproductions of original documents on the broad theme of *Women's Labour Activism in Eastern Europe and Internationally from the Age of Empires to the 1990s*, https://zarah-ceu.org/zarah-db/; have invited colleagues to contribute to our ZARAH Guest Blog Series, https://zarah-ceu.org/blog/; and aim to support and publicize research on the broad theme discussed in this volume in a variety of other ways.

At the same time, we believe that through collaboration and engagement with each other's work, we can promote a *new socio-political history* of women's labour activism that examines women's labour struggles through a critical lens. Collaboration helps overcome three inclinations that are often found in the early phases of establishing new fields in social movement history, namely empiricism (without a sophisticated interpretation), limited contextualization, and a celebratory tendency. This is not to say that the historiography of women's labour struggles can or should simply bypass the recuperative effort. Without significantly expanding our empirical knowledge, we cannot move the field forward. We also acknowledge that the sympathies of women's and gender historians toward the agendas and actions of women in the past have been an important driving force behind the recuperative effort of restoring both history to women—by denaturalizing women's inferior status in society—and women to history—by considering women as agents in the making of history.[168]

Still, we argue that the historiographical and conceptual discussions on women's struggles for the improvement of women's social and economic rights and the position of working women and their communities in the region studied in this volume should move beyond recuperative efforts. We consider this to be particularly necessary for the debate on "women's agency" in the state-socialist countries of Central and Eastern Europe as well as the communist-aligned international organizations that flourished during the period. In this debate, those working within the "feminist revisionist paradigm" have associated scholarship indebted to the "totalitarian" model with "ongoing Cold War paradigms," pointing to the undeniable fact that anticommunism has played an important role in devaluing anything women did under state socialism.[169] Indeed, some of the scholarship inclined toward the "totalitarian" or, to put it more bluntly, the anticommunist model has denied women the status of being historical agents in state-socialist contexts unless they confronted and directly challenged the state-socialist system. This anticommunist model, in fact, reverberated with how mainstream historical scholarship treated women and their activism before women's and gender historians restored women to history. It also suffered from biases—similar to those in old-school imperial and colonial histories—which have resulted in ignoring, marginalizing, and/or

168 On these two key moves, see Kelly-Gadol 1976.

169 De Haan 2010. A good introduction to the debate in English is the "Forum" published in 2016 with contributions by Francisca de Haan (as editor), Chiara Bonfiglioli, Krassimira Daskalova, Alexandra Ghiţ, Kristen Ghodsee, Magdalena Grabowska, Jasmina Lukić and Raluca Maria Popa, see De Haan 2016.

devaluing the actions and perspectives of non-Western populations, deeming them irrelevant for the course of history. In return, some of the "feminist revisionist" scholarship aimed at restoring "agency" to women living and acting in state-socialist contexts, has, not without reason, been characterized as celebratory.[170] From the perspective of a critical history of women's labour activism, both the "totalitarian" and much of the "feminist revisionist" scholarship, we argue, can indeed be characterized as lacking full historical contextualization and a fully reflective analysis of women's activism in these state-socialist contexts and communist-aligned movement organizations more generally. The take of some of the "feminist revisionist" scholarship on women's action and agency under state socialism can be characterized as having much in common with the classical recuperative women's history and with scholarship glorifying social movement history.

It is against the combined backgrounds outlined above that we advocate for an integrative and critical approach to the history of women's labour activism. This approach helps put into perspective the debate on women's activism under state socialism and calls for a more contextualized and critical stance. With this approach, we join an emergent cluster of scholarship that goes beyond the "feminist revisionist" tendency by fully including the study of political problem zones and the historical shortcomings of these activisms.[171] We argue, in other words, that while insisting on the historical relevance of women's activism in state-socialist contexts (just as the "feminist revisionist" scholarship does), we should think in a conceptually and historically specific manner about these activisms. We must conceive of this activism as an important dimension of an enlarged, global constellation of activisms and as integral to the global history of women's activism—all currents of which should be analyzed critically. This can be done, we suggest, by developing our analyses with reference to three key sets of historical circumstances.

First, we need to build our analysis on a clear delineation of the type of state (political system) a specific type of women's labour activism developed in and with whom and what much of this activism interacted, whether in closer or looser alignment. When building such an analysis, it is important to not lose sight of the state as part of a global typology of political systems. The state-socialist political system differed markedly from the (idealized) political constitution of the Western world. In state socialism, civic social movements were largely absent while the state claimed to embody the interests of the working

170 In her blurb on the back of Kristen Ghodsee's *Second World, Second Sex* (2019), historian Maria Bucur writes that Ghodsee "makes visible and celebrates" these actors.

171 Recent examples in English include Donert 2022; Todorova 2021; Valiavicharska 2021.

class, including the interests of working women. This stood in contradistinction to non-socialist states, at least in the earlier decades of the Cold War era. At the same time, despite its claim to represent women's quest for emancipation, the state-socialist state was also a deeply masculinist one, and it sustained and reproduced the masculinist traditions of the labour movement. It also commanded limited material resources, many of which it reserved for economic catch-up policies within the global capitalist-dominated economy.

Put in the larger, global perspective, when determining the structural conditions of women's power to act, it is important to consider the place that different types of states, including classical bourgeois, social/democratic, colonial, and state-socialist, allotted to the vision and practice of emancipation for women belonging to lower social stratas.[172] The state-socialist regime—the far-reaching qualifications and limitations just mentioned notwithstanding—was, we claim, relatively more open to and keen on considering working women's issues. This was an important factor that contributed to the willingness of women who identified with working women's problems to closely engage with this state. The fact that the state-socialist period can be regarded as "the climax of the Eastern European state" further undergirded this tendency. In the second half of the twentieth century, women not only in Eastern Europe but also in countries like Turkey and Austria regarded the expansive state as a privileged site through which to pursue their agendas of socio-economic improvement for women. Thus, research on women's social and political action to improve the lot of working women in the Eastern European state-socialist context should consider these historically specific conditions of women's activism when developing a critical analysis of its character in terms of both its involvement with a non-democratic political system and its agendas, achievements, and failures.

Second, and moving on to the study of specific cases of such activisms, we need to explore more thoroughly the determining factors and political dynamics that shaped women's (labour) activism within the expansive and layered state-socialist political system. How exactly were women functionaries, women experts and professionals, women trade unionists at every level (from the shop floor to the highest reaches of government), and ordinary working women—women so variably positioned in a diverse network of political actors—involved in formal and informal processes of decision making? Which rights did national women's committees, factory-based shop stewards, and many other groups of activists, functionaries, and institutions involved with

172 Zimmermann 2021, 681–686.

the politics of women's work acquire, and to what extent were they able to exercise these rights? What material resources did they command, and what was the scope of possibilities available to them when using these material resources? How did women aim to exploit the ever-shifting opportunities to advance agendas they regarded as their own within the variable and changing policy frameworks afforded by the state-socialist regimes? How did they explain and react when they failed to achieve certain goals?

In other words, we need to engage in a deep analysis of the formal and informal power relations in which women actors were involved and to which they contributed and establish the strategies they employed, the variations in their room to maneuver, their modes of activism, and the effectiveness of their actions. Effectiveness was impacted not only by power relations and the status of an actor(s) alone but also by the compatibility of women actors' views and policy templates with those of other actors in any given policy field, including the leading players in the state-socialist political regime. Scholars who focus on the history of expert and professional women in state-socialist countries, as Natalia Jarska and Marie Láníková do in their chapters in this volume, have begun to address these and related questions through an exploration of women's activism rooted in a critical gendered re-reading of governmentality in state-socialist societies.[173] A lot can be learned also from a transregional perspective, when we examine simultaneously and from a comparative perspective the history of women's labour activism in political systems that, in certain ways, resembled state-socialist systems in terms of political economy and/or governmentality. This is one reason we embrace the corporatist and, from the 1970s onward, social democratic Austrian state as well as the Kemalist and developmentalist Turkish state when aspiring to deepen our understanding of women's labour activism.

Finally, we need to investigate and situate within a global framework the state-socialist model of women's emancipation, the related debates in which women during the state-socialist period engaged, and the variegated policy templates—which were linked to the state-socialist model—for which they advocated. Discussing West-East interactions, Dorothy Sue Cobble has noted that labour feminists from both sides of the Iron Curtain entertained similar women's (labour) rights agendas in substance and variety, debate

173 Large-scale projects advancing this research agenda are now underway, including "ExpertTurn: Expertise in Authoritarian Societies. Human Sciences in the Socialist Countries of East-Central Europe," n.d., https://expertturn.fss.muni.cz/team, with team members Šárka Caitlín Rábová, Annina Gagyiova, Natalia Jarska, Eva Kicková, and José Luis Aguilar López-Barajas.

notwithstanding.[174] Women labour functionaries and activists under state socialism regarded women's paid work as a liberatory force, paid close attention to women's involvement in and their attachment to care work, and went a long way to ease the tension between women's paid and unpaid labour—although without fundamentally challenging the unequal relationship between both or critically evaluating the latter's function in modern economic development. Their plans for a more women-friendly politics of women's work formed part of the long-term global trend of increasing women's involvement in paid employment (and, in the Global South, in paid work as such). Rather than interrogating the overarching meaning and implications of this trend, many women engaged in the state-socialist politics of women's work aimed to counterbalance its negative effects on large groups of working women. With the critical perspective we advocate, it is possible to move beyond the emphasis on—in global comparison—the "advanced" agenda of the state-socialist politics of women's work and contextualize it within the history of women's work in the twentieth century as it played out on both sides of the Iron Curtain and in the Global South. This can contribute to the evaluation of larger trends in the history of women's work; discussions about the embeddedness of the state-socialist politics of women's work in these larger trends; and the establishment of a more reflective view on the contributions as well as limitations of women labour functionaries and activists within this larger context. In turn, approaching women's labour struggles in the (state-)socialist context in such a manner can contribute to the advancement of integrative and critical approaches to the history of women's labour struggles in other parts of and across the world.

174 Dorothy Sue Cobble speaks explicitly about the "shared women's rights agenda" of labour feminists on both sides of the Iron Curtain in the 1950s. See Cobble 2021, 326. While focusing on "democratic equality" feminists, i.e., those not on the state-socialist side of the global history of women's activisms, the book provides a tremendously rich foundation for a global history of the politics of "full rights feminists" in the twentieth century, with important information on the role of state-socialist actors in shaping the relevant East-West encounters. See also Zimmermann 2023c.

Bibliography

Akal, Emel. 2003. *Kızıl Feministler. Bir Sözlü Tarih Çalışması* [Red feminists: A study of oral history]. Istanbul: Tüstav.

Akbulut, Erden. 2016. *Zülal Kılıç Arşiv Fonundan. TKP Kadın Bürosu 1984–1986* [From the Zülal Kılıç Archive Fond: TKP Women's Bureau 1984–1986]. Istanbul: Sosyal Tarih Yayınları.

Akgöz, Görkem. 2021. "Experts, Exiles, and Textiles: German 'Rationalisierung' on the 1930s Turkish Shop Floor." *International Review of Social History* 66, no. 2: 179–216. doi: 10.1017/S0020859020000589.

Akkaya, Gülfer. 2008. *Unutulmasın Diye ... Demokratik Kadın Derneği* [Not to forget ... Democratic Women's Association]. Istanbul: Fitne Fücur Kitaplığı.

Alpern, Sara, Joyce Antler, Elisabeth Israels Perry, and Ingrid Winther Scobie. 1992. *The Challenge of Feminist Biography: Writing the Lives of Modern American Women.* Urbana: University of Illinois Press.

Appelt, Erna. 1985. *Von Ladenmädchen, Schreibfräulein und Gouvernanten: Die weiblichen Angestellten Wiens zwischen 1900 und 1934* [Shop girls, typists and governesses: Vienna's female employees between 1900 and 1934]. Vienna: Verlag für Gesellschaftskritik.

Aranyossi, Magda. 1978. *Rendszertelen önéletrajz* [Disorderly autobiography]. Budapest: Kossuth Könyvkiadó.

Aranyossi, Magda. 1963. *Lázadó asszonyok: A magyar nőmunkásmozgalom története, 1867–1919* [Rebellious women: The history of the Hungarian woman workers' movement, 1867–1919]. Budapest: Kossuth.

Arbore-Ralli, Ecaterina. 1908. *Femeile în revoluțiunea din Rusia* [Women in the revolution in Russia]. 2nd edition. Bucharest: Editura Institutului de Arte Grafice "Minerva."

Archer, Rory. 2022. "Inside the Factory, Outside the Party-State: The Agency of Yugoslav Women Workers in Late Socialism (1976–1989)." In *Women, Work and Activism*, edited by Eloisa Betti, Leda Papastefanaki, Marica Tolomelli and Susan Zimmermann, 167–185. Budapest: CEU Press.

Arik, Hülya, Selin Çağatay, Mia Liinason, and Olga Sasunkevich. 2022. "Unsettling the Political: Conceptualizing the Political in Feminist and LGBTI+ Activism Across Russia, the Scandinavian Countries, and Turkey." *International Feminist Journal of Politics*, published online on 01 November 2022. doi: 10.1080/14616742.2022.2130806.

Arruzza, Cinzia. 2016. "Functionalist, Determinist, Reductionist: Social Reproduction Feminism and Its Critics." *Science and Society* 60, no. 1: 9–30.

Artwinska, Anna, and Agnieszka Mrozik, eds. 2020. *Gender, Generations, and Communism in Central and Eastern Europe and Beyond.* New York and London: Routledge.

Asztalos Morell, Ildikó. 1999. *Emancipation's Dead-End Roads? Studies in the Formation and Development of the Hungarian Model for Agriculture and Gender (1956–1989)*. Uppsala: Acta Universitatis Upsaliensis.

Atay, Korhan. 2021. *Serteller* [The Sertels]. Istanbul: İletişim Yayınevi.

Augeneder, Sigrid. 1987. *Arbeiterinnen im Ersten Weltkrieg: Lebens- und Arbeitsbedingungen proletarischer Frauen in Österreich* [Women workers in World War One: Living and working conditions of proletarian women in Austria]. Vienna: Europaverlag.

Aydın, Zafer. 2010. *Kanunsuz Bir Grevin Öyküsü: Kavel 1963* [The story of an illegal strike: Kavel 1963]. Istanbul: Sosyal Tarih Yayınları.

Azak, Umut, and Henk de Smaele. 2016. "National and Transnational Dynamics of Women's Activism in Turkey in the 1950s and 1960s: The Story of the ICW Branch in Ankara." *Journal of Women's History* 28, no. 3 (September 8): 41–65. doi: 10.1353/jowh.2016.0024.

Bahenská, Marie, and Jana Malínská, eds. 2014. *Ženy a politika 1890–1938* [Women and politics 1890–1938]. Prague: Masarykův ústav AV ČR.

Bahenská, Marie, Libuše Heczková, and Dana Musilová. 2014. *O ženské práci: dobové (sebe)reflexe a polemiky* [On women's work: Contemporary (self-)reflections and polemics]. Prague: Masarykův ústav a Archiv AV ČR.

Bahenská, Marie, Libuše Heczková, and Dana Musilová. 2011. *Iluze spásy: české feministické myšlení 19. a 20. století* [Illusion of salvation: Czech feminist thought in the nineteenth and twentieth centuries]. České Budějovice: Veduta.

Balkanski, Grigor. 1982. *Libération nationale et révolution sociale: À l'exemple de la révolution macédonienne* [National liberation and social revolution: The example of the Macedonian revolution]. Paris: Volonté anarchiste.

Balsoy, Gülhan. 2009. "Gendering Ottoman Labour History: The Cibali Régie Factory in the Early Twentieth Century." *International Review of Social History* 54, no. S17: 45–68. doi: 10.1017/S002085900999023X.

Banaszak, Lee Ann, and Anne Whitesell. 2017. "Inside the State: Activism within Legislative and Governmental Agency Forums." In *The Oxford Handbook of U.S. Women's Activism*, edited by Holly McCammon, Verta Taylor, Jo Reger, and Rachel Einwohner, 487–506. New York: Oxford University Press.

Bauer, Ingrid. 2015. *"Tschikweiber haums uns g'nennt…": Die Zigarrenfabriksarbeiterinnen von Hallein: Frauen, Arbeit, Geschichte* ["They called us Tschikweiber…": The women workers of the cigarette factory in Hallein: Women, labour, history]. Berlin: Die Buchmacherei. First published 1988.

Bednářová, Věra. 1984. "Josef Hybeš a brněnské ženské hnutí" [Josef Hybeš and the women's movement in Brno]. *Vlastivědný věstník moravský* [Journal of local Moravian history] 36, no. 1: 100–103.

Benería, Lourdes. 2010. "Globalization, Women's Work, and Care Needs: The Urgency of Reconciliation Policies." *North Carolina Law Review* 88, no. 5: 1502–1526.

Beoković, Mila. 1967. *Žene heroji* [Women heroes]. Sarajevo: Svjetlost.

Bereni, Laure, and Anne Revillard. 2018. "Movement Institutions: The Bureaucratic Sources of Feminist Protest." *Politics and Gender* 14, no. 3: 407–432.

Betti, Eloisa. 2021. "Equal Pay and Social Justice: Women's Agency, Trade Union Action and International Regulations. Italy, the ILO and the EEC in the Global Context (1951–1977)." *The International History Review* 44, no. 3: 577–594.

Betti, Eloisa. 2018. "Unexpected Alliances: Italian Women's Struggles for Equal Pay, 1940s–1960s." In *Women's ILO: Transnational Networks, Global Labour Standards and Gender Equity, 1919 to Present*, edited by Eileen Boris, Dorothea Hoehtker, and Susan Zimmermann, 276–299. Studies in Global Social History 32. Leiden: Brill.

Betti, Eloisa, Leda Papastefanaki, Marica Tolomelli, and Susan Zimmermann. 2022. "Introduction: Thinking the History of Women's Activism into Global Labour History." In *Women, Work, and Activism: Chapters of an Inclusive History of Labour in the Long Twentieth Century*, edited by Eloisa Betti, Leda Papastefanaki, Marica Tolomelli and Susan Zimmermann, 1–31. Budapest: CEU Press.

Bhattacharya, Tithi. 2015. "How Not To Skip Class: Social Reproduction of Labor and the Global Working Class." *Viewpoint Magazine*, 31 October 2015. https://www.viewpointmag.com/2015/10/31/how-not-to-skip-class-social-reproduction-of-labor-and-the-global-working-class/.

Biçer-Deveci, Elife. 2017. *Die osmanisch-türkische Frauenbewegung im Kontext internationaler Frauenorganisationen: Eine Beziehungs- und Verflechtungsgeschichte von 1895 bis 1935* [The Ottoman-Turkish women's movement in the context of international women's organizations: A relational and entangled history from 1895 to 1935]. Ottoman Studies/Osmanistische Studien 4. Göttingen: V&R unipress and Bonn University Press.

Birtek, Faruk. 1985. "The Rise and Fall of Etatism in Turkey, 1932–1950: The Uncertain Road in the Restructuring of a Semiperipheral Economy." *Review (Fernand Braudel Center)* 8, no. 3: 407–438.

Bjelić, Krste, Seada Hodžić, Jovo Popović, Darko Stuparić, and Radule Vasović. 1980. *Heroine Jugoslavije* [Heroines of Yugoslavia]. Zagreb: Spektar.

Bluhm, Katharina, Gertrud Pickhan, Justyna Stypinska, and Agnieszka Wierzcholska, eds. 2021. *Gender and Power in Eastern Europe: Changing Concepts of Femininity and Masculinity in Power Relations*. Cham: Springer.

Bock, Gisela. 1989. "Women's History and Gender History: Aspects of an International Debate." *Gender and History* 1, no. 1: 7–30.

Bogdanova, Elena [Богданова, Елена]. 1969. *Вела Благоева: Биографичен очерк* [Vela Blagoeva: Biographical essay]. Sofia: BKP.

Bohachevsky-Chomiak, Martha. 1988. *Feminists Despite Themselves: Women in Ukrainian Community Life, 1884–1939*. Edmonton: University of Alberta.

Bonfiglioli, Chiara. 2020. *Women and Industry in the Balkans: The Rise and Fall of the Yugoslav Textile Sector*. London: I.B. Tauris.

Bonfiglioli, Chiara. 2018. "Feminist Translations in a Socialist Context: The Case of Yugoslavia." *Gender and History* 30, no. 1: 240–254.

Bonfiglioli, Chiara. 2017. "A Working Day That Has No End. The Double Burden in Socialist Yugoslavia." *Themenportal Europäische Geschichte*, www.europa.clio-online.de/essay/id/fdae-1705.

Bonfiglioli, Chiara. 2012. "Cold War Internationalisms, Nationalisms and the Yugoslav-Soviet Split: The Union of Italian Women and the Antifascist Women's Front of Yugoslavia." In *Women's Activism: Global Perspectives from the 1890s to the Present*, edited by Francisca de Haan, June Purvis, Margaret Allen, and Krassmira Daskalova, 59–73. London: Routledge.

Boris, Eileen. 2019. *Making the Woman Worker: Precarious Labor and the Fight for Global Standards, 1919–2019*. New York: Oxford University Press.

Boris, Eileen, Dorothea Hoehtker, and Susan Zimmermann, eds. 2018. *Women's ILO: Transnational Networks, Global Labour Standards, and Gender Equity, 1919 to Present*. Studies in Global Social History 32. Leiden and Boston: Brill.

Boris, Eileen, and Carolyn Herbst Lewis. 2006. "Caregiving and Wage-Earning: A Historical Perspective on Work and Family." In *The Work and Family Handbook: Multi-Disciplinary Perspectives and Approaches*, edited by Marcie Pitt-Catsouphes, Ellen Ernst Kossek, and Stephen Sweet, 73–97. New York: Routledge.

Bosch, Mineke. 2009. "Gender and the Personal in Political Biography." *Journal of Women's History* 21, no. 4: 13–37.

Bozeva, Aneliia [Бозева, Анелия]. 1981. *Женското движение в България от Освобождението до наши дни* [Women's movement in Bulgaria from the Liberation until the present day]. Sofia: Glavno upravlenie na arkhivite pri Ministerski Suvet.

Bracke, Maud Anne. 2022. "Women's Rights, Family Planning, and Population Control: The Emergence of Reproductive Rights in the United Nations (1960s–70s)." *The International History Review* 44, no. 4: 751–771.

Bradinska, Radka [Брадинска, Радка]. 1969. *Възникване и оформяне на женското социал-демократическо движение в България, 1885–1915* [The emergence and development of the women's social democratic movement in Bulgaria, 1885–1915]. Sofia: Izdatelstvo na Natsionalnia suvet na Otechestvenia Front.

Briskin, Linda, and Lynda Yanz, eds. 1983. *Union Sisters: Women in the Labour Movement*. Toronto: Women's Educational Press.

Brown, Carolyn A., Marcel van der Linden, Franco Barchiesi, Peter Winn, Jürgen Kocka, Dorothy Sue Cobble, and Prasannan Parthasarathi. 2012. "Scholarly

Controversy: Defining Global Labour History." *International Labor and Working-Class History*, no. 82: 53–113.

Brunnbauer, Ulf. 2022. "How and Where Do We Write the History of State Socialism? Some Preliminary Reflections." In *Everyday Socialism: Promises, Realities, and Strategies*, edited by Ana Luleva, Ivanka Petrova, Petar Petrov, Svetla Kazalarska, Zlatina Bogadnova, and Yana Yancheva, 7–25. Sofia: Prof. Marin Drinov Publishing House.

Buckley, Mary. 1989. *Women and Ideology in the Soviet Union*. Toronto, Sydney, and Tokyo: Harvester Wheatsheaf.

Bujaković, Minja. 2021. "*Reinvestigating Communist Women's Activism in the Interwar Kingdom of Yugoslavia*." MA thesis, Central European University.

Burek, Jan Antoni. 2017. "From Party Leaders to Social Outcasts: Women's Political Activism During the Establishing of Communist Power in a Polish Industrial Town (Żyrardów, 1945–1948)." *History of Communism in Europe* 8: 167–188.

Caine, Barbara. 1994. "Feminist Biography and Feminist History." *Women's History Review* 3, no. 2 (June 1): 247–261. doi: 10.1080/09612029400200049.

Çakır, Serpil. 1994. *Osmanlı Kadın Hareketi* [Ottoman women's movement]. Istanbul: Metis Yayınları.

Câncea, Paraschiva. 1976. *Mişcarea pentru emanciparea femeii în România* [The movement for women's emancipation in Romania]. Bucharest: Editura Politică.

Çağatay, Selin. "Gendering Adult Education in the Developing World: Vocational Training of Women in Turkey, 1960s–1990s." Paper presented at the 14th European Social Science History Conference, Gothenburg, 12 April 2023.

Çağatay, Selin. 2022. "Turkey and Eastern Europe: Historicising Geopolitical Convergences in Gender Politics." In *Decolonising (Knowledge on) Euro–Mediterranean Relations: Insights on Shared Histories and Futures*, edited by Daniela Huber and Lorenzo Kamel, 43–54. Istituto Affari Internazionali (IAI) Research Studies 7. Rome: Edizioni Nuova Cultura.

Çağatay, Selin. 2017. "*The Politics of Gender and the Making of Kemalist Feminist Activism in Contemporary Turkey (1946–2011)*." PhD diss., Central European University.

Celasun, Zehra. 1946. *Tarih Boyunca Kadınlık* [Womanhood throughout history]. Istanbul: Ülkü Kitabevi.

Çelik, Birten. 2013. "Sweatshops in the Silk Industry of the Bursa Region and the Workers' Strikes in 1910." *Turkish Historical Review* 4, no. 1: 26–56. doi: 10.1163/18775462-00401002.

Chevigny, Bell Gale. 1983. "Daughters Writing: Toward a Theory of Women's Biography." *Feminist Studies* 9, no. 1: 79–102. doi: 10.2307/3177684.

Cobble, Dorothy Sue. 2021. *For the Many: American Feminists and the Global Fight for Democratic Equality*. Princeton, NJ: Princeton University Press.

Cobble, Dorothy Sue. 2005. *The Other Women's Movement: Workplace Justice and Social Rights in Modern America*. Princeton, NJ: Princeton University Press.

Constantinescu-Iaşi, Petre. 1952. *Organizaţii de massă legale conduse de Partidul Comunist din România în anii 1932–1938* [Legal mass organizations led by the Communist Party of Romania in the years 1932–1938]. Bucharest: Editura Academiei Republicii Populare Române.

Çınar, Sercan. 2023. "A Transnational History of Left Feminism in Turkey (1974–1979): Relations and Exchanges between the IKD and the WIDF." In "A Century of Gender Equality Struggles in Turkey: Feminist History Revisited," edited by Elife Biçer-Deveci and Selin Çağatay, special issue, *Diyâr. Journal of Ottoman, Turkish and Middle Eastern Studies* 4, no. 1: 72–99. doi: 10.5771/2625-9842-2023-1.

Cucu, Alina-Sandra. 2019. *Planning Labour: Time and the Foundations of Industrial Socialism in Romania*. New York: Berghahn Books.

Cvetić, Bosa [Цветић, Боса], ed. 1975. *Жене Србије у НОБ* [Women of Serbia in the People's Liberation Struggle]. Belgrade: Nolit.

Dalos, György. 1984. *A cselekvés szerelmese: Duczynska Ilona élete* [In love with action: The life of Ilona Duczynska]. Budapest: Kossuth Könyvkiadó.

Daskalova, Krassimira. 2016. "A Woman Politician in the Cold War Balkans: From Biography to History." *Aspasia: International Yearbook for Women's and Gender History of Central, Eastern and Southeastern Europe* 10: 63–88.

Daskalova, Krassimira [Даскалова, Красимира]. 2012. *Жени, пол и модернизация в България 1878–1944* [Women, gender and modernization in Bulgaria 1878–1944]. Sofia: Universitetsko izdatelstvo "Sv. Kliment Ohridski."

Daskalova, Krassimira, and Susan Zimmermann. 2017. "Women's and Gender History." In *The Routledge History of East Central Europe Since 1700*, edited by Irina Livezeanu and Árpád von Klimó, 278–322. London and New York: Routledge.

Davaz, Aslı. 2020. "An Annotated Archive of Entangled European Feminist History: The Union of Turkish Women, the Second Balkan Conference and Cécile Brunschvicg's Visit to Balkan Feminists (1923–1935)." *Feminist Encounters: A Journal of Critical Studies in Culture and Politics* 4, no. 2 (September 8): 28. doi:10.20897/femenc/8516.

David, Katherine. 1991. "Czech Feminists and Nationalism in the Late Habsburg Monarchy: 'The First in Austria.'" *Journal of Women's History* 3, no. 2: 26–45.

De Haan, Francisca, ed. 2023. *The Palgrave Handbook of Communist Women Activists around the World*. Basingstoke: Palgrave Macmillan.

De Haan, Francisca, ed. 2016. "Forum 'Ten Years After: Communism and Feminism Revisited.'" *Aspasia: The International Yearbook of Central, Eastern, and Southeastern European Women's and Gender History* 10, no. 1: 102–168.

De Haan, Francisca. 2010. "Continuing Cold War Paradigms in the Western Historiography of Transnational Women's Organisations: The Case of the Women's

International Democratic Federation (WIDF)." *Women's History Review* 19, no. 4 (September): 547–573.

De Haan, Francisca, Krassimira Daskalova, and Anna Loutfi, eds. 2006. *Biographical Dictionary of Women's Movements and Feminisms in Central, Eastern, and South Eastern Europe: 19th and 20th Centuries*. Budapest and New York: CEU Press.

Demirdirek, Aynur. 1993. *Osmanlı Kadınlarının Hayat Hakkı Arayışının Bir Hikayesi* [A history of the Ottoman women's quest for the right to life]. Ankara: İmge Kitabevi.

Devinatz, Victor G. 2019. "The CPUSA's Trade Unionism during Third Period Communism, 1929–1934." *American Communist History* 18, no. 3–4: 251–268. doi: 10.1080/14743892.2019.1608710.

Diadiuk, Myroslava [Дядюк, Мирослава]. 2011. Український жіночий рух у міжвоєнній Галичині: Між гендерною ідентичністю та національною заангажованістю [The Ukrainian women's movement in interwar Galicia: Between gender identity and national engagement]. Lviv: Astrolabiia.

Dimitrova, Snezhana [Димитрова, Снежана]. 2018a. "'Дайте ни мъжете, пуснете ги да си дойдат и те ще ни намерят всичко, което ни трябва': Първата световна война, женските бунтове и политиките на женска еманципация" ["Give us back our men, let them come back home, and they will give us everything we need": World War One, women's revolts, and the policies of women's emancipation]. *Sotsiologicheski problemi* [Sociological problems] 50, no. 2: 631–674.

Dimitrova, Snezhana. 2018b. "Hunger, Diseases, and Bulgarian Women's Revolts (1916–1918)." In *Der Erste Weltkrieg auf dem Balkan: Geschichtliches Ereignis, Erfahrung und Erinnerung* [World War One in the Balkans: Historic event, experience and memory], edited by Wim van Meurs and Wolfgang Höpken, 116–161. Munich: Peter Lang.

Donert, Celia. 2022. "Women's Rights and Global Socialism: Gendering Socialist Internationalism during the Cold War." *International Review of Social History* 67, no. S30 (April): 1–22.

Donert, Celia. 2013. "Women's Rights in Cold War Europe: Disentangling Feminist Histories." *Past and Present* 218, no. 8: 180–202.

Dudeková, Gabriela. 2011. "Konzervatívne feministky? Ženské hnutie na Slovensku v kontexte. Uhorska a medzinárodných aktivít" [Conservative feminists? Women's movement in Slovakia in the context of Hungary and international activities]. In *Na ceste k modernej žene: kapitoly z dejín rodových vzťahovna Slovensku* [On the road toward a modern woman: Chapters from the history of gender relations in Slovakia], edited by Gabriela Dudeková et al., 232–257. Bratislava: Veda.

Dudeková, Gabriela et al. 2011. *Na ceste k modernej žene: Kapitoly z dejín rodových vzťahov na Slovensku* [On the road toward a modern woman: Chapters from the history of gender relations in Slovakia]. Bratislava: Veda.

Duma, Veronika. 2019. *Rosa Jochmann: Politische Akteurin und Zeitzeugin* [Rosa Jochmann: Political actor and historical witness]. Vienna: Verlag des ÖGB.

Đurović, Bosa [Ђуровић, Боса], Zoran Lakić [Зоран Лакић], and Bosa Vuković [Боса Вуковић], eds. 1960. *Жене Црне Горе у револуционарном покрету 1919–1945* [Women of Montenegro in the revolutionary movement 1919–1945]. Titograd: Glavni odbor Saveza ženskih društava Crne Gore.

Ecevit, Yıldız. 1986. "*Gender and Wage Work: A Case Study of Turkish Women in Manufacturing Industry.*" PhD diss., Kent University.

Ehmer, Josef. 1981a. "Frauenarbeit und Arbeiterfamilie in Wien: Vom Vormärz bis 1934" [Women's work and working-class family in Vienna: From the Vormärz period to 1934]. *Geschichte und Gesellschaft* [History and society] 7, no. 3–4: 438–473.

Ehmer, Josef. 1981b. "Frauenerwerbsarbeit in der industriellen Gesellschaft" [Women's gainful employment in industrial society]. *Beiträge zur historischen Sozialkunde* [Contributions to historical social studies] 11, no. 1: 97–106.

Ekmekçioğlu, Lerna, and Melissa Bilal, eds. 2006. *Bir Adalet Feryadı: Osmanlı'dan Türkiye'ye Beş Ermeni Feminist Yazar, 1862–1933* [A cry for justice: Five Armenian feminist writers from the Ottoman Empire to the Turkish Republic, 1862–1933]. Istanbul: Aras Yayıncılık.

Fábián, Katalin, Janet Elise Johnson, and Mara Lazda, eds. 2021. *The Routledge Handbook of Gender in Central-Eastern Europe and Eurasia.* New York: Routledge.

Federici, Silvia. 2012. *Revolution at Point Zero: Housework, Reproduction, and Feminist Struggle.* Oakland: PM Press.

Feinberg, Melissa. 2006. *Elusive Equality: Gender, Citizenship, and the Limits of Democracy in Czechoslovakia, 1918–1950.* Pittsburgh: University of Pittsburgh Press.

Fidelis, Małgorzata. 2010. *Women, Communism and Industrialization in Postwar Poland.* New York: Cambridge University Press.

Filtzer, Donald A., Wendy Goldman, Gijs Kessler, and Simon Pirani, eds. 2008. *A Dream Deferred: New Studies in Russian and Soviet Labour History.* Bern: Peter Lang.

Fonó, Zsuzsa. 1978. *A magyar munkásnők helyzete és szervezettsége a két világháború között* [The situation and organization of Hungarian women workers between the two world wars]. Budapest: Szakszervezetek Elméleti Kutató Intézete.

Fonó, Zsuzsa. 1975. *A magyarországi szocialista nőmozgalom történetéhez, 1895–1918* (*A mozgalom és a szociális összetétel konfliktusai*) [On the history of the Hungarian socialist women's movement, 1895–1918. (Conflicts of movement and social composition)]. Budapest: Szakszervezetek Elméleti Kutató Intézete.

Frader, Laura L. 2008. *Breadwinners and Citizens: Gender and the Making of the French Social Model.* Durham, NC: Duke University Press.

Fraser, Nancy. 2016. "Contradictions of Capital and Care." *New Left Review*, no. 100: 99–117.

Friss, Mrs. István. 1974. *A textilmunkások sztrájkjairól a két világháború között* [On the textile workers' strikes between the two world wars]. Budapest: Szakszervezetek Elméleti Kutató Intézete.

Gehmacher, Johanna, and Natascha Vittorelli, eds. 2009. *Wie Frauenbewegung geschrieben wird: Historiographie, Dokumentation, Stellungnahmen, Bibliographien* [Writing the women's movement: Historiography, documentation, positions, bibliographies]. Vienna: Löcker Verlag.

Georgescu, Elena, and Titu Georgescu. 1975. *Mişcarea democratică şi revoluţionară a femeilor din România* [The democratic and revolutionary movement of women from Romania]. Craiova: Editura Scrisul Românesc.

Gerk, Stana, Ivka Križnar, and Štefanija Ravnikar-Podbevšek. 1970. *Slovenke v narodnoosvobodilnem boju: zbornik dokumentov, člankov in spominov* [Slovenian women in the People's Liberation Struggle: A collection of documents, articles and memoirs]. Ljubljana: Zavod 'Borec'.

Ghiţ, Alexandra. 2021. "Solidarity and Inequality: European Socialist Women's International Organizing in the Interwar Period." *ZARAH Blog*, 6 December 2021. https://zarah-ceu.org/solidarity-and-inequality-european-socialist-womens-international-organizing-in-the-interwar-period/.

Ghiţ, Alexandra. 2018. "Professionals' and Amateurs' Pasts: A Decolonizing Reading of Post-War Romanian Histories of Gendered Interwar Activism." *European Review of History: Revue européenne d'histoire* 25, no.1: 21–44. doi: 10.1080/13507486.2017.1376619.

Ghiţ, Alexandra. (under review, a). "State Labor Control and Women's Resistance in Austro-Hungarian Transylvania Tobacco Manufacturing, 1890s–1918."

Ghiţ, Alexandra. (under review, b). "Biography and Context—Ecaterina Arbore: The Working Woman in the Struggle Towards Emancipation."

Ghiţ, Alexandra, Veronika Helfert, Ivelina Masheva, Zhanna Popova, Jelena Tešija, Eszter Varsa, and Susan Zimmermann. 2023. "Women and the Gendered Politics of Work in Central and Eastern Europe, and Internationally, in the Twentieth Century: Activism, Governance, and Scale." *Journal of Contemporary Central and Eastern Europe* 31, no. 2.: 227–240. doi: 10.1080/25739638.2023.2227512.

Ghodsee, Kristen. 2019. *Second World, Second Sex: Socialist Women's Activism and Global Solidarity during the Cold War*. Durham, NC: Duke University Press Books.

Ghodsee, Kristen. 2012. "Rethinking State Socialist Mass Women's Organizations: The Committee of the Bulgarian Women's Movement and the United Nations Decade for Women, 1975–1985." *Journal of Women's History* 24, no. 4: 49–73. doi: 10.1353/jowh.2012.0044.

Glickman, Rose L. 1986. *Russian Factory Women: Workplace and Society, 1880–1914*. Berkeley: University of California Press.

Gnydiuk, Olga. 2022. "In the Web of a Male-Dominated Trade Union International: Women and the World Federation of Trade Unions." *ZARAH Blog*, 3 February 2022. https://zarah-ceu.org/blog/.

Göhring, Walter, ed. 1998. *Anna Boschek: Erste Gewerkschafterin im Parlament: Biographie einer außengewöhnlichen Arbeiterin* [Anna Boschek: The first female trade unionist in Parliament: Biography of an extraordinary woman worker]. Vienna: Verlag des ÖGB.

Goldman, Wendy Z. 2002. *Women at the Gates: Gender and Industry in Stalin's Russia*. Cambridge and New York: Cambridge University Press.

Grabowska, Magdalena. 2017. "Bits of Freedom: Demystifying Women's Activism under State Socialism in Poland and Georgia." *Feminist Studies* 43, no. 1: 141–168. doi: 10.1353/fem.2017.0008.

Gradskova, Yulia. 2022. "The WIDF's Work for Women's Rights in the (Post)colonial Countries and the 'Soviet Agenda.'" *International Review of Social History* 67, no. 30: 155–178. doi: 10.1017/S0020859022000062.

Gradskova, Yulia. 2021. *The Women's International Democratic Federation, the Global South, and the Cold War: Defending the Rights of Women of the "Whole World?"* London: Routledge.

Grama, Adrian. 2019. *Laboring Along. Industrial Workers and the Making of Postwar Romania*. Berlin and Boston: De Gruyter.

Grandner, Margarete. 1995. "Special Labor Protection for Women in Austria, 1860–1918." In *Protecting Women: Labor Legislation in Europe, the United States, and Australia, 1880–1920*, edited by Ulla Wikander, Alice Kessler-Harris, and Jane Lewis, 150–187. Urbana: University of Illinois Press.

Grubački, Isidora. 2020. "Communism, Left Feminism, and Generations in the 1930s: The Case of Yugoslavia." In *Gender, Generations, and Communism in Central and Eastern Europe and Beyond*, edited by Anna Artwińska and Agnieszka Mrozik, 45–65. London: Routledge.

Gülenç, Nuran. 2022. "DISK ve Kadın İşçiler: Gecikmiş Bir Buluşma (1967–1980) [DISK and women workers: A delayed encounter (1967–1980)]." In *DISK Tarihi. Dayanışma, Direniş, Umut. Cilt 2* [*DISK history. Solidarity, resistance, hope. Vol. 2.*], *1975–1980*, edited by Aziz Çelik, 591–617. Istanbul: DISK Yayınları.

Gyáni, Gábor. 1989. *Women as Domestic Servants: The Case of Budapest, 1890–1940*. New York: Institute on East Central Europe, Columbia University.

Hacker, Hanna. 1998. *Gewalt ist: keine Frau: Der Akteurin oder eine Geschichte der Transgressionen* [Violence is: Not a woman: The actor or a history of transgressions]. Königstein and Taunus: Ulrike Helmer Verlag.

Hadzhinikolov, Veselin [Хаджиниколов, Веселин], Mito Isusov [Мито Исусов], Angel Georgiev [Ангел Георгиев], and Vasil Vasilev [Васил Василев]. 1960. *Стачните борби на работническата класа в България* [Strike struggles of the working class in Bulgaria]. Edited by Dragoi Kodzheikov [Драгой Коджейков] and Veselin Hadzhinikolov [Веселин Хаджиниколов]. Sofia: Profizdat.

Hann, Edith. 1988. "'Durch die Weiber kann man viel, sehr viel ausrichten': Frühformen der Arbeiterinnenorganisation" ["With women a lot can be achieved": Early forms of women workers' organization]. *Archiv: Jahrbuch des Vereins für Geschichte der Arbeiterbewegung* [Archive: Yearbook of the Association for the History of the Labour Movement] 4: 66–85.

Hauch, Gabriella. 2012. "'Against the Mock Battle of Words.' Therese Schlesinger, Neé Eckstein (1863–1940), a Radical Seeker." In *Austrian Lives*, edited by Günter Bischof, Fritz Plasser, and Eva Maltschnig, 71–91. New Orleans: Uno Press.

Hauch, Gabriella. 2009. "'Arbeite Frau! Die Gleichberechtigung kommt von selbst'? Anmerkungen zu Frauen und Gewerkschaften vor 1914" ["Work woman! Equal rights will come automatically"? Annotations to women and labour unions before 1914]. In *Frauen bewegen Politik, Österreich 1848–1938* [Women move politics, Austria 1848–1938], edited by Gabriella Hauch, 105–127. Innsbruck: Studienverlag.

Hauch, Gabriella. 2003. "'Wir, die viele Geschichten haben:' Zur Genese der historischen Frauenforschung im gesellschaftlichen und wissenschaftlichen Kontext ['We who have many stories:' On the genesis of women's historical research in a social and scientific context]." In *Frauen- und Geschlechtergeschichte: Positionen/Perspektiven* [Women's and gender history: Positions/perspectives], edited by Johanna Gehmacher and Maria Mesner, 21–36. Innsbruck: Studien Verlag.

Hauch, Gabriella. 1986. "'Revolutionäre im Schlafrock' und 'Instrumente des Klassenkampfes': Konsumgenossenschaften in der österreichischen Arbeiterbewegung bis 1914" ["Revolutionaries in robes" and "Instruments of class struggle": Consumer cooperatives in the Austrian labour movement until 1914]. In *Arbeiterbewegung in Österreich und Ungarn bis 1914: Referate des österreichisch-ungarischen Historikersymposiums in Graz vom 5.–9. September 1986* [Workers' movement in Austria and Hungary until 1914: Papers presented at the Austro-Hungarian historians' symposium in Graz, 5–9 September 1986], edited by Wolfgang Maderthaner, 216–225. Vienna: Europaverlag.

Heindl, Waltraud, Edit Király, and Alexandra Millner eds. 2006. *Frauenbilder, feministische Praxis und nationales Bewusstsein in Österreich-Ungarn 1867–1918* [Envisioning women, feminist practice, and national consciousness in Austria-Hungary 1867–1918]. Tübingen and Basel: Francke Verlag.

Helfert, Veronika. 2021. *Frauen, wacht auf! Eine Frauen- und Geschlechtergeschichte von Revolution und Rätebewegung in Österreich, 1916–1924* [Women, wake up! A women's and gender history of the Austrian Revolution and Council Movement, 1916–1924]. Göttingen: Vandenhoeck & Ruprecht.

Helfert, Veronika. 2015. "Eine demokratische Bolschewikin: Ilona Duczynska Polanyi (1897–1978)" [A democratic bolshevik woman: Ilona Duczynska Polanyi (1897–1978)]. *Österreichische Zeitschrift für Geschichtswissenschaft/Austrian Journal of Historical Studies* 26, no. 2: 166–189.

Helfert, Veronika (under review). "Radical and Utopian or Partnership between Men and Women? Austrian Trade Union Women, Autonomous Feminists and Labour Related Concerns, 1970s–1980s".

Hemmings, Clare. 2018. *Considering Emma Goldman: Feminist Political Ambivalence and the Imaginative Archive*. Durham, NC: Duke University Press Books.

Hillyar, Anna, and Jane McDermid. 2000. *Revolutionary Women in Russia, 1870–1917: A Study in Collective Biography*. Manchester and New York: Manchester University Press.

Hîncu, Adela. 2022. "Ambivalentes Empowerment: Sozialwissenschaftliche Forschung über die Ungleichstellung von Frauen im spätsozialistischen Rumänien" [Ambivalent empowerment: Social science research on the unequal position of women in late socialist Romania]. In *Jahrbuch für Historische Kommunismusforschung* [Yearbook for historical research on communism] 29: 105–126.

Holečková, Božena. 1978. *Komunistická novinářka Jožka Jabůrková* [The communist journalist Jožka Jabůrková]. Prague: Novinář.

Holubec, Stanislav. 2021. *Nešťastná revolucionářka: myšlenkový svět a každodennost Luisy Landové-Štychové (1885–1969)* [An unhappy revolutionary: The ideas and everyday life of Luisa Landová- Štychová]. Prague: NLN.

Homenco, Suzana, and Elisabeta Ioniță. 1975. *Suzana Pârvulescu*. Bucharest: Editura Politică.

Hüchtker, Dietlind. 2021. *History as Performance: Political Movements in Galicia Around 1900*. New York: Routledge.

Iankova, Mariia [Янкова, Мария]. 1980. *Люба Ивошевич-Димитрова: Биографический очерк.* [Liuba Ivoshevich-Dimitrova: Biographical essay]. Sofia: Sofia-Pres.

Ignácz, Károly. 2020. "The Emergence of the Outskirts of Budapest as a New Administrative District through the Organisation of the Food Supply, 1917–1919." *Südost-Forschungen* [Southeast research] 79: 71–95.

Ilic, Melanie. 1999. *Women Workers in the Soviet Interwar Economy: From "Protection" to "Equality."* New York: Palgrave Macmillan.

Ilıcak, H. Şükrü. 2002. "Jewish Socialism in Ottoman Salonica." *Southeast European and Black Sea Studies* 2, no. 3: 115–146. doi: 10.1080/14683850208454706.

Ioniță, Elisabeta. 1980. "Uniunea Femeilor Muncitoare din România" [The Union of Working Women from Romania]. *Revista de istorie* [History review] 33, no. 10: 1905–26.

Ioniță, Elisabeta. 1973. *Ecaterina Arbore*. Bucharest: Editura Politică.

Jarska, Natalia. 2015. *Kobiety z marmuru. Robotnice w Polsce w latach 1945–1960* [The marble women: Women workers in Poland, 1945–1960]. Warsaw: Instytut Pamięci Narodowej.

Jinga, Luciana M. 2015. *Gen și reprezentare în România comunistă: 1944–1989* [Gender and representation in communist Romania: 1944–1989]. Iași: Polirom.

Jobst, Vinzenz. 1999. *Marie Tusch: Lebensbild einer Tabakarbeiterin* [Marie Tusch: Life portrait of a woman tobacco worker]. Klagenfurt: Archiv der Kärntner Arbeiterbewegung.

Jovanović, Miroslav, and Slobodan Naumović, eds. 2004. *Gender Relations in South Eastern Europe: Historical Perspectives on Womanhood and Manhood in the 19th and 20th Century*. Graz: Lit Verlag.

Kaplan, Temma. 1996. *Crazy for Democracy: Women in Grassroots Movements*. London: Routledge.

Kaplan, Temma. 1987. "Women and Communal Strikes in the Crisis of 1917–1922." In *Becoming Visible: Women in European History*, edited by Renate Bridenthal, Claudia Koonz, and Susan Stuard, 430–446. Boston: Houghton Mifflin.

Karakışla, Yavuz Selim. 2015. *Osmanlı İmparatorluğu'nda Savaş Yılları ve Çalışan Kadınlar. Kadınları Çalıştırma Cemiyeti (1916–1923)* [War years and working women in the Ottoman Empire: Society for the employment of women (1916–1923)]. Istanbul: İletişim Yayınları.

Karakışla, Yavuz Selim. 2002. "Uşak'ta Kadın Halı İşçileri'nin İsyanı (1908)" [The revolt of woman carpet weaving workers in Uşak (1908)]. *Toplumsal Tarih* [Social history], no. 99 (March): 54–57.

Kazgan, Gülten. 1981. "Labour Force Participation, Occupational Distribution, Educational Attainment and Socio-Economic Status of Women in the Turkish Economy." In *Women in Turkish Society*, edited by Nermin Abadan-Unat, 131–159. Leiden: Brill.

Kecman, Jovanka. 1978. *Žene Jugoslavije u radničkom pokretu i ženskim organizacijama 1918–1941* [Women of Yugoslavia in the labour movement and women's organizations 1918–1941]. Belgrade: Narodna knjiga.

Kelly-Gadol, Joan. 1976. "The Social Relation of the Sexes: Methodological Implications of Women's History." *Signs: Journal of Women in Culture and Society* 1, no. 4: 809–823.

Kessler-Harris, Alice. 1990. *A Woman's Wage: Historical Meanings and Social Consequences*. Lexington: University Press of Kentucky.

Koenker, Diane P. 1995. "Men against Women on the Shop Floor in Early Soviet Russia: Gender and Class in the Socialist Workplace." *The American Historical Review* 100, no. 5 (December): 1438–1464. doi: 10.2307/2169865.

Kofman, Eleonore. 2012. "Rethinking Care Through Social Reproduction: Articulating Circuits of Migration." *Social Politics* 19, no. 1: 142–162.

Kolar-Dimitrijević, Mira. 1977. "Najnovije knjige o sudjelovanju žena u radničkom pokretu i NOB-u" [The latest books on women's participation in the labour movement and People's Liberation Struggle]. *Časopis za suvremenu povijest* [Journal of contemporary history] 9, no. 3: 127–131.

Koller, Christian. 2009. *Streikkultur: Performanzen und Diskurse des Arbeitskampfes im schweizerisch-österreichischen Vergleich (1860–1950)* [Culture of strike: Performances and discourses of industrial action in Swiss-Austrian comparison (1860–1950)]. Vienna: Lit Verlag.

Konstantinova, Yura. 2018. "The Role of Bulgarians for the Spread of National, Anarchist and Socialist Ideas in Ottoman Salonica." *Études Balkaniques* [Balkan studies] 54, no. 3: 508–535.

Kosova, Zehra. 1996. *Ben İşçiyim* [I am a worker]. Istanbul: İletişim Yayınları.

Kovačević, Dušanka, ed. 1972. *Borbeni put žena Jugoslavije* [The combat path of women of Yugoslavia]. Belgrade: Leksikografski zavod "Sveznanje."

Kraft, Claudia. 2018. "Spaces of Knowledge and Gender Regimes: From Double Marginalization to a Gendered History of Knowledge in Central and Eastern Europe." *Acta Poloniae Historica* 117 (October 10): 7–25. doi:10.12775/APH.2018.117.01.

Kučera, Rudolf. 2016. *Rationed Life: Science, Everyday Life, and Working-Class Politics in the Bohemian Lands, 1914–1918*. New York and Oxford: Berghahn Books.

Laskova, Pavlina [Ласкова, Павлина]. 1974. "Тютюноработниците в България през периода 1934–1939" [Tobacco workers in Bulgaria in 1934–1939]. *Godishnik na Sofiiskiia universitet: Ideologicheski katedri* [Sofia University yearbook: Ideological departments] 63: 45–194.

Laslett, Barbara, and Johanna Brenner. 1989. "Gender and Social Reproduction: Historical Perspectives." *Annual Review of Sociology* 15: 381–404.

Lazitch, Branko, and Milorad M. Drachkovitch. 1986. *Biographical Dictionary of the Comintern*. Stanford: Hoover Institution Press.

Levy, Robert. 2001. *Ana Pauker: The Rise and Fall of a Jewish Communist*. Berkeley: University of California Press.

Lichtblau, Albert, and Sabine Jahn, eds. 1995. *Prive Friedjung: "Wir wollten nur das Paradies auf Erden": Die Erinnerung einer jüdischen Kommunistin aus der Bukowina* [Prive Friedjung: "We just wanted heaven on earth": The memories of a Jewish communist woman from Bukovina]. Vienna: Böhlau Verlag.

Livezeanu, Irina, with June Pachuta Farris, eds. 2007. *Women and Gender in Central and Eastern Europe, Russia, and Eurasia: A Comprehensive Bibliography*. Vol. 1, *Southeastern and East Central Europe*. Armonk: M.E. Sharpe.

Lóránd, Zsófia. 2022. "International Solidarity as the Cornerstone of the Hungarian Post-War Socialist Women's Rights Agenda in the Magazine *Asszonyok*." *International Review of Social History* 67, no. S30: 103–129.

Lovenduski, Joni. 2005. *Feminizing Politics*. Cambridge, UK and Malden, MA: Polity Press.

Lozovskii, A. [Лозовский, А.], ed. 1930. *Десять лет Профинтерна в резолюциях, документах и цифрах* [Ten years of the Profitern in resolutions, documents and numbers]. Moscow: Izdatelstvo VTsSPS.

Lukasser, Carina. 2002. "*Frauen in den freien Gewerkschaften Österreichs: Ihre Stellung und Bedeutung von 1918 bis 1932*" [Women in the free trade unions of Austria: Their position and significance from 1918 to 1932]. Diploma Thesis, Vienna University of Economics and Business.

Magyar Munkásmozgalmi Intézet (from 1956 A Magyar Szocialista Munkáspárt Központi Bizottságának Párttörténeti Intézete), ed. 1951–1960. *A magyar munkásmozgalom történetének válogatott dokumentumai* [Selected documents of the history of the Hungarian workers' movement], vols. 1–6. Budapest: Szikra.

Makal, Ahmet, and Gülay Toksöz, eds. 2012. *Geçmişten Günümüze Türkiye'de Kadın Emeği* [Women's labour in Turkey from past to present]. Ankara: Ankara Üniversitesi Yayınları.

Malečková, Jitka. 2004. "The Emancipation of Women for the Benefit of the Nation: The Czech Women's Movement." In *Women's Emancipation Movements in the Nineteenth Century: A European Perspective*, edited by Sylvia Paletschek and Bianka Pietrow-Ennker, 167–188. Stanford, CA: Stanford University Press.

Malínská, Jana. 2013. *"My byly, jsme a budeme!": české ženské hnutí 1860–1914 a idea českého národa* ["We existed, exist, and will exist!": Czech women's movement 1860–1914 and the idea of the Czech nation]. Prague: Nakladatelství Lidové Noviny.

Mamadouh, Virginie, and Martin Müller. 2017. "Political geography and geopolitics." In *European Regions and Boundaries: A Conceptual History*, edited by Diana Mishkova and Balázs Trencsényi, 258–279. New York: Berghahn Books.

Manley, John. 2005. "Moscow Rules? 'Red' Unionism and 'Class Against Class' in Britain, Canada, and the United States, 1928–1935." *Labour/Le Travailleur* 56: 9–50.

Marian, Maria. 1965. "Greva lucrătoarelor de la Regie din august 1906" [The strike of the Regie women tobacco workers from August 1906]. *Studii: Revista de istorie* [Studies: History review] 18, no. 1: 75–87.

Marinova, Mariia [Маринова, Мария]. 1989. "Комунистическият интернационал и възникването на международното женско комунистическо движение" [The Communist International and the emergence of the international women's communist movement]. *Izvestia na durzhavnite arkhivi* [Notices of the state archives] 57: 5–25.

Markova, Ina. 2019. *Tilly Spiegel: Eine politische Biographie* [Tilly Spiegel: A political biography]. Vienna: New Academic Press.

Masheva, Ivelina. (forthcoming). "Renegotiating Skills, Wages and the Right to Work: On the Gender of Labour Activism around Rationalization in the Bulgarian Tobacco Industry in the Early 1930s." *International Labor and Working-Class History.*

Massino, Jill. 2019. *Ambiguous Transitions: Gender, the State, and Everyday Life in Socialist and Postsocialist Romania*. New York: Berghahn Books.

Massino, Jill. 2009. "Workers under Construction: Gender, Identity, and Women's Experiences of Work in State Socialist Romania." In *Gender Politics and Everyday Life in State Socialist Eastern and Central Europe*, edited by Shana Penn and Jill Massino, 13–31. New York: Palgrave Macmillan.

Mazohl-Wallnig, Brigitte, ed. 1995. *Bürgerliche Frauenkultur im 19. Jahrhundert* [Bourgeois women's culture in the nineteenth century]. Vienna: Böhlau Verlag.

McAuley, Alistair. 1981. *Women's Work and Wages in the Soviet Union*. London: Allen and Unwin.

McBride Stetson, Dorothy E., and Amy Mazur, eds. 1995. *Comparative State Feminism*. Thousand Oaks: Sage Publications.

Mihăilescu, Ștefania. 2006. *Din istoria feminismului românesc: Studiu și antologie de texte* [From the history of Romanian feminism: Study and text anthology]. Bucharest: Polirom.

Milkman, Ruth, ed. 1985. *Women, Work, and Protest: A Century of U.S. Women's Labor History*. London: Routledge.

Morgan, Kevin. 2012. "Comparative Communist History and the 'Biographical Turn.'" *History Compass* 10, no. 6: 455–466.

Moriarty, Theresa. 2002. "'Who Will Look after the Kiddies?' Households and Collective Action during the Dublin Lockout." In *Rebellious Families: Household Strategies and Collective Action in the Nineteenth and Twentieth Century*, edited by Jan Kok, 110–124. New York: Berghahn Books.

Musabegović, Jasmina, ed. 1977. *Žene Bosne i Hercegovine u narodnooslobodilačkoj borbi 1941–1945 godine: Sjećanja učesnika* [Women of Bosnia and Herzegovina in the People's Liberation Struggle 1941–1945: Memoirs of the participants]. Sarajevo: Svjetlost.

Nacar, Can. 2019. *Labor and Power in the Late Ottoman Empire: Tobacco Workers, Managers, and the State, 1872–1912*. London: Palgrave Macmillan.

Nacar, Can. 2014. "The Régie Monopoly and Tobacco Workers in Late Ottoman Istanbul." *Comparative Studies of South Asia, Africa and the Middle East* 34, no. 1: 206–219.

Nagy, Margit Sárdi, ed. 1997. *Szerep és alkotás: Női szerepek a társadalomban és az alkotóművészetben* [Role and creative work: Women's roles in society and the creative arts]. Debrecen: Csokonai Kiadó.

Naples, Nancy A. 1998. *Grassroots Warriors: Activist Mothering, Community Work, and the War on Poverty*. London: Routledge.

Nazŭrska, Georgeta [Жоржета Назърска]. 2003. *Университетското образование и българските жени, 1879–1944* [University education and Bulgarian women, 1879–1944]. Sofia: IMIR.

Nečasová, Denisa. 2013. "Women's Organizations in the Czech Lands, 1948–89. An Historical Perspective." In *The Politics of Gender Culture under State Socialism: An Expropriated Voice*, edited by Hana Havelková and Libora Oates-Indruchová, 57–81. London and New York: Routledge.

Neudorflová, Marie L. 2010. "Problematika žen a placená práce v ženských časopisech na přelomu 19. a 20. století" [Women's problems and paid work in women's journals at the turn of the nineteenth and twentieth centuries]. *Historická demografie* [Historical demography] 34, no. 1: 2–13.

Neunsinger, Silke. 2018. "The Unobtainable Magic of Numbers: Equal Remuneration, the ILO and the International Trade Union Movement." In *Women's ILO: Transnational Networks, Global Labour Standards, and Gender Equity, 1919 to Present*, edited by Eileen Boris, Dorothea Hoehtker, and Susan Zimmermann, 121–148. Studies in Global Social History 32. Leiden: Brill.

O'Brien, Tia, and Nur Deris, eds. 2019. *The Struggle for Modern Turkey: Justice, Activism and a Revolutionary Female Journalist*. Translated by David Selim Sayers and Evrim Emir-Sayers. London and New York: I.B. Tauris.

Ortutay, Zsuzsa. 1960. *A nagy évforduló előtt (A nemzetközi nőmozgalom történetéből)* [Before the big anniversary (Of the history of the international women's movement)]. Budapest: Kossuth Kiadó Sokszorosító Üzeme.

Papp, Claudia. 2004.*"Die Kraft der Weiblichen Seele": Feminismus in Ungarn 1918–1941* ["The strength of woman's soul": Feminism in Hungary, 1918–1941]. Münster: Lit Verlag.

Paskaleva, Virginia [Паскалева, Вирджиния]. 1953. "За живота и дейността на Анна Маймункова" [On the life and activity of Anna Maimunkova]. *Istoricheski pregled* [Historical review], no. 4: 399–423.

Pasteur, Paul. 1986. "*Femmes dans le mouvement ouvrier autrichien 1918–1934*" [Women in the Austrian labour movement, 1918–1934]. 2 vol. PhD diss., Université de Rouen.

Penn, Shana, and Jill Massino, eds. 2009. *Gender Politics and Everyday Life in State Socialist Eastern and Central Europe*. New York: Palgrave Macmillan.

Pervan, Muazzez. 2013. *İlerici Kadınlar Derneği 1975–1980: Kırmızı Çatkılı Kadınların Tarihi* [Progressive women's association 1975–1980: The history of women with red headbands]. Istanbul: Tarih Vakfı Yayınları.

Pittaway, Mark. 2014. *From the Vanguard to the Margins: Workers in Hungary, 1939 to the Present. Selected Essays*. Edited by Adam Fabry. Leiden: Brill.

Pokorný, Jiří. 2006. "Odborářka. Příklad Karly Pfeiferové" [A trade unionist. The example of Karla Pfeiferová]. In *Člověk na Moravě v první polovině 20. století* [Man in Moravia in the first half of the twentieth century], edited by Lukáš Fasora, Jiří Hanuš, Jiří Malíř, and Libor Vykoupil, 419–431. Brno: Centrum pro studium demokracie a kultury.

Popa, Raluca. 2009. "Translating Equality between Women and Men across Cold War Divides: Women Activists from Hungary and Romania and the Creation of International Women's Year." In *Gender Politics and Everyday Life in State Socialist Eastern and Central Europe*, edited by Shana Penn and Jill Massino, 59–74. New York: Palgrave Macmillan.

Popova, Zhanna. (under review). "Halina Krahelska: Transnational Encounters of a Labour Activist, 1919–1939."

Popova, Zhanna, and Veronika Helfert. 2021. "Putting Activists Center Stage: An Introduction to the ZARAH Blog Series II." *ZARAH Blog*, January 2021. https://zarah-ceu.org/blog/.

Próchnik, Adam. 1948. *Kobieta w polskim ruchy socjalistycznym* [Woman in the Polish socialist movement]. Warsaw: Spółdzielnia wydawnicza "Wiedza."

Quataert, Donald. 1991. "Ottoman Women, Households, and Textile Manufacturing, 1800–1914." In *Women in Middle Eastern History: Shifting Boundaries in Sex and Gender*, edited by Nikki Keddie and Beth Baron, 161–176. New Haven, CT: Yale University Press.

Rajković, Ana. 2021. *Dugi ženski marš: Položaj radnica i ženski aktivizam u Hrvatskoj između dvaju svjetskih ratova* [The long women's march: The position of women workers and women's activism in Croatia between the two world wars]. Zagreb: DAF.

Rath, Brigitte. 2010. "Olga Misař oder: Die Vielfalt der Grenzüberschreitungen" [Olga Misař or: multiple transgressions]. *Ariadne—Forum für Frauen- und Geschlechtergeschichte* [Ariadne—Forum for women's and gender history] 57 (May): 44–47.

Réti, László. 1980. *A magyarországi textilipari munkásmozgalom* [The labour movement in the Hungarian textile industry]. Budapest: Textilipari Dolgozók Szakszervezete and Táncsics Könyvkiadó.

Rigler, Edith. 1976. *Frauenleitbild und Frauenarbeit in Österreich: Vom ausgehenden 19. Jahrhundert bis zum Zweiten Weltkrieg* [Female norm and women's work in Austria from the end of the nineteenth century to World War Two]. Munich: De Gruyter Oldenbourg.

Robinson, Fiona. 2011. *The Ethics of Care: A Feminist Approach to Human Security*. Philadelphia, PA: Temple University Press.

Romanian Workers' Party. 1949. *Căzute în luptă* [Fallen in the struggle]. Bucharest: Editura Partidului Muncitoresc Român.

Rose, Sonya O. 1988. "Gender Antagonism and Class Conflict: Exclusionary Strategies of Male Trade Unionists in Nineteenth-Century Britain." *Social History* 13, no. 2: 191–208.

Sachse, Carola. 2002. *Der Hausarbeitstag: Gerechtigkeit und Gleichberechtigung in Ost und West 1939–1994* [The domestic workday: Justice and equality in East and West 1939–1994]. Göttingen: Wallstein.

Sarıtaş, Ezgi, and Yelda Şahin Akıllı. 2015. "Feminist History of Periods of 'Stagnation': Women's Movement in the 1950s." Paper presented at the International Conference on Knowledge and Politics in Gender and Women's Studies, Ankara: Orta Doğu Teknik Üniversitesi, 9–11 October 2015.

Satı, Büşra. 2021. "Working-Class Women, Gender, and Union Politics in Turkey, 1965–1980." *International Labor and Working-Class History* 100: 87–108. doi: 10.1017/S0147547921000119.

Saygılıgil, Feryal. 2021. *Kadınlar Hep Vardı: Türkiye Solundan Kadın Portreleri* [Women were always there: Women portraits from the Turkish left]. Ankara: Dipnot Yayınları.

Schadt, Mária. 2003. *"Feltörekvő dolgozó nő." Nők az ötvenes években* ["Aspiring working woman." Women in the 1950s]. Budapest: Pro Pannonia Kiadói Alapítvány.

Schenk, Frithjof Benjamin. 2017. "Eastern Europe." In *European Regions and Boundaries: A Conceptual History*, edited by Diana Mishkova and Balázs Trencsényi, 188–209. New York: Berghahn Books.

Schindler, Christine, ed. 1993. *Der Forschungsstand zum Thema "Klasse und Geschlecht" in Zentral- und Osteuropa* [The state of research on the theme "class and gender" in Central and Eastern Europe]. Vienna: ITH.

Scott, Joan W. 1987. "On Language, Gender, and Working-Class History." *International Labor and Working-Class History*, no. 31: 1–13.

Sekyrková, Milada. 2010. "K sebereflexi pracujících žen na přelomu 19. a 20. století" [The self-examination of working women at the turn of the nineteenth and twentieth centuries]. *Historická demografie* [Historical demography] 34, no. 1: 30–44.

Silver, Beverly J. 2003. *Forces of Labor: Workers' Movements and Globalization since 1870.* Cambridge: Cambridge University Press.

Sklevicky, Lydia. 1984a. "Karakteristike organiziranog djelovanja žena u Jugoslaviji u razdoblju do Drugog svjetskog rata (I)" [Characteristics of women's organized activities in Yugoslavia in the period up to World War Two (I)]. *Polja* [Fields] 308: 415–417.

Sklevicky, Lydia. 1984b. "Karakteristike organiziranog djelovanja žena u Jugoslaviji u razdoblju do Drugog svjetskog rata (II)" [Characteristics of women's organized activities in Yugoslavia in the period up to World War Two (II)]. *Polja* [Fields] 309: 454–456.

Šoljan, Marija, ed. 1967. *Žene Hrvatske u radničkom pokretu do aprila hiljadu devetsto četrdeset prve* [Women of Croatia in the labour movement until April 1941]. Zagreb: Konferencija za društvenu aktivnost žena Hrvatske.

Šoljan, Marija, ed. 1955. *Žene Hrvatske u Narodnooslobodilačkoj borbi: Knjiga prva* [Women of Croatia in the People's Liberation Struggle: Volume 1]. Zagreb: Glavni odbor Saveza ženskih društava Hrvatske.

Šolle, Zdeněk. 1960. *Dělnické stávky v Čechách v druhé polovině 19. století* [Workers' strikes in the Czech lands in the second half of the nineteenth century]. Prague: ČSAV.

Stegmann, Natali. 2000. *Die Töchter der geschlagenen Helden: "Frauenfrage," Feminismus und Frauenbewegung in Polen 1863–1919* [The daughters of the beaten heroes: "Woman question," feminism, and women's movement in Poland, 1863–1919]. Wiesbaden: Harrassowitz.

Stibbe, Matthew, Ingrid Sharp, Clotide Faas, Veronika Helfert, Mary McAuliffe, and Corinne Painter. 2022. "Socialist Women and the Great War, 1914–21: Protest, Revolution and Commemoration." In *Socialist Women and the Great War,*

1914–21: Protest, Revolution and Commemoration, edited by Corinne Painter, Ingrid Sharp, and Matthew Stibbe, 1–30. London: Bloomsbury Academic.

Stites, Richard. 1978. *The Women's Liberation Movement in Russia: Feminism, Nihilism, and Bolshevism 1860–1930*. Princeton, NJ: Princeton University Press.

Studer, Brigitte. 2015. *The Transnational World of the Cominternians*. Basingstoke: Palgrave Macmillan.

Studer, Brigitte. 2008. "Arbeit am Selbst im Arbeiterstaat: Neue Quellen des Stalinismus und ihre Deutung" [Working on the self in the workers' state: New sources of Stalinism and their interpretation]. *Jahrbuch für Historische Kommunismusforschung* [Yearbook for historical research on communism] 8: 223–230.

Szegvári-Nagy, Katalin. 1981. *Út a nők egyenjogúságához* [The road to women's equality]. Budapest: Magyar Nők Országos Tanácsa: Kossuth Könyvkiadó.

Szegvári-Nagy, Katalin. 1969. *A nők művelődési jogaiért folytatott harc hazánkban (1777–1918)* [The struggle for women's educational rights in our home country (1777–1918)]. Budapest: Közgazdasági és Jogi Könyvkiadó.

Talay Keşoğlu, Birsen. 2007. "*Socialist Women's Organizations in Turkey, 1975–1980*." PhD diss., Boğaziçi Üniversitesi.

Taşkıran, Tezer. 1973. *Cumhuriyetin 50. Yılında Türk Kadın Hakları* [Turkish women's rights on the 50th anniversary of the republic]. Ankara: Başbakanlık Basımevi.

Tatar Kırılmış, İlknur. 2014. *Yaşar Nezihe Bükülmez*. Ankara: Gece Kitaplığı.

Tešija, Jelena. 2014. "*The End of the AFŽ – The End of Meaningful Women's Activism? Rethinking the History of Women's Organizations in Croatia, 1953–1961.*" MA thesis, Central European University.

Todorova, Maria. 2020. *The Lost World of Socialists at Europe's Margins: Imagining Utopia, 1870s–1920s*. New York: Bloomsbury Academic.

Todorova, Miglena. 2021. *Unequal under Socialism: Race, Women, and Transnationalism in Bulgaria*. Toronto: University of Toronto Press.

Todorova, Rada [Тодорова, Рада], Nedialka Karalieva [Недялка Каралиева], Nadia Gancheva [Надя Ганчева], Sonia Bakish [Соня Бакиш], and Mariia Dobreva [Мария Добрева], eds. 1960. *На предни линии: Спомени и очерци из историята на женското социалистическо движение в България* [On the front lines: Memoires and essays on the history of the women's socialist movement in Bulgaria]. Sofia: BKP.

Todorova, Tsveta [Тодорова, Цвета]. 1982. *Българската комунистическа партия и женското комунистическо движение в България (1919–1944)* [The Bulgarian Communist Party and the women's communist movement in Bulgaria (1919–1944)]. Sofia: Otechestven Front.

Toksöz, Gülay, and Seyhan Erdoğdu. 1998. *Sendikacı Kadın Kimliği* [Trade union women's identity]. Ankara: İmge Kitabevi.

Tóth, Eszter Zsófia. 2009. "'My Work, My Family, and My Car:' Women's Memories of Work, Consumerism, and Leisure in Socialist Hungary." In *Gender Politics and Everyday Life in State Socialist Eastern and Central Europe*, edited by Shana Penn and Jill Massino, 33–44. New York: Palgrave Macmillan.

Trausmuth, Gernot. 2019. *"Ich fürchte niemanden": Adelheid Popp und der Kampf für das Frauenwahlrecht* ["I fear nobody": Adelheid Popp and the fight for women's suffrage]. Vienna: Mandelbaum Verlag.

Tudoran, Georgeta. 1987. "Din lupta socialistă pentru afirmarea politică a femeii în anii premergători făuririi Partidului Comunist Român (III)" [From the socialist struggle for women's political affirmation in the years preceding the forging of the Romanian Communist Party (III)]. *Revista de istorie* [History review] 40, no. 5: 493–514.

Tudoran, Georgeta. 1986. "Din lupta socialistă pentru afirmarea politică a femeii la începutul secolului al XX-lea" [From the socialist struggle for women's political affirmation in the beginning of the twentieth century]. *Revista de istorie* [History review] 39, no. 2: 162–179.

Tudoran, Georgeta. 1985. "Din lupta socialistă pentru afirmarea femeii la sfârșitul secolului trecut" [From the socialist struggle for women's affirmation during the previous century]. *Revista de istorie* [History review] 38, no. 2: 128–144.

Tunçay, Mete, and Erik Jan Zürcher. 1994. *Socialism and Nationalism in the Ottoman Empire and Modern Turkey*. London and New York: Bloomsbury Publishing PLC.

Tutavac, Vesela, and Ilse Korotin, eds. 2016. *"Wir wollen der Gerechtigkeit und Menschenliebe dienen": Frauenbildung und Emanzipation in der Habsburgermonarchie—der südslawische Raum und seine Wechselwirkung mit Wien, Prag und Budapest* ["We want to serve justice and the love of mankind": Women's education and emancipation in the Habsburg Monarchy—The South Slavic region and its interaction with Vienna, Prague, and Budapest]. Vienna: Praesens Verlag.

Uhrová, Eva. 2008. *České ženy známé a neznámé* [Czech women we know and we don't know]. Prague: Mediasys.

Uhrová, Eva. 1984. *Po nevyšlapaných stezkách: z dějin ženského hnutí a jeho žurnalistiky do roku 1921* [Toward untrodden paths: From the history of the women's movement and their press until 1921]. Prague: Mona.

Urhan, Betül. 2014. *Sendikasız Kadınlar Kadınsız Sendikalar* [Women without trade unions, trade unions without women]. Istanbul: KADAV.

Valiavicharska, Zhivka. 2021. *Restless History: Political Imaginaries and Their Discontents in Post-Stalinist Bulgaria*. Montreal: McGill-Queen's University Press.

Van Duin, Pieter C. 2009. *Central European Crossroads: Social Democracy and National Revolution in Bratislava (Pressburg), 1867–1921*. New York: Berghahn.

Van Os, Nicole A. N. M. 1997. "Bursa'da Kadın İşçilerin 1910 Grevi" [Women workers' 1910 strike in Bursa]. *Toplumsal Tarih* [Social history] 7, no. 39: 7–10.

Varsa, Eszter. 2023. "'The Rulers Are the Causes of the War [...] They Are the Reason There Is No Bread in Our Town:' Women's Food Riots in the Hungarian Countryside, 1917–1918." *Journal of Contemporary Central and Eastern Europe* 13, no. 2: 279–299. doi: 10.1080/25739638.2023.2227515.

Varsa, Eszter. (under review). "The Women of Viharsarok [the Stormy Corner]: Peasant Women's Labour Activism in 1890s Hungary."

Vasilev, Vasil. 1970. [Василев, Васил], Mariia Chervendineva [Мария Червендинева], Mariia Ereliiska [Мария Ерелийска], and Petur Tsanev [Петър Цанев]. *Текстилци: Организация и борби на текстилните работници в България 1878–1944* [Textile workers: Organization and struggles of the textile workers in Bulgaria 1878–1944]. Sofia: Profizdat.

Verginella, Marta, ed. 2017. *Slovenka: Prvi ženski časopis (1897–1902)* [Slovenka: The first women's newspaper (1897–1902)]. Ljubljana: Filozofska fakulteta.

Veskoviḱ-Vangeli, Vera [Весковиќ-Вангели, Вера], and Marija Jovanoviḱ [Марија Јовановиќ], eds. 1976. *Зборник на документи за учеството на жените од Македонија во народноослободителната војна и револуцијата, 1941–1945* [Collection of documents on the participation of the women of Macedonia in the People's Liberation War and Revolution 1941–1945]. Skopje: Institut za nacionalna istorija.

Vodenicharova, Zdravka [Воденичарова, Здравка], and Nevena Popova [Невена Попова]. 1972. *Революционното женско движение в* България [The revolutionary women's movement in Bulgaria]. Sofia: Otechestven Front.

Wohlgemuthová, Renata. 1965. "Účast žen v české sociální demokracii." [The participation of women in Czech social democracy]. *Československý časopis historický* [Czechoslovak historical journal] 13, no. 3: 403–418.

Wood, Elizabeth. 1997. *The Baba and the Comrade: Gender and Politics in Revolutionary Russia*. Bloomington: Indiana University Press.

Yici, Özkal. 2010. *Kırk Bir Uzun Gün: Berec Grevi* [Forty-one long days: Berec strike]. Istanbul: Sosyal Tarih Yayınları.

Yılmaz, İlkay. 2021. "Conspiracy, International Police Cooperation and the Fight against Anarchism in the Late Ottoman Empire, 1878–1908." In *Age of Rogues: Rebels, Revolutionaries and Racketeers at the Frontiers of Empires*, edited by Ramazan Hakkı Öztan and Alp Yenen, 208–234. Edinburgh: Edinburgh University Press.

Zalai, Katalin. 2017a. "Háborús 'nőügyek'" [The case of women during the war]. In *Háborús mindennapok—mindennapok háborúja: Magyarország és a Nagy Háború—ahogy a sajtó látta (1914–1918)* [Everyday life during the war—The war of the everydays: Hungary and the Great War—As seen through the press (1914–1918)], edited by Eszter Kaba, 224–288. Budapest: Politikatörténeti Intézet, Napvilág Kiadó.

Zalai, Katalin. 2017b. "A nők 'baljós' térfoglalása: A nők gazdasági mobilizációja az első világháború idején" [The alarming occupation of public space by women: Women's economic mobilization during World War One]. In *1916 a fordulat éve? Tanulmányok a Nagy Háborúról* [1916, the year of change? Studies on the Great War], edited by Gábor Egry and Eszter Kaba, 229–266. Budapest: Napvilág.

Żarnowska, Anna, and Andrzej Szwarc, eds. 2000. *Kobieta i praca. Wiek XIX i XX. Zbiór studiów* [Woman and work. Nineteenth and twentieth centuries. A collection of studies] Warsaw: DiG.

Zihnioğlu, Yaprak. 2003. *Kadınsız İnkılap: Nezihe Muhiddin, Kadınlar Halk Fırkası, Kadın Birliği* [Revolution without women: Nezihe Muhiddin, the Women's People's Party, the Women's Alliance]. Istanbul: Metis Yayınları.

Zimmermann, Susan. 2023a. "Dance Around a 'Sacred Cow:' Women's Night Work and the Gender Politics of the Mass Worker in State-Socialist Hungary and Internationally." In *State Socialism: History, Theory, Anti-Capitalist Alternatives*, edited by Eszter Bartha, Tamás Krausz, and Bálint Mezei, 79–127. Basingstoke: Palgrave Macmillan.

Zimmermann, Susan. 2023b. "The Changing Politics of Women's Work and the Making of Extended Childcare Leave in State-Socialist Hungary, Europe, and Internationally: Shifting the Scene." In *Life Course, Work and Labour: Historical, Sociological and Anthropological Perspectives*, edited by Josef Ehmer and Carola Lentz, 225–257. Berlin: De Gruyter.

Zimmermann, Susan. 2023c. "Spurring Women to Action? Communist-Led Women's Trade Unionism Between the Hungarian Shopfloor and Top-Level Internationalism, 1947 to 1959." *Journal of Contemporary Central and Eastern Europe 31*, no. 2: 339–362. doi: 10.1080/25739638.2023.2227518.

Zimmermann, Susan. 2022. "Introducing Magda Aranyossi: Notes on Her Life, Writings, and the Politics of History." In *The Forgotten Revolution: The 1919 Hungarian Republic of Councils*, edited by András B. Göllner, 157–165. Montreal and Chicago: Black Rose/ University of Chicago Press.

Zimmermann, Susan. 2021. *Frauenpolitik und Männergewerkschaft: Internationale Geschlechterpolitik, IGB-Gewerkschafterinnen und die Arbeiter- und Frauenbewegungen der Zwischenkriegszeit* [Women's politics and men's trade unionism: International gender politics, women IFTU-trade unionists and the workers' and women's movements of the interwar period]. Vienna: Löcker Verlag.

Zimmermann, Susan. 2020a. "'It Shall Not Be a Written Gift, But a Lived Reality': Equal Pay, Women's Work, and the Politics of Hungary." In *Labor in State-Socialist Europe, 1945–1989: Contributions to a History of Work*, edited by Marsha Siefert, 337–372. Budapest: CEU Press.

Zimmermann, Susan. 2020b. "Framing Working Women's Rights Internationally: Contributions of the IFTU Women's International." In *The Internationalisation of the Labour Question. Ideological Antagonism, Workers' Movements and the ILO since 1919*, edited by Stefano Bellucci and Holger Weiss, 95–117. Houndsmills and New York: Palgrave Macmillan.

Zimmermann, Susan. 2018. "The Agrarian Working Class Put Somewhat Centre Stage: An Often Neglected Group of Workers in the Historiography of Labour in State-Socialist Hungary." *European Review of History/Revue européenne d'histoire* 25, no. 1: 79–100. doi: 10.1080/13507486.2017.1374926.

Zimmermann, Susan. 2014. "In and Out of the Cage: Women's and Gender History Written in Hungary in the State-Socialist Period." *Aspasia: International Yearbook for Women's and Gender History of Central, Eastern and Southeastern Europe* 8: 125–149. doi: 10.3167/asp.2014.080107.

Zimmermann, Susan. 2006. "Reich, Nation, und Internationalismus: Konflikte und Kooperationen der Frauenbewegungen der Habsburgermonarchie" [Empire, nation, and internationalism: Conflict and cooperation among the women's movements of the Habsburg Monarchy]. In *Frauenbilder, feministische Praxis und nationales Bewusstsein in Österreich-Ungarn 1867–1918* [Images of women, feminist praxis and national consciousness in Austria-Hungary 1867–1918], edited by Waltraud Heindl, Edit Király, and Alexandra Millner, 119–167. Tübingen and Basel: A. Francke Verlag.

Zimmermann, Susan. 2005. "The Challenge of Multinational Empire for the International Women's Movement: The Case of the Habsburg Monarchy." *Journal of Women's History* 17, no. 2: 87–117.

Zimmermann, Susan. 1999. *Die bessere Hälfte? Frauenbewegungen und Frauenbestrebungen im Ungarn der Habsburgermonarchie 1848 bis 1918* [The better half? Women's movements and women's aspirations in Hungary under the Habsburg Monarchy 1848–1918]. Vienna and Budapest: Promedia Verlag and Napvilág Kiadó.

Zimmermann, Susan, Birgitta Bader-Zaar, Ágoston Berecz, Jitka Gelnarová, Alexandra Ghit, and Michaela Königshofer. 2018. "Women and Social Movements in the Habsburg Empire." In *Women and Social Movements in Modern Empires since 1820*, edited by Kathryn Kish Sklar and Thomas Dublin. Alexander Street Press. https://search.alexanderstreet.com/wasg.

Zirin, Mary, and Christine D. Worobec, eds. 2007. *Women and Gender in Central and Eastern Europe, Russia, and Eurasia: A Comprehensive Bibliography*. Vol. 2, *Russia, the Non-Russian Peoples of the Russian Federation, and the Successor States of the Soviet Union*. Armonk: M.E. Sharpe.

PART 1

Women's Struggles and Men-Dominated Trade Union and Labour Movements: Rethinking a Complex Relationship

CHAPTER 2

On Unity and Unions

St. Petersburg Women Printers and Labour Activism in the Trade Union Paper The Printers' Herald, *1906*

Sophia Polek

Abstract

In 1906—immediately after the Russian Revolution of 1905—a remarkable debate developed on the pages of *The Printers' Herald* (*Вестник Печатников*), the official trade union journal of the St. Petersburg Printers' Union. An anonymous woman typesetter published an article entitled "The Voice of the Woman Worker," sparking a debate about gendered experiences in the workplace and the resulting problems for unity in unions. Seven contributions published in *The Printers' Herald* between May and July 1906 form the core source base of this chapter. A feminist reading of these articles reveals a variety of attitudes towards unionism, including the voices of the anonymous woman typesetter as well as that of Tat'iana Abramovna Rubinchik, a woman printer, editor of the trade union journal, and a member of the executive committee of the St. Petersburg Printers' Union. This analysis expands our understanding of printers' political attitudes, showing how their conceptualization of class, which was based on their belief in the moral superiority of workers, failed to incorporate the experiences of those who were marginalized within this broader group and therefore threatened the unity of the printers' union. This chapter challenges the heretofore masculine focus of research on the printers—one of the most influential groups in the imperial Russian workers' movement—and uncovers the voices of women print unionists.

Keywords

access to unions – print unionism – Russian Revolution 1905 – St. Petersburg Printers' Union – Tat'iana Abramovna Rubinchik – *Вестник Печатников* (*The Printers' Herald*) – trade union journal – voices of women printers

 | DOI:10.1163/9789004682481_003

"With your attitude toward us, women, you make us alienate ourselves from you. Out of this comes, discord, disunity, and the result is division."[1] Such were the words of a woman typesetter in an article for the trade union paper of the St. Petersburg Printers' Union (Союз рабочих печатного дела) in May 1906. She wrote them during the development of the first legal trade unions in the Russian Empire. It was a "transitional period" between the legalization of trade unions in April 1906 following the mass strikes of the revolutionary year 1905 and the reaction of the imperial government in June 1907, which sought to put an end to union organizing.[2] During these months, the St. Petersburg printers, like workers in many other industries, consolidated their union (and resumed it after a temporary closure by the government) and campaigned for the improvement of working conditions. The printers were one of the most powerful groups of workers in St. Petersburg as well as Moscow, with a high level of unionization.[3] There is research on various aspects of the internal organization of the St. Petersburg and Moscow Printers' unions, such as delegate councils, trade union journals and the underlying common values and goals, but no scholar has addressed the inclusion of women printers. This may be due to the small number of women printers and women print unionists within an otherwise highly unionized profession. Exact numbers are difficult to find. For Moscow in 1907, it is estimated that women printers made up 1.5 percent of union membership, while they constituted between 6 and 10.8 percent of the print work force.[4] In this chapter, I show that by attentively reading trade union papers and other journals, the marginalized voices of women printers can still be found.[5]

After an introduction to the printing industry of late imperial Russia and the start of legal print unionization after the Revolution of 1905, I will present two micro-herstories.[6] In the first, I will analyze a debate in the printers' trade union

1 Naborshchitsa 1906, 3. All translations from Russian into English are mine.

2 Bonnell 1983, 315–321.

3 Zelnik 2006, 620; Engelstein 1982, 73. Between 1906 and 1907, out of a total of 18,048 printers in St. Petersburg, 12,000 were union members (peak membership), corresponding to a unionization rate of 66 percent. At the same time in Moscow, 8,000 out of 12,384 printers were union members, which corresponds to a 65 percent unionization rate. Bonnell 1983, 208–209.

4 Bonnell 1984, 216–217; Sher 1911, 44–45.

5 A newly released anthology about women in print production tackles the "challenges of rescuing these lives from obscurity" by using other sources such as wills or company archives, see Moog 2022, 2. One contribution uses census data and vital records in order to track the employment of women especially in typesetting in Perth, Scotland, see Williams 2022, 173–192.

6 Contributing to what Rochelle Goldberg Ruthchild calls "telling Russia's herstory": see Ruthchild 2016, 173. For works on women's lives in imperial Russia, see Muravyeva and

paper *The Printers' Herald* (*Вестник Печатников*) about unity and union in the printers' movement that was sparked by a woman typesetter's criticism and threats concerning women's separate organizing. In the second micro-herstory, I will turn towards the pragmatic incentives used to entice women printers to join the union, again as expressed in print. Here, I will furthermore introduce Tat'iana Abramovna Rubinchik, a woman print unionist who has been overlooked thus far, to the scholarship on the printers' movement in the "transitional period" of unionization in imperial Russia (1906–1907). I will use a close-reading approach for the article analysis in order to capture sometimes quite subtle issues in this rather limited set of sources. Inspired by gender-oriented narratology, I will pay special attention to the performance of the narrators in the articles, their agency and relationship to the actors they discuss, as well as the line and structure of their argumentation.[7] This chapter is, thus, a study of women printers' labour activism in print and facets of the notions of unity and union advanced in the union paper *The Printers' Herald* in reaction to one woman printer's critique. It offers insight into print unionist ideology in the context of the transitional phase of unionization in imperial Russia after the revolution of 1905.

1 Labour Organization in Late Imperial Russia

The history of workers in the Russian Empire—peasant serfs, miners, workers in cottage industry, urban artisans, and factory workers—did not begin in the nineteenth or even twentieth century, of course. However, due to forced industrialization in the 1870s and 1890s and simultaneous urbanization, an industrial workforce developed in the industrial hotspots of the empire.[8] Numerically speaking, this was a small group: in the 1897 national census, the industrial workforce numbered about two million persons out of a population of over 128 million. Nevertheless, despite their relatively small numbers, industrial workers gained social and political prominence in the late Russian

---

Novikova 2014; Clements 2012; Engel 2004, 1994, 1983; Bisha 2002; Edmondson 2001; Norton and Gheith 2001; Worobec, Engel, and Clements 1991. This is not an exhaustive list.

7 Gymnich 2010, 255–259; Allrath and Gymnich 2004, 33–48.

8 Zelnik 2006, 619–621; Ananich 2006, 408–417; Palat 2007, 307–312. Such hotspots were St. Petersburg, Moscow, Baku, the Don basin, the Urals, parts of Congress Poland, and the port cities of Riga and Odesa. It is important to note that the category of "industrial workers" is an elusive one.

Empire.[9] Workers' organization in the form of mutual aid funds, neighborhood associations, trade journals, clubhouses, libraries, and assemblies were established, although trade unions remained illegal until 1906.[10]

Labour unrest, including work stoppages, became increasingly visible and political, especially when it took place in the industrial political centers of St. Petersburg and Moscow. Workers frequently connected their deteriorating working conditions with the structural problems of the imperial administration, and unrest was reported in the growing commercial periodical press. The decade leading up to the 1905 Revolution saw widespread strike actions in the St. Petersburg textile and metal industries (1896–1897 and 1901, respectively), in the Moscow printing industry (1903), and elsewhere in the empire.[11] From the first organized factory strike actions in the 1870s on, members of the radical *intelligentsia* interacted with workers. Above all, the Marxist-influenced groups of the Social Democrats, which split into the Menshevik and Bolshevik wings in 1903, and the Socialist-Revolutionaries became involved in labour unrest and the organized labour movement.[12] In the Jewish Pale of Settlement, the socialist "Bund" (algemeyner yidisher arbeter-bund in lite, poyln un rusland) organized workers. In order to prevent such activity, the tsarist authorities even came up with their own workers' organization administered by police officers. The idea was to sponsor associations and activities among workers that were intensively surveilled by the police and distanced members from other oppositional political groups. The experiments of Sergei Zubatov and Father Gapon are the most famous examples of this strategy of "ideological subservience."[13]

In 1904, the Russian Empire entered into a disastrous and unpopular war with Japan, which led to open criticism of the government across the political spectrum and caused economic conditions to deteriorate. In the early days of

9 Mayoraz 2021, 76–80; Zelnik 2006, 620–621, 627–631; Steinberg 1994, 76; Steinberg 1992, 323; Ruud 1981, 383–384; Sher 1911, 460.

10 Koenker 2005, 19–20; Steinberg 1992, 525–551; Bonnell 1983, 73–97.

11 Mayoraz 2021; Zelnik 2006, 621–624; Bovykin, Borodkin, and Kiryanov 1988; Bonnell 1983, 80–81.

12 Mayoraz 2021, 30–31; Zelnik 2006, 623–624; Engelstein 1982, 73–96. However, this does not mean that all strikes or trade union activities were necessarily revolutionary in character.

13 Palat 2007, 337–341; Zelnik 2006, 625–627; Daly 2006, 644; Bonnell 1983, 80–93. Zubatov worked for the Department of the Police, and in the late 1890s, he came up with the program of police-sponsored workers' clubs in major cities of the empire that addressed the material life conditions of workers. A spin-off of Zubatov's experiment was the organization of tearooms and social clubs by Father Gapon in St. Petersburg in 1904. Both initiatives were meant to drive the workers away from revolutionary groups and activities. This strategy did not go according to plan for the tsarist government as the events of late 1904 and early 1905 show.

January 1905, the situation at home escalated. One hundred thousand workers in St. Petersburg went on strike to protest the arbitrary dismissal of four workers at the Putilov Iron Works Factory. The unrest culminated in a march of tens of thousands of workers on 9 January led by the Orthodox priest Father Gapon, who had founded numerous social clubs for workers in St. Petersburg that had enjoyed the support of local authorities since 1904. The plan was to march peacefully to the Winter Palace and present the tsar with a petition describing inhumane working conditions and demanding civil rights, such as the freedom of assembly and speech, the right to participate in politics, and an end to the war with Japan. However, soldiers opened the fire on the unarmed workers. "Bloody Sunday" was the kick-off for the revolutionary year of 1905. Strikes and unrest spread from St. Petersburg to cities across the empire and to the countryside. It was not only industrial workers and peasants who revolted against the tsarist regime; marines, students, and the oppositional liberal *zemstvo* movement also demonstrated. These months were marked by the establishment of new unions, new group identification, mass movements on the streets, and the awakening and hope, but there was also street fighting, pogroms, and a brutal reaction against these developments by the tsarist armed forces and the far-right paramilitary "Black Hundreds" groups.[14]

One of the most influential groups of industrial workers involved in the unrest of 1905 were the printers, who had de facto control over the print production of the empire, that is, a vital part of the empire's communication infrastructure. Their Moscow strike in September and October 1905, for example, led to the complete closure of printing plants and paralyzed all newspaper operations for a fortnight, causing a news blackout.[15] There is some evidence of printers refusing to set and print articles that ran counter to their political views in the dailies or refusing to hand over newspaper issues to censorship officers.[16] Printers also set and printed articles against the wishes of editors.[17] In October 1905, tsar Nikolai II (1868–1918) finally had to give in to the pressure of the protestors and some of his advisers. In the 1905 "October Manifesto," he was forced to grant a series of civil and political rights, including freedom of assembly, and the introduction of a State Duma (the lower house of the legislative assembly) with elected delegates.[18] After the major strike actions of 1905,

14 Aust 2017, 23–55; Smith 2017, 9–59; Steinberg 2017, 47–59, 132–138, 170–215; Lieven 2015, 46–224; Figes 2014, 27– 47; Aust 2007; Sprotte 2007; Ascher 2004.

15 Engelstein 1982, 97–113; Ruud 1981, 387; Sher 1911, 160–182.

16 Engelstein 1982, 97– 113, Ruud 1981, 390; Sher 1911, 211–222.

17 As in the case of the "finance manifesto" in December 1905, see Ruud 1981, 390–395.

18 Aust 2017, 23–55; Smith 2017, 60–71; Dahlmann 2009; Ascher 2004.

the printers of St. Petersburg, Moscow, and many other cities transformed their strike committees and mutual aid assemblies into trade unions. Trade unions were legalized in the "Temporary Regulations on Unions and Societies" issued by the tsarist government on 4 March 1906, and the broad development of a trade union organization got underway.[19] However, this "transitional period" ended in the summer of 1907. The tsar felt threatened by the political program of Duma delegates and dissolved two elected State Dumas in July 1906 and June 1907. On 3 June 1907, prime minister Petr Arkad'evich Stolypin (1862–1911) changed the electoral law to ensure that the third Duma would be dominated by conservative delegates. This "coup" was also the beginning of a government campaign to break the power and structures of trade unions.[20] The debates analyzed in this chapter take place in the period between the legalization of trade unions in March 1906 and the government reaction after the "coup" of June 1907.

2 The Printers' Unions

The printers overwhelmingly belonged to the factory labour force within the manufacturing sector. In the last decades of the nineteenth century and the early years of the twentieth, the printing trade of imperial Russia went from being a small, skilled handicraft into a factory-based industry that produced printed materials for a mass market.[21] In factories, the mechanization as well as the division of printing labour became more advanced.[22] A highly hierarchical organization based on "skill, training, and authority" became dominant, leading to constant tension between master printers, supervisors, assistants, skilled printers, apprentices, semi-skilled or unskilled press workers, and folders. Unskilled peasant boys came into industrial centers to work in the lowest

19 Bonnell 1984, 194–209. In St. Petersburg alone, 72 unions were registered between 1906 and the summer of 1907.

20 Solov'ev 2021; Aust 2017, 23–55; Smith 2017, 71–100; Figes 2014, 49–69; Dahlmann 2009; Bonnell 1984, 315–349.

21 Steinberg 1994, 76; Steinberg 1992, 323; Sher 1911, 460.

22 This development was not unique to the Russian printing trade. For the British case, see, for instance, Score 2014. Compared to the British printing trade, setting machines were introduced in the Russian Empire only in the early years of the twentieth century and were not as successfully adopted as elsewhere because labour was cheaper than the purchase and maintenance of the machines. See Koenker 2005, 31.

ranks of the printing industry, as did many peasant women.[23] Print workers were not a homogeneous group, and even within subgroups, there were major differences in terms of levels of literacy and income.[24] Among typographers, for instance, typesetters were the most highly skilled workers and earned a significantly higher income than printers working at printing presses. Since no apprenticeship was required to operate the machines, it was mostly women who worked at the printing presses and, thus, in the largest industrial printing plants. Smaller print shops that could not afford such machinery employed significantly more children as cheap, unskilled labour.[25] In the 1870s, a normal working day for both women and men printers lasted fourteen to fifteen hours; after the strikes of 1903, ten hours; and after the 1905 Revolution, nine hours. The conditions in printing plants were exceptionally unhealthy and dangerous due to the large machinery, the chemicals used for printing, and the lead dust that sloughed off the typesetting letters. Typesetters especially suffered from eating disorders, lead poisoning, consumption, and myopia.[26] Women printers also experienced abuse, harassment, and gender discrimination perpetrated by their fellow workers, foremen, and employers.[27] Taking into account differences in wages between various groups working in printing plants, women printers received about 40 percent of male printers' wages. In certain areas such as folding or lacquering, the percentage was even lower. Women typesetters earned about 66 percent of the wages of their male counterparts; this was the narrowest wage gap in the industry. However, the proportion of women employed in highly skilled typesetting work was very low. Women printers were also more likely to be illiterate than men, and they tended to be older than men at the time of their initial employment in the printing industry.[28] Compared to other professional groups, however, printers as a group were disproportionately literate and also enjoyed relatively high incomes.

---

23 Koenker 2005, 26; Engel 2004, 95–100; Steinberg 1992, 323–342. In the 1880s, women made up 22 percent of the overall factory work force in the central part of the empire; by 1914, this figure was 32 percent, see Clements 2012, 136–138.

24 In 1900, a Petersburg machine master in the typographic department earned 72 rubles per month, whereas a feeder in the same department earned 24 rubbles. A news compositor earned 51 rubbles, and a book compositor 31 rubles. Binding workers had an average income of 26 rubbles. See McDermid and Hillyar 1998, 35, 45, 86–88; Steinberg 1992, 366–374.

25 Sher 1911, 55; Dmitrieva 1909. For the British context, see Score 2014.

26 Sher 1911, 47–54.

27 Mayoraz 2021, 65; Engel 2004, 96–97; Smith 2002, 99; McDermid and Hillyar 1998, 44–45, 111; Glickman 1984, 204–208. Working women in general were often forced to engage in prostitution because their income was not high enough to support their families.

28 Clements 2012, 136–137; Glickman 1984, 86–87; Sher 1911, 55–57; Dmitrieva 1909.

Before the legalization of trade unions in 1906, the printers of imperial Russia had been organizing in mutual aid societies for decades. Their main aim was to financially support members in case of illness or accident, and they rarely voiced concerns related to working conditions or factory legislation. Employers actively participated in these associations at the administrative level. Print workers usually did not hold offices in the mutual aid societies, but they were still able to gain experience in running associations. These voluntary societies were not yet mass-membership organizations. Trade festivals organized in collaboration with employers were also common among printers, as were printing industry trade journals. In 1902, the first worker-oriented trade union journal *The Typesetter* (*Наборщик*) was inaugurated by the St. Petersburg typesetters and their mutual aid society. Articles in *The Typesetter* addressed issues related to working conditions and proposed reforms.[29] Among the radical *intelligentsia,* it was the Social Democrats and, after their split in 1903, above all the Mensheviks who participated in printers' organizations, similar to their involvement in many other workers' organizations.[30] Nevertheless, *The Typesetter* and the Petersburg printers who organized around that paper and the mutual aid society followed a "moral-communitarian" approach to organizing. They saw themselves and the (good) employer both as parts of a "single human community." In order to overcome the suffering of workers, it was not class struggle or revolution that was needed; rather class collaboration would lead to the "moral transformation of personal and social relationships."[31]

After the mass strikes of the 1905 Revolution and the legalization of trade unions, many mutual aid societies, factory committees, and strike committees were transformed into trade unions. General unionization developed across the Russian Empire. Printers organized themselves into industrial unions, unifying the various craft-based groups such as typesetters, press-workers, lithographers, folders, and bookbinders.[32] In August 1905, the St. Petersburg Union of Print Workers (Союз рабочих печатного дела) was founded, and its leaders organized around the new class-oriented and more militant trade union paper *The Print Herald* (*Печатный вестник*).[33] After the official registration

29 Steinberg 1994, 67–68; Bonnell 1984, 76–80.

30 Steinberg 1994, 81; Bonnell 1984, 160–164. Vasilii Vladimirovich Sher (1883–1940), author of the study on the Moscow printers' movement from 1911, was a Menshevik himself. Several articles in the printers' press also explicitly express their sympathy for the Social Democrats. See, for instance, Orlov 1906, 7.

31 Steinberg 1994, 67.

32 Koenker 2005, 18–19; Steinberg 1992; Bonnell 1984, 106–151.

33 Steinberg 1994, 76; Steinberg 1992; Bonnell 1984, 129–130.

of the union following the "Temporary Regulations" of 4 March, 1906, the trade union paper was renamed *The Printers' Herald* and appeared under the editorial supervision of G. S. Zhuravlev from April 1906 until its closure by government officials in July 1906. The printers immediately restarted the paper with basically the same content under a new name: *The Printer's Voice* (*Голос Печатника*) and with new acting editors T. A. Rubinchik and I. Kh. Babichev.

Trade union journals in general were financed by the unions, usually ran eight to sixteen pages, and normally contained an amalgam of features of newspapers and thematic magazines, both in form and content.[34] The editors of *The Printers' Herald* declared that their journal was a union organ, and as such, it would look out for the needs of printers as well as explain and defend their interests.[35] As *The Printer's Voice* was clearly a continuation of *The Printers' Herald*, the same purpose and objectives can be assumed for *The Printer's Voice*. The editors of both papers included advertisements, job postings, and articles about the most important developments in their profession in the Russian Empire and abroad. There were reports about the trade union executive committee meetings, articles about the labour and civil rights policies of the imperial government, and candidate recommendations for State Duma elections. The printers' trade union journals had a circulation of approximately 10,000 copies, an impressive figure compared to the print run of other St. Petersburg dailies during the same time.[36] But the activities of the St. Petersburg Printers' Union were not limited to publishing a trade union paper in the period between legalization in spring 1906 and the tsarist "coup" in 1907. The union also fought for the introduction of a Sunday rest day for all printers and a single *tarif* for all Petersburg printing plants, and union leaders entered into negotiations with employers and publishers.[37]

---

34 Sliadneva 2016, 166–169.

35 "Ot redaktsii" 1906a. Additionally, there were organizations and journals for specific crafts within the printing industry. See Koenker 2005; Steinberg 1992.

36 In two incidents, authorities ordered that all 10,000 copies of an issue of *The Printer's Voice* were to be confiscated. Therefore, I assume *The Printers' Herald* had the same or a similar print run. As noted in the official censorship documentation, the printers managed to save 75 percent and 100 percent, respectively, of the copies by the time the inspectors arrived: Document No. 1791, 8 February (22 February) 1907, str. 68, d. 196, op. 9, f. 776, RGIA, St. Petersburg, Russia; Document No. 1186, 19 February (4 March) 1907, str. 72–72ob, d. 196, op. 9, f. 776, RGIA, St. Petersburg, Russia. The St. Petersburg dailies *Новое Время* (*The New Time*) and *Речь* (*Speech*) had print runs of 60,000 and 40,000, respectively, for the year 1905. See McReynolds 1991, appendix.

37 Bonnell 1984, 298–304.

In principle, the printers' unions of both St. Petersburg and Moscow did not exclude women from membership or from holding an office. All groups of print workers could join the unions: skilled and unskilled workers, apprentices and women. Non-members could sit in the meetings too, and even workers from outside print factories were welcome. Only non-proletarian (or metaphorical) "print workers" such as writers were explicitly denied entrance.[38] The demands of a petition drawn up by the print workers of the Sytin printing plant in Moscow and submitted to their employer in September 1905 show an awareness of the difficult situation of women printers. The printers called for the introduction of a workers' delegation consisting of men and women printers in each factory and equal wages within all departments, as well as maternity leave (four weeks before and six weeks after birth), a break every three hours to breastfeed, and the introduction of childcare facilities in factories.[39] In this way, the union sought to provide incentives for women printers to join.

Still, due to a lack of sources, it remains difficult to assess how accessible strike committees and trade unions were for women printers in practice. Apart from possible ideological differences, one can imagine there were several obstacles preventing women from joining the union. As equal wages were not a reality, it is likely that it was far more difficult for women workers to pay the union membership fee. Further, strike committee meetings often took place in locations that were not always accessible to women such as pubs and restaurants. The Moscow printers' strike of 1903, for example, was organized during unofficial meetings involving several hundred participants in a restaurant in Moscow, and later, for security reasons, at locations outside the city.[40] In general, attending meetings—especially in the evening—would likely have been far more difficult for women workers to attend since many had to care for children after finishing their factory work. And then there is the question of how the workplace culture at printing plants influenced women printers' decisions to unionize or not. As mentioned above, research has described the "masculinized culture of the capitalist workplace" among male workers—also present at the printing plants of St. Petersburg—which included intense peer pressure, heavy drinking, vulgar language, explicit boasts about sexual exploits, as well

38 Sher 1911, 189. The pre-revolutionary Zubatov and Gapon societies, for instance, excluded women from leadership positions, see Wood 1997, 27.

39 "Революция 1905 г. Петиция типографских рабочих, от департамента полиции (хроника событий), Забастовка типо-литографов" [The Revolution of 1905. Petition of printing workers, from the police department (a chronicle of events), the strike of printers], 19 September (2 October) 1905, e. kh. 26, k. 26, f. 259, Russian State Library. Manuscript Department (Российская государственная библиотека, Отдел рукописей), Moscow, Russia.

40 Sher 1911, 115–119.

as comments about looks, derogatory names, and vulgar jokes directed toward their female colleagues.[41] Kopeliovich, the author of one of the articles published in *The Printers' Herald* analyzed this culture in the paper; he speaks of the "humiliation" (*унижение*) of women printers and the "unjust, senseless mockery and persecution" (*несправедливые, бессмысленные насмешки и гонения*) they faced.[42] Often times, such misogynist behavior was instrumentalized by male workers to prove one's status through the "subordination of women."[43] In addition to this article, this masculine workplace culture was criticized by "conscious" male workers, who saw this behavior as a "moral vice," based on the belief that women were human beings to who deserve respect, dignity, and protection.[44] It was in this context that a debate about unity and union with regard to women printers unfolded on the pages of *The Printers' Herald* in 1906.

3 The Voice of the Woman Worker Debate

Especially after 1905, trade union journals were used by women workers to publicly "confront not only management and society but men comrades as well" due to their experiences of gender-based discrimination and harassment.[45] The article "The Voice of the Woman Worker" by Naborshchitsa is one such example of this.[46] As the title already suggests, the article functions as a speech in essay form, and it was published in the 20 May (2 June) issue of *The Printers' Herald* in 1906.[47] The self-proclaimed motivation for the essay was to make the voices of women printers heard as they had not yet been represented

41 Smith 2002, 98–99. Williams speaks of "'male' practices" in print shops in Great Britain, including rituals for "marking the transition from apprentice to journeyman" (women were officially excluded from apprenticeships in print shops) and a drinking culture, see Williams 2022, 178.

42 Kopeliovich 1906, 3.

43 Mayoraz 2021, 65; Engel 2004, 96–97; Smith 2002, 98–99; McDermid and Hillyar 1998, 44–45, 111; Steinberg 1992, 78, 242; Glickman 1984, 204–208. Also, the idea that leadership was a male prerogative continued to be prevalent in the labour movement of the early twentieth century, preventing women workers from joining unions. See Clements 2012, 138.

44 Smith 2002, 98–99; Steinberg 1994, 82.

45 Glickman 1984, 204.

46 Since the activist signed her article with the pseudonym "Naborshchitsa," meaning "woman typesetter," I will treat this pseudonym as her name in the following analysis.

47 Naborshchitsa 1906, 3.

in the trade union journal.[48] The essay is arranged symmetrically, opening with an exclamatory salutation and a *captatio benevolentiae*, followed by the first argument, and culminating in a prolepsis. Then comes the second argument and finally several slogans forming a *finis benevolentiae*.

Naborshchitsa opens the essay by using classical rhetorical techniques to address the audience: "Comrades!" During the essay, it becomes clear that by "comrades," she specifically means her "politically conscious" fellow men printer-unionists.[49] She repeats this apostrophe eight times in the essay, using it as her refrain and emphasizing the pressing nature of her words. Naborshchitsa introduces herself as a reader of "our journal" in the first sentences, creating a political and emotional connection between herself and her addressees. With this unifying *captatio benevolentiae*, Naborshchitsa paves the way for her following accusation: Male comrades do not want to recognize their female colleagues as human beings or as comrades. She demands a collegial relationship because: "First and foremost, we are human beings." The male comrades must prepare for the presence of women in the world of work and, thus, in the public sphere because this is where things are heading. Due to a sudden change in tense, this prolepsis clearly stands out as the climax of the speech and takes on a threatening tone: If men comrades do not change their behavior, Naborshchitsa warns, women workers will form their own organization. According to her, such a split would be a crime against the whole proletarian liberation movement, and men comrades would bear the blame. Naborshchitsa explains that due to the uncooperative and condescending attitude of male workers toward their female colleagues, the latter are not likely to get involved in proletarian organizations. They avoid contact with men workers, which results in their alienation from the struggle for proletarian goals, ultimately damaging the common proletarian cause. But Naborshchitsa is determined not to accept this situation: "No, comrades, it cannot go on like this; it must not!" The finale is, again, typical for speeches. It uses slogans and a call to action: "Down with this old relic! It must be recognized that our enemies are our exploiters. And our comrades are those who work honestly without exploiting others and do not live at the expense of others." With this *finis*

48 Here, Naborshchitsa touches on the issue of the representation of marginalized voices in the media. Most press institutions are not structured to include women's voices (or those of other marginalized groups), resulting in the under-representation of their opinions and experiences in journalistic products. See, for instance, Hall 2021; Allan 2010, 145–191.

49 Usually "politically conscious" meant active oppositional thinking or activity, in this specific case, I assume it meant union membership.

benevolentiae, Naborshchitsa re-creates a sense of unity with the addressees against the common class enemy.

Naborshchitsa's essay is clear, self-confident, and passionate, offering moments of group identification, harsh criticism, and direct calls to action. Two main, interrelated themes can be identified in it: what I call "unity" and "union." The same themes, in different variations, were taken up in the reactions to Naborshchitsa's article published in *The Printers' Herald*. Naborshchitsa observes class unity as linking her and all other printers. It is a unity that builds on the existence of a common enemy: the exploiters. However, she postulates an additional, yet unrealized type of unity: unity among human beings. The following sentence exemplifies her notion of this dual unity:

> No matter how hard and painful it is, one has to admit that the plight of the woman worker is so bad because her comrades do not want to acknowledge in her the human being, the comrade who is as capable as them to think, fight, and hope for liberation from exploitative oppression.[50]

Naborshchitsa constructs a moral basis for class unity, which was a characteristic of printers' unionism after 1905, but turns a key argument of the movement against male print unionists. She explicitly addresses the immoral behavior (disrespect and condescension directed toward women printers) of readers of *The Printers' Herald,* the trade union organ—in other words, the behavior of "conscious printers." In Naborshchitsa's eyes, this attitude is the direct cause of women workers' lack of participation in the Printers' Union and, thus, disunity among print workers. Naborshchitsa's idea of a "union" on the other hand, is a proletarian trade union that crosses gender lines to unite workers in the fight against exploiters. In her essay, she repeatedly emphasizes her most important concern: the continuation of a united workers' movement. Her remark about organizing women printers into a "special group" is a threat, not an aspiration. Her warning is explicit: "among the working class [the woman worker] will occupy a major place. She will have to be reckoned with, life will force you to reckon with her."[51] Separate union organizing along this line of thinking is merely a strategy to bind women printers to proletarian organizations despite the behavior of men printers and unionists, it is *not* a goal.[52] To ensure unity and union, Naborshchitsa does not demand change from women printers but

50 Naborshchitsa 1906, 3.
51 Naborshchitsa 1906, 3.
52 On the differentiation between "degrees of separateness," see Briskin 1993, 90–91.

rather from male print unionists.[53] Her motivation for advocating that women join the Printers' Union is strengthening the proletarian movement, and the main obstacle she identifies is the moral double standard prevalent among men printers and unionists.

Naborshchitsa's insistence on the importance of drawing women printers into proletarian organizations such as the Printers' Union is indicative of the broader political context of the time in which she was writing. It was a time when women workers had several potential allies from which to choose. In fact, in the Russian Empire at the beginning of the twentieth century, liberal and left-wing parties, philanthropic women's groups, the women's rights movement, conservative circles, and trade unions, among others, competed with each other for the support of workers, especially working women.[54] Socialist groups, for instance, were afraid that women's rights groups would lead women workers away from socialism. Social Democrats, who were the most influential group in printers' organizations, were generally opposed to separate women's organizations because they believed that "feminism" would divert attention away from the class struggle. According to this argument, the "woman question" would be solved automatically as soon as the class struggle was won. Therefore, Naborshchitsa's threat of separate women's organizations and her statement that such segregation would be a betrayal of the proletarian cause collates with the socialist commitment to unified organizing. Naborshchitsa also identifies the limits of this position in her description of women's real-life experiences in the workplace.

The challenge to "make sense of gender, as well as class inequalities and oppression"[55] was confronted not only by Naborshchitsa and the left-wing parties of imperial Russian but by socialists in other countries as well.[56] However, as Rochelle Goldberg Ruthchild stresses in her study of the fight for full women's suffrage in the Russian Empire, the "boundaries between feminism and socialism were permeable and shifting."[57] For instance, by 1906, the League of Working Women in Finland (then a Grand Duchy governed as an autonomous part of the Russian Empire) had organized hundreds of suffrage meetings and demonstrations, aligned with the Social Democratic Party of Finland,

53 On "women changing" and "unions changing," see Briskin 1993, 95.

54 Zelnik 2006, 624; Wood 1997, 30–33. On the suffrage movement in the Russian Empire, see, for instance, Ruthchild 2010; Iukina 2007.

55 Hannam and Hunt 2002, 57.

56 Zimmermann 2014, 101–126 (for the German context); Hannam and Hunt 2002, 57–78, 105–133 (for the British context); Wood 1997, 30–33 (for the imperial Russian context).

57 Ruthchild 2010, 242–243.

and eventually achieved its goal in the summer 1906: Nicholas II had to accede to the Finnish proposal for men's and women's suffrage.[58] Additionally, at the First All-Russian Women's Congress (Первый всероссийский женский съезд) held in 1908, Social Democrat Aleksandra Mikhailovna Kollontai (1872–1952) joined a group of women workers in a boycott of the congress against the explicit instructions of the Russian Social Democratic Labour Party (Российская социал-демократическая рабочая партия). Aleksandra Kollontai still organized a group of women workers and drafted a list of resolutions to prevent bourgeois suffrage activists from exerting too much influence on the female proletariat.[59] In 1914, the first socialist journals for working women were published by socialist women activists who actually opposed "feminism" because of its potential to split the working class and its individualism, but they organized these journals and events to secure social democrats' influence on working women.[60] Therefore, given the influence of the social democrats on the trade unionism of printers, it was highly unlikely that women's separate organizing would have been supported. Nevertheless, Naborshchitsa's critiques of unity and union were taken up and addressed by readers of *The Printers' Herald*.

4 Reactions

The initial reaction to Naborshchitsa's criticism was an editorial comment that accompanied the essay. The editors responded to Naborshchitsa's claim that the voices of women printers were not represented in *The Printers' Herald*. They agreed that "in the pages of our professional organ [...] the very important topic of women workers [...] has not been raised."[61] Additionally, they immediately offered up the trade union journal as a place to discuss such issues. And the editors kept their word: in the following issues of *The Printers' Herald*, there were five articles on questions related to women workers.

The 28 May (10 June) 1906 issue contains an article by a certain Ia. Kopeliovich.[62] In "It is Time: On the Occasion of the Article 'The Voice of the Woman Worker,'" Kopeliovich salutes the comrade woman typesetter for her

58 Blanc 2017, 1–18.

59 Roelofs 2018; Ruthchild 2010, 102–145; Iukina 1998. During the discussion of full women's suffrage, the Congress reached its high point; this group left the Congress in protest.

60 Ruthchild 2012, 8–9; Wood 1997, 13–39.

61 "Ot redaktsii" 1906b, 3. In my perusal of *The Printers' Herald*, I found very few editorial comments, underlining the exceptionality of this case.

62 Kopeliovich 1906, 3.

courage and stresses that it was time for her voice to be heard in *The Printers' Herald.* Kopeliovich's article touches on the themes of unity and union as well. He expresses confusion about the discrepancy between his observations of gender-based workplace harassment such as the humiliation, senseless mockery, and persecution of women by men workers—not managers or supervisors—and proper proletarian ethics. He condemns such behavior and explicitly speaks of the inconsistency and criminality of "our [men workers'] behavior." In his line of thinking, everyone who fights for the liberation of the working class is a comrade. Kopeliovich continues on, arguing that since the proletariat itself uses morality and human dignity as arguments in its struggle against exploiters, he cannot understand why male workers act immorally and fail to treat women with dignity. Kopeliovich identifies the same moral double standard among print workers as Naborshchitsa did, but he communicates his personal confusion and, possibly, his insecurity concerning group identity. Kopeliovich's confusion is an indicator of a flaw in print unionists' moral construction of social judgement of which he could make no sense: How can those who claim moral superiority act immorally? In any case, he, too, calls for change in the attitudes of male printers as a greater good is at stake, namely the union. Kopeliovich sees separate women's organizing as a betrayal of the workers' cause, but one for which male printers should be blamed.

A different perspective on unity and union in response to Naborshchitsa was expressed by a bookbinder called P. Bogushevich, whose "Answer to the 'Voice of the Woman Worker'" was published in *The Printers' Herald* on 11 June (24 June) 1906.[63] In Bogushevich's eyes, Naborshchitsa is mistaken about disunity among printers: The proletarian movement regards women as fellow comrades and, therefore, it is not possible that men printers treat their female colleagues in the disrespectful manner described by Naborshchitsa. His line of reasoning is simple: Since such behavior does not conform to proletarian ethics, it does not—cannot—exist among workers. It can only exist among the immoral bourgeoisie or maybe among unconscious and, therefore, morally imperfect workers, but certainly not among print unionists. Indeed, in an earlier article by the same author entitled "Men Workers and Women Workers," he points out the exploitative work conditions in the Kirkhner bookbinding and printing factory where only profit rules and describes workplace inequality and harassment (meager salaries, vulgar jokes, and abuses of power) women and girls must endure in order to have enough to eat. However, according to Bogushevich, this harassment comes from managers and supervisors only, i.e.,

63 Bogushevich 1906b, 3.

from members of the exploiter class who have power over women and girls and turn them into the most disadvantaged social group.[64] Therefore, the politically conscious proletariat—with which he himself identifies—must offer women and girls a helping hand.[65] In this patronizing strategy, Bogushevich sees three advantages for print unionists. Morally, standing up for women's dignity awakens a sense of justice in oneself; so, bringing women into the union is an act of moral self-advancement. Economically, by defending women's economic interests, men simultaneously protect their own economic interests. With equal pay, there would be no cheap female labour force that could threaten the jobs of men. Indeed, working women in most sectors were frequently perceived as competition by male workers because they were cheaper to employ and they—rather than factory owners and other employers—were accused of taking jobs away from men, which caused disunity and hostility.[66] Finally, Bogushevich offers a strategic reason for women's inclusion in the Printers' Union: The proletariat profits by drawing women workers inside because a cleavage in the proletarian movement would be undesirable. This last reason is linked to the unionist movement's fear of losing women workers to the bourgeois women's movement, as discussed above.

Regarding Naborshchitsa's experience with print workers, however, Bogushevich disagrees vehemently. In his "Answer to the 'Voice of the Woman Worker,'" Bogushevich writes that Naborshchitsa has misunderstood something fundamental, and the "facts" prove her wrong, although the "right facts" are simply based on his own experience. He undermines and discredits Naborshchitsa's perception of reality by stating that she imagines things and alleges that his own experience represents the true story in a classical example of gaslighting. Bogushevich then declares that Naborshchitsa is the problem, not the victim, adding that if some women workers experience condescension from their male colleagues, it is because they are politically unconscious and therefore in the wrong, which implicitly suggests that in such a case, men's intrusive and degrading behavior is acceptable.[67] Bogushevich's article makes very clear the consequences of the ideological deadlock, about which Kopeliovich is confused: A moral construction of class unity not only excludes "less developed" printers who are still "unconscious" but is also incapable of

64 Bogushevich, 1906a, 2.

65 Bogushevich, 1906a, 2.

66 Mayoraz 2021, 65, 105–111, 330; McDermid and Hillyar 1998; Dmitrieva 1909, 143–144. In other states, there was the same dispute, see Score 2014, 280–286.

67 The concept of punishing "bad women" is a common feature of misogyny, as described by today's scholars and feminists, see Manne 2018, 80; Marchese 2018.

accommodating experiences of "immoral" or "uncultivated" behavior among the allegedly morally superior print unionists. What follows in Bogushevich's article, then, is a straightforward negation of marginalized perspectives such as Naborshchitsa's. This exclusionary dynamic must be part of our discussion of print unionist ideology in late imperial Russia.[68] It is a perspective that can be tempered only if historians acknowledge the biases of their sources and work to complement the dominant experience with voices from the margins, as this chapter demonstrates.

Finally, a completely new aspect of unity and union among printers was introduced a couple of weeks after the publication of Naborshchitsa's essay. A certain Pavel published an article entitled "Something about the Woman Worker" in *The Printers' Herald* on 1 July (14 July) 1906.[69] First, Pavel acknowledges the importance of the subject of women's labour and supports the call to overcome the old conceptualization of women as "lesser beings." In the rest of his article, however, Pavel is very much preoccupied with introducing the element of class into discussions concerning union. For example, he describes the exploitation of women by the management of two printing factories in St. Petersburg: Marks and Kirkhner. In the Marks factory, women workers are tyrannized by a woman supervisor, while in the Kirkhner factory, they endure cynical remarks and vulgar behavior by a male supervisor. In the eyes of Pavel, the problem is the supervisors' status (or class), not their gender. In other words, women from the exploiter class are no better than men from the same class. The solution to this problem, in Pavel's eyes, is to exchange the entire management with persons elected by the printers themselves. Following this line of reasoning, there is no way to account for gender-based harassment among workers.

Pavel also identifies another source of disunity in the social relationships among workers in general, namely their aspiration to adapt to bourgeois culture. If a woman worker tries to dress nicely and disrespects a male worker in a dirty shirt, Pavel writes, this can only lead to mockery and jokes, which then culminate in fights. The influence of the "cursed bourgeoisie" also causes other conflicts. For example, when working girls see bourgeois women in their fancy dresses, they understandably work overtime to buy nice clothes to hide their miserable living conditions. Male workers, however, try to forget their depressing situations by drinking. According to Pavel, both phenomena are the result of an oppressive regime that can only be successfully opposed by a unified

68 This is the one point on which Steinberg's otherwise very careful study falls short, see Steinberg 1994.

69 Pavel 1906, 2–3.

proletariat. Pavel calls on workers to unite and especially calls on women to bravely join the struggle for a common victory. More explicitly than any other participant in the debate, Pavel uses class as prism through which he analyzes the social conditions of and relationships within the working class.

His article serves as yet another example of the socialists' fear of "losing" workers to the bourgeoisie, but he goes further, addressing the dangers (excessive) consumption poses to workers' unity and prosperity. Here, Pavel reacts to yet another aspect of the everyday life of urban workers in late imperial Russia. The last decades of the Russian Empire saw the rapid growth of a consumer culture in urban centers. Commerce was the main engine of economic life, and it remained the sector most responsible for the expansion of the urban economy (more than large-scale industry) until the end of the century. Streets were filled with shops, stores, open markets, hawkers, and peddlers.[70] There were also theaters, concert halls, circuses, clubs, societies, and outdoor stages, which offered commercialized entertainment for a low price.[71] At the beginning of the twentieth century, nearly 40 percent of the space in commercial newspapers were dedicated to advertisements.[72] There are many reports about workers longing for fashionable objects, just like Pavel described in his article; many women workers spent their small incomes on fancy dresses and traveled to their villages to show them off. However, contrary to what Pavel suggests, both women and men workers aspired to the "bourgeois" lifestyle.[73] The "loss" of workers to middle-class consumer culture seemed to have been yet another worry for trade unionists in late imperial Russia. The debate sparked by Naborshchitsa in *The Printers' Herald* in the summer of 1906 shows the multiple points of tension in discussions concerning workers' unity and women's labour activism, as well as the social, political, and economic context in which unionization after 1905 evolved.

70 Ananich 2006, 395–425; Smith and Kelly 1998, 108; Kimerling Wirtschafter 1997, 143–144; Brower 1990, 33–36.

71 For a discussion of the social function and symbolic meaning of specific forms of entertainment and consumer goods in the Russian Empire, see Brooks 2019; Dralyuk 2012; West 2011; McReynolds 2003; Smith and Kelly 1998; Engelstein 1992; Kelly 1990.

72 Neuberger 1993, 52; West 2011, 19–61; Zhirkov 2014, 120.

73 Engel 2004, 97; Smith and Kelly 1998, 111–113; Gerasimov 2018.

5 Joining the "Fraternal Ranks" as a Coping Strategy

One last contribution to the debate in *The Printers' Herald* hints at the practical rather than ideological incentives for women printers to join the Printers' Union. The article "Woman—Into the Fraternal Ranks!" was published by T. Rubinchik on 11 June (24 June) 1906.[74] At one point in the article, Rubinchik calls readers "sisters," leading to the conclusion that Rubinchik was a woman printer.[75] Her article, again as the title already suggests, is similar to Naborshchitsa's in terms of style, but this time it was addressed to the "woman comrade." Rubinchik uses short, sharp sentences to describe the miserable life of a young woman worker who has never known anything else but poverty, hunger, and shame.[76] This woman is constantly stepped on, and it never occurs to anyone to offer her a helping hand. According to Rubinchik, the only solution is that she rises up on her own and joins the proletarian fight and the fraternal ranks of the trade union. This essay is very short and does not contain any detailed arguments or explanation. But the description of the wretched life of the typical young woman worker speaks to a greater disillusionment or perhaps frustration. Rubinchik clearly does not put any trust in fellow women workers, male workers, or bourgeois women's groups. The only pragmatic option for the woman worker is to join the union. Rubinchik seems to link two incentives women printers have for joining the union: unionization as a coping strategy in a hostile environment, and unionization as a contribution to the proletarian struggle.

Beyond the printers' trade union paper, there is evidence that women workers had other pragmatic motives for joining the union. I will point to two articles published in the feminist journal *The Women's Union* (*Союз Женщин*), edited by Maria Alekseevna Chekhova (1866–1937), who was the co-founder and secretary of the All-Russian Union for Women's Equality (Всероссийский союз равноправия женщин). *The Women's Union* was an organ of the "bourgeois" women's movement, and its main objective was securing equal political rights

74 Rubinchik 1906a, 3. The surname "Rubinchik" does not reveal the gender of the person. Whether the article title uses the adjective "fraternal" on purpose or without a hidden agenda, I cannot say.

75 Indeed, in the imprint of *The Printer's Voice*—the successor of *The Printers' Herald* after its closure in July 1906—I found T. Rubinchik as "editor-publisher" ("редактор-издательн.") The grammatic female ending of the Russian noun confirms that T. Rubinchik was a woman printer.

76 Another word for prostitution.

for women, above all women's suffrage.[77] *The Women's Union* did not usually deal with women workers or the question of unions. Between 1907 and 1909, there were only two (unknown) authors who raised these issues. They were not regular contributors to the journal, and both offer pragmatic arguments for why women workers should join unions. In a two-part article entitled "The Woman Question and Trade Unions," a certain S. D. writes that women workers have no capacity for self-organization.[78] Special women organizations outside general unions are, therefore, unrealistic. The author sees the economic dependence of working women on a "side income"—the wages of a husband, a lover, or prostitution—as the main problem. Women workers cannot earn enough to support themselves and their families. They earn less than male workers and lose income because of fines, for instance, when they have to leave work early in order to pick up their children from the nursery. The only option they are left with, S. D. writes, is joining unions and working together with their comrades. In the second lengthy article entitled "Women Printers," also published in *The Women's Union*, a certain Dmitrieva (most likely a woman printer herself) describes the hardship of printers, especially women printers.[79] She gives figures on the gender wage gap and describes workplace harassment. Dmitrieva argues that the situation of women printers is highly dependent on the general economic situation. Since unions advocate for equal pay in economically difficult times, in order to prevent the exploitation of cheap female labour and the attendant high unemployment of men, it is only union membership that offers workers—both women and men—stability and security.

The statements by Rubinchik, S. D. and Dmitrieva do not exclude the possibility that union membership can serve as a coping strategy as well as an act of proletarian unity. At least in Rubinchik's case, there is enough evidence to suggest that despite the pragmatism of her arguments, she was an ardent supporter of the Printers' Union. Indeed, thanks to four articles and one speech transcript published by Rubinchik, one comment about her in the printers' union paper, as well as several entries about her in censorship files, it is clear that the typesetter Tat'iana Abramovna Rubinchik was a print unionist. She was a member of the St. Petersburg Printers' Union executive committee during the transitional period between the legalization of trade unions and

77 Ruthchild 2010; McDermid and Hillyar 1998, 108. Famous representatives of the imperial Russian women's movement contributed to *The Women's Union,* such as Liubov' Iakovlevna Gurevich, Anna Pavlovna Filosofova, and Ariadna Vladimirovna Tyrkova.

78 S. D. 1907a; S. D. 1907b. I cannot say whether the abbreviation S. D. refers to the author's affiliation to the Social Democrats.

79 Dmitrieva 1909.

the government reaction in 1907.[80] In April 1906, the printers of St. Petersburg declared Sunday a day of rest for all printers. This specifically concerned the printing factories of daily newspapers because a Sunday off for printers meant that there would be no newspapers on Mondays. Many non-official, commercial dailies of St. Petersburg agreed to the printers' demand, with one exception: Aleksei Alekseevich Suvorin (1862–1937), publisher and editor of the daily newspaper *Rus'* (*Русь*)—at times called *Twentieth Century* (*XX Век*)—opposed the demand, fired all printers, and refused to negotiate with the St. Petersburg Printers' Union on the pretext that it was (to him) an "unknown organization."

The printers called for a boycott of Suvorin's successful newspaper *Twentieth Century* in order to pressure him to introduce Sunday as a day of rest. All the other trade unions in the city joined the boycott in an unusual act of workers' solidarity. The tense situation did not abate for weeks, until both sides agreed on an arbitration tribunal to settle the matter.[81] Both parties—the Printers' Union and *Twentieth Century*—appointed three judges and three representatives. Rubinchik acted as one of three representatives for the Printers' Union, the only women among the otherwise exclusively male panel.[82] *The Printers' Herald* closely followed all seven sessions of the tribunal. Rubinchik's speech was published in its entirety. In that speech, Rubinchik introduces herself as experienced unionist: "Out of the dozens of everyday conflicts I dealt with as representative [female ending] of a trade union, the present conflict is especially interesting to me."[83] She then addresses the structural disadvantages of the exploited class and declares that the printers are taking a revolutionary stance in this regard: "We know that Russian laws are completely on the side of the owners, the gentlemen engineers, and the lawyers who defend their interests; this is exactly why we fight against these laws and their creators." The printers' advantage is their moral superiority. Rubinchik says that the printers behaved properly, whereas those who claim to be "well educated knights who see themselves as the salt of the earth and representatives of art and literature" did the opposite. They used insulting language and violence, oppressed workers by threatening to dismiss them, and forbade self-organization. In a

80 I found her full name in a censorship document: Document No. 9191, str. 4, d. 196, op. 9, f. 776, RGIA, St. Petersburg, Russia. Her membership in the union's executive committee is mentioned in the announcement "The First Session of the Arbitrational Court" 1906, 1. Her profession is given in a short note by fellow compositors about Rubinchik's exile: "Among Printers" 1907, 10. I have not found Rubinchik mentioned in any scholarly publication to date.

81 Sliadneva 2016, 178; Steinberg 1992, 645–666; Bonnell 1984, 298–299; "Boikot gazete" 1906, 1.

82 "1-e zasedanie" 1906, 1.

83 Rubinchik 1906b, 4.

dramatic finale, Rubinchik calls on the judges to choose between the "noble knights" or the "ignorant workers."

Tat'iana Rubinchik and the St. Petersburg Printers' Union won a sensational victory against publisher Suvorin, who was ordered to reintroduce the Sunday Rest for the printers in his factory. But the printers' victory did not last long. In July 1906, the tsarist police raided the St. Petersburg Printers' Union's offices, arresting many unionists and confiscating trade union papers, documents, and funds. The union and *The Printers' Herald* were officially closed.[84] Only weeks later, the printers re-opened both, and Rubinchik took over as editor of the "new" union paper, *The Printer's Voice*. In her articles, Rubinchik reminded her fellow printers of past victories, the morality of their proletarian cause, and the executive committee's ongoing activities in an effort to keep spirits up and fortify the sense of unity and strength.[85] In five months, Rubinchik oversaw the publication of seventeen issues of *The Printer's Voice*, and two cases against her were referred to the district court by the Main Administration of Press Affairs (Главное управление по делам печати). In a period of political oppression, constant searches, and imprisonments, Rubinchik continued to hold a very public position in the union. But in the end, she paid for her activism. In an announcement in the re-launched *The Printers' Herald* from March 1907, the typesetters of the Slovo print factory in St. Petersburg announced Rubinchik's deportation. They, as well as the executive committee of the union, supported Rubinchik from the day of her arrest on, and they collected money to give Rubinchik on her way into exile. "Com. Rubinchik," wrote her fellow printers and unionists, "is a restless spokesperson for the idea of trade unionism in society, and for this, the Suvorins and Shebuevs hate her."[86]

6 Conclusion

During the transitional period of unionization in the Russian Empire (1906–1907), St. Petersburg women printers engaged in labour activism using the Printers' Union paper. Naborshchitsa raised her voice in *The Printers' Herald* to show that workplace harassment, which even "conscious" men printers engaged in, discouraged women printers from joining the union and might eventually force them to organize and fund their own union.

84 Bonnell 1984, 299.

85 Rubinchik 1906c; Rubinchik 1906d.

86 "Sredi pechatnikov" 1907, 10. In January 1907, *The Printer's Voice* was closed by tsarist authorities. I could not trace what happened to Rubinchik after her deportation.

In the debate sparked by her essay, other printers expressed their understanding of unity and union, decrying separate organizing as a betrayal of the working class, suggesting the possibility of immoral behavior among morally superior workers, and denouncing the powerful lure of "bourgeois" consumer culture and non-socialist political movements. An analysis of this debate in *The Printers' Herald* not only provides insight on the internal organization of one of the most important professional unions in late imperial Russia; it also shows how the dominant notion of class among printers, which regarded moral superiority as *the* defining feature of the working class, not only excluded "uncultured" workers but also negated the existence of misogynist behavior among "conscious" print workers, usually unionists. This aspect of print unionist ideology during the transitional phase of imperial Russian unionization has been overlooked by scholars so far.

In addition to the ideological justifications for unionism, there were also pragmatic arguments for unionization specifically directed at women workers; these were usually based on women's lack of financial resources and time to organize a separate women's union. Bringing these two strands together, Tat'iana Abramovna Rubinchik was a pragmatic, yet convinced, print unionist. As a member of the St. Petersburg Printers' Union executive committee during the transitional period, Rubinchik represented the union in arbitration and served as editor of the trade union paper *The Printer's Voice,* thereby making publishing itself part of her broader labour activism. However limited the sources, the voices and figures discussed in this chapter—like Naborshchitsa's and Rubinchik's—belong to the history of the imperial Russian printers' movement and, thus, to its historiography.

Bibliography

"1-e zasedanie treteiskogo suda" [1-е заседание третейского суда; The First Session of the Arbitration Court]. 1906. *Вестник Печатников* [The printers' herald], 20 May (June 2) 1906, 1.

Allan, Stuart. 2010. *News Culture.* Maidenhead: McGraw-Hill/Open University Press.

Allrath, Gaby, and Marion Gymnich. 2004. "Neue Entwicklungen in der *gender*-orientierten Erzähltheorie" [New developments in gender-oriented narrative theory]. In *Erzähltextanalyse und Gender Studies* [Narrative text analysis and gender studies], edited by Vera Nünning and Ansgar Nünning, 33–48. Stuttgart/Weimar: Verlag J.B. Metzler.

Ananich, Boris. 2006. "The Russian Economy and Banking System." In *The Cambridge History of Russia*. Vol. 2: *Imperial Russia, 1689–1917*, edited by Dominic Lieven, 394–425. Cambridge: Cambridge University Press.

Ascher, Adam. 2004. *The Revolution of 1905: A Short History*. Stanford: Stanford University Press.

Aust, Martin. 2017. *Die russische Revolution: Vom Zarenreich zum Sowjetimperium* [The Russian Revolution: From the tsarist rule to the Soviet Empire]. Munich: C. H. Beck.

Aust, Martin, and Ludwig Steindorff, eds. 2007. *Russland 1905: Perspektiven auf die erste Russische Revolution* [Russia 1905: Perspectives on the first Russian Revolution]. Frankfurt am Main: Peter Lang.

Bisha, Robin. 2002. *Russian Women, 1698–1917: Experience and Expression. An Anthology of Sources*. Bloomington: Indiana University Press.

Blanc, Eric. 2017. "'Comrades in Battle'. Women Workers and the 1906 Finnish Suffrage Victory." *Aspasia. The International Yearbook of Central, Eastern and Southeastern European Women's and Gender History* 11: 1–18.

Bogushevich, P. [Богушевич, П.]. 1906a. "Рабочие и работницы" [Men workers and women workers]. *Вестник Печатников* [The printers' herald], 28 May (June 10) 1906, 2.

Bogushevich, P. [Богушевич, П.]. 1906b. "Ответ на 'голос женщины-работницы'" [Answer to "The Voice of the Woman Worker"]. *Вестник Печатников* [The printers' herald], 11 June (24 June) 1906, 3.

"Boikot gazete XX Vek" [Бойкот газете XX Век; Boycott of the Newspaper 20th Century]. 1906. *Вестник Печатников* [The printers' herald], 20 May (2 June) 1906, 1.

Bonnell, Victoria. 1983. *Roots of Rebellion. Workers' Politics and Organizations in St. Petersburg and Moscow, 1900–1914*. Berkeley: University of California Press.

Bovykin, V. I., L. I. Borodkin, and Y. I. Kiryanov. 1988. "Strikes in Imperial Russia, 1895–1913: A Quantitative Analysis." In *Strikes, Wars, and Revolutions in an International Perspective: Strike Waves in the Late Nineteenth and Early Twentieth Centuries*, edited by Leopold H. Haimson and Charles Tilly, 197–216. Cambridge: Cambridge University Press.

Briskin, Linda, and Patricia McDermott, eds. 1993. *Women Challenging Unions. Feminism, Democracy, and Militancy*. Toronto: University of Toronto Press.

Brooks, Jeffrey. 2019. *The Firebird and the Fox: Russian Culture under Tsars and Bolsheviks*. Cambridge: Cambridge University Press.

Brower, Daniel R. 1990. *The Russian City between Tradition and Modernity, 1850–1900*. Berkeley: University of California Press.

Clements, Barbara Evans. 2012. *A History of Women in Russia: From Earliest Times to the Present*. Bloomington: Indiana University Press.

Dahlmann, Dittmar, Pascal Trees, Christian Hacke, Klaus Hildebrand, Christian Hillgruber, Joachim Scholtyseck. 2009. *Von Duma zu Duma: Hundert Jahre russischer Parlamentarismus* [From Duma to Duma: One hundred years of Russian parliamentarism]. Göttingen: V&R unipress.

Daly, Jonathan W. 2006. "Police and Revolutionaries." In *The Cambridge History of Russia.* Vol. 2: *Imperial Russia, 1689–1917,* edited by Dominic Lieven, 637–654. Cambridge: Cambridge University Press.

Dmitrieva [Дмитриева]. 1909. "Женщины-типографщицы" [Women printers]. *Союз Женщин* [The women's union], April 1909, 5–8.

Dralyuk, Boris. 2012. *Western Crime Fiction Goes East: The Russian Pinkerton Craze 1907–1934.* Leiden: Brill.

Edmondson, Linda Harriet. 2001. *Gender in Russian History and Culture.* Basingstoke: Palgrave.

Engel, Barbara Alpern. 1994. *Between the Fields and the City: Women, Work, and Family in Russia, 1861–1914.* Cambridge: Cambridge University Press.

Engel, Barbara Alpern. 1983. *Mothers and Daughters: Women of the Intelligentsia in Nineteenth-Century Russia.* Cambridge: Cambridge University Press.

Engel, Barbara Alpern. 2004. *Women in Russia, 1700–2000.* Cambridge: Cambridge University Press.

Engelstein, Laura. 1992. *The Keys to Happiness: Sex and the Search for Modernity in Fin-de-Siècle Russia.* Ithaca, NY: Cornell University Press.

Engelstein, Laura. 1982. *Moscow, 1905: Working-Class Organization and Political Conflict.* Stanford: Stanford University Press.

Figes, Orlando. 2014. *Revolutionary Russia, 1891–1991.* London: Pelican.

Gerasimov, Ilia. 2018. *Plebeian Modernity: Social Practices, Illegality, and the Urban Poor in Russia, 1906–1916.* Rochester: University of Rochester Press.

Glickman, Rose L. 1984. *Russian Factory Women: Workplace and Society, 1880–1914.* Berkeley: University of California Press.

Gymnich, Marion. 2010. "Methoden der feministischen Literaturwissenschaft und der Gender Studies" [Methodology of feminist literary studies and gender studies]. In *Methoden der literatur- und kulturwissenschaftlichen Textanalyse. Ansätze—Grundlagen—Modellanalysen* [Methods of literary and cultural text analysis. Approaches, foundations, model analysis], edited by Vera Nünning and Ansgar Nünning, 251–269. Stuttgart/Weimar: Verlag J. B. Metzler.

Hall, Stuart. 2021. "The Whites of their Eyes: Racist Ideologies and the Media." In *Stuart Hall: Selected Writings on Race and Difference,* edited by Paul Gilroy and Ruth Wilson Gilmore, 97–120. Durham/London: Duke University Press.

Hannan, June, and Karen Hunt. 2002. *Socialist Women. Britain, 1880s to 1920s.* London: Routledge.

Iukina, Irina Igorevna [Юкина, Ирина Игоревна]. 2007. *Русский феминизм как вызов современности* [Russian feminism as a challenge to modernity]. St. Petersburg: Aleteia.

Iukina, Irina Igorevna [Юкина, Ирина Игоревна]. 1998. "Первый всероссийский женский съезд" [The First All-Russian Women's Congress]. *Вы и мы. Диалог женщин* [You and we. Women's dialogue], no. 6: 13–16.

Kelly, Catriona. 1990. *Petrushka: The Russian Carnaval Puppet Theatre.* Cambridge: Cambridge University Press.

Kimerling Wirtschafter, Elise. 1997. *Social Identity in Imperial Russia.* DeKalb: Northern Illinois University Press.

Koenker, Diane P. 2005. *Republic of Labour: Russian Printers and Soviet Socialism, 1918–1930.* Ithaca, NY: Cornell University Press.

Kopeliovich, Ia. [Копелиович, Я.]. 1906. "Пора. По поводу статьи 'голос женщины-работницы'" [It's time. Regarding the article "The Voice of the Woman Worker"]. 1906. *Вестник Печатников* [The printers' herald], 28 May (10 June) 1906, 3.

Lieven, Dominic. 2015. *Towards the Flame. Empire, Wars and the End of Tsarist Russia.* London: Penguin Books.

Manne, Kate. 2018. *Down Girl: The Logic of Misogyny*. New York: Oxford University Press.

Marchese, David. 2018. "In Conversation: Chimamanda Ngozi Adichie. The Novelist on Being a 'Feminist Icon,' Philip Roth's Humanist Misogyny, and the Sadness in Melania Trump," *Vulture*, 9 July 2018. https://www.vulture.com/2018/07/chimamanda-ngozi-adichie-in-conversation.html.

Mayoraz, Sandrine. 2021. *Streik! Fabrikunruhen, jüdische Gesellschaft und staatliche Behörden in den nordwestlichen Gouvernements des Russischen Reiches 1895–1904. Eine mikrohistorische Perspektive* [Strike! Factory riots, Jewish society, and state authorities in the northwestern governments of the Russian Empire 1895–1904. A microhistorical perspective]. Cologne: Böhlau Verlag.

McDermid, Jane, and Anna Hillyar. 1998. *Women and Work in Russia, 1880–1930. A Study in Continuity through Change.* London: Longman.

McReynolds, Louise. 2003. *Russia at Play: Leisure Activities at the End of the Tsarist Era.* Ithaca, NY: Cornell University Press.

McReynolds, Louise. 1991. *The News Under Russia's Old Regime: The Development of a Mass-Circulation Press.* Princeton, NJ: Princeton University Press.

Moog, Christine. 2022. "Introduction." In *Women in Print.* Vol. 2: *Production, Distribution and Consumption,* edited by Caroline Archer-Parré, Christine Moog, and John Hinks, 1–6. Oxford, New York: Peter Lang.

Muravyeva, Marianna, and Natalia Novikova, eds. 2014. *Women's History in Russia: (Re) establishing the Field.* Newcastle upon Tyne: Cambridge Scholars Publishing.

Naborshchitsa [Наборщица]. 1906. "Голос женщины-работницы" [The voice of the woman worker]. *Вестник Печатников* [The printers' herald], 20 May (2 June) 1906, 3.

Neuberger, Joan. 1993. *Hooliganism: Crime, Culture, and Power in St. Petersburg, 1900–1914*. Berkeley: University of California Press.

Norton, Barbara T., and Jehanne M. Gheith, eds. 2001. *An Improper Profession: Women, Gender, and Journalism in Late Imperial Russia*. Durham, NC: Duke University Press.

Orlov, P. [Орлов, П.]. 1906. "Независимая чушь" [Independent nonsense]. *Голос печатника* [The printer's voice], 9 September (22 September) 1906, 7.

"Ot redaktsii" [От редакций; From the editors]. 1906a. *Вестник Печатников* [The printers' herald], 21 April (4 May) 1906, 1.

"Ot redaktsii" [От редакций, From the editors]. 1906b. *Вестник Печатников* [The printers' herald], 20 May (2 June) 1906, 3.

Palat, Madhavan K. 2007. "Casting Workers as an Estate in Late Imperial Russia." *Kritika: Explorations in Russian and Eurasian History* 8, no. 2: 307–348.

Pavel [Павел]. 1906. "Кое-что о женщине-работнице" [Something about the woman worker]. *Вестник Печатников* [The printers' herald], 1 July (14 July) 1906, 2–3.

Roelofs, Joan. 2018. "Alexandra Kollontai: Socialist Feminism in Theory and Practice." *International Critical Thought* 8, no. 1: 166–175.

Rubinchik, T. [Рубинчик, Т.]. 1906a. "Женщина в братские ряды!" [Woman—into the fraternal ranks!]. *Вестник Печатников* [The printers' herald], 11 June (24 June) 1906, 3.

Rubinchik, T. [Рубинчик, Т.]. 1906b. "Речь тов. Рубинчик на заседании третейского суда с XX Веком" [Speech by comr. Rubinchik at a session of the arbitration court against twentieth century]. *Вестник Печатников* [The printers' herald], 7 July (20 July) 1906, 4.

Rubinchik, T. [Рубинчик, Т.]. 1906c. "Существует ли Союз?" [Does the union exist?]. *Голос Печатника* [The printer's voice], 16 August (29 August) 1906, 6–7.

Rubinchik, T. [Рубинчик, Т.]. 1906d. "Что же дальше?" [What's next?]. *Голос Печатника* [The printer's voice], 24 August (6 September) 1906: 7–8.

Ruthchild, Rochelle Goldberg. 2016. "Telling Russia's Herstory." *Aspasia. International Yearbook for Women's and Gender History of Central, Eastern and Southeastern Europe* 10: 169–174.

Ruthchild, Rochelle Goldberg. 2012. "From West to East: International Women's Day, the First Decade." *Aspasia. International Yearbook for Women's and Gender History of Central, Eastern and Southeastern Europe* 6: 1–24.

Ruthchild, Rochelle Goldberg. 2010. *Equality and Revolution. Women's Rights in the Russian Empire, 1905–1917*. Pittsburg, PA: University of Pittsburgh Press.

Ruud, Charles. 1981. "Printing Press as Agent of Political Change in Early Twentieth Century Russia." *The Russian Review* 40, no. 4: 378–395.

S. D. [С. Д.]. 1907a. "Женский вопрос и профессиональные союзы" [The women's question and trade unions]. *Союз женщин* [The women's union], August–September 1907: 7–8.

S. D. [С. Д.]. 1907b. "Женский вопрос и профессиональные союзы" [The women's question and trade unions]. *Союз женщин* [The women's union], November 1907: 7–10.

Score, Melissa. 2014. "Pioneers of Social Progress? Gender and Technology in British Printing Trade Union Journals, 1840–64." *Victorian Periodicals Review* 47, no. 2 (Summer): 274–295.

Sher, Vasilii Vladimirovich [Шер, Василий Владимирович]. 1911. *История профессионального движения рабочих печатного дела в Москве* [History of the professional movement of print workers in Moscow]. Moscow: Nauka.

Sliadneva, O. V. [Сляднева, О. В.]. 2016. "Профессиональные издания 1906–1914 гг." [Trade union journals 1906–1914]. In *Петербург газетный 1711–1917* [Newspaper Petersburg 1711–1917], edited by E. S. Sonina [Сонина, Е. С.], 166–185. St. Petersburg: Svoe izdatel'stvo.

Sloane, Nan. 2018. *The Women in the Room. Labour's Forgotten History.* London: I. B. Tauris.

Smith, S. A. 2002. "Masculinity in Transition: Peasant Migrants to Late-Imperial St. Petersburg." In *Russian Masculinities in History and Culture,* edited by Barbara Evans Clements, Rebecca Friedman, and Dan Healey, 94–112. Basingstoke: Palgrave.

Smith, S.A. 2017. *Russia in Revolution. An Empire in Crisis, 1890 to 1928.* Oxford: Oxford University Press.

Smith, Steve, and Catriona Kelly. 1998. "Commercial Culture and Consumerism." In *Constructing Russian Culture in the Age of Revolution: 1881–1940,* edited by Catriona Kelly and David Shepherd, 106–164. Oxford: Oxford University Press.

Solov'ev, Kirill Andreevich. 2021. "Правительство и избирательные кампании в Государственную думу" [The government and the election campaigns to the state Duma]. In *Российская Империя между реформами и революциями, 1906–1916. Коллективная монография* [The Russian Empire between reform and revolutions, 1906–1916. Collective monograph], edited by Aleksei Il'ich Miller and Kirill Andreevich Solov'ev, 73–99. St. Petersburg: Kvadriga.

Sprotte, Maik Hendrik, Wolfgang Seifert, and Heinz-Dietrich Löwe, eds. 2007. *Der Russisch-Japanische Krieg 1904/1905: Anbruch einer neuen Zeit?* [The Russo-Japanese War 1904/1905: Dawn of a new era?]. Wiesbaden: Harrassowitz.

"Sredi pechatnikov" [Среди печатников; Among printers]. 1907. *Вестник Печатников* [The printers' herald], 20 March (2 April) 1907, 10.

Steinberg, Mark D. 2017. *The Russian Revolution, 1905–1921.* Oxford: Oxford University Press.

Steinberg, Mark D. 1994. "Vanguard Workers and the Morality of Class." In *Making Workers Soviet. Power, Class, and Identity*, edited by Lewis H. Siegelbaum and Ronald Grigor Suny, 66–84. Ithaca, NY: Cornell University Press.

Steinberg, Mark D. 1992. *Consciousness and Conflict in a Russian Industry: The Printers of St. Petersburg and Moscow, 1855–1905.* Ann Arbor, MI: University Microfilms International.

West, Sally. 2011. *I Shop in Moscow: Advertising and the Creation of Consumer Culture in Late Tsarist Russia.* DeKalb: Northern Illinois University Press.

Williams, Helen S. 2022. "'Dangerous Intruders': Women Compositors and Nineteenth-Century Print Trade Unionists—the Case of Perth." In *Women in Print.* Vol. 2: *Production, Distribution and Consumption,* edited by Caroline Archer-Parré, Christine Moog, and John Hinks, 173–192. Oxford, New York: Peter Lang.

Wood, Elisabeth A. 1997. *The Baba and the Comrade: Gender and Politics in Revolutionary Russia.* Bloomington: Indiana University Press.

Worobec, Christine, Barbara Alpern Engel, and Barbara Evans Clements, eds. 1991. *Russia's Women: Accommodation, Resistance, Transformation.* Berkeley: University of California Press.

Zelnik, Reginald E. 2006. "Russian Workers and Revolution." In *The Cambridge History of Russia.* Vol. 2: *Imperial Russia, 1689–1917,* edited by Dominic Lieven, 617–636. Cambridge: Cambridge University Press.

Zimmermann, Susan. 2014. "A Struggle over Gender, Class and the Vote: Unequal International Interactions and the Formation of the 'Female International' of Socialist Women (1905–1907)." In *Gender History in a Transnational Perspective. Networks, Biographies, Gender Orders,* edited by Oliver Janz and Daniel Schönpflug, 101–126. New York: Berghahn.

Zhirkov, Gennadii Vasil'evich [Жирков, Геннадий Васильевич]. 2014. *Журналистика России: от золотого века до трагедии. 1900–1918 гг.* [The journalism of Russia: from golden age to tragedy. 1900–1918]. Izhevsk: Institut komp'uternykh issledovanii.

CHAPTER 3

Women's Labour Activism

The Case of Bank Clerks in Central Europe, 1900–1920

Mátyás Erdélyi

Abstract

The chapter examines the labour activism of women clerks in the late Habsburg Monarchy (Austria, Hungary, the Czech lands) between 1900 and 1914. By 1900, women clerks had begun to be employed by banks, and they represented around 10 to 15 percent of clerks by 1914. Their numerical growth in the sector coincided with increasing discrimination on multiple levels: in professional education, on the job market, in matters of welfare benefits, and in labour unions. This chapter analyzes the strategy and methods women clerks used to cope with their (often disadvantageous) social and economic status and battle discrimination on multiple fronts. Their strategies varied from joining male-dominated labour unions to establishing women-only structures, as well as relying on peaceful demonstrations and democratic elections and denouncing their mistreatment in the press. Their history showcases the malleable nature of class relations. Women clerks confronted middle-class gender roles and assumptions at the workplace, which were used to justify women clerks' lower salaries, smaller pension benefits, and lesser job protections. At the same time, men clerks tried to demote women clerks from higher positions to protect their own privileges in the workplace. Women clerks, therefore, had to choose between less welcoming male-dominated labour unions or the establishment of women-only associations in their fight against gender discrimination and their battle to ultimately achieve middle-class status.

Keywords

bank clerks – educational inequalities – gender-pay gap – gender discrimination – Habsburg Monarchy – old-age pensions – women clerks

Leopoldina Anderl applied for the job of office clerk at the affiliate of the Foncière insurance company in Pozsony/Bratislava/Pressburg just before the Great War. Her story is representative of female employees' place in the

 | DOI:10.1163/9789004682481_004

bureau in the two decades after the turn of the twentieth century. Born in 1898, Anderl graduated from a middle school (*Bürgerschule*) and completed her professional training in Zsolna/Žilina/Sillein; she also spoke three languages fluently: Magyar, German, and Slovak. Upon receiving Anderl's application, the branch office demanded authorization from the Budapest headquarters to employ the young woman. There was a lack of trained workforce in the city—there was no secondary trade school in Zsolna—and junior clerks with a trade-school education were "immediately employed at the local factory for 100–120 krones a month." The affiliate office in Pozsony had no other option, its managers argued, but to hire a "*demoiselle*" for a starting salary of 50 krones per month, and her responsibility would only consist in keeping the bureau in good order.[1] This short excerpt from a company personnel file enumerates many of the challenges women clerks faced on the job market at the time: inadequate education, menial office jobs, no opportunities for career advancement, low salaries, and so forth.

Gendered hierarchies and discrimination against women at work unfolded in the context of ongoing industrialization and capitalist modernization in the Habsburg Monarchy, which also resulted in similar patterns as those that had emerged in Western Europe in the nineteenth century.[2] Systematic discrimination against women in the educational system in general and in vocational education in particular and the employment and wage discrimination practices of employers caused a functional differentiation and a gendered allocation of duties and roles in the bureau.[3] Employers willingly profited from discrimination against women: women clerks, in their eyes, represented a cheap workforce that could carry out the multiplying administrative tasks in private companies. The significantly different and heavily disadvantageous position of women clerks in the labour market meant that women labour activists had aims that were distinct from those of male labour activists. Male clerks were mainly interested in securing their own economic and social position even at the price of excluding women from male-dominated labour unions. From the early 1910s on, male clerks' attitudes changed when the number of women clerks grew too high to be ignored, and male-dominated associations began to integrate women clerks and their interests into their programs.

1 File 2, Fonciere Általános Biztosító Intézet (1865–1949) [Fonciere General Insurance Company], Z 171 Személyzeti osztály (1892–1949) [Personnel department], Magyar Nemzeti Levéltár Országos Levéltára [National Archives of Hungary].

2 Adams 2002.

3 Gardey 2001; Gardey 1996; Fehrer 1989.

This chapter analyzes the labour activism of women bank clerks in the late Habsburg Monarchy (Austria, Hungary, the Czech lands) with an emphasis on the way women clerks reacted to ongoing gender discrimination in both the workplace and, as we will see, in the labour unions of private clerks. The chapter therefore reveals the work-related problems specific to women clerks and explores avenues of labour activism in the world of banking, which was quite distinct from the world of the working classes, and which was characterized by a gradual change in the gender composition of the workforce during the period in the decades after the turn of the century. Additionally, this chapter provides a dual perspective of women's labour activism, showcasing the activism of both men-dominated and women-only labour unions.

The structure of the chapter proceeds from a general introduction, to the social position of women clerks in the late Habsburg Monarchy, to an analysis of specific labour unions' activities. The first part of the chapter, therefore, introduces the socio-economic status of women clerks in banking and identifies the causes of gender inequality and discrimination at work. The second part presents the different types of labour unions in banking that took up the specific issues of women clerks, including both male-dominated and women-only unions. The last section of the chapter analyzes how women clerks approached and coped with gender discrimination at work, in society, and in labour unions in particular. This section is based on select case studies (educational qualification, the gender pay-gap, marriage clauses, and old-age pensions) that are representative of the issues faced by women clerks and which demonstrate the particularities of bank clerk labour movements.

1 Women Bank Clerks after the Turn of the Century

The turn of the century was in many aspects a revolutionary period for office work, but it entailed a revolution for gender as well.[4] Throughout much of the nineteenth century, the clerk was a man and the office a male universe. This began to change at the turn of the century with the increase of women employed by private bureaus, and by the 1930s, the clerk was essentially a woman.[5] Women started to enter the offices of private companies in the second half of the nineteenth century, and the first women were employed as clerks at private railway companies, postal offices, and postal savings banks.[6]

4 Gardey 2008.
5 Gardey 2001, 6, 53.
6 Appelt 1996, 121.

Banks employed a female workforce in clerk positions considerably later. The Austrian-Hungarian Bank (Österreichisch-ungarische Bank) recruited women workers (*Arbeiterinnen*) into banknote production starting in 1878, but the first women clerks (*Beamtinnen*) were only hired by the bank in 1919.[7] In the Czech lands, the Prague-based Trade Bank (Živnostenská Banka, ŽB) employed the first women clerks to manage telephone service at their Vienna affiliate only in 1899 and at their Prague headquarters in 1900. It is paradigmatic that the first two women clerks at Živnostenská Banka had basic elementary-level qualifications and left the labour market within a decade: one got married in 1910 at the age of 42, and the other was pensioned off in 1909, probably also as a result of her marriage.[8]

By 1905, most banks began hiring women clerks, but the majority of women employees held lower-level positions as typewriters, telephone operators, correspondents, delivery assistants, or only performed "light" bookkeeping. The Länderbank in Vienna, for example, confirmed the growing number of women employees—by 1905 there were around fifty women clerks working at the bank—but claimed that women could not fill senior positions and were unable to carry out "independent" tasks.[9] In both halves of the Habsburg Monarchy, the exponential growth of women clerks in the financial sector was a plain fact in the years before the Great War. The most important growth took place in Vienna: the proportion of women clerks increased from 4.4 percent (banking) and 2.1 percent (insurance) in 1890 to 19.2 percent and 20.3 percent, respectively, by 1910. This was remarkable growth, yet it was in line with the sectoral growth of women employees in Austria: in trade and transportation, the proportion of women clerks (*Angestellte*) was 7.8 percent in 1890 (8,405 persons), which increased to 21.8 percent (36,811 persons) by 1910.[10] Budapest and Prague were less progressive in terms of the proportion of women clerks in the workforce: in Prague, the proportion of women clerks reached 10.2 percent (banking) and 11.4 percent (insurance) by 1910, while in Budapest, the proportion of women clerks was 12.5 percent (banking and insurance combined) in 1910.[11]

7 Ulbrich 2018, 70–71, 89.

8 Entry 253 and 292, book 424, Osobní oddělení [Personnel department, hereafter OD] 1869–1945 (1950), Fond Živnostenská banka v Praze [Trade Bank in Prague, hereafter Fond ŽB], Archiv České Národní Banky [Archive of the Czech National Bank, hereafter ČNB].

9 *Stenographisches Protokoll* 1905, 3, 23, 27, 31.

10 Fehrer 1989, 85.

11 *Magyar Statisztikai Közlemények* 1914, 30. *Österreichische Statistik* 1916b, 151.

Women were generally engaged in lower-level positions that encompassed unskilled office work—typing, copying, and basic calculations, and companies overtly excluded them from upper-level positions. Women were therefore also denied access to the *Beamten* ranks until the turn of the century or later, as in the case of the Österreichisch-ungarische Bank. There was an unbridgeable gap between the rank and status of the *Beamten* (official, *tisztviselő* in Hungarian, *úředník* in Czech) and the *Diener* (servant, *szolga*, *služba*); furthermore, upward mobility from the rank of *Diener* to *Beamten* was very limited. The two categories were set apart from each other in terms of education (secondary school vs. elementary level education), salary (monthly, annual salary vs. a daily wage), old-age pensions, length of notice period, holidays, etc. In addition, *Beamten* belonged to the gentlemanly middle classes, whereas *Diener* formed part of the working classes. Although women were often entitled "*Beamtinnen*" in the bureau, they did not benefit from the privileges associated with the status in terms of old-age pensions, holidays, a notice period, and annual salary;[12] therefore, they had a specific set of work-related problems that were significantly different from the issues addressed by men-only professional associations.

The mechanisms that maintained the social and gender-based division of labour were quite universal in Europe in the nineteenth century and would be targeted by women clerks in labour unions. Alice Salomon, the social reformer, women's activist, and founder of social work as an academic discipline, suggested that the causes of the wage gap between men and women had to do with the low self-esteem of women, the fact that men were considered the sole breadwinner of the family, the inadequate education of women, and the shorter careers of women as compared to those of men.[13] The historiography of women clerks clearly identified these factors in the long nineteenth century. Erna Appelt, for instance, has argued that the "feminization of poverty" in general was the result of educational differences, the gender-specific allocation of tasks in the bureau, and the exclusion of women from all positions having to do with power in general.[14] Rosemarie Fehrer enumerated the disadvantages faced by women clerks in comparison to their male counterparts as follows: fewer educational qualifications, different professional duties and positions within firms, lower average ages, differences in lifestyle expectations, and the existence of a marriage barrier, which referred to the practice of dismissing women after marriage.[15] These differences actively contributed to the

12 Appelt 1996; Appelt 1985.

13 Salomon 1906.

14 Appelt 1985, 10, 15.

15 Fehrer 1989, 176–177.

creation of a gender-pay gap in the bureaus of private companies. In our case, the vocational school system (the so-called trade schools) actively contributed to the relative under-schooling of women clerks: in Hungary, women could only attend elementary-level trade schools until 1906, while in Cisleithania, only the lowest two grades of secondary trade schools were accessible to women.[16] Higher-level vocational schools across the Monarchy began to open their ranks to women at approximately the same period with some notable exceptions. The higher "academic" course of the Budapest Academy of Trade granted the right of admission to women after 1908;[17] the Teacher Training Institute for Trade Schools also accepted women candidates—the first enrolled in 1907—but only with ministerial permission;[18] and other institutions, like the Oriental Academy of Trade in Budapest, did not accept women as regular students throughout the entire period.[19]

The salaries of women clerks were considerably lower than those of men. The statistics of the central pension institute in Vienna provide a general overview of the gender pay gap in 1909. The average annual pay was 956 krones for women clerks and 1,791 krones for male clerks. While 70.3 percent of female employees received less than 1,200 krones per year, only 21.4 percent of male clerks received a wage this low.[20] The gender pay gap was the result of various factors: it was partly due to seniority and partly due to the generally higher educational qualifications of male clerks. Yet, data based on the salary books of the Živnostenská banka in Prague demonstrate that women were underpaid even when they held the same educational qualifications and seniority. For instance, among men, the starting salary of commercial high school graduates was 906 krones, while women were paid only 778 krones.[21] The overall gender pay gap was, thus, also the result of gender discrimination on the part of employers in banking.

Women's labour activism in banking had a twofold goal between 1900 and 1920. First, women advocated for better labour conditions and renumeration alongside male clerks. Besides fighting for gender equality at work and in labour unions, these women also embraced the general goals of male-dominated

16 Erdélyi 2019, 24–69.

17 Szuppán 1908, 7, 54.

18 Dengl 1925, 24.

19 Felügyelőbizottsági jegyzőkönyvek [Minutes of the Supervisory Board of the Oriental Academy of Trade], 6 May 1915, Fond 2/a 3 Keleti Kereskedelmi Akadémia iratai [The archive of the Oriental Academy of Trade], Budapesti Corvinus Egyetem Levéltár [University Archives of the Corvinus University of Budapest].

20 Leichter 1930, 209.

21 Erdélyi 2019, 204; Books 423–424, OD, Fond ŽB, ČNB.

associations. These included a significant salary increase, the introduction of official service regulations including the regulation of holidays, no work on Sunday, the establishment of old-age pensions, and so forth. Second, women had to combat social prejudice and gender discrimination at work and in society. Activists all over the Habsburg Monarchy thus tried to find ways to elevate the educational qualifications of women to obtain equal status in labour unions and in the workplace. For this reason, women's labour activism in both types of labour unions (women-only and mixed sex) is addressed in this chapter because women activists were present in both types of associations.

2 Labour Unions of Bank Clerks: Male-Dominated Associations and Women's Movements

In Cisleithania, the most influential bank clerk association was the Reich Association of Bank and Savings Bank Clerks (Reichsverein der Bank- und Sparkassenbeamten, hereafter the Reichsverein). Its precursor, the Club for Clerks at the Wiener Bank and Credit Institute (Klub der Beamten der Wiener Bank- und Credit-Institute, hereafter the Klub) was established as a casino in 1888; the premises of the Klub hosted a library to "cultivate" members and provide a place to read the daily press and play card games; of course, at this time, only male clerks could participate in the activities of the Klub.[22] The Klub was transformed into a labour union at the end of 1906, and the leaders proposed the organization of a *Bankbeamtentag* every year in order to have regular contact with bank management, to establish a savings banks for private clerks, and to fight for the regulation of old-age pensions and legally guaranteed service regulations.[23] The Reichsverein was a politically neutral organization and was not at all radical: it was claimed that the association was so moderate that it was impossible to become more moderate.[24] This openly proclaimed neutrality was extremely important for the bank clerk association as they had to navigate between competing ideologies. As part of the middle classes, they had to set themselves apart from socialist associations, but they also opposed "yellow" unionization in which employees and employers came together to form a labour union as in the case of bank clerks in Germany. Instead, the Reichsverein excluded employers from participating in their association. By doing so, they agreed with one of the core political principles of

22 Landertshammer 1927, 7–8; *Klub der Beamten der Wiener Bank- und Credit-Institute* 1893, 1.
23 "Der Aufruf des Aktionskomitees" 1906, 2.
24 "Sind wir radikal?" 1908, 8–10.

labour unions: namely, that the interests of employees and employers were incompatible and, consequently, employers should not participate in the management of labour unions.[25] The neutrality of the Reichsverein was also discernable in the diverse political affiliations of their allies in the Imperial Council (Reichsrat).

The initial charter of the Reichsverein did not specify whether women clerks could become members or not, but women were not admitted to the association, and the question of women members was discussed relatively late, only in 1909, due to the numerical growth of women clerks in banking. At this point, the presence of women in the bureau was already considered detrimental because they were blamed for ruining the wages of male clerks.[26] *The Austrian Bank Clerk* (*Der Österreichische Bankbeamte*), the official journal of the association, began publishing editorials about the issue. Otto Glöckel, a social democrat, was particularly candid about the problems faced by private clerks.[27] The real issue for him was the arbitrariness of employers, which equally affected both women and men. He expressed pragmatism concerning the question of women clerks; they had two options: either join the existing association or establish women-only clerk associations, and from these two options, the former option was more desirable for labour unions in general. The Reichsverein decided to admit women into the association in 1910 in order to enhance the overall strength of the movement. By 1916, 14.8 percent of members were women,[28] a number that appropriately reflected the proportion of women clerks in the entire banking sector (banks, savings banks, credit cooperatives), which was 12.6 percent according to the 1910 census.[29] The Reichsverein also guaranteed gender equality in elections and in administrative matters. Women clerks paid the same membership dues and were entitled to all the support services of the association such as the resistance fund, legal aid, library services, and the consumer association.[30]

Women bank clerks could join the Association of Working Women (Vereinigung der arbeitenden Frauen, AWW), which was established in 1902 and had a division for private clerks and trade employees (Fachgruppe der Privatbeamtinnen und Handels-Angestellten). The AWW had three basic goals: to improve the general and professional education of women; to

25 Landertshammer 1927, 33.
26 "Die Organisation und die weiblichen Angestellten" 1909.
27 "Die Organisation und die weiblichen Angestellten" 1909, 2.
28 Allina 1916, 6.
29 *Österreichische Statistik* 1916a, 9.
30 "Die Beamtinnenfrage" 1910, 1–3.

represent the class interests of women employees; and to improve the economic situation of women employees.[31] It had altogether 3,512 members in 1911 and had a wide network of branch associations in Brno (210 members), Czernowitz/Chernivtsi (351 members), Graz (280 members), and Troppau/Opava (191 members). Their official journal *Papers of the Association of Working Women* (*Mitteilungen der Vereinigung der arbeitenden Frauen*) and later *Austrian Women's Magazine* (*Österreichische Frauenrundschau*) often dealt with the specific issues of women clerks, and women bank clerks specifically. The activities of the association included the establishment of a club library, the organization of professional courses, the establishment of a recruitment office, and the AWW also ran a restaurant for members.[32]

Although both the Reichsverein and the AWW were active in the Czech lands, a similar women-only association, the Czech Woman Association of Production (Ženský výrobní spolek český), had been established in the Czech lands in 1871. The main activity of this association was to organize professional education for women: the most popular courses were language instruction and trade courses. The association also established an employment bureau to help women find appropriate jobs. Most influential in the association was Eliška Krásnohorská, who was responsible for the school's prestigious reputation and became the editor of *Woman Papers* (*Ženské listy*).[33] Krásnohorská also played a crucial role in the foundation of the Minerva Society, which helped establish the first girls' gymnasium in the Habsburg Monarchy in 1890.[34] The Czech Woman Association of Production established other services to help women employees, which were similar to the AWW. They created an employment agency that mediated between employees and employers and favored graduates of the commercial school funded by the Czech Woman Association of Production. The association organized a lecture series to further the education of all working women because the education of both men and women was considered the source of the nation's strength.[35]

In Hungary, the main association of bank clerks was the National Association of Bank Clerks (Pénzintézeti Tisztviselők Országos Egylete, NABC); it was established in 1893 as a social club, and like the Reichsverein, it had a large library and supported the cultural life of its members. For fifteen years, "directors and ordinary clerks spent their free time playing cards and chess in the rooms of

31 Die Vereinsleitung 1906, 2–4; "Was will die 'Vereinigung'" 1913, 6–9.
32 Hauch 2009; Friedrich 1995; Hahn 1912, 5–7.
33 Bahenská 2004.
34 De Haan, Daskalova and Loutfi 2006, 262–266.
35 Volet-Jeanneret 1988, 221–222.

the club."[36] In 1908, the growth in the number of bank clerks and the parallel decline of their economic standing prompted members to transform the club into an interest-group association, and the association was finally transformed into a labour union in 1912. The demands of bank clerks had a clear middle-class character: old-age pensions, fixed and uninterrupted working hours, and proper service regulations. Bank clerks, like the Reichsverein, advocated for political neutrality and presented themselves as a bourgeois association, but during the Great War, their political orientation moved to the left: they initiated their first strike on the occasion of a conflict between clerks and the Hungarian Commercial Credit Bank (Magyar Kereskedelmi Hitelbank), which ended successfully with the improvement of inflation raises.[37] Shortly after the Aster Revolution in 1918, the association joined the Council of Labour Unions (Szakszervezeti Tanács).

The NABC realized the importance of women for the movement and invited them to join the association in 1912. However, in 1913, the association started to complain about women's lack of engagement despite the fact that women were granted full membership and *one* female clerk was elected to the general board of the association to "prove their [the board's] liberalism." It was also acknowledged that equal work should be compensated equally, regardless of the clerk's gender, and the bank clerk association advocated for full equality in terms of service regulations and pension rights.[38] As was often the case in male-dominated associations, this pledge for gender equality was not implemented, and the association remained quite indifferent to the problems of women in practice.

In Hungary, the most influential women-only association was the National Association of Women Office Workers (Nőtisztviselők Országos Egyesülete, NAWOW), established in 1897. It represented the professional interests of both private and public employees. The NAWOW organized professional courses for clerks, had an employment bureau, provided aid for unemployed women clerks, opened a library, had a holiday camp, in addition to offering other services. By 1913, it had nearly 4,000 members, and by 1917, the membership was estimated at 6,000 women clerks. The NAWOW established provincial branches in Nagyvárad/Oradea/Großwardein, Szombathely, Arad, and Temesvár/Timișoara/Temeswar.[39] Members of the NAWOW established the Feministák Egyesülete (Feminists' Association, FA) in 1904, and together the associations

36 Kabos and Sipos 1975, 97.
37 "Hitelbank" 1917.
38 "Kartársnőink és a szervezet" 1913, 11–12.
39 Zimmermann 1999, 38–39.

published the journal *Woman and Society* (*A Nő és a Társadalom*) starting in 1907.[40] The NAWOW also launched an independent journal in 1915 called *Journal of Women Clerks* (*Nőtisztviselők Lapja*). The NAWOW belonged to the "camp of individualist modernizers"[41] and differed fundamentally in their political stance from social democratic women's associations like the Association of Hungarian Woman Workers (Magyar Munkásnők Egyesülete) in the sense that they did not want to combine the feminist agenda with their fight against gender inequalities in society, economy, and politics, nor did they want to subordinate it to other ideological or class-based interests. In contrast to the Association of Hungarian Woman Workers, it was equally important for the NAWOW to remain an independent organization, which explains their refusal to join the ranks of bank or insurance clerk associations. The case of the women clerk association in Pécs provided evidence to justify the NAWOW's position. Instead of joining the NAWOW, local women clerks joined the male association of trade employees in 1909. As a result, they lost their financial independence and their ability to campaign, and the women clerks' association was soon completely dissolved.[42]

Women clerks had other reasons not to join the "little particular associations,"[43] as they put it, such as NABC and the association of insurance clerks. As Szidónia Willhelm claimed in *Nő és a Társadalom*, the NAWOW had successfully defended the interests of the whole group of women clerks for almost two decades, whereas these newly founded associations had not yet proved their worth. Additionally, until gender equality existed in all spheres of society, women had to fight separately for their rights and for gender equality in general, and according to Willhelm, male associations never cared about the improvement of women's situation. Last but not least, women clerks had their own special issues to deal with, and the differences between women clerks and men clerks were greater than the differences between bank clerks, insurance clerks, and so forth.[44]

The specific demands of the NAWOW were in line with the feminist agenda that sought equality between the sexes. The main goal of the NAWOW was radically different from men-only clerk associations as their solution to the poor position of women clerks was to improve the education women received; thus, they promoted the abolition of the one-year trade course and the establishment of secondary women's trade schools.[45] Other demands included the

40 Kereszty 2013.
41 Zimmermann 1999, 42–43.
42 "A Nőtisztviselők Országos Egyesülete" 1909, 106–107.
43 Willhelm 1913, 173.
44 Willhelm 1913.
45 Zimmermann 1999, 127–136.

abolition of marriage clauses in service regulations, better and equal pay for women clerks, and gender-neutral pension regulations. Once gender equality was established, the NAWOW would willingly join with men clerks to advocate as a profession. For instance, having abolished gender discrimination in the regulations of the private clerk pension fund—married female clerks lost their membership upon marriage until 1910—the NAWOW began to intensively campaign among women clerks to encourage them to join the pension fund.[46] Gender equality was a key concern in relation to other issues as well. The NAWOW opposed the idea of regulating Sunday office hours differently for men and women clerks for a specific reason: if legal regulations protected women separately, the principle of gender neutrality in the office might become unattainable. Women, for example, would be unable to reclaim equal pay.[47]

3 Gender Pay Gap, Education, Marriage Clauses, and Old-Age Pensions

Private clerks' unions and activists focused on a number of specific problems of women bank clerks, including gendered educational inequalities, the gender pay gap, marriage clauses, and old-age pension access. As Leopoldina Anderl's story in the introduction demonstrated, gender-based educational inequalities played a crucial role in the pay gap between men and women clerks and in the general position of women employees of banks and private companies. Education, therefore, quickly became a focal point of the activism around women clerks. A woman clerk from Prague described the situation of women in trade and industry at a session of the Federation of Austrian Women's Associations (Bund Österreichischer Frauenvereine) as follows: women clerks were often the daughters of middle-class families, had little professional education, and received small salaries. In Prague, the average salary of male clerks varied between 90 and 100 krones per month, whereas it only reached 50 to 70 krones for female clerks. Yet, according to this report, which was often parroted by clerks of both genders, women clerks themselves were partly responsible for this situation. This narrative suggested that women clerks lived with their parents, had meager needs (they only needed pocket money), and thus only needed small salaries. The biggest issue in tackling women's lower pay, however, was their lack of education: higher positions in the office hierarchy

46 -ly-a 1913; Wilhelm 1911; "A Nőtisztviselők Országos Egyesülete" 1910, 108.
47 Grossmann 1908, 160.

could be achieved only if one had an appropriate professional education.[48] In this spirit, the AWW in Cisleithania actively engaged in creating educational opportunities for women. Until 1906, it offered eighty-five courses attended by approximately 2,400 women employees.[49]

Hungarian women, too, quickly realized that the inadequate education of women was the main factor that relegated them to menial tasks in the office and ruled out any possibility of climbing the office hierarchy. Janka Grossmann, a private clerk and later the president of the NAWOW, claimed that this was not a war between the two sexes but a conflict between clerks with different levels of education and salaries. Grossmann called for the introduction of coeducational courses and equality in the professional education of boys and girls.[50] This was clearly an effort on the part of Grossmann to separate class and gender inequalities and to push for the improvement of women's education. Education was, therefore, an ever-present topic on the pages of *A Nő és a Társadalom*. Grossmann's claim was repeated several times in the pages of the journal between 1907 and 1908.[51] The proposed solution was the reform of the ten-month, lower-level trade courses, and the NAWOW was engaged in widespread agitation in support of this comprehensive reform. In a petition sent to the Ministry of Religion and Public Education, the NAWOW argued that mixed-sex education could prevent the depression of wages; thus, male clerks would profit from these measures as well.[52] The ten-month course was not enough to teach all the material that male students learned in their three-year secondary trade school course. NAWOW activists argued that the existence of officially certified trade courses prevented authorities from abolishing fake trade schools that offered shorter courses and fake qualifications. Uneducated girls flooded the labour market, and this contributed to the proletarianization of women clerks, resulted in salary decreases for both men and women clerks, and reduced the general moral value of the work performed by private clerks.[53] Graduates were also too young and could seemingly not bear the hardships of working in a bureau.

Another issue to be tackled by private clerk associations was the wage gap between men and women employees. This problem could not be separated from the depression of the salaries of private clerks in general, and, for

48 Stepanek 1906.
49 Die Vereinsleitung 1906, 3.
50 Grossmann 1905.
51 "A tisztviselőpálya megrontói" 1908; "A magyar nőtisztviselők szervezkedése" 1907, 165.
52 "Felirat a közoktatásügyi miniszterhez" 1907, 112.
53 Zimmermann 1999, 129; "A leányok kereskedelmi szakoktatása" 1909.

example, the Reichsverein addressed the issue by publishing the salary scheme of banks and savings banks. These publications were meant to pinpoint bad and good employers, those that increased salaries and supplemental income and those that refused to consider the effects of inflation on clerks' livelihood. Overall, the salaries of women clerks ranged between four-fifths and half the salary of male clerks at the time when the wage gap was at its historical peak in the second half of the nineteenth century.[54] The gap was the smallest during the first few years of employment and gradually widened as the number of service years grew. The existence of a salary cap for women employees further enlarged this gap at many companies.[55] The Lower Austrian Discount Company (Niederösterreichische Escompte-Gesellschaft), for example, paid male junior clerks 800 krones and women junior clerks 720 krones (80 percent of men's salaries), but by the fifth year of employment, women clerks only received 60 percent of the salary of male clerks (1,620 krones and 3,350 krones, respectively), and this declined to 52 percent by the twentieth year of service (3,270 krones and 6,315 krones, respectively).[56] *Der Österreichische Bankbeamte* often drew attention to the gender salary gap and demanded salary increases for women employees as well as for men.

The Reichsverein displayed a constructive attitude concerning *Beamtinnen* in banking. Misogynist arguments were caricatured from the very beginning. "How could an intelligent person question [the idea] that the same work deserves the same salary?" asked one contributor.[57] But other justifications for the gender pay gap were equally challenged: if not women, then uneducated apprentices would do the office work for meager salaries; if married male clerks deserved a higher salary to provide for their family, single men should also get smaller salaries. The latter disputed the idea that salaries should be set according to the needs of the employee instead of merit and performance. Moreover, the legal and social definition of the private clerk did not make any reference to gender. In addition to full equality within the association, equality at the workplace was also envisioned by contributors to *Der Österreichische Bankbeamte*.

54 Eder 2015.

55 See the salary schemes published in *Der Österreichische Bankbeamte* and the service regulations of the *Živnostenská banka* (*Služební řád pro úředníky Živnostenské banky v Praze* [Service regulations for the clerks of the Živnostenská banka in Prague], box 4830/1, OD, Fond ŽB, ČNB).

56 "Lombard- und Escompte-Bank" 1914. I refer to the overall salary of clerks including the basic salary, quarterly remuneration, and the inflation allowance (*Teuerungsbeitrag*), but do not include exceptional remuneration and pension contributions.

57 "Die Damen" 1910, 2.

They also pledged that women would no longer be salary ruiners (*Lohndrückerinnen*) if they received the same salaries as men. To achieve this goal, minimum age and qualification requirements were proposed for women clerks as well as the abolition of forced female celibacy.[58] The Reichsverein vowed to fight for total equality in employment conditions: the inflation allowance, the quarterly allowance, the residence allowance, yearly remuneration, access to the pension scheme, and the notice period.[59] Despite these demands, according to a commentator, there was not much change in terms of gender equality until the outbreak of the Great War. However, women clerks' attitudes toward their work changed "for the good" during the war, as the bad economic conditions reshaped the purpose of women's work. This meant that the salary of women clerks became indispensable to the family budget, and wages no longer served as merely "pocket money" for women. Moreover, the number of women clerks who married declined precipitously during the war, which resulted in a more stable staff.[60]

In connection to these developments, the ideology of the "surplus woman" made the Czech discourse distinctively misogynist.[61] The concept of the "surplus woman" primarily referred to demography: the reason for the flood of women clerks in private bureaus was the growing number, i.e., "surplus" of unmarried women. According to this logic, "Men could not marry because they were too poor. What caused this? Salary-ruining women!"[62] Women were by nature more numerous than men, argued the *Clerks' Papers* (*Úřadnické listy*); there were 1,047 women for every 1,000 men in Cisleithania according to the 1900 census.[63] But by the turn of the century, the "back-up" institutions for unmarried women—the convents and asylums established in the Middle-Ages—were declining in numbers and did not take charge of the many unmarried women.[64] In the narrative of male clerks, the problem became more pressing around 1900 because unmarried women entered the banking sector and ruined the salaries of male clerks. This influx of women into the profession, in turn, impoverished male clerks, prevented them from marrying, and thus created a vicious cycle.

58 "Die Beamtinnenfrage" 1910.

59 "Die Beamtinnen" 1912.

60 "Frauenarbeit im Kriege" 1916.

61 "Otázka zaměstnání žen v ústavech peněžních" 1910; Fanta 1907; "K otázce ženských úřadnic soukromých" 1904; "K ženskě otázce" 1902; "Bankovní úřednictvo—ženy" 1898.

62 "Ženy jakožto konkurentky soukromých úředníků" 1902.

63 Fanta 1901, 2.

64 "Otázka zaměstnání žen v ústavech peněžních" 1910, 222.

Male clerks at the turn of the century also advanced a discourse that women lacked the "determination" to get married on their own. Accordingly, with the decline of organized marriage, women looked for lust, "walking princes," or a comfortable urban life instead of stable marriage proposals.

> The essence of the "woman question" is always simply about the man: the impossibility for women to get a man, and all the consequences of this. Every step that ensures that a larger number of men are married contributes to finding a solution to the woman question.[65]

The solution to the problem, therefore, was the free marriage of male bank clerks to marry and the improvement of their financial circumstances.[66]

On the point of marriage, the frustration of men clerks was not baseless. Marriage clauses in the contracts of clerks often contained marital restrictions: for example, the service regulations of the Živnostenská Banka stated that male clerks could only marry if they reached the eighth rank on the salary scale, which amounted to a basic yearly pay of 3,240 krones in 1914, a salary level that male clerks reached in the ninth year of employment unless promoted in the meantime.[67] Additionally, specific marriage patterns in urban settings contributed to the restriction of marriage opportunities: marriages occurred later and less frequently in cities than in the countryside, and the dissolution of the traditional marriage circle further decreased opportunities to wed.[68] Still, the imbalance of the sexes was more imagined than a genuine social reality, and male clerks actually connected imagined demographic changes and their consequences to morality.[69]

The other motif recurrent in Czech discourse was the unnaturalness of the bureau environment for women. Not only did women carry out tasks ill-suited for their natural characteristics but they also were unable to work independently and creatively. Women had always been dependent on men—formerly the husband—until they confronted the unprecedented social relations that defined the bureau. Although the wife was subordinate to the husband within the family, she could always rely on him, and they could establish a secure relationship with one another. The relationship between managers and women clerks involved a new type of subordination: the boss regarded

65 Fanta 1907, 27.

66 "K ženskě otázce" 1902, 2–3.

67 *Služební řád pro úředníky Živnostenské banky v Praze.*

68 Dollard 2009, 78–79.

69 Dollard 2009, 83.

the female clerk merely in terms of profit, as a cheap workforce, and exploited her to the fullest extent.[70] A recurring theme was that women were regarded by employers as a form of capitalist merchandise, making them the victims of the rationalization process in urban capitalism. Women were also inexperienced in the public sphere and, consequently, could not defend themselves against exploitation. This was coupled with the assertion that women did not want to join professional associations and pay membership fees because they spent their money on things like gloves.[71] Furthermore, women's lack of experience in the public sphere was the reason women clerks willingly stayed in the bureau after the end of office hours and happily brought home their unfinished work, concluded the narrative of male clerks.

For the *Österreichische Frauenrundschau*, the most crucial issue was the ability to lead a middle-class lifestyle, which was hampered by the small salaries of clerks. The average monthly salary of women clerks varied between 70 krones and 120 krones; however, an annual salary of at least 2,200 krones was needed to be able to sustain a middle-class household. Overall, this budget included meals, clothing, a one-room apartment in the outer districts of Vienna, and additional expenses like pension contributions, personal income taxes, and cultural expenditures.[72] Having a fixed salary, the only option for women clerks was to reduce their needs, both material and cultural.

In Hungary, one of the means used by the NAWOW to fight the pay gap was the creation of an employment bureau to negotiate between employers and job applicants. The experience of this bureau demonstrated that the lack of adequate professional training indeed resulted in a shortage of qualified women workers and caused the oversupply of underqualified applicants. The so-called ten-month trade courses provided training in typing, correspondence, and basic political arithmetic, but these courses did not provide sufficient training—on an equal level with secondary trade school for boys—to be able to take up higher positions in the bureau hierarchy.[73] Between 1903 and 1905, the NAWOW advertised 854 positions, and there were 410 applicants; still, 160 candidates were rejected because of inadequate qualifications.[74]

An important component of employers' discrimination against women was the practice of forced female celibacy. The topic moved to the center of discussion in 1913, when the Magyar Kereskedelmi Hitelbank revised their service

70 "Otázka zaměstnání žen v ústavech peněžních" 1910, 222.
71 "K ženskě otázce" 1902, 2.
72 Gronemann 1910.
73 Zimmermann 1999, 122–136.
74 "A szellemi proletariátus" 1907, 35.

regulations and curtailed their clerks' rights. The regulations stated that the marriage of women clerks would result in their immediate dismissal. All women clerks at the bank revolted against the proposal, and the board agreed to postpone the implementation of the new rule and created the possibility of receiving permission to marry at the discretion of the management.[75] The issue was widely discussed in the press and drew further attention to the challenges faced by women private clerks.[76]

The campaign against marriage restrictions in Budapest was successful. But the female celibacy requirement was not a problem unique to the women clerks in Budapest. A similar clause was included in the service regulations of both the Österreichisch-ungarische Bank and the Živnostenská Banka, and data about the women employees of the latter showed that marriage almost exclusively meant dismissal for women clerks.[77] In those cases, there is no evidence that bank clerk associations initiated a fight for the right of women to marry. Both Hungarian and Austrian associations paid attention only to the problem in relation to male clerks: according to bank regulations, if male clerks did not meet the salary criteria, they were banned from marrying.

The case of the Austrian old-age pension law for private clerks further illustrates how the male clerk became the proxy to assess the situation of all clerks—including women—and the reactions of men and women clerks to changes in the system. Here, the male, middle-class orientation of the pension law angered many women clerks. The main issue, in short, was that the law discriminated against women, especially unmarried women, in pension provisions. From the outset, the survey conducted by the Ministry of Internal Affairs was designed to serve the needs of male clerks: it compiled statistics on, for example, the average age of only *male* clerks in combination with the average age of their wives and children.[78] The law set the financial contributions of women clerks too high and collected the same premiums from women clerks for lower pension distributions, and single women clerks could not profit from widow's pensions. Additionally, the children of married women clerks were only entitled to 50 percent of the pension amount, while the rate was 75 percent for the offspring of male clerks. The rationale was that female clerks, if they had children, were surely married to a male clerk, whereas male clerks

75 "Nőkongresszus" 1913.

76 "Gondolatok a Kereskedelmi Bank" 1913; "A Kereskedelmi Bank szolgálati szabályzata" 1913; "A Kereskedelmi Bank uj szolgálati szabályzata" 1913.

77 See the personal files and salary sheets of women employees at the Živnostenská Banka: books 420–424, OD, Fond ŽB, ČNB.

78 Ministerium des Innern 1898, I: 120–131.

with children were most often married to women who were not employed. The law thus blended motives of social class and habitus with financial reasoning. The only relief for women was that in contrast to the illegitimate children of male clerks, the illegitimate children of female clerks were entitled to educational allowances.[79] These directives actually were not relevant for women clerks due to banks' practices of requiring women clerks to quit their jobs after marrying. Overall, then, the main demand of women clerks was to ensure "equal services for equal premiums."[80]

The AWW wanted to stop discrimination and achieve recognition for women clerks as employees in their own right and not as the employed wife of a male clerk. The organization drew attention to the many shortcomings of the pension law. In the case of marriage, the pension institute reimbursed all the premiums paid by both the employee and the employer to women clerks; single women clerks who left their position of their own will were only entitled to receive their own payments. Similarly, if a widow remarried, she was no longer entitled to the widow's pension and instead received a compensation sum.[81] The payments of women clerks were illusory for the most part. The retirement age, reached after altogether 480 months of employment, could not be attained by women in most cases due to periods of unemployment, early death, and for the fact that compulsoriness according to law usually started later in a woman clerk's career. Starting salaries were considerably lower among women, and they also had to go through a longer period of (unpaid) training than male clerks. In conclusion, this was basically an "annuity that was not paid to women."[82] Furthermore, pregnancy and early childcare, family events associated with women, were not included at all in discussions concerning pension reform.

The particular demands of women included cheaper premiums, shorter waiting periods, voting rights for women in pension institutes, and the annulment of illusory payments.[83] The reaction of Richard Kaan, chief secretary of the Universal Pension Institute for Clerks (Allgemeine Pensionsanstalt für Angestellte) in Vienna, to the complaints of Adele Rosenberg, a member of the AWW, was typical. According to Rosenberg, it was misleading to provide women clerks with a cheaper option to buy "insurance years" because women clerks could not build enough of a savings to be able to take advantage of the

79 "Das Pensionsversicherungsgesetz" 1907; Rosenberg 1909.
80 Rosenberg 1909b, 61, 5.
81 Rosenberg 1909b, 61, 4.
82 C. G. 1906.
83 "Das Pensionsversicherungsgesetz" 1907, 8.

opportunity. Instead, she argued, women clerks should enjoy shorter waiting periods and smaller premium payments, and women's relatives, like parents, sisters, and brothers, should be able to receive pension allowances upon a woman clerk's death. When Rosenberg confronted Kaan with these issues in 1909, he merely replied: "Aren't you happy that at least once, women are taken into account?"[84] Nevertheless, some of the demands of women clerks were addressed prior to the Great War. Further amendments to the law reduced the number of years women clerks needed to work before retirement: from the initial forty years to thirty-five years 1913;[85] and the relatives of single women were also entitled to pension allowances after 1914.[86]

There was no compulsory old-age pension for private clerks in Hungary, but similar discriminatory practices were put into effect by individual employers. Women, for instance, most often lost their premium payments if they quit their jobs due to marriage. The NAWOW started a campaign against gender discrimination in the charter of the National Old-Age Pension Association for Private Clerks (Magántisztviselők Országos Nyugdíj-Egyesülete). When they succeeded in abolishing gender discrimination in 1910, the NAWOW started to organize among women clerks and encourage them to join the fund as the only viable alternative to company-funded pension institutes.[87]

4 Conclusion

One of the sources of gender inequality proved to be the limited ability of women clerks to defend their professional interests against the potential exploitation of companies, and in this respect, male clerks were better equipped than their female colleagues by far. Men, for example, had voting rights and could protest injustices at work through a number of different channels. Male clerks also were successful in certain areas: they were able to improve their salaries and received inflation allowances, pension provisions, and so forth. Male clerks could easily utilize the public sphere to advance their own interests and fight against the unfair dismissal of a colleague or the curtailment of their right to assembly. Changes in the attitude of male-dominated associations took place after 1910: they started to publicly criticize the unfair

84 "Sind Sie froh, daß man die Frauen wenigstens in einer Hinsicht berücksichtigt"; Rosenberg 1909b, 60, 8.

85 Abelles 1913.

86 Von einer staatlichen Kanzleigehilfin 1914, 5.

87 Willhelm 1913; Willhelm 1911; A Nőtisztviselők Országos Egyesülete 1910.

treatment of women clerks, for example, in the case of the institutionalized marriage clause or in the case of the unfair dismissal of a woman clerk because the boss "learned something about her" but refused to elaborate.[88]

Male-dominated clerk associations became more engaged in the problems of their female counterparts when the number of women became too significant to ignore. Starting in the early 1910s, these associations gradually welcomed women clerks but only represented the interests of women clerks to a limited extent. The main problem here was the fact that regulations in general—the old-age pension system was the most notable example—regarded the situation of the male clerk as representative of the experience of all clerks. Consequently, there were protests for properly regulated holidays, office hours, and demands for salary increases, but the existing and prevailing differences between women and men employees were rarely addressed. The gender wage gap, or the discussion about the "salary-destroying women" in contemporary parlance, was addressed mostly from the perspective of male clerks, who only considered how the low salaries of women would affect the salaries of male clerks. This perspective, of course, limited the solutions male-dominated associations could offer.

In contrast to the associations led by their male colleagues, the main goal of women clerks' associations was to battle gender discrimination by addressing inequality within the educational system. Under-educated women could not claim equal status, and the lack of training damaged the prestige of educated women and undermined their fight for proper treatment in the office. Accordingly, the NAWOW actively criticized the ten-month trade courses in Hungary that could only produce lower-level office employees, and the AWW also advocated for equality in secondary vocational education. Both associations established a recruitment office to help their members find appropriate jobs and to force employers to offer fair labour conditions to women clerks; they also offered courses and lectures to improve the professional qualification of members. Overall, women clerks' associations tackled gender inequalities in work and society and aimed to establish women as independent economic actors at the *fin-de-siècle*. The main arenas of labour activism concerning the status of women clerks remained the public sphere and particularly the press, and advocacy efforts were quite successful. Women clerks were able to address and remedy some forms of gender discrimination—most notably the marriage clause at certain banks—through protests covered by the press.

88 "A tisztviselőnő becsülete" 1915.

The labour unions of women bank clerks in the Habsburg lands were similar in many respects. They differed from workers' trade unions in their political neutrality—bank clerks were often forbidden to join political parties or be elected to any office—and in the form of their activism. Bank clerks refrained from general strikes, with the first held only after the Great War in the Czech lands in 1921,[89] and they lobbied for their interests only through more pacific means like press releases, rallies, or open letters to the directorate. The strike scene of *Gentlemen Clerks* (*Hivatalnok urak*), a play by Béla Földes,[90] captures the difference between unions composed of workers and those of bank clerks very well. The former went on strike after the directorate dismissed two workers, and the workers refused to start the machines that day. The clerks of the company silently watched the scene from the window of the office upstairs, also embittered because a fellow accountant was dismissed the same day due to his considerable debts. Threatened by the director, the clerks promptly returned to work and were even ready to work overtime because clerks have "feelings of responsibility." It is also notable that the Resistance Fund (*Widerstandsfond*) of the Reichsverein was most often used to sponsor bank clerks discharged for simply joining the association because bank management actively tried to prevent the unionization of clerks. Even though state borders (and an independent legal system) separated Hungary and Cisleithania, the problems of women bank clerks and the way they addressed them were astonishingly similar regardless of ethnic affiliation or region, although one significant difference is visible in the Czech case, where male clerks expressed a particularly misogynist attitude toward their female counterparts. Nevertheless, these similarities explain efforts to write a history of the *Gesamtmonarchie*.

Bibliography

Abelles, Olga. 1913. "Die Novelle zum Pensionsversichurngs-Gesetz" [The amendment of the old-age pensions law]. *Österreichische Frauenrundschau* [Austrian women's magazine] x, 109: 3–4.

Adams, Carole Elizabeth. 2002. *Women Clerks in Wilhelmine Germany: Issues of Class and Gender*. Cambridge: Cambridge University Press.

Allina, Heinrich. 1916. "Rechenschafts- und Tätigkeitsbericht des Zentralvorstandes für die Vereinsperiode 1914/1916" [Accounting report and activities of the Central

89 Charous 1953.

90 Földes 1908.

Board of the Association for the period between 1914 and 1916]. *Der Österreichische Bankbeamte* [The Austrian bank clerk] X, no. 9: 1–7.

Appelt, Erna. 1985. *Von Ladenmädchen, Schreibfräulein und Gouvernanten: Die weiblichen Angestellten Wiens zwischen 1900 und 1934* [Shop girls, typists and governesses: Vienna's female employees between 1900 and 1934]. Vienna: Verlag für Gesellschaftskritik.

Appelt, Erna. 1996. "The Gendering of the Service Sector in Late Nineteenth-Century Austria." In *Austrian Women in the Nineteenth and Twentieth Centuries: Cross-Disciplinary Perspectives*, edited by David F. Good, Margarete Gradner and Mary Jo Maynes, 115–131. Providence, RI: Berghahn Books.

"Der Aufruf des Aktionskomitees" [The call of the committee]. 1906. *Der Österreichische Bankbeamte* [The Austrian bank clerk] I, no. 1: 2.

Bahenská, Marie. 2004. "Ženský výrobní spolek český" [Czech Woman Association of Production]. *Český lid* [The Czech people] 91, no. 3: 253–271.

"Bankovní úřednictvo—ženy" [Bank clerks—women]. 1898. *Bank-beamte–Bankovní úředník* [Bank clerk—bank clerk] I, no. 8: 2–3.

"Die Beamtinnenfrage" [The question of woman clerks]. 1910. *Der Österreichische Bankbeamte* [The Austrian bank clerk] IV, no. 5: 1–3.

"Die Beamtinnen" [The woman clerks]. 1912. *Der Österreichische Bankbeamte* [The Austrian bank clerk] VI, no. 5: 8–9.

C., G. 1906. "Die Pensionsversicherung der Privatbeamten" [The old-age pension insurance of private clerks]. *Mitteilungen der "Vereinigung der arbeitenden Frauen"* [Papers of the Association of Working Women] 4, no. 33: 2–4.

Charous, Jaromír. 1953. "Bankovní stávka 1921" [Bank strike in 1921]. *Sborník archivních prací* [Almanac of archival works] III, no. 1–2: 168–347.

"Die Damen" [The women]. 1910. *Der Österreichische Bankbeamte* [The Austrian bank clerk] IV, no. 3: 2–4.

Dengl János. 1925. *A hazai felső kereskedelmi iskolai tanárok képzésének és képesítésének múltja és jelen állapota: az érvényben lévő szabályzatokkal* [The past and present of the training and qualification of teachers for commercial high schools in the country: Including the relevant regulations]. Budapest: Lampel R. könyvkereskedése.

Dollard, Catherine Leota. 2009. *The Surplus Woman: Unmarried in Imperial Germany, 1871–1918*. New York: Berghahn Books.

Eder, Ernst Gerhard. 2015. "Gravierende Einkommensunterschiede und die patriarchalische Struktur in den Arbeitswelten des 18., 19. und frühen 20. Jahrhunderts" [Significant income differences and patriarchal structures in the world of labour in the eighteenth, nineteenth and early twentieth centuries]. In *Sozialgeschichte Wiens 1740–2010: Soziale und ökonomische Ungleichheiten, Wanderungsbewegungen, Hof, Bürokratie, Schule, Theater* [The social history of Vienna 1740–2010: Social and economic inequalities, migration, the court, education, and theater], edited by

Andreas Weigl, Peter Eigner, and Ernst Gerhard Eder, 63–260. Innsbruck: Studien Verlag, 2015.

Erdélyi, Mátyás. 2019. *Experts in the Bureau: Private Clerks and Capitalism in the Late Habsburg Monarchy*. Phd diss., Central European University.

Fanta, J. Karel. 1907. "Ženská soutěž soukromých úřadníků" [The competition of women among private clerks]. *Úřadnické listy* [Clerks' papers] XIV, no. 2: 25–27.

Fanta, Karel Jindř. 1901. "Ženy—naše konkurentky" [Women—Our competition]. *Úřadnické listy* [Clerks' papers] VIII, no. 8: 2–3.

Fehrer, Rosemarie. 1989. *Die Frau als Angestellte in Wirtschaft und Verwaltung Österreichs: ihr sozialer Aufstieg seit dem letzten Drittel des 19. Jahrhunderts* [The woman as a clerk in the economy and in administration of Austria: Their social assent since the last third of the nineteenth century]. Linz: Trauner.

"Felirat a közoktatásügyi miniszterhez" [Petition to the Minister of Public Education]. 1907. *A Nő és a Társadalom* [Woman and society] I, no. 6: 112.

Földes, Imre.1908. *Hivatalnok urak: színmű* [Gentlemen clerks: A drama]. Budapest: Lampel.

"Frauenarbeit im Kriege" [Woman's work in the war]. 1916. *Der Österreichische Bankbeamte* [The Austrian bank clerk] X, no. 2: 1–2.

Friedrich, Margret. 1995. "'Vereinigung der Kräfte, Sammlung des kleinen Gutes zu einem gemeinschaftlichen Vermögen, kurz die Assoziation ist hier die einzige Rettung'. Zur Tätigkeit und Bedeutung der Frauenvereine im 19. Jahrhundert in Metropole und Provinz" [Joining forces, the collection of small goods into a common fortune, in short, association is the only salvation! On the activity and significance of women's associations in the nineteenth century in the capital and the provinces]. In *Bürgerliche Frauenkultur im 19. Jahrhundert* [Bourgeois women culture in the nineteenth century], edited by Brigitte Mazohl, 125–174. Vienna: Böhlau.

Gardey, Delphine. 1996. "Du veston au bas de soie: identité et évolution du groupe des employés de bureau (1890–1930)" [From the man's jacket to stockings: The identity and evolution of office workers (1830–1930)]. *Le Mouvement social* [The social movement], no. 175: 55–77.

Gardey, Delphine. 2001. *La dactylographe et l'expéditionnaire: histoire des employés de bureau: 1890–1930* [The typist and the copyist: The history of clerks: 1890–1930]. Paris: Belin.

Gardey, Delphine. 2008. *Ecrire, calculer, classer: comment une révolution de papier a transformé les sociétés contemporaines (1800–1940)* [Writing, calculating, classifying: How the revolution of paper transformed contemporary societies]. Paris: Découverte.

"Gondolatok a Kereskedelmi Bank uj szolgálati szabályzatat körül" [Thoughts about the new service regulations of the Trade Bank]. 1913. *Pénzintézeti Tisztviselők Lapja* [The journal of bank clerks] VI, no. 4: 1–7.

Gronemann, Caroline. 1910. "Das Budget der weiblichen Angestellten" [The budget of woman clerks]. *Österreichische Frauenrundschau* [Austrian women's magazine] VIII, no. 78: 3–5.

Grossmann, Janka. 1905. "Nemek harca" [War of the sexes]. *Magántisztviselők Lapja* [Journal of private clerks] XIII, no. 21: 6–7.

Grossmann, Janka. 1908. "Vasárnapi munkaszünet" [Holiday on Sunday]. *A Nő és a Társadalom* [Woman and society] II, no. 10: 160.

De Haan, Francisca, Krassimira Daskalova, and Anna Loutfi, eds. 2006. *Biographical Dictionary of Women's Movements and Feminisms: Central, Eastern, and South Eastern Europe, 19th and 20th Centuries*, 1st ed. Budapest: CEU Press.

Hahn, Ida. 1912. "Vor zehn Jahren" [Ten years ago]. *Österreichische Frauenrundschau* [Austrian women's magazine] X, no. 96: 5–7.

Hauch, Gabriella. 2009. "'Arbeite Frau! Die Gleichberechtigung kommt von selbst'? Anmerkungen zu Frauen und Gewerkschaften vor 1914" ["Work woman! Equal rights will come automatically"? Annotations to women and labour unions before 1914]. In *Frauen bewegen Politik, Österreich 1848–1938* [Women move politics, Austria 1848–1938], edited by Gabriella Hauch, 105–127. Innsbruck: Studienverlag..

"Hitelbank" [Credit bank]. 1917. *Pénzintézeti Tisztviselők Lapja* [The journal of bank clerks] X, no. 6–7: 2–3.

Kabos, Ernő, and Péter Sipos, eds. 1975. *Az egység útján: a Kereskedelmi-Pénzügyi és Vendéglátóipari Dolgozók Szakszervezetének története* [On the road to unification: The history of labour unions of workers in trade, finances, and in the hospitality industry]. Budapest: Táncsics Kiadó.

"Kartársnőink és a szervezet" [Our female colleagues and the organization]. 1913. *Pénzintézeti Tisztviselők Lapja* [The journal of bank clerks] VI, no. 12: 11–12.

"A Kereskedelmi Bank szolgálati szabályzata" [The service regulations at the Trade Bank]. 1913. *A magánalkalmazott* [The private employee] XII, no. 5: 13.

"A Kereskedelmi Bank uj szolgálati szabályzata és a Pénzintézeti Tisztviselők Országos Egyesülete" [The new service regulations at the Trade Bank and the National Association of Bank Clerks]. 1913. *Pesti Hírlap* [Pest news], 30 April 1913.

Kereszty, Orsolya. 2013. "A Great Endeavor: The Creation of the Hungarian Feminist Journal A Nő és a Társadalom (Woman and Society) and Its Role in the Women's Movement, 1907–1913." *Aspasia. International Yearbook for Women's and Gender History of Central, Eastern and Southeastern Europe* 7: 92–107.

Klub der Beamten der Wiener Bank- und Credit-Institute. Bericht über das V. Vereinsjahr [The club for clerks at the Wiener Bank and Credit Institute. Report of the fifth year of the association]. 1893. Vienna: Verlag des Klub der Beamten der Wiener Bank- und Credit-Institute.

"K otázce ženských úřadnic soukromých" [About the question of woman private clerks]. 1904. *Úřadnické listy* [Clerks' papers] XI, no. 3: 1–2.

"K ženské otázce" [About the woman question]. 1902. *Úřadnické listy* [Clerks' papers] IX, no. 5: 2–3.

Landertshammer, Franz. 1927. *Der Reichsverein der Bank- und Sparkassenbeamten Österreichs in den Jahren 1907 bis 1927: anläßlich der 20. Wiederkehr des Gründungstages* [The Imperial Association of Bank and Savings Bank Clerks in Austria from 1907 to 1927: On the occasion of the twentieth anniversary of its foundation]. Vienna: Reichsverein der Bank- und Sparkassenbeamten.

"A leányok kereskedelmi szakoktatása" [Trade education of girls]. 1909. *A Nő és a Társadalom* [Woman and society] III, no. 7: 117–119.

Leichter, Käthe. 1930. *Handbuch der Frauenarbeit in Österreich* [Handbook of women's work in Austria]. Vienna: Kammer für Arbeiter und Angestellte.

-ly-a. 1913. "Márkus Dezső a magántisztviselőkért" [Dezső Márkus in the interest of private clerks]. *A Nő és a Társadalom* [Woman and society] VI, no. 1: 10–11.

"Lombard- und Escompte-Bank" [Lombard and Escompte Bank]. 1914. *Der Österreichische Bankbeamte* [The Austrian bank clerk] VIII, no. 1: 2–3.

"A magyar nőtisztviselők szervezkedése" [The unions of woman clerks]. 1907. *A Nő és a Társadalom* [Woman and society] I, no. 10: 165–166.

Magyar Statisztikai Közlemények, Új sorozat [Hungarian statistical publication, New series], Vol. 52: *A Magyar Szent Korona Országainak 1910. évi népszámlálása. Harmadik rész. A népesség foglalkozása részletesen és a vállalati statisztika* [The 1910 census in the countries of the Hungarian Kingdom. Third Part. The occupation of the population in detail and company statistics]. 1914. Budapest: Athenaeum.

Ministerium des Innern. 1898. *Die Ergebnisse der über die Standesverhältnisse der Privatangestellten im Jahre 1896 eingeleiteten amtlichen Erhebungen* [The results of the official survey about the status of private clerks carried out in 1896], vol. 1. Vienna: Staatsdruckerei.

"Nőkongresszus" [Congress of women]. 1913. *A Nő és a Társadalom* [Woman and society] VII, no. 6: 122.

"A Nőtisztviselők Országos Egyesülete választmányának évi jelentése" [The yearly report of the Committee of the National Association of Woman Office Workers]. 1909. *A Nő és a Társadalom* [Woman and society] III, no. 6: 103–110.

"A Nőtisztviselők Országos Egyesülete választmányának évi jelentése" [The yearly report of the Committee of the National Association of Woman Office Workers]. 1910. *A Nő és a Társadalom* [Woman and society] IV, no. 6: 108.

"Die Organisation und die weiblichen Angestellten" [The organization and the female staff]. 1909. *Der Österreichische Bankbeamte* [The Austrian bank clerk] III, no. 1: 2–4.

"Otázka zaměstnání žen v ústavech peněžních" [The question of woman employees in financial institutinos]. 1910. *Peněžní obzor* [Financial review] III, no. 11: 221–224.

Österreichische Statistik, Neue Folge [Austrian statistics, New series]. *Band 3, Heft 1, Berufstatistik nach den Ergebnissen der Volkszählung vom 31. Dezember 1910 in*

Österreich. 1. Heft des dritten Bandes der Volkszählungsergebnisse. Hauptübersicht und Besprechung der Ergebgnisse [Occupational statistics of the census conducted on 31 December 1910 in Austria. First issue of the third volume of census results. Overview and assessment of results]. 1916a. Vienna: Hof- und Staatsdruckerei.

Österreichische Statistik, Neue Folge [Austrian statistics, New series]. *3. Band, 8. Heft, Berufsstatistik nach den Ergebnissen der Volkszählung vom 31. Dezember 1910 in Österreich. 8. Heft des dritten Bandes der Volkszählungsergebnisse. Böhmen* [Occupational statistics of the census conducted on 31 December 1910 in Austria. Eighth issue of the third volume of census results. Bohemia]. 1916b. Wien: Hof- und Staatsdruckerei.

"Das Pensionsversicherungsgesetz" [The law on old-age pensions]. 1907. Mitteilungen der "Vereinigung der arbeitenden Frauen" [Papers of the Association of Working Women] 5, no. 44: 4–8.

Rosenberg, Adele. 1909. *Aktuelles über das Privatbeamten-Pensionsversicherungs-Gesetz. Vortrag* [Current information about the law on the insurance of private clerks. A presentation]. Vienna: Strauss.

Rosenberg, Adele. 1909b. "Das Privatbeamten-Pensionsversicherungsgesetz" [The old-age pensions law for private clerks]. Mitteilungen der "Vereinigung der arbeitenden Frauen" [Papers of the Association of Working Women] 7, no. 60, 61: 3–11, 2–12.

Salomon, Alice. 1906. *Die Ursachen der ungleichen Entlohnung von Männer- und Frauenarbeit* [The causes of the unequal pay between male and female work]. Leipzig: Duncker und Humblot.

"Sind wir radikal?" [Are we radical?]. 1908. *Der Österreichische Bankbeamte* [The Austrian bank clerk] II, no. 3: 8–10.

Stenographisches Protokoll der im k.k. arbeitsstatistischen Amte durchgeführten Vernehmung von Auskunftspersonen über die Arbeitszeit in Banken, Kredit- und Versicherungsanstalten [Abbreviated transcript of the interrogation about working hours in banks, credit and insurance companies, carried out by the employment statistics office]. 1905. Wien: Hölder.

Stepanek, Maria. 1906. "Die Frau im Handel und Gewerbe" [The woman in trade and industry]. Mitteilungen der "Vereinigung der arbeitenden Frauen" [Papers of the Association of Working Women] 4, no. 35, 36: 1–4, 4–6.

"A szellemi proletariátus" [The intellectual proletariat]. 1907. *A Nő és a Társadalom* [Woman and society] I, no. 3: 35–36.

Szuppán, Vilmos, ed. 1908. *A BKA ötvenegyedik évi jelentése az 1907–1908-ik iskolai évről* [Report of the Budapest Academy of Trade on the 1907–1908 academic year]. Budapest: Pesti Könyvnyomda Részvénytársaság.

"A tisztviselőnő becsülete" [The honor of the woman clerk]. 1915. *Pénzintézeti Tisztviselők Lapja* [Journal of bank clerks] VIII, no. 10–12: 16–17.

"A tisztviselőpálya megrontói" [The spoilers of the clerk's career]. 1908. *A Nő és a Társadalom* [Woman and society] II, no. 3: 52.

Ulbrich, Elisabeth. 2018. "Qualification: Frau, Arbeiterinnen und Büromanipulantinnen der Oesterreichisch-ungarischen Bank 1878–1922" [Education: Woman, female workers and female office workers at the Austrian-Hungarian Bank, 1878–1922]. MA Thesis, University of Vienna.

Die Vereinsleitung. 1906. "Fünf Jahre Vereinsarbeit" [Five years of club activity]. Mitteilungen der "Vereinigung der arbeitenden Frauen" [Papers of the Association of Working Women] 4, no. 38: 2–4.

Volet-Jeanneret, Helena. 1988. *La femme bourgeoise à Prague 1860–1895: de la philanthropie à l'émancipation* [The bourgeois woman in Prague between 1860 and 1895: From philanthropy to emancipation]. Geneva: Editions Slatkine.

Von einer staatlichen Kanzleigehilfin. 1914. "Die Bedeutung der Dienstpragmatik für die Beamtinnen bei den staatlichen Behörden" [The significance of service regulations for women in the public sphere]. *Österreichische Frauenrundschau* [Austrian women magazine] XI, 118: 5–8.

"Was will die 'Vereinigung der arbeitenden Frauen?'" [What does the Association of Working Women want?]. 1913. *Österreichische Frauenrundschau* [Austrian women's magazine] X, no. 116: 6–9.

Willhelm, Szidónia. 1911. "A nőtisztviselő jövője" [The future of the women clerks]. *A Nő és a Társadalom* [Woman and society] V, no. 5: 74–75.

Willhelm, Szidónia. 1913. "Hol szervezkedjenek a nőtisztviselők" [Where should woman clerks organize themselves]. *A Nő és a Társadalom* [Woman and society] VII, no. 10: 172–174.

"Ženy jakožto konkurentky soukromých úředníků" [Women as competitors among private clerks]. 1902. *Všeobecné Úřadnické listy* [Clerks' general papers] VII, no. 6 (207): 1–2.

Zimmermann, Susan. 1999. *Die bessere Hälfte? Frauenbewegungen und Frauenbestrebungen im Ungarn der Habsburgermonarchie 1848 bis 1918* [The better half? Women's movements and women's aspirations in Hungary under the Habsburg Monarchy 1848–1918]. Vienna and Budapest: Promedia Verlag and Napvilág kiadó.

CHAPTER 4

"Approached as a Force for Labour"

Communist Women's Fight for Women Workers' Rights in the Comintern, the Profintern, and Eastern Europe in the 1920s

Daria Dyakonova

Abstract

The Communist Women's Movement (CWM) emerged in 1920 following the foundation of the Communist International (the Comintern). The CWM's program for women's emancipation included total equality of rights, universal suffrage, and the participation of women in national and municipal governments. The economic emancipation of women and women's rights at the workplace, however, were core points of the communists' agenda. Communist women were active within the Red International of Labour Unions (or Profintern), a Comintern auxiliary organization established to coordinate communist activities in trade unions. Using unpublished archival sources and the press, this chapter recovers numerous unknown facets of communist women's activities within the Profintern. It focuses on two aspects in particular: communist's women's activism within the Profintern, and the complex relationship between men and women within the trade union international of the communist movement. I demonstrate that organized communist women played a crucial role in setting up structures for women within the Profintern. These organizational bodies became particularly active in 1927–1928 and took up and promoted the specific demands of women workers. Their efforts were only partially successful, however, due to the lack of cooperation and sometimes open sexism of the male-dominated Profintern structures and leadership.

Keywords

Comintern – communist women's movement – International Trade Union Committee of Women Workers of the Profintern – interwar period – Profintern – sexism – women's economic emancipation

 | DOI:10.1163/9789004682481_005

The Communist Women's Movement (CWM), as it was often referred to by its members, emerged in 1920 following the foundation of the Communist International (or the Comintern).[1] The Comintern was founded a year earlier, in 1919, on Vladimir Lenin's initiative to replace the (Second) Socialist International, which had discredited itself by its militarist and nationalist policies during World War One. The "woman question" had long been an important issue on the socialist agenda—both the Socialist and Communist Internationals had argued for women's emancipation. Within the Comintern, structures for communist women were integrated into communist parties but had special agitation units for women (to which men could belong as well) that were to coordinate work by local women's committees on the branch level. By 1922, almost all European countries where communists could legally operate would indeed set up such party structures. On the international level, an International Women's Secretariat (IWS) associated with the Executive Committee of the Comintern (ECCI) was established. A member of the IWS was also a member of the ECCI. The Secretariat had its offices first in Moscow, then briefly in Berlin, and again in Moscow. Its goal was to recruit women into communist parties and train them as cadres and leaders so they could, together with men, work to bring about socialist transformation, an integral component of which would be the emancipation of women workers.

The CWM's program for women's emancipation was quite ambitious for the time and included total equality for women in law and practice, universal suffrage, and women's right to participate in national and municipal governments. It also contained the struggle for equal pay for men and women, women's access to equal and free education; social measures intended to ease the burden of childcare and housework for women, and many other goals. Communist women were particularly active within labour movements and labour politics as they prioritized the fight for the rights and interests of women workers. Since 1921, they promoted the struggle for these rights within the Red International of Labour Unions (commonly known as the Profintern), another Comintern auxiliary organization established in 1921 to coordinate communist activities in the arena of trade unions worldwide.

Scholarly studies on communist women and the Comintern's gender policy in a transnational perspective are still rare. Historians of the Soviet Union have made important contributions to our understanding of the work of the women's department of the Russian Communist Party, the Zhenotdel (Женотдел)

1 The name (Communist Women's Movement) was not an official term and is rarely used in the Comintern's documents. But this was how communist women commonly spoke of it. See, for example, Riddell 2012, 838.

and some notable women's leaders.[2] A few works have discussed interwar communist women's efforts in different countries, mostly in Europe.[3] Several scholars have explored communist women's activities in China during the interwar period.[4] Few contributions have engaged with the global history of the movement.[5]

Studies of the Profintern, scarce as they are, have not focused on women's issues or women's participation in the international communist labour movement.[6] I use the work of Albert Resis and Reiner Tosstorff as key references for the history of the Profintern. Resis, who analyzed the origins of the Red International and its early activities, has pointed out that the Comintern conceived of this organization as a major rival to the International Federation of Trade Unions (IFTU) in Amsterdam. He has also emphasized the importance of debate in the early Profintern, noting the modification and sometimes rejection of policies proposed by Moscow by a number of its member states. Following Resis's argument, this chapter also highlights the conflicts and divisions that characterized the Profintern in the 1920s, specifically those related to women's participation in the organization. Tosstorff's work, anchored in archival data unavailable to Resis at the time, is an invaluable source of information on the Profitern between 1921 and 1937. But because Tosstorff's work is a general study and is not informed by a gender-historical approach, the author has limited himself to summarizing the contents of the resolutions related to women workers passed during Profintern congresses. However, despite its limitations, Tosstorff's study provides a strong foundation for the analysis included in this chapter.

Historians who have analyzed women's participation in international labour movements and trade unions such as the IFTU have not yet addressed the role of women within the Profintern. That said, Susan Zimmermann has made a ground-breaking contribution to the discussion of competing policies and competition over proletarian women between the Profintern and the IFTU Women's Committee.[7] Zimmermann's argument serves as the primary

2 Ruthchild 2010; Alpern-Engel 2003; Scheide 2001; Clements 1997 and 1979; Wood 1997; Goldman 1996 and 1993; Elwood 1992; Farnsworth 1980; Porter 1980.
3 Sewell 2012; Bard 2011; Hunt and Worley 2004; Bard and Robert 1998; Gibson 1998; Grossmann 1998; Weitz 1997.
4 Hershatter 2007; Young 2001; Gilmartin 1995.
5 Studer 2021, 2015a and 2015b; Bayerlein 2007 and 2006; Marie 2003; Waters 1989; Carr 1964.
6 Tosstorff 2004; Adibekov 1971; Resis 1964.
7 Zimmermann 2021, 218–225.

analytical framework for my research, as this chapter discusses the attitudes of communist women toward their rivals in the IFTU.

This study also makes use of the methodological insights of recent scholarship on Cold War era communist women's activities in communist and socialist countries.[8] These studies have nuanced liberal historians' criticism of socialist and communist feminism,[9] demonstrating that such scholars have "underestimated the extent to which the program of women's emancipation was a fundamental component of the overall communist program for rapid modernization," which communist/ socialist women believed was the best path to women's autonomy.[10] Kristen Ghodsee, for example, has contended that communist women working in state women's and international socialist organizations strategically chose to align their programs with the larger goals of communist parties. This alignment resulted in significant successes for women in terms of legal equality and family law, education, and labour force participation. Francisca de Haan underlined the progressive character of important achievements in the Women's International Democratic Federation (WIDF), an organization that brought together left-leaning feminists from around the world and achieved important results in the promotion of peace, women's rights, antiracism, and anticolonialism. Susan Zimmermann has analyzed the complex gender regime and gender struggles in Hungary during the Cold War, pointing out the conflicts at different levels provoked by the struggle against men's privileges in various spheres. Zheng Wang has also shown how socialist state feminists in China skillfully navigated male–female relationships to advance the cause of gender equality, often facing opposition from party leadership.

This chapter adopts de Haan and Ghodsee's "revisionist" perspective, applying it to the interwar period and the labour and trade union activities of communist women. It further develops Zimmermann's and Zheng's methodological insights in order to scrutinize the antagonistic gender dynamics within the Profintern. It also builds on my own recent articles and a co-edited documentary collection on the international CWM, which analyze the wider scope of policies, activities, and efforts in which the CWM engaged during the early 1920s.[11]

Using the archives of the Comintern and Profintern, this study seeks to offer a deeper analysis of the Profintern's engagement with women's issues and

---

8 Ghodsee 2016, 2014, 2012; Zheng 2016, 2010, 2005; De Haan 2012, 2010; Zimmermann 2010.

9 Partridge 2012; Einhorn, 2010; Brunnbauer 2009; Jancar 1978.

10 Ghodsee 2016, 115.

11 Dyakonova 2023; Taber and Dyakonova 2022.

to recover virtually unknown facets of communist women's activities within the Profintern. The overarching objective of this chapter is to complicate and advance both the scholarship on communist women's activism and the struggle to address working women's concerns that contemporary feminist labour activists continue to pursue.

I focus on two aspects in particular: communist women's activism within the Profintern, and the complex relationship between men and women within the trade union international communist movement. I argue that the Communist Women's Movement played a crucial role in setting up structures for women within the Profintern. These structures became particularly active in 1927–1928 and took up the demands of specific women workers. Their efforts were, however, only partially successful because of the lack of cooperation and sometimes open sexism on the part of men Profintern activists. The Profintern's women's section was active until early 1936 and fought for women's unionization and women's specific workplace demands. Developments during the 1930s lay outside the scope of this research. That said, the abundance of archival data on Profintern activities at the Russian State Archive for Social and Political History (RGASPI) leaves space for further research on Profintern women in the future.

1 "The Trade Unions Should Become the Center to Which the Attention of the Women's Section Is Directed": The CWM and the Profintern

When the CWM's delegates convened in Moscow for their founding conference in July 1920, labour relations between the sexes and the participation of women in the labour movement and trade unions were core points on the agenda. All delegates who took the floor pointed out the growing importance of women workers within trade unions, which was the result of women's mass entry into industries during World War One. Indeed, women became important actors in labour politics particularly after 1914. Things, however, changed once the war ended and men workers returned to their workplaces. Trade Unions, then, as the French delegate Alfred Rosmer pointed out, "seemed not only indifferent to the task of organizing women workers, but even showed hostility," discouraging "in every possible way those who came to the trade unions and spoke for the women, asking for help with organizing women workers."[12] Some

12 Kollontai and Vinogradskaia 1921, 50.

federations, Rosmer added—quoting the example of the printer's union in France—refused to admit women workers as members of the union. The situation in France was not unusual. Many trade unions worldwide were reluctant to admit or support women workers.[13]

The young Soviet state intended to fight such tendencies in Soviet trade unions and encouraged women's entry and participation in the organizations, including in leadership positions. However, changes were slow, which is why the First Conference's "Guidelines"—a blueprint for the CWM's activities drafted by Clara Zetkin and amended later by a specially appointed commission—encouraged "countries such as Russia, where the proletariat has already conquered state power [...], to draw all employed women into full participation in the work of economic reconstruction through the soviets, the trade unions, and the cooperatives and their various institutions." In capitalist countries, the CWM called on parties to "enlist women as members with equal rights and duties in the Communist Party and in the economic organizations of the proletariat for the class struggle," meaning that wherever communists had influence within trade unions, they were to promote women's participation and leadership in these structures.[14]

The conference call for the Second CWM's Conference, which convened in 1921, encouraged parties and unions to send CWM's representatives to both the Comintern's Third Congress and the Founding Congress of the Red International of Labour Unions—the Profintern.[15] Women delegates were indeed present at the first Profintern international meeting in Moscow, which opened two weeks after the closure of the women's gathering. Clara Zetkin, *de facto* leader of the women's movement and head of its international secretariat, was one of the key participants and leaders of the Profintern's Founding Congress as well. Solomon Lozovsky, a seasoned Russian revolutionary who would become the Profintern's general secretary and hold this position until its dissolution in 1937, gave a speech on behalf of the international trade union movement at the opening of the Second Communist Women's Conference. Lozovsky highlighted the important role played by Russian revolutionary women "in all the practical work of our economic life, in the party, in the trade unions, and on the military front with rifle in hand"[16] and encouraged delegates to organize

13 Hunt 2012; Miller Jacoby 1994; Frances 1993.

14 Riddell 1991, 988–990.

15 "The Second International Communist Women's Conference" 1921, 1–2.

16 During the Civil War, some 60,000 women fought as combatants; almost 2,000 died in combat or were taken prisoner. In addition, 20,000 women served as Red Nurses, and 30,000 were performing administrative work.

women workers worldwide and draw them into trade unions by promising them all kinds of support from the future Red Trade Union International.[17]

The economic and labour integration of women became one of the key themes of the Second Conference. Alexandra Kollontai, the prominent Russian communist and women's rights activist, the first woman minister (People's Commissar of Social Welfare), and the head of the Soviet Zhenotdel, was also a major leader in the international CWM, and in her "Report on Forms and Methods of Communist Work Among Women," she underlined that economic struggle was the focus of broader communist movement, and specifically the women's communist movement. Reflecting the perspective of the Workers' Opposition, Kollontai[18] characterized trade unions as "organizations that embody the proletariat as a whole" and asserted that winning them over was the most important task for communist parties.[19] Regarding the women's organization, she argued:

> Trade unions should become that center, to which the attention of the women's section should be directed. The trade union ought to become the center of the struggle for controlling the national economy, its regulation, and control over production.
>
> Every one of us understands that the old system of capitalist production kept the woman dependent and deprived of all rights, and that only communism will bring about her emancipation. But the importance of the revolution for a woman does not lie in the fact of granting her political rights equal to those of a man, but in the fact that the social collective began to need her work. And the greatest day for the woman was not

17 "Заседание второй конференции коммунисток" [Meeting of the Second Conference of Communist Women], Стенограмма первого дня второй международной конференции коммунисток [Minutes of the first day of the Second Conference of the CWM], 9 June 1921, f. 507, op. 1, d. 3, ll. 6–7, Российский государственный архив социально-политической истории [Russian State Archive for Socio-Political History] (hereafter RGASPI), Moscow, Russia.

18 Alexandra Kollontai was one of the leaders of the Workers' Opposition in the Soviet Communist Party at the time. This opposition emerged in 1920 as a fraction within the CPSU that opposed what it perceived as over-bureaucratization of the party and urged the transfer of economic management to trade union organizations. Kollontai presented her views at the Comintern's Third Congress. See Riddell 2015, 679–682.

19 "Отчет о формах и методах коммунистической работы среди женщин" [Report on forms and methods of communist work among women], Стенограмма третьего дня второй международной конференции коммунисток [Minutes of the third day of the Second Conference of the CWM], 12 June 1921, f. 507, op.1, d. 6., l. 62. RGASPI, Moscow, Russia.

> when she was acknowledged as having equal rights according to law but when the universal obligation to labour was established across the entire Soviet Republic. That day was a magnificent event in relation to the condition of woman, second to none in the whole history of humanity. Being enrolled on the registration list inasmuch as the national economy is concerned, the woman is no longer responsible only to her husband or family but to the collective, and from this naturally follows a new attitude toward her on the part of the state and society, and she is approached as a force for labour.[20]

In other words, Kollontai pointed out how the economic and labour integration of women liberated them more than did political emancipation linked to voting rights. Despite its distinct Workers' Opposition perspective, the Comintern supported Kollontai's ideas on the importance of women's economic integration, as did communist Parties worldwide.[21]

A few delegates who spoke after Kollontai at the Second Conference again underscored the importance of work among women within trade unions and special measures and methods the future international Red Union should adopt in order to address the position of women within the labour movement. German delegate Gertrude Faber urged participants of the second conference to approach the forthcoming Profintern congress and encourage the future Profintern to consider the "woman question." As a result of these efforts, the conference adopted a resolution calling for such action, and the Profintern adopted a "Resolution on the Woman Question" at its Founding Congress in July 1921.

At the Profintern's Founding Congress,[22] it was Hertha Sturm, an active German delegate at the CWM's international gatherings and a member of the International Women's Secretariat in Berlin in 1921–1924, who delivered a "Report on Women in the Trade Unions" in which she stressed that women made up a large part of the proletarian masses. She then spoke about the divisions within the proletariat and specifically the trade union movement on the question of women's employment and their integration into the labour movement. She mentioned the need for the new communist labour organization—the Profintern—to do away with practices that discriminated against women.

20 "Отчет о формах и методах коммунистической работы среди женщин" [Report on forms and methods of communist work among women], Minutes of the third day, 12 June 1921, f. 507, op. 1, d. 6., l. 63. RGASPI, Moscow, Russia.

21 Riddell 2015, 1028–1029.

22 Tosstorff 2004, 348–421.

Sturm also spoke of the need to use all possible means to attract working women and bring them into the Profintern, including addressing issues that concerned only working women or those that were particularly relevant for them such as Sunday work, night work, and maternity protections. The speaker cited the Soviet example, where night and Sunday work was legally prohibited for women (and, in fact, for most workers) and where sixteen weeks of paid maternity leave was introduced by decree in 1918.[23] Sturm also argued that it was vital that the Profintern address the needs of housewives, a demand that was in line with discussions that took place within the CWM and which promoted the transformation of housework and the domestic economy into paid forms of social labour.

Following Sturm's report, a commission consisting of women delegates was appointed to develop a resolution regarding the "woman question" that could be adopted by the congress. The document declared the importance of women within the proletarian movement and called on the Profintern to, first, gather and engage working women using all means of agitation and organization, and, second, make women "take an active part in all forms of trade-union life and activity" in shop committees, agitation, wage-rate committees, executive committees, etc. The resolution also urged members of the Profintern to "energetically fight the efforts of capitalist employers, aided by governments, to increase their profits and strengthen and maintain their industries by utilizing the cheap labour of unorganized women." This latter point reiterated the significance of struggle for equal pay for equal work and the improvement of working conditions for women, as well as legal protections for women workers and working mothers. Finally, the Profintern instructed its members to fight against the antiwomen tendencies of workers within the rival socialist Amsterdam International—the International Federation of Trade Unions.[24] This resolution, thus, carried the seeds of the competition between socialists and communists over working-class women that would only increase throughout the 1920s.

After reading out the resolution at the Profintern's congress, Swiss CWM activist Rosa Bloch highlighted the importance of *acting* on the resolution and *translating principles into specific actions* that would protect the interests of

23 The 1918 Labour Code also provided at least one paid 30-minute break every three hours to feed a baby, factory rest facilities for working mothers, free pre- and post-natal care and allowances. See Sazhina 2013; Kiselev 2010; Goldman 1993, 52.

24 The International Federation of Trade Unions (also known as the Amsterdam International) was an international organization of trade unions founded in 1919. The organization had close ties with the Socialist International.

women. In addition to this specific resolution, the First Profintern Congress added points concerning women workers into two other documents: the "Resolution on the Tasks and Tactics of the Trade Unions" and the "Resolution on the Organizational Question." The former called for "firm resistance" to a "split in the ranks of the labour movement," that is, the tendency of some trade unions to expel women in order to increase men's wages or employment opportunities instead of fighting against employers who exploited cheap women's labour and, in turn, hurt working men. The latter demanded the inclusion of women in trade union work as equal members with equal rights (guarding against separate women's organizations within the workers' movement), which promised to "increase the army of the social revolution."[25]

At the Profintern's Founding Congress, women were still a tiny minority. Those who attended were mainly women organized within the CWM and coordinated by the IWS; though small, they immediately began implementing the goals laid out in the Profintern's resolutions. However, toward the end of the year, German delegates had to admit that this work had not advanced much. The situation was similar in other countries. Almost a year later, in October 1922, the conference of specially appointed communist women delegates from most European countries that met in Berlin reported certain improvements in trade union work. The reports stated that not only parties but also the trade union press in different countries had begun publishing so-called women's pages—articles and news items concerning women's activities. At the same time, the conference had to acknowledge that turning resolutions into reality was a slow process, and in most countries, "comrades have, as yet, hardly embarked on conscious and systematic activity in the trade unions at all, let alone considered a special focus on working women."[26] At the same time, the reporter on the trade union question, Austrian communist Isa Strasser, pointed out successes in specific countries. One of these countries was Bulgaria, where communists controlled almost the entire trade union movement at the time. According to Bulgarian communist Tina Kirkova's report, the women's committee within the Bulgarian party closely cooperated and sent its members to trade unions to organize women and fight for their specific demands. The party and its women's department also formed so-called educational or information groups, which assembled women sympathizers, including members of trade unions. It goes without saying that the international CWM viewed Soviet Russia as the country where women were the most active and effective in the

25 Taber (forthcoming).
26 Sturm 1922, 662.

trade union sphere. Indeed, in 1922, women constituted 38 percent of the total trade union membership in the Soviet Union, a number that had been steadily growing since 1917.[27]

When the Second Profintern Congress convened in November 1922, Hertha Sturm pointed out the low level of organizing among women. Lozovsky, by that time the head of the Profintern, agreed and urged the Profintern to earnestly take up issues related to women workers.[28] However, once again, it was up to the IWS (rather than the Profintern) to formulate the specific modes of women's work within the Red International and, most importantly, to bring the project to life. At a meeting in Berlin in January 1923, the IWS worked out a plan for the Profintern's activism among women workers. The objective was familiar: involving women in all of the proletariat's political and economic struggles. At the same time, the plan included some very specific, new, and ambitious (for the time) demands such as the abolition of Saturday afternoon work for women; a decrease in the working hours for women agricultural workers, domestic servants, nurses, and other "female professions" not covered by the legislation for industrial workers; the abolition of overtime for women; a reduction of working hours in dangerous and hazardous industries; fourteen fully paid days off; health and accident insurance and allowances; measures to ease the burden of housework for housewives, and the establishment of facilities that would transform housework into collective work such as laundries, canteens, etc. by employers; day care and school facilities for children and youth; sixteen weeks of maternity leave; a six-hour working day for nursing mothers and breaks to breastfeed at the workplace; and the creation of special inspections to ensure employer compliance with these measures. Communist women demanded equal pay for equal work and the abolition of take-home work for fully employed women workers.[29] Lozovsky again spoke of the need to engage women in trade union work at the Third Profintern Congress held in July 1924. The resolution on women worked out by the congress integrated most of the demands formulated during the CWM's meeting in Berlin, adding

27 "Стенограмма восьмого заседания третьей сессии Центрального совета Профинтерна" [Minutes of the eighth sitting of the third session of the Central Council of the Profintern], July 1923. f. 534, op. 2, d. 9, l. 21. RGASPI, Moscow, Russia.

28 Tosstorff 2004, 577 and 579.

29 "Тезисы и письмо МЖК в Берлине о революционной профсоюзной работе среди работниц, отправленное исполкому Профинтерна" [Theses and letter of the IWS in Berlin on revolutionary trade union work among women workers sent to the EC of the Profintern], "Стенограмма заседания Международного женского комитета (МЖК) в Берлине" [Minutes of the meeting of the IWS in Berlin], January 1923, f. 534, op. 3, d. 52, ll. 15–26. RGASPI, Moscow, Russia.

to them equality for men and women in unemployment insurance and the fight against the alleged IFTU policy of dismissing working women from their jobs in factories after they married.[30] The Profintern also decided to hold its own separate international trade union women conferences moving forward.[31]

For the next few years, the IWS remained the major body charged with the implementation—as far as possible—of the decisions of the Profintern. It was only in 1928, just before the Profintern's Fourth Congress, that the Red International itself established a special women's committee within its structures.[32] At the beginning of 1928, the Comintern was about to take the "Left Turn"—a new policy strategy formulated in late 1927 and adopted by the Sixth Congress of the Comintern convened in Moscow from 17 July through 1 September 1928. The new policy prohibited communists around the world from collaborating with reformist labour unions and social democratic organizations and, thus, directly targeted Profintern activities.[33] Moreover, this meant that communists within trade unions were to mobilize and radicalize in order to unmask social democrats and reformists.[34] Greater mobilization implied better organized and disciplined structures, which pushed the Profintern to set up a number of new secretariats, first to lead trade union work in colonial and semi-colonial countries and contexts—a Pan-Pacific Secretariat, a Latin American Trade Union Confederation (Confederación Sindical Latinoamericana), and an International Trade Union Committee for Negro Workers. Women were also included in the plans for organizational expansion envisioned in the Left Turn. In February 1928, a special (at first temporary) body was created within the Executive Committee of the Profintern specifically to work among women.[35]

30 "Проекты резолюций, резолюции и обращения к Третьему Конгрессу Профинтерна" [Projects of resolutions and resolutions, addresses of the 3rd Congress of the Profintern], Тезисы о работе среди женщин [Theses on work among the women], July 1924, f. 534, op. 1, d. 44. l. 66. RGASPI, Moscow, Russia.

31 Zimmermann 2021.

32 Zimmermann 2021 has outlined this turn in the politics of the Profintern (using printed and non-Russian language sources).

33 International developments in 1926–1927 seemed to confirm the new analysis. In 1927, the Chinese revolution suffered a serious setback that led to the systematic extermination of the Chinese communists. Britain severed its ties with the Soviet Union. Austrian Social Democrats ignored a call for a general strike by communists in Vienna in the summer of 1927. In the autumn of the same year, British trade unionists dissolved the Anglo-Russian Trade Union Committee. The reformist and moderate Left appeared to turn its back on the "Reds." The radicalization of the international communist movement seemed inevitable and imperative.

34 McDermott and Agnew 1996, 71–74.

35 "Стенограммы заседаний, отчеты, планы и другие материалы Международного профсоюзного комитета работниц Профинтерна" [Minutes of meetings, reports,

Naturally, its cadres came from the CWM. At first, the new body did not have a name and acquired one only in April.

At the beginning, the new permanent body, which was called the International Trade Union Committee of Women Workers of the Profintern (ITUCWWP), had representatives from Britain, the United States, China, France, Germany, Czechoslovakia, Mexico, Italy, Poland, Norway, the USSR, and Bulgaria, Romania, and Yugoslavia.[36] In cooperation with the IWS, the Lenin School in Moscow,[37] the Soviet All-Union Central Council of Trade Unions, as well as the Central Committee of the Communist Party of the Soviet Union (CPSU), the ITUCWWP developed a resolution regarding women workers for the Fourth Congress of the Profintern. In line with "Left Turn" rhetoric, this resolution blamed reformist unions (including social democratic ones, which would soon be called "social-fascist" unions by Comintern members) for "the weak organization of women workers" and for "sidetracking them from the questions of the class struggle."[38] It nevertheless recognized its own deficiency, admitted that the work done by the Profintern among women had been insufficient, and appealed to its members "to extend it as far as possible," declaring that such work was "one of the fundamental tasks" of the RILU.[39] The resolution encouraged the integration of women into Profintern structures at every level and promoted women as trade union leaders. Moreover, admitting that many male Profintern members "underestimated the importance of women's work," it suggested resorting to "special explanatory propaganda efforts" to spell out to members the importance of women's labour and trade union organizing.[40]

---

plans and other materials of the ITUCWWP]. Стенограмма первого заседания [Minutes of the first meeting], 12 April 1928, ll. 1–2, f. 534, op. 3, d. 360. RGASPI, Moscow, Russia.

36 "Воззвание к работницам всего мира" [Appeal to working women of the whole world], 5 May 1928, l. 28. f. 534, op. 3, d. 360. RGASPI, Moscow, Russia.

37 The Lenin school was founded by the Comintern in 1926 to teach Marxist-Leninist theory and Soviet history to foreign communist militants and instruct them on activism in their countries.

38 "Проекты резолюций и резолюции Четвертого Конгресса Профинтерна. Резолюция о работе среди работниц" [Draft resolutions and resolutions of the Fourth Congress of the Profintern. Resolution on work among women workers], April 1928, f. 534, op. 1, d. 81, ll. 171–172. RGASPI, Moscow, Russia.

39 "Проекты резолюций и резолюции Четвертого Конгресса Профинтерна. Резолюция о работе среди работниц" [Draft resolutions and resolutions of the Fourth Congress of the Profintern. Resolution on work among women workers], April 1928, f. 534, op. 1, d. 81, l. 172. RGASPI, Moscow, Russia.

40 "Резолюция о работе среди женщин" [Resolution on work among women workers], April 1928, RGASPI, f. 534, op. 1, d. 81, l. 176 and 177. RGASPI, Moscow, Russia.

Regarding specific demands, the Fourth Congress's resolution articulated an even more radical program: it called for a seven-hour workday (six hours in dangerous industries) and a four-hour workday on Saturday; one month of paid holiday, as well as the previously mentioned prohibitions on women's night work and overtime; sixteen weeks of paid maternity leave and employer-supported daycare facilities; facilities and breaks for nursing mothers; and equal unemployment benefits for men and women. A new addition to this list was the demand to install women-only dressing rooms, washrooms, and showers at factories and anywhere else women worked for wages.[41] In May 1928, the new ITUCWWP issued an "Appeal to Working Women of the Whole World" that encouraged women workers and employees to join in the fight for even more radical demands contained in the Fourth Congress' resolution on women.[42] In countries where the Profintern was not present, the ITUCWWP recommended joining socialist trade unions (to build cooperation from below) in order to unmask and "remove from leadership reformist traitors and replace them by tested and true comrades, both men and women."[43]

As a part of the Profintern's Executive Committee, the ITUCWWP could (or at least hoped to) have access to greater resources, both financial and human. It planned to collect very detailed information about the situation of women workers in different countries and designed pamphlets for different countries that outlined a concrete plan for organizing among working women. As part of the Red Unions Executive, the woman's body also believed that several points on the agenda that were related to the work being done among women and by women were to be integrated into the "Thesis of the Agitprop [agitation and propaganda] Department" of the Profintern and, in accordance with the Fourth Congress's resolution, expected national Profintern sections to issue a special mass paper for women. The new work plan also included sending special instructors from the Soviet Union to work with women in trade unions in other countries.[44]

---

41 "Резолюция о работе среди женщин" [Resolution on work among women workers], April 1928, f. 534, op. 1, d. 81, l. 173. RGASPI, Moscow, Russia. See also Zimmermann 2021, 122.

42 "Воззвание к работницам всего мира" [Appeal to working women of the whole world], 5 May 1928, f. 534, op. 3, d. 360, ll. 27–28. RGASPI, Moscow, Russia.

43 "Воззвание к работницам всего мира" [Appeal to working women of the whole world], 5 May 1928, f. 534, op. 3, d. 360, l. 28. RGASPI, Moscow, Russia.

44 "Стенограммы заседания Международного профсоюзного комитета работниц Профинтерна 15 сентября" [Minutes of the meeting of the ITUCWWP on 15 September 1928], ll. 3–4; "Стенограммы заседания Международного профсоюзного комитета работниц Профинтерна 13 ноября" [Minutes of meeting on 13 November 1928], ll. 14–16. f. 534, op. 3, d. 360. RGASPI, Moscow, Russia.

The newly founded ITUCWWP coordinated work on the international level. The Fourth Congress's resolution instructed national sections of the Profintern to create "commissions of women workers as auxiliary organizations for assisting unions in carrying out work among women."[45] Women's sections within parties were also to participate in trade union work and coordinate their efforts with the Profintern's national sections and communist parties. It was, however, one thing to adopt a policy as part of a resolution at an international congress, but quite another for local leaders and rank-and-file members to put the policy into effect on the ground.

2 "Completely Sabotaged by the Central Trade Union Department": Rank-and-File vs. Leaders and Women vs. Men in the Profintern

The leadership of Profintern sections and parties, which was overwhelmingly male, were to encourage and support women's efforts within their structures in all possible ways, an approach in line with all the resolutions of Profintern congresses and with other Profintern programmatic documents. In reality, support and cooperation, or even the coordination of efforts, had been highly contentious issues from the very beginning of the Profintern.

Attitudes within the Profintern, in fact, reflected the broad sexism of and prejudice against women on the part of men comrades within the communist movement, which has been discussed in a number of historical studies on the complex gender dynamics within communist parties in the Soviet Union as well as in other (national) contexts.[46] This was one of the questions the CWM discussed at all of its meetings, and women delegates made impassioned

45 "Резолюция о работе среди женщин" [Resolution on work among women workers], April 1928, f. 534, op. 1, d. 81, l. 175. RGASPI, Moscow, Russia.

46 Studer examines the masculinist culture that limited most Comintern women's career opportunities and maintained the sexual double standard for men and women (Studer, 2015b). Anne E. Gorsuch (1996) and Seth Bernstein (2017) have looked into complexities of gender relations within the Soviet Komsomol, and more broadly among Soviet youth. Susan Zimmermann (2010), in her article on state socialism and gender in post-Second World War Hungary, discussed the tendency to reduce direct attacks on the privileged position of men promoted by the state. The 2016 *Aspasia* "Forum" also examined the issue of male resistance to women's activism in socialist countries during Cold War era (De Haan 2016). Wang Zheng discussed the fierce opposition of the male-dominated Communist Party leadership to women's rights activists' struggles in post-World War Two China (Zheng 2016).

speeches on the relations between the Executive Committee of the Comintern and the CWM as well as between the male leadership and women's structures within communist parties. On the one hand, many communist men viewed gender-based claims with suspicion, fearing that such claims called into question Marxist class-based analysis; on the other hand, despite the Comintern's and Profintern's official egalitarian discourse, a number of communist men found it challenging to reconcile this discourse with traditional male sexism and chauvinism.

Within the Profintern, the case of the communist trade union movement in Poland is both revelatory and relevant. In a report to the ITUCWWP dated July 1928, the Polish trade union delegate comrade Kalina mentioned the significant presence of women employed in the industrial and agricultural sectors of the country.[47] Indeed, according to Kalina, women constituted 35 percent of the workforce. In the textile industry, they represented 60 percent of all workers, and in tobacco industry, up to 90 percent. Kalina reported that women earned only 60 percent of men's wages and worked ten to sixteen hours a day, often in hazardous and toxic conditions. Legislation protecting women (such as prohibitions on women's night work, the protection of motherhood, and employer-provided day care facilities) existed only on paper. In short, there was much work to be done to remedy Polish women workers' deplorable conditions. And yet, Kalina stated, work among women in trade unions was deficient even in those unions where communists were influential. She explained this by pointing to the lack of contact and coordination between the trade union department of the communist party and the party's women's section on both the national and local levels, except in a few locations such as Łódź. Kalina complained that a number of important campaigns including the fight for maternity protections and the celebration of International Women's Day were "completely sabotaged by the central trade union department [of the Party]."[48] Despite the women's section's demands and complaints to the Central Committee of the party, she argued, the trade union department's inaction persisted as far as work among women was concerned. During the first half of 1928, the department had sent a representative to a women's section meeting only once. While women hoped that this would be the start of true coordination, in reality, such collaboration remained unrealized.

Despite the fact that Polish women workers were active and effectual in strikes—and for this the ITUCWWP praised them on a number of occasions—it

47 "Отчет делегата Польши Калиной" [Report by Kalina, Poland], July 1928, f. 534, op. 3, d. 360, ll. 92–96. RGASPI, Moscow, Russia.

48 "Report by Kalina, Poland," July 1928, f. 534, op. 3, d. 360, l.95. RGASPI, Moscow, Russia.

was only in big industrial centers that the party supported them. In smaller places like Belsk and Częstochowa, Kalina reported, women had to act on their own. In its conclusion, the report suggested taking a few concrete steps to ensure organizing women received sufficient attention and resources: assigning special paid activists (preferably women) to work among women; improving coordination and communication on all levels; providing training for women in trade unions so that they could be promoted to leadership positions; creating a press organ for women workers as well as creating women's pages in the trade union press and wall newspapers.[49] These efforts came to naught. Two other reports dated by April and May 1929 admitted that the situation had not improved since July 1928, and the party and Profintern department had not been giving women sufficient assistance, a state of affairs that pushed women toward social democratic movements and other political forces, including the liberal feminist movement.[50]

The Polish case was not unique, of course. Similar reports came from Austria, where "prejudices against women" were still strong.[51] Even the Central Council of the Profintern had to recognize "insufficient interest directed toward the work of women's trade union commissions" in France, Bulgaria, and Czechoslovakia.[52] At its regular meeting held in May 1929, the central secretariat of the ITUCWWP emphasized the importance of coordinating the work of the EC of the Profintern, the IWS, the Lenin School, and the Communist

49 "Report by Kalina, Poland," July 1928, f. 534, op. 3, d. 360, l.96. RGASPI, Moscow, Russia.

50 "Отчет о профсоюзной работе среди работниц в Польше" [Report on trade union work among women workers in Poland]. Стенограммы собраний, резолюции, отчеты о работе среди женщин в Австрии, Британии, Польше, США, в странах Дальнего Востока и другие материалы Международного профсоюзного комитета работниц Профинтерна. [Minutes of meetings, resolutions, reports on activities among women in Austria, Britain, Poland, USA, in countries of the Far East and other materials of the ITUCWWP], 1 May 1929, f. 534, op. 3, d. 449, ll. 91–92; "Отчет центрального женского секретариата КПП" [Report of the Central Women's Secretariat of the CPP], Отчеты и письма Международного профсоюзного комитета работниц Профинтерна ЦК КПП о работе среди женщин [Reports and letters of the ITUCWWP to the CC of the Communist Party of Poland on Work among Women], November 1928 to April 1929, f. 534, op. 7, d. 429, ll. 13–14. RGASPI, Moscow, Russia.

51 "Отчет о работе в Австрии" [Report on work in Austria], March 1929, f. 534, op. 3, d. 449, l. 30. RGASPI, Moscow, Russia.

52 "Работницы в экономической борьбе и задачи революционного профсоюзного движения" [Women workers in the economic struggle and tasks of revolutionary trade union movement], Тезисы и резолюции шестой сессии Центрального Совета Профинтерна [Theses and resolutions of the Sixth Session of the Central Council of the Profintern], December 1929, f. 534, op. 2, d. 55, ll. 50–55. RGASPI, Moscow, Russia.

Academy (the future Academy of Sciences), and later integrated such efforts as part of its agenda for the period between October 1929 and January 1930.[53]

At the joint meeting of the ITUCWWP and a delegation of foreign women workers who traveled to the Soviet Union for the celebration of the twelfth anniversary of the October Revolution, Ekaterina Arbore-Ralli, the Swiss CWM's representative and an ITUCWWP activist of Romanian descent, described the attitude toward women's work observable time and again in the following way:

> What can one say about workers that scowl with disdain when women are elected to factory and plant committees [...] and who think that womankind is not ready to assume elected office or leadership? [...] This does not mean there are no instructions and directives that urge women's involvement in trade union work. There are more than enough resolutions, statements, and directives. The problem is that our organizations do not carry them out. It is time to do away with this vicious situation.[54]

Comrade Asher, who represented Britain, then spoke about the strength of such tendencies within the British branch of the Profintern and even maintained that women workers could only find support from women leaders.[55]

This situation resulted in the creation of a special commission to "examine" the ITUCWWP, which assembled representatives of the latter, as well as the Comintern and the Soviet All-Union Central Council of Trade Unions. Comrade Gerber, representing the ITUCWWP, spoke about the unsatisfactory work of the Women's Committee due to scarce financial and human

53 "Заседание секретариата Международного профсоюзного комитета работниц Профинтерна" [Meeting of the Secretariat of the ITUCWWP], 22 May 1929, f. 534, op. 3, d. 449, l. 4; "План работы Международного профсоюзного комитета работниц Профинтерна, октябрь 1929-январь 1930" [Plan of work of the ITUCWWP for October 1929 through January 1930], f. 534, op. 3, d. 449, l. 8. RGASPI, Moscow, Russia.

54 "Стенограмма совместного заседания секретариата Международного профсоюзного комитета работниц Профинтерна и делегации иностранных работниц в СССР по случаю празднования двенадцатой годовщины Октябрьской Революции" [Minutes of the joint meeting of the ITUCWWP and Delegation of Foreign Women Workers to the USSR for the celebrations of the 12th anniversary of the October Revolution], November 1929, f. 534, op. 3, d. 449, l. 137. RGASPI, Moscow, Russia.

55 "Стенограмма совместного заседания секретариата Международного профсоюзного комитета работниц Профинтерна и делегации иностранных работниц в СССР по случаю празднования двенадцатой годовщины Октябрьской Революции" [Minutes of the joint meeting of the ITUCWWP and Delegation of Foreign Women Workers to the USSR for the celebrations of the 12th anniversary of the October Revolution], November 1929.

resources and high staff turnover, the lack of support or direction on the part of the Profintern; and the "well-known disparagement of the work among women workers."[56] Comrade Perevoznikov, a representative of the Comintern, objected, arguing that "there [was] no disparagement but rather a lack of confidence in the performance of the Committee" on the part of the Profintern. He argued that the Committee "had to show more initiative and had to more frequently turn to the Profintern for advice and instructions in order to make the Profintern hear women workers' concerns."[57] Comrade Voitkevich, chair of the examining commission, disagreed with Perevoznikov and pointed out that women were not entirely responsible for the lack of coordination. In the end, these differences in opinion were resolved by the Executive Committee of the Profintern, which adopted a document "On the Work of the Secretariat of the ITUCWWP," in which it admitted its own poor leadership and lack of support for working women's trade union work.[58]

At its Sixth session held in December 1929, the Central Council of the Profintern returned to the "woman question." Its resolution on the topic was somewhat contradictory. While noting the important role played by women workers in all recent economic disputes, and women's independent role in initiating many strikes (including the Czechoslovakian miners' strike in Kladno, as well as strikes in the United States, Japan, France, China, and in British colonies), the Central Council declared that the fundamental reasons for the weak organization of women workers were the "treachery of the reformist unions"; "the general political backwardness of women workers"; and "the lack of systematic activities among the women on the part of RILU," i.e., the Profintern.[59] According to the resolution, only Germany could boast of some progress, but even there, women were rare among leaders of red trade union organizations.

---

56 "Стенограмма заседания комиссии по Международному профсоюзному комитету работниц Профинтерна" [Minutes of the meeting of the Commission to examine the ITUCWWP], 14 November 1929, f. 534, op. 3, d. 449, l. 14.

57 "Стенограмма заседания комиссии по Международному профсоюзному комитету работниц Профинтерна" [Minutes of the meeting of the Commission to examine the ITUCWWP], 14 November 1929, f. 534, op. 3, d. 449, l. 14.

58 "Стенограмма заседания комиссии по Международному профсоюзному комитету работниц Профинтерна" [Minutes of the Meeting of the Commission to examine the ITUCWWP], 14 November 1929, f. 534, op. 3, d. 449, l. 15.

59 Резолюция "Работницы в экономической борьбе и задачи революционного профсоюзного движения" [Resolution "Women Workers in the Economic Struggle and Tasks of Revolutionary Trade Union Movement"] December 1929, f. 534, op. 2, d. 55, ll. 50–55. RGASPI, Moscow, Russia. See also Zimmermann 2021, 221–224 (who, while referring to the decision to establish the ITUCWWP in 1928, gives the end of 1929 as date of the formal foundation of the Committee, a date based on published sources).

In July 1930, the Fifth (and last) Congress of the Profintern convened in Moscow. It seemed that this time, the Profintern tried its best to solve the problem of the underrepresentation of women in its ranks. The selection criteria for delegates, for example, included specific quotas for young people and women.[60]

3 Afterword and Conclusion

Research on women in the Comintern has noted the deradicalization of the CWM from the mid- to late 1920s. Elizabeth Waters has argued that by the end of the 1920s, "the movement's aim was no longer the advancement of women but their mobilization for the advancement of the Comintern."[61] The movement became weaker as the Comintern downgraded the IWS from a semi-autonomous body to a department of the Executive Committee. Scholars have attributed this weakening and subsequent de-radicalization to the Comintern's Left Turn, brought about by the rise of the Stalinist system in the Soviet Union; the CPSU's domination of the international communist movement; as well as the increasing centralization of the Comintern's apparatus.[62] These interpretations reveal important truths about the history of the CWM. By the mid-1930s, the CPSU would become a major—although not omnipotent—decision-maker within the Comintern. Simultaneously, in the Soviet Union, there was a revival of the old conservatism that led to significant retreat as far as women's rights were concerned—the most important of which were, perhaps, the closure of the Zhenotdel in 1930 and the re-criminalization of abortion in 1936. The Soviet retreat from its emancipatory agenda would indeed affect the CWM, both its international apparatus and the national communist parties. Moreover, shifts in Soviet Foreign policy and, perhaps more importantly, the adoption of the Popular Front policy by the Comintern significantly affected the work of women. The Comintern then sought alliances with a very broad spectrum of antifascist political movements, including center-left and even bourgeois forces, and tried to avoid antagonizing potential allies with a radical gender agenda. Consequently, the Comintern's women's agenda was often revised and deradicalized for the sake of unity with more traditional (in terms of gender) political forces within the mass Popular Front movement. The search for a broad alliance with "all women," which then became a major element of the CWM's strategy, meant the adoption of a weaker gender agenda that would

60 Tosstorff 2004, 769.
61 Waters 1989, 51.
62 Waters 1989; Bayerlein 2007, 2006.

unite women across the political spectrum. In November 1935, the women's department of the ECCI was formally dissolved.

National women's sections, however, continued to function in most communist parties. And women involved in these sections continued the struggle for women's rights on the national and local levels. During the interwar period, communist women advocated for the creation of broader non-party women's organizations that would appeal to wider audiences. In Norway, communist women established the Housewives Organization, which assembled non-party working-class housewives. Until the late 1930s, this organization engaged in efforts related to everyday women's demands such as solutions to housing problems, unemployment, food prices, and the legalization of abortion. The Norwegian "Mothers' Clinics," established in 1924 as a collaborative effort by three socialist parties, were active throughout the interwar period. In Denmark, up until 1934, the Working Women's Association—the women's organization of the Communist Party—fought for gender equality in civil rights, in the workplace, and in the home.[63]

Although it was also an auxiliary organization of the Comintern, the Profintern followed a slightly different path. The RILU started genuinely supporting women only in spring 1928, when the International Trade Union Women Workers Committee was founded as part of the Profintern's Executive Committee. The turn coincided and was arguably encouraged by the Comintern's "Left Turn" and the increased competition between the Profintern and the IFTU over women workers. Women still faced numerous difficulties after the body was established: the lack of support on the part of trade union leadership, discrimination against women's separate organizations, and ordinary sexism. That said, women in the Profintern were reluctant to ignore these difficulties. On the contrary, they pushed the Profintern leadership to fight against such attitudes within its ranks and effectively promoted their specific agenda.

The ITUCWWP was rather short-lived. With the Comintern's adoption of the Popular Front policy, the Profintern became an obstacle to trade union unity. The new strategy called for the coordination of efforts among all trade unions, including reformist ones. In early 1936, the Profintern was transformed into a department of the Comintern's Executive Committee. Its major task was now to achieve the unification of different trade union organizations, not to be an alternative international revolutionary union. Accordingly, all parts of

63 For more information on communist and left-wing women's movements in Norway, Denmark, and Germany, see Blom 1998; Christensen 1998; and Grossmann 1998.

the Profintern's apparatus that were not necessary for achieving this purpose, such as the youth, women's, agitation, and propaganda sections, had to be liquidated.[64] The Red International itself did not last long after the liquidation of the women's committee. In late 1937, by which point the Profintern was already extremely weak and nearly inactive, the ECCI secretariat made the decision to dissolve it.

Bibliography

Adibekov, G.M [Адибеков Г. М.]. 1971. *Красный интернационал профсоюзов: Очерки истории Профинтерна* [The Red International of trade unions: Studies in the history of the Profintern]. Moscow: Profizdat. Translated into German as *Die Rote Gewerkschaftsinternationale*. Berlin, 1973.

Alpern-Engel, Barbara. 2003. "Women in Revolutionary Russia, 1861–1926." In *Political and Historical Encyclopedia of Women,* edited by Christine Fauré, 383–411. New York: Routledge.

Bard, Christine. 2011. "A Bitter-sweet Victory: Feminisms in France (1918–1923)." In *Aftermaths of War: Women's Movements and Female Activists, 1918–1923*, edited by Ingrid Sharp and Matthew Stibbe, 197–220. Leiden: Brill.

Bard, Christine, and Robert, Jean-Louis. 1998. "The French Communist Party and Women, 1920–1939." In *Women and Socialism/Socialism and Women*, edited by Helmut Gruber and Pamela Graves, 321–347. New York: Berghahn Books.

Bayerlein, Bernhard H. 2006. "Zwischen Internationale und Gulag. Präliminarien zur Geschichte der internationalen kommunistischen Frauenbewegung (1919–1945)" [Between the International and the gulag. Preliminary notes on the history of the international communist women's movement]. *The International Newsletter of Communist Studies Online* 12, no. 19: 27–47.

Bayerlein, Bernhard H. 2007. "Zu Aufbau und Destruktion einer Fraueninternationale" [On the construction and destruction of a women's International]. *The International Newsletter of Communist Studies Online* 13, no. 20: 102–104.

Bernstein, Seth. 2017. *Raised under Stalin: Young Communists and the Defense of Socialism*. Ithaca, NY: Cornell University Press.

Blom, Ida. 1998. "A Double Responsibility: Women, Men, and Socialism in Norway." In *Women and Socialism/ Socialism and Women*, edited by Helmut Gruber and Pamela Graves, 450–477. New York: Berghahn Books.

64 Tosstorff 2004, 805.

Brunnbauer, Ulf. 2009. "'The Most Natural Function of Women': Ambiguous Party Policies and Female Experiences in Socialist Bulgaria." In *Gender Politics and Everyday Life in State Socialist Eastern and Central Europe,* edited by Shana Penn and Jill Massino, 77–96. New York: Palgrave Macmillan.

Carr, Edward Hallett. 1964. *Socialism in One Country, 1924–1926,* vol. 3, part II. London: Macmillan.

Christensen, Hilda Romer. 1998. "Socialist Feminists and Feminist Socialists in Denmark, 1920–1940." In *Women and Socialism/Socialism and Women,* edited by Helmut Gruber and Pamela Graves. New York: Berghahn Books.

Clements, Barbara Evans. 1997. *Bolshevik Women.* Cambridge: Cambridge University Press.

Clements, Barbara Evans. 1979. *Bolshevik Feminist: The Life of Aleksandra Kollontai.* Bloomington: University of Indiana Press.

Dyakonova, Daria. 2023. "'Through the Dictatorship of the Proletariat in All Countries, Onward to the Complete Emancipation Of Women!': The Transnational Networks of Communist Women's Movement in the Early 1920s." *Journal of Women's History* 35 no. 1: 11–33.

Einhorn, Barbara. 2010. "Mass Dictatorship and Gender Politics: Is the Outcome Predictable?" In *Gender Politics and Mass Dictatorship,* edited by Jie-Hyun Lim and Karen Petrone, 34–62. New York: Palgrave MacMillan.

Elwood, Ralph Carter. 1992. *Inessa Armand: Revolutionary and Feminist.* Cambridge: Cambridge University Press.

Farnsworth, Beatrice. 1980. *Aleksandra Kollontai: Socialism, Feminism and the Bolshevik Revolution.* Stanford, CA: Stanford University Press.

Frances, Raelene. 1993. *The Politics of Work: Gender and Labour in Victoria 1880–1939.* Cambridge: Cambridge University Press.

Funk, Nanette, and Magda Mueller. 1993. *Gender Politics and Post-Communism.* New York: Routledge.

Ghodsee, Kristen. 2016. "State-Socialist Women's Organizations in Cold War Perspective: Revisiting the Work of Maxine Molyneux." *Aspasia. International Yearbook for Women's and Gender History of Central, Eastern and Southeastern Europe* 10: 111–121.

Ghodsee, Kristen. 2014. "Research Note: The Historiographical Challenges of Exploring Second World-Third World Alliances in the International Women's Movement." *Global Social Policy* 14, no. 2: 244–264.

Ghodsee, Kristen. 2012. "Rethinking State Socialist Mass Women's Organizations: The Committee of the Bulgarian Women's Movement and the United Nations Decade for Women, 1975–1985." *Journal of Women's History* 24, no. 4 (Winter): 49–73.

Gibson, Mary. 1998. "Women and the Left in the Shadow of Fascism in Interwar Italy." In *Women and Socialism/Socialism and Women*, edited by Helmut Gruber and Pamela Graves, 381–411. New York: Berghahn Books.

Gilmartin, Christina. 1995. *Engendering the Chinese Revolution: Radical Women, Communist Politics, and Mass Movements in the 1920s*. Berkeley: University of California Press.

Goldman, Wendy Z. 1996. "Industrial Politics, Peasant Rebellion, and the Death of the Proletarian Women's Movement in the USSR." *Slavic Review* 55: 46–77.

Goldman, Wendy Z. 1993. *Women, the State and Revolution*. Cambridge: Cambridge University Press.

Gorsuch, Anne E. 1996. "'A Woman Is Not a Man': The Culture of Gender and Generation in Soviet Russia, 1921–1928." *Slavic Review* 55, no. 3 (Fall): 636–660.

Grossmann, Atina. 1998. "German Communism and New Women: Dilemmas and Contradictions." In *Women and Socialism/Socialism and Women*, edited by Helmut Gruber and Pamela Graves, 135–170. New York: Berghahn Books.

De Haan, Francisca. 2012. "The Women's International Democratic Federation (WIDF): History, Main Agenda, and Contributions, 1945–1991." In *Women and Social Movements (WASI) Online Archive*, eds. Thomas Dublin and Kathryn Kish Sklar. Alexandria, VA: Alexander Street. http://alexanderstreet.com/products/women-and-social-movements-international.

De Haan, Francisca. 2010. "Continuing Cold War Paradigms in the Western Historiography of Transnational Women's Organizations: The Case of the Women's International Democratic Federation (WIDF)." *Women's History Review* 19, no. 4: 547–573.

De Haan, Francisca, Kristen Ghodsee, Krassimira Daskalova, Magdalena Grabowska, Jasmina Lukić, Chiara Bonfiglioli, Raluca Maria Popa, and Alexandra Ghit. 2016. Forum "Ten Years After" *Aspasia. International Yearbook for Women's and Gender History of Central, Eastern and Southeastern Europe* 10: 102–168.

Hershatter, Gail. 2007. *Women in China's Long Twentieth Century*. Santa Cruz: University of California.

Hunt, Cathy. 2012. "Sex Versus Class in Two British Trade Unions in the Early Twentieth Century." *Journal of Women's History* 24, no. 1 (Spring): 86–110.

Hunt, Karen, and Matthew Worley. 2004. "Rethinking British Communist Party Women in the 1920s." *Twentieth Century British History* 15, no. 1: 1–27.

Jancar, Barbara Wolfe. 1978. *Women under Communism*. Baltimore: Johns Hopkins University Press.

Kiselev, I. Ya. [Киселев И.Я.]. 2010. *Трудовое право России* [Labour law in Russia]. Moscow: Norma. http://www.hist.msu.ru/Labour/Law/kodex_18.htm#f1.

Kollontai, Alexandra, and Polina Vinogradskaia, eds. 1921. *Отчет о Первой международной конференции коммунисток* [Report on the first international conference of communist women]. Translated by Sonja Franeta, 19–20. Moscow: Gosizdatel'stvo.

Marie, Jean-Jacques. 2003. "The Women's Section of the Comintern, from Lenin to Stalin." In *Political and Historical Encyclopedia of Women*, edited by Christine Fauré, 424–442. New York: Routledge.

Mc Dermott, Kevin, and Jeremy Agnew. 1996. *The Comintern. A History of International Communism from Lenin to Stalin*. London: Macmillan.

Miller Jacoby, Robin. 1994. *The British and American Women's Trade Union Leagues 1890–1925: A Case Study of Feminism and Class*. New York: Carlson.

Porter, Cathy. 1980. *Alexandra Kollontai: A Biography*. London: Virago.

Partridge, Damani. 2012. *Hypersexuality and Headscarves: Race, Sex and Citizenship in the New Germany*. Bloomington: Indiana University Press.

Resis, Albert. *The RILU: Origins to 1923*. PhD dissertation, Columbia University, 1964.

Riddell, John, ed. 2015. *To the Masses: Proceedings of the Third Congress of the Communist International, 1921*. Leiden: Brill.

Riddell, John, ed. 2012. *Toward the United Front: Proceedings of the Fourth Congress of the Communist International, 1922*. Leiden: Brill.

Riddell, John, ed. 1991. *Workers of the World and Oppressed Peoples, Unite!: Proceedings and Documents of the Second Congress, 1920*, vol. 2. New York: Pathfinder.

Ruthchild, Rochelle Goldberg. 2010. *Equality & Revolution: Women's Rights in the Russian Empire, 1905–1917*. Pittsburgh: University of Pittsburgh Press.

Sazhina, N. S. [Сажина Н. С.]. 2013. "Социальная политика в отношении материнства и детства в первые годы советской власти" [Social policy on motherhood and childhood during the early years of the Soviet Union]. *Vestnik BGU* 2. https://cyberleninka.ru/article/n/sotsialnaya-politika-v-otnoshenii-materinstva-i-detstva-v-pervye-gody-sovetskoy-vlasti.

"The Second International Communist Women's Conference." 1921. *Die Kommunistische Fraueninternationale* [The Communist Women's International], no. 2/3 (May–June): 1–2.

Scheide, Carmen. 2001. "'Born in October': The Life and Thought of Aleksandra Vasil'evna Artyukhina, 1889–1969." In: Ilič, M. (eds) *Women in the Stalin Era. Studies in Russian and East European History and Society* edited by Melanie Ilič, 9–28. Basingstoke: Palgrave Macmillan.

Sewell, Sara Ann. 2012. "Bolshevizing Communist Women: The Red Women and Girls' League in Weimar Germany." *Central European History* 45, no. 2 (June 2012): 268–305.

Studer, Brigitte. 2015a. "Communisme et féminisme" [Communism and feminism]. *Clio. Femmes, Genre, Histoire* 41: 139–152.

Studer, Brigitte. 2015b. *The Transnational World of the Cominternians*. London: Palgrave Macmillan.

Studer, Brigitte. 2021. *Reisende der Weltrevolution. Eine Globalgeschichte der Kommunistischen Internationale.* Berlin: Suhrkamp.

Sturm, Hertha. 1922. "Second Conference of International Women's Correspondents." *Die Kommunistische Fraueninternationale* [The Communist Women's International] 9/10 (September/October): 662.

Taber, Mike. Forthcoming 2023. *The Founding of the Red Trade Union International: Proceedings and Resolutions of the First Congress, 1921.* Leiden: Brill.

Taber, Mike, and Daria Dyakonova, eds. 2022. *The Communist Women's Movement, 1920–1922. Proceedings, Resolutions, and Reports.* Leiden: Brill.

Tosstorff, Reiner. 2016 [2004]. *The Red International of Labour Unions (RILU) 1920–1937.* Translated by Ben Fowkes. Leiden: Brill.

Waters, Elizabeth. 1989. "In the Shadow of the Comintern: The Communist Women's Movement, 1920–1943." In *Promissory Notes: Women in the Transition to Socialism*, edited by Sonia Kruks, Rayna Rapp, and Marillyn Blatt Young, 29–56. New York: Monthly Review Press.

Weitz, Eric. 1997. "The Gendering of German Communism." In *Creating German Communism 1890–1990: From Popular Protests to Socialist State.* Princeton, NJ: Princeton University Press.

Wood, Elizabeth. 1997. *The Baba and the Comrade: Gender and Politics in Revolutionary Russia.* Bloomington: Indiana University Press.

Young, Helen Praeger. 2001. *Choosing Revolution: Chinese Women Soldiers on the Long March.* Champaign: University of Illinois Press.

Zheng, Wang. 2016. *Finding Women in the State: A Socialist Feminist Revolution in the People's Republic of China, 1949–1964.* Berkeley: University of California Press.

Zheng, Wang. 2010. "Creating a Socialist Feminist Cultural Front: Women of China (1949–1966)." *The China Quarterly* 204 (December): 827–849.

Zheng, Wang. 2005. "'State Feminism'? Gender and Socialist State Formation in Maoist China." *Feminist Studies* 31, no. 3 (Fall): 519–551.

Zimmermann, Susan. 2010. "Gender Regime and Gender Struggle in Hungarian State Socialism." *Aspasia. International Yearbook for Women's and Gender History of Central, Eastern and Southeastern Europe* 4: 1–24.

Zimmermann, Susan. 2021. *Frauenpolitik und Männergewerkschaft. Internationale Gewerkschaftspolitik, IGB-Gewerkschafterinnen und die Arbeiter- und Frauenbewegungen der Zwischenkriegszeit* [Women's politics and men's trade unionism. International gender politics, women IFTU trade unionists and the workers' and women's movements of the interwar period]. Vienna: Löcker.

CHAPTER 5

Forgotten Women

Slovak Communist Women's Struggle for Reproductive Rights on the Pages of Proletárka *in the 1920s*

Denisa Nešťáková

Abstract*

This chapter discusses the activism of women associated with the Communist Party in Czechoslovakia and the newspaper *Proletárka* (*Proletarian Woman*), which was published in Slovakian and addressed Slovak women. An analysis of *Proletárka*, one of the most important sources of information on the activism of communist women in the Slovak lands, sheds light on the journal's program of social and gender justice, its criticism of women's position on the labour market and women's second shift, its pioneering approach to sexual liberalization, and its treatment of nationalism. The chapter investigates how communist women connected their demands for access to contraception and abortion to class struggle and working women's double burden, focusing on the main arguments for understanding the sexual liberation of women as a working-class issue advanced on the pages of *Proletárka*. The chapter points out the difficulties faced by the communist women's movement in Slovakia as its activism moved beyond mainstream party goals and exposed the tension between reproductive rights and class struggle.

Keywords

abortion – birth control – communist party – class struggle – Czechoslovakia – feminism – nationalism – *Proletárka* (*Proletarian Woman*) – sexual liberation – Slovakia – women's movement

---

* The research for this article was conducted thanks to the generous support of the project ZARAH: Funding from the European Research Council (ERC) under the European Union's Horizon 2020 research and innovation programme (Grant agreement No. 833691—ZARAH), and within the project "Family planning" in East Central Europe from the 19th century until the approval of the "pill," funded by Ministry of Education and Research, BMBF, FKZ 01UC1902.

 | DOI:10.1163/9789004682481_006

> A woman can be freed from sexual slavery only if she is freed from class slavery. That is why the communists consider the fight for liberation of women as a necessary part of the class struggle of the entire proletariat.

In 1989, the American sociologist Arlie Russell Hochchild published a book called *The Second Shift: Working Parents and the Revolution at Home*, in which she talks about the so-called double burden of mothers employed in the United States.[1] The book set off a wave of public debate and controversy and became a bestseller shortly after its publication. Introduced by Arlie Hochschild, the term "second shift" describes work done at home after paid work in the public sector. Yet the notion of a second shift or "double burden" was nothing new. Slovak communist women had been discussing these issues a hundred years ago, i.e., sixty years before the publication of Hochchild's book. This article examines the activism of women associated with the Communist Party of Czechoslovakia (Komunistická strana Československa, KSČ) and its newspaper *Proletárka* (*Proletarian Woman*) (see Figure 5.2), which was dedicated to Slovak women. An analysis of *Proletárka*, one of the most important sources of information about the activism of communist women in the region of Slovakia, sheds light on its commitment to social and gender justice, its criticism of the labour market and women's second shift, and its pioneering work in the field of sexual liberation.

Based on an in-depth analysis of *Proletárka*, this article examines how Slovak communist women's struggle for improved access to contraception and abortion drew on their understanding of class struggle and the Slovak national issue. I show that the distinct discourse that emerged around the issues of abortion and contraception reflected the dynamic interaction between three pillars: class struggle, reproductive rights, and nationalism, and explain how this discourse shaped communist women's writing.

Communist perceptions of family planning, birth control, and sexuality were closely connected with the class struggle and, thus, stood in opposition to the pronatalism of the newly established Czechoslovak republic, which the party saw as an instrument for the capitalist exploitation of working-class. The arguments made by Slovak communist women in support of sexual liberation shaped the official party discourse on birth control and abortion; they even affected the work of scientists who had begun to study how the lack of women's access to contraceptives led working-class women to seek out dangerous, criminal abortions, which often had harmful effects on their health, including

1 Russell Hochchild 1989.

infertility. The yearning for women's sexual liberation and social emancipation was omnipresent among the women within the Czechoslovak Communist Party in the 1920s. Yet, while gender equality was a major issue for communist women, it was perceived as a means to liberate women from poverty, which was a more critical societal matter. Additionally, the women's agenda embraced by Slovak women active in the Communist Party pitted them against not only the so-called bourgeois women's movement; facing persecution by the authorities and rejection in the political sphere, communist women also confronted resistance from their own comrades.

This chapter analyzes communist women's political and educational activism in *Proletárka* in the 1920s. I focus specifically on their demands for access to contraception and abortion as means to help women from disadvantaged backgrounds and as an issue related to working-class liberation, while considering how their arguments reflect particularities of Slovak nationalism as represented by the party. In the first section, I briefly introduce the status of women's health and reproductive rights in Czechoslovakia; the struggle between national self-determination and centralized leadership within the Communist Party of Czechoslovakia; and the specific conditions in which the communist women's movement developed in Slovakia. The second section of the article analyzes the main arguments for women's sexual emancipation, including debates on access to birth control and safe, professional abortion as discussed in *Proletárka*, which were considered the chief concerns for working-class women in Slovakia. Through this analysis, this chapter reveals the challenges faced by the communist women's movement, whose activism was supposed to reflect the party's general goals. However, I argue that Slovak women in the Communist Party often found themselves caught between a politics of reproductive rights and a commitment to class struggle specific to Slovak national circumstances. This eventually led to their marginalization in the movement and their absence from the broader history of communist women's activism.

1 New Nation—Old Woman?

The parliamentary democracy of Czechoslovakia tended to represent more liberal and progressive attitudes toward gender equality compared to Dual Monarchy to which Czechoslovakia had previously belonged. However, regarding population policy, it fell back into old habits. Despite its goal to halt demographic decline, throughout its entire existence, even during the period of stabilization in the 1920s, the Czechoslovak republic never managed to increase the birth rate. Additionally, the multinational state decided to promote a single

Czechoslovak nation instead of two distinct Czech and Slovak nations to ensure its political stability; otherwise, the German inhabitants of the new state—a historic population concentrated in the Czech lands and Slovakia which was now a minority of around three million persons—would outnumber Slovaks.[2] This fragile demographic situation created a sense of uncertainty, which was embodied in the pervasive fear of the extinction of the nation that was particularly popular among political elites, religious circles, and intellectuals. In addition to the fear of a disappearing nation, a significant part of Czechoslovak society and its political representatives signified the continuity of a pre-1918 conservativism closely connected to Catholic religious dogma.[3] And while the Czechoslovak republic sought to create a unique identity and culture of family and wanted to distinguish itself from its new neighbors—Hungary and Austria, especially—it also inherited from the former Austro-Hungarian Dual Monarchy the particularities of its regulation of family life and family planning, including the criminalization of abortion.[4] The Czechoslovak maintenance of Austro-Hungarian abortion laws and the state's persistent promotion of demographic growth stood in contrast to calls for the country's development and its most pressing social issues, notably the call for the emancipation of Czechoslovak women, whose voices, especially those of socialist and communist women, called for social justice, gender equality, and the freedom of choice in family planning.[5]

Because some believed that "[Czechoslovakia] emancipated not only all the Czechoslovak people but especially its women, to whom it granted suffrage [in 1920], and otherwise essentially placed on the same level as men in public life," many politicians assumed there was no place or reason for any further measures to advance the equality of women.[6] Indeed, Czech and Slovak women involved in the prewar women's movement recognized the urgency of and their responsibility and role within the Czech and Slovak movements for national liberation. Their women's agenda and commitment to the international feminist movement was secondary.[7] The Czech and Slovak national liberation movements emerged in the nineteenth century as counterparts

2 See Bakke 2011, 247–268; Šuchová 2011.

3 For instance, Slovak Catholic priest Jozef Tiso became Minister of Health and Sports in 1927; he strongly opposed any proposals related to sexual liberation. See Fabricius 2002.

4 Nešťáková 2020, 31–51; Aláč 2017, 90–154; Repková 2014, 147–173; Šubrtová 1991, 9–46; Šubrtová 2002, 233–244.

5 See Krylova 2017, 434; Falisová 2013, 51–65; Zavacká 2001, 23–30.

6 Scheinost 1932.

7 About the feminist movement in Czechoslovakia, see Škorvanková 2021b, 62–80; Adams 2014; Kodymová and Haburajová-Ilavská 2014, 81–86; Dudeková 2011; Feinberg 2006, 20–40.

to the ruling German and Hungarian-speaking population of the Austro-Hungarian Monarchy. While the national revival movements of the Czech and Slovak nations differed from each other, there was relative unity and agreement between men and women in both the Czech lands and Slovakia because the national struggle against German and Hungarian elements increased the unity of all individuals who identified themselves as Slovaks and/or Czechs. Subsequently, Czech and Slovak men understood the importance of woman for the national struggle. Encouraging the education of women and supporting women's suffrage meant that many Slovak and Czech men regarded women as their allies in a shared struggle for independence.[8] At the same time, the nature of women's inclusion in the national struggle differed in the Czech lands and in Slovakia, and it generally did not go beyond a more conservative and patriarchal understanding of women's roles in society.

When public, political, and scientific debates on women's unequal position in marriage, lack of access to employment opportunities, and sexual emancipation in Czechoslovak society began, they met with suspicion, scorn, and denunciation. However, an increasing number of women became active in politics and entered the National Assembly and Senate in Czechoslovakia, and most of the female MPs represented the most progressive force within the Czechoslovak legislature, especially on topics related to women's employment, gender equality, health care for women and children, and family planning.[9] Some of the most radical proponents of sexual liberation and reproductive rights for women were women associated with the Communist Party. Their work primarily grew out of the postwar social situation, the development of an independent Czechoslovak society, the Austro-Hungarian past, and most importantly, communist theories of women's emancipation. Recognizing the despair of working-class women burdened by their childcare responsibilities and social inequality, communist women activists reached out to the marginalized female masses.[10] However, women in different regions of Czechoslovakia

8 Clearly, there were also persons who opposed women's suffrage, e.g., Milan Rastislav Štefánik, one of the leading Slovak members of the Czechoslovak National Council who contributed decisively to the cause of Czechoslovak sovereignty, opposed women's right to vote. For further reading, see Šiklová, 1997, 264. See also Lengyelová 2004; David 1991, 26–45.

9 About women in Czechoslovak politics, see Musilová 2007.

10 About the socialist women's movement in Czechoslovakia, see Škorvanková 2021b, 62–80; Kodymová and Haburajová-Ilavská 2014, 81–86; Dudeková 2011; Feinberg 2006, 20–40. See also Lengyelová 2004; David 1991, 26–45.

FIGURE 5.1 Slovak press committee of the communist party. On the left, the chief editor of *Proletárka* Barbora Rezlerová Švarcová, and on the right author Hermína Pfeilmayerová
SOURCE: PHOTOGRAPH (ARCHIV NÁRODNÍHO MUZEA PRAHA [ARCHIVE OF THE NATIONAL MUSEUM PRAGUE]), FOND VERČÍK, BOX 4, FILE 166.

faced distinct challenges, so communist women had to ensure their arguments reflected accurate knowledge of women's needs within the national framework.

2 Slovak Communists and the National Question

The young communist movement emerged in the newly founded Czechoslovak state in the early post-World War One period, and the Czechoslovak Communist Party was formally established in 1921. At the time, it was one of the largest communist parties in the world. This strength was reflected in its position in domestic politics. As early as 1925, in the first election in which the party could participate, it gained 13.2 percent of all votes and became the second largest party in the Czechoslovak parliament.[11]

While the national issue was consistently present from the very beginning, it did not seem to be one of the party's most pressing problems. However, Prague soon became the center of the party, and its practices proved to be strongly centralist and inattentive to the needs and goals of Slovak communists in the eastern part of the country. The Czech leadership abolished the relatively autonomously formed local cells in the national party as well as the trade union organs and called for a united and centralized party.[12] Additionally, Czech communists strongly opposed the autonomist proposals submitted by the Slovak nationalist camp within the party. Meanwhile, Slovak communists pointed out the economic neglect of the eastern part of the Czechoslovak republic and the marginalization of the Slovak nation, which soon produced a sense of grievance that undermined the Czechoslovak consensus.[13] Slovak communists were also concerned about the underfunding of the movement's regional structures and the unbalanced representation of Czech communist officials in Slovakia. Július Verčík (see Figure 5.1), a functionary of the party in Slovakia and an editor of the party's newspapers, criticized the party for filling all the important leadership positions in Slovakia with "their people," i.e., Czechs, "as if they did not trust us Slovaks."[14] Furthermore, for Slovak communists, the Communist Party's attention to the national question effectively co-opted the core agenda of the nationalist and conservative Slovak People's Party.[15] Therefore, Slovak communists had to fight on two fronts—in Slovakia, they competed with the Slovak People's Party for votes; and within the Communist Party, they struggled against Czech communists for recognition.

In 1924, the 5th Congress of the Communist International adopted the Leninist position on the recognition of the right of all nationalities to self-determination, which explicitly rejected the "fictional Czechoslovak nation" and described Czechoslovakia as the "new small imperialist state"; in response, Slovak communists became eager supporters of Lenin's national theses.[16] Those Slovak men and women who resisted the doctrine of Czechoslovakism

11 Rupnik 2003, 42, 60.

12 Hertel 2006, 53. See also Rychlík 2012, 306–316.

13 See Benko and Hudek 2021, 313–342.

14 Archív Národního muzea (ANM) Praha, Fond Verčík, Box 1, Archival Unit 2c, Július Verčík, *Životopis*, p. 73.

15 Benko and Hudek 2019, 289.

16 See Theses on the National Question by Lenin 1977, 243–251. See also Kopeček 2012, 123 and Fowkes 2008, 215.

and the political centralism of the Czechoslovak Communist Party in the interwar republic became known as Slovak national communists. Starting in the mid-1920s, Slovak communists gathered around Július Verčik, the main representative of Slovak national communism, placed the issue of Slovakia's position within the state at the center of their political agenda.[17] Starting in the early 1920s, almost immediately after the party's establishment, Slovak communists portrayed Slovakia as the colonial prey of the Czech bourgeoisie's economic interests.[18] Already in 1925, a resolution of the Slovak branch of the communist party claimed that "national minorities are suppressed, [and] a colonial regime rules in Slovakia and Subcarpathian Russia."[19] The radical, emotional, and even inflammatory programmatic document discussing the national issue entitled "Vypracte Slovensko!" (Get Out of Slovakia!), which was published by Slovak communists in Verčík's circle in 1926, similarly declared: "Without the destruction of bourgeois colonial rule in Slovakia, there is no social and truly national liberation of working people."[20] Women were well represented in this debate: for example, Gizela Kolláriková, a Slovak national and Communist Party MP, reacted, proclaiming some Czech MPs love for the Slovak nation while harshly criticizing corrupt Czech politicians willing to impoverish Slovaks in exchange for bribes offered by businesses, corporations, or lobbyists: "a fat bakshish is nicer [...] than even ten Slovak nations, even if this Slovak nation will starve to death."[21] One of the most significant publications to address the matter of Slovakia's colonization by Czechs entitled *Slovensko. Oběť česko-kapitalistické kolonisace* (*Slovakia—A victim of Czech-Capitalist Colonization*) was written by the Czech communist Barbora Rezlerová-Švarcová (see Figure 5.1), who served as the regional secretary of the Communist Party organization Slovenské ženy (Slovak Women) and was the editor-in-chief of the Slovak women's communist bi-weekly periodical *Proletárka* in early 1920s.[22] Thus, while class struggle was formed the core of the national party's agenda, for Slovak communists, the national question was fundamental and, consequently, it shaped Slovak communist women's discourse on reproductive rights.

17 Benko and Hudek 2019, 286.

18 See Hudek 2015, 51–68; Rapoš 1957, 50–52; Gottwald 1951, 45–57.

19 "Martin—zhromaždenie Komunistickej strany (rezolúcia)" [Martin—Meeting of the Communist Party (Resolution)], 1 May 1925, Fond Okresný úrad Turčiansky Sv. Martin, ŠA ZAM.

20 "Vypracte Slovensko (odpis)" [Get Out of Slovakia!], 1926, Fond Okresný úrad Turčiansky Sv. Martin, ŠA ZAM.

21 Kolláriková 1927.

22 See Švarcová 1925. See also Juráňová 2006, 467–469.

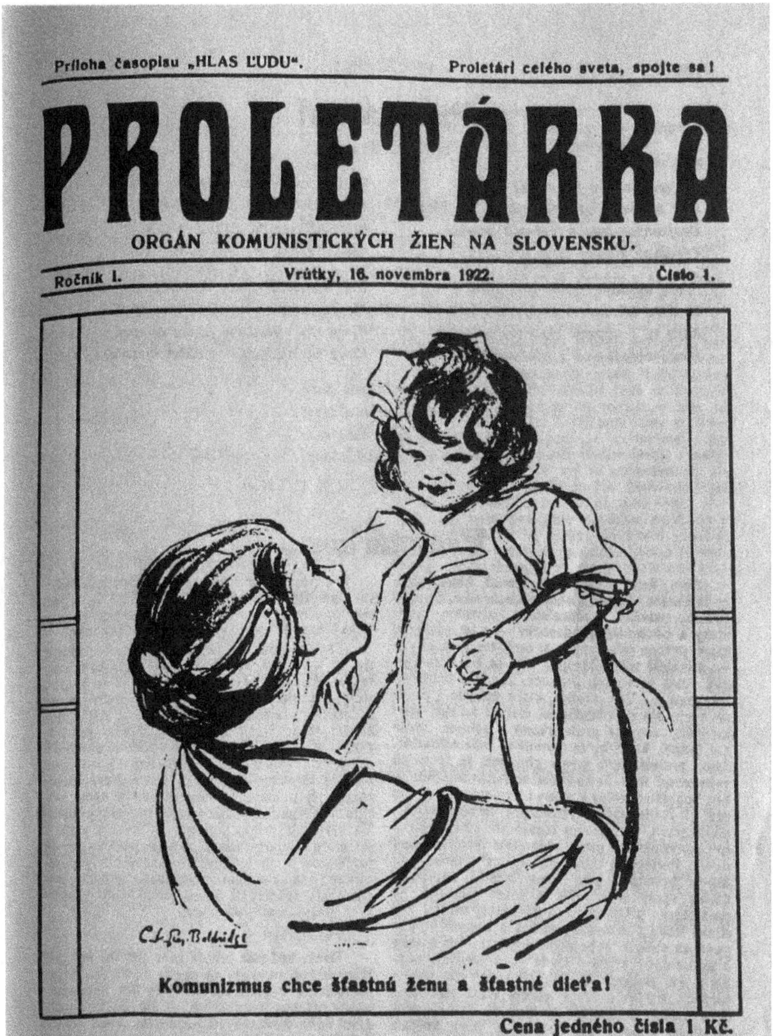

FIGURE 5.2 "Komunizmus chce šťastnú ženu a šťastné dieťa!" [Communism wants a happy woman and a happy child]
SOURCE: *PROLETÁRKA*, TITLE PAGE, 16 NOVEMBER 1922

3 "Angry" Communist Women

Women's public roles in the new Czechoslovak state reflected the legacy of states to which the territories had formerly belonged. Given the impact of prewar Magyarization policies and "restrictions on educational opportunities that had existed during Austro-Hungarian rule prior to 1914, women's as well as men's educational levels remained lower in Slovakia than in Czech lands."[23] Nevertheless, women's share of the labour force increased dramatically in Czechoslovakia during the interwar period, as the country became the seventh largest industrial power in the world. In 1921, women accounted for 30.2 percent of the labour force in the whole of the country; in Slovakia specifically, they represented 24 percent of workers.[24] These numbers did not include women's unpaid domestic work or family members who engaged in agricultural labour. Despite the increase in women's educational levels and employment outside the home, and regardless of the fact that large numbers of women voted, women only rarely ran for or were elected to political office. Women accounted for 4.1 percent of the deputies elected to the lower house of parliament in 1924, and 3.3 percent in 1930. Among the 150 senators in the upper house, three (2 percent) were women in 1924, increasing to only five (3.3 percent) in 1935.[25]

Notwithstanding the relatively low number of female political representatives, Czech, Slovak, German, Hungarian, Jewish, and Ruthenian women began to participate in political parties, and the Social Democratic Party and the Communist Party boasted the highest number of female members.[26] In the 1920s, the Czechoslovak Communist Party had the highest proportion of women members: 24 percent. This proportion was higher than in Germany and Russia, where in the 1920s, women's share was 17 percent and 14 percent, respectively; in France and Italy, women represented just around 2 percent of Communist Party members in both countries.[27] Since many women (as well as men) had become active in politics, especially in the Social Democratic Party, following the establishment of Czechoslovakia, a communist women's movement coalesced at the same time the Slovak Communist Party was established in 1921, and the first regional conference of communist women took place in Vrútky in 1922.[28]

---

23 See Wolchik 1996, 525–538; Johnson 1985.

24 Garver 1985, 71–78.

25 Wolchik 1996, 530.

26 Musilová 2007, 96–121.

27 Studer 2015b, 26 and 48; Sewell 2012, 280; Bayerlein 2006, 27–47; Grossmann 1998, 139; Waters 1989, 29–56.

28 "Konferencia komunistických žien vo Vrútkach 1922 /1. zemská konferencia" [The Conference of Communist Women in Vrútky 1922/ 1st Land Conference], 1923, Signature1136/23, Box 6, Fond Magistrát Banská Bystrica 1850–1922 [Municipality Banská Bystrica 1850–1922], ŠA BB. See also Malá and Křenová 1921, 11–15; Bahenská, Heczková, and Musilová 2010.

Slovak communist women confronted numerous adversaries: from competing women's movements in the region, political elites, and local authorities, as well as opponents within their own party. First, Slovak communist women sought to define their interpretation of the woman question within the communist framework and against the so-called bourgeoise women's movement—i.e., feminism.[29] Competing with well-established women's organizations such as the Slovak women's organization Živena, founded in 1869, communist women embedded their solution to women's inequality in the class struggle.[30] Thus, they accused women's organizations of engaging in counter-productive work as they considered the charity initiatives of such organizations as harming rather than helping:

> These women are dominated by a childish belief that charity, diligence, and goodwill on all sides are the means to remove social misery from the world. [...] it is offensive to give alms to social disadvantaged people from whom humble thanks and a hunched back are required. [...] Alms remain alms.[31]

Most importantly, communist women claimed that their activism was not "a struggle against men, but a struggle against a common enemy: the capitalist model of production."[32] For this reason, they regarded feminism's opposition to working-class women as "a dangerous enemy of workers and an obstacle on the road to resolving the question of the female proletariat."[33] Asserting the ideology of what we define as Marxist feminism, contributors to *Proletárka* claimed that women were exploited through capitalism, and women's liberation could only be achieved by dismantling the capitalist system.[34]

Second, Czechoslovak authorities investigated and persecuted both women and men who were active in the Communist Party. For example, Anna Jurisová (Slezáková), a leader of communist women in Trnava, was called an

29 Braunová 1924.

30 *Proletárka* never openly nor explicitly attacked any Czechoslovak women's organizations; it kept its criticism very general. About the rather voluntarily and charitable work of Živena, see Kodajová 2019.

31 "Beseda. Dopis ploretárskej žene" 1924.

32 "Beseda. Dopis ploretárskej žene" 1924.

33 "Beseda. Dopis ploretárskej žene" 1924.

34 For more about Marxist Feminism, see Ferguson and Hennessy 2010. See also foundational works on women's position in society, for example, Engels 1962 and works by Clara Zetkin and Alexandra Kollontai.

"angry communist" by Czechoslovak authorities.[35] Hermína Pfeilmayerová (see Figure 5.1), one of the most prominent and active figures in the socialist and later the communist women's movement in Slovakia, a contributor to *Proletárka*, and a participant in the Fifth Communist International in Moscow in 1924, was described as follows by Czechoslovak authorities: "[she has a] wrathful nature, and she likes to provoke."[36] Eventually, in 1925, she was found guilty for inciting another person(s) to commit a criminal offense and sentenced to fourteen days in prison; the same year, she was again tried for defaming the republic and sentenced to ten days of imprisonment.[37] The authorities went even further; because of their repeated arrests and prosecution, Barbara Rezlerová-Švarcová and her husband Ladislav Švarc were forced to move to Prague in 1925, and they ultimately emigrated to the Soviet Union year later.[38]

Third, communist women in Slovakia had to confront resistance from their own comrades, whose activism and political and ideological beliefs often retained a patriarchal understanding of woman's role in society. Whereas the party proclaimed that only a communist society would ensure women's full equality, in practice, enthusiastic communist women found it difficult to incorporate gender-specific issues into the class-based political agenda of the party, and they were distressed by the strong objections of some of their comrades, who suggested that the party did not need a women's movement because a woman belonged in the kitchen.[39] Indeed, many men were active members of the party only because their wives took on all domestic tasks, child care, and even paid work.[40] For instance, during the meeting of the executive committee in 1925, Mária Bachratá emphasized that most of the women present had to make sacrifices to attend the meeting: they had to leave their families and children and stay up late even though they needed to wake up early in the morning to go to work. She then argued that instead of dealing with urgent matters, a boring resolution had been discussed for four hours, and the discussion on women's issues had been postponed.[41] At the same meeting, Maria

35 "Komunistická strana v Trnava" [Communist Party in Trnava], Box 303, Fond PR, SNA.

36 "V. Kongres komunistickej internacionály v Moskve" [5th Congress of the Communist International in Moscow], Fond Župný úrad Turčiansky Sv. Martin [County Office Turčiansky Sv. Martin], ŠA ZAM.

37 "Hermína Pfeilmayerová—žiadosť o milosť" [Hermína Pfeilmayerová—request for pardon], 1925, Fond Okresný úrad Turčiansky Sv. Martin [Regional Office Turčiansky Sv. Martin], ŠA ZAM.

38 See Švarcová 1925. See also Juráňová 2006, 467.

39 See Krylova 2017, 435.

40 Uhrová 2004, 27–40.

41 "Schôdza výkonného výboru 20. Kraja" [The Meeting of Executive Committee of the 20th region], 5 March 1925, File 271/25, Fond PR, SNA.

Kocsisová talked about the cruelty of men and working women who were "constantly oppressed in factories by employers, in household by husbands, and at today's meeting, men oppress the women participating by forcing them to sit for four hours and listen to their rubbish discussions."[42] Women active in the Communist Party in Slovakia continually protested that "[women] comrades as well as the [woman] Comrade Secretary face difficulties in their work and very often have to face the resistance of their [male] comrades too."[43] Such comments and descriptions of women's experiences clearly reveal that the predominantly male leadership of the Communist Party in Slovakia had very little understanding of issues that their women colleagues considered crucial. However, many Slovak communist women were able to become political players on the local, regional, and national Czechoslovak scene in spite of the challenges they faced.[44]

Slovak communists' disappointment and frustration with the Czechoslovak Communist Party's Czech centralism was also prevalent among communist women. For this reason, *Proletárka* was first published in November 1922 as an appendix to the Slovak newspaper *Hlas ľudu* (*Voice of People*), and only later as a separate bi-weekly newspaper starting in January 1924.[45] Its contents did not mirror its Czech equivalent *Komunistka* (*Woman Communist*). The guidelines for agitation among communist women published in the 29 March 1927 issue of *Proletárka* suggest that one of the duties of women in party cells was to subscribe to a women's magazine, and men were encouraged to buy such magazines for their wives and sisters. The guidelines also encouraged women to subscribe to the Slovak *Proletárka*, the German *Die Kommunistin* (*Communist Woman*), or the Hungarian *Nömunkás* (*Woman Worker*), but, perhaps in line with anti-Czech sentiments, avoided mentioning equivalent Czech magazines

42 "Schôdza výkonného výboru 20. Kraja," 5 March 1925, File 271/25, Fond PR SNA.

43 "Župný úrad vo Zvolene; Predmet Komunistické hnutie žien v ČSR" [County Office in Zvolen; Subject: the Communist Women's movement in Czechoslovakia], 1924, Signature 1559/2488, Box 12, Fond Magistrát Banská Bystrica 1850–1922 [Municipality Banská Bystrica 1850–1922], ŠA BB.

44 See Studer 2015a, 136.

45 In 1927, *Proletárka* ceased to exist as a separate paper due to financial difficulties and the persecution of its editors. Subsequently, starting in August 1927, it was published as an appendix to the newspaper *Pravda* [Truth] once a week. Similar newspapers dedicated to communist women were *Komunistka* for Czech women, with a circulation of 10,000 copies; *Die Kommunistin* for German speakers with a circulation of 10,500 copies; *Žena* for women in Moravia and Silesia with a circulation of 7,000 copies, *Proletárka* for Slovak women with a print run of 2,300 copies; and *Nömunkás* for Hungarian-speaking women with a circulation of 300 copies. For more about communist women in Czech Lands, see Matysková 2011; Jahodářová 2015, 102–118.

FIGURE 5.3 Poster for International Women's Day, 1926
SOURCE: POSTER (SLOVENSKÝ NÁRODNÝ ARCHÍV [SLOVAK NATIONAL ARCHIVE], FOND POLICAJNÉ RIADITEĽSTVO, BOX 271, FILE 56)

as an option.[46] Therefore, even in their journalism, Slovak communist women did not abandon the battle for the nation, which led to a formulation of and discourse on reproductive rights that was quite independent from that of the Czech party.

46 "Komunistická strana, hnutie žien" [The Communist Party, women's movement], Fond Župný úrad Turčiansky Sv. Martin [County Office Turčiansky Sv. Martin], ŠA ZAM.

Communist women activists in Slovakia were well-traveled and/or boasted extensive networks of communist activists (both women and men). Consequently, they were well informed about developments abroad. For this reason, they preferred to rely on their international contacts and sources rather than simply copy or adapt material from the Czech *Komunistka*. Numerous investigations and reports by Czechoslovak authorities suggest that Slovak women active in the Communist Party traveled across Europe and were in touch with communists who visited Slovakia from the United Kingdom, Germany, Austria, Italy, Macedonia, Romania, France, Ukraine, Hungary, Poland, and the Soviet Union; they even made connections with Jewish communists in Palestine (see Figure 5.3). While most of the foreign communist functionaries who visited were men, they often arrived with their wives, who were also involved in party politics. For this reason, police surveilled communist women—both the Slovak and foreign women, because they were considered a dangerous element.[47] Eventually, harassment by local authorities, along with other challenges including competition from bourgeois feminist organizations; the struggle with the male communist leadership; national interests; and transnational knowledge transfer came together to shape the Slovak communist women's movement. *Proletárka* was the rich and well-articulated representation of their thoughts. The newspaper was, on the one hand, heavily dependent on communist ideology and understood the woman question through that lens; on the other hand, *Proletárka* represents a unique source of the communist women's movement in Slovakia, which reveals how the movement addressed problems and debates in the local (Slovak) context as well as the broader international sphere.

4 The Sexual Liberation of Women—a Vital Issue for the Working Class

Women communist politicians and activists in the interwar period tried to promote a new model of family that fundamentally reorganized relations between men and women and reconceived child-rearing duties. They referred to the work of Friedrich Engels and Vladimir Lenin, who supported the legalization of divorce, demanded the abolition of all laws punishing abortion,

47 "Robotnícke hnutie a dejiny KSČ" [Labour movement and history of the Czechoslovak Communist Party], Fond Okresny úrad v BB 1923–1945 [Regional Office Banská Bystrica 1923–1945], ŠA BB.

and supported the expansion and promotion of contraception.[48] At the same time, Lenin called on the leading representative of the German communist women's movement Clara Zetkin and other women comrades to avoid debates on sexual issues and marriage and instead focus entirely on class struggle.[49] In Czechoslovakia, communist women, full of enthusiasm for the situation in Soviet Union, began to talk about marriage as an "institution of free love" rather than an economically motivated union of man and woman.[50] As an outgrowth of their understanding of social justice and the working-class struggle, women members of the Communist Party in Slovakia advocated for the introduction of sex education in schools, equal rights for unmarried mothers and children born out of wedlock, the abolition of prostitution, the adoption of more liberal legislation on abortion, and the expansion of contraception and health care for mothers and newborns.[51] Fueled by their professional solidarity and their common commitment to social justice and sexual liberation, communists, together with social democrats, overcame otherwise bitter political differences and rivalries and submitted several proposals to reform legislation on marriage, women's working conditions, and abortion.[52] Due to the lack of support by other parties, these proposals never succeeded in Parliament, but thanks to the communist press, working-class women became aware of these issues; so too did the editors of *Proletárka*.[53]

Heretofore, *Proletárka* has not received much scholarly attention apart from a recent study by Eva Škorvanková. In general, the newspaper is believed to have been fully subordinated to the goals of the Communist Party, first and foremost, the class struggle.[54] This misinterpretation of the paper's position has led to ignorance about its content, which consisted not only of ideological texts and articles that uncritically praised the situation of women and children in the Soviet Union but also included candid descriptions of the actual condition of working-class women and children in Slovak national discourse. The

48 See Lenin 1984, 321–324; Marx, Engels, and Lenin 1973; Engels 1962. See also Brown 2012; Slušná 1988.

49 Zetkinová 1973, 207–230. See also Nečasová 2013, 107–115; Ashwin 2000.

50 Malá-Křenová 1921, 8.

51 Musilová 2007, 77. See also Škorvanková 2021a, 162–168.

52 For the similarity with the German case, see Grossmann 1995, 19.

53 For more about history of *Proletárka*, see Ruttkay 1987, 132–134; Darmo 1966, 462–467.

54 Škorvanková 2014, 17–44. About Czech women in the Communist Party, there are numerous works, among them, Báhenská, Heczková, and Musilová 2013; Musilová 2007; Uhrová 2004, 27–40.

FIGURE 5.4 Matka s dvomi deťmi [Mother with two children]
SOURCE: DRAWING. ARNOLD PETER WEISZ-KUBÍNČAN, 1920–1929 (SLOVENSKÁ NÁRODNÁ GALÉRIA [SLOVAK NATIONAL GALLERY], K 19099)

women who contributed to and published *Proletárka* were at the forefront of the struggle to build a more just society.[55]

Additionally, *Proletárka* is an invaluable source for understanding the specific local experiences of Slovak women and the agency of Slovak communist women, since most of their political activism was limited to the Slovak context. They understood that they must address the needs of women in Slovakia not only as a class issue but also as a (Slovak) national issue, since Slovakia brought its past, connected to the Kingdom of Hungary and its legacy, into

55 See Just 2004, 153–161.

the Czechoslovak state. Among other things, this legacy was embodied in the reproductive behavior of Slovaks as well as the socioeconomic conditions of women in the region. For instance, Slovakia continued to have a much higher birth rate (380 newborns per 1,000 women in 1921) compared to the Czech part of the republic (250 newborns per 1,000 women). It also had a much higher infant mortality rate; together with Hungary, Slovakia's infant mortality rate was one of the highest in Europe (167 per 1,000 live births in Slovakia and 168 per 1,000 in Hungary; contrast this to 133 per 1,000 newborns in the Czech lands or 119 per 1,000 in Austria in 1925).[56]

Communist women politicians had limited access to Czechoslovak high politics, which translated to a low number of Slovak women MPs in Parliament.[57] Thus, communist women's formal agency was limited. In fact, the activism of Slovak communist women generally remained confined to the local Slovak context, and *Proletárka* serves as crucial evidence of their work. Many of the texts published in *Proletárka* offered concrete advice and assistance for working-class women and children. Among the issues most frequently addressed by the newspaper were women's unequal position in the workplace, women's "second shift," the sexual exploitation of women, and the effects of women's lack of access to sexual education and contraception within the specific Slovak context.[58] Some of these issues were also on the agendas of numerous feminist organizations in Slovakia and abroad, but the communist women's movement refused to identify as feminist because of communists' hostility toward "bourgeois" women's movements.[59] On the contrary, communist women saw the chance to define themselves in opposition to feminism to gain more supporters because according to them, the bourgeois women's movement was unable to address the everyday problems of working-class women.[60] At the same time, the authors and editors of *Proletárka* sought to address working-class women's issues independently from the Czech party core.

Proletárka published articles on issues that had a direct impact on working-class women in Slovakia, and reported on state policies and how

56 Šprocha and Tišliar 2008, 29–30, and Chura 1936, 82.

57 Throughout the existence of the interwar Czechoslovak republic, only two women MPs from Slovakia represented the party: Gisela Kolláriková and Irena Kaňová. The latter woman represented Social Democracy in the *Revolučné národné zhromaždenie* [Revolutionary National Assembly] in 1919–1920, and only afterward, in 1921, did she join the Communist Party. See Musilová 2007, 96–121.

58 About birth control in the interwar Slovakia, see Falisová 2013, 51–65; Falisová 2011, 29–36.

59 Studer 2015a, 132.

60 About Marxist feminism, see Lokaneeta 2001, 1405–1412. For its interpretation among Slovak communist women, see Braunová 1924, 3.

they affected women's material circumstances and their legal dependence on men. For instance, in her talk during a meeting of communist women in 1925, N. Kollárová, a communist functionary from Žilina, encouraged women to prevent men, especially their husbands, from enslaving them and to secure their own daily bread so they could "cease to be men's prostitutes."[61] Beyond their criticism of women's position in marriage, communist women protested the significantly lower wages women received for the same jobs men did, which limited women's roles in public and only increased women's economic dependence on men.[62] Criticism of the "double burden" of women was voiced at public events organized by the party and was published in *Proletárka*. "separated from their housework all day long,"[63] women returned home after working a shift in the factory, the field, or after a long day working as a maid in someone else's home and then were solely responsible for childcare and housework. The newspaper repeatedly ran articles that criticized the double burden or women's "second shift." Pointing out their 8-hour workday outside the home, contributors estimated that women workers worked 4 to 5 hours more per day on average than their husbands because of their unpaid childcare responsibilities and food preparation and housekeeping duties.[64] Contributors to *Proletárka* also spared no criticism of the dearth of state institutions that could provide childcare for working-class mothers in Slovakia.[65]

Among the crucial questions related to the status of women in the class struggle was whether sexual emancipation was vital for working-class women's broader liberation? The Marxist perception of women's labour, family planning, birth control, and sexuality were a part and parcel of the class struggle. Unlike idyllic, propagandistic portraits of patient mothers surrounded by many children, communist women understood motherhood differently. An article entitled "Is it smart to have many children?" declared, "what a misfortune it is for the poor to have many children," referencing numerous foreign authors.[66] Although Slovak communist women often referenced the Soviet Union as the example to be followed, their writings also suggest that it was equally important to address any author—woman or man—whose work

61 "Vrútky, zhromaždenie komunistických žien" [Vrútky, Meeting of communist women], 1925, Okresný úrad Turčiansky Sv. Martin [Regional Office Turčiansky Sv. Martin], ŠA ZAM.

62 See, for example, "Medzinárodný týždeň žien" [International week of women], 1925, Box 291, Fond PR, SNA.

63 K. 1924.

64 K. 1924.

65 See Dudeková-Kováčová 2019, 99–140.

66 "Je múdre mať veľa detí?" 1924.

supported their understanding of the woman question within the class struggle, such as (U.S.) American socialist writer Upton Sinclair; Swedish physician Seved Ribbing, who wrote about sexual hygiene and ethics; German gynecologist Heinz Zikel, whose work focused on sexuality; English physician and feminist Mary Scharlieb; and French writer and communist Henri Barbusse.[67] Thus, *Proletárka* was an important channel for Slovak women to access the latest information about the women's movement, sexual liberation, eugenics, contraception, and abortion laws in numerous countries in Europe and beyond. Indeed, due to their socioeconomic background, girls and women in Slovakia very often lacked any form of higher education that allow them to gain knowledge about their bodies and learn how to prevent unwanted pregnancies. *Proletárka* developed its own narrative about reproduction—influenced by the Soviet model promoted by the party, the American birth control movement, and European representatives of sexual reform and social hygiene—and sought to disseminate it among Slovak women.[68]

Proletárka also published information about abortion laws in Czechoslovakia and abroad and provided instruction on which contraceptive methods and products to use and how to use them correctly to prevent unwanted pregnancies. In several texts, they pointed out that limited access to safe and affordable contraceptives led many women to seek out abortions, performed in secret, unsanitary conditions that might result in life-threatening illness and even death because abortion remained illegal and criminalized in interwar Czechoslovakia:[69] "uneducated women sometimes do insane things with their bodies to protect themselves from motherhood."[70] While authors of *Proletárka* strongly discouraged women from undergoing life-threatening illegal abortions, they also described the desperate social circumstances in which working-class women and families raised children: "In the current economic crisis and poverty, [...] it is no wonder women avoid or reject motherhood. Every new addition to the family means a financial catastrophe." (see Figure 5.4)[71] Unequal access to contraception and safe abortion were presented as problems related to poverty that were intentionally caused by the capitalist system (see Figure 5.6). Indeed, the lack of access to medically induced abortion was omnipresent on the pages of *Proletárka*, which included stories about wealthy and middle-class women bribing physicians to safely terminate their

67 "Je múdre mať veľa detí?" 1924.
68 See the similar case of Weimar Germany in Grossmann 1995, 37.
69 Nešťáková 2023.
70 "Matka a dieťa" 1923.
71 "Matka a dieťa" 1923.

FIGURE 5.5 Bieda [Misery]
SOURCE: DRAWING. MIKULÁŠ GALANDA, 1928–1929 (SLOVENSKÁ NÁRODNÁ GALÉRIA [SLOVAK NATIONAL GALLERY], K 592)

pregnancies: "Although rich ladies have good medical care, a poor woman cannot pay several hundred crowns for such an operation."[72] The role of corruption and poverty in shaping access to abortion and contraception remained strong arguments for viewing family planning, birth control, and sexuality more generally as related to the class struggle.[73] While women from socially disadvantaged backgrounds were forced to seek out illegal abortions provided in unhygienic and life-threatening conditions, women from the middle and upper classes—albeit still illegally—enjoyed professional, science-based medical care.[74]

The Communist Party viewed the Czechoslovak state's positions on family planning as clear evidence of capitalist exploitation of the working classes, as did scientists, who understood the dire situation of many working-class women. For instance, in August 1934, an international congress of the Medical

72 Stopes 1925c.
73 See Feinberg 2006.
74 See Žáčková 2016, 55–78.

Women's International Association (MWIA) took place in Stockholm and addressed the topic of birth control within the framework of physical education.[75] In a report about the congress written by Czechoslovak ophthalmologist Ludmila Dewetterová, a representative of Czechoslovak medicine, the main findings of the congress concerning the birth control were discussed.[76] Dewetterová was not a communist; she was a member of the Women's National Council (Ženská národní rada),[77] where she was responsible for the activities of the "Mother and Child" department, which considered abortion an urgent issue.[78] Dewetterová's report discusses several matters regarding family planning as discussed within the Central Europe Committee of the congress, which included Austria, France, Hungary, Poland, and Czechoslovakia. The committee debated the importance of birth control and the need to educate couples on contraceptive methods, but it also pointed out many flaws in the family policies of their respective states. Representatives agreed that working-class women in cities and rural areas were especially disadvantaged when it came to accessing contraception and knowledge about methods of birth control compared to women from the middle and upper classes.[79] Thus, scientists, especially physicians, acknowledged that working-class women suffered the most from the criminalization of abortion not only in their rates of prosecution but also due to health problems—even death—caused by illegal abortion.[80] At the same time, communist women were part of a minority that fought for the decriminalization of abortion and the ability of all women to access safe abortion procedures performed by proper medical professionals, based on their own, individual decision:

> We are of the opinion that this prohibition is also incorrect, that a law that does not protect children from poverty cannot and should not prohibit abortion. On the contrary, it should be ensured that medical care is

75 The Medical Women's International Association is a non-governmental organization founded in 1919 with the purpose of representing women physicians worldwide. See Bornholdt 2008.

76 Dewetterová 1935, 507–510.

77 The Women's National Council was the most significant feminist organization in the interwar period. Its members fought for the reform of marriage laws and against employment restrictions on women. It was founded by Františka Plamínková, a Czech feminist and suffrage activist and member of the Czechoslovak Socialist Party, who was elected to the National Assembly and Senate Chair.

78 Chlapcová-Gjorgjevičová 1932, 193–194.

79 Dewetterová 1935, 507–510.

80 See Panýrek 1932, 628–630.

> available, and that a woman has the free will to decide whether she wants to have a child or not.[81]

However, *Proletárka* did not regard legalized abortions as a good solution, and the periodical warned women to avoid them: "We do not recommend abortions, [...] Any abortion is harmful to women's health, and every woman can avoid it if she is well informed about the means of protection."[82] Understanding the dangers of illegal and unprofessional abortion, *Proletárka* called for the translation of books by American birth control activist, sex educator, writer, and nurse Margaret Sanger—especially *Family Limitation*—and by the British author, paleobotanist, and eugenics and women's rights campaigner Marie Stopes, including *Wise Parenthood: A Treatise on Birth Control or Contraception* and *Married Love or Love in Marriage*. The newspaper even provided an abbreviated Slovak translation of a book about birth control by Swiss physician Fritz Brupbacher.[83] Authors of *Proletárka* also added further information and instructed women about methods of birth control, especially condoms, despite their high price: "[W]e can only advise our women on what has already been said here—caution and the use of means that prevent conception. These products are sold in pharmacies and drugstores and are not prohibited."[84]

As far as it was able, *Proletárka* took part in informal sexual education dedicated to Slovak working-class women due to its belief that preventing multiple pregnancies would help their socioeconomic situation. This was especially emphasized in Slovak communist discourse because women in Slovakia had more children than women in the Czech lands, and communists considered the Slovak part of Czechoslovakia to be the main supplier of new workers for the state.[85] *Proletárka*'s contributors also never missed a chance to explain how the criminalization of abortion and the lack of reliable and accessible contraception was the result of the capitalist exploitation of female bodies: "The immorality of the bourgeoisie lies in its relationship with women, requiring a woman to become a mother to satisfy a man, often because of a simple urge and not out of an overwhelming and mutual desire to have a child."[86] Similarly, the paper highlighted the hypocrisy of religious and bourgeois circles who, on

81 Stopes 1925c.
82 "Je múdre mať veľa detí?" 1924.
83 See, for example, Stopes 1925a; Stopes 1925b; Stopes 1925c. For more about the work of Marie Stopes, see Debenham 2018. See also Brupbacher 1925.
84 Stopes 1925c.
85 See Malá 1926.
86 Braunová 1924.

the one hand, moralized about sexual behavior, and on the other hand, refused to provide any sex education and, thus, became party to the intentional restriction of contraception and safe abortion: "Bourgeois society is demonizing abortion, but it does not guarantee the safety of the human being already born, it drives millions of young people to the slaughter of imperialist wars, and it leaves thousands to die of disease and poverty."[87]

Proletárka stated that only those who were in charge of pronatalist propaganda benefited from large working-class families, such as "legislators of the capitalist state, Catholic priests who themselves were not allowed to marry or have children, or Protestant pastors who had fewer and fewer children, or backward thinking individuals."[88] When discussing family planning, despite protecting the national agenda and interests of the Slovak Communist, *Proletárka* rejected any political notions of extinction of the nation as the work of capitalists seeking to achieve a high birth rate among working-class women in order to "expand the army of workers and soldiers."[89] The authors opposed the state's pronatalism—demands for an increase in the birth rate—as a capitalist demand for cheap labour supplied by the working class. As, according to communist women, the society did not provide working-class women with material security for motherhood, it should not demand that any woman take on the burden of unwanted motherhood.[90]

5 Forgotten Women?

> In order to truly help women and their children from the scourge of poverty and infant mortality, women must first fight together with men for the dictatorship of the proletariat and only then will they construct better protections for motherhood and children according to the communist program as needed for the benefit of their class.[91]

Anna Malá, a Communist MP, published these words in *Proletárka*, expressing her position on the incorporation of gender-specific issues into the class-based political agenda of the party. Clearly, women affiliated with the Communist Party, whose work and activities are analyzed above, represent

87 "Beseda. Dopis ploretárskej žene" 1924.
88 "Je múdre mať veľa detí?" 1924.
89 See Malá 1926.
90 See Grossmann 1995, 36.
91 Malá 1924.

FIGURE 5.6 Čo mohol poskytnúť takýto domov tejto rodine? [What could such a home provide for this family?]
SOURCE: PHOTOGRAPH. ILJA JOZEF MARKO, 1936–1937 (SLOVENSKÁ NÁRODNÁ GALÉRIA [SLOVAK NATIONAL GALLERY] OF—MARKO, I. J—17)

one of the most significant actors concerning matters related to gender equality in Czechoslovak society. They sought to influence political debates about family planning going on at the highest levels of policymaking, such as those on questions related to acceptable methods of birth control, the legalization of abortion, in addition to the legal and social inequality of women in work and marriage. Yet, they refused to be associated with feminism because they considered it a bourgeois ideology, and because they positioned the fight for women's reproductive and sexual rights within a broader framework of social justice. While gender equality and women's sexual liberation was a critical issue for communist women, it was part of a broader politics focused on the alleviation of women's poverty, which was considered a more pressing social issue (see Figure 5.5).

By designating class struggle as the highest priority, *Proletárka*'s authors were able to tackle distinctive issues related to Slovak nationalism within the party, specifically those matters that directly impacted their activism and writing on reproductive rights. Due to Slovak communist women's limited political influence in Czechoslovak high politics, Slovak communist women activists focused their attention on the local Slovak context. They specifically addressed Slovak working-class women as women and, at the same time, communicated their understanding of Slovak women's underprivileged socioeconomic situation as well as their disadvantaged position as Slovak nationals within the Czechoslovak republic; this strategy was mirrored in communist women's discourse on reproductive rights. The activism and writing of Slovak communist women were then shaped by their ability to recognize matters that troubled Slovak working-class women in particular. Because Slovak communist women were forced to focus on the local (Slovakian) context, *Proletárka* is a key piece of evidence of their work and agency and demonstrates their role in shaping Slovak discourse.

But despite their predominantly local focus, the women editors of and contributors to *Proletárka* were politicians, activists, and talented journalists familiar with politics, feminism, and different women's movements in Western and Eastern Europe and beyond. While they wrote about the position and problems of women in Slovakia in the 1920s, their reflections, opinions, and attitudes were also characteristic of the international communist women's movement.[92] The historical experience of national struggle against Austria-Hungary, too, taught both Slovak and Czech women to see men as allies. This clearly did not mean that women held the same position and performed the same roles as men, but it does show that the participation of women was considered essential for the achievement of national goals. Additionally, following communist ideology, Slovak communist women did not understand their activism as a struggle against men, but "a struggle against the common enemy: the capitalist model of production."[93] Articulating positions of what we would call Marxist feminism today, the contributors of *Proletárka* claimed that women were exploited through capitalism, and that women's liberation could only be achieved by dismantling the existing system.[94] Stemming from their political affiliation and ideological focus on class struggle, authors of *Proletárka* understood equal payment, the fair division of child care and domestic work, and women's health and reproductive rights within a broader context of social justice.[95] Therefore, legal access to reliable contraceptive and the legalization of abortion were understood as matters related to not only the "woman question" but also to class struggle.

92 See Krylova 2017, 427.

93 Malá 1924.

94 See, for example, Ferguson 2010.

95 About equal payment, see also Bahenská, Heczková, and Musilová 2014, 187–189.

However, concerns that could be described as feminist but were not generally identified as such, which had previously been accepted, began to disappear from the political agenda under Soviet influence.[96] In 1927, *Proletárka* ceased to exist as an independent newspaper due to financial problems and the ongoing persecution of its authors, and it eventually became just a short section within the newspaper *Pravda* (*Truth*). By the 1930s, several leading figures of the communist women's movement were persecuted, imprisoned, or had emigrated. While eagerly fighting for social justice and equal rights for women—including the health and sexual rights, I argue that communist women in Slovakia were forced to compete with the existing so-called bourgeois women's movement while, at the same time, they confronted gendered limits on involvement in state-level politics, persecution by local authorities, marginalization among the Czech leadership of the Communist Party, and the ignorance of their Slovak party comrades on gender-related issues. Additionally, after 1948, women's activism and radicalism in the form represented by the authors on the *Proletárka* had no place in either the Slovak or the Czechoslovak context, as the state-socialist regime declared the women's question solved. After the regime change in 1989, women's activism as embodied in *Proletárka* was stigmatized because of these women's affiliation with the Communist Party. Furthermore, as the Czech pioneering gender scholar Jiřina Šiklová has suggested, feminists from the former Eastern bloc enthusiastically rejected all things "Eastern" and celebrated everything "Western."[97] The legacy of the Cold War and the persistence of the cultural division between East and West despite their formal political unification through the EU has led to either the vilification of the communist women's movement or its absence from the historical record altogether.[98] Indeed, existing narratives that cast Central and Eastern Europe as a sexual wasteland defined by backwardness and reaction rooted in the Cold War era restrict scholars' attempts to examine the emancipatory potential and women's agency within communist women's organizations.[99]

The activism of Slovak communist women around *Proletárka* was not an exact replica of the women's movement in the West or the East. One the one hand, it was produced within the communist movement, and it reflected dominant political, scientific, and ideological thinking in the wider European context—both West and East; on the other hand, it reflected the local Slovak

96 Studer 2015a, 132.
97 Šiklová 1997, 262. See also Kusá 1996, 129–137.
98 See Olse 1997, 2218.
99 See Kościanska 2020, 22–23.

environment and, consequently, accepted methods for solving the distinct social problems of Slovak society at the time. Despite the marginalization of the ideas and work of women members and sympathizers of the Communist Party in Slovakia and the persistent limitations on women's involvement in politics in interwar Czechoslovakia, the case of Slovak communist women and *Proletárka* demonstrates that reproductive rights were politicized earlier by communist women in Eastern Europe than by feminist women in the West.[100] Indeed, Slovak communist women's ability to simultaneously address the needs of working-class Slovak women and formulate their own arguments within a broader international context made their activism for the sexual emancipation of women in Slovakia and beyond truly pioneering.

Bibliography

Adams, Jad. 2014. *Women and the Vote. A World History*. Oxford: Oxford University Press.

Aláč, Ján. 2017. "Jednodetstvo. Rozprávanie o pustých školách a prázdnych dvoroch" [One-childness: Talking about deserted schools and empty courtyards]. In *Tajní vrahovia* [Secret murderers], edited by Samuel Činčurák, 90–154. Krná: Miloš Hric.

Ashwin, Sarah, ed. 2000. *Gender, State and Society in Soviet and Post-Soviet Russia*. London: Routledge.

Báhenská, Marie, Libuše Heczková, and Dana Musilová. 2014. *O ženské práci: Dobové (sebe)reflexe a polemiky* [About women's labour: Period self-reflections and polemics]. Prague: Masarykův ústav AV ČR.

Báhenská, Marie, Libuše Heczková, and Dana Musilová. 2013. *Iluze spásy: České feministické mýšlení 19. a 20. století* [An illusion of salvation. Czech feminist thinking in the 19th and 20th centuries]. České Budejovice: Veduta.

Bahenská, Marie, Libuše Heczková, and Dana Musilová. 2010. *Ženy na stráž! České feministické myšlení 19. a 20. Století* [Women on guard! Czech feminist thinking in 19th and 20th centuries]. Prague: Masarykův ústav a Archiv AV ČR.

Bakke, Elisabeth. 2011. "Czechoslovakism." In *Slovakia in History*, edited by Mikuláš Teich, Dušan Kováč, and Martin D. Brown, 247–268. Cambridge: Cambridge University Press.

Bayerlein, Bernhard H. 2006. "Zwischen Internationale und Gulag. Präliminarien zur Geschichte der internationalen kommunistischen Frauenbewegung (1919–1945)" [Between the Communist International and the gulag. Preliminary findings on

100 About domestication of East Central Europe, see Myslinska 2021, 271–307.

the history of the international communist women's movement]. *International Newsletter of Communist Studies Online* XII, 19: 27–47.

Benko, Juraj, and Adam Hudek. 2019. "Ideológia čechoslovakizmu a slovenskí komunisti" [The Ideology of Czechoslovakism and Slovak communists]. In *Čechoslovakizmus* [Czechoslovakism], edited by Adam Hudek, Michal Kopeček, and Jan Mervart, 281–309. Prague: Ústav pro soudobé dějiny.

Benko, Juraj, and Adam Hudek. 2021. "Slovak Communists and the Ideology of Czechoslovakism." In *Czechoslovakism: Routledge Histories of Central and Eastern Europe*, edited by Adam Hudek, Michal Kopeček, and Jan Mervart, 313–342. London: Routledge.

"Beseda. Dopis ploretárskej žene." 1924. *Proletárka* [Proletarian woman], 1 September 1924.

Bornholdt, Kerstin. 2008. *Medical Women's International Association—A Space for Generating International Knowledge and an International Medical Identity?* https://drexel.edu/~/media/Files/legacy-center/fellowships/drexel-legacy-center-gloeckner-2008-bornholdt.ashx?la=en.

Braunová, Lily. 1924. "Meštianske hnutie žien/Feminizmus." *Proletárka* [Proletarian woman], 1 September 1924.

Brown, Heather A. 2012. *Marx on Gender and the Family. a Critical Study*. Leiden: Brill.

Brupbacher, Fritz. 1925. *Kindersegen, Fruchtverhütung, Fruchtabtreibung* [The blessing of children, contraception, abortion]. Berlin: Neuer Deutscher Verlag.

Chlapcová-Gjorgjevičová, Julka. 1932. "Pátý mezinárodní sexuologický kongres" [Fifth International Congress of Sexology], *Ženská rada* [Women's council] 8, no. 10: 193–194.

Chura, Alojz. 1936. *Slovensko bez dorastu?* [Slovakia without youth?]. Bratislava: Publikácie roľníckej osvety v Bratislave.

Darmo, Jozef. 1966. *Slovenská žurnalistikaa 1918–1938* [Slovakian journalism: 1918–1938]. Martin: Matica slovenská.

David, Katherine. 1991. "Czech Feminists and Nationalism in the Late Habsburg Monarchy: 'The First in Austria.'" *Journal of Women's History* 3, no. 2 (Fall): 26–45.

Debenham, Clare. 2018. *Marie Stopes' Sexual Revolution and the Birth Control Movement*. London: Palgrave Macmillan.

Dewetterová, Ludmila. 1935. "Zpráva o Birth Control" [Report on birth control]. *Praktický lékař. Časopis pro další vzdělávání lékařů* [Practitioner: Journal of advanced medical education] 15, no. 22: 507–510.

Dudeková-Kováčová, Daniela. 2019. "Živena v politických režimoch 19. a 20. Storočia" [Živena in the political regimes of the 19th and 20th centuries]. In *Živena. 150 rokov spolku slovenských žien* [Živena. 150 Years of the Union of Slovak Women], edited by Daniela Kodajová et al., 99–140. Bratislava: Slovart.

Engels, Friedrich. 1962. *Pôvod rodiny, súkromného vlastníctva a štátu* [The origins of family, private property and the state]. Bratislava: Vydavateľstvo politickej literatúry, 1962.

Fabricius, Miroslav, ed. 2002. *Jozef Tiso. Prejavy a články 1 (1913–1938)* [Jozef Tiso. Speeches and writings (1913–1938)]. Bratislava: AEP.

Falisová, Anna. 2013. "Remeslo či milosrdenstvo: Kriminálne potraty v medzivojnovom období" [Craft or compassion: Criminal abortions in the interwar period]. In *Storočie procesov. Súdy, politika a spoločnosť v moderných dejinách Slovenska* [The century of court trials. Courts, politics and society in the modern history of Slovakia], edited by Valerián Bystrický and Jaroslava Roguľová, 51–65. Bratislava: Veda.

Falisová, Anna. 2011. "Spoločnosť proti pohlavným chorobám na Slovensku v medzivojnovom období" [Society against venereal diseases in interwar Slovakia]. *Forum Historiae* [Historical forum] 5, no. 1: 29–36.

Feinberg, Melissa. 2006. *Elusive Equality: Gender, Citizenship, and the Limits of Democracy in Czechoslovakia, 1918–1950*. Pittsburgh: University of Pittsburgh Press.

Ferguson, Ann, and Rosemary Hennessy. 2010. "Feminist Perspectives on Class and Work." *The Stanford Encyclopedia of Philosophy*, edited by Edward N. Zalta (Winter). Accessed 11 November 2021. http://plato.stanford.edu/archives/win2010/entries/feminism-class/.

Fowkes, Ben. 2008. "To Make the Nation or to Break It: Communist Dilemmas in Two Interwar Multinational States." In *Bolshevism, Stalinism and the Comintern: Perspectives on Stalinization, 1917–1953*, edited by Norman LaPorte, Kevin Morgan, and Matthew Worley, 206–225. New York: Palgrave Macmillan.

Gabriela, Dudeková. 2011. *Na ceste k modernej žene* [On the road to a modern woman]. Bratislava: Veda.

Garver, Bruce M. 1985. "Women in the First Czechoslovak Republic." In *Women, State and Party in Eastern Europe*, edited by Sharon L. Wolchik and Alfred G. Meyer, 71–78. Durham, NC: Duke University Press.

Grossmann, Atina. 1998. "German Communism and New Women." In *Women and Socialism: Socialism and Women,* edited by Helmut Gruber and Pamela Graves, 135–170. New York: Berghahn Books.

Grossmann, Atina. 1995. *Reforming Sex. The German Movement for Birth Control and Abortion Reform 1920–1950*. New York: Oxford University Press.

Hertel, Maroš. 2006. "Komunisti, ľudáci a maďarská irredenta" [Communists, autonomists, and Hungarian irredentists]. In *Komunisti a ľudáci* [Communists and Ľudáks], edited by Xénia Šuchová, 53–60 Prešov: Universum.

Hochchild Russell, Arlie. 1989. *The Second Shift: Working Parents and the Revolution at Home*. New York: Viking.

Hudek, Adam. 2015. "Národná otázka v myslení prvej generácie slovenských komunistických intelektuálov" [The National Question in the thinking of the first generation of Slovak communist intellectuals]. In *Ideológia naprieč hranicami: Myšlienkové transfery v Európe a na Slovensku v 1. polovici 20. storočia* [Ideology across borders: Ideological transfers in Europe and Slovakia during the first half of the 20th century], edited by Matej Hanula and Linda Osyková, 51–68. Bratislava: Historický ústav SAV.

Jahodářová, Lucie. 2015. "Zpátky k plotně? Ženský komunistický tisk a kritika úsporných opatření ve veřejné správě (1932–1933)" [Back to the stove? Women's communist press and a critique of austerity measures in public administration (1932–1933)]. *Forum Historiae* [Historical forum] 9, no. 2: 102–118.

"Je múdre mať veľa detí?" [Is it wise to have many children?]. 1924. *Proletárka* [Proletarian woman], 15 March 1924.

Johnson, Owen. 1985. *Slovakia, 1918–1938: Education and the Making of a Nation.* New York: Columbia University Press.

Juráňová, Jana. 2006. "Rezlerová-Švarcová, Barbora (1890–1941)." In *A Biographical Dictionary of Women's Movements and Feminisms. Central, Eastern, and South Eastern Europe, 19th and 20th Centuries,* edited by Francisca De Haan, Krassimira Daskalova, and Anna Loutfi, 467–469. Budapest: Central European University Press.

Just, Peter. 2004. "Ženy v parlamentu v meziválečném Československu: komparace se Spojenými státy americkými a Švédskem" [Women in parliament in interwar Czechoslovakia: A comparison with the United States and Sweden]. In *Sféry ženy. Právne, politické a ekonomické vedy* [Spheres of women. Legal, political and economic sciences], edited by Jana Lasicová, 153–161. Zvolen: Fakulta humanitných vied Univerzity Mateja Bela v Banskej Bystrici a Sociologický ústav Akadémie vied Českej republiky v Prahe.

K. 1924. "Ťažkosti ženskej organizačnej práce" [Difficulties of women's organizational work]. *Proletárka* [Proletarian woman], 1 September 1924.

Klement, Gottwald. 1951. *Spisy I* [Writings I]. Bratislava: Svoboda.

Kodajová, Daniela, et al. 2019. *Živena. 150 rokov spolku slovenských žien* [Živena. 150 years of the Union of Slovak Women]. Bratislava: Slovart.

Kodymová, Pavla, and Haburajová-Ilavská Lenka. 2014. "Vesna a Živena—spolky významné pro rozvoj sociální práce jako profese" [Vesna and Živena—Associations important for the development of social work as a profession]. *Fórum sociální práce* [Forum of social work] 1: 81–86.

Kolláriková, Gizela. 1927. 80. schůze. 5. května 1927 [Gizela Kolláriková. Meeting no. 80, 1927-05-05]. In Poslanecká sněmovna Parlamentu České republiky. Digitalni repozitar [Chamber of Deputies of the Parliament of the Czech Republic. Digital repository]. https://www.psp.cz/eknih/1925ns/ps/stenprot/080schuz/s080015.htm.

Kolláriková, Gizela. 1927. Speech in the Czechoslovak Parliament, May 5, 1927. https://www.psp.cz/eknih/1925ns/ps/stenprot/080schuz/s080015.htm.

Kopeček, Michal. 2012. "Historical Studies of Nation-building and the Concept of Socialist Patriotism in East Central Europe 1956–1970." In *Historische Nationsforschung im geteilten Europa 1945–1989* [Historical national research in divided Europe 1945–1989], edited by Pavel Kolář and Miloš Řezník, 135–150. Cologne: SH-Verlag.

Kościanska, Agnieszka. 2020. *Gender, Pleasure, and Violence. the Construction of Expert Knowledge of Sexuality in Poland.* Bloomington: Indiana University Press.

Krylova, Anna. 2017. "Bolshevik Feminism and Gender Agendas of Communism." In *The Cambridge History of Communism.* Vol. 1: *World Revolution and Socialism in One Country 1917–1941*, edited by Silvio Pons and Stephen A. Smith, 424–448. Cambridge: Cambridge University Press.

Kusá, Zuzana. 1996. "The Immune Deficiency Acquired of Inherited?" *Replica, Hungarian Social Science Quarterly*, Special Issue, edited by Miklós Hadas and Miklós Vörös: 129–137.

Lengyelová, Tünde, ed. 2004. *Žena a právo. Právne a spoločenské postavenie žien v minulosti* [Woman and law. Legal and social status of women in the past]. Bratislava: Academic Electronic Press.

Lenin, Vladimir Iljič. 1984. "Robotnícka trieda a novomaltuzovstvo" [Working-class and Neo-Malthusianism]. In *Zobrané spisy: marec—september 1913, zv. 23* [Collected works: March–September 1913, vol. 23]. Bratislava: Pravda.

Lenin, Vladimir. 1977. *Collected Works*, vol. 19. Moscow: Progress Publishers. https://www.marxists.org/archive/lenin/works/1913/jun/30.htm#fwV19E085.

Lokaneeta, Jinee. 2001. "Alexandra Kollontai and Marxist Feminism." *Economic and Political Weekly* 36, no. 17: 1405–1412.

Malá, Anna. 1924. "Matka a dieťa [Mother and child]." *Proletárka* [Proletarian woman], 1 August 1924.

Malá, Anna. 1926. "Materstvo a zárobková práca žien" [Motherhood and paid work of women]. *Proletárka* [Proletarian woman], 15 May 1926.

Malá, Anna, and Anna Křenová. 1921. *Program, organisace a taktika komunistických žen* [The program, organization and tactics of communist women]. Prague: Svoboda v Kladne.

Marx, Karl, Friedrich Engels, Vladimir Iljič Lenin. 1973. *K ženské otázce* [On the woman question]. Prague: Nakladatelství Svoboda.

"Matka a dieťa. Ochrana pred materstvom." 1923. *Proletárka* [Proletarian women], 25 January 1923.

Matysková, Hana. 2011. "Komunistky ve 20. Letech" [Communist women in '20s.]. PhD diss., Charles University, 2011.

Musilová, Dana. 2007. *Z ženského pohledu: Poslankyně a senátorky Národního shromáždění Československé republiky 1918–1939* [From women's perspective: Women deputies and senators of the National Assembly of the Czechoslovak Republic 1918–1939]. České Budejovice: Veduta.

Myslinska, Dagmar Rita. 2021. "Not Quite Right: Representations of Eastern Europeans in ECJ Discourse." *International Journal of Politics, Culture and Society* 34: 271–307. 10.1007/s10767-020-09368-2.

Nečasová, Denisa. 2013. "'Bez žen nic nevybojujeme.' Lenin a ženská otázka" ["Without women we would win nothing." Lenin and Woman Question]. In *Lenin: Kontinuita a/nebo diskontinuita ruských dějin*? [Lenin: Continuity and/or discontinuity of Russian history], edited by Jiří Hanuš, Kateřina Hloušková, Vít Hloušek, Radomír Vlček, Petr Horák, Denisa Nečasová, Ivana Ryčlová and Zbyněk Vydra, 107–115. Brno: Centrum pro studium demokracie a kultury.

Nešťáková, Denisa. 2023. "Between Creation of Czechoslovak Nation and Sexual Liberalization (1918–1939)." *Journal for Family History* 48, no. 3: 309–322.

Nešťáková, Denisa. 2020. "Žena proti štátu. 'Kriminálne' potraty v čase Slovenskej republiky 1939–1945" [Woman against the state. "Criminal" abortions in Slovak Republic 1939–1945]. In *Tisovi poza chrbát* [Behind Tiso's back], edited by Jozef Hyrja, 31–51. Bratislava: Hadart.

Olse, Frances Elisabeth. 1997. "Feminism in Central and Eastern Europe: Risks and Possibilities of American Engagement." *The Yale Law Journal* 106, no. 7 (May): 2215–2257.

Panýrek, D. 1932. "V. medzinárodní sjezd Světove ligy pro sexualni reformu na vědeckém zakladě v Brne. 20–26 září 1932" [5th International Congress of the World League for sexual reform on a scientific basis held in Brno, 20–26 September 1932]. *Praktický lékař. Časopis pro další vzdělávání lékař* [Practitioner. Journal of advanced medical education] 12, no. 21: 628–630.

Rapoš, Pavol. 1957. *Priemysel Slovenska za kapitalizmu* [Industry of Slovakia during capitalism]. Bratislava: Slovenské vydavateľstvo politickej literatúry.

Repková, Eva. 2014. "Abort a infanticídium v novovekom uhorskom trestnom práve" [Abortion and infanticide in modern Hungarian criminal law]. *Societas et Iurisprudentia* [Society and jurisprudence] 1, no. 2: 147–173.

Rupnik, Jacques. 2003. *Dějiny Komunistické strany Československa* [History of the Communist Party of Czechoslovakia]. Prague: Academia.

Ruttkay, Fraňo. 1987. *Slovenský život a žurnalistika* [Slovak life and journalism]. Martin: Osveta.

Rychlík, Jan. 2012. "Slovenský národní komunismus a slovenští národní komunisté" [Slovak national communism and the Slovak national communists]. In *Český a slovenský komunismus (1921–2011)* [Czech and Slovak communism (1921–2011)], edited by Jan Kalous and Jiří Kocian, 306–316. Prague: Ústav pro soudobé dějiny AV ČR.

Sewell, Sara Ann. 2012. "Bolshevizing Communist Women: the Red Women and Girls' League in Weimar Germany." *Central European History* 45, no. 2 (June): 268–305.

Slušná, Nataša. 1988. *Postavení ženy ve společnosti: K problematice postavení ženy v socialistické společnosti* [The position of women in society: On the issue of the position of women in socialist society]. Prague: Charles University.

Stopes, Marie. 1925a. "Ochrana pred tehotenstvom" [Protection against pregnancy]. *Proletárka* [Proletarian woman], 15 January 1925.

Stopes, Marie. 1925b. "Ochrana proti tehotenstvu" [Pregnancy prevention]. *Proletárka* [Proletarian woman], 15 February1925.

Stopes, Marie. 1925c. "Ochrana proti tehotenstvu" [Pregnancy prevention]. *Proletárka* [Proletarian woman], 1 March 1925.

Studer, Brigitte. 2015a. "Communism and Feminism." *Clio. Women, Gender, History*, no. 41, "Real socialism" and the Challenge of Gender: 126–139.

Studer, Brigitte. 2015b. *The Transnational World of the Cominternians*. London: Palgrave Macmillan.

Ščheinost, Jan. 1932. "Paragraf 144" [Paragraph 144]. *Lidové Listy* [The people's paper], 29 June 1932.

Šiklová, Jiřina. 1997. "Feminism and the Roots of Apathy in the Czech Republic." *Social Research* 64, no. 2: 258–280.

Škorvanková, Eva. 2021a. "Sexuálny život budovateliek socializmu" [Sexual life of women builders of socialism]. In *Moc Sexu. Sex a sexualita v moderných dejinách Slovenska* [The power of sex. Sex and sexuality in the modern history of Slovakia], edited by Denisa Nešťáková, 162–168. Bratislava: Paradigma Publishing.

Škorvanková, Eva. 2021b. "New Slovak Woman. The Feminine Ideal in the Authoritarian Regime of the Slovak State, 1939–1945." In *If This Is a Woman. Studies on Women and Gender in the Holocaust*, edited by Denisa Nešťáková, Katja Grosse-Sommer, Borbála Klacsmann, and Jakub Drábik, 62–80. Boston: Academic Studies Press.

Škorvanková, Eva. 2014. "Otázka regulácie pôrodnosti v období prvej Slovenskej republiky (1939–1945)" [Regulating fertility in 1939–1945 Slovakia]. In *Populačné štúdie Slovenska 4* [Studies of the population of Slovakia 4], edited by Pavol Tišliar and Terézia Šprochová, 53–122. Bratislava: Muzeológia a kultúrne dedičstvo.

Šprocha, Branislav, and Pavol Tišliar. 2008. *Vývoj úmrtnosti na Slovensku v rokoch 1919–1937* [The development of mortality in Slovakia in 1919–1937]. Bratislava: Stimul.

Šubrtová, Alena. 1991. "Kontracepce, aborty a infanticida v pramenech k předstatistickém období [Contraception, abortion, and infanticide in sources of the prestatistical period]." *Historická demografie* [Historical demography] 15: 9–46.

Šubrtová, Alena. 2002. "Umělé potraty v diskusích meziválečného období v Československu (1918–1938) [Induced abortions in the discussions of the interwar period in Czechoslovakia (1918–1938)]." *Demografie* [Demography] 44, no. 4: 233–244.

Šuchová, Xénia. 2011. *Idea československého štátu na Slovensku 1918–1939: Protagonisti, nositelia, oponenti* [The idea of the Czechoslovak state in Slovakia 1918–1939: Protagonists, bearers, opponents]. Bratislava: Historický ústav SAV.

Švarcová, Barbora. 1925. *Slovensko. Oběť česko-kapitalistické kolonisace* [Slovakia. The victim of Czech-capitalist colonization]. Prague: Kommunistické knihkupectví a nakladatelství.

Uhrová, Eva. 2004. "Ženy v KSČ a textilné dělnice v Čechách ve 20. letech. Ze stránek komunistického tisku pro ženy" [Women in the Communist Party and textile workers in Bohemia in the 1920s. From the pages of the women's communist press]. In *Bolševismus, komunismus a radikální socializmus v Československu*, vol. 2 [Bolshevism, communism and radical socialism in Czechoslovakia, vol. 2], edited by Zdeněk Kárník and Michal Kopeček, 27–40. Prague: Ústav pro soudobé dějiny AV ČR.

Waters, Elizabeth. 1989. "In the Shadow of the Comintern: the Communist Women's Movement, 1920–1943." In *Promissory Notes: Women in the Transition to Socialism*, edited by Sonia Kruks, Rayna Rapp, and Marillyn Blatt Young, 29–56. New York: Monthly Review Press.

Wolchik, Sharon L. 1996. "Czech and Slovak Women and Political Leadership." *Women's History Review* 5, no. 4: 525–538.

Žáčková, Zdeňka. 2016. "Boj o paragraf 144. Potraty a legislativa za první republiky" [The struggle for Paragraph 144. Abortions and legislation during the First Republic]. *Acta historica Universitatis Silesianae Opaviensis* [Journal of the history of the Silesian University of Opaviensis] 9: 55–78.

Zavacká, Katarína. 2001. "Prerušenie tehotenstva v práve na území Slovenska" [Abortion in Slovakian law]. In *Možnosť voľby. Aspekty práv a zodpovednosti: Zborník príspevkov* [Freedom of choice. Aspects of rights and responsibilities, edited volume], edited by Jana Ciková and Jana Juráňová, 23–30. Bratislava: Aspekt.

"Ženy, komunisti a voľby." 1925. *Proletárka* [Proletarian woman], 15 September 1925.

Zetkinová, Klára. 1973. "Ze zápisníku: Vzpomínky na Lenina" [From the diary: Memories of Lenin]. In *K ženské otázce* [About the woman question], by Karl Marx, Friedrich Engels, and Vladimir Iljič Lenin, 207–230. Prague: Nakladatelství Svoboda.

CHAPTER 6

"Women as Workers"

Discussions about Equal Pay in the World Federation of Trade Unions in the Late 1940s

Johanna Wolf

Abstract

With the end of World War Two opposing political factions, such as social democrats and communists joined forces, placing issues relating to marginalized groups on the political agenda, such as the inclusion of colonized peoples and the role of women in society. Since women's legal equality was closely related to their economic role, the matter of equal pay for women was also discussed. The debate gained momentum when several international organizations began to look more closely at this issue. The role of the World Federation of Trade Unions (WFTU), which put the issue on the agenda of the UN Economic and Social Council (ECOSOC) in 1948, has not yet been explored systematically. Using the WFTU's archive, the chapter argues that the WFTU played a major role in the debate on equal pay for equal work in the international community. It analyzes the discussions concerning the WFTU's call for equal pay for equal work during the ECOSOC's 6th session in February 1948. In the second part, the internal discussions of the WFTU are analyzed by looking at the Executive Committee meeting that took place in May 1948. As the records of this meeting reveal, it was a woman, Nina Vasil'evna Popova—the vice-president of the Women's International Democratic Federation (WIDF) and secretary of the All-Union Council of Trade Unions (ACCTU)—who pressed the issue in the discussion. Since the role of women in the WFTU is unexplored, the chapter begins to fill this lacuna by focusing on the contributions of this woman activist.

Keywords

Cold War – Commission on the Status of Women (CSW) – Economic and Social Council (ECOSOC) – equal pay – International Labour Organization (ILO) – international trade union movement – international women's movement – women's employment – Women's International Democratic Federation (WIDF) – World Federation of Trade Unions (WFTU)

 | DOI:10.1163/9789004682481_007

Research on women's roles in the international trade union movement is not new. Heretofore, the focus has been mainly on their position and importance in male-dominated organizations.[1] Consequently, it has become clear that women within the trade union movement organized themselves into their own networks, developing close relationships with women in other international organizations such as the Joint Consultative Committee on Women Workers' Questions of the International Trade Secretariats (ITS) and the International Confederation of Free Trade Unions (ICFTU),[2] which were in contact with the Commission on the Status of Women (CSW) at the United Nations (UN) and the Correspondence Committee on Women's Work at the International Labour Organization (ILO).[3] However, it is striking that this research mainly refers to networks in the Global North/West and movements in the East and Global South are addressed separately. In the case of global organizations where East and West came together on equal terms, eastern European and Soviet actors are discussed, but often from a Western perspective, which can be explained by the limited access to sources and, perhaps, by the specific research interests and background of the researcher.[4] This is particularly evident in the case of the World Federation of Trade Unions (WFTU) at the end of the 1940s.

For only four years, between 1945 and 1949, the World Federation existed as a united movement of social democratic and communist trade unions. This period has been studied in detail by Anthony Carew, who relied on British and U.S. materials and was mainly interested in the reasons for organization's split into two camps.[5] This approach, which foregrounds emerging Cold War division, not only creates an imbalance in perspectives but also reproduces certain narratives and interpretations. Thus, the WFTU of the 1940s is viewed only through the lens of ideological conflict (between communists and anti-communists), and the communists' dominant position in the organization is blamed for the failure of the organization. This narrative then reappears—mostly unquestioned—in the work of other scholars, such as in Eileen Boris's

1 This article is the revised version of the article: Johanna Wolf, "'Women as Workers.' Diskussionen über die Berufstätigkeit von Frauen und Lohngleichheit in der internationalen Gewerkschaftsbewegung der späten 1940er Jahre." In *Gender Pay Gap, Vom Wert und Unwert von Arbeit in Geschichte und Gegenwart*, edited by Rainer Fattmann, Johanna Wolf, and Wiebke Wiede (Bonn: Dietz, forthcoming). Zimmermann 2021; Zimmermann 2020, 95–117. "Women as Workers" was a section title in the brochure WFTU [1957].

2 Neunsinger 2018, 121–148.

3 Boris 2018, 97–120.

4 This is not only the case for trade union research; Francisca de Haan has confirmed this for international women's organizations as well. See De Haan 2010, 547–573.

5 Carew 2000, 167–185; Carew 2018.

work on the Commission on the Status of Women (CSW), in which the WFTU had observer status and is mentioned in connection to an equal pay resolution. In her article, Boris writes that the WFTU "lacked the capacity to provide such information [for an equal pay resolution, JW] and only pledged its cooperation,"[6] but does mention that the World Federation was dominated by communists at the time.

There are of course authors who approach trade union internationalism differently. In *Imagining Internationalism in American and British Labor*, Victor Silverman writes that there is much to be learned about the ambitions of the WFTU in the 1940s. It was not actually impacted by the nascent Cold War until the late 1940s. Before that, it was a very ambitious movement attempting to address many pressing issues and find a position in the emerging postwar world order.[7] Following Silverman, I argue that the World Federation played a major role in the debate on equal pay for equal work in the international community.[8] In this chapter, I analyze the discussions about the WFTU's call for equal pay for equal work that took place in the Economic and Social Council (ECOSOC) of the UN in 1948. I approach these discussions from the perspective of the WFTU and reconstruct the resistance of certain members of the ECOSOC to the WFTU. I will then analyze the discussions on women's employment and equal pay that took place *within* the WFTU during a meeting of the WFTU Executive Committee in Rome in May 1948. It is not surprising that this debate was already affected by the Cold War. It is interesting, however, that in the 1940s, the "Western" trade union movement, which was generally seen as progressive, struggled with the idea of equal pay for equal work for women and vigorously argued against the Soviet claim that economic equality for women had been established with the victory of the October Revolution in the Soviet Union (SU).

The debates on the issue during the Rome meeting can be read as a condensed version of wider discussions about women's employment taking place worldwide at the time, and as such, this analysis demonstrates how different political interests overlapped on substantive issues and shows how difficult it was for participants to critically reflect on their ideological perspective. As Francisca de Haan writes, the Cold War was more than an argument about the arms race and space race; it was a conflict over living standards in which there was a strong ideological clash over the question of what defined a good

6 Boris 2018, 106.

7 Silverman 2000.

8 In her most recent work, Zimmermann shows that these discussions began much earlier. See Zimmermann 2021, 34–49.

life.[9] Both sides were convinced that their system was better for women; thus, Cold War conflict also impacted views on women's work and women's role in society. My analysis does not take sides but rather clarifies how women's struggle for equal pay was fought in a particular arena characterized by multidimensional tensions.

The readjustment of the global trade union international also entailed the inclusion of new members. The attention to political and trade union conditions in colonial and politically independent countries in the post-1945 period went far beyond the scope of issues taken up by the international trade union movement during the interwar period.[10] The main criticism of the International Federation of Trade Unions (IFTU) had always been its lack of global representation, and a few Afro-Asian unions had joined the organization in the 1930s.[11] This lack of global representation was not only due to a lack of contacts; rather, the decolonizing world did not see the IFTU as willing or able to address its concerns. While the communist Red International of Labour Unions (also known as Profintern) did explicitly support anticolonial and anti-imperial struggles, "the IFTU was much more cautious, avoiding any clear statements on the issue."[12] Carolien Stolte notes that this legacy of the interwar period lived on after World War Two and was reflected in the discussions on equal pay that took place at the Executive Committee meeting. Delegates from the Global South used the forum to address the labour situation and issue of fair wages in their countries, pointing out that this issue was not just a matter of gender but also race. The fact that some delegates were still deeply entangled in the colonial system of their countries rendered them incapable of responding.

This study is based on sources held in the WFTU Archives at the International Institute of Social History (IISH) in Amsterdam,[13] especially the "Report on the Activity of the WFTU Concerning the Principles of Equality of Wages for Equal Work between Male and Female Labour,"[14] which included a "Declaration of

9 De Haan 2012.

10 Pohrt 2000, 254.

11 Stolte 2019, 333.

12 Stolte 2019, 333.

13 I would like to thank Research Director Karin Hofmeester and all the staff of the library for supporting my stay at the International Institute of Social History during the pandemic. I would also like to thank the German Research Foundation, which made this research financially possible.

14 "Report on the activity of the W.F.T.U. concerning the principles of equality of wages for equal work between male and female labour," Folder 79, WFTU Archives, International Institute of Social History, Amsterdam (hereafter IISH).

Principle on the Retribution of Female Labour"—presented and discussed at the ECOSOC meeting[15]—and a "Survey on the Question of the Retribution of Female Labour"—prepared and conducted by the Secretariat in cooperation with the Social and Economic Department of the WFTU.[16] In the second part of this analysis, I refer to WFTU records of the meeting of the Executive Committee in May 1948.[17] In order to contextualize the statements of the trade unionists involved in the Executive Committee meeting, I rely on scholarship that has examined debates on women's employment and gender pay gaps in relevant national contexts.

Returning to the introduction, whereas researchers have examined the role of women in the trade union movement, the specific role of women in the World Federation has not yet been researched—neither during the period between 1945 and 1949 nor after the split in 1949, when the WFTU continued to exist but with only communist and state-socialist trade unions as members.[18] I pay special attention to the work of a woman activist who not only advocated for women's issues in the WFTU but was active in many international (women's) organizations: Nina Vasil'evna Popova (1908–1994). She was one of the founders of the Antifascist Committee of Soviet Women in 1941, a vice-president of the Women's International Democratic Federation (WIDF) starting in 1945, and a secretary of the All-Union Central Council of Trade Unions (ACCTU, Всесоюзный центральный совет профессиональных союзов) between 1945 and 1957. She played a crucial role in the debate on the gender pay gap that took place at the WFTU Executive Committee meeting in Rome in May 1948.

I will start this analysis by briefly presenting the history of the WFTU. In the second section, I will discuss its position in ECOSOC and the memorandum on equal pay for equal work. In the third section, I examine the internal debate on

15 "Declaration of principle on the retribution of female labour," In Appendix "Statement of principle and examination of the question of the remuneration of female labour of the report on the activity of the W.F.T.U. concerning the principles of equality of wages for equal work between male and female labor," Folder 79, WFTU Archives, IISH.

16 "Survey on the question of the retribution of female labour," In Appendix "Statement of principle and examination of the question of the remuneration of female labour of the report on the activity of the W.F.T.U. concerning the principles of equality of wages for equal work between male and female labor," Folder 79, WFTU Archives, IISH.

17 Reports on the Session of the Executive Committee, Rome, 4 May to 10 May 1948, Folder 83, WFTU Archives, IISH.

18 Olga Gnydiuk is running a project: "A Story of Women's International Endeavor: The Politics of Women's Paid and Unpaid Work in and beyond the World Federation of Trade Unions, 1940s to 1980" as part of the ZARAH project. See https://zarah-ceu.org/wp-content/uploads/2022/02/ZARAH_Component_Study_Olga_Gnydiuk_Short_Description.pdf.

the issue during the 1948 WFTU Executive Committee meeting in Rome and analyze the role Nina Popova played in it.

1 The World Federation of Trade Unions in the Late 1940s

The idea for a common and unified international trade union movement emerged during World War Two. The British Trades Union Congress (TUC) and the Soviet ACCTU had established contact with each other in 1941; they agreed that there was a need for world peace and that civil society would need to be reconstructed in fascist countries.[19] In cooperation with the U.S. Congress of Industrial Organizations (CIO), the grassroots desire for unity was fulfilled and, after an exploratory conference in London, the WFTU was founded in Paris in the autumn of 1945.[20] Although political, economic, and social programs had been sidelined during the war to promote broad-based cooperation among all trade unions, these questions were now up for debate and quickly led to disputes. Many trade unionists who had been active in the IFTU worked to overcome politicization within the movement, integrate various forms of organization—e.g., national trade union federations as well as international trade secretariats—and geographically extend the organization beyond Europe.[21]

Due to a lack Soviet source material, or rather due to the fact that it has not yet been analyzed, one can only speculate about the Soviet trade union's ambitions for membership in the WFTU. However, the Soviet resolution, introduced during negotiations on a trade union international in 1943, makes it clear that the dissolution of the Communist International (Comintern) in May 1943 had left the Soviet trade union with the task of filling a gap in the Soviet Union's foreign policy propaganda.[22] Yet, during the establishment of the trade union international, East and West did not initially confront each other as might be assumed. The main tension related to political affiliation, which crossed geographic boundaries. During the preparations for the conference in London, a communist-progressive grouping had formed in opposition to the British bloc; in addition to the Soviet trade union, this grouping included the communist minority of the CIO, the French General Confederation of

19 Carew 2000, 167; Schevenels 1956, 303–304.

20 Cooperative discussions with the second most important U.S. union, the American Federation of Labor (AFL), failed and it did not join the WFTU in 1945. Pohrt 2000, 29–41.

21 Lewis and Stolte 2019, 1–19.

22 Pohrt 2000, 52.

Labour (Confédération générale du travail, CGT), the Confederation of Latin American Workers (Confederación de Trabajadores de América Latina, CTAL), and the trade union federations of Mexico, Australia, and Czechoslovakia.[23] This polarity remained for some time, with the CIO increasingly emerging as a mediator between positions, distancing itself from the communist-progressive bloc on fundamental issues and moving closer and closer to the TUC.[24]

When the Marshall Plan was announced in the summer of 1947, the split in the WFTU began, though the dispute over the American aid program merely deepened pre-existing cleavages and intensified antagonisms within the organization.[25] For this reason, the WFTU's split must be understood within the context of the overall development of the East–West conflict that affected the European Left as a whole.[26] In January 1949, the WFTU finally fractured when the British, U.S., and Dutch delegates left the Executive Bureau. The social democrats merged into the ICFTU, along with the AFL, while the state-socialist unions remained in the WFTU together with the communist unions of Western Europe and those of the Global South.

2 WFTU and Equal Pay Discussions in the ECOSOC and CSW

As an important organ of the UN, the ECOSOC became the main structure used for implementing global trade union policy.[27] Representatives of both political blocs valued having a voice here. The council was composed of eighteen member states. Various regional and functional commissions were affiliated with it, including the CSW. After persistent and lengthy negotiations, the WFTU, as a non-governmental organization, achieved so-called Category A consultative status in the ECOSOC, which allowed it to participate in discussions and granted it the right to submit items directly to the UN agenda. After an initial submission concerning the free exercise of trade union rights in 1947, the WFTU put the issue of equal pay on the agenda of the ECOSOC in February 1948.[28] Preparations for this had been underway since 1946. The WFTU, with

23 Windmuller 1954, 40.

24 Pohrt 2000, 112.

25 Pohrt 2000, 314.

26 Weiler 1988, 125.

27 Dessau 1956, 6.

28 Pohrt 2000, 301. Other issues in 1947 and 1948 included the abolition of national and racial discrimination, full employment and the fight against unemployment, and immigration policy.

the participation of its trade union members, launched an inquiry "for the purpose of ascertaining the situation of female wage earners,"[29] which resulted in a detailed report.

Almost simultaneously, similar debates had been going on in the CSW. As Boris documents, at the first session of the CSW in February 1947, a Russian lawyer and trade unionist[30] had pushed for a questionnaire on the economic rights of women.[31] This demand triggered a dispute over who was responsible for carrying out such a study, the ECOSOC or the ILO. As Boris explains, behind this institutional question was a political one: delegates from the Western European and U.S. context considered the ILO responsible for carrying out such a survey, whereas delegates from state-socialist countries hoped that the ECOSOC would be able to exert greater influence on the content of the study. There was, however, also a practical reason behind the latter's reliance on the ECOSOC: the Soviet Union had no influence in the ILO because they had left the organization in 1940.[32]

In January 1948, not much happened to advance the issue of equal pay in the CSW. The members declared their support and invited the ILO as well as non-governmental organizations "to compile memoranda setting out what action they are taking to provide equal pay for men and women."[33] And it was agreed that the topic would be discussed further at the next meeting. The WFTU, too, was allowed to submit proposals. Against the background of these decisions, Boris' conclusion is somewhat misleading. She states that the Byelorussian delegate attempted to get the WFTU involved, but the WFTU "lacked the capacity to provide such information and only pledged its cooperation."[34] According to the records, no representative of the WFTU was present at that meeting, and as we have seen, the WFTU submitted its proposal to the ECOSOC only a month later. So, the WFTU's proposal concerning equal pay must have been in preparation but was intended for the ECOSOC. At the next meeting of the CSW

29 "Report on the activity of the W.F.T.U. concerning the principles of equality of wages for equal work between male and female labour," p. 1, Folder 79, WFTU Archives, IISH.

30 Her name was Elizavieta Alekseevna Popova. In the scholarship on the CSW, she is mentioned as a founding member of the commission. So far, I have not found any further biographical details. Since she has the same surname as Nina V. Popova and I do not want to cause confusion, I do not mention her by name in the text. See Adami 2019, 78; Lambertz 2012.

31 Boris 2018, 105.

32 Boris 2018, 100.

33 "Draft resolution submitted by the Resolution Committee on equal pay," 14 January 1948, E/CN.6/70, CSW. https://digitallibrary.un.org/record/1474103?ln=en.

34 Boris 2018, 106.

in Beirut in 1949, the WFTU sent a representative who defended the WFTU's proposal, which I will discuss at the end of the chapter.

The WFTU's demands to the ECOSOC in 1948 called for equal pay for women and men as well as an end to discrimination against women in hiring, education and training, part-time work, and against older women workers.[35] These points were based on the resolution adopted at the founding congress of the WFTU, which called for "freedom from every form of exploitation and social or economic discrimination based on race, creed, colour or sex."[36] The issue of equal pay was addressed in point one of the demands the WFTU submitted to the ECOSOC:

> As a result of the extension of large scale industry and mechanisation, the improvement of implements, the emancipation of women, two world wars, and the ever more extensive industrialization of backward countries, the number of women wage earners has increased considerably during the XXth century. [...] Without seeking to pass judgment of any kind on the development we have just mentioned, we feel obliged to state that it appears to us impossible to reverse this development and that, consequently, women wage earners must be guaranteed, in their own interests as well as in those of workers in general and in the interests of economic and social progress, wages equal to those paid to male workers for an equal quantity and quality of work.[37]

It is clear what form of work the WFTU had in mind here. It was about women in industry, a field trade unions originally allocated to the white, male worker. In this sector, the text added in point two, "female labour is paid less than the rate fixed for male labour"[38] in most countries. In piecework, the difference was even more pronounced. But the "lessons of industrial psychology" had shown that a woman can, "by reasons of her natural talents, such as skill, dexterity, etc. furnish an excellent output, in no way inferior to the output provided by male labour."[39] The report called for a "re-grade" of women's wages "on the basis of the quantity and quality of the work performed, so as to eliminate present

35 Dessau 1956, 26.

36 "Report on the activity of the W.F.T.U. concerning the principles of equality of wages for equal work between male and female labour," p. 1, Folder 79, WFTU Archives, IISH.

37 "Declaration of principle on the retribution of female labour," Folder 79, p. 1, WFTU Archives, IISH.

38 "Declaration of principle on the retribution of female labour," Folder 79, p. 1.

39 "Declaration of principle on the retribution of female labour," Folder 79, p. 2.

differences between the rate of wages paid to women workers and the market value of their production."[40] Jobs essentially performed by women would also have to be re-evaluated on the basis of a reasonable comparison with similar work performed by men. For this re-evaluation, women labour inspectors would have to be appointed in cooperation with trade union organizations, shop stewards, and works councils. The inspectors would also be responsible for monitoring wages. Of course, the demand for an increase in women's wages was also about avoiding competition with male workers, a motivation that was not concealed. The text also called for equal conditions in training, pay during maternity leave and after the birth of a child, the reduction of domestic responsibilities through the establishment of nurseries, kindergartens, canteens, and laundries, which would be supervised by trade unions or works councils and established through financial subsidies provided by the public purse.[41] Finally, the text emphasized the need to organize women in trade unions, especially in "dependent territories or in territories held under trusteeship."[42]

The declaration, thus, covered both the potential problems associated with calculating fair wages and the general support of women in the labour market. It was influenced by socialist concepts in that it did not question women's employment in general, and it addressed the concern of possible competition from women workers as well contradicted the idea that women were responsible only for domestic work, a prevailing view in some Western countries—like the Netherlands or Great Britain—as will be seen in the discussion at the WFTU Executive Committee meeting. The socialist line was also obvious in the demand for public support for childcare facilities and women's education and in the declaration of support for trade unionism in colonial countries, which will be addressed later as well.

The sources document the opposition delegates of the WFTU faced at the ECOSOC meeting and the arguments it had prepared to allay the concerns of some state representatives about possible inflation or competition in the labour market from an increase in women's employment. While all the members of the council agreed in principle, representatives of New Zealand and Great Britain balked at the immediate implementation of these proposals, claiming that these reforms would lead to an increase in inflation. WFTU delegates sought to counter this concern arguing that "measures should lead, in practice, to rationalisation in the use of women's labour and consequently should serve to reduce the disequilibrium between methods of payment and

40 "Declaration of principle on the retribution of female labour," Folder 79, p. 2.
41 "Declaration of principle on the retribution of female labour," Folder 79, p. 3.
42 "Declaration of principle on the retribution of female labour," Folder 79, p. 4.

productivity."[43] In the end, despite the dissenting votes from Britain, New Zealand, and abstentions from Australia, Canada, and the Netherlands, the WFTU's memorandum was successful. The ECOSOC passed a resolution adopting a recommendation on "equal pay for equal work" and "equal remuneration for work of equal value." It decided to transmit the memorandum of the WFTU to the ILO, inviting the latter to proceed as rapidly as possible on the further consideration of this subject.[44] The member states had to implement these principles and were requested to report to the ILO and the ECOSOC. The WFTU was aware that its work did not end here.

3 The WFTU Executive Committee Meeting in Rome, May 1948

The discussions in the World Federation continued three months later, in May 1948, at the WFTU Executive Committee meeting held in Rome. The committee was confident it could put its own resolutions into action and, with its twenty-six members, was geographically broad-based. Most delegates came from the Soviet Union, which held five seats, followed by the United States and Canada, which sent a total of four delegates. France had three seats, and Great Britain two. The remaining delegates mostly represented larger regions such as Latin America, India, and what was then Ceylon, Africa, Scandinavia, and Western, Southern, Central, and Eastern Europe. China, Australia, and New Zealand were also represented. In addition to the core leaders of the WFTU—including President Arthur Deakin, General Secretary Louis Saillant, and two of Saillant's three deputies Walter Schevenels and Rombert Chambeiron—the head of the Economic and Social Department G. Fischer, who was responsible for the paper in cooperation with Saillant, was also present. Shortly before, a meeting of the Executive Bureau, the central organ of the WFTU, had taken place. This meeting was already dominated by the dispute over Marshall Plan aid, and this conflict affected the overall mood of the Executive Committee meeting, which was further exacerbated by the presence of Saillant, who had

43 "Report on the activity of the W.F.T.U. concerning the principles of equality of wages for equal work between male and female labour," p. 2–3, Folder 79, WFTU Archives, IISH.

44 "Report on the activity of the W.F.T.U. concerning the principles of equality of wages for equal work between male and female labour," p. 5, Folder 79, WFTU Archives, IISH. On the adjustments, see also "Principle of equal pay for equal work for men and women workers," 6th session, 1948, Lake Success, N.Y., E/RES/121(VI), ECOSOC, https://digitallibrary.un.org/record/212044?ln=en.

become the "key and irritating figure" in the dispute due to his public positioning against Marshall Plan aid.[45]

The basis of the debates was the 27-page survey that had been part of the memorandum presented to the ECOSOC in February and which was now being discussed internally by the members of the Executive Committee. The introduction to the report explained that it was a "general statement, which tries to state the question and to provide the elements of solution."[46] The primary and most crucial point raised by the survey was the issue of women's wages. The survey used figures and a variety of arguments to justify the WFTU's demands. It contained a chapter on historical context, which explained the development and conditions of women workers, the employment of women in specific sectors in different countries, the level of wages, and the provision of public funds for kindergartens, nurseries, etc. The text mainly attempted to counter narratives that had developed in trade unions regarding women's employment. For example, it argued that for "the mother of a family [...] carrying on a job does not generally mean that her household is neglected";[47] stressed that women employees' absenteeism could be reduced by nurseries and kindergartens; and asserted that the "greater physical strength" of men could be supplemented through "other qualities" like "dexterity and exactness."[48] Finally, the last chapter dealt with the issue of equal pay for equal work in detail. The first step was to define the meaning of this concept:

> Whenever a woman replaces a man and performs the same work, she should receive the same wage. [...] The woman must be capable of working and carrying on production under the same conditions as a man she has replaced, without any additional supervision or assistance.[49]

In the very next sentence, the text admitted that this situation was rare. But when the work of the woman is very similar, a method should be developed whereby the woman is paid "according to the true values of her work and not

45 Saillant belonged to the communist-progressive bloc. Even during his appointment, Saillant was criticized by many Western trade unionists for his lack of neutrality—although he was never officially a communist party member and despite the support of the non-communist French CGT leader Léon Jouhaux. McIlroy 2013; Pohrt 2000, 118.

46 "Survey on the question of the retribution of female labour," p. 1, Folder 79, WFTU Archives, IISH.

47 "Survey on the question...," p. 6, Folder 79, WFTU Archives, IISH.

48 "Survey on the question...," p. 19, Folder 79, WFTU Archives, IISH.

49 "Survey on the question...," p. 19, Folder 79, WFTU Archives, IISH.

according to a prejudice against women in employment," the WFTU claimed.[50] For the evaluation of work considered "feminine," a system would have to be developed to estimate the value of work, "allowing for a revaluation of women's wages on a scientific basis."[51] This revaluation should be based on a comparison between the work performed by men and women. "When the exact value of a job has been estimated and equality in wages for men and women has been attained, these new wages are to be applied in the various industries."[52]

Finally, the text made clear that the implementation of this re-evaluated work would have to be implemented by governments, trade unions, and by society. The ILO had begun taking steps on this issue in 1944, but "we must not lose sight of the immediate reality and content ourselves with mere paper reforms."[53] The WFTU Executive Committee meeting was now focused on discussing the proposal, sharing experiences, and planning further actions. After General Secretary Saillant had talked about the results at the ECOSOC meeting, he invited discussion.

Nina Popova was the first to speak. Before delving into an analysis of the position she took in the discussion, I want to briefly introduce her. Popova played a dual role here. She was invited as a delegate of the ACCTU, but as vice-president of the WIDF, she also spoke as an activist of a women's organization. Like many international organizations, the WIDF was established after World War Two to give institutional expression to the euphoria around the end of the war and the successful fight against fascism. As Francisca de Haan writes, many of the actors had suffered trauma as well as personal losses during the war, as had Popova, who had been involved in the defense of Moscow[54] and had lost her husband "in the fight for Berlin."[55] The WFTU and WIDF were similar in that they both aimed their activism at the working class. The WIDF explicitly distinguished itself from conservative and liberal women's associations and

50 "Survey on the question…," p. 20, Folder 79, WFTU Archives, IISH.

51 "Survey on the question…," p. 20, Folder 79, WFTU Archives, IISH.

52 "Survey on the question…," p. 21, Folder 79, WFTU Archives, IISH.

53 "Survey on the question…," p. 22, Folder 79, WFTU Archives, IISH.

54 In 1941, Popova became head of the Krasnopresneskiy district in Moscow and started to mobilize all material and human resources against the war. She "especially encouraged and cherished women's mobilization, which in her eyes was a central part of the district's defense program. […] She not only encouraged and mobilized others, but was herself planning and preparing to go underground in 1942, in case Moscow fell to Nazi occupation." Archivnaia sparavka [Archival note] 18/07/65, Party Archive of the Institute of Party History, cited in Borisova 2005, quoted in Knopova 2011, 60.

55 De Haan 2009, 243. Knopova-Ziferblat, in reference to Borisova, refers to the letters between Nina Popova and her husband Vladimir Orlov from 1942 to 1945, Borisova 2005, 206–208, quoted in Knopova 2011, 60.

defined itself as a "left feminist organization which saw the active participation of the mass of working women as a prerequisite for fundamental social change."[56] The aim was not only to speak for and with working-class women but also to prepare them to take up leadership positions, as was the case for Popova, who was born to a working-class family in Yelets, Russia in 1908.[57]

In her role as the international representative of Soviet women, Popova was highly respected within the Soviet Union, and in subsequent years, she was appointed to and promoted in other important political institutions.[58] Yana Knopova, who has studied the Soviet Women's Committee, called Popova "one of the most influential Soviet women figures of her time."[59] Because she held so many international positions, Popova had access to a lot of information and had insight into discussions taking place at the international level, where she, of course, also had the opportunity to express her convictions. Since Popova was politically active during the Stalinist period, one must ask to what extent she was a follower of the political line; convinced of what the state apparatus represented; or merely a puppet in the Stalinist state apparatus. Alexandra Talaver has recently examined this question, analyzing Popova's political writings as well as her letters and personal records. She concludes that these questions are not so easy to answer since "there are no sources available to make a reliable guess about Popova's views on Stalin. But her biography demonstrates a controversial positionality. On the one hand, her career growth was probably partly due to the repression that "freed" up jobs, which was typical for people of her generation. On the other hand, she experienced the injustice and randomness of the purges in her personal life."[60] It was not surprising, then, that at the WFTU Executive Committee meeting, she began her official (and recorded remarks) by promoting the achievements of Soviet society and defending the equal rights of women in the SU:

---

56 De Haan 2009, 244. A comparison of as well as the connections between these two international organizations has not been researched so far, but it would be interesting not only in terms of their members—who, as in the case of Popova, were members of both organizations or used both networks for their political activities—but also in terms of their historical development and political goals.

57 Borisova 2005, 22–23, quoted in Knopova 2011, 58.

58 She served as the chairwoman of the Presidium of the Union of Soviet Societies for Friendship and Cultural Relations with Foreign Countries (1958–1975) and was also member of the Central Committee of the Communist Party (1961–1976). See Knopova 2011, 58.

59 Knopova 2011, 57. For insight into her personal life with some photos, see the website of the museum in the city she was born: https://hudotdel.eletsmuseum.ru/нина-васильевна-попова-жизнь-ка/. I thank Olga Gnydiuk for this reference.

60 Talaver 2023. I thank Alexandra Talaver for making her manuscript available to me before publication.

> The principle of equal pay for equal work was one of the most long-standing claims of the working class, one of the conditions of true democracy and a guarantee for the vital interests of the workers. In the USSR, complete equality had long existed in fact for women; from the earliest days of the Revolution in 1917, the principle of equal pay for equal work had been effectively applied. [...] If one wished to be objective, it was clear that the liberation of women presupposed, as an essential condition, their employment in productive work, and their freeing from the drudgery of the kitchen and the nursery and from economic dependence and household slavery.[61]

Popova was quite clear on how this could be achieved: women's liberation was possible through the abolition of private ownership of the means and instruments of production, as had been achieved in the Soviet Union. A year later, she summarized her ideology concerning a discrimination-free Soviet Union and voiced her commitment to socialism in *Women in the Land of Socialism*, in which she saw Soviet women as the "vanguard of the struggle of women all over the world." In the context of the international women's movement, she wrote: "They take the lead in the efforts to strengthen cooperation among women of all freedom-loving nations."[62]

But what was the situation like in the Soviet Union? What was the employment ratio of women? Did women's wages really correspond to those of men, as Popova proclaimed? First, women's participation in the labour force was regarded as a key dimension of the industrialization drive and the achievement of Soviet economic goals dating from the late 1920s.[63] The Soviet constitution of 1936 explicitly granted men and women the equal right to work and equal pay for equal work—one of the earliest examples of gender equality legislation.[64] Beyond legislation, there had been a marked increase in women's

---

61 Reports on the Session of the Executive Committee, Rome, 4 May to 10 May 1948, p. 91–92, 94, Folder 83, WFTU Archives, IISH.

62 Popova 1949.

63 Ofer and Vinokur 1985, S330. For references to literature in this paragraph, I would like to thank Marcel van der Linden. As Olga Gnydiuk has rightly pointed out, the following figures come from studies conducted in the 1980s. Unfortunately, I have not found any current statistics. If one follows Katarina Katz's statement, these statistics were rarely compiled in the USSR. In her 1997 article, she writes that "official data on the gender wage gap were published only once in the history of the USSR, in 1989 (Goskomstat [SSSR] 1989. [Narodnoe Khoziaistvo SSSR v 1989 g., Moscow, Finansy I statistika]) and not at all so far in the Russian Federation." Katz 1997, 431.

64 Katz 1997, 431.

employment—a higher level of women joined the work force combined with women's greater penetration of occupations previously considered *male*.[65] According to statistics on women's employment in the 1960s, 77 percent of the Soviet Union's female working-age population was employed.[66] This figure was far different from those of Western countries. While Sweden followed with 51 percent, the figures for other countries represented at the WFTU Executive Committee lagged far behind (e.g., Britain, with 43 percent; and Italy, with 35 percent).[67]

However, the relatively small difference in women's labour force participation in the Soviet Union did not equate to a small gender wage gap. Soviet women earned between 60 percent and 65 percent of the average salary of men and about 70 percent of men's hourly wages,[68] which was not much different or was even lower than women's wages in Western countries. For example, Swedish women earned 72 percent of men's earnings in 1960; Italian women, 73 percent; and British women, at least 61percent.[69] So, in terms of Soviet women's employment, there was a foundation on which Popova could launch her campaign, but this foundation was far shakier than her arguments for equal pay suggested.

A point that is still disputed today is the consequence(s) of the unequal distribution of unpaid (care) work within the household. Some argue that the main responsibility for care work continued to fall on women. This double burden was one of the reasons women entered into more flexible employment relationships in white-collar occupations, which were relatively low-paid in the Soviet wage structure.[70] The question of whether the distribution of domestic work is the primary reason women were over-represented in low-paid jobs cannot be clearly answered. However, the measures taken by the Soviet state show that officials tried to counteract this situation. They provided support

65 Ofer and Vinokur 1985, S330.

66 Mincer 1985, S2. If one looks at the figures from a more comparative perspective, even more concrete statements emerge. Ofer and Vinokur recorded the numbers of working women who were actually of working age (16–55 years). Here, the figure for 1959 was 87.4 percent. And they also stated that already in 1950, the "participation rates of women between the ages of 15 and 54 [...] were around 70%." Ofer and Vinokur 1985, S333; S335.

67 Mincer 1985, S2.

68 As indicated by various scholars, there were statistics on wages in the Soviet Union, but they not differentiated by sex. The figures given here come from Ofer and Vinokur, but the figures are not very concrete, as the Ofer and Vinokur also write that the wage gap was narrower within occupational groups. Ofer and Vinokur 1985, S337.

69 Gunderson 1989, 47.

70 Katz 1997, 432–433.

for women through the construction of a universal childcare system—a comprehensive network of nurseries and kindergartens—and made an enormous effort to increase women's access to education. While in 1939, only 10 percent of all women aged 10 or older had more than seven years of schooling, in 1979, this had risen to 80 percent of working women, and 60 percent of all women 10 years old or older.[71]

In addition to propagandizing the Soviet model, Popova also made a statement regarding international discussions about the issue and the WFTU's declaration on equal pay. Therefore, she used the knowledge she obtained from her network and included her reflections on the negotiations at the ECOSOC and CSW meetings in her WFTU speech. Although she had not been present at either meeting, she was able to refer to the discussion. She complained about Britain's and New Zealand's resistance to the proposal of the WFTU during the ECOSOC meeting in February 1948. To convince British trade unionists, she condemned the speech of Mary Sutherland, who as a British CSW Commission member in January 1948 had not insisted on the introduction of equal pay for women. It was up to British women to decide whether this statement was an accurate reflection of their opinion, Popova said, but this statement was certainly not in the interest of the TUC, which had defended women's labour on many occasions.[72]

Popova's critical attitude toward the liberal feminist movement was obvious. Sutherland was the Chief Woman Officer of the British Labour Party since 1932 and, as a Western feminist, was definitely in favor of gender equality but was restrained on the issue of female employment. Even during the war, when many women had to work to survive, Sutherland expressed the view that married women should not be obliged to work outside the home: "the priority remained the 'living wage' for men, and only those married women who were free should volunteer for work."[73] Sutherland also represented this position during the CSW's international discussions. Here, she explained that collective bargaining would be the only "democratic method" and "factor that entered into any international regulation on equal pay."[74]

At the WFTU Executive Committee meeting in Rome, President Deakin supported his comrade Sutherland and, thus, challenged Popova, who had called on him to take a stand on Sutherland's position:

71 Ofer and Vinokur 1985, S337.

72 Reports on the Session of the Executive Committee, Rome, 4 May to 10 May 1948, p. 93, Folder 83, WFTU Archives, IISH.

73 Pugh 1992, 280.

74 Boris 2018, 108.

> Miss Sutherland was right when she said that the principle [equality of wages, JW] had not been abandoned, but that it had been decided to restrict its application. An acceptance in principle had been obtained from the Government in regard to equality of men's and women's wages but it was impossible to obtain its full application for the time being.[75]

Deakin also believed that British women, far from seeing it as a duty to go to work, expected their husbands to secure the livelihood for the entire family. In Britain, as in many countries, the number of women employed in jobs outside the home had increased considerably during World War Two.[76] But because of the double burden of employment and care work, working women were viewed unfavorably in Britain.[77] The increase in women's employment also had sparked discussion on equal pay. Some trade unionists advocated for it in principle, but did so only half-heartedly.[78] Deakin, who had taken over the presidency of the WFTU from Walter Citrine in 1946, "worked strenuously to counteract Soviet influence in the World Federation and Communist activity in the unions."[79] This attitude was reflected in his reaction to Popova's speech. However, he demonstrated his resistance not only toward Popova's political attitude but also toward her status as a woman:

> When one told a woman where to go, she went as a rule in the opposite direction; it was therefore difficult to impose direction of women's labour. The discussion had strayed too far from the facts, and at certain times, it had even become ridiculous and undignified. One should not try to turn the question of equal wages into a political which would completely distort the problem.[80]

Deakin's comment was not the only disparaging remark made by male colleagues about women's gainful employment. Dutch delegate Evert Kupers claimed that Dutch women could not work (for wages outside the home)

75 Reports on the Session of the Executive Committee, Rome, 4 May to 10 May 1948, p. 105–106, Folder 83, WFTU Archives, IISH.

76 By late 1943, 46 percent of all women aged 14–59 years were employed. Pugh 1992, 271.

77 The trade unions were also restrained. They blocked women's claim to apprenticeships, accepted the increase of women in the union, but excluded them from positions of responsibility. Pugh 1992, 274.

78 Pugh 1992, 275.

79 Silverman 2000, 108.

80 Reports on the Session of the Executive Committee, Rome, 4 May to 10 May 1948, p. 105–106, Folder 83, WFTU Archives, IISH.

because they had to take care of their large houses, wheras such employment was possible for Soviet women because of their smaller one-room apartments.[81] With his comment comparing the size of households of Dutch and Russian women, Kupers also articulated a view of women's work widely embraced by Dutch society. After World War Two, the male breadwinner model continued to exist there for some time; it began to be replaced by the government only in the early 1970s with the introduction of a dual labour market and state support for women's part-time work. In line with the idea that women's tasks were primarily domestic, women's income was also seen as *extra income* and inequality, therefore, was not considered problematic.[82]

The Polish delegate Kazimierz Witaszewski clearly criticized Kupers's arguments.[83] He declared that he would inform all the women in Poland, and through the WIDF, all the women of the world of Kupers's attitude toward women workers. How dare he make such a statement when women had been fighting against fascism as well racist discrimination in colonies for decades, he said.[84] In the opinion of Witaszewski:

> Equal pay for equal work was a yardstick of social progress. Whoever was opposed to this principle was opposed at the same time to social justice in the world. Absence of such legislation was the result of capitalist exploitation. Russian women had worked during the war and contributed to the victory over fascism. This was perhaps the reason why comrade Kupers was still alive.[85]

81 Reports on the Session of the Executive Committee, Rome, 4 May to 10 May 1948, p. 100, Folder 83, WFTU Archives, IISH. Kupers, like most of those present, had been a trade unionist on the international stage for many years. The tailor, born in 1885, who organized himself in the textile industry, was a member of both the Social Democratic Labour Party and of several trade unions. He was, first and foremost, the first secretary of the Dutch Confederation of Trade Unions (Nederlands Verbond van Vakverenigingen). He had been involved in founding the International Garment Workers' Federation at the beginning of the twentieth century and had been delegate of the ILO since 1922. Reinalda 2001.

82 De Groot 2021, 764.

83 Witaszewski, who in the early postwar years was a communist rank-and-file trade unionist, was involved in drafting the February Decree in 1947, which would guarantee works councils certain rights of participation beyond the communist party and union, Burek 2021, 47–48; 53; 75. I thank Jan A. Burek for making his manuscript available to me before publication.

84 Reports on the Session of the Executive Committee, Rome, 4 May to 10 May 1948, p. 102, Folder 83, WFTU Archives, IISH.

85 Reports on the Session..., p. 102, Folder 83, WFTU Archives, IISH.

Witaszewski pointedly asked Kupers "what he would propose to do for women whose husbands had been shot by the fascists, especially those women who earned the families' livelihood; must they be left unprotected?"[86] Apart from this provocative statement, Witaszewski brought up a point that was pertinent for many women in the Eastern bloc in the immediate postwar period: the participation of women in the workforce was necessary for the economic reconstruction of the country. Even when the men eventually returned from war, economic scarcity meant that in many cases, both men and women had to work.[87]

Even if Witaszewski was on the "side of the women" here, it was clear that trade unionists held misogynistic attitudes in addition to ideological convictions, and this tendency was not criticized because women were absent from the leadership of trade union bodies at both the national and international levels. Thus, the only woman present on the Executive Committee was Nina Popova, who addressed the problem of women's lack of representation: She hoped that the time would come when, in the WFTU, the Executive Committee, and the delegations of the CIO, the TUC, the French CGT, and in the organizations of still other National Centres, women would be given suitable representation.[88]

The fact that the issues of women's employment and remuneration were dealt with differently by male delegates than by female ones is demonstrated by the example of Italy. Italy was represented on the WFTU Executive Committee by Guiseppe di Vittorio, the secretary of the Italian General Confederation of Labour (Confederazione Generale Italiana del Lavororo—CGIL). He was known for his rather left-wing positions. When di Vittorio discussed the situation of women's employment in Italy and praised the progressiveness of the country, he did not mention at any point who had been involved in achieving this status.[89] According to historian Eloisa Betti, it was, in fact, mainly Italian women's associations that demanded that "a woman has the same rights and, for equal work, the same remuneration as a man."[90] It was they who mobilized inside and outside Parliament and "repeatedly denounced the fact that women

86 Reports on the Session..., p. 102, Folder 83, WFTU Archives, IISH.

87 Fidelis 2010, 22–23.

88 Reports on the Session of the Executive Committee, Rome, 4 May to 10 May 1948, p. 99, Folder 83, WFTU Archives, IISH.

89 Reports on the Session..., p. 110, Folder 83, WFTU Archives, IISH.

90 According to Betti, the most important women's organizations were the Women's Defense Group and the Union of Italian Women (UDI). It was they, together with some women trade unionists, who called for equal pay in those years. See Betti 2018, 278–279.

workers still experienced unequal remuneration, notwithstanding constitutional guarantees."[91] Di Vittorio appeared confident at the WFTU meeting, but he failed to understand the actual concerns of the Italian women's movement:

> It was not only a question of protecting women, which was already a high and noble task, and obligatory for all, trade-unionists or not, but of protecting them in their work. The question went much further and on to a higher plane, for in protecting women in this way one prevented their labour from being used in competition with the work of men. The Italian trade unions had fought against that for 30 or 35 years. At the same time, they had succeeded in preventing women from being employed in work that was too heavy for them.[92]

This statement supports Betti's analysis. Even in left-wing organizations, the model of the male breadwinner prevailed, and women's wages were seen as secondary and complementary to those of their male counterparts. In the CGIL, the equal-pay principle existed only on the level of discourse until the second half of the 1950s.[93]

President Deakin, who as chairman of the committee played the role of moderator, intervened in the debate between Kupers and Witaszewski, expressing his support for his Dutch colleague: "Comrade Kupers may have adopted a bantering tone, but had Comrade Witaszewski lost his sense of humour to the extent that he did not perceive the irony of his words?"[94] Deakin claimed he did not want to use his speech for political purposes, but then he did:

---

91 Betti 2018, 276. For instance, at its first congress in 1945, the Union of Italian Women (UDI), which was close to the Italian Communist Party (PCI), raised the demand for equal pay for equal work. In contrast, Italian trade unions did not mention the issue at that time. "Until the late 1950s, women workers were not a priority in the political strategy of the Italian CGIL, or the PCI, even though leaders like Giuseppe Di Vittorio [...] thought of themselves as enlightened" (Betti 2018, 281).

92 Reports on the Session of the Executive Committee, Rome, 4 May to 10 May 1948, p. 110–111, Folder 83, WFTU Archives, IISH.

93 Betti 2018, 281. Betti also mentions a woman who was present at the international level and could easily have been sent as a delegate for WFTU instead of di Vittorio. Terese Noce was general secretary of the Italian Federation of Textile Workers and President of the International Union of Textile and Clothing Workers between 1949 and 1958. At the Second Congress of the WIDF in 1948, she represented the Italian trade unions. Betti 2018, 284.

94 Reports on the Session of the Executive Committee, Rome, 4 May to 10 May 1948, p. 104, Folder 83, WFTU Archives, IISH.

> It was not their aim to establish slavery for women. [He] had, himself, seen in the Soviet Union women do certain types of work which they would not be allowed to do in England. [...] If it was necessary in Poland and in the USSR for the carrying out of the Five-Year Plan, to put women on to work they would not be given to do in Britain, this was the concern of comrades in those countries, but they should not give this as a model to be copied by every country.[95]

President Deakin's support for Kupers was certainly not only related to the issue of women's employment but was also of a more general nature. Kupers was on the side of those who welcomed the Marshall Plan.

Both trade unionists acted similarly with regard to anticolonial policy and were reticent to criticize their governments—another tendency evident at the Executive Committee meeting.[96] When Sugiswara Abeywardena Wickremasinghe came to the stage to inform the group about the status of labour relations and the trade union movement in Ceylon (today, Sri Lanka), which had just gained independence just four months before the WFTU Executive Committee meeting took place, Deakin and Kupers remained silent.[97] In Wickremasinghe's speech, he described the very fragile trade union movement in his country and the many persecutions his colleagues faced. The economy of the former colony—based on tea and rubber—was still largely dependent on British industry and international cartels, he said, and both men and women were paid miserable wages. He appealed to the British and Dutch delegates to put pressure on their governments to eliminate "this inequality of wages," this "cheap labour." Wickremasinghe regretted that "certain speakers had adopted a tone of moral superiority. They had, no doubt a right to be proud of high standard of living in their country, but he would like to bring them back to a more correct sense of their responsibilities."[98] Brian Goodwin,[99] a

95 Reports on the Session..., p. 104, Folder 83, WFTU Archives, IISH.

96 At the congress in Paris in 1945, Kupers criticized possible interference by the WFTU in the Indonesian revolution. Despite that, when the Dutch military became active in Indonesia in July 1947, the WFTU supported the admission of Central All-Indonesian Workers Organization (Sentral Organisasi Buruh Seluruh Indonesia). See Pohrt 2000, 273; Hearman 2016.

97 Wickremasinghe belonged to the Ceylon Trade Union Federation (CTUF) and was an official delegate to the WFTU in 1948. The CTUF was formed in 1941 and was the trade union arm of the Communist Party of Ceylon. See Office of International Labor Affairs 1958.

98 Reports on the Session of the Executive Committee, Rome, 4 May to 10 May 1948, p. 115, Folder 83, WFTU Archives, IISH.

99 Money 2015.

trade unionist from Northern Rhodesia, a British protectorate formed in 1911 that gained independence in 1964, took a similar line. He argued that British trade unions bore at least some responsibility for their colleagues and workers in (former) colonies, and that the issue of pay equality was related not only to gender but also to race:

> The Rhodesian trade unions insisted that the work done should be paid for in the same way as they demanded the same wages for men and for women irrespective of colour when they did the same work. The TUC should bring pressure to bear on the British Government in order that this principle be accepted in colonial administration.[100]

That there was no discussion following this emphatic statement was mainly because there was no unity within the WFTU regarding (anti)colonial policies at the time.[101] The fact that substantive colonial issues were swept under the rug, however, was due to the avoidance tactics used by union delegates from states that still maintained colonial empires. President Deakin ended the speeches of Wickremasinghe and Goodwin without any debate and only mentioned that there were plans for a conference in Asia where these issues could be discussed.[102]

The last speaker of the WFTU Executive Committee meeting on equal pay was Nina Popova. She attacked President Deakin and Western trade unionists, summarizing her position: "Why is the president submitting the issue of wage equality to the ECOSOC if capitalism is paradise for working men and women?" she asked, highlighting what she regarded as a contradiction.[103] To calm Popova down and put an end to the discussion, Deakin blamed the disagreement between delegates on poor translation. He emphasized that there was agreement on the report as well as the resolution. Since the latter required

---

100 Reports on the Session of the Executive Committee, Rome, 4 May to 10 May 1948, p. 114, Folder 83, WFTU Archives, IISH.

101 The Colonial Department, which was in the hands of the CIO, was directed by Elmer Cope since the end of 1947. Cope had a decidedly anticommunist stance and tried to push back communist influence on the WFTU's anticolonial activities. See Pohrt 2000, 260–261. There is a lack of research on the WFTU's anti-colonial policies and its role in the Global South. I am currently working with Immanuel R. Harisch on communist trade unionists from the Global South within the WFTU.

102 This conference did not take place during the period when the WFTU was unified but only after the split in Beijing in 1949. See Pohrt 2000, 266–272, 276–277.

103 Reports on the Session of the Executive Committee, Rome, 4 May to 10 May 1948, p. 118, Folder 83, WFTU Archives, IISH.

some improvements, he proposed a smaller commission "for the purpose of drawing up a definite text in which these remarks were taken into account."[104]

4 The Aftermath of the WFTU Executive Committee Meeting

In Beirut in March 1949, equal pay was discussed again at the CSW. This time, the now-divided WFTU submitted a declaration. Marie Couette, a trade unionist from the French CGT, represented the WFTU. In France, Couette had been known for her struggle for equal pay since the 1920s, and she had supported the formation of a women's commission in the CGT.[105] In addition to the WFTU declaration, proposals were submitted by the delegates of China, the Soviet Union, and the United States. They were discussed and partly included in the CSW resolution. Regarding the WFTU proposal, the records states: "The proposal of the World Federation of Trade Unions was rejected paragraph by paragraph."[106] The reasons for this were matters related to protocol and content. For example, it was not appropriate to accept the proposal of one non-governmental organization and exclude others. The material distributed by the WFTU also contained serious inaccuracies about some countries.[107] Couette reported afterward that only the Soviets supported the resolution of the WFTU, and that the negative attitude of the others had been evident even before the meeting.[108]

Finally, the resolution adopted by the CWS affirmed "the principle of equal pay for equal work for men and women workers" and wanted to continue the process of implementation. This responsibility was attributed primarily to the ILO, which was asked to prepare a study on this issue. ECOSOC was requested to promote this project to member states and called on them to act.[109] This development shows that by 1949, any cooperation between the Cold War blocs

104 Reports on the Session of the Executive Committee, Rome, 4 May to 10 May 1948, p. 118.

105 Liszek 2020.

106 Report of the 3rd session of the Commission on the Status of Women, 21 March to 4 April 1949, pp. 12–13, E/1316, E/CN.6/124, CSW, https://digitallibrary.un.org/record/824970?ln=en.

107 Summary record of the 52nd meeting held at Beirut, Lebanon, on Tuesday, 29 March 1949, p. 2, E/CN.6/SR.52, CSW, https://digitallibrary.un.org/record/3844750?ln=en.

108 Couette 1949, 16–17.

109 Summary record of the 52nd meeting held at Beirut, Lebanon, on Tuesday, 29 March 1949, p. 8, E/CN.6/SR.52, CSW, https://digitallibrary.un.org/record/3844750?ln=en.

had ended. The issue went to the ILO and resulted in ILO Convention no. 100 "Equal Remuneration for Male and Female Workers for Work of Equal Value" in 1951.[110] While the WFTU was able to act as an important initiator in 1948, they were no longer involved in shaping the content of international directives just one year later due to the split in the international trade union movement and the escalating conflict of the Cold War.

5 Conclusion

This chapter has shown that the WFTU played a significant role in debates on equal pay for men and women in the late 1940s. They took up the issue, which was omnipresent in many countries at the time, and attempted to put the question at the forefront of the agenda related to the improvement of working women lives. The aim of the WFTU was, on the one hand, to make their voice heard internationally as the first globally active trade union movement and, on the other hand, to address a subject that was being debated in national women's and trade union's movements and offer a transnational solution to an omnipresent problem. The higher rates of female employment during World War Two generated the question of their remaining in the labour force after the end of the conflict.

Looking at the declaration prepared by the general secretary and the Economic and Social Department, it was not difficult to see that the WFTU Secretariat was primarily following the (state) socialist model. Women's employment was assumed to be essential, and the male breadwinner model was not addressed or given preference in any way. The WFTU's conceptualization of the issue attempted to bring together the debates on women's employment and equal pay that had taken place at the national context and at the international level. The demand for equal pay for equal work was considered self-evident; regarding the problem of evaluating genuinely female occupations, a method was to be developed that did not discriminate against women. In order to support women in their gainful employment, the WFTU demanded the improvement of training and support for women in their care work.

The failure of this program at the ECOSOC—where the WFTU had placed the issue on the agenda in 1948—is clear from the later discussion that took place at the WFTU Executive Committee meeting. What made this meeting special was, first, that it was the last time West, East, and South met to

110 On the development of the Recommendation 100 at the ILO, see Boris 2018, 108–111.

negotiate the topic before the WFTU's split. But the meeting was already held during the final days of the joint international trade union. Cold War divisions had already appeared in other arenas and were now apparent at this meeting.

The topic would probably not have received such attention if Nina Popova had not appeared as a representative of the ACCTU. She was both a socialist as well as a women's activist, who, through her membership in other international women's organizations, attached special importance to the discussion. Popova, however, did not use the forum only to advocate women's occupation but also transformed her speeches into propaganda in which the Soviet solution appeared as the only real choice for women. One can only speculate about whether the debate could have been different had it involved other women who knew more about the topic than their male colleagues. But as indicated by Sutherland and the discussion in the CSW, the debates among women's movements reflected similar lines of confrontation.

The economic situation was precarious in both Eastern and Western European countries in the postwar period. However, the models proposed to address it differed considerably with regard to women's employment. While the double-earner model was introduced in the Eastern bloc, in Western Europe, the tried-and-true model of the male breadwinner had to be protected; changing it would call the entire social structure of states into question, especially in connection with the allocation of responsibility for care and housework. This debate took place primarily within a European context. Non-European issues, such as pay inequality in relation to race, were marginalized, as the example of Wickremasinghe and Goodwin reveals. That the WFTU came to an end with this discussion is shown by what happened next in the negotiations at the CSW in Beirut in 1949. The WFTU contribution never make it into the final resolution. A discussion on the issue seemed obsolete because of the conflicts taking place out in the open.

Bibliography

Adami, Rebecca. 2019. *Women and the Universal Declaration of Human Rights*. New York: Taylor & Francis.

Betti, Eloisa. 2018. "Unexpected Alliances: Italian Women's Struggles for Equal Pay, 1940s–1960s." In *Women's ILO. Transnational Networks, Global Labour Standards, and Gender Equity, 1919 to Present*, edited by Eileen Boris, Dorothea Hoethker, and Susan Zimmermann, 276–299. Leiden: Brill.

Boris, Eileen. 2018. "Equality's Cold War. the ILO and the UN Commission on the Status of Women, 1946–1970s." In *Women's ILO. Transnational Networks, Global Labour*

Standards, and Gender Equity, 1919 to Present, edited by Eileen Boris, Dorothea Hoethker, and Susan Zimmermann, 97–120. Leiden: Brill.
Borisova, Natalya [Борисова, Наталья]. 2005. *Нина Попова: Жизнь как созидание* [Nina Popova: life as creation]. Yeletzskii gosudarstvennyi universitet.
Burek, Jan A. 2021. *Communists and Workers in a "Red Town." A Microhistory of Party Politics and Shopfloor Relations in a Polish Industrial Centre from a Trans-War Perspective, 1926–1951*. PhD diss., European University Institute Florence.
Carew, Anthony. 2018. *American Labour's Cold War Abroad: From Deep Freeze to Detente, 1945–1970*. Edmonton: Athabasca University Press.
Carew, Anthony. 2000. "A False Dawn: The World Federation of Trade Unions (1945–1949)." In *The International Confederation of Free Trade Unions*, edited by Anthony Carew, Michel Dreyfus, Geert van Goethem, Rebecca Gumbrell-McCormick, and Marcel van der Linden, 167–185. Bern: Peter Lang.
Couette, Marie. 1949. "Der WGB verteidigt die Arbeiterinnen in der OVN" [The WFTU defends the women workers in the CSW]. *Die Weltgewerkschaftsbewegung* [World trade union movement]. German edition, no. 1 (May): 16–17.
Dessau, Jan. 1956. *Ten Years' Activity of the World Federation of Trade Unions in the United Nations*. London: WFTU Publications.
Fidelis, Malgorzata. 2010. *Women, Communism, and Industrialization in Postwar Poland*, Cambridge: Cambridge University Press.
De Groot, Timon. 2021. "Making Part-time Work a Fully-Fledged Alternative: How the Dutch Social Partners Responded to a Dual Labour Market, 1966–1993." *Labor History* 62, no. 5–6 (2021): 762–780.
Gunderson, Morley. 1989. "Male-Female Wage Differentials and Policy Responses." *Journal of Economic Literature* 27, no. 1: 46–72.
De Haan, Francisca. 2012. "Women as the 'Motor of Modern Life'. Women's Work in Europe West and East since 1945." In *Women and Gender in Postwar Europe: From Cold War to European Union*, edited by Joanna Regulska and Bonnie G. Smith, e-book. London: Taylor & Francis Ltd.
De Haan, Francisca. 2010. "Continuing Cold War Paradigms in Western Historiography of Transnational Women's Organizations: The Case of the Women's International Democratic Federation (WIDF)." *Women's History Review* 19, no. 4: 547–573.
De Haan, Francisca. 2009. "Hoffnungen auf eine bessere Welt: Die frühen Jahre der Internationalen Demokratischen Frauenföderation (IDFF/WIDF) (1945–1950)" [Hopes for a better world: The early years of the International Democratic Women's Federation (IDFF/WIDF) (1945–1950)]. *Feministische Studien* 2: 241–257.
Hearman, Vannessa. 2016. "Indonesian Trade Unionists, the World Federation of Trade Unions and Cold War Internationalism, 1947–65." *Labour History* 111: 1–16.
Katz, Katarina. 1997. "Gender, Wages and Discrimination in the USSR: A Study of a Russian Industrial Town." *Cambridge Journal of Economics* 21: 431–452.

Knopova, Yana. 2011. *The Soviet Union and the International Domain of Women's Rights and Struggles: A Theoretical Framework and a Case Study of the Soviet Women's Committee (1941–1991)*. MA thesis, Central European University, Budapest. http://www.etd.ceu.edu/2011/knopova_yana.htm.

Lambertz, Jan. 2012. "'Democracy Could Go No Further': Europe and Women in the Early United Nations." In *Women and Gender in Postwar Europe: From Cold War to European Union,* edited by Joanna Regulska and Bonnie G. Smith. London: Taylor & Francis.

Lewis, Su Lin, and Carolien Stolte. 2019. "Other Bandungs: Afro-Asian Internationalisms in the Early Cold War." *Journal of World History* 30, no. 1–2: 1–19.

Liszek, Slave. 2020. "Couette, Marie. Née Bluet, Marie, Jeanne." *Le Maitron. Dictionnaire Biographique Mouvement Ouvrier. Mouvement Social* [The master. Labour movement biographical dictionary. Social movement]. https://maitron.fr/spip.php?article20828.

McIlroy, John. 2013. "Léon Jouhaux, Louis Saillant and the National and International in Transnational Trade Unionism." *Labor History* 54, no. 5: 554–576.

Mincer, Jacob. 1985. "Intercountry Comparisons of Labor Force Trends and of Related Developments: An Overview." *Journal of Labor Economics* 3, no. 1: S1–S32.

Money, Duncan. 2015. "The World of European Labour on the Northern Rhodesian Copperbelt, 1940–1945." *International Review of Social History* 60, no. 2: 225–255.

Neunsinger, Silke. 2018. "The Unobtainable Magic of Numbers: Equal Remuneration, the ILO and the International Trade Union Movement 1950s–1980s." In *Women's ILO. Transnational Networks, Global Labour Standards, and Gender Equity, 1919 to Present,* edited by Eileen Boris, Dorothea Hoethker, and Susan Zimmermann, 121–148. Leiden: Brill.

Ofer, Gur, and Aaron Vinokur. 1985. "Work and Family Roles of Soviet Women: Historical Trends and Cross-Section Analysis." *Journal of Labor Economics* 3, no. 1: S328–S354.

Office of International Labor Affairs of the U.S. Department of Labor. 1958. *Directory of Labor Organizations Asia and Australia.*

Pugh, Martin. 1992. *Women and the Women's Movement in Britain 1914–1959*. Basingstoke a. o.: Palgrave Macmillan.

Pohrt, Oliver. 2000. *Die Internationale Gewerkschaftsbewegung zwischen Einheitswunsch und Kaltem Krieg. Der Weltgewerkschaftsbund (WGB) von der Gründungsphase bis zu seiner Spaltung (1941–1949)*. [The international trade union novement between the desire for unity and the Cold War. The World Federation of Trade Unions (WFTU) from its founding phase to its split (1941–1949)]. Regensburg: Roderer.

Popova, Nina V. 1949. *Women in the Land of Socialism*. Moscow: Foreign Languages Publishing House. https://www.revolutionarydemocracy.org/archive/WomSoc.htm.

Reinalda, Bob. 2001. "Evert Kupers." *Biografisch Woordenboek van het Socialisme en de Arbeidersbeweging in Nederland* (BWSA) 8: 132–140. https://socialhistory.org/bwsa/biografie/kupers.

Schevenels, Walter. 1956. *Forty-Five Years International Federation of Trade Unions: 1901–1945. A Historical Precis*, edited by Walter Citrine. Brussels: Board of Trustees.

Silverman, Victor. 2000. *Imagining Internationalism in American and British Labor, 1939–49. The Working Class in American History*. Urbana: University of Illinois Press.

Stolte, Carolin. 2019. "Introduction: Trade Union Networks and the Politics of Expertise in an Age of Afro-Asian Solidarity." *Journal of Social History* 53, no. 2: 331–347.

Talaver, Alexandra. 2023. "Nina Vasilievna Popova (1908–1994): 'Woman in the Land of Socialism.'" In *The Palgrave Handbook of Communist Women Activists Around the World*, edited by Francisca de Haan, 245–269. Cham: Palgrave Macmillan.

Weiler, Peter. 1988. *British Labour and the Cold War*. Stanford, CA: Stanford University Press.

Windmuller, John P. 1954. *The American Labor and the International Labor Movement 1940 to 1954*. Ithaca, NY: The Institute of International Industrial and Labor Relations, Cornell University.

WFTU. [1957]. *The W.F.T.U. and the Struggle of Women Workers. Forward to the Fourth World Trade Union Congress.*

Zimmermann, Susan. 2021. *Frauenpolitik und Männergewerkschaft. Internationale Gewerkschaftspolitik, IGB-Gewerkschafterinnen und die Arbeiter- und Frauenbewegungen der Zwischenkriegszeit* [Women's politics and men's trade unionism: International gender politics, women IFTU-trade unionists and the workers' and women's movements of the interwar period]. Vienna: Löcker.

Zimmermann, Susan. 2020. "Framing Working Women's Rights Internationally: Contributions of the IFTU Women's International." In *The Internationalisation of the Labour Question*, edited by Stefano Bellucci and Holger Weiss, 95–117. London: Palgrave Mcmillan.

CHAPTER 7

Women's Activism, Vocational Training, and Cultural Exchanges between East and West

The Case of Cold War Italy (1948–1962)

Eloisa Betti

Abstract

Women's vocational training was a key topic in women's debates in Cold War Italy. Between the 1950s and 1960s, women started to mobilize around the reform of the secondary school system and vocational training schemes in order to create new opportunities for women workers in line with the new phase of industrial development. Women unionists, along with women MPs and officials of women's associations, played a crucial role in pushing for a less gender-stereotypical system of vocational and technical high schools as well. Drawing on archival material, conference proceedings, parliamentary speeches, and women's and union magazines, this chapter analyzes the role played by Italian women in pushing for a more inclusive and less stereotypical form of vocational training in Cold War Italy. It takes into consideration the period between 1945 and 1968, which saw widespread debate and mobilization around the issue of vocational training and which has never been properly investigated. The chapter connects different scales (local, national, and international) of political engagement, highlighting the circulation of ideas on vocational training in Cold War Europe. The relevance of the Italian case in the Cold War context is demonstrated by the different international actors, from both the West and the East, who participated in Italian conferences as well as the organization of international congresses in Italian cities.

Keywords

Cold War – cultural exchange – equal pay – equal remuneration – International Labour Organization (ILO) – International Association for Social Progress (IASP) – Italy – technical institute – vocational training – women's activism – women's right agenda

Women's vocational training was a key topic in women's debates and mobilization in Cold War Italy and in the Global Cold War due to its relevance

 | DOI:10.1163/9789004682481_008

in and beyond the blocs.[1] Women's associations and trade unions, together with philanthropic organizations, were active in promoting vocational training courses.[2] Nevertheless, in postwar Italy, such training was implemented in a very traditional manner as women were mainly trained as nurses, seamstresses, and maids, all highly feminized professions. Only between the 1950s and 1960s did women begin to mobilize in favor of reforms to the secondary school system as well as the vocational training scheme for adult women; they did so in order to create new opportunities for women workers in line with the industrial development that occurred during the so-called Italian economic miracle (1958–1963).[3] Women unionists along with women MPs and officials of women's associations played a crucial role in pushing for a less stereotyped system of vocational and technical high schools, inspired by the circulation of imaginaries and models related to socialist women workers especially prominent in the left-wing milieu.

The debate on women's vocational training in Cold War Italy was closely related to the ongoing mobilization around equal pay and the equal value of women's work, which has a transnational character, as revealed by recent studies.[4] The principles of equality between women and men as well as equal pay were written into the text of the Republican Constitution in 1948, which states that "a woman worker has the same rights and, for equal work, the same remuneration as a man" and recognized the right to vocational training.

In the first half of the 1950s, both equal pay and vocational training were discussed in congresses promoted by Italian women's associations such as the Union of Italian Women (Unione Donne Italiane, UDI); conferences devoted to women and women workers organized by political parties including the Italian Communist Party (Partito Comunista Italiano, PCI); and by trade unions like the Italian General Confederation of Labour (Confederazione Generale Italiana del Lavoro, CGIL). The three organizations shared a common agenda on women's rights that was advanced by activists and officials who were often involved in more than one of these organizations. Increasing the effectiveness

1 This contribution has been realized within the project "Genere, lavoro e cultura tecnica" [Gender, labour and technical culture] promoted by UDI of Bologna and supported by the Emilia-Romagna Region and Fondazione del Monte di Bologna e Ravenna. See https://generelavoroculturatecnica.it/. See, for instance, Laot 2022; Richards 2018.

2 See, for instance, Betti, Campigotto, and Grandi 2019; Cosmai 2017; Della Campa 2003.

3 Ginsborg 1990.

4 On equal pay in the Italian context, see Betti 2021 and 2018. On the equal pay struggle from an international perspective, see Neunsinger and Warrier 2019; Neunsinger 2018; Määttä 2008. On equal pay in Eastern Europe, see Zimmermann 2020.

of women's vocational training became a shared goal in left-wing organizations in the second half of the decade.

In 1959, the Committee of Female Associations for Equal Remuneration, established after the ratification of the ILO Convention no. 100, organized a conference wholly devoted to women's vocational training.[5] Several national and international speakers took the floor, including representatives of Italian women trade unionists and workers and officials of the Women's International Democratic Federation (WIDF).[6] A few years earlier, in 1956, Italy had hosted the Congress of the International Association for Social Progress (IASP), which approved—under the leadership of Marguerite Thibert and Margarita Schwarz-Gagg—a resolution on women's work that included vocational training and equal pay as key topics.[7]

Drawing on a number of archives, especially those of women's associations (e.g., UDI), conference proceedings on women's vocational training, parliamentary speeches, women's and union magazines (e.g., *Noi donne* [*We Women*]), this chapter analyzes the role played by Italian women, especially communists and socialists, in pushing for a more inclusive and less stereotypically gendered model of vocational training in Cold War Italy. In doing so, it will highlight how the Italian debate was shaped by the state-socialist model of women workers and women's vocational training from Eastern Europe and Soviet Union as portrayed in women's magazines. It focuses on the period between 1948 and 1962, during which there was significant debate and mobilization on women's vocational training but which has never been systematically studied. In March 1948, the National Congress for Female Vocational Education, promoted by the General Office for Technical Training of the Education Ministry,[8] marked the resumption of a debate that had its roots in the late nineteenth and early twentieth century.[9] After the inauguration of the new middle school model in 1962,[10] women's access to technical and technical-industrial institutes in particular was broadened within the scope of the more general development of mass schooling which occurred during the 1960s and 1970s.[11]

The chapter necessarily engages with different levels of analysis (local, national, and international), illuminating the circulation of ideas on women's

5 Società Umanitaria di Milano 1959.
6 On the history of WIDF, see De Haan 2012.
7 "Progetto di risoluzione sul lavoro delle donne," 123–124.
8 Ministry of Education 1948.
9 Soldani 1991.
10 Gaudio 2019.
11 Galfré 2017.

vocational training in Cold War Europe before 1965, when both the ILO and UNESCO recognized it as a priority.[12] In fact, different international actors from both the West and East participated in Italian conferences, and international congresses were held in Italian cities, providing the necessary foundation for this circulation. The Italian case also shows the role played by both national and international women's associations (UDI and WIDF) as well as by international organizations like the ILO and IASP in the vocational training debate.

The first section addresses vocational training and women's work in the Cold War imaginary, underscoring the distance between opposing models in postwar Italy. On the one hand, the traditional model of the female worker and gendered vocational training inherited from the Fascist regime was still in place; on the other hand, the model of Soviet women workers was being advanced by Italian communist women and left-wing women's magazines. The second section analyzes the debate on equal pay and vocational training in the 1950s, taking into account the conferences and congresses promoted by women's association and trade unions, with particular focus on the role played by international organizations such as WIDF. The third section reconstructs women's advocacy for more inclusive vocational training in the years known as economic miracle (1958–1963), focusing on major Italian conferences concerning women's work and training. The role of international organizations and trade unions such as the ILO, UNESCO, IASP, WFTU is explicitly explored in order to understand the connection between the local, national, and international dimensions of the debate on women's vocational training in Cold War Europe and beyond.

1 Vocational Training, Women's Work, and the Cold War Imaginary in Post-World War Two Italy

In the aftermath of World War Two, a nationwide debate was initiated on vocational training for women in Italy, as testified by the Convegno nazionale per l'istruzione professionale femminile (National Congress for Female Vocational Training), which was held in Florence in March 1948 and promoted by the General Secretariat for Technical Education of the Ministry of Public Education.[13] At that congress, the results of the questionnaires sent to the schools and other institutions and actors involved in women's vocational

12 Laot 2022.

13 Ministry of Education 1948.

training were discussed, along with the measures proposed by the ministry itself. In the years following the war, the structure of vocational training introduced by the Fascist regime was still in force;[14] it established two-year or three-year vocational training schools for women. In 1950, the curricula of these programs were still those ratified in 1936,[15] which proposed a traditional conception of a woman's role in the family, society, and the world of work that was in line with Fascist ideology.[16]

Home economics was still one of the cornerstones of the curricula of vocational schools for women. The theoretical lessons on the home and family wardrobe were combined with exercises related to proper cleaning, the management of crockery and cookware, laundry and ironing, managing and purchasing groceries, and, lastly, food preparation. The declared aim of these lessons and exercises was to "prepare the pupil to run the domestic company alone, following rational norms of economics and hygiene."[17] The syllabus was completed through activities deemed to be distinctively feminine tasks defined as "women's work": laundry, sewing, needlework, lacework, and lacemaking. The practical workshops completed at these schools were supposed to provide girls with the appropriate training to independently carry out at least two of the above tasks.

Girls' vocational teacher training schools and other related vocational schools for women were revamped only in the second half of the 1950s. Law no. 782, passed in 1956, transformed them into five-year technical institutes for women whose stated objective—"to be prepared for the exercise of the technical activities best suited to women"[18]—revealed a traditional conceptualization of women's roles, with home economics and female work (e.g., needlework) still the pillars of such schools. The diploma in "vocational qualification in women's technical activities" reiterated the same alleged difference between male and female technical applications.[19] The program of the girls' technical institutes bore a strong resemblance to girls' vocational institutes launched during the Fascist regime; one of the few innovations was represented by the

14 Bonafede and Causarano 2019, 219–254; Pironi 2019, 287–318.
15 *Orari e programmi della scuola professionale femminile* 1950.
16 De Grazia 1993.
17 *Orari e programmi della scuola professionale femminile* 1950.
18 Law passed on 8 July 1956, no. 782, "Trasformazione delle scuole di magistero professionale per la donna e delle annesse scuole professionali femminili in istituti tecnici femminili" [Transformation of professional schools for women and attached female vocational schools in female technical schools], *Gazzetta Ufficiale*, no. 192 dated 2 August 1956.
19 See De Maria 2021.

introduction of subjects like "social legislation and social services."[20] In the preface to the short volume drafted by the Ministry of Public Education on the technical institute for girls, the Minister for Education Giuseppe Medici nicely summed up the concept of female education prevalent among the leadership during postwar economic boom:

> However, it is not always easy to reconcile the new social function of the woman with the traditional tasks that placed her and still put her at the heart of family and domestic life. Finding the right balance between the two forms of activity is a very difficult task because it is a question of running a house and educating one's children—that is, holding together a family—and at the same time, if necessary, ultimately practicing a trade or a profession. The natural way to achieve this dual purpose is to develop as far as possible specifically female aptitudes on both the empirical level, through imitation, and on a technical level. This will facilitate both a more rational organization of family life and the application of the techniques acquired beyond the domestic sphere, in productive companies.[21]

This was not the only model of womanhood, women workers, and female vocational training circulating in postwar Italy. Foreign cultural models and practices, exchanges and networks with the Soviet Union and socialist Eastern European countries were, in fact, crucial for advancing a different, modern idea of women in Italy, one that was based on emancipation through paid work and equal rights.[22] Women were observers and promoters of such a model, which they reproduced both publicly and privately. At the same time, they espoused the imaginary of equality and the models of emancipation propagated by real socialism[23] that was reasserted in Italy by the Communist Party, the Union of Italian Women, and, to some extent, by the Italian General Confederation of Labour. The paradigm of the working mother, the main reference point for left-wing women influenced by the ideal of the communist/Soviet woman, was fortified and legitimized in Italy.[24]

20 Ministry of Education 1960.

21 The quotation has been translated for the purpose of this article from the original Italian appearing in Medici 1960, 5–6.

22 On networks and exchanges during the Cold War, see Babiracki and Zimmer 2014; Ilic 2011, 157–174; Autio, Humphreys, and Miklóssy 2010.

23 Navailh 1996.

24 See Betti 2020.

A number of Italian left-wing women had first-hand knowledge about women's lives on the other side of the Iron Curtain thanks to official trips to the Soviet Union and other communist countries in Eastern Europe. A continuous exchange of delegations was promoted by the Association Italy-USSR, and some women-only delegations were hosted by, for instance, the Soviet Women's Committee. This was the experience of UDI women in the mid-1950s. In 1954, more than twenty UDI women from all over Italy made a trip to the Soviet Union, visiting several cities including Moscow, St. Petersburg (formerly Petrograd, Leningrad), Volgograd (formerly Stalingrad), and Minsk, among others. During their trip, the Italian delegation had a chance to visit schools, nurseries, universities, as well as a car factory in Moscow, the summer camp of communist children's organization Pioneer, and a farm with agricultural workers in Georgia. From the perspective of the Soviet Union, the trip had a dual purpose: to show off Soviet modernity, and showcase the main Russian tourist attractions such as the Kremlin.[25]

"Women are everywhere," according to the memoirs published by members of the Italian delegation, a sentiment repeated in their correspondence and photographs dated 1954 (to be catalogued) in the UDI Archive of Bologna, which was probably rather impressive for a Italian woman in the 1950s. Soviet women were blue-collar workers in automobile factories, agricultural workers, and street cleaners, but they also held a leading position in highly sensitive sectors, such as the underground system in Moscow. The modernity of transportation, together with the health system, was highly regarded by Italian women, who considered these sectors to be highly advanced. The 1954 trip was neither the last nor probably the first of such trips, but it gave Italian women from UDI a taste of how Soviet women lived. Equality was surely one of the impressions that emerged from the writing of these women. Private accounts of the trip were much less rhetorical than the letter sent by UDI women to the Soviet Women's Committee, but Italian women were genuinely impressed by their encounter with the Eastern bloc.[26]

UDI was inspired by the Soviet emancipation model, especially in the so-called "Red Regions" such as Emilia-Romagna, which was locally governed by the Communist Party.[27] Nevertheless, in a Catholic country like Italy, the Soviet model had to be restyled, preserving the crucial role of the family and

25 "Note di viaggio dall'Unione Sovietica," [Travel notes from the Soviet Union] (to be catalogued), UDI Archive of Bologna.

26 Correspondence and photographs dated back to 1954 (to be catalogued), UDI Archive of Bologna.

27 On Soviet culture in the Emilia-Romagna Region, see also Fincardi 2007.

incorporating the reassuring model of the working mother as the ideal woman so as not to undermine the traditional basis of Italian culture and morality.[28] The communist press and the left-wing women's press, in publications such as *Noi Donne*, were the dedicated channel for promoting such models, publishing articles with pictures (both photographs and drawings) describing the Soviet Union as the "promised land" for workers and their families.[29]

In 1950, *Noi Donne* hosted the feature "Conversations on the Soviet Union," penned by Rita Montagnana. The communist leader and vice president of the WIDF answered readers' questions about the working and living conditions in the USSR, from trends in prices,[30] to children's education, and social services. One article, for example, was dedicated to the condition of Soviet maids, renamed "house workers," testifying to the rights attributed to them as full-fledged workers: from the working hours set at eight hours per day, to weekly rest-days and holidays.[31] It was emphasized that this type of work would soon be superseded by the use of electrical appliances commonly owned. Besides Rita Montagnana, other important communist leaders of UDI and the WIDF wrote reports on their journeys to the Soviet Union, turning their attention to the roles played by women in Soviet society. Maria Maddalena Rossi underlined that women made up 50 percent of the workforce of the Soviet railways, mentioning that the general director of the Moscow underground was a woman, Zinaida Trotskaia.[32] The Italian leader shed light on other ordinary women workers, but above all were women who had achieved high-level positions; among these was the vice president of the Anti-Fascist Committee of Soviet Women Zinaida Gagarina, who was not only a politician but also a scientist and the vice rector of the University of Moscow.

Other reports published in the journal addressed the female condition in both the Soviet Union and in other countries in Eastern Europe. Some testimonies published not only by women but also by men[33] in the magazine *Noi Donne* document that women constituted the majority of the labour force in some factories and were present all the way up the hierarchy to executive roles. It was stressed that in the USSR, equality was so deeply rooted that there were no doubts as to the "executive and managerial capacities of women." The profile of the factory manager emerged in the reports and in a specifically

28 See, for instance, Guerra 2000.
29 "Da un lato impetuoso sviluppo dall'altro continuo regresso" 1952.
30 Montagnana 1950a.
31 Montagnana 1950b.
32 Rossi 1950.
33 Pieraccini 1950.

dedicated column: a woman who started as an ordinary manual worker and had risen through the ranks to become a food engineer thanks to her studies and after having filled several management roles in other factories, had become the director of the Mikonian candy factory. The column stressed that this manager's path was not unique but rather served as an example for other workers who studied to become industrial technicians and engineers after they finished their workday. The theme of education was discussed in terms of gender stereotypes, and it was clear that education was women's springboard to management positions. The social and recreational structures adjacent to the factory, in particular nurseries, were not overlooked. In an effort to reassure Italian readers—both men and women—that "equal rights did not mean masculinization or fighting against the family," precisely the family and the role of "bride and mother" was explicitly identified as the foundation the Soviet system. Other "atypical" workers recalled in the reports were women stationmasters, tram drivers, policewomen, and company directors.

> Here we move to the matriarchy, one of our delegates said jokingly after coming across numerous women factory managers, executives, employees, and scientists in the Soviet Union. In actual fact, in no other country had gender equality become such a concrete and living reality as in the Soviet Union.[34]

2 The Debate on Equal Pay and Vocational Training at Conferences in the 1950s

Communist and socialist women belonging to UDI used these international models to assert local claims and to call for the advancement of rights for women in the working and social sphere despite their awareness that these very same models were idealized, as recent publications show.[35] In communist-led Bologna, for instance, the Declaration of Bolognese Women's Rights clearly addressed the issue of women's education and vocational training, promoting the creation of "a women's vocational skills center for unemployed young women and, across the Province, new vocational courses of various kinds (for sewing, dressmaking, ironing; for shops assistants, farmworkers, etc.)."[36] The issue of paid work was at the heart of both the Italian and international

34 Pieraccini 1950.
35 See, for instance, Ilic 2011.
36 Consiglio delle donne bolognesi 1953.

"Declaration of Women's Rights": the latter clearly states that education and vocational training were to be considered fundamental women's rights. The Italian document was ratified at the National Congress of Italian Women organized by UDI[37] in 1953 on the basis of the results of local congresses taking place across Italy, which were well attended by women workers.

The connection between the local, national, and international levels was relevant not only in the drafting of the document(s) but also in its worldwide promotion. Communist MP and high-ranking trade unionist Teresa Noce[38] publicly supported the international document, which the WIDF was trying to disseminate. UDI also played a key role in defining a national and, to some extent, global agenda for women's rights thanks to its affiliation to the Women's International Democratic Federation.[39] UDI was a key member of the federation itself, and several UDI women served as officials in its ranks, such as the communist MPs Rita Montagnana and Maria Maddalena Rossi; the former was the president of UDI, and the latter became vice president of the WIDF in the 1950s.[40] In 1951, Rina Picolato, UDI's representative at the WIDF, gave the executive committee of the WIDF in Bucharest[41] a well-documented account of the conditions of Italian women workers and the numerous battles promoted together with women's associations and trade unions, raising also the issue of vocational training in relation to equal pay. In 1953, Teresa Noce published an article on her participation in the 3rd Congress of the World Federation of Trade Unions, mentioning explicitly that she raised the issue of equal pay and providing information about the mobilization on the issue that she was leading in Italy.[42] Equal pay and vocational training were discussed jointly at two other two events in the mid-1950s.

The National Conference of Women's Workers held in Florence in January 1954 was another important venue for mobilization around the issue of women's vocational training. The 1954 conference put the battle for wage equality and the fight against exploitation at the center of CGIL's strategy for women workers. Across the whole of Italy, 20,000 preparatory assemblies for the National Conference of the Women Workers were held; of these gatherings, 4,000 were organized for labourers, 6,000 for sharecroppers, and over 10,000

37 "La voce di tutte" 1953.

38 On Teresa Noce, see Betti and Migliucci 2023.

39 De Haan 2012.

40 On Carmen Zanti, see Ledda 2018, 58–66; Nava and Ruggerini 1987.

41 XIII session of Executive Committee of the WIDF (Bucharest, July 18–20, 1952), box. 11, f. 50, Thematic Section "Donne nel mondo" [Women in the world], UDI National Archive.

42 Noce 1953.

for those belonging to other categories of workers. Over 1.5 million altogether participated in these assemblies.[43] In Bologna, in preparation for the national conference, the Costituente della Donna Lavoratrice Bolognese was held on 26 April 1953 and was chaired by Teresa Noce, among others. The improvement of women's working and living conditions and women's equality constituted the core themes, and there was a particular emphasis on the relationship between working conditions and social rights. At the end of the work period, the "Carta Costituente della donna lavoratrice bolognese" (Constituent Charter of the Working Woman of Bologna) was passed; it included these demands: the right to work, an increased standard of living, the need to fight against exploitation, wage equality, vocational training courses for young women, respect for the needs of women workers in the workplace; adequate old-age pensions; insurance against injuries and illnesses equal to that of men, access to all careers and professions, and proper protections for mothers and infant children.[44]

One year later, the Second Communist Women's Conference (Rome, 1955) affirmed the existence of a common women's rights agenda, while the importance of the role of UDI, CGIL, and the cooperative movement was declared a pillar of the project to emancipate women.[45] Although women workers were the main focus of the PCI's strategy, housewives were also mentioned explicitly, as in the second half of the 1950s, when the campaign "Pensions for Housewives" was launched. Equal pay was a key topic at the conference and was addressed by several delegates including Marisa Rodano, Ines Pisoni Cerlesi, and General Secretary of the Italian Communist Party Palmiro Togliatti himself. Pisone Cerlesi, a key figure in the mobilization for equal pay along with Teresa Noce and Marisa Rodano, explicitly mentioned the 1956 conference of the World Federation of Trade Unions, which was devoted to women workers and had placed the issue of equal pay at the top of its agenda.[46] The equal-pay principle was clearly stated in the final resolution of the conference together with the immediate goal of the reduction of the pay gap between men and women workers. The Communist Women's Conference held in Rome in October 1955 was preceded by an intense discussion and wide-ranging debate that led to some interesting developments among the women from Emilia-Romagna and Bologna in particular, who continued to expand on them within the scope of numerous branch conferences (*sezione*) and hundreds of local conferences (*cellula*). Many reports testified to the poor labour conditions of

43 CGIL 1954.
44 "Le rivendicazioni di tutte le lavoratrici" 1953; Noce 1953.
45 PCI 1956.
46 Pisoni Cerlesi in PCI 1956, 172–180.

women workers in the provinces. On the one hand, the elevated rates of female unemployment and the dismissal of thousands of workers following the demobilization of Italian factories in the postwar years was highlighted; on the other hand, the conditions in which the Bolognese women were forced to work were described, including aspects of precarity, disparate levels of exploitation, and discrimination that were widely reported in the concluding conference and effectively summarized in an article published in *La lotta* (*The Fight*).[47]

At the 1956 UDI Congress, the "right to work" was voiced by Italian women through the so-called "referendum on women's rights"; this referendum was launched by the association in preparation for the congress in order to better understand women's working and living conditions.[48] Maria Maddalena Rossi's speech clearly referenced the 1944 ILO Declaration of Philadelphia,[49] as evidenced by the relevance UDI attributed to the actions of international institutions, namely the International Labour Organization.[50] Demands related to women's work clearly emerged such as equal pay and the equal value of women farmworkers, access to all professions and jobs (including the judiciary, from which Italian women were still excluded in the late 1950s), the safeguarding of maternity and women's health, the fight against the dismissal of married women, unemployment and health insurance for every woman, and last but not least, pension rights for housewives. In the speech given by representatives of the Young Women's Commission of UDI, vocational training for girls and young women was clearly identified as a matter of concern. Not only was existing vocational training considered outdated; it was also regarded as discriminatory toward women because it was based on sex. Also addressed was the lack of vocational training schools in 785 of Italian municipalities with fewer than 3,000 inhabitants. These concerns were reinforced with data: "Between 1952 and 1953, 4,171 of these courses were delivered, with the participation of 185,000 pupils: of these, 60,000 were girls, most of whom attended commercial or handicraft courses; women's participation in agro-industrial courses was close to zero."[51] In the concluding speech delivered by Rosetta Longo, the

47 "La 2° Conferenza delle donne comuniste apre i suoi lavori sabato alla Farnese" 1955.

48 "Un grande referendum sui diritti della donna" 1956.

49 The 1944 Declaration of Philadelphia stated that "labour is not a commodity" and "freedom of association and of expression are essential to sustained progress." In addition, it extended the scope of the the ILO's work by affirming the centrality of human rights for all people: "all human beings, irrespective of race, creed or sex, have the right to pursue both their material well-being and their spiritual development in conditions of freedom and dignity, of economic security and equal opportunity." Maul 2019.

50 UDI 1956.

51 UDI 1956, 55.

general secretary of UDI, equal pay was clearly reinstated as one of the main priorities, along with structural reform of the school system to address the issue of women's vocational training. Several delegates of the women's association and branches from Eastern Europe were hosted (from Poland, Albania, Yugoslavia, the USSR, Czechoslovakia), demonstrating the exchanges between Italian women and their counterparts from state-socialist countries. President of the WIDF Eugénie Cotton took the floor to emphasize once more the close relationship between UDI and the WIDF, recalling the 1953 Declaration of Women's Rights.

3 Toward More Inclusive Vocational Training: Italian Women's Activism during the Economic Miracle

In the mid-1950s, the socio-economic and politico-cultural situation in Italy changed significantly. The industrial growth during the years of the so-called economic miracle (1958–1963) generated new employment opportunities for women, in particular younger women who entered the factories and offices of the industrial cities of the north and elsewhere *en masse*.[52] Together with the new visibility of women's work captured, for example, by the television documentary *La donna che lavora* (*The Working Woman*),[53] a renewed female leadership emerged in the mid-1950s and coalesced around the important battle for wage equality.[54] In addition to the UDI Congress, two significant events took place in 1956: the ratification of the ILO Convention no. 100 "Equal Remuneration for Male and Female Workers for Work of Equal Value" and the Congress of the International Association for Social Progress. The latter was held in Milan in March 1956; it was hosted by the Società Umanitaria (Humanitarian Society) of Milan and was partly dedicated to women's employment.[55]

The resolution of the Commission for Women's Labour, chaired by two experts on working women's problems—Margherite Thibert and Margarita Schwarz-Gagg[56]—effectively summarized some of the key elements of the national and international debate on technical and vocational training. The

52 Betti 2020; Betti 2010.

53 The documentary consisting of eight episodes was released in 1959 thanks to the contributions of journalist Ugo Zatterin and director Giovanni Salvi.

54 Betti 2018, 276–299.

55 "Progetto di risoluzione sul lavoro delle donne" 1957, 123–124.

56 On Margherite Thibert, see Thébaud 2017; on Margarita Schwarz-Gagg, see Mantilleri and Hervé 2005.

links between vocational training, wage equality, and the fair evaluation of women's work emerged in the discussion together with the need to professionalize women's work and give women equal access to managerial positions in order to adapt the company to the demands of the women workers and establish social services promoted by the public authorities. The national sections of the International Association for Social Progress were also called upon to conduct studies and exchange results by making them available to the International Labour Organization.

It was the Società Umanitaria of Milan, the headquarters of the Italian section of the IASP, and its president Riccardo Bauer that played a strategic role in creating research and discussion opportunities on the issues of wage equality and women's vocational training/education during the boom years. A few months after the Milan congress of the IASP, the ratification process of ILO Equal Remuneration Convention no. 100 was completed. Starting on 8 June 1956, Italy was on the list of countries that had ratified international norms concerning "equal remuneration for work of equal value." Recommendation no. 90, combined with Convention no. 100, explicitly referred to the importance of vocational training for the achievement of equal pay, highlighting the need for the equal training of workers of both sexes and adopting appropriate measures to facilitate women's vocational training.

In October 1957, a committee of eleven women's associations ranging from mass organizations that were part of the left-wing milieu like UDI, to associations like the Unione Femminile Nazionale (National Women's Union) of Milan, to religious and professional groups,[57] organized the congress "Retribuzione equale per un lavoro di valore uguale" (Equal Remuneration for Work of Equal Value). The congress was hosted and supported by the Società Umanitaria of Milan and addressed the political, economic, and legal implications of the ratification of ILO Convention no. 100 in Italy.[58] On this occasion, Leone Diena, the director of the Center for Social Studies of the Società Umanitaria, gave a lecture that dealt with women's vocational training[59] in relation to the goal of wage equality. Diena highlighted the complexity of the issue and the

57 The Conference was promoted by: Alleanza Femminile Italiana, Associazione Nazionale Donne Elettrici, Consiglio Nazionale delle Donne Italiane, Consociazione Nazionale Infermiere Professionali ed Assistenti Sanitarie, Federazione Italiana di Arti, Professioni e Affari (FIDAPA), Federazione Italiana Donne Giuriste, Federazione Italiana Laureate e Docenti Istituti Superiori (FILDIS), Unione Cristiana delle Giovani d'Italia (YWCA), Unione Donne Italiane (UDI), Unione Giuriste Italiane, Unione Femminile Nazionale di Milano.

58 On the Società Umanitaria di Milano, see Della Campa 2003; Colombo 2002.

59 Diena 1958, 177–204.

fragmented nature of the data available, stressing the challenges women faced when attempting to attain up-to-date professional qualifications, an issue closely related to the (in)adequacy of existing vocational schools.

The cooperation between women's associations that had begun with the ratification of Convention no. 100 did not conclude at the congress in 1957. As president of UDI—the association that played a pivotal role both in the organization of the congress mentioned above and in the battle for wage equality between the 1940s and 1950s[60]—Marisa Rodano officially proposed transforming the organizing committee of the congress into a permanent structure. In 1959, the Committee of Female Associations for Equal Remuneration under the patronage of the Società Umanitaria of Milan once again promoted a national congress specifically dedicated to the theme of women's vocational training.[61] The starting point was the assertion that the "search for better and greater professional qualifications would allow for a broader and more fruitful inclusion of women into productive activity and a just acknowledgment of women's work."[62] In the opening speech, Riccardo Bauer argued that women's vocational training was directly connected to the more general role of women in the labour and social sphere and influenced by the numerous, persistent, and widespread stereotypes and prejudices that would affect future women workers. Bauer critiqued the recent reform measures concerning vocational schools for women, which reiterated the concept of "typically female activities" in a context of profound technological transformation and industrial growth.

Statistician Nora Federici[63] provided important data for the discussion, highlighting how, by the late 1950s, "the low average level of education and the near-absolute exceptionality of adequate technical-vocational preparation undoubtedly constitute major obstacles to the broader and, above all, the more extensive participation of women in the economic life of the country." The actions to be undertaken, in her opinion, needed to include the reform of schools for both workers and the unemployed; such reforms must avoid confining women to traditional fields of female craftwork and address the needs of new generations of women workers/students. Economist Luciano Barca dealt with the more general relationship between women's employment, vocational training and professional development, highlighting the very diverse socio-economic conditions of Italian regions grouped in two main areas, namely the under-developed southern regions and the industrial-driven northern

60 UDI 1957.

61 Società Umanitaria di Milano 1959.

62 Dal Pozzo 1959.

63 Federici in Società Umanitaria di Milano 1959, 23–77.

regions.[64] According to Barca, increasing the qualifications of the female workforce could help reduce regional imbalances.[65]

Several teachers from vocational schools and professors from universities, along with trade unionists, economists, pedagogues, officials of women's associations, and government officials participated in the three-day conference. Among the topics discussed were the level of primary education and women's education; the need to respect compulsory schooling for everyone and in particular women; women's employment prospects; the school structure and nature of vocational training; proposals for vocational institutes and retraining courses; and wider reforms to technical and vocational education.[66] There were numerous discussions regarding women's vocational training in specific sectors: industry, agriculture, the tertiary sector. The theme of technological progress and the improvement of female qualifications resurfaced in many speeches and was dealt with directly by Ines Pisoni Cerlesi, who emphasized the need to improve women's vocational training by adapting it to the new boom economy and the professions that were emerging as a result.[67] As indicated by Pisoni Cerlesi's speech, unionists were crucial for an equal determination of wages and, ultimately, for the achievement of equal pay.

A detailed analysis of women's apprenticeships was made. In 1958, over 170,000 young women had been involved in this type of training and work, representing about 30 percent of the total apprentices. The speech by MP Giuseppina Palumbo, National Secretary of the Italian Federation of Garment Workers,[68] referenced more negatives than positives in the condition of apprentices during the boom years. The violation of the norms established by the law on apprenticeships no. 25 passed in 1955[69] was also a consequence of the lack of training content of the complementary teaching courses delivered to apprentices. Technical-practical traineeships called for a decisive improvement which, according to the unionist, should occur through a concerted effort on the part of unions. Palumbo also referenced the relationship between qualifications, training, and equal pay, arguing that in the case of apprentices, their relative youth often generated inequality in terms of an even greater pay differential.

64 Lutz 1958; Graziani 1962; Cafagna 1989.
65 Barca in Società Umanitaria di Milano 1959, 75–110.
66 Dal Pozzo 1959.
67 Pisoni Cerlesi in Società Umanitaria di Milano 1959, 394–405.
68 Palumbo in Società Umanitaria di Milano 1959, 387–393.
69 Zago 2016, 107–123.

At the congress, UDI presented the results of a large-scale study of women workers (employed in industry, agriculture, the public sector, commerce), unemployed women, and women searching for their first job. The talk given by Baldina Berti Di Vittorio of the National Secretariat of UDI[70] shed light on the methodology used: 240,000 copies of a questionnaire was distributed to girls aged between 14 and 21 and to adult and elderly women, both single and married. Overall, around 56,000 questionnaires were collected, representing twenty-four different Italian provinces. Of the submitted questionnaires, 6,450 were completed by adolescents 14 to 18 years of age, and 12,150 by girls between 18 to 21 years old; of the total 18,600 girls who submitted questionnaires, 2,130 were already married by the age of twenty-one (11 percent of the total). The schooling rates of girls were low according to the UDI survey: 67.1 percent of the girls had completed primary school, just 3.69 percent had finished middle school, and 12.9 percent had completed high school; 14 percent had not even finished primary school. Overall, 77.8 percent of the women examined in the study held no professional qualifications, while the few (12.8 percent) who had completed some vocational training reported that those courses were in dress-making, knitting, and handicrafts.[71]

At the center of the questionnaire was the topic of education and women's vocational training, but the questions also mapped out the familial status, employment situation, level of education, and, finally, the respondent's aspirations, desires, and opinions about the job. Berti Di Vittorio emphasized the need to reassert some of the key principles in the hoped-for reform of women's vocational training and education: the abolition of limits on women's access to training activities; the expansion of new training/work opportunities; the creation of a coordinating commission that would include representatives from unions and women's associations; and the consolidation and reform of the territorial consortia for technical and vocational education.

The 1959 conference clearly showed how the Italian discussion on women's vocational training fit into the broader global context. In his speech, engineer Marco Pantaleo referred to key national and international achievements of the 1950s, recalling the Conference on Public Education organized by the International Bureau of Education and UNESCO and held in Geneva in 1952. This conference focused in particular on recommendation no. 34, "Access of Women to Education,"[72] which represented a document of special significance because it not only asserted the general principle that "general education for

70 Berti Di Vittorio in Società Umanitaria di Milano 1959, 139–159.

71 Berti Di Vittorio 1959, 141–144.

72 Azara 2021.

girls should be equal in value and status to that for boys" but also provided a series of recommendations to the education ministers of participating countries intended to facilitate women and girls' access to education and vocational training. Thus, the relationship between the national and international levels of discussion at the 1959 conference also emerged in connection with UNESCO to the extent that resolution no. 34 was included in the conference proceedings.

The international situation was also inserted into the communications of the Women's International Democratic Federation, which underlined how the "profound transformations that occur in society and are reflected in the work of women requiring their upskilling, pose the urgent problem of vocational training of girls and women."[73] The 1959 Italian conference was regarded as a model by WIDF delegates as it showed the possibility of collaboration between different organizations and very different actors all united around the goal of ensuring that "laws and institutions allow women to exercise their right to education and vocational training." The communiqué of the WIDF representative expressed the relations between their organization and specific international organizations—first and foremost the ILO—active in these matters and committed to improving women's vocational training as well as equal pay claims. In this regard, the 1956 "Recommendations Concerning Vocational Training in Agriculture" was mentioned with respect to the topic of vocational training for women in agriculture.

The WIDF communiqué clearly expressed how the ILO Recommendation had in actual fact embraced the proposals on women's vocational training formulated at the WFTU World Conference on Women Workers held in Budapest in 1956. The WIDF also stated that it had underwritten the UNESCO report approved at the 12th Session of the UN Commission on the Status of Women in 1958. Lastly, the communiqué emphasized the role of education and vocational training within the broader emancipatory vision of the WIDF: "The WIDF has always considered the education and vocational training of women, without discrimination, to be one of the elements of women's emancipation. In the Charter of Women's Rights, passed by the Congress of Copenhagen in 1953, the WIDF placed vocational training among the fundamental rights of women."[74]

The 1962 conference marked an important step in the discussion of and mobilization around women's vocational training and women's work in general. From the institutional perspective, the theme of vocational training was reiterated by the "National Commission for Working Women." Established on

73 "Comunicazione della Federazione Democratica Internazionale delle donne" 1959, 367–373.

74 "Comunicazione della Federazione Democratica Internazionale delle donne" 1959, 369.

1 February 1962 by the Ministry of Employment and National Insurance,[75] and chaired by Riccardo Bauer (president of the Società Umanitaria of Milan), by statute the commission was supposed to deal with the orientation and vocational training of women; the placement and emigration of women workers; the regulation and protection of women's employment; and insurance and social care for particular groups of workers. It could also call for special inquiries and investigations.[76] The members of the commission and the respective institutions it was related to[77] sent reports to the commission that included remarks on the most critical aspects of women's employment. Both the Italian Confederation of Trade Unions (Confederazione Italiana Sindacati Lavoratori, CISL) and CISL stressed the importance of women's professional training with a view to achieve wage parity, employment stability and job guarantees.[78]

That same year, a single middle school was set up (law no. 1859 dated 31 December 1962) which would give graduates access to all secondary schools. This reform had an impact on vocational training schools and technical-industrial schools and ended up triggering a broader reorganization of vocational schools. This did not result in an instant change because until the end of the 1960s, the traditional role of the woman was emphasized in the regulations relating to training in technical applications, which were subdivided into male technical applications and female technical applications.[79] For women, dressmaking, embroidery, knitting, and home economics were core subjects. However, women's access to technical institutes, and to the technical-industrial

75 *La Commissione Nazionale per le donne lavoratrici presso il Ministero per il lavoro e la Previdenza Sociale, ha iniziato i suoi lavori*, [The National Commission for women workers at the Ministry for Labour and Social Security has begun its works] "Posta della Settimana" [Weekly post], 10–11 (1962), 5–9; box 7, f. 4, Thematic Section "Diritto al Lavoro" [The right to work], UDI National Archive.

76 Commissione nazionale per le donne lavoratrici, *Appunto per l'onorevole Ministro* [The National Commission for women workers, *Note to the Honorable Minister*] [1962], box 7, f. 4, Thematic Section "Diritto al Lavoro" [The right to work], UDI National Archive.

77 The president of the Commission was Riccardo Bauer, and the vice president was Maria Eletta Martini. The secretariat of the commission was set up in the Ministry for Labour and Social Security and was directed by Elena Gatti Caporaso. Cfr: Ministerial decree, *Nomina del presidente e dei componenti la Commissione nazionale per le donne lavoratrici* [Appointment of the president and the members of the national Commission for women workers], passed on 23 August 1962, published in the *Gazzetta Ufficiale* [Official gazette] no. 228 on 10 September 1962.

78 *Memorie presentate dai componenti la Commissione nazionale per le donne lavoratrici—Indicazioni in ordine ad un primo programma di lavoro della* Commissione [Memorandum presented by the members of the National Commission for women workers. Indications concerning an initial working programme of the Commission] [CISL], box 7, f. 4, Thematic Section "Diritto al Lavoro," [The right to work], UDI National Archive.

79 De Maria 2021.

institutes in particular, increased within the more general scope of the development of mass education that occurred in the 1960s.

It was precisely in a red region like Emilia-Romagna—characterized by forms of local communism and a process of industrialization in which women were present in significant numbers—where the issue of vocational training for women took on an important role in the public debate and in the actions of both women's associations and the local authorities. Vocational training had been addressed at the regional conference of the Emilian women workers promoted by the Emilia-Romagna UDI branches in 1962. The conference attendees welcomed the opening of the first courses for women chemists and electronics experts initiated by the Aldini-Valeriani technical institute in Bologna and held at the technical-vocational institute Elisabetta Sirani. At the same conference, the fact that most of the existing professional courses were still overly oriented toward "typically female" competencies was heavily criticized, and speakers declared their hope that reforms were in the offing.[80] A petition containing the main demands of the Emilian women workers was circulated at the conference.[81] Among these was the demand for equal pay for equal work and the reorganization of vocational education. After thousands of women in the region signed the petition, it was sent to the Ministry of Labour and the National Commission for Women Workers: no direct reply appears in the archives, however. In Emilia-Romagna, and specifically in Modena, the first electronics technician earned her diploma in 1963.[82]

80 UDI Regione Emiliana, *Parità, libertà, dignità sul luogo di lavoro, formazione professionale, servizi sociali, assistenza all'infanzia* [Equality, liberty, dignity in the workplace, vocational training, social services, childcare services] (Bologna, 14 October 1962) in particular: *Onorevole Marisa Rodano: conclusioni alla Conferenza regionale delle lavoratrici del 14-10-1962* [Marisa Rodano MP: conclusions to the regional conference of women workers], box. 3, f. 1962III, UDI Archive of Bologna.

81 UDI Regione Emiliana, *Parità, libertà, dignità sul luogo di lavoro, formazione professionale, servizi sociali, assistenza all'infanzia* [Equality, liberty, dignity in the workplace, vocational training, social services, childcare services] (Bologna, 14 October 1962) in particular: *Onorevole Marisa Rodano: conclusioni alla Conferenza regionale delle lavoratrici del 14-10-1962* [Marisa Rodano MP: Conclusions to the regional conference of women workers on 14.10.1962], box. 3, f. 1962III, UDI Archive of Bologna.

82 Ascari 1963.

4 Conclusion

This chapter demonstrates the relevance of the debate on women's vocational training in Cold War Italy in the first fifteen years following the establishment of the Italian Republican Constitution (1948–1962). Several conferences and congresses organized by women's associations, political parties, and trade unions, along with philanthropic associations, debated the intersection of women's work, equal pay, and vocational training. This chapter identifies three major periods: the postwar years (1948–1953), the mid-1950s (1954–1957), and the economic boom years (1958–1963). Whereas in the first period, vocational training and equal pay were discussed mainly at congresses promoted by women's associations and trade union organizations, during the second period, women's work and equal pay began to be discussed in ad hoc conferences thanks in part to the ratification of the 1951 ILO Equal Remuneration Convention no. 100. In the third period, due to the changes occurring in the Italian labour market, namely the increase in women's employment, the issue of women's vocational training became topical, and women began to mobilize in support of a less stereotypical and gender-oriented model of training.

Two subsequent conferences promoted by the Committee of Female Associations for Equal Remuneration and the Società Umanitaria of Milan held in 1957 and 1959, respectively, discussed the links between equal pay and vocational training in the debate as well as within the scope of women's activism. The struggle to implement the principle of equal remuneration for work of equal value in Italy led to a new awareness of the importance of improving women's vocational training, thereby overcoming the gender divide in professional education. In particular, the 1959 conference on women's vocational training displays the scope of the debate which involved teachers, university professors, trade unionists, economists, pedagogues, officials of women's associations, and government officials. Moreover, the 1959 conference revealed that the Italian discussion on women's vocational training was linked to broader international debates around the issue from two different perspectives. On the one hand, foreign delegations, especially those from Eastern bloc state-socialist countries and related organizations were hosted by Italian organizations; on the other hand, globally relevant documents concerning women's vocational training promoted by international organizations such as UNESCO were referenced and taken into account in Italy.

Bibliography

Ascari, Terenzio. 1963. "Prima in elettronica" [First in electronics]. *Noi Donne* [We women], 12 October 1963.

Associazione Internazionale per il Progresso Sociale. 1957. *Congresso Internazionale di Milano (24–27 marzo 1956)* [International Congress of Milan (24–27 March 1956)]. Milan: Giuffrè.

Autio, Sari, Brendan Humphreys, and Katalin Miklóssy, eds. 2010. *Winter Kept Us Warm: Cold War Interactions Reconsidered*. Helsinki: Aleksanteri Institute.

Azara, Liliosa. 2021. "Genere, istruzione e formazione nell'Unesco: diritti, politiche, prospettive" [Gender, education and training in UNESCO: Rights, policies, prospects]. In *Genere, lavoro e formazione professionale nell'Italia contemporanea* [Gender, work, and vocational training in contemporary Italy], edited by Eloisa Betti and Carlo De Maria, 253–279. Bologna: Bononia University Press.

Babiracki, Patryk, and Kenyon Zimmer, eds. 2014. *Cold War Crossings. International Travel and Exchange across the Soviet Bloc, 1940s–1960s*. Arlington: Texas A&M University Press, 2014.

Barca, Luciano. 1959. "Prospettive dell'occupazione, qualificazione femminile nell'attività economica italiana" [Prospects of employment, women's qualifications in Italian economic activity]. In *La preparazione professionale della donna. Atti del Convegno organizzato dal Comitato di associazioni femminili per la parità di retribuzione. Milano, 3–4–5 aprile 1959* [The professional preparation of the woman. Proceedings of the conference organized by the committee of women's associations for equal pay. Milan, 3–4–5 April 1959], edited by Società Umanitaria di Milano, 75–110. Florence: La Nuova Italia.

Berti Di Vittorio, Baldina. 1959. "Risultanze di un'inchiesta condotta dall'Unione Donne Italiane fra le lavoratrici e le giovani in cerca di prima occupazione" [Outcomes of a survey conducted by the Italian Union of Women among the women workers and young girls seeking their first job]. In *La preparazione professionale della donna. Atti del Convegno organizzato dal Comitato di associazioni femminili per la parità di retribuzione. Milano, 3–4–5 aprile 1959* [The professional preparation of the woman. Proceedings of the conference organized by the committee of women's associations for equal pay. Milan, 3–4–5 April 1959], edited by Società Umanitaria di Milano, 139–159. Florence: La Nuova Italia.

Betti, Eloisa. 2020. *Le ombre del fordismo. Sviluppo industriale, occupazione femminile e precarietà del lavoro nel trentennio glorioso (Bologna, Emilia-Romagna, Italia)* [The Shadows of Fordism, industrial development, female employment and precarity of employment in the glorious thirty-year period (Bologna, Emilia-Romagna, Italia)]. Bologna: Bononia University Press.

Betti, Eloisa. 2018. "Unexpected Alliances: Italian Women's Struggles for Equal Pay, 1940s–1960s." In *Women's ILO: Transnational Networks, Global Labour Standards and Gender Equity, 1919 to Present*, edited by Eileen Boris, Dorothea Hoehtker, and Susan Zimmermann, 276–299. Leiden: Brill.

Betti, Eloisa. 2010. "Il lavoro femminile nell'industria italiana. Gli anni del boom economico" [Women's work in Italian industry. The economic boom years]. *Storicamente* [Historically], no. 6: https://storicamente.org/lavoro_femminile_donne.

Betti, Eloisa, and Debora Migliucci. 2023 "Teresa Noce (1900–1980): A Communist 'Professional Revolutionary' in 20th-Century Italy." In *The Palgrave Handbook of Communist Women Activists around the World*, edited by Francisca de Haan. London: Palgrave Macmillan.

Betti, Eloisa, and Carlo De Maria, eds. 2021. *Genere, lavoro e formazione professionale nell'Italia contemporanea* [Gender, work and vocational training in contemporary Italy]. Bologna: Bononia University Press.

Betti, Eloisa, Antonio Campigotto, and Maura Grandi, eds. 2019. *Formazione professionale, lavoro femminile e industria a Bologna (1946–1970)* [Vocational training, women's work and industry in Bologna]. Bologna: Bononia University Press.

Bonafede, Paolo, and Pietro Causarano. 2019. "Istruzione tecnica e formazione professionale" [Technical education and vocational training]. In *Manuale di storia della scuola italiana. Dal Risorgimento al XXI secolo* [Textbook of the history of the Italian school: From the Risorgimento to the 21st century], edited by Fulvio De Giorgi, Angelo Gaudio, and Fabio Pruneri, 219–254. Brescia: Morcelliana-Scholé.

Cafagna, Luciano. 1989. *Dualismo e sviluppo nella storia d'Italia* [Dualism and development in the history of Italy]. Venice: Marsilio.

CGIL. 1954. *L'emancipazione delle lavoratrici italiane. Atti della Conferenza nazionale della donna lavoratrice. Firenze 23–24 gennaio 1954* [The emancipation of Italian women workers. Proceedings of the national conference of the woman worker. Florence, 23–24 January 1954]. Florence: CGIL.

Colombo, Arturo, ed. 2002. *Il coraggio di cambiare. L'esempio di Riccardo Bauer* [The courage to change. The example of Riccardo Bauer]. Milan: Franco Angeli.

"Comunicazione della Federazione Democratica Internazionale delle donne." 1959. In *La preparazione professionale della donna. Atti del Convegno organizzato dal Comitato di associazioni femminili per la parità di retribuzione. Milano, 3–4–5 aprile 1959* [The professional preparation of the woman. Proceedings of the conference organized by the committee of women's associations for equal pay. Milan, 3–4–5 April 1959], edited by Società Umanitaria di Milano, 367–373. Florence: La Nuova Italia.

Consiglio delle donne bolognesi. 1953. *Carta dei diritti delle donne bolognesi* [Bolognese women's Charter of Rights]. Bologna: Steb.

Cosmai, Franca. 2017. "L'Unione Donne Italiane e il Centro Italiano Femminile dalla Resistenza agli anni Sessanta tra centro e periferia (1943–1964)" [The Union of Italian Women and the Italian Women's Centre from the Resistance to the 1960s, between center and periphery 1943–1964]. PhD dissertation, Università degli studi di Padova.

"Da un lato impetuoso sviluppo dall'altro continuo regresso" [On one side impetuous growth, on the other, regression]. 1952. *La Lotta* [The fight], 7 March 1952.

Dal Pozzo, Giuliana. 1959. "La scuola alleata del lavoro" [School an ally of work]. *Noi Donne* [We women], 19 April 1959.

Della Campa, Massimo, ed. 2003. *Il modello Umanitaria* [The humanitarian model]. Milan: Edizioni Raccolto-Umanitaria.

Diena, Leone. 1958. "La preparazione professionale della Donna" [Women's vocational preparation]. In *Retribuzione eguale per un lavoro di valore eguale. Atti del convegno di studio svoltosi nel Salone degli Affreschi dal 4 al 6 ottobre 1957* [Equal pay for work of equal value. Proceedings of the study conference held in the Salone degli Affreschi from 4 to 6 October 1957], edited by Società Umanitaria, 177–204. Milan: Giuffré.

Federici, Nora. 1959. "Situazione della istruzione generale e professionale della donna in relazione all'occupazione femminile" [Situation of women's general and vocational education in relation to female employment]. In *La preparazione professionale della donna. Atti del Convegno organizzato dal Comitato di associazioni femminili per la parità di retribuzione. Milano, 3–4–5 aprile 1959* [The professional preparation of the woman. Proceedings of the conference organized by the committee of women's associations for equal pay. Milan, 3–4–5 April 1959], edited by Società Umanitaria di Milano, 23–77. Florence: La Nuova Italia.

Fincardi, Marco. 2007. *C'era una volta il mondo nuovo. La metafora sovietica nello sviluppo emiliano* [There once was the new world. The Soviet metaphor in Emilian development]. Rome: Carocci.

Galfrè, Monica. 2017. *Tutti a scuola! L'istruzione nell'Italia del Novecento* [All off to school! Education in twentieth-century Italy]. Milan: Carocci.

Ginsborg, Paul. 1990. *A History of Contemporary Italy. Society and Politics, 1943–1988.* London: Penguin books.

De Giorgi, Fulvio, Angelo Gaudio, and Fabio Pruneri, eds. 2019. *Manuale di storia della scuola italiana. Dal Risorgimento al XXI* secolo [Handbook of the history of Italian schools: From the Risorgimento to the 21st century]. Brescia: Morcelliana-Scholé.

De Grazia, Victoria. 1993. *How Fascism Ruled Women: Italy, 1922–1945*. Berkeley: University of California Press.

Graziani, Augusto. 1963. "Dualismo e sottosviluppo nell'economia italiana" [Dualism and underdevelopment in the Italian economy]. *Nord e Sud* [North and south], no. 38: 24–32.

Graziani, Augusto. 1962. "Dualismo e sottosviluppo nell'economia italiana" [Dualism and underdevelopment in the Italian economy]. *Nord e Sud* [North and south], no. 2.

Guerra, Elda. 2000. "Soggettività individuale e modelli del femminile: il desiderio della politica" [Individual subjectivity and female models]. In *Donne, guerra, politica. Esperienze e memorie della resistenza* [Women, war, politics. Experiences and memories of the resistance], edited by Dianella Gagliani, Elda Guerra, and Fiorenza Tarozzi, 169–189. Bologna: Clueb.

De Haan, Francisca. 2012. "The Women's International Democratic Federation (WIDF): History, Main Agenda and Contributions (1945–1991)." In *Women and Social Movements (WASI) Online Archive*, edited by Thomas Dublin and Kathryn Kish Sklar. Alexandria, VA: Alexander Street. http://alexanderstreet.com/products/women-and-social-movements-international.

Ilic, Melanie. 2011. "Soviet Women, Cultural Exchange and the Women's International Democratic Federation." In *Reassessing Cold War Europe*, edited by Sari Autio-Sarasmo and Katalin Miklóssy, 157–174. Oxon: Routledge.

"La 2° Conferenza delle donne comuniste apre i suoi lavori sabato alla Farnese" [The second Communist Women's Conference begins its work on Saturday at the Farnese]. 1955. *La Lotta* [The fight], 30 September 1955.

Laot, Françoise F. 2022. "French Trade Unionists Go International: The Circulation of Ideas about Women Workers' Education and Training in the 1950s and 1960s." In *Women, Work, and Activism. Contributions to an Inclusive History of Labor in the Long Twentieth Century*, edited by Eloisa Betti, Leda Papastefanaki, Marica Tolomelli, and Susan Zimmermann. Budapest: Central European University Press.

"Le rivendicazioni di tutte le lavoratrici esposte dalla compagna Teresa Noce" [Demands for all women workers expressed by Comrade Teresa Noce]. 1953. *L'Unità. Cronaca di Bologna* [The Unit. Chronicle of Bologna], 27 April 1953.

Ledda, Rachele. 2018. "'Sorelle in un'altra terra'. Carmen Zanti tra internazionalismo, pace e diritti delle donne" [Sisters in another land. Carmen Zanti between internationalism, peace and women's rights]. In *Biografie, percorsi e networks nell'Età contemporanea. Un approccio transnazionale tra ricerca, didattica e Public History* [Biographies, paths and networks in the contemporary age. A transnational approach between research, teaching and public history], edited by Eloisa Betti and Carlo De Maria, 53–66. Rome: Bradypus.

Lutz, Vera. 1958. "The Growth Process in a Dual Economic System." In *Banca Nazionale del lavoro Quarterly Review* [National Labour Bank quarterly review] 9: 279–324.

Määttä, Paula. 2008. *The ILO Principle of Equal Pay and Its Implementation.* Tampere: Tampere University Press.

Mantilleri, Brigitte, and Florence Hervé. 2005. *Histoires et visages de femmes* [Stories and faces of women]. Yens sur Morges: Editions Cabédita.

De Maria, Carlo. 2021. "Presenze e assenze: donne e istruzione tecnico-professionale dall'Unità alla seconda metà del Novecento" [Presence and absences: Women and technical-vocational education from unification to the late twentieth-century]. In *Genere, lavoro e formazione professionale nell'Italia contemporanea* [Gender, work and vocational training in contemporary Italy], edited by Eloisa Betti and Carlo De Maria, 27–52. Bologna: Bononia University Press.

Maul, Daniel. 2019. *The International Labour Organization: 100 years of Global Social Policy*. Berlin: DeGruyter.

Medici, Giuseppe. 1960. "Prefazione" [Preface]. In *L'Istituto Tecnico femminile. Caratteristiche, orari, programmi* [The Women's Technical Institute. Features, timetables, programs], edited by Ministero della Pubblica Istruzione. Florence: Tip. E. Ariani e L'arte della stampa.

Ministerial decree. 1962. *Nomina del presidente e dei componenti la Commissione nazionale per le donne lavoratrici* [Nomination of the President and Members of the National Commission for Women Workers]. Passed on 23 August 1962. *Gazzetta Ufficiale*, no. 228 (10 September).

Ministry of Education, Direzione generale per l'Istruzione tecnica. 1948. *Atti del Convegno nazionale per l'istruzione professionale femminile (Florence, 4–8 March 1948)* [Proceedings of the National Congress for Women's Vocational Education]. Turin: Giuseppe Vigliardi Paravia.

Ministry of Education, Ministero della Pubblica Istruzione. 1960. *L'Istituto Tecnico femminile. Caratteristiche, orari, programmi* [The Women's Technical Institute. Features, timetables, programs]. Florence: Tip. E. Ariani e L'arte della stampa.

Montagnana, Rita. 1950a. "Colloqui sull'Unione Sovietica" [Conversations on the Soviet Union]. *Noi Donne* [We women], 10 December 1950°.

Montagnana, Rita. 1950b. "Colloqui sull'Unione Sovietica" [Conversations on the Soviet Union]. *Noi Donne* [We women], 31 December 1950.

Nava, Paola, and Maria Grazia Ruggerini. 1987. *Carmen Zanti. Una biografia femminile* [Carmen Zanti: A woman's biography]. Cavriago: Comune di Cavriago.

Navailh, Francoise. 1996. "The Soviet Model." In *History of Women in the West*. Vol. 5, *Toward a Cultural Identity in the Twentieth Century*, edited by Françoise Thébaud, 226–259, Cambridge, MA: Harvard University Press.

Neunsinger, Silke. 2018. "The Unobtainable Magic of Numbers: Equal Remuneration, the ILO and the International Trade Union Movement 1950s–1980s." In *Women's ILO. Transnational Networks, Global Labour Standards, and Gender Equity, 1919 to Present*, edited by Eileen Boris, Dorothea Hoehtker, and Susan Zimmermann, 121–148. Leiden: Brill.

Neusinger, Silke, and Shoblana M. V. Warrier. 2019. "Transnational Activism and Equal Remuneration in India During the Twentieth Century." In *The Internationalisation of the Labour Question. Ideological Antagonism, Workers' Movements and the ILO since 1919*, edited by Stefano Bellucci and Holger Weiss, 329–350. London: Palgrave Macmillan.

Noce, Teresa. 1953. "A uguale lavoro-uguale salario. Garantire alla donna tutte le carriere sociali" [Equal work, equal pay. Guaranteeing all social careers to women]. *La Voce dei Lavoratori* [The voice of the worker], 1 May 1953.

Orari e programmi della scuola professionale femminile e della scuola di magistero professionale per la donna [Schedules and syllabi of women's vocational schooling and teacher-training for women]. 1950. Milan: L. di G. Pirola.

Palumbo, Giuseppina. 1959. "La situazione dell'apprendistato femminile in Italia" [The situation of female apprenticeships in Italy]. In *La preparazione professionale della donna. Atti del Convegno organizzato dal Comitato di associazioni femminili per la parità di retribuzione. Milano, 3–4–5 aprile 1959* [The professional preparation of the woman. Proceedings of the conference organized by the committee of women's associations for equal pay. Milan, 3–4–5 April 1959], edited by Società Umanitaria di Milano, 387–393. Florence: La Nuova Italia.

Parca, Gabriella. 1953. "La voce di tutte" [The voice of all women]. *Noi Donne* [We women], 12 April 1953.

PCI. 1956. *Seconda Conferenza nazionale delle donne comuniste. Documenti e risoluzioni. (Roma, 20–23 ottobre 1955)* [Second National Congress of Communist Women. Documents and Resolutions. Rome 20–23 October 1955]. Rome: La Stampa moderna.

Pieraccini, Giovanni. 1950. "140 tonnellate di caramelle" [140 tons of candies]. *Noi Donne* [We women].

Pironi, Tiziana. 2019. "Le donne a scuola" [Women at school]. In *Manuale di storia della scuola italiana. Dal Risorgimento al XXI secolo* [Textbook of the history of the Italian school. From the Risorgimento to the 21st century], edited by Fulvio De Giorgi, Angelo Gaudio, and Fabio Pruneri, 287–318. Brescia: Scholé.

Pisoni Cerlesi, Ines. 1959. "Il valore del lavoro femminile nel settore industriale e necessità dell'adeguamento della preparazione professionale femminile al progresso tecnologico" [The value of female work in the industrial sector and the need to adapt female professional training to technological progress]. In *La preparazione professionale della donna. Atti del Convegno organizzato dal Comitato di associazioni femminili per la parità di retribuzione. Milano, 3–4–5 aprile 1959* [The professional preparation of the woman. Proceedings of the conference organized by the committee of women's associations for equal pay. Milan, 3–4–5 April 1959], edited by Società Umanitaria di Milano, 394–405. Florence: La Nuova Italia.

Pisoni Cerlesi, Ines. 1956. "Ines Pisoni della Commissione femminile della CGIL" [Ines Pisoni from the Female Commission of the CGIL]. *Seconda Conferenza nazionale delle donne comuniste. Documenti e risoluzioni. (Roma, 20–23 ottobre 1955)* [Second National Conference of Communist Women. Documents and resolutions. (Rome, 20–23 October 1955)], PCI, 172–180. Rome: La Stampa moderna.

"Progetto di risoluzione sul lavoro delle donne" [Draft resolution on women workers]. 1957. In *Congresso Internazionale di Milano (24–27 marzo 1956)* [Milan International Congress (March 24–27, 1956)], edited by Associazione Internazionale per il Progresso Sociale, 123–124. Milan: Giuffrè.

Richards, Yevette. 2018. "Transnational Links and Constraints: Women's Work, the ILO and the ICFTU in Africa, 1950s–1980s." In *Women's ILO. Transnational Networks, Global Labour Standards, and Gender Equity, 1919 to Present*, edited by Eileen Boris, Dorothea Hoehtker, and Susan Zimmermann, 121–148. Leiden: Brill.

Rossi, Maria Maddalena. 1950. "Note da un taccuino di viaggio" [Note from a travel diary]. *Noi Donne* [We women].

Società Umanitaria di Milano. 1959. *La preparazione professionale della donna. Atti del Convegno organizzato dal Comitato di associazioni femminili per la parità di retribuzione. Milano, 3–4–5 aprile 1959* [Women's vocational training. Proceedings of the congress organized by the Female Associations for Equal Pay. Milan 3–4–5 April 1959]. Florence: La Nuova Italia.

Soldani, Simonetta. 1991. "The Construction of a New Feminine Identity in Italy through the School from the Unification to Fascism." In *Education and the Construction of Gender*: 26–40.

Thébaud, Françoise. 2017. *Une traversée du siècle. Marguerite Thibert, femme engagée et fonctionnaire international* [Across the century. Marguerite Thibert, a committed woman and international civil servant]. Paris: Belin.

UDI. 1957. *La voce della Donna* [The woman's voice]. 1 March 1957.

UDI. 1956. *Atti del V Congresso della donna italiana (Roma, 12–15 aprile 1956)* [Proceedings of the 5th Congress of Italian Woman]. Rome: n. p.

"Un grande referendum sui diritti della donna" [A great referendum on women's rights]. 1956. *Noi Donne* [We women], 29 January 1956.

Zago, Giuseppe. 2016. "La riforma dell'apprendistato nell'Italia della ricostruzione: fra politica, economia e pedagogia" [The reform of apprenticeships in Italy during the Reconstruction era: Between politics, economics and pedagogy]. *Rivista di storia dell'educazione* [Educational history magazine] 1: 107–123.

Zatterin, Ugo, and Giovanni Salvi. 1959. *La donna che lavora* [The working woman]. Rai Italia. https://www.raiplay.it/programmi/ladonnachelavora.

Zimmermann, Susan. 2020. "'It Shall Not Be a Written Gift, but a Lived Reality': Equal Pay, Women's Work, and the Politics of Labor in State-Socialist Hungary, Late 1960s to Late 1970s." In *Labor in State-Socialist Europe, 1945–1989: Contributions to a History of Work*, edited by Marsha Siefert, 337–372. Budapest: Central European University Press.

CHAPTER 8

"Long Live Our Father"

The Culture of Solidarity, Kinship, and Marriage in Labour Unions, 1964–1965

Büşra Satı

Abstract

In the winter of 1964, the workers of the Berec Battery Factory in Turkey, most of whom were women from rural areas of the country or migrants from the Balkans, initiated a strike under the leadership of the Petroleum, Chemical and Rubber Industry Workers' Union of Turkey (Türkiye Petrol Kimya Lastik İşçileri Sendikası, Petrol-İş). Through relations and acts of kinship, workers and union delegates forged a culture of solidarity and co-constructed the labour union as a family. Working-class women engaged with labour activism within this framework of family and kinship. Women's labour activism in Turkey has not received adequate attention from labour historians or feminist scholars. By analyzing the discursive and material practices of union leadership, employers, and workers during the Berec strike, the chapter explores a different dimension of women's activism by focusing on labour women's experiences. It argues that during the 1960s, participation in labour unions became an effective mechanism to unite the family and labour-based identities of working-class women who were torn between the demands of wage labour and the desire to start or maintain families. Utilizing the publications of Petrol-İş, labour newspapers, and magazines documenting the strike, the chapter foregrounds the familial relationship between workers and labour unions, paying particular attention to women workers.

Keywords

Berec – Petroleum, Chemical and Rubber Industry Workers' Union of Turkey (Türkiye Petrol Kimya Lastik İşçileri Sendikası, Petrol-İş) – family – kinship – labour unions – marriage – petroleum – solidarity – strike

"The moment Ziya Hepbir stepped into the room, he was lifted onto the shoulders of male workers. Women were crying, and girls were clapping until their palms hurt, cheering 'long live our father!' The historical leader of the historical

 | DOI:10.1163/9789004682481_009

strike was floated to the stage."[1] These were the words Özkal Yici, the deputy general secretary of Türkiye Petrol Kimya Lastik İşçileri Sendikası (Petroleum, Chemical, and Rubber Industry Workers' Union of Turkey, hereafter Petrol-İş), used to describe the atmosphere after Petrol-İş announced the end of the Berec Strike because the union and Berec management had finally come to agreement on a new contract. It remains unclear to what extent Yici's gendered narration accurately represents how workers actually expressed their joy and celebrated the day. More remarkable in this description is that workers, specifically girls, called the union leader Ziya Hepbir "father." Why would workers think of a union leader as a father? What does this form of addressing a union delegate imply about the relations of labour, family, and gender in the context of Turkish labour activism?

The analogy of family relations in Petrol-İş provides clues as to how union bureaucracy and working-class communities in Turkey conceptualized trade unionism during the 1960s. The understanding of union activism within the framework of family and kinship is an essential but overlooked aspect of unionism in Turkey. While many scholars have noted the ubiquity of kinship networks in the organization of Turkish economic life, they have often focused on recruitment practices in industry and the ways kinship ties disguised exploitation at the workplace.[2] Other scholars have explored the role of kinship through migrant solidarity networks in community formation in the public and private spheres through the organization of squatter neighborhoods, *hemşehri* (those from the same village or region) associations, and other informal practices.[3] Scholars have thus shown that both the industrial workplace and migrant solidarity networks were shaped by kinship relations. Yet, even though labour unions operated at the intersection of these two spheres as they predominantly targeted migrant labourers employed in industrial workplaces, they have not been conceptualized as organizations where kinship had any significant influence.

Attention to labour solidarity characterized by specific discourses and practices during the 1960s can expand our understanding of the connection between kinship networks and labour organizations. An analysis of the Berec strike shows that utilizing diverse practices, trade union officials formed fictive kinship ties with workers. Although these relations of kinship were significant for all workers, they prove especially useful for highlighting women's labour activism in Turkey. Analyzing family as a central tenet of labour politics

1 Yici 2010, 112.
2 White 2004, 2000; Nichols, Sugur, and Sugur 2003; Dubetsky 1976.
3 Mura 2021; Erder 2003; Erman 1996.

refines our understanding of the unique contours of women's trade unionism in Turkey.

This chapter explores the culture of solidarity in Turkish labour unions during the mid-1960s, focusing on the history of a women's strike organized by Petrol-İş in the Berec Battery Factory located in Istanbul. Shortly after Petrol-İş organized workers in the Berec Battery Factory, workers, most of whom were women, went on strike asking for salary increases and employment benefits. After forty-one days of striking, Petrol-İş signed a collective agreement in January 1965 that secured higher wages and more comprehensive benefits for all workers. Analyzing the Berec strike not only highlights women's labour activism in Turkey but also foregrounds the role of kinship-based networks of solidarity in collective labour action.

By analyzing Petrol-İş publications that documented the strike and labour newspapers and magazines from the period, I explore the discursive and material practices of union leadership, employers, and workers during the strike. Drawing on scholarship concerning the anthropology of labour, such as Lazar, Leviestad, Kepesea and Mcnamara, and Soul, I argue that during the 1960s, labour unions in Turkey operated as extensions of kinship networks.[4] Through an analysis of gender relations and the reproductive realm, I show that kinship ties, both actual and fictitious, formed the basis of solidarity during the strike. Attention to these relations may enhance our understanding of women's labour activism in Turkey.

The Berec strike shows that women workers' collective action was motivated by the conflicting demands of industrial work and their family lives. Women workers strategically used the kin-like relations they had developed with labour union leaders to carve out a space for themselves within the patriarchal structures of labour and public life. The relations and discourse of kinship helped ease women workers' interactions with otherwise strangers and justified their visibility in the public space as sisters, daughters, and wives of male workers. Specifically, the act of marriage during the strike helped women acquire respect, dignity, and virtue, which were often denied to women from rural backgrounds who had to engage in work for wages.

The contribution of this chapter is twofold. First, it contributes to the historiography of women's labour in Turkey by recuperating a moment of successful labour organizing by women. Women's trade unionism in Turkey before the 1980s has been overlooked by both labour historians and feminist scholars. An analysis of the Berec strike demonstrates how labour activism went beyond

4 Leivestad 2021; Kapesea and McNamara 2020; Soul 2020; Lazar 2018.

the factory floor and spilled into the household, neighborhood, and community; thus, working-class women participated in labour activism as workers, wives, mothers, and daughters.

Second, this chapter contributes to the flourishing scholarship on the prevalence of kinship in labour unions by developing an analysis that accounts for gender and reproductive labour. Conceptualizing kinship as a relationship constituted through acts,[5] I discuss various acts of kinship performed by workers, their families, and union officials in the course of the Berec strike. I highlight working-class marriage as a key focal point for union officials and workers, using multiple examples that show the collision of marriage and labour union activism. Focusing on family and marriage-related issues that took place during the Berec strike, this article examines a unique feature of Turkish trade unionism that has not been explored.

An analysis of the Berec strike emphasizes the dialectical relationship between kinship ties and labour politics in Turkey. During the 1960s, labour politics was not limited to the shopfloor or the public sphere. Indeed, as a result of relations within the family, labour activism entered the household. Working-class identity and culture were transferred from one generation to the next through practices of kinship. Women and children were radicalized as family members because the demands of industrial capitalism disrupted the gendered order of the household. Concurrently, workers extended kinship relations into the factory and on the picket line, re-making family relations in the public sphere. Through the help of union officials, working-class women elevated their status from "factory girls" to respectable members of a large union family.

Labour unions became an effective mechanism for uniting family and labour-based identities through fictive kinship ties between union officials and workers; in other words, productive and reproductive labour converged, and the family was transformed into an institution that produced labour activism while the factory was reconfigured as a space for cultivating kinship bonds. Even though labour activism has historically been a part of households across the world, this situation was heightened in the Turkish context, where rapid urbanization and the lack of social protections by the state strengthened family and community ties.

In the first part of the chapter, I provide the historical context and a conceptual framework to understand the fundamental conditions underlying the extensive use of kinship terms and practices by workers and trade unionists

5 Lambek 2013, 2011.

in Turkey. The second section discusses the history of the Berec strike and the composition of the workers who went on strike. Utilizing interviews conducted with workers for a magazine article, I examine the testimonies of women workers to understand the sources of their mobilization. These interviews provide insight into women's lives, desires, and challenges beyond the workplace and bring marriage, family, and reproductive labour issues to the fore. In the third section, employing Lambek's concept of acts of kinship, I discuss marriage and other kinship practices performed by workers and labour union officials, highlighting their importance for working-class women. Finally, I discuss the limits of labour politics structured around kinship, pointing out the tensions that arose during and after the strike. Because I rely on union publications and pro-labour magazines to reconstruct the history of the Berec strike, it is challenging to highlight workers' points of view concerning the effectiveness of Petrol-İş in improving their work and household lives. Despite this limitation, I conclude by raising several issues that point to conflicts between workers and Petrol-İş.

1 Conceptualizing Labour Unions as Family

Against the assertion that kinship lost its significance with the emergence of modernity, current anthropological research demonstrates the persistence of kinship in modern capitalist societies.[6] Scholars have shown that kinship continues to play a decisive role in the organization of economic relations, even under neoliberal conditions. Similarly, a fruitful line of research has emerged within the scholarship on the anthropology of labour, which focuses on the intimate relationship between kinship and labour unions. Scholars argue that kinship networks shape labour unions and, relatedly, labour activism. As Kapesea and McNamara argue, in this understanding, collective action "represents a flow from kinship into politics, rather than vice versa, with political action inspired by personal relationships and obligations."[7] In other words, how workers and unionists relate to each other is influenced and shaped by their current understanding of personal relationships within the family, community, and workplace.

Scholars have demonstrated how values, morality, and mutual obligations derived from kinship define workers' collective identity—as expressed through

6 Lambek 2013; McKinnon and Cannell 2013.

7 Kapesea and McNamara 2020, 157.

labour unions—in diverse contexts such as Argentina, Spain, and Zambia.[8] This conceptualization of labour unions is particularly helpful in examining the class solidarity required for collective actions like strikes. Following Edelman, I would like to emphasize solidarity "as a highly variable thicket of obligations and emotional ties, which is deeply rooted in the soil where it springs to life."[9] Regarding the success of the Berec strike, my argument is that relations and practices of kinship among workers and union leaders constituted the roots of solidarity and played a role in the strike's success.

Such an understanding of unionism is productive for examining modern Turkish history. Since its foundation, the Turkish nation-state itself has been characterized by what feminist scholar Nükhet Sirman calls "familial citizenship."[10] The social order of the Ottoman Empire was identified with the familial order in which "the head of the house is at once the father and the sovereign"[11] The mutually constitutive character of politics and kinship continued under the new republican regime, which perceived the family as a site of intervention for establishing a modern order. The new republican order relied on a model that centered on the modern patriarchal nuclear family, which employs "love" as a binding agent, obscuring hierarchies of gender, ethnicity, and age. The universal laws of citizenship can, thus, co-exist with familial citizenship[12] while maintaining the hegemony of the familial order as an organizing principle for social life.

Similarly, the welfare system in Turkey has been categorized with familialist Mediterranean welfare regimes.[13] Familialism is defined "as a heavy reliance on a gendered and intergenerationally structured family solidarity" that characterizes Southern European welfare regimes.[14] In Turkey, as throughout the Global South, the import-substitute industrialization (ISI) model became dominant beginning in the 1950s. With dissolution of the petty commodity production in the rural economy, migration from rural to urban areas accelerated. Such rapid and large-scale urbanization exacerbated the importance

---

8 Leivestad 2021; Kapesea and McNamara 2020; Soul 2020; Lazar 2018.

9 Edelman 2003, 3.

10 Sirman 2005, 148.

11 Sirman 2005, 155.

12 Sirman 2005, 164–165.

13 Emerging after World War Two, familialism has been a persistent feature of the Turkey's welfare system. However, the rise of neoliberalism and the AKP's conservative policies have changed institutional arrangements regarding care provisions. For an overview of the transformations in the Turkish welfare regime, see Akkan 2018; Eder 2010; Buğra and Keyder 2006.

14 Saraceno 2016, 315.

of kinship networks for the new rural migrants.[15] In the absence of an adequate state mechanism of social protection, migrants had to rely on kinship networks for their basic needs such as housing, employment, and access to limited social services, including healthcare and education. These networks of assistance and self-help based on kinship and rural ties forged a "culture of solidarity" that can be characterized as "a social encasement for the expression of working-class solidarity, an emergent cultural form embodying the values, practices, and institutional manifestations of mutuality."[16] This mutuality was evident in working-class communities in Turkey during the 1960s, the peak years of rural-urban migration.

Feminist scholars have noted women's pivotal role in creating or reinforcing class solidarity through women's networks that forge community in diverse contexts.[17] Women's relationships with each other occurring in the neighborhood, outside of productive relations, significantly influence relationships at the workplace. Women's informal networks and their support for one another create a community that exceeds the limits of formal kinship networks. In the context of Turkey, scholars note a similar pattern where women's close relationships in working-class neighborhoods contribute to people seeing each other as part of the same community.[18] Women played a significant role in reinforcing this culture of solidarity as they performed unpaid domestic labour that benefited the broader community and not just their own families. Uyar Mura, for example, highlights "women's network-maintaining role," as they shouldered the responsibility for hosting overnight guests from rural areas.[19] When new migrants first came to cities, they relied on other women from their hometowns for lodging while searching for jobs and housing. Women's unpaid labour was central to cementing these intra-household relations and creating a working-class community in the urban context.

In the Turkish case, women's informal relations continued to be significant when employed in industry. Women utilized their existing ties to organize at the workplace to advocate for the improvement of their salaries and working conditions. Scholars of labour have often overlooked women's union activism due to women's low labour force participation and unionization in Turkey. However, women were not entirely absent from the scene. Despite the lack of representation in the leadership of labour unions, working-class women

15 Mura 2021; Buğra and Keyder 2006; Erder 2003; Kalaycıoğlu and Tılıç 2000.

16 Fantasia 1989, 25.

17 Cameron 2013; Guglielmo 2010.

18 Mura 2021; Erman 1997; Erman 1996.

19 Mura 2021, 5.

participated in labour activism on the shop floor during the 1960s and 1970s.[20] Rather than presuming that women were rarely interested in labour unions, we must understand the conditions under which women workers chose to organize.[21] In this vein, the Berec strike, which was organized mainly by women, is significant for exploring women's experiences in labour movements in Turkey. An analysis of the Berec strike highlights the need to look beyond the workplace for sources of discontent and past the male worker as the agent of labour activism. Indeed, if we are to understand women's labour activism, we must include the family and household in the study of labour politics.

In an early article advocating the need to bridge the gap between household history and labour history, Marcel van der Linden argues that working-class households have four primary survival and improvement strategies that involve asking for help from external sources. Households may ask for the help of their relatives (relations of kinship); they can utilize personal communities that may function like fictitious kinship networks; they may request the assistance of more powerful individuals (patronage), and finally, they can form or participate in social movement organizations (such as trade unions).[22] In this chapter, I demonstrate that for Berec workers, joining Petrol-İş was an amalgamation of these different strategies.

Workers had family and kinship networks that extended to the squatter neighborhood and factory. In other words, there was significant overlap between family members, neighbors, fellow workers, and union members. Furthermore, union officials themselves were considered powerful father figures vis-à-vis workers. Therefore, participating in a labour union and enhancing salaries and working conditions through collective agreements did not merely benefit one worker's status but also helped the entire household and community. Through marriage, the use of kinship terms, expectations of care, and gift-giving, workers (together with their families) and union delegates formed a (fictive) kin group that reinforced mutual commitments and obligations. Therefore, through these acts of kinship, workers and union officials co-constructed the labour union as a family, including the reproduction of gender and age-based hierarchies.

20 Satı 2021, 88, 93–94.
21 Milkman 1990, 92.
22 Van der Linden 1993, 170–171.

2 Women's Labour and Labour Union Activism

The Berec Battery Factory was established by two Jewish businessmen in Gaziosmanpaşa (Taşlıtarla) in 1954. Gaziosmanpaşa emerged as a resettlement neighborhood when the Turkish state sponsored the construction of two thousand houses for Bulgarian Turks migrating to Turkey in 1953.[23] Migration from Bulgaria, Yugoslavia, and rural parts of Turkey continued in the decades that followed,[24] and Gaziosmanpaşa quickly became a *gecekondu* (built overnight) town. According to one estimate, by 1965, there were thirty thousand houses and almost ninety thousand people living in the neighborhood.[25] During the 1950s and 1960s, Gaziosmanpaşa was often described as an underfunded, poverty-ridden neighborhood that lacked infrastructure.[26]

Given the lack of housing provided by the state during the 1960s and subsequent decades, migrants, with the help of family networks, began to build their own houses on public lands on the peripheries of cities that were close to factories.[27] The Turkish state usually tolerated migrants squatting on public land because they were a source of cheap labour for the ongoing industrialization efforts.[28] Many workers employed in the Berec Factory resided in Gaziosmanpaşa, and most of them were young migrant women from the Balkans[29] and rural areas of Turkey.

Women composed most of the workforce of the Berec Battery Factory despite the falling rates of women's labour force participation during the 1960s (from 72 percent in 1955, to 56 percent in 1965).[30] Women rural-to-urban migrants lost their employment status when they withdrew from agricultural production and moved to urban areas. In other words, in Turkey, as throughout the world, women were excluded from and marginalized in industrial production.[31]

---

23 Karahasanoğlu 2013, 26.

24 Between the foundation of the Turkish Republic in 1923 and 1997, over 1.6 million migrants settled in Turkey. İçduygu and Sert 2015, 91. Most of these migrants came from Greece, Bulgaria, Yugoslavia, and Romania and settled in Turkey due to political reasons.

25 Karahasanoğlu 2013, 27.

26 See Türeli 2010; Kemal 2021.

27 Erman 2001, 985.

28 Erman 2001, 985.

29 Koçak 2014a, 8.

30 Makal 2001,122.

31 This global trend changed after transitioning from ISI to export-led industrialization in most places. Pearson 1998, 173–174. However, Turkey has been isolated from this trend to this date, with an ongoing low female labour force participation rate (32.2 percent in 2020, according to the World Bank). See İlkkaracan 2012, 9–10 for a global comparison.

Within this period of marginalization, there was a slight increase in the percentage of women in the workforce in cities with over ten thousand residents: from 7.8 percent in 1960, to 8.8 percent in 1965.[32] The chemical industry, which includes battery production, did not employ an exceptionally high number of women workers. For example, in 1957, the percentage of women workers employed in the chemical industry was less than 10 percent.[33] For this reason, women's overrepresentation in workforce of the Berec Factory requires explanation. First, the concentration of Bulgarian and Yugoslavian migrants in Gaziosmanpaşa could explain the high number of women employees in the Berec Factory. Researchers have noted that migrants from the Balkans were often more open to and eager for women to work outside the home.[34] Second, the statistics concerning women's labour can be misleading and may not represent the full picture of women's labour force participation in urban areas.[35] Some researchers noted that many women in squatter neighborhoods held jobs outside the home. However, men in the household tended to hide this fact due to widespread negative perceptions of women's employment outside the home, and this tendency resulted in misleading statistics.[36]

During the early Republican period, the Turkish state encouraged women's employment in certain professions as part of the modernization project.[37] However, women employed in low-skill, working-class jobs did not enjoy the same prestige as their middle-class counterparts. Moreover, the male breadwinner model dominant in Turkey further marginalized women's employment outside the home. As feminist scholar Ferhunde Özbay argues, during the 1960s, being an urban housewife was considered a status symbol among rural migrant women in cities.[38] Consequently, gender discourses surrounding women's employment attached a stigma to women who worked in factories, which threatened women's reputation, respectability, and virtue.[39] Participation in labour union activism and strike activity further exacerbated these concerns. As I demonstrate below, the women workers of Berec resisted

32 Makal 2001, 128.

33 Makal 2001, 147.

34 A study examining the Bulgarian workers in Bursa during the 1990s notes that Bulgarian women, including married women, often took jobs outside the home, and they did not meet with any opposition from their husbands and families, as opposed to Turkish women workers. Nichols, Sugur, and Sugur 2003, 48.

35 Nichols, Sugur, and Sugur 2003, 123.

36 Nichols, Sugur, and Sugur 2003, 123.

37 See White 2003; Özbay 1995.

38 Özbay 1995, 102.

39 See Sarıoğlu 2016; White 2000.

this stigma by strategically cultivating and deploying kinship ties with male workers and union officials.

This period of industrialization and urbanization was marked by the power of labour movements in Turkey.[40] The right to strike had just become legal in the 1961 constitution, and it was enacted through the Collective Bargaining, Strike, and Lockout Law, no. 275 in 1963, thanks to the pressure workers generated through protests, strikes, and meetings.[41] It was in this context, defined by the newly acquired right to strike and a strong labour movement, that Petrol-İş officials began to organize Berec workers in 1964.

Petrol-İş officials noted the low wages and lack of social benefits of workers employed at the Berec factory. As more workers unionized, Petrol-İş officially invited the management to begin collective bargaining on 27 March 1964.[42] However, the management and the union could not agree on terms during the negotiations. Failing to achieve any results, Petrol-İş organized a strike vote by secret ballot on 11 September 1964 and reported that 813 out of 823 participating workers voted in favor of the strike action.[43] The union announced that the strike would begin on 7 December 1964, the first strike action that Petrol-İş took since its establishment in 1950.[44]

During the strike, Petrol-İş generously supported the workers. Besides utilizing its own strike fund, Petrol-İş also received assistance from its affiliated confederations: the Confederation of Turkish Trade Unions (Türkiye İşçi Sendikaları Konfederasyonu, Türk-İş) and the International Federation of Petroleum and Chemical Workers (IFPCW).[45] Petrol-İş used its funds to provide weekly stipends and bi-weekly food assistance (in pre-made food boxes) to workers. Moreover, Petrol-İş planned creative recreational activities to boost workers' morale and build solidarity. For instance, Petrol-İş took workers to a famous play entitled *Keşanlı Ali Destanı* (*The Ballad of Ali of Keshan*).[46] The

40 See Mello 2013; Ahmad 1994.

41 Kaya 2018; Turgay 2017.

42 Yici 2010, 21.

43 "900 İşçi" 1964.

44 "Petrol-İş'in BEREC'deki Grevi," 1964.

45 Petrol-İş decided to join Türk-İş and IFPCW (IFPW before 1963) during its eighth General Assembly held in 1958. Both Türk-İş and IFPCW were founded in the 1950s and were heavily influenced by the Cold War. Both confederations embraced American-style unionism, avoided radical militant political actions, and had a strong anticommunist agenda. For a review of the history of Türk-İş, see Kaleağası Blind 2007; Berik and Bilginsoy 1996; Ahmad 1994. For the international activities of the IFPCW, see Williams 2010.

46 Kalmuk 1964. Described as an epic, *Keşanlı Ali Destanı* was written by Haldun Taner. The play was a social commentary on social inequality and poverty.

importance of these provisions was not lost on the workers themselves. When a leftist magazine of the period *Yön* (*Direction*) conducted interviews with several striking workers, one of the workers, Münevver Kaya, stated:

> We are always in debt. Our stomach was filled properly for the first time after the food aid provided by the union last week. We went to the theater; it was for the first time for most of us. The play was about our lives. Ali of Keşan was able to break a single sticks. But he couldn't break eight–ten sticks. So, he meant no one could take you down if you unite.[47]

On another day during the strike, the union co-organized a dance performance by the National Turkish Students Association (Milli Türk Talebe Birliği) Folk Dance Group. *Worker's Post* (*İşçi Postası*) noted that after the dance performance, a group of striking workers from Üsküp (the Turkish name for Skopje) took the stage and performed their folk dance, which cheered up the workers, who clapped along late into the night.[48]

The interviews *Yön* magazine conducted with striking workers provide valuable insight into the contentious relationship between workers and management, as workers hinted at the reasons for their participation in the strike. For example, a woman worker named Fatma Aydın noted, "My dad was a construction worker. He has lung disease. When he got sick, I went to the manager and requested some money. Because I am in the union, he didn't give me an advance on my wages."[49] Others mentioned the difficulty of their work, its adverse effects on their health and well-being, and their poor living conditions, implicating their low salaries as the culprit. For example, one worker named Hayrettin İçli stated, "I work in the part of the factory near the furnace. The furnace gets very hot, making you sweat like a sausage. One day I got cold when I went outside. I have second-degree tuberculosis. [...] I know I should eat meat. Believe me, none of us are able to eat 250 grams of meat a month."[50] By sharing these details, workers held the factory management responsible for their experiences of hardship, including poor health, debt, and food insecurity, justifying their decision to strike.

During the Berec strike, women workers' militancy surprised the public, state, and union officials. For example, when the İstanbul governor Niyazi Akı came to visit the striking workers and the factory management, two women

47 Akalın and Okay 1964.
48 "Berec Grevinde" 1964.
49 Akalın and Okay 1964.
50 Akalın and Okay 1964.

workers were picketing at the gates of the Berec Factory. Women did not let him in as they did not know who he was.[51] Decades later, this was a memory of the strike the union president Hepbir recalled fondly. According to Hepbir, the governor was so impressed with a migrant worker named Fikriye that he called Hepbir and said, "Your workers are very conscientious. A woman worker didn't let me in."[52] Hepbir also mentions that Fikriye became part of the militant group formed during the strike.[53] The weekly newspaper published by Petrol-İş confirms this, reporting that Fikriye visited the United States for a six-week transnational union program in 1966.[54]

Petrol-İş and workers' media frequently emphasized women's lack of experience, claiming that most workers did not even know what a trade union was. However, some women told a completely different story.

> I am Sevinç Gülsuna, a sixteen-year-old worker girl from Çarşamba, Samsun working at the Berec Battery Factory, number 2612. We came to Istanbul in 1960. I could go to school only until the fifth grade. With my salary from the factory, I take care of seven people. My father was a worker like me. I mean, I've become a worker just like my father. He used to work at the General Textile Machines Factory. Because he was unionized in Metal-İş, he got fired five months ago, and now he is unemployed.[55]

Sevinç's self-introduction using her factory identification number and emphasizing her similarity to her father indicates a strong occupational and class-based identity. I believe she was not alone in inheriting a working-class identity and culture of labour activism from her father. During the 1960s and 1970s, working-class women were primarily involved in labour politics through their families. During this period, many women took active roles in strikes, protests, and other forms of labour activism as wives and children. The Kavel Strike organized in 1963 and the Paşabahçe Strike in 1966 are two examples where the spouses and children of workers showed enthusiastic support for the strikes, picketed with the striking workers, and clashed with the police.[56]

Neither scholars nor union officials have recognized the relevance of women's productive and reproductive work for enhancing the strength of labour

51 Yici 2010, 97, 169.
52 Koçak 2014a, 82–83.
53 Koçak 2014a, 83.
54 "Grevci Kız Fikriye" 1966.
55 Akalın and Okay 1964.
56 For the history of Paşabahçe strike in 1966, see Koçak 2014b.

politics. While women's unpaid domestic work contributed to the formation of working-class culture, their participation in strikes and protests as wives, daughters, or workers produced a class consciousness. For example, the wives of Paşabahçe workers threatened to divorce their husbands if they prematurely ended their strike due to pressure from their employer.[57] For working-class women, the stability of the marriage and household was closely tied to the success of a strike, crystallizing the intimate relationship between labour activism and family. When we understand the family, not the male worker, as the actor in labour politics, we can make better sense of women's militant labour activism despite the relatively short duration of women's working lives (as most of them withdrew after getting married or having children); their overall lower levels of labour force participation; and their lack of experience in formal union membership in Turkey.

In the *Yön* magazine interviews, workers mentioned their inability to plan and prepare for marriage due to intense financial pressures. The prospect of marriage was simply unattainable for some workers. Seventeen-year-old Safiye Sarıoğlu explained her experience: "Our house is forty-five minutes from the factory. I commute with my good friend Sevinç. Sevinç and I make lace on Sundays. We don't make it for our trousseau, though. We do it for money."[58] Safiye's words demonstrate how some working-class women combined their formal jobs as factory workers with other income-generating activities. In Turkey, young girls were expected to assemble a trousseau that required labour-intensive, elaborate needlework and operated as a status symbol, showcasing their skills and industriousness.[59] However, the demands of wage labour meant that some women had to give up traditional forms of reproductive labour, such as preparing a trousseau.

Another woman worker also talks about marriage as an impossible goal:

> My mom, dad, me, my two siblings in school, and my two brothers who are completing their military service all live on this [her] salary. We send money to my brothers too … How can I even think of getting married? Who is going to take care of our household if I get married? My current duty is picketing. Even if we starve, we will continue to strike.[60]

57 "Paşabahçe İşvereni İşçileri" 1966.
58 Akalın and Okay 1964.
59 White 2000, 129.
60 Akalın and Okay 1964.

These interviews show that the pressures of wage labour disrupted the traditional gendered division of labour in working-class households and made it difficult for young working-class women to start their own families. When working-class women managed to get married and have children, their work experiences continued to diverge from those of male workers. Another worker, Münevver Kaya, discussed the pressures pregnant women faced at the workplace and alluded to the distance between women's legal rights and their lived experiences.

> I'm Münevver Kaya, 19 years old. I've been working in Berec for six years […] Maybe the bosses in our factory are good, but those managers … You have no idea what kind of things they do to us. When a woman colleague is pregnant, they ask her to do heavy work. She had to work these heavy jobs so she would have a miscarriage. Because if she gives birth, they [managers] need to give her maternity leave.

This interview highlights the challenges women experienced as expectant mothers and workers. Considering that pregnancy itself is a form of reproductive labour,[61] it is possible to see the difficulty Berec's women workers had in trying to reconcile their productive and reproductive labour. Furthermore, Münevver shared problems other women experienced at the workplace, which indicates that managers' practices promoted a collective sense of injustice among women workers. This group identification may have played a role in women's mobilization in support of collective action.

One of the men workers mentioned the difficulties he encountered when he wanted to marry a woman who was a worker in the same factory and the support he received from Petrol-İş.

> I am Sadık Balaban. My friends call me "groom." Why? My wife works here too. We have liked each other for two years. I asked for permission from her parents many times. They want two thousand lira as the bridewealth. Where am I supposed to find that kind of money? So, I kidnapped her. We will get married, but her parents refuse to give us her identification card. So, we have applied for a new one. Once we have it, we will do the official marriage. Our union will perform our wedding.[62]

61 Mullin 2005.

62 Akalın and Okay 1964.

In addition to Sadık and his wife Necibe, there was another couple who eloped during the strike. Furthermore, other strikes also witnessed workers getting married without their families' approval while striking. This trend of eloping could be due to the sense of freedom and empowerment that the collective action promoted. Furthermore, for workers who were unable to meet the conditions traditionally required for marriage (e.g., trousseau, bride-wealth, family/parental approval), the support of labour unions and class-based identities might have been meaningful enough to disregard some of these traditions while transforming others.

At the convergence of productive and reproductive labour, working-class women adopted relations and discourses of family in their interactions with union officials. Under the pressure of stigma attached to their workplace identities, women carried marriage and kinship relations from the private sphere of the household into the workplace and onto the picket line. In other words, women workers reconfigured the factory as a space that produced kinship, and they turned to the labour union to help them decrease conflicts and balance the needs of the home and workplace.

3 Marriage and Other Acts of Kinship

Following Lambek, I conceptualize kinship as a relationship that is constituted through specific acts.[63] Focusing on the acts of kinship performed during the Berec strike, such as using kin terms to address union officials, getting married during the strike, organizing wedding and circumcision ceremonies, naming practices, gift-giving, and other forms of care, I investigate the nature of the relationship between workers and union delegates. Lambek argues that "kinship does not simply convey meaning as a symbol or set of symbols [...] but is also carried out in acts that are *meant* and that have meaningful consequences."[64] Through the performance of these acts, union delegates and workers co-constructed the union as a kin group where all parties submitted to "an order of kinship."[65] As Lambek puts it, these "acts produce commitments and inform people with, and of, their commitments to one another, thereby determining not practice itself but the meanings that are attributed to it. In other words, such acts establish kinship as an ethical domain."[66] The culture of

63 Lambek 2011, 2013.
64 Lambek 2013, 247. Emphasis in original.
65 Lambek 2013, 248.
66 Lambek 2013, 248.

solidarity that emerged through the Berec strike and other instances of labour activism should be conceptualized within this ethical domain.

One of the most significant themes that emerged from the testimonies of Berec workers published in *Yön* magazine was marriage. The dual demands of productive and reproductive labour made it difficult for women workers to manage both. The issue of marriage exemplifies the pressures that industrial capitalism placed on all workers. When we pay close attention to the marriage-related issues of workers and the union's involvement in workers' private lives, we see a dialectical relationship between kinship and labour politics through which they transform one another. Acts of kinship, specifically those involving marriage, allowed workers and union officials to forge a culture of solidarity during the Berec Strike.

During the Berec strike, seven couples decided to get married and turned to Petrol-İş officials for support. As Lambek argues, marriage is a "ritual enactment of kinship,"[67] and marrying as an act involves not only those who get married but also "mediators, officiates, and witnesses" that reproduce kinship as a relationship.[68] Petrol-İş officials acted as mediators and witnesses, supported workers' decision to get married, and provided financial support for the new couples. For example, union official Mücahit Teoman assumed responsibility when he learned that one of the women workers' parents did not allow her to marry another worker from the Berec Factory. Teoman visited the woman's parents and convinced her father to consent to the engagement.

Moreover, union officials were invited to the wedding ceremonies. For example, when Necibe Çeltikçi and Sadık Balaban married during the strike, the wedding witness was one of the union officials. Many workers and union leaders attended the couple's marriage ceremony at the city hall. The newly married workers refused to go home after the ceremony and instead returned to the picket line,[69] blending union activism and the celebration of marriage, clearly demonstrating the intersection of the public and private spheres.

President Hepbir promised that the union would organize a collective wedding for all the couples in a sports center and bear the expenses.[70] Hepbir also declared that the union would help the engaged workers with marriage-related costs (e.g., furniture, domestic appliances). By taking over a responsibility that often falls to the parents, workers may have considered Hepbir as deserving of the nickname of "father." Hepbir's wife was also involved in taking up these

67 Lambek 2013, 258.

68 Lambek 2013, 247.

69 "Berec Grevinde" 1965.

70 Yici 2010, 98.

tasks; *İşçi Postası* published a photograph showing the newly married workers kissing the hand of Mrs. Hepbir.[71] Hand kissing is considered a sign of respect for elders, and the practice marks significant days and reinforces social ties.

Considering that migrants frequently utilized solidarity networks to find employment, it is plausible that multiple people from the same family, neighborhood, or community worked together in the Berec Factory. Even if most workers had no actual kinship relations, the cultural values and practices of kinship that characterized migrant working-class communities shaped how workers formed relationships with each other and with union officials. As Sirman argues, "relations between strangers in the public sphere are converted into fictive kinship through the use of kinship terms."[72] In the absence of any other moral order that regulates relationships in the public arena, kinship imaginaries persist.[73] The cultural practices that govern everyday life reflect this point. Strangers with no blood or family ties frequently call each other sister, sister-in-law, brother, niece, aunt, uncle, mother, and father. These kinship terms are especially useful in facilitating social interaction between men and women who are not related to each other, "signaling the sexually neutral character of interactions."[74] Women workers addressing the union president Ziya Hepbir as "Ziya Father" and their fellow workers as "brothers" illustrates this point.

Kinship terms were used by workers and unionists alike to evoke emotions, articulate expectations, and (re)produce affection during the strike. In this understanding, unionism is conceptualized through "kinship, where actions are motivated by mutual inter-dependence, within self-defining hierarchies and identity structures."[75] Thus, calling Hepbir "father" was not merely a symbolic gesture. Instead, workers expected him and other union officials to help and support them with material concerns and other issues. During an interview, one of the striking workers said, "Ziya Hepbir is such a man that he did more for all of us than our own fathers."[76] In other words, care among the unionists and workers shaped the union as a kin-like group.[77]

The naming practices of workers and unionists, and especially the process of collectively naming children, illustrates the construction of labour- and

71 "Grevciler 3üncü Parti" 1964.
72 Sirman 2005, 161.
73 Sirman 2005, 166.
74 Kandiyoti 1997, 126. Also see Duben 1982.
75 Kapesea 2020, 155.
76 Karagöz 1964, 4.
77 Lazar 2018, 266.

union-centered identity and its transmission to the next generation. On the one hand, when two workers welcomed new babies during the strike, Mrs. Hepbir visited the families in their homes, right across from each other, and gave the newborn babies union's gold coins with blue beads to protect against the evil eye.[78] On the other hand, both couples named their newborn children "Grev" (strike) to honor the Berec strike, demonstrating their commitment to labour politics.[79] Similarly, Hepbir's son was named "Akar," referring to the first name of Petrol-İş, İstanbul Akaryakıt İşçileri Sendikası. There was at least one more delegate whose son was named "Türkiş" after the name of the confederation Türk-İş. With regard to both Akar and Türkiş, other union officials proposed these names in the congresses of Petrol-İş and Türk-İş, and they were voted on and officially decided in union meetings.[80] The naming practices of workers, therefore, took communal forms and unified family and labour identities while strengthening the ties between workers and the union.

The Berec workers expected union officials to care for them if and when they needed it. For example, a woman named Hanife Akarsu was a migrant from Yugoslavia, and when the driver of her employer hit her during the strike, she was hurt. She expressed her frustration with her employers saying that "Even in Yugoslavia, they didn't do such things to us ... Now they want to have me run over by a bus as if I am infidel [*gavur*]."[81] Hanife was a single mother with six children, so she added, "who would look after my children if I died?" Then, she said, "Well, I am sure our leader Ziya Hepbir and others would look after them."[82] These expectations of familial care indicate shared values of family and kinship.

When the factory management dismissed two workers for organizing other workers and inciting discontent during the strike, Petrol-İş immediately hired the union activists. Similar to the networks of kinship that assisted people in finding employment, Petrol-İş took similar responsibility for their members. Furthermore, the substantive strike fund, supplemented by Türk-İş and the IFPCW, generously supported workers with cash and food packages. All these

78 Lazar 2018, 266. Giving gifts of gold jewelry and coins during significant (and costly) life events such as birth and marriage is an old tradition practiced in different parts of Asia, including China, India, and Turkey. In monetary terms, gold coins are standardized and can easily be converted to cash when the need arises; thus, this specific form of gift giving has both economic and social value. It is typically family, relatives, close neighbors, and friends who give each other gold coins. See Ertimur and Sandıkcı 2014, 204.

79 "Grevciler 3üncü Parti" 1964.

80 Sülker 1986, 49.

81 Karagöz 1964, 4.

82 Karagöz 1964, 4.

care practices performed by the union drew workers and union delegates closer to each other.

The expectations and demands of workers regarding personal and family issues played a role in unions' organizational strategies and tactics. Especially in the absence of the right to strike, the union operated similar to a mutual aid society. For example, Petrol-İş decided to establish a "social support fund" as early as 1954, i.e., when strikes were still illegal, as a temporary solution for the arbitrary dismissal of workers. Social support included lending money, providing access to cheap foods items, and direct monetary assistance in case of a death in the family.[83] Moreover, the union management was authorized to organize recreational activities such as picnics and circumcision ceremonies for workers' children.[84] Intended to gain workers' loyalty and strengthen bonds among their members, these recreational activities extended to include workers' children and other family members. Traditional and religious rituals also found a place in the activities of organized labour. For example, when multiple workers died in work accidents, several labour unions pooled their resources for an Islamic memorial to be broadcasted over the radio.[85]

Religion served as another potential grounds for establishing solidarity and producing kinship bonds among workers. Religious identity was especially significant for those who had migrated from the Balkans as they had faced intense pressure to secularize under the communist regimes of Yugoslavia and Bulgaria.[86] However, by the 1960s, the non-Muslim population in Turkey had declined significantly due to a series of violent, ultra-nationalist policies.[87] For a Sunni Muslim workforce, having non-Muslim employers may have been influential in their mobilization and their exclusion of their employers from their shared understanding of kinship.[88] There is some evidence supporting this claim, for example, the use of the term *gavur* by some workers.

Gavur was used by the Ottoman Empire to refer to non-Muslim Ottoman populations, and it had pejorative connotations. Muslim populations in the

83 Sülker 1986, 50.

84 Sülker 1986, 49.

85 According to Petrol-İş publications, this was enthusiastically supported by U.S. labour organizations, which recommended inviting Islamic religious figures to the union's general meetings. See Sülker 1986, 59.

86 For a detailed account of socialist regimes' policies concerning Muslim women, see Ballinger and Ghodsee 2011.

87 For an overview of the impact of geopolitical conflict and violence on the development of historical capitalism since the late Ottoman Empire, see Karatasli and Kumral 2019.

88 It is not clear whether antisemitism played a role in the workers' perception of their employers.

Balkans used the term derogatorily to refer to the non-Muslim majority. For example, Yugoslavian migrant Hanife mentioned the aggressive incident she had with the driver by saying, "they try to run me over as if I am *gavur*."[89] In another newspaper article discussing the conditions of Berec workers, the author reports that "most of the workers sold all their property to regain their homeland. They [workers] say we escaped from the *gavur*['s land] and came to our homeland; we came to our brothers. It is one thing to experience these things in the land of *gavur*, but we will not accept slavery in our own homeland."[90] Hence, migrant workers using the word *gavur* and emphasizing their *own homeland*, knowing that their employers were non-Muslims, could be intentional and may suggest religious-nationalist sentiments expressed as class conflict.

All in all, working-class communities participated in labour activism partly because it helped them maintain their traditions, family practices, and reproduce kinship in the public sphere. By looking at all these acts of kinship and the caring practices of the union, it is possible to argue that the function of labour unions far exceeded protecting the rights of workers on the shop floor. These relations are particularly important for understanding women's labour activism during this period. It was critical for the small group of women who held industrial jobs to find strategies to unify their work identity with their family lives. With the labour union's assistance, women workers were able to merge social relations of kinship and work, which were otherwise in tension. Acts of kinship (including the popular practice of getting married during the strike) and kin-like relations with their union delegates helped women workers attain respect and maintain the status derived from having a family.

4 Conclusion

The Berec Strike lasted for forty-one days, with almost the full participation of the workforce, resulting in a two-year collective agreement signed on 15 January 1965. In addition to salary increases, Petrol-İş also secured social benefits such as child allowances, a death benefit, and a one-time bonus payment after the birth of each child.[91] The union officials, workers, and media outlets enthusiastically welcomed the contract.

89 My emphasis. Karagöz 1964, 4.

90 Çeliksoy 1964.

91 BEREC PİL ve Batarya San. T. A.Ş. (1965) Collective Agreement, Box 40, Folder 414, Petrol-İş Archive, Istanbul, Turkey.

Family metaphors were noticeable in the language of employers as well. One of the employers, Nesim Afumado, gave a speech when the strike ended. He said, "you all are our children who were absent from the factory for forty-one days."[92] On the first day back to work after the strike, the employers organized a Ramadan *iftar* in the factory to celebrate. As workers, union leaders, and employers shared this meal, "labour peace" was restored with the help of commensality.[93] Both union leaders and employers emphasized that now was the time to "work in family intimacy."[94] Because labour peace meant cooperation between labour and capital, employers were also drawn into practices of solidarity. Petrol-İş and employers agreed to share the expenses of engaged couples. Hepbir announced that Mr. Afumado promised to pay all the marriage-related costs of engaged women, and he (Hepbir) would cover the men's expenses. Hepbir repeated that the union would organize the wedding for all seven couples, just as it had promised earlier.[95]

The so-called labour peace secured after the strike, however, was short-lived. Berec workers went on strike again in 1975, this time under the leadership of the Petroleum, Chemical and Rubber Industry Workers' Union of Turkey (Türkiye Petrol Kimya ve Lastik İşçileri Sendikası, Petkim-İş), which was affiliated with the Confederation of Progressive Trade Unions of Turkey (Devrimci İşçi Sendikaları Konfederasyonu, DISK). When the police attempted to disperse the strikers, the workers clashed with the police, resulting in the wounding of several police officers and workers and the arrest of sixteen workers.[96] Workers' unionization in the rival labour union, which had a more radical and political agenda, indicates the increasing militancy of workers and the collapse of kinship ties between workers and the leaders of Petrol-İş in the 1970s.

The labour politics formed around fictive kinship structures had its limits in terms of improving women's status in the workplace and/or in society. As gender hierarchies in the household and workplace were subsumed into the bonds of kinship, women workers found limited opportunities for improving gender equality in the workplace. For instance, some of the concerns raised by women workers were not included in the collective agreement signed between Petrol-İş and the Berec management. A woman worker employed in the coal department complained that while men took showers with hot water, women

92 "Petrol-İş Grevi Kazandı" 1965.
93 "Berecde Mesut Günler" 1965.
94 "Berecde Mesut Günler" 1965.
95 "Petrol-İş Grevi Kazandı" 1965.
96 Çelik 2012, 57.

workers had to use cold water.[97] Although union officials included clauses addressing seemingly minor issues such as the menu offered to workers in the factory canteen, women's demands for equal working conditions were ignored in negotiations. Similarly, in the subsequent decades, working-class women struggled to make their concerns a priority for labour unions. Even when labour unions added working-class women's issues to their agenda, such as the demand for childcare centers at the workplace, they failed to make meaningful changes. As I have shown elsewhere, working-class organizations also missed the opportunity to challenge the unequal gendered division of labour at home.[98] While labour unions eased women's participation in labour politics and provided informal support through kinship ties, they were unable to effect a broader change in women's status in Turkey.

The Berec strike was not the only example in which family and labour politics were fused. For instance, after fifty-three couples married during the strike organized in Kula Mensucat Factory, the Textile, Knitting, and Clothing Workers' Union of Turkey (Türkiye Tekstil Örme ve Giyim Sanayii İşçileri Sendikası, TEKSİF) formed a committee composed of elderly women workers. Following New Year's Eve and the religious holiday, the "wedding committee" visited the newlyweds and brought flowers for the brides.[99] There were many other instances of workers visiting the picket line right after their wedding ceremonies. These examples show that kinship, and specifically marriage, was an integral part of doing labour politics in Turkey during the 1960s.

The Berec strike is significant because it demonstrates women's presence and militancy within the labour movement of Turkey. My analysis of the Berec strike also provides some insight into the sources of women's mobilization and the specific form of their labour activism. This chapter has explored the working-class solidarity that developed through kinship relations, as labour politics became an integral part of the household, kin group, and community. Women with rural ties who were recently incorporated into industrial wage labour had a strong desire to marry and start a family. However, for many women, it was challenging to do so. It was in this context women workers employed various strategies to extend the family into the factory through acts of kinship. Marrying fellow workers or eloping during strikes illustrates this relationship. One of the strategies women workers utilized was membership in labour unions, through which they formed kin-like relations with union delegates, whom they could ask for support in matters of marriage. Through

97 Akalın and Okay 1964.
98 Satı 2021, 103.
99 "53 Günlük Grev" 1966.

labour union officials' support in matters such as obtaining parental approval, organizing wedding ceremonies, acting as wedding witnesses, gift-giving, and organizing religious rituals, labour union leaders were transformed into father figures. A successful strike action was deemed the achievement of the labour union, which was a family headed by its president. For these reasons, it is understandable that the victory celebration for a strike was blended with the celebration of family, as women workers declared, "long live our father!"

Bibliography

"53 Günlük Grev Süresinde Tanışan 53 Çift Evlendi" [53 couples, met during the 53-Day strike, got married]. 1966. *Petrol-İş*, 28 January 1966.

"900 İşçi Adına Petrol-İş Grev Oylaması Yaptı" [Petrol-İş organized a strike vote for 900 Workers]. 1966. *İşçi Postası* [Workers' post], 14 September 1964.

Ahmad, Feroz. 1994. "The Development of Working-Class Consciousness in Turkey." In *Workers and Working Classes in the Middle East: Struggles, Histories, Historiographies*, edited by Zachary Lockman, 133–163 Albany, NY: SUNY Press.

Akalın, S., and Ö. Okay. 1964. "Berec'in Grevci İşçileri Arasında" [Among the strikers of Berec]. *Yön* [Direction], 25 December 1964.

Akkan, Başak. 2018. "The Politics of Care in Turkey: Sacred Familialism in a Changing Political Context." *Social Politics: International Studies in Gender, State and Society* 25, no. 1: 72–91. doi: 10.1093/sp/jxx011.

Aşçıoğlu, Adil. 1964. "Berec Grevi Başladı [Berec strike has begun]." *Yön* [Direction], 11 December 1964.

Ballinger, Pamela, and Kristen Ghodsee. 2011. "Socialist Secularism: Religion, Modernity, and Muslim Women's Emancipation in Bulgaria and Yugoslavia, 1945–1991." *Aspasia. International Yearbook for Women's and Gender History of Central, Eastern and Southeastern Europe* 5: 6–27. doi: 10.3167/asp.2011.050103.

"Berec Grevinde" [In Berec strike]. 1964. *İşçi Postası* [Workers' post], 11 December 1964.

"Berec Grevinde Sevişen Yedi Çiftten İlki Dün Evlendi" [The First of the seven couples involved in the Berec strike got married Yesterday]. 1965. *İşçi Postası* [Workers' post], 9 January 1965.

BEREC PIL ve Batarya San. T. A.Ş. 1965. Collective Agreement, Box 40, Folder 414, Petrol-İş Archive, Istanbul, Turkey.

"Berecde Mesut Günler Başladı" [Happy days started at Berec]. 1965. *İşçi Postası* [Workers' post], 21 December 1965.

Berik, Günseli, and Cihan Bilginsoy. 1996. "The Labor Movement in Turkey: Labor Pains, Maturity, Metamorphosis." In *The Social History of Labor in the Middle East*, edited by Ellis Jay Goldberg, 37–64. Boulder, CO: Routledge.

Buğra, Ayşe, and Çağlar Keyder. 2006. "The Turkish Welfare Regime in Transformation." *Journal of European Social Policy* 16, no. 3 (August): 211–228. doi: 10.1177/0958928706065593.

Cameron, Ardis. 2013. "Bread and Roses Revisited: Women's Culture and Working-Class Activism in the Lawrence Strike of 1912." In *Women, Work, and Protest: A Century of U.S. Women's Labor History*, edited by Ruth Milkman, 42–61. London: Taylor & Francis Group.

Çelik, Aziz. 2012. "ABD Diplomatik Yazışmalarında Türkiye Sendikal Hareketi 1973–1976" [Turkish unionism in U.S. Diplomatic correspondence, 1973–1976]. *Çalışma ve Toplum* 2, no. 33: 49–74.

Çeliksoy, Cahit. 1964. "Bu İnsanlar Ne Yer, Ne İçer, Nerede Oturur" [What do these people eat, what do they drink, where do they live]. *İşçi Postası* [Workers' post], 14 December 1964.

Duben, Alan. 1982. "The Significance of Family and Kinship in Urban Turkey." In *Sex Roles, Family and Community in Turkey*, edited by Çiğdem Kağıtçıbaşı and Diane Sunar, 73–99. Bloomington: Indiana University Press.

Dubetsky, Alan. 1976. "Kinship, Primordial Ties, and Factory Organization in Turkey: An Anthropological View." *International Journal of Middle East Studies* 7, no. 3 (July): 433–451. doi: 10.1017/s0020743800025745.

Edelman, Birgitta. 2003. "Brothers or Mates? Identity and Trust in Two Railway Trades." *Anthropology of Work Review* 24, no. 3–4: 3–14.

Eder, Mine. 2010. "Retreating State? Political Economy of Welfare Regime Change in Turkey." *Middle East Law and Governance* 2, no. 2: 152–184. DOI: 10.1163/187633710x500739.

Erder, Sema. 2003. "Urban Migration and Reconstruction of Kinship Networks: The Case of Istanbul." In *Autonomy and Dependence in the Family: Turkey and Sweden in Critical Perspective*, edited by Rita Liljestrom, 117–136. Abingdon: Routledge. DOI: 10.4324/9780203461129.

Erman, Tahire. 2001. "The Politics of Squatter (Gecekondu) Studies in Turkey: The Changing Representations of Rural Migrants in the Academic Discourse." *Urban Studies* 38, no. 7 (June): 983–1002. doi: org/10.1080/00420980120080131.

Erman, Tahire. 1997. "Squatter (Gecekondu) Housing versus Apartment Housing: Turkish Rural-to-Urban Migrant Residents' Perspectives." *Habitat International* 28, no. 1: 91–106. DOI: 10.1016/s0197-3975(96)00048-3.

Erman, Tahire. 1996. "Women and the Housing Environment." *Environment and Behavior* 28, no. 6 (November): 764–798. doi: 10.1177/001391659602800603.

Ertimur, Burçak, and Özlem Sandıkcı. 2014. "Alienable Gifts: Uses and Meanings of Gold in Turkey." *Journal of Consumer Behaviour* 13, no. 3: 204–11. doi: org/10.1002/cb.1479.

Fantasia, Rick. 1989. *Cultures of Solidarity: Consciousness, Action, and Contemporary American Workers*. Berkeley: University of California Press.

"Grevci Kız Fikriye Odaman Amerika'ya Gitti" [The girl striker Fikriye Odaman has gone to the U.S.]. *Petrol-İş*, 15 July 1966.

"Grevciler 3üncü Parti Yardım Aldı" [The strikers have received aid for the third time]. 1964. *İşçi Postası* [Workers' post], 28 December 1964.

Guglielmo, Jennifer. 2010. *Living the Revolution: Italian Women's Resistance and Radicalism in New York City, 1880–1945*. Chapel Hill: The University of North Carolina Press.

İçduygu, Ahmet, and Deniz Sert. 2015. "The Changing Waves of Migration from the Balkans to Turkey: A Historical Account." In *Migration in the Southern Balkans from Ottoman Territory to Globalized Nation States*, edited by Hans Vermeulen, M. Baldwin-Edwards, and R. Boeschoten, 85–104. Springer, Cham. 2015. doi: org/10.1007/978-3-319-13719-3_5.

İlkkaracan, İpek. 2012. "Why so Few Women in the Labor Market in Turkey?" *Feminist Economics* 18, no. 1 (January): 1–37. doi: org: 10.1080/13545701.2011.649358.

Kalaycıoğlu, Sibel, and Helga Rittersberger-Tılıç. 2000. "Intergenerational Solidarity Networks of Instrumental and Cultural Transfers within Migrant Families in Turkey." *Ageing and Society* 20, no. 5 (September): 523–542. doi: 10.1017/s0144686x99007916.

Kaleağası Blind, Peride. 2007. "A New Actor in Turkish Democratization: Labor Unions." *Turkish Studies* 8, no. 2 (June): 289–311. doi: org/10.1080/14683840701312260.

Kalmuk, Fikret. 1964. "Petrol-İş Taşlıtarlayı Otobüsle Beyoğlu'na Taşıdı" [Petrol-İş has brought Taşlıtarla to Beyoğlu]. *İşçi Postası* [Workers' post], 17 December 1964.

Kandiyoti, Deniz. 1997. "Gendering the Modern: On Missing Dimensions in the Study of Turkish Modernity." In *Rethinking Modernity and National Identity in Turkey*, edited by Sibel Bozdoğan and Reşat Kasaba, 113–132. Seattle: University of Washington Press.

Kapesea, Robby, and Thomas McNamara. 2020. "'We Are Not Just a Union, We Are a Family' Class, Kinship and Tribe in Zambia's Mining Unions." *Dialectical Anthropology* 44, no. 2: 153–172. doi: 10.1007/s10624-019-09578-x.

Karagöz, Abdullah. 1964. "Berec Grevcileri İle Geçen Bir Gecenin İlginç Hikayesi" [The interesting story of a night with Berec workers]. *İşçi Postası* [Workers' post], 16 December 1964.

Karahasanoğlu, Selim. 2013. *Küçükköy, Taşlıtarla, Gaziosmanpaşa: Bir İlçenin Öyküsü* [Küçükköy, Taşlıtarla, Gaziosmanpaşa: The story of a county]. Istanbul: Gaziosmanpaşa Belediyesi, 2013. https://www.gaziosmanpasa.bel.tr/det/415/bir-ilcenin-oykusu.

Karatasli, Sahan Savas, and Sefika Kumral. 2019. "Capitalist Development in Hostile Conjunctures: War, Dispossession, and Class Formation in Turkey." *Journal of Agrarian Change* 19, no. 3: 528–549. doi: 10.1111/joac.12317.

Kaya, Muzaffer. 2018. "'We Too Have a Word to Say.'" *The Journal of Interrupted Studies* 1, no. 1: 48–68. doi: 10.1163/25430149-00101002.

Kemal, Orhan. 2021. *İstanbul'dan Çizgiler* [Lines from Istanbul]. Istanbul: Everest.

Koçak, M. Hakan, ed. 2014a. *O Hep Sendikacıydı: Ziya Hepbir'in Yaşam Öyküsü* [He was always a unionist: The life story of Ziya Hepbir]. Istanbul: Sosyal Tarih Yayınları.

Koçak, M. Hakan. 2014b. *Camın İşçileri: Paşabahçe İşçilerinin Sınıf Olma Öyküsü* [The workers of glass: The story of Paşabahçe's workers becoming a class]. Istanbul: İletişim.

Lambek, Michael. 2013. "Kinship, Modernity, and the Immodern." In *Vital Relations: Modernity and the Persistent Life of Kinship*, edited by Susan McKinnon, Fenella Cannell, Laura Bear, Barbara Bodenhorn, Janet Carsten, and Gillian Feeley-Harnik. 241–260. Santa Fe, NM: SAR Press.

Lambek, Michael. 2011. "Kinship as Gift and Theft: Acts of Succession in Mayotte and Israel." *American Ethnologist* 38, no. 1: 2–16. doi: 10.1111/j.1548-1425.2010.01288.x.

Lazar, Sian. 2018. "A 'Kinship Anthropology of Politics'? Interest, the Collective Self, and Kinship in Argentine Unions." *Journal of the Royal Anthropological Institute* 24, no. 2: 256–274. doi: 10.1111/1467-9655.12809.

Leivestad, Hege Høyer. 2021. "Kinship on the Waterfront: Logistics Labour in a Global Port." *Journal of the Royal Anthropological Institute* 27, no. 3: 518–533. doi: 10.1111/1467-9655.13548.

Makal, Ahmet. 2001. "Türkiye'de 1950–1965 Döneminde Ücretli Kadın Emeğine İlişkin Gelişmeler" [Developments in women's paid labor in Turkey, 1950–1965]. *Ankara Üniversitesi SBF Dergisi* 56, no. 2 (February): 117–155.

McKinnon, Susan, and Fenella Cannell. 2013. "The Difference Kinship Makes." In *Vital Relations: Modernity and the Persistent Life of Kinship,* edited by Susan McKinnon, Fenella Cannell, Laura Bear, Barbara Bodenhorn, Janet Carsten, and Gillian Feeley-Harnik, 3–38. Santa Fe, NM: SAR Press, 2013.

Mello, Brian. 2013. *Evaluating Social Movement Impacts: Comparative Lessons from the Labor Movement in Turkey*. New York: Bloomsbury Academic.

Milkman, Ruth. 1990. "Gender and Trade Unionism in Historical Perspective." In *Women, Politics and Change,* edited by Louise Tilly and Patricia Gurin, 87–107. New York: Russell Sage Foundation.

Mullin, Amy. 2005. *Reconceiving Pregnancy and Childcare: Ethics, Experience, and Reproductive Labor*. New York: Cambridge University Press.

Mura, Elif S Uyar. 2021. "Hosting Overnight Guests: Gendered Unpaid Work as a Solidarity Mechanism of Migrants in the Process of Urbanization in Turkey." *Social Politics: International Studies in Gender, State and Society* (April): 1–24. doi: 10.1093/sp/jxab002.

Nichols, Theo, Nadir Sugur, and Serap Sugur. 2003. "Muhacir Bulgarian Workers in Turkey: Their Relation to Management and Fellow Workers in the Formal

Employment Sector." *Middle Eastern Studies* 39, no. 2 (April): 37–54. doi: 10.1080/00263200412331301597.

Özbay, Ferhunde. 1995. "Changes in Women's Activities Both Inside and Outside the Home." In *Women in Modern Turkish Society: A Reader*, edited by Şirin Tekeli, 89–111. London: Zed Books. 1995.

"Paşabahçe İşvereni İşçileri Tehdit Ediyorİ" [The Paşabahçe employer threatens the workers]. *Petrol-İş*, 22 April 1966.

Pearson, Ruth. 1998. "'Nimble Fingers' Revisited: Reflections on Women and Third World Industrialisation in the Late Twentieth Century." In *Feminist Visions of Development: Gender Analysis and Policy*, edited by Cecile Jackson and Ruth Pearson, 171–189. London: Routledge.

"Petrol-İş'in BEREC'deki Grevi Pazartesi Başlıyor" [The strike by Petrol-İş begins on Monday in BEREC]. *İşçi Postası* [Workers' post], 2 December 1964.

"Petrol-İş Grevi Kazandı" [Petrol-İş won the strike]. 1965. *İşçi Postası* [Workers' post], 18 January 1965.

Saraceno, Chiara. 2016. "Varieties of Familialism: Comparing Four Southern European and East Asian Welfare Regimes." *Journal of European Social Policy* 26, no. 4: 314–326. doi: 10.1177/0958928716657275.

Sarıoğlu, Esra. 2016. "New Imaginaries of Gender in Turkey's Service Economy: Women Workers and Identity Making on the Sales Floor." *Women's Studies International Forum* 54: 39–47. doi: 10.1016/j.wsif.2015.10.006.

Satı, Büşra. 2021. "Working-Class Women, Gender, and Union Politics in Turkey, 1965–1980." *International Labor and Working-Class History* 100 (November): 87–108. doi: 10.1017/s0147547921000119.

Sirman, Nükhet. 2005. "The Making of Familial Citizenship in Turkey." In *Citizenship in a Global World: European Questions and Turkish Experiences*, edited by Fuat Keyman and Ahmet İçduygu, 147–172. London: Routledge.

Soul, Julia. 2020. "'The Union Is like a Family Father, the Chief'. Working-Class Making and (Re) Making and Union Membership Experiences in Two Generations of Argentinian Metalworkers." *Dialectical Anthropology* 44, no. 2: 137–151. doi: 10.1007/s10624-019-09576-z.

Sülker, Kemal. 1986. *36 Yaşında Genç Bir Sendika: Petrol-İş, 1950–1986* [A 36 year-old young union: Petrol-İş, 1950–1986]. Istanbul: Petrol-İş Yayınları.

Türeli, İpek. 2010. "Ara Güler's Photography of 'Old Istanbul' and Cosmopolitan Nostalgia." *History of Photography* 34, no. 3 (August): 300–313. doi: 10.1080/03087290903361373.

Turgay, Feyza. 2017. "1960–1963 Dönemi İşçi Eylemlerine Aşağıdan Bakmak." *İnsan ve İnsan* [Human and human] 4, no. 13: 253–263. doi: 10.29224/insanveinsan.298800.

Van der Linden, Marcel. 1993. "Connecting Household History and Labour History." *International Review of Social History* 38, no. S1 (April): 163–173. doi: 10.1017/s0020859000112350.

White, Jenny B. 2004. *Money Makes us Relatives: Women's Labor in Urban Turkey*. London: Routledge.

White, Jenny B. 2003. "State Feminism, Modernization, and the Turkish Republican Woman." *NWSA Journal* 15, no. 3: 145–159.

White, Jenny B. 2000. "Kinship, Reciprocity and the World Market." In *Dividends of Kinship: Meanings and Uses of Social Relatedness*, edited by Peter P. Schweitzer, 124–150. London: Routledge.

Williams, Brandon Kirk. 2010. "Labor's Cold War Missionaries: The IFPCW's Transnational Mission for the Third World's Petroleum and Chemical Workers, 1954–1975." *Labor* 7, no. 4: 45–69.

Yici, Özkal. 2010. *Kırkbir Uzun Gün: Berec Grevi* [Forty-one long days: The Berec strike]. İşçi Hareketi Dizisi [Labour movement series] 4. Istanbul: Sosyal Tarih Yayınları.

PART 2

Women's Ways of Action: New Perspectives on Repertoires and Agendas

CHAPTER 9

From Anonymity to Public Agency

The Women's Publishing Cooperative in St. Petersburg, 1863–1879

Masha Bratishcheva

Abstract

The history of the Women's Publishing Cooperative (Женская издательская артель, WPC) is an important example of a women's professional coalition in nineteenth-century Russia. Its founders pursued the twin goals of pursuing women's right to engage in publicly visible work and providing women with jobs. During its fifteen years of existence, the WPC published books for children as well as books addressed to women professionals. The enterprise represents a branch of the Russian feminist movement that is usually neglected in discussions about the conflicts between nihilists and aristocrats. Reconstructing the full list of WPC publications, members' biographies, and analyzing the organizational particularities of the enterprise, this chapter explores the limits of women's participation and representation in the print market. Further, by using book history to explore the history of Russian feminism, the author discusses the strategies for transforming the individual precarious intellectual worker into a collective agent that might create an imagined community based on gender.

Keywords

book history – imagined community – Russian feminism in the nineteenth century – women's collective agency – Women's Publishing Cooperative (Женская издательская артель, WPC) – women translators

When we think about book history carefully, we begin to question the processes behind the physical cover and the printed pages inside. What are the publisher's reasons for choosing a specific book? What motivates an editor's choice of one translator over another? Robert Darnton presented the system of relationships between authors, publishers, editors, and booksellers as a cornerstone of

 | DOI:10.1163/9789004682481_010

the development of the Enlightenment.[1] But Michelle Levy criticized Darton's failure to include gender in his analysis and pointed to the extensive archival record through which women's participation in the print market might be traced.[2] Following on Levy's critiques, I go further and claim that women's participation in book production went unnoticed by historians for reasons beyond men's monopolization of the printing process. The most important reason for historians' neglect of women's publishing unions is the refusal to understand them as *imagined communities*.[3] Benedict Anderson coined this term to explain the emergence of national identities—humans' sense of belonging to a community based on territory instead of religion. An affinity with a particular community becomes possible due to the shared experience of knowledge consumption. Such shared knowledge is, according to Anderson, more significant than personal connections or sharing the same geographical space. Drawing on Andersons's ideas, I argue that the protagonist of my essay, the Women's Publishing Cooperative (Женская издательская артель, WPC), was a gender-based imagined community. I explore how this union of women combined motherhood and moneymaking, influencing generations of mothers and women professionals. I also show how a group of anonymous individuals can become a visible, unified actor in the public sphere.

1 Women's Imagined Community

In 1875, Nadezhda Belozerskaia, a 37-year-old journalist and translator, received an offer to collaborate with the journal *Ancient and New Russia* (*Древняя и Новая Россия*). The editor appreciated her style, diligence, and attention to detail. He had only one condition: Belozerskaia had to use the editor's name to sign her work because "the public would not accept [a female name]; a woman, the first case"[4] Having declined the humiliating offer, Belozerskaia nevertheless agreed to publish under the pseudonym Without Fury (Б. Гнв). In the eight years that followed, she signed her real name, N. Belozerskaia, to the article "Royal Weddings in Russia" ("Царское венчание в России").[5] That

1 The author dedicates the chapter to all invisible women of the Feminist Antiwar Resistance. Darnton 1990, 107–135.
2 Levy 2014, 309–310.
3 Anderson, 2006.
4 Belozerskaia 1913, 933.
5 Belozerskaia 1896.

same year, she published a volume about the eighteenth-century writer Vasily Narezhny, for which she received a prize from the Russian Academy of Science.

In the mid-nineteenth century, Belozerskaia was a rare example of a woman journalist who demanded that her texts be properly attributed. Most women who worked in the print market as authors, journalists, rewriters, and translators in the mid-nineteenth century remained silent, unnamed, and excluded from the historical record and the public sphere. The phenomenon of remaining unidentified in the public sphere was not unique to Russia: Nineteenth-century Canada, for example, was characterized by women's exceptional anonymous participation in the printing market.[6] Like their Russian counterparts, Canadian women were highly engaged in book production as translators, bookbinders, and authors. In both countries, they promoted philanthropic initiatives rather than fought for political rights as suffragists.[7] They predominantly published literature for children and rarely intervened in political debates or discussions. The result of their labour was not appreciated publicly; in exceptional cases, critics emphasized the accuracy of a translation, but for the most part, women's work in the publishing industry remained unnoticed. George Eliot highlighted the gender-specificity of translators' work, advising her colleagues, that is, "*all young women* [italics, MB] and some middle-aged gentlemen": "We had meant to say something of the moral qualities especially demanded in the translator—the patience, the rigid fidelity, and the sense of responsibility in interpreting another man's mind."[8]

The main feature that made Russian women translators different from their Canadian counterparts was that Russians found a way to institutionalize their labour activity. They created the Women's Publishing Cooperative, a union of anonymous intellectuals who nevertheless identified themselves as women. With the concept of imagined community, Anderson underlined the importance of shared individual experience.[9] Incapable of expressing their agency (and identities) openly, translators, illustrators, and editors replicated their individual experiences in the books they published. The shared anonymous working experience addressed the challenge of women's inclusion in the public sphere better than the public debates around the so-called "woman question" (женский вопрос).[10] Nameless as individuals, women entered a hitherto

---

6 Gersons 2010. See the chapter "Women and Print in Canadian Colonies."

7 Fraisse 2015, 84.

8 Eliot 1855, 1014–1015.

9 Anderson 2006, 37–40.

10 In Russia, the "woman question" was an umbrella term that united all spheres of life not marked as men's: childbirth, family, women's education, marital legal rights, and prostitution. I oppose applying the concept of the "woman question" to the WPC's activities

male-dominated business. United through the enterprise, the same women who created this imagined community also endeavored to prove women's ability to be public actors with visible influence on their respective societies. The sum of the individual efforts of each anonymous translator resulted in the development of a women's movement that claimed broader civil and legal rights.

As a gender-based imagined community, the WPC relates to the concept of self-definition through the establishment of book standards. In order to go into production, a book had to be attractive for children and ease the teaching process for mothers. Before the WPC decided to translate a book, the original volume had to be approved by the WPC's informal scientific board. It had to reflect the latest scientific discoveries in history, geography, and physics and communicate it in age-appropriate ways. For the first five years of its existence, the WPC focused exclusively on the publication of children's literature. Later, it published works that would provide a comparative perspective on women's labour conditions and professional lives. By addressing women as professionals and organizing the labour process as an enterprise, the WPC moved away from the established representation of women as mothers. As individuals, the Russian women translators who were members of the WPC were very similar to their anonymous Canadian colleagues. As a community, the WPC pursued the goal of helping women enter the public sphere. In this respect, they acted like British feminists, who openly fought for their rights. The Russian case study allows for a better understanding of the transformation of the anonymous precarious intellectual worker into a collective public actor and the creation of an imagined community based on gender.

The WPC was first mentioned in an article by historian Josef Barenbaum.[11] Barenbaum traced the WPC's connections with the revolutionary print market and revealed that the same shops that sold WPC books were also involved in the publication of uncensored literature. Beyond Barenbaum, the WPC is mentioned only in the memoirs of members. The first was a biography of Nadezhda Stasova, one of the most active members of the WPC and a prominent lobbyist for women's higher education.[12] Referring to Stasov, other memoirs mention the artel occasionally as one of the symbols of the liberal era during the reign of Alexander II, without analyzing the nature of the union. In this chapter, I draw on the correspondence between WPC members, which is preserved in

because in Russia, "the question" was publicly posed and resolved without attention to the perspective of women who joined the discussion. See, for instance, Stites 1978, 29–64.

11 Barenbaum 1965.

12 Stasov 1899.

the Institute of Russian Literature (IRLI) and reconstruct members' impact on the enterprise using the official reports of the organization. Access to the Russian State library catalogue allowed me to reconstruct a complete list of books published by the WPC. Along with Stasov's memoirs, I also refer to two biographies: a 1915 biography of Anna Filosofova,[13] and a relatively recent biography of Anna Engelhardt, published by Eleonora Mazovetskaia in 2001.[14]

2 Prototypes

Known today as the Women's Publishing Cooperative, the Women Translators Publishing House (издательство переводчиц), the Women Translators' Artel (work collective) (женская издательская артель), and the Stasova and Trubnikova Publishing House (издательство Стасовой и Трубниковой) were different names of the same enterprise that existed in St. Petersburg (later Petrograd, Leningrad, now St. Petersburg again) between 1863 and 1879.[15] This initiative was the realization of another project that had remained only on paper. In 1861, Anna Engelhardt, a chemist and the first Russian woman to work as a seller in a bookshop, and Petr Lavrov, one of the founders of Russian socialism, developed the founding principles for a future society that would offer women of any social class the opportunity to become independent breadwinners. They called it the Women's Labour Society (Общество женского труда) and drafted the charter:

1. Women occupy one of the most unfortunate positions in our society.
2. Most jobs are inaccessible to women. This is the case because of the discomfort of society related to encountering women in men's spaces rather than women's inability to do these jobs.
3. The consequences of women occupying this [unfortunate] position negatively influence the social order.
4. Women's difficulty in achieving financial security degrades them in the eyes of man. He looks at woman as a dependent, a lesser creature. All

13 Tyrkova 1915.

14 Mazovetskaia 2001.

15 Women's Translation Artel was the name used by its members between 1863 and 1867. Stasova and Trubnikova Publishing House was the official name of the WPC between 1867 and 1879. The Women's Publishing House was the name mostly used by critics and memoirists. The Oxford Encyclopedia *Women in World History* translates the title as Women's Publishing Cooperative. To avoid misunderstanding, I use the Oxford translation in the text.

> these troubles—ethical and economic—provoke us to establish a society that will organize women's workplaces on [the basis of] equitable principles.[16]

Engelhardt and Lavrov saw the Women's Labour Society as a prototype for a women's labour union. The enterprise was considered an experiment that would prove women's ability to do the same jobs as men. Although numerous wives helped their husbands write and edit books (Anna Dostoevskaia, for example), this job was considered a reliable wife's responsibility rather than a professional job deserving of payment. The founders believed that the idea that women were incapable of performing *men's* work was a product of social bigotry and had nothing to do with any innate attributes of women. The Society planned to open a bookbindery and publishing houses for children's literature and academic scholarship. The emergence of an enterprise run exclusively by women could move the discussion concerning women's rights to a new level. The problem was that both Engelhardt and Lavrov were considered disloyal to the Russian government and could not receive permission from the censor's office to initiate such enterprise; thus, the project was never realized.

Organizational experiments related to women's employment were not unique to the Russian Empire. In 1860, Emily Faithfull organized the Victoria Press, a London-based printing house where women worked. The goals of both projects were so similar, they could only be distinguished from each other by the name of their founder. Faithfull's printing and editing house Victoria Press was an example of an enterprise run by women, with equitable salaries, professional training opportunities, and progressive labour conditions.[17] Moreover, Faithfull met the same resistance from the conservative segments of British society as Engelhardt and Lavrov did. She wrote about that period:

> When I proposed, in 1859, to open a printing-office for women, I was told that setting up type would degrade and injure them, and that I could scarcely suggest a more suitable employment; yet, even while these warnings were being given, girls were extensively employed, in an inferior capacity, in printing establishments as machine feeders; a branch of the business which appeared to me so unsuitable, that I never allowed it to be undertaken by girls in the office I eventually started for female compositors.[18]

16 Mazovetskaia 2001, 53–54.

17 Okeson 2017.

18 Faithfull 1871, 6.

Faithfull regularly appeared in the news; articles about her views on women's employment appeared in London newspapers right under the news from Russia.[19] Both Engelhardt and Lavrov had access to these newspapers. Although we do not have written evidence of their awareness of the English project, Lavrov and Engelhardt were likely inspired by the British example.

3 The Women's Publishing Cooperative

Various features of the unrealized Women's Labour Society became the starting points for another activist, Mariia Trubnikova (1835–1897). The daughter of Camille Le Dentu,[20] a translator and a mother of four children, Trubnikova was fully aware of Engelhardt and Lavrov's unsuccessful attempt to organize a women's union. Still, she believed that a similar project was feasible. Trubnikova was a member of the so-called Female Triumvirate (Женский триумвират), the informal alliance of three women: Nadezhda Stasova, Anna Filosofova, and Mariia Trubnikova.

Nadezhda Stasova (1820–1896) was known as the sister of music critic Vladimir Stasov, the latter of whom advocated for musical realism and the Five (Могучая Кучка)[21] in the press. Sometimes she is remembered as the daughter of architect Vasily Stasov. Another relative, Dmitry Stasov, was a lawyer who defended Karakozov's group.[22] As for her mother, we know that she died of cholera when Nadezhda was a little girl. In 1859, after returning from a European voyage, during which Stasova had been treated for depression, she engaged in charity work and later joined the struggle for women's access to higher education.

Anna Filosofova (1837–1912) was the daughter of Anna Sulmenova and Pavel Diagilev, members of the hereditary nobility. As she later wrote, she joined Trubnikova's circle out of curiosity: she had not received a decent education during her childhood and was trying to fill in the gaps. In 1855, she married

19 See, for instance, Public Opinion, 39.

20 Camille Le Dentu is known for following her husband Vasilii Ivashev into exile after the Decembrist revolt of 1825 (Pavliuchenko 1986, 69–70).

21 The union of five composers: Mily Balakirev, César Cui, Modest Mussorgskii, Nikolai Rimsky-Korsakov, and Alexander Borodin.

22 Dmitry Karakozov was an early Russian terrorist who attempted to kill tsar Alexander II in 1866.

Vladimir Filosofov, the first chief of the military attorney and the architect of the army reforms of the 1860s.[23]

Trubnikova suggested a humble but more feasible plan as compared to Engelhardt and Lavrov's proposal. She designed a cooperative for women translators. The charter of her project contained five paragraphs:

1. The maximum number of members of the Women's Publishing Cooperative is 100.
2. Members elect, by mutual agreement, two head managers, a secretary, and an accountant who will manage the Cooperative's affairs.
3. The Cooperative's principal affairs consist of publishing academic and children's books, both original and translations.
4. At its founding, each member of the Cooperative should make a deposit.
5. The deposit may be paid in money or labour: original or translated articles are acceptable.[24]

Mariia Trubnikova and Nadezhda Stasova were elected the managers of the WPC. Trubnikova was responsible for managing relationships with authors and editors, and Stasova organized the work of bookbindery and book distribution. Trubnikova's sister, Vera Cherkesova (Ivasheva), worked as an accountant.

The difference between Lavrov's and Trubnikova's initiatives was scale. Lavrov and Engelhardt were interested in a grand experiment that would lead to a renewed society. Although theoretically achievable, the project ended before the realization of the plan because of a lack of practical organizational skills: organizers could not reach agreement on the question of whether noblewomen could join the Women's Labour Society. Trubnikova, on the contrary, was not a prolific theoretician of women's labour; rather, she was invested in efforts to employ women in her close circle and to publish books for children. In terms of practical questions concerning the creation of distinct positions, WPC members did not openly declare gender independence or class equality. While exclusively women performed the translation work, men participated in other stages of production.[25] The gradual inclusion of women into male institutions met with less resistance from the conservative public because it addressed the woman question more subtly than the open confrontation

23 The military reforms included, among other things, the abolition of physical punishment in the army and a transformation of the nature of service: Instead of recruits who served in the army for 20 years, the reforms called for a period of conscription ranging from 1 to 12 years depending on the educational level and family status of the conscript.

24 Barenbaum 1965, 227–228.

25 Compare with Faithfull, who also did not exclude male labour in her factory and emphasized that a working woman should still be a benevolent mother and a loyal wife.

Engelhardt and Lavrov promoted. Instead of defending the idea of women's equality, the WPC tended to mimic men, avoiding conflict altogether. Initiated as a translation enterprise, the WPC soon brought women into each stage of book production: editing, printing, coloring, binding, and selling. Because they knew the principal market players, cooperative members could reach agreements with typographers and bookshops. Through artel mediation, at least two women whose surnames were Vistelius and Glenn held positions as typesetters in typography. Surrounded by men, they suffered from misogyny, but typography still paid better than private teaching.[26]

The choice of the cooperative as the form of corporation was natural for the organizers: a fair salary based on workers' contributions and collective management of the enterprise was a key feature of organizations of this type.[27] Stasova's brother recalled: "All [new] enterprises tended to take this form … Partnership and equality was the maxim of the era."[28] Another reason for choosing to work collectively was that it was subject to relatively simple regulations. Though the term cooperative (*артель*) had existed in Russia since the 1830s, this form of enterprise was most popular among peasants or seasonal workers.[29] Because collective agricultural work or mutually beneficial construction projects (like watermills) were private affairs and did not interfere with the state's interests, the legal regulation of artels was *laissez-faire*. In the case of the WPC, however, the relaxed regulation enjoyed by other cooperative enterprises remained elusive because WPC organizers stepped into a politically sensitive field: the government zealously controlled book printing. Multiple bureaucrats scrutinized each stage of the publishing process. A censor could remove pages from a printed book, prohibit the circulation of a released book, and destroy all copies. A permit for the organization of the enterprise had to be acquired.

The case of this exclusively female cooperative was help up in bureaucratic red tape for three years, and the decision was ultimately unfavorable. Although the censorship bureau of the Third Department of Imperial Chancellery did not find any reason to prevent the establishment of the cooperative in principle, the Minister of Internal Affairs rejected the WPC's application: "The minister does not accept it as possible to solicit the approval of a society established

26 Stasov 1899, 127.

27 Isaev 1881, I–VI. The author follows the transformation of the term *artel* from collective work in which all members were united by their lower class origins and their common goal to finish work to the form of an enterprise based on the principles of equality, joint capital, and collective physical effort.

28 Stasov 1899, 122–123.

29 Isaev 1881, III.

on such broad bases and orders the announcement that the applicants' petition is not subject to approval."[30] By the time of the decision, the WPC had already been operating for three years and had published four books under the name The Women Translators' Edition (Издание переводчиц). After 1867, when the official rejection was received, the Cooperative was renamed. The new title was Stasova and Trubnikova's Publishing House. Stasova and Trubnikova explained the renaming by citing their concern for the workers; the latter could face legal problems by working for an unregistered company. The new name did not influence the character of the enterprise. It functioned as a cooperative until its closure, and all members shared costs and dividends. By 1879, WPC members were supposed to receive bonuses according to their impact on the enterprise (see Appendix 2).

4 Members

The precise number of women translators who joined the artel fluctuated annually. Barenbaum mentioned thirty-six women,[31] Cherkesova, twenty-seven women,[32] while Shtakenshnaider mistakenly counted one hundred members[33]—the artel never reached the limit defined by the charter. In 1865, according to Tyrkova, there were fifty-four women members,[34] and in the opinion of Iukina, there were fifty-three members.[35] Poliksena Stasova, a WPC member, gives the following numbers:

Vladimir Stasov identified "the most active translators and editors" as follows: Nadezhda Belozerskaia, Anna Engelhardt, Anna Filosofova, Mariia Ermolova, Elizaveta Beketova, Alexandra Markelova, Vera Pechatkina, Poliksena Stasova, Mariia Men'zhinskaia, Vera Ivasheva, Anna Shakeeva, [no name given] Tiblen, Olga Butakova, Elena Shtakenshnaider, Anna Shulgovskaia. In his list of *the most active* members, Stasov included only those members of the artel who were part of the Russian nobility. He did not mention those who were not members of the old nobility or those who could compromise the enterprise's liability.[36] Submitted as a list without commentary, WPC members symbolize

30 Barenbaum 1965, 226.
31 Barenbaum 1965, 226.
32 Cherkesova 1899, 27.
33 Shtakenshnaider 1934, 332.
34 Tyrkova 1915, 136.
35 Iukina 2007, 179.
36 Stasov 1899, 125.

TABLE 9.1 Membership of the Women's Publishing Cooperative

Year	Members
1863	36
1864	54
1865	63

SOURCE: STASOVA, POLIKSENA [СТАСОВА, ПОЛИКСЕНА]. 1900. "ИЗДАТЕЛЬСКОЕ ДЕЛО" [THE PUBLISHING BUSINESS]. *ЖЕНСКОЕ ДЕЛО* [WOMEN'S BUSINESS], MAY 1900, 24–30

the invisible territory of Russia during the period. Though their names were given, many details about their personalities remain lost to history. With several exceptions, members' biographies and professional impact can be restored only from dispersed fragments left in memoirs, newspaper articles, and obituaries. In some notable cases, they are described as ancestors of famous men, such as Elizaveta Beketova (1834–1902), who was until recently mentioned in sources as Alexander Block's grandmother. Only in 2020 did her translation work became the subject of in-depth comparative analysis.[37]

A closer look at the list of translators paints a picture that does not fit the existing coordination system proposed by Richard Stites and which was taken for granted by historians of the Russian women's movement. Stites finds the conflict between "aristocrats" and "nihilists" to be one of the definitive characteristics of the Russian women's movement.[38] Borrowed from fictional literature, this division obscures the long period of coordination that was based on gender solidarity rather than political alliances or social origin. The WPC united women from across the socio-political spectrum. For example, at one pole, we find the aristocrat Mariia Ermolova (1825–1905). A socialite, as Tyrkova describes her,[39] Ermolova was appointed the first inspector of medical courses in St. Petersburg. Her presence in the field guaranteed that medical courses would be seen as respectable in the eyes of the conservative public. Considered by organizers as someone who would enforce moral conduct, Ermolova was not taken seriously by liberal critics. A humorist wrote the following about her:

37 Samorodnitskaia 2020.

38 Stites 1990, 64–115.

39 Tyrkova 1915, 135.

Though she had outstanding morality,
And displayed every skill and ability,
To the ladies in her own academy,
She taught nothing except servility.[40]

At the middle of the spectrum was Alexandra Markelova-Karrik (1832–1916), the partially deaf daughter of a middle-class nobleman and a single mother. After moving to St. Petersburg, she joined the Znamenskaia commune, the most well-known Fourierist experimental community in Russia. Her ties to the commune and single motherhood raised suspicions among tsarist authorities, and she was placed under police surveillance permanently. At the same time, Poliksena Stasova considered Markelova-Karrik one of "the most important and active members" of the artel.[41] Apart from working for the WPC, Markelova-Karrik also translated for *St. Petersburg News* (*Ведомости*). She worked at the newspaper daily, including Sundays. In a letter to Polinksena Stasova, she wrote that she is a "hunted nag," overwhelmed by the amount of work at the newspaper.[42] In another letter, apologizing for unfinished work, she called herself "the animal, prohibited in Talmud. I could refer to work, to my 'unhealthy heart,' as you ironically wrote, but anyone could remind me that I had had to complete the work [the text] beforehand and do not bother people, from whom I've never seen anything less than compassion."[43] These letters reveal her modesty, which is less the hysterical humility of a desperate person but rather the sardonic modesty of a self-respecting woman who realizes the limits of her potential and yet continues to conduct herself with dignity.

The other pole of the spectrum was occupied by Mariia Mariia Beteva-Turgeneva (before 1839–1892), one of the first revolutionaries in Russia.

40 Mart'ianov 1891, 87. In original: Благотворить она умела/ И знала всяческое дело/ Но женские взяв в руки курсы/ Создала что-то вроде бурсы. I'm grateful to Katya Knyazeva for an appropriate translation.

41 Stasova 1900, 28.

42 Письма от Каррик Александры Григорьевны к Поликсене Степановне Стасовой [Letters from Karrik, Alexandra Grigorievna to Poliksena Stepanovna Stasova] Case 294, Inventory 5, Fond 294, Institute of Russian Literature, IRLI (Институт Русской Литературы, ИРЛИ), St. Petersburg.

43 Письма от Маркеловой Александры Григорьевны к Поликсене Степановне Стасовой [Letters from Markelova, Alexandra Grigor'evna to Poliksena Stepanovna Stasova]. Case 292, Inventory 5, Fond 294, IRLI.

According to Valentin Ovsiannikov,[44] Mariia Apollos'evna Turgeneva moved to St. Petersburg in the mid-1860s and joined Trubnikova's circle.[45] In 1870, she applied to the University of Zurich[46] but returned after one semester and opened three schools in villages in the Stavropol region. A year later, she organized courses for future teachers. In 1872, she invited Sofia Perovskaia[47] to work in one of her schools, after which she was placed under permanent police surveillance. Accused of planning the peasants' revolt, Turgeneva was supposed to be arrested, but fled the country. She spent the rest of her life in Zurich, working as a cleaner in a Russian canteen.

Comparing these three members' lives and experiences demonstrates that the WPC cannot be described as a proto-political enterprise whose members held similar political views. Furthermore, it is not true that women united exclusively for financial independence. Nadezhda Stasova and Mariia Menzhinskaia were wealthy enough already and did not need to work. Still, for most members, the WPC was one of the only opportunities they had to work. Along with joining the WPC, they also worked for multiple newspapers. Such was the case of Nadezhda Belozerskaia; after her divorce, she wrote: "I didn't want to ask for child support. With youthful cockiness, I decided to raise them by myself and give them secondary and higher education [the last was achievable in her sons' case only, MB]. And I did."[48] She combined her work in the WPC with her position as Nikolai Kostomarov's secretary; he was a prominent—and prolific—historian.

Because of the symbolic discontinuity resulting from the tradition of changing surnames after marriage, another WPC member, Ekaterina Il'ina-Tsenina-Zhukovskaia (1841–1913), might be mistaken for three different people in the sources. Ekaterina Il'ina became Tsenina to escape from her parents. As Tsenina, she joined the WPC[49] and Znamenskaia commune. She joined the commune after she fled from her first husband. Later, as Zhukovskaia

44 Ovsiannikov 1999, 266–277. Though Ovsiannikov's text corresponds with other sources, his essay does not contain any references or bibliography and should be treated with caution.

45 Other sources confirm that Beteva was Trubnikova's cousin. Serno-Solovievich writes in a letter to Mariia Trubnikova that "In Zurich, they definitively don't ask for any records or diplomas to listen the lecture. Please, discuss it with M. Turgeneva" (Serno-Solovievich 1935, 400).

46 Pavluchenko 1988, 228–229.

47 Sofia Perovskaia: Russian terrorist, the organizer of the successful assassination of tsar Alexander II (1881). The first woman in Russia executed by hanging.

48 Belozerskaia 1913, 925–941.

49 Pavliuchenko 1988, 133.

she became part of the family of the Head of the State Bank of the Russian Empire and wrote *The Notes* (*Записки*)[50] about the period when she identified as a nihilist. Describing the history of the Znamenskaia commune, Kornei Chukovskii gave Zhukovskaia an exclusively negative assessment, calling her a pretentious woman who treated Sleptsov, the head of the commune, as an intellectual equal.[51] Apart from her memoirs about the 1863–1864 period, Il'ina-Tsenina-Zhukovskaia also left behind articles on economics she published in the *Europe Newsletter* (*Вестник Европы*), but scholars have never analyzed this part of her past.

What united these very different women? The key threads that tied them together were gender solidarity and their shared need to confront prejudices about women's lack of "fitness" for institutionalized intellectual work. The note "Women's Publishing Edition" printed on the book cover was a means to highlight women's exit from the private sphere while simultaneously proclaiming their public agency. Through this imprint, the WPC absorbed the names of all its individual members and promoted the labour of the entire gender. At the same time, individual members preserved their traditional roles as mothers, concealing the agentic dimensions of their public identities. This blend of the traditional and activist roles of women is important for understanding the nature of an imagined community: whereas motherhood was visible, only a few devoted members emphasized their translation work. In WPC correspondence, members explained their absence from meetings by citing sick children and, in the very same letters, debated whether or not to pay dividends. In other words, anxiety about a child's health was combined with a discussion about the health of the enterprise. The integration of motherhood into activism was also reflected in the WPC's selection of books to publish, which I will discuss below.

Cross-referencing archival data makes it possible to confirm who worked on specific books. The challenge, however, is that even for a double translation (a translation made from another translation instead of the original), whereas the name of the English or German translator is listed in the introduction, the female translator remained anonymous,[52] despite the fact that male translators were usually identified in books in the nineteenth century.[53] The WPC did not mention translators' names on the cover or front pages or in the editorial

50 Zhukovskaia 1930.

51 Chukovskii 1967, 311.

52 For the reconstructed list of translators, and the sum of members' dividends, see Appendix 2.

53 Levin 1985, 9–10. According to Levin, the translator's anonymity was a specific feature of the 17th and 18th centuries but not later.

introductions of the books it published. Given its commitment to activism, one can only speculate about the reasons for this omission. Was it because of the widespread prejudice against women's work? Or did this practice emerge from the principle of collectivism? Or would it be too challenging to list all the translators? None of the members of the artel left any evidence of the WPC's reasons for not including translators' names. Nevertheless, individual anonymity allowed the WPC to foreground women's collective agency without specifying which women had joined the enterprise.

While the translators' names remained unknown, the WPC benefited from its association with famous men. In some cases, the inability to list a man's name on the book cover was grounds for refusing to translate an important text. For example, the WPC did not translate William Kampenter's book because the most famous Russian physiologist, Ivan Sechenov, did not share his view. Sechenov agreed to supervise the translation anonymously, but the WPC decided that without his name on the cover, the book would sell poorly and did not translate it in the end.[54] The single exception to the rule of anonymity might be *An Old-Fashioned Girl* by Louisa May Alcott. The Russian State Library Catalog lists Elizaveta Beketova as translator. Still, all the original copies of that edition are lost, and we cannot confirm whether Beketova's name was actually on the cover page.

5 Why Did It Last So Long?

How was the Women's Publishing Cooperative able to operate for as long as it did despite its status as a partially unofficial enterprise? Statistics offer one possible answer to this question. Despite the common belief that rural men represented the majority of migrants to St. Petersburg after the abolition of serfdom, this was not the case. In 1860, the population of the city was 464,656 people. Of this number, only 176,320 (38 percent) persons were women. Five years later, the number of women had increased to 221,415 (41 percent), whereas the number of men remained almost the same (318,060). So, 45,000 women migrated to the capital within five years,[55] and these women were looking for jobs. We do not know how many were literate, but the increasing number of women's magazines proves the active participation of women in the economic life of the city. Most of these magazines did not cover politics or social problems,

54 Barenbaum 1965, 231–232.

55 Karnovich 1865, 61.

but their existence clearly indicates there was an attempt to address women's social needs: articles addressed questions of women's manners, fashion, and housekeeping.[56] Women's inclusion in the economy coincided with the idea of rehabilitating Russian society after the loss of the Crimean War, and the book trade was one sign of recovery. Within five years, between 1850 and 1855, the Russian publishing market released 6,036 books. This number almost doubled in the next five years, up to 10,924.[57]

Another answer concerns the flourishing print market. New typographic technologies drastically decreased the costs of printing. The WPC's books cost between ten kopecks and two to three rubles and were affordable for the literate citizenry.[58] The cooperative, thus, was part of a movement that transformed books into instruments of enlightenment rather than symbols of prosperity or a hobby. The government included WPC books on the official list of literature recommended to schoolteachers. This decision was only partially an economic choice; mostly, this inclusion was a genuine attempt on the part of the state to increase opportunities for mothers and future generations of women. Poliksena Stasova, a WPC member, linked the lack of appropriate literature to the low level of girls' primary education and their consequent exclusion from public life; she saw it as her duty to fill this lacuna.[59]

The third answer to the question of why the WPC was able to operate for ten years, whereas other similar enterprises operating at the same time barely survived for two years was the organizers' wealth and connections. Family ties did not guarantee financial prosperity, but they did give the whole enterprise a certain level of stability other corporations did not enjoy. The cooperative was never criticized for being (too) radical, and its success was partially due to the support it received from moderately progressive men. There were also some rather famous men among the WPC's scientific advisers: Dmitry Mendeleev, Ivan Sechenov, and Andrey Beketov, whose names appeared on the title pages or in the prefaces of WPC books. Collaboration with famous men played a dual role in the destiny of the enterprise. On the one hand, WPC academic advisers were the most advanced professors in Russian higher education. The enterprise shielded itself due to the presence of men and stood above reproach because of these men's pro-emancipatory goals. On the other hand, men's

56 Tishkin 1984, 127.

57 Kufaev 2003, 157.

58 Strahov 1937, 118–119.

59 Stasova 1918, 5–7; "Мои воспоминания" [My memoirs], Folder 4, Case 286, Fond 2711 Российский государственный архив литературы и искусства (Russian State Archive of Literature and Arts, RGALI), Moscow.

symbolic presence overshadowed women's roles in book history (and history more broadly): the presence of famous scientists rendered the work of translators' invisible.

6 What Did the WPC Publish?

The first book released by the WPC was Hans Christian Andersen's *Fairytales* (1864). Often mentioned in memoirs and research, this book is considered the most significant achievement of the cooperative. The first Russian edition of *Fairytales* that came out was missing two tales—"Heaven's Garden" and "Angel"—because of censorship. Furthermore, all illustrations of angels, queens, and kings had to be redrawn because their crowns and wings had to be removed.[60] Despite these difficulties, *Fairytales* received a great deal of public interest. Released right before the New Year holidays, the first edition sold within a month, and two more editions were published, with an overall print run of 6,800 copies. The book also received favorable reviews from critics, who remarked on the quality of the translation and Anderson's style and language. The influential journal in the Russian Empire *The Contemporary* (*Современник*) remarked that this book was the first Russian book to be produced entirely by women. WPC members carried out all aspects of the process, from the translation, to the illustrations and editing, to the printing and binding.[61] The enterprise repeated its success in 1868 by releasing *New Fairytales*.

The following three books also addressed children education: translations of Augustin Thierry's *Stories of Time Merovingian* (1864), Hermann Wagner's *In Nature* (1864), and Henry Walter Bates *The Naturalist on the River Amazons* (1865). The challenge of choosing specific books to translate was dictated by limited sources that overlapped with ambitious goals. The cooperative volumes aimed to address the need to disseminate an accurate and deep knowledge of European history, the foundations of geography and life science, but at the same time, they had to be captivating works. Educators understood the lack of such readings.[62] The artel met this challenge. Critics wrote about the translation of Thierry that it was "a brilliant volume on the time of the first French kings, which combines a deep historical excavation of sources and vivid narration."[63] Bates' volume soon became famous because of the news that Charles

60 Stasov 1899, 135.
61 Stasov 1899, 131.
62 Stasova 1918, 7.
63 Stasov 1899, 137.

Darwin advised Bates to publish it. Wagner's book became a botanical handbook for primary schools. Three out of the four first volumes were included in the state catalogue of "valuable" books for women's educational institutions.

The next volume, *Tales of Ancient People* (1865), was written by Ivan Khudiakov, a folklorist and future revolutionary. *Tales* included five booklets on history, starting with Ancient Rome, and the WPC published three of them. The book, addressing the social order of ancient times, contained thoughts on the welfare state, social order, and the nature of power. Discussing Massalia, one of the ancient Greek colonies, Khudiakov mentioned: "This city was perfectly organized. There was no king but a people's government."[64] Underlying the idea of the commonwealth, the author constantly referred to differences between ancient and modern times in favor of modern-day civilization that "tends to educate hundreds of millions of people, whereas Greek society was limited to hundreds of thousands."[65] Though memoirists do not doubt the authorship of these booklets, the book itself did not contain author's name; only the titles, "Women Translators' Edition" and "O. I. Bakst Printing House," were printed on the cover page.

Next, the WPC released *The Book of Travel Novels,* a series of stories based on Theodor Dielitz's writing (1868), and Otto Ule's *Why and Because* (1868), an illustrated physics encyclopedia for children. This book answered questions about the nature of heating, crystallization, mixtures, etc. The last two books, which published for children, were two novels by Louisa May Alcott: *An Old-Fashioned Girl* (translated in 1875) and *Little Women* (translated in 1876).

It is difficult to accurately access the WPC's impact on the market because the book history of the Russian Empire does not have enough data concerning print runs of works published in the mid-nineteenth century. However, there are a few examples that might be useful as points of comparison: in 1864, forty-one books for children were printed in the Russian Empire, and the WPC published three of them.[66] As for the number of copies printed, in some cases, WPC editions were comparable to copies of *The Contemporary,* the most famous magazine of the time,[67] and exceeded the number of copies of Herzen's *The Bell* (*Колокол*), which had print runs of 500 to 2,500 copies, respectively, between 1857 and 1867.[68]

---

64 Khudiakov 1865, 22.

65 Khudiakov 1865, 8.

66 Frolova 1988, 28.

67 In 1861, more than 7,000 copies of *The Contemporary* were printed; 6,800 copies of the WPC's Andersen's *Fairytales* were printed. For details, see Appendix 1.

68 Frolova 1988, 60.

7 Politics and the WPC

Two books diverged from the general book selection policy of the WPC and addressed women as professionals. *Women's Labour* and *A Handbook for Hospital Sisters* were some of the first examples of Russian nonfiction literature "for women" that neither addressed motherhood nor offered moralizing advice on women's public behavior. Further, there has been no analysis of these works, which prompted me to take a closer look at their content.

Women's Labour by Anton Daul (1868) was an extension of the *American Employments of Women: A Cyclopœdia of Woman's Work* by Virginia Penny (1863). The success of Penny's work inspired Daul; he added practical information about the kinds and conditions of women's labour in European countries. He calculated standard salaries and types of women's labour unions and described the professional help available for women who had lost their jobs. In some fields, Daul mentioned cases where workers' rights had been violated and workers abused. The artel translated this volume in 1869, and Piotr Tkachev, a critic and future revolutionary theorist, wrote the introduction. In the anonymous preface, the Russian publishers explained their reasons for publishing this work:

> On the one hand, the book introduces the reader to the current conditions in different industries in which women can work. On the other hand, [the volume] demonstrates women's roles in many fields of work and proves that it is possible to expand women's labour rights and use women's labour power in different types of technological industries. The weakness of the book is the absence of a rational understanding of the woman's question. The book points out the realistic chances that women will gain the equal right to work in different industries. Still, it misses the consequences of such equality, and how women themselves may contribute to an ultimate solution to the woman question.[69]

As with the WPC's other books, translators' names remain unknown to the public. Only the authorship of the introductory article is mentioned: Petr Tkachev.

The content of articles, which would have been approved by Trubnikova and Stasova, merits attention: Tkachev revised Julie-Victoire Daubié's work *Poor Woman of the Nineteenth Century* (*La femme pauvre du XIX siècle* [1869]). The first French woman to receive a university degree after the Revolution,

69 Daul 1869, I.

Daubié wrote a historical review of women's occupations and legal restrictions starting in the Middle Ages. Using a similar approach as Penny's work and Daul's research on the Russian context, Tkachev extensively drew from Daubié's discussion of women's occupations far beyond the scope of the Russian imagination in the mid-1860s. He quoted examples of women participating in warfare as commanders, soldiers, and knights: "using political rights, women also performed the duties that stemmed from these rights: if need be, they rode horses, united their vassals, and led them, repelling attacks by internal and external enemies."[70] For Russian women largely excluded from participation in any aspect of public life except for charitable work, this discussion of thirteenth-century women in the military was a revelation. Tkachev also referenced women's ability to elect and be elected to parliament during the early medieval period. Moving to the fifteenth century, Tkachev mentioned that although women could not be elected as judges or members of parliament anymore, they still were able to hold office as civil servants: "our lawyers still remember Mrs. Calonne, who held the office of archivist in the Seine department archive at the beginning of the century. She worked for 42 years and was famous for her incredible memory, resourcefulness, and ability to find the needed document in the mountain of folios."[71] Tkachev devoted several pages to women's skills in the field of medicine; among other facts, he mentioned women's expertise in midwifery. Prohibited for French men, midwifery required several years of theoretical and practical preparation and required passing a final exam: "In official ceremonies, midwives enjoyed the same rights as other physicians; they sat with other doctors altogether in the same room, and midwives had their own uniforms, suits, and badges."[72] Unlike the French case described by Tkachev, in the Russian Empire, midwives' training was not conducted in universities until 1872.[73] Analyzing the reasons for the decline of women's influence on social processes, Tkachev identifies the transformation of the character of labour as the cause.

> When labour was a difficult, unavoidable responsibility, men tried to avoid it and shifted [work] to women, or at least did not exclude women from the labour market. When labour became "a right," one began to feel

70 Daul 1869, XIII.
71 Daul 1869, XVI.
72 Daul 1869, XXIV–XXV.
73 Zlatkovskii 1875, 10.

> the lack of it; women had to leave the market, and their ability to compete with men was taken away.[74]

As one of the first Russian Marxists, Tkachev expanded the definition of inequality to include gender and proposed that women's opportunities be understood in terms of rights rather than obligations. He placed gender inequality in labour on a similar level as class inequality—and was harshly criticized for it. Aleksei Suvorin (under the name Stranger [Незнакомец]) accused Tkachev of amateurism and a lack of knowledge of French history. He shamed Trubnikova and Stasova for cooperating with a revolutionary romantic.[75] The popular journal *Fatherland Notes* (*Отечественные записки*) criticized the book for unnecessary theorization, asserting that the books by Penny and Daul were written as reference books with useful addresses and numbers, whereas the Russian edition criticized the current social order without providing any guidance for women looking for work.[76] In response to critics, Tkachev insisted on the economic basis of women's oppression and desperately attempted to link gender inequality with women's economic conditions.[77] He formulated what we would call intersectional oppression—overlapping class and gender oppression—the concept Gayatri Spivak introduced to political and cultural theory in the twentieth century.[78]

Vladimir Stasov, Nadezhda's brother and a reliable memoirist, meticulously traced Stasova's life path. Still, he mentioned the publication of Daul's and Penny's volumes only once, providing the translators' names: Mariia Malysheva, Nadezhda Belozerskaia, A. N. Shulgovskaia, and Olga Pushkareva.[79] The absence of any mention of the scandalous public debate involving all the liberal newspapers in the capital must have been an intentional omission. Tkachev had a reputation as a radical, whereas Stasov described the artel as a progressive charitable and educational enterprise without a revolutionary bent.

A Handbook for Hospital Sisters (1877) by Florence Sarah Lees was the second book published by the artel that was addressed to female professionals rather than to mothers. Lees wrote this book after years of practicing under Florence Nightingale's supervision. It was the first professional literature for nurses

---

74 Daul 1869, XXXIV.
75 Stranger 1869.
76 "Zhenskii trud" 1869.
77 Tkachev 1990 [1869], 393–405.
78 Spivak 1988.
79 Stasov 1899, 146.

published in the Russian Empire, though memoirists, including Vladimir Stasov, forgot about it. The translation was published at the beginning of the Russo–Turkish War (1877)—the first military conflict in which Russian women participated as physicians.[80] Women who did not pass their training course in the Medical Academy[81] could not perform doctors' duties in the battlefield but could volunteer as nurses. *A Handbook* was translated for the latter group of women as its target audience. It included general guidelines for nursing: it outlined proper hygiene practices, provided instructions for the necessary tasks nurses should be able to perform, and it distinguished between the types of operations nurses could perform and those that only physicians should do.

The erasure of the single book that addressed women's professional problems from public memory is significant. The question of education and children's literature was frequently discussed in the media and attracted considerable public attention. Theoretical discussions about women's moral destiny were also of interest to men. What stayed hidden from the public eyes, then, were women's professional lives. Medicine was a new profession open to women; public concerns about women in the field included proposals to dress corpses during anatomy classes to ensure the maintenance of moral standards.[82] The fact that the WPC addressed the book to female medical professionals and not mothers has heretofore been ignored by historians.

8 Conclusion

The Women's Publishing Cooperative existed from 1863 until 1879, when its board decided to officially shut down the enterprise because the artel had not published a single book for two years. The cooperative boasted several features that determined the destiny of the enterprise and the direction of the Russian feminist movement that emerged in the 1860s. Attaining public visibility without open confrontation was one of them. The Female Triumvirate tended to remain in the shadows of men, following traditional patterns established by women engaged in public life, i.e., charity work. But their interpretation of charity work went far beyond its typical conceptualization. Instead

80 Abramov 1886, 9.

81 Women had voluntarily participated in wars as sisters of mercy since the Crimean War (1853–1856). In 1872, four years before the Turkish war, the first women's medical course was established at the Medical Academy. One of the WPC's members, Mariia Ermolova, became its first director.

82 Svatikov 1916, 13.

of supporting the material survival of women, the WPC endeavored to include women in economic relations as equal participants and helped women become visible as independent economic actors. The WPC succeeded in creating a union based on solidarity rather than income, family status, or political preference. Contemporaries and most historians interpret the WPC as a quasi-charitable organization that helped women find jobs.[83] Neither contemporaries nor scholars have recognized the WPC's attempts to create a language and an environment in which only gender mattered. Its members appealed to individuals with similar values and virtues through their selection of books and the tone of their introductory articles. Parallel to conventional historical narratives about the artel, a unified history of these women revises our understanding of women's place in the public sphere of the Russian Empire.[84] The WPC framed language and shaped norms for the contemporary woman, especially her educational background and life interests. Instead of moralizing, the WPC tackled the issue of women's agency, creating a new gender-based imagined community. The cooperative set a high standard: the WPC was among the first to publish children's books explicitly designed to increase young people's interest in science and their social environment rather than focus on the memorization of the Bible or grammar lessons. For the first time, they addressed women primarily as professionals and not as wives or mothers. The WPC viewed women as specialists who needed to be supported intellectually rather than financially.

The Women's Publishing Cooperative was not a single enterprise initiated by pioneers of the Russian feminist movement. The artel also successfully lobbied for the establishment of the first university for women. By opening up opportunities for women to study and work, the WPC improved the lives of the next generation of Russian women and taught and supported them. In a stance that was unimaginable for men, they resisted the myth that there was a perpetual conflict between parents and children, signaling their readiness for the changes their future daughters—both real and symbolic—were going to make to the existing system. The generation of the Figner sisters and Vera Subbotina, the best-known women rebels, was raised by the women who published books and organized study courses rather than by the men who dreamed about new utopias.

The case of the WPC offers a broader perspective on the history of women's unions in the nineteenth century. It encourages researchers to revise the existing chronology of the feminist movement and search for other evidence

83 For instance, Iukina and Guseva 2004, 109–112; Likhacheva 1899, 483–487.

84 About parallel historical narratives, see Anderson 2006, 204.

of women's collective participation in public life as political actors instead of objects.

Appendixes. From Anonymity to Public Agency: The Women's Publishing Cooperative in Saint Petersburg, 1863–1879

Appendix 1.

TABLE 9.2 Translators' names and number of books copies[85]

Title	Year	Translators	# of copies
Hans Christian Andersen, *Fairytales*	1864	Mariia Malysheva Alexandra Markelova Anna Shulgovskaia Anna Engelhardt Ekaterina Tsenina	6800 (including two additional editions)
Augustin Thierry, *Stories Of Time Merovingian*	1864	No data	4000 (including additional edition)
Hermann Wagner, *In Nature*	1864	Kudinovich (no name given), Elena Vistelius, Dzichkovskaia (no name given) Anna Engelhardt	4800 (including additional edition)
Henry Walter Bates, *The Naturalist on the River Amazons*	1865	Anna Shulgovskaia, Schults, Munt, Babkina	4000 (including additional edition)

85 The table is created based on a compilation of several sources. The first is Poliksena Stasova's article about the WPC (1900). The second set of sources includes invoices preserved in Stasova's archive (Case 349, Inventory 5, Fond 294, IRLI) and the WPC financial report (case 242, inventory 5, Fond 294, IRLI). The third source is Stasov's memoirs (1899). Since none of sources is complete, I have included the translator's name in the list in case it is mentioned in at least one source.

TABLE 9.2 Translators' names and number of books copies (*cont.*)

Title	Year	Translators	# of copies
Ivan Khudiakov, *Tales of Ancient People*	1865	No data	3000
Hans Christian Andersen, *New Fairytales*	1866	Alexandra Markelova Anna Shulgovskaia Ekaterina Tsenina Mariia Ermolova Mariia Malysheva	2000
Theodor Dielitz, *The Book of Travel Novels*	1868	Alexandra Markelova	2000
Otto Ule, *Why and Because*	1868	Anna Shulgovskaia Anna Engelhardt Nadezhda Belozerskaia Mariia Malysheva	6000
Anton Daul, *Women's Labour*	1869	Mariia Malysheva Olga Pushkareva Nadezhda Belozerkaia A. N. Shulgovskaia	1200
Louisa May Alcott, *An Old-Fashioned Girl*	1875	Elizaveta Beketova	No data
Louisa May Alcott, *Little Women*	1877	Alexandra Markelova Olga Klark	No data
Florence Sarah Lee, *A Handbook for Hospital Sisters*	1877	No data	No data
Total number of copies			33 800

Appendix 2.

TABLE 9.3 Women's Publishing Cooperative members' financial contributions

No	Name	Initial contribution in rubles[86]	Dividends in rubles in 1872
1	N. A. Belozerskaia	75	38.79
2	M. G. Ermolova	60	31.04
3	A. N. Engelhardt	120.46	62.32
4	A. P. Filosofova	75	38.79
5	M. S. Olhina	75	38.79
6	M. V. Trubnikova	72	37.24
7	V. V. Cherkesova	62	32.23
8	M. A. Menzhinskaja	77	39.82
9	O. A. Kobeko	60	31.04
10	M. V. Turgeneva	45	23.26
11	E. I. Tsenina	33	26.96
12	P. S. Stasova	75	38.79
13	M. E. Markelova	15	7.77
14	V. I. Pechatkina	100	51.72
15	E. A. Shtakenshnaider	77	39.82
16	N. V. Stasova	60	38.79
17	E. G. Beketova	30	15.53
18	Livotova (no name given)	60	31.04
19	Rostovtseva (no name given)	60	31.04
20	A. N. Shulgovskaia	75	38.79
21	L. I. Stasulevich	75	38.79
22	E. N. Voronina	60	31.04
23	O. N. Butakova	45	23.28
24	A. I. Ivanova	15	16.56
25	M. I. Malysheva	45	23.28
26	E. I. Vistelius	15	7.77
27	[Mariia] Babkina	45	No data
28	O. I. Ivanova	32	7.77

86 Рукописи Поликсены Стасовой об артели. Дело 352, опись 5, фонд 294, ИРЛИ [Poliksena Stasova's notes about the artel. Case 352, Inventory 5, Fond 294, IRLI]. Two separate pages of contributions are preserved. Apparently, the first part of the list (Belozerskaia-N. V. Stasova, lines 1–16) reflects the very first contributors. The second part of the list (Beketova-Ivanova, lines 17–28) is titled "Contribution of those who were WPC members from 1863 until 1869." The second part of the list should be interpreted as a list of those who joined WPC when it was already operating.

Bibliography

Abramov, Iakov [Абрамов, Яков]. 1886. *Женские врачебные курсы* [Medical courses for women]. St. Petersburg: Pechatnia S. P. Iakovleva.

Anderson, Benedict. 2006. *Imagined Communities: Reflections on the Origin and Spread of Nationalism*. ACLS Humanities E-Book. London, New York: Verso.

Barenbaum, Iosif [Баренбаум, Иосиф]. 1965. "Из истории русских прогрессивных издательств 60–70х годов XIX века (Женская издательская артель М.В. Трубниковой и Н.В. Стасовой)" [From the history of Russian progressive publishing houses of 1860s–1870s (M. V. Trubnikova and N. V. Stasova's Women's Publishing Cooperative)]. In *Книга. Исследования и материалы. Сборник XI* [The book: Research and materials], 223–241. Moscow: Kniga.

Belozerskaia, Nadezhda [Белозерская, Надежда]. 1913. "Надежда Александровна Белозерская, урожденная Ген (автобиография)" [Nadezhda Alexandrovna Belozerskaia, née Gen: An autobiography]. *Исторический вестник* [Historical newsletter], no. 6: 925–941.

Belozerskaia, Nadezhda [Белозерская, Надежда]. 1896. *Царское венчание в России. Исторический очерк* [Royal wedding in Russia. A historical essay]. St. Petersburg: Baikov i K.

Cherkesova, Vera [Черкесова, Вера]. 1899. "Мария Васильевна Трубникова" [Maria Vasil'evna Trubnikova]. *Женское дело* [Women's business] (December): 15–37.

Chukovskii, Kornei [Чуковский, Корней]. 1967. *Собрание сочинений, том 5* [Collected works, volume 5]. Moscow: Khudozhestvennaia literatura.

Darnton, Robert. 1990. *The Kiss of Lamourette: Reflections in Cultural History*. New York: W. W. Norton.

Daul, Anton. 1869. *Женский труд в применении к различным отраслям промышленной деятельности* [Women's labour applying to different fields of industrial activity]. St. Petersburg: Izdanie Trubnikovoi i Stasovoi.

Eliot, George. 1855. "Translations and Translators." *Leader* (October 20): 1014–1015.

Engelhardt, Anna [Энгельгардт, Анна]. 1870. "Очерки институтской жизни былого времени. (Из воспоминаний институтки)" [Essays on the institute's life (From memoirs)]. *Заря* [Sunrise], no. 8: 107–149.

Faithfull, Emily. 1871. *Woman's Work: With Special Reference to Industrial Employment*. London: Victoria Press.

Fraisse, Geneviève. 2015. *История женщин на Западе. Том 4. Возникновение феминизма. От Великой французской революции до Мировой войны* [History of women in the West, vol. IV: Emerging feminism from the French revolution to the World War]. St. Petersburg: Aleteia.

Frolova, Irina [Фролова, Ирина]. 1988. *Книга в России, 1861–1881* [The book in Russia, 1861–1881], vol. 1. Moscow: Kniga.

Gerson, Carole. 2010. *Canadian Women in Print, 1750–1918.* Waterloo: Wilfrid Laurier University Press.

Gorlova, Elena [Горлова, Елена]. 2018 "Доктор, Лечивший Поэта Кольцова" [The doctor who healed poet Kol'tsov]. *Вороженский Государственный Медицинский Университет Им. Бурденко* [Voronezh State Medical University named after N. N. Burdenko], 19 April 2018. http://vrngmu.ru/news/2018-god/15268/.

Isaev, Andrei [Исаев, Андрей]. 1881. *Артели в России* [Artels in Russia]. Yaroslavl: Pechatnia Gubernskogo pravleniia.

Iukina, Irina [Юкина, Ирина]. 2007. *Русский феминизм как вызов современности* [Russian feminism as challenge]. St. Petersburg: Aleteia.

Iukina, Irina, and Guseva, Iulia [Юкина, Ирина; Гусева, Юлия]. 2004. *Женский Петербург* [Women's Petersburg]. St. Petersburg: Aleteia.

Karnovich, Evgeniĭ [Карнович, Евгений]. 1865. *О Развитии женского труда в России* [About the development of female labour in Russia]. St. Petersburg: Tipografiia V. Bezobrazova.

Kartsev, Nikolaĭ [Карцев, Николай]. 1897. *Мариинский институт: 1797–1897. Исторический очерк.* [Mariinsky Institute: 1797–1897. A historical essay]. St. Petersburg: Tipografiia Sankt-Peterburgskogo gradonachal'stva.

Khudiakov, Ivan [Худяков, Иван]. 1865. *Рассказы о старинных людях* [Tales of ancient peoples]. St. Petersburg: O. I. Bakst.

Khvoshchinskaia, Sof'ia [Хвощинская, Софья]. 1861. "Воспоминания институтской жизни" [Memoirs of the institute's life]. *Русский вестник* [Russian newsletter], no. 9–10.

Komarova, Aleksandra [Комарова, Александра]. 1881. *Одна из многих: из записок нигилистки* [One of many: A nihilist's notes]. St. Petersburg: Tipografiia E. Mettsiga.

Kufaev, Mikhail [Куфаев, Михаил]. 2003. *История русской книги* [The history of the Russian book]. Moscow: Pashkov Dom.

Levin, Iurii [Левин, Юрий]. 1985. *Русские переводчики XIX века и развитие перевода* [Russian translators of the nineteenth century and the development of translation]. Leningrad: Nauka.

Levy, Michelle. 2014. "Do Women Have a Book History?" *Studies in Romanticism* 53, no. 3, (Fall): 297–317.

Likhacheva, Elena [Лихачева, Елена]. 1899. *Материалы для истории женского образования в России, (1086–1856)* [Materials for the history of women's education in Russia (1086–1856)]. St. Petersburg: Tipografiia M. M. Stasiulevicha.

Malysheva, Mariia [Малышева, Мария]. 1875. *Природа и Жизнь: научно-литературный сборник для детей старшего возраста* [Nature and life: Scientific handbook for teenagers]. St. Petersburg: Tipografiia tovarishchestva "Obshchestvennaia pol'za".

Mart'ianov, Petr [Мартьянов, Петр]. 1891. *Словарь-альбом русских деятелей XIX века в силуэтах, кратких характеристиках, надписям к портретам и эпитафиям* [Dictionary-album of Russian figures of the nineteenth century in silhouettes, brief descriptions, portrait inscriptions and epitaphs]. St. Petersburg: Tipo-litografiia R. Golike.

Mazovetskaia, Eleonora [Мазовецкая, Элеонора]. 2001. Анна Энгельгардт (Санкт-Петербург второй половины XIX века) [Anna Engelhardt (St. Petersburg in the second half of the nineteenth century)]. St. Petersburg: Akademicheskii proekt.

Mogilianskii, Aleksandr [Могилянский, Александр]. 1968. "Неизвестный автор 'Современника'" [The unknown author of *Sovremennik*]. *Русская Литература. Историко-литературный журнал* [Russian literature: History and literature journal], no. 1: 203–204.

Nekrasova, Elena [Некрасова, Елена]. 1887. *Из прошлого женских курсов* [From the past of women's courses]. Moscow: n. p.

Okeson, Taylor. 2017. "A Woman's Right to Work: Emily Faithfull and the Victoria Press." *The Journal of Publishing Culture* 7: 1–11.

Ovsiannikov, Valentin [Овсянников, Валентин]. 1999. *Ставрополь—Тольятти. Страницы истории. Часть II. Дела и люди* [Stavropol'-Tol'iatti. History pages, part II, deeds and people]. Tol'iatti: Sovremennik.

Pavliuchenko, Eleonora [Павлюченко, Элеонора]. *В добровольном изгнании. О женах и сестрах декабристов.* [In voluntary exile. About the wives and sisters of the Decembrists]. Moscow: Nauka, 1986.

Pavliuchenko, Eleonora [Павлюченко, Элеонора]. 1988. *Женщины в русском освободительном движении. От Марии Волконской до Веры Фигнер* [Women in the Russian liberation movement: From Mariia Volkonskaia to Vera Figner]. Moscow: Mysl'.

Public Opinion. 1862. 2, no. 29 (12 April).

Samorodnitskaia, Ekaterina [Самородницкая, Екатерина]. 2020. "'Плеяда равнодушных ремесленников': как в России переводили Джордж Элиот" ["A constellation of indifferent artisans": How George Eliot was translated in Russia]. In *Shagi/Steps* 6, no. 3: 137–151. doi: 10.22394/2412-9410-2020-6-3-137-151.

Serno-Solov'evich, Aleksandr [Серно-Соловьевич, Александр]. 1935. "Пятнадцать неопубликованных писем с приложением записки А.А. Серно-Соловьевича об его имущественном положении. Предисловие О.К. Булановой-Трубниковой и Б.П. Кузьмина" [Fifteen unpublished letters, accompanied by a note by A. A. Serno-Solov'evich on his property status. Preface by O. K. Bulanova-Trubnikova and B. P. Kuzmin]. In *Звенья. Сборник материалов и документов по истории литературы, искусства и общественной мысли XIX века* [Links. A collection of materials and documents on the history of literature, art, and public thought in the nineteenth century], 374–415. Moscow-Leningrad: Akademiia.

Shtakenshnaider, Elena [Штакеншнайдер, Елена]. 1934. *Дневники и Записки (1854–1886)* [Diary and notes (1854–1886)]. Moscow-Leningrad: Akademiia.

Spivak, Gayatri Chakravorty. 1988. *Can the Subaltern Speak?* Basingstoke: Macmillan.

Stasov, Vladimir [Стасов, Владимир]. 1899. *Моя сестра Надежда Стасова* [My sister Nadezhda Stasova]. St. Petersburg: Tipografiia M. Merkusheva.

Stasova, Poliksena [Стасова, Поликсена]. 1900. "Издательское Дело" [The publishing business]. *Женское Дело* [Women's business], May 1900, 24–30.

Stasova, Poliksena [Стасова, Поликсена]. 1918. "Мои воспоминания" [My memoirs], Folder 4, Case 286, Fond 2711 Российский государственный архив литературы и искусства [Russian State Archive of Literature and Arts, RGALI], Moscow.

Stites, Richard. 1978. *Women's Liberation Movement in Russia: Feminism, Nihilism, and Bolshevism, 1860–1930*. Princeton, NJ: Princeton University Press.

Strakhov, Vasilii [Страхов, Василий]. 1937. "Пушкин и массовый читатель. Библиографический очерк" [Pushkin and the mass reader. A bibliographical essay]. In *А. С. Пушкин. 1837–1937, сборник статей и материалов* [A. S. Pushkin. 1837–1937, Articles and materials], 115–123. Saratov: n. p.

Stranger [Незнакомец]. 1869. "Недельные очерки и картинки" [Weekly novels and pictures]. *Sankt-Peterburgskie Vedomosti*, 24 November.

Svatikov, Sergei [Сватиков, Сергей]. 1916. "Русские студентки (1860–1915)" [Russian women students (1860–1915)]. *Путь студенчества* [Students' path]. Moscow, 90–111.

Tishkin, Grigorii [Тишкин, Григорий]. 1984. *Женский вопрос в России. 50–60 годы XIX* [The woman question in Russia, 1850s–1860s]. Leningrad: Izdatel'stvo LGU.

Tkachev, Petr [Ткачев, Петр]. 1990. *Кладези мудрости российских философов* [Treasure troves of wisdom of Russian philosophers]. Moscow: Pravda.

Tyrkova, Ariadna [Тыркова, Ариадна]. 1915. *Сборник памяти Анны Павловны Философовой* [Anna Pavlovna Filosofova's collection of memories]. Petrograd: T-vo R. Golike i E.A. Vil'borg.

"Zhenskii trud v primenenii k razlichnoi otrasli promyshlennoi deiatel'nosti" [Женский труд в применении к различной отрасли промышленной деятельности; Women's labour applied to different kinds of industries]. 1869. *Отечественные записки* [Fatherland notes], no 1: 107–114.

Zhukovskaia, Ekaterina [Жуковская, Екатерина]. 1930. *Записки: брак по принципу, Знаменская коммуна, Плещеев, Некрасов, Салтыков-Щедрин* [Notes: Marriage in principle, Znamenskaia Kommuna, Pleshcheev, Nekrasov, Saltykov-Shchedrin]. Leningrad: Izdatel'stvo pisatelei v Leningrade.

Zlatkovskii, Mikhail [Златковский, Михаил]. 1875. *Женское специальное образование в Петербурге. Настольная книжка для учащихся женщин, равно как и для других лиц, нуждающихся в свведениях по этому предмету* [Women's special education in St. Petersburg. Handbook for female students and others, who need knowledge on this subject]. St. Petersburg: Tipografiia Balasheva.

CHAPTER 10

"Each Woman Must Join the Trade Union of Her Profession!"

Women's Labour Activism in the Austro-Hungarian Bourgeois-Liberal, Feminist Associations and Their Press

Dóra Fedeles-Czeferner

Abstract

How did the two most influential Austrian and Hungarian bourgeois-liberal, feminist women's organizations use their press to try to convince their followers (members, readers of their journals, and supporters) to join trade unions and (actively) participate in labour activism? How did the official press organs of these associations function as an important forum and scene for labour activism? How were women's labour activism and the exploitation of women workers interpreted in the articles? The chapter seek answers to these questions based on a qualitative and quantitative analysis of the official organs of the General Austrian Women's Association (Allgemeiner Österreichischer Frauenverein, GAWA, Vienna, 1893–1922) and the Hungarian Feminists' Association (Feministák Egyesülete, FA, Budapest, 1904–1942; 1946–1949). The official organ of GAWA, *Neues Frauenleben* (*New Women's Life*) was published between 1902 and 1918 in Vienna, and FA's *A Nő és a Társadalom* (*Woman and Society*) appeared in Budapest between 1907 and 1913. This chapter examines how these journals covered issues related to the integration of middle-class and working women from the lower classes into trade unions and their concrete efforts to facilitate such integration before the outbreak of World War One.

Keywords

Austro-Hungarian Monarchy – content analysis – bourgeois-liberal and feminist organizations – discourse analysis – middle-class women – women's labour activism – working-class women

The political, economic, and social transformation of the final two decades of the nineteenth century led to an increasing number of working women and to

 | DOI:10.1163/9789004682481_011

a parallel rise in women's emancipation movements in Austria and Hungary. In 1900, 41 percent of women were engaged in paid work in Austria; this proportion was 27.6 percent in Hungary.[1] Structural transformation of the economy resulted in the feminization of certain professions and led to the decline of their prestige. In Hungary, the majority of working women employed before 1914 worked in the food processing and printing industries, tobacco and match manufacturing, the chemical industry, and in factories producing building materials and brickworks. In Austria too, these were the most important sectors that relied on female labour, along with the clothing and textile industry. Women in larger numbers started working in both countries as schoolteachers; female clerks in banks, post offices, telegraph offices, and the railways; and in commerce. A majority of the female workforce was young, unmarried, and childless.[2] For these reasons, a growing number of newly established women's associations, which became differentiated along ideological lines at the turn of the century,[3] began to fight for equal rights for women working in intellectual professions as well as in the agricultural, industrial, and service sectors of the economy; they also began to promote women's labour activism. These organizations also engaged in struggles for women's right to be employed in professions that had heretofore been exclusively male.

In this chapter, I argue that the two leading Austrian and Hungarian bourgeois-liberal and feminist associations promoted women's labour activism based on similar principles in their periodical press before the outbreak of World War One. Both organizations treated their official press organs as particular forums and platforms for women's labour activism through which they could constantly communicate with their followers. In the Austrian context, I focus on the labour activism of the General Austrian Women's Association (Allgemeiner Österreichischer Frauenverein, GAWA) and its official organ entitled *New Women's Life* (*Neues Frauenleben*). GAWA was founded in Vienna in 1893 and was active until 1922. It began publishing *New Women's Life*, its second monthly journal, in 1902 and managed to keep it alive until 1918. For the Hungarian context, I focus on the labour activism carried out by the Feminists' Association (Feministák Egyesülete, FA) and its two official organs. FA was founded in Budapest in 1904 and operated until 1949. Its first journal was *Woman and Society* (*A Nő és a Társadalom*), published between 1907 and

1 Rigler 1976, 54–55; Sullerot 1972, 143.

2 For more details, see Gyáni 2020; Maderthaner 1986; Appelt 1985.

3 Anderson 1992, 35–38. For the history of women's organizations in Austria and Hungary, see, e.g., Hauch 2006, 965–1003; Zimmermann 1999.

1913, which was followed by *The Woman: A Feminist Journal* (*A Nő. Feminista Folyóirat*), published between 1914 and 1928.

GAWA and FA, representing the radical left-wing of women's organizations, had basically the same aims, profiles, and the backgrounds of their membership—(upper) middle-class women—was similar. They approached the challenges working women faced almost identically, and the strategies they developed to support working women were also similar. I demonstrate that the communication and discursive strategies both associations employed to encourage working women to join trade unions and urge them to fight for the equal rights of women in the labour market paralleled each other. I also argue that, contrary to the accusations of the social democratic and Christian-socialist women's associations of both countries, GAWA and FA encouraged the employment of not only (upper) middle-class women and defended the interests of women workers from these groups but did so also for women in the lower classes. However, their means to achieve the latter goal were limited. Additionally, I evaluate how successful the two organizations were in using their press to convince their female followers (members, readers of the journals, and their supporters) to join trade unions and (actively) participate in labour activism.[4]

Organized on the basis of modern ideals, GAWA and FA rejected the principles of traditional women's organizations of the early nineteenth century. Instead of charity work, they made an effort to use practical tools to support women. They pursued a rich variety of politics related to women's work and carried out a wide range of activities related to job placement and the protection of working women's interests, which has been an under-studied dimension of these organizations in scholarship on both countries thus far.[5] There are also several identical features of these organizations' journals in relation to their profile, structure, and content, including the strategies of their respective editorial offices. Furthermore, it is possible to identify a group of Austrian and Hungarian publicists who published articles in all three journals and shared their thoughts on working women's status and their labour activism in both countries.

4 This research is based on my PhD dissertation, in which I analyzed the history and the press activity of GAWA and FA between 1893 and 1918: Czeferner 2020. For the results of this research as it relates to press history, see Czeferner 2021.

5 In Hungary, the lack of focus on this subject is partly because of the preoccupation of the secondary scholarship with female suffrage. For some exceptional studies dealing with this rich variety of politics, see Hauch 2006, 965–1003; Bader-Zaar 1999, 365–383; Zimmermann 1999; Mucsi 1980, 333–342.

Using a comparative perspective to explore this history is necessary for three reasons. First, the histories of Austria and Hungary had been inseparable from each other for centuries. Nevertheless, even at the beginning of the 2020s, research comparing the diplomatic, economic, and social history of the Monarchy as a whole is scant. Second, from its establishment, FA regarded GAWA and its work as a model, and FA's association's press activities and strategies for promoting women's labour activism reveal a sense that the organization was following its Austrian predecessor's example. Thus, GAWA stimulated the labour activism carried out by FA. Despite these similarities, however, there were some differences in the two organizations' strategies, which are discussed below. Third, the Austrian-Hungarian comparison provides a much more relevant context concerning the history of the Hungarian feminist movement and its press than does the Hungarian movement's relations with the Anglo-Saxon movement, which has heretofore been over-emphasized in the scholarship. Indeed, I argue that there were significantly more direct and indirect links between the Austrian and Hungarian bourgeois-liberal and feminist movements, i.e., between GAWA and FA, than between Hungarian and British or U.S. activism. Therefore, in order to understand pre-World War One women's labour activism in Hungary, it is more relevant to compare it to activism in Austria than to activism in the United Kingdom or the United States. Although, these countries are known as the birthplaces of radical feminism, their economic and social development differed significantly from that of Hungary; thus, such a comparison does not yield analytically relevant research results. For this reason, I plead for a more inclusive approach to the history of Austria-Hungary rather than a continuation of nationally divided historiographies that emerged with the collapse of the Monarchy.

1 Sources, Methodology

The basis of my arguments is my analysis of *New Women's Life*, *Woman and Society*, and *The Woman: A Feminist Journal*, which uses the methods of critical discourse analysis and content analysis.[6] I analyzed every issue of the three journals published between January 1907 and the military mobilization of early August 1914 from both a quantitative and qualitative perspective. In total, this investigation included 98 issues (2,889 articles) from the Hungarian journals

6 I relied on the principles of Allan Bell and Teun A. van Dijk, who developed critical discourse analysis. van Dijk 2006; Bell 1991. These principles were adapted to my sources.

and 89 issues (1,941 articles) from the Austrian periodical. Furthermore, I relied on archival sources i.e., the documentation of GAWA, FA, and the estates of their leaders, who were also the editors of these journals.

In addition to enabling me to thoroughly analyze the structure and content of the journals, these methods helped reveal that the press activity of GAWA and FA focused primarily on the general protection of women's interests, specifically those of working women, as opposed to women's suffrage. Furthermore, examining the discursive strategies employed by publicists is essential because linguistic-rhetorical and stylistic devices played a fundamental role in shaping the opinions and identities of working women.[7] In the longer term, persuasive strategies were a crucial means of encouraging women to organize. Such an analysis, therefore, demonstrates that both the Austrian and Hungarian editorial offices of the above journals gave prominence to articles covering the economic emancipation of women living outside the Dual Monarchy, which can be explained by the transnational embeddedness of GAWA and FA.

2 Aims of the Two Organizations in the Field of Labour Activism and Working Women's Protection and Their Related Press Activity before 1914

In addition to the commonality of their objectives, working methods, membership, and the characteristic features of their press activities, many other strands directly linked GAWA and FA. The two associations originated in the middle- and partly upper-class milieu of educated women (teachers, doctors, female office workers, and university students of Jewish origin, as well as the wives of aristocrats and the *grande* bourgeois) and had strong relationships with each other. Furthermore, both GAWA and FA were directly or indirectly linked to several transnational women's organizations, e.g., the International Council of Women (1888–, Washington, DC) and the International Woman Suffrage Alliance (IWSA, 1904–, Berlin). However, FA was more successful in the international arena during the period examined here.

GAWA began its activity in fin de siècle Vienna due to the initiative of Auguste Fickert (1855, Vienna–1910, Maria Enzersdorf, Austria), a middle-class teacher, women's rights activist, and devoted pacifist, who was the future editor-in-chief (*Herausgeberin*) of *New Women's Life*. She was not only a leading figure of the radical (progressive) left-wing Austrian bourgeois-liberal ("*bürgerlich-liberal*")

7 On this, see von La Roche 2008; van Dijk 2006, 116–120.

women's movement and president of GAWA; she also cooperated with proletarian women's organizations and took an active role in campaigns around education and legal protection for working-class women.[8] GAWA, apart from a brief period immediately after its foundation, was led by Fickert until her death. In terms of Austrian law, there was no legal way to prevent the association's promotion of women's labour activism, which, according to GAWA, was closely connected to educational rights. The leadership of GAWA believed that the "comprehensive solution to the women's question" was attaining "the economic independence of women," which would require access to adequate (vocational) education.[9]

In comparison to other contemporary Austrian women's associations, the radicalism of GAWA was most obvious in its treatment of the closely interconnected issues of the plight of domestic servants and prostitution. Regarding the latter issue, GAWA members did not believe that the legislation in place would restrict commercial sex. Meanwhile, in every arena, they sought to stress the importance of sexual education for children, which they represented as a partial solution for the problems related to the handling of domestic servants, i.e., to the "misery of maids," as it was framed at the time. They called for the introduction of working women's maternity support and the reform of marital legislation. From its very beginning, GAWA advocated for the reform of the entire civil law code (*Allgemeines Bürgerliches Gesetzbuch*), which had been in effect since 1811.[10]

After the death of Auguste Fickert, Leopoldine Kulka (1872, Vienna–1920, Vienna), a journalist, board member of GAWA, co-editor of *New Women's Life*, and one of Fickert's "best students" (*Schülerin*), was elected vice-president in 1911. She filled this position until her death. After 1910, the presidency remained vacant. As a devoted pacifist, Kulka actively participated in the establishment of the Austrian Branch of the Women's International League for Peace and Freedom (Österreichischen Zweiges der Internationalen Frauenliga für Frieden und Freiheit, 1920–1938, Vienna) and formulated close contacts with the leaders of FA.[11] During her tenure as the leader of GAWA and editor of *New Women's Life*, Kulka was able to rely on Christine Touaillon (1878, Jihlava, Bohemia–1928, Graz), a GAWA board member. In addition to these two women, another board member, Adele Gerber (1863, Vienna–1937, Vienna) is worth mentioning; she

8 Hacker 2006, 131–133.
9 Stenographishes Protokoll 1893, 12.
10 Stenographishes Protokoll 1893, 8–13.
11 Malleier 2001, 48–59.

was responsible for the publication of *New Women's Life* and served as managing editor from 1902 until 1918.

FA was founded in 1904 at the international initiative of IWSA.[12] Aletta Jacobs (1854, Sappemeer, Netherlands–1929, Baarn, Netherlands), a leading member of IWSA and the Dutch progressive women's movement in 1902, was the leading voice behind its establishment, although at this stage, she was still thinking in terms of a joint Austro-Hungarian organization.[13] In the end, FA established as an independent Hungarian auxiliary organization of IWSA. It was led by Vilma Glücklich (1872, Vágújhely/Nové Mesto nad Váhom/Neustadt an der Waag–1927, Vienna) and Rosika Schwimmer (1877, Budapest–1948, New York), two prominent activists involved in the Hungarian and international women's and peace movements at the time. As a young bookkeeper, Schwimmer participated in the establishment and in the leadership of another progressive Hungarian organization dedicated to protecting woman office workers: the National Association of Women Office Workers (Nőtisztviselők Országos Egyesülete, NAWOW, Budapest, 1896–1919).[14] Schwimmer chaired the political committee of FA between 1904 and 1920. She had been well embedded in the international women's movement since the beginning of the 1900s, and she also became an internationally renowned publicist during these years. She was one of the first Hungarian women to earn a living from her journalism.[15] Because of her experience in publishing, she was elected editor of *Woman and Society*, and in 1914, she became the managing editor of *The Woman: A Feminist Journal*. Vilma Glücklich, the first women to receive a degree at the University of Budapest, a teacher, and the closest colleague and friend of Schwimmer, served as president of FA from its establishment almost until her death. She also took on an essential role in the organization of the women's international peace movement during and after World War One.[16]

---

12 Letter from Auguszta Rosenberg to Rosika Schwimmer, 4 December 1904, Rosika Schwimmer Papers [RSP], Box 6, New York Public Library Manuscripts and Archives Division [NYPL], General Correspondence I.A. MssCol6398.

13 Letter from Aletta Jacobs to Rosika Schwimmer, 1 August 1902, RSP, Box 6, NYPL, General Correspondence I.A. MssCol6398.

14 It must be noted at this point, that besides FA, NAWOW was also involved in the publication of *Woman and Society* and *The Woman: A Feminist Journal* until 1915. The cornerstone of their cooperation, dominated by FA, will not be discussed here as they are of little relevance to the topic of this chapter. For the objectives of NAWOW, see A Nőtisztviselők Országos 1909.

15 Zimmermann and Major 2006, 484–491.

16 Zimmermann 2006, 162–166.

Similar to GAWA, FA aimed to support women's rights in the labour market, education, civil rights, politics, family life, motherhood, and prostitution. In their 1905 work plan, they also detailed their goals related to women's work:

> We wish for a woman to acquire economic independence, such that she does not have to be restricted by financial considerations when selecting her life partner [...], or the financial rewards of her work, so she may spend her own income, and that of her parents or her husband, on acquiring goods of genuine value.[17]

Besides the protection of working women' interests (including industrial workers, agricultural employees, and domestic servants, along with those employed in the liberal professions), FA's goals included the campaign for the extension of women's institutional education and the battle against prostitution and the trafficking of girls. FA also struggled to prevent the exploitation of female labourers and solve the legally unsettled situation of domestic servants.[18] Related to these issues, like GAWA, FA allocated space in its official organs to discuss issues related to prostitution and the trafficking of girls, topics that were still considered taboo in the press of the Austrian and Hungarian social democratic and Christian socialist movements.[19]

Vienna, under the leadership of the Christian socialist politician Karl Lueger (1844, Vienna–1910, Vienna; mayor 1897–1910), was by no means an idyllic setting for a women's association that wanted to promote the radical emancipation of women. In addition to ensuring GAWA would receive publicity, Auguste Fickert and her fellow women were constantly fighting against what they branded the "Christian socialist scourge."[20] Unlike their Austrian counterpart, FA managed to win the support of the city administration of Budapest shortly after its establishment. As mayor of the Hungarian capital, István Bárczy (1866, Pest–1943, Budapest; mayor between 1906–1919), a member of National Democratic Civil Party, contributed considerable sums to fund FA's operations, and more specifically to support its labour exchange. The contrast

17 Tájékoztatás a Feministák Egyesületének céljairól és munkatervéről [Report on the objectives and plan of work of the Feminists' Association], 1905, Feministák Egyesülete [Feminists' Association, hereafter FA], item a, P999, Magyar Nemzeti Levéltár Országos Levéltára [National Archives of Hungary, MNL OL].

18 As outlined in the document referenced in footnote 17.

19 Czeferner 2021.

20 Fickert even published a mocking poem entitled "Dignity of Women" (Würde der Frauen) to criticize Karl Lueger and Christian socialist women's organizations. Ehmer 1996, 73–92.

between antagonistic environment in Vienna and the supportive milieu in Budapest help explain a few differences between the working strategies and press activity of GAWA and FA, as well as their overall effectiveness. At this point, however, neither GAWA nor FA had (publicly) committed themselves to any Austrian and Hungarian political party, which in practice meant that they were willing to accept the support of any and all political groupings that supported their aims.

An important aspect of this analysis is that the three journals essentially capture the moment when a self-conscious but not yet politically empowered group of (upper) middle-class Austrian and Hungarian women stepped out of obscurity and began leaving their mark on public life, in part through the press. *New Women's Life*, *Woman and Society*, and *The Woman: A Feminist Journal* are distinctive because they were the first modern feminist journals in the Austro-Hungarian Monarchy that gave women the space to make their voices heard on issues of labour activism. Their editors created an entirely new discursive space in which women's work and women's labour activism played central roles. The two associations and their journals closely collaborated, and publishing and communicating with their respective supporters and the general public through the periodicals were important dimensions of their labour activism. All the three periodicals, however, had a relatively restricted readership (compared to e.g., more popular family journals or fashion magazines). In terms of their social background, subscribers and readers of the journals, similar to the membership of the associations, were composed of (upper) middle-class women and men living in Vienna and Budapest and, primarily in the case of Hungary, in a few economically and socially more developed provincial cities.

In addition to the similarities between the journals (their structure, content, communication strategies, advertising policies, and use of images) and the indirect contacts between the associations within the framework of transnational women's organizations, the editorial offices of GAWA and FA were closely connected. Schwimmer's first publications outside Hungary were published in the first official organ of GAWA entitled *Documents of Women* (*Dokumente der Frauen*, 1899–1902, Vienna) and later in *New Women's Life*, which she began contributing to regularly, publishing articles on the situation and perspectives of working women in Hungary. GAWA and later FA considered it crucial to secure their press, and they made significant financial sacrifices to keep their journals alive. Their strategies to achieve this were shared in letters Auguste Fickert, Adele Gerber, and later Leopoldine Kulka exchanged with Rosika Schwimmer. Schwimmer turned to her Austrian colleagues for guidance several times when FA started planning the publication of *Woman and Society*. Occasionally she asked practical questions related to publishing and funding *New Women's Life*, whereas at other times, she recruited authors who were either GAWA-members or had previously published in the Austrian journal. On other occasions, she requested information about the Austrian women's movements and their labour activism. The intensity of cooperation between associations and editorial offices was further deepened through personal meetings of activists, which often occurred during congresses of the international women's movement, and by Schwimmer's regular visits to Vienna.[21]

3 Female Work and Women's Labour Activism in the Journals of GAWA and FA

A content analysis of articles published in the press organs of GAWA and FA[22] reveals that the Austrian and Hungarian journals devoted the greatest attention to women's work and women's labour activism in their thematic content.[23] During the period between January 1907 and August 1914, 29 percent (556 articles) of the articles appearing in *New Women's Life* and 35 percent (1,021 articles) of articles published in the Hungarian periodicals discussed these issues. Compared to this, the proportion of articles on female suffrage in the Hungarian journals was 15 percent.[24] The proportion was 12 percent in *New Women's Life*, which is partly the result of §30 of the law on associations (*Vereinsgesetz*). This law was enacted in Austria in 1867 and excluded women from membership in political associations and prohibited (theoretically) women's organizations from publishing on female suffrage in their journals until 1918. Board members of GAWA and the editorial office of *New Woman's Life* worked to get around this law, and in addition to engaging in political activism, they published articles on the issue. Nevertheless, the number of articles about

---

21 Gehmacher 2011, 58–64.

22 For the searchable Excel database of articles from the three journals between 1907–1918, see SchwimmerBlog, Cikkadatbázisok [Article database], https://schwimmerblog.com/cikkadatbazisok/.

23 Categorization of the articles was based on their subject-matter and by the selection of words of primary importance (key words) in their texts (Andor 2009). According to my classification, articles were published on the following topics: alcoholism, actualism, general women's rights, family law, fashion, high cost of living, child protection, war/peace/pacifism, literature, white slavery, women's labour and women's labour activism, sexuality, women's movements in general, education, prostitution, and women's suffrage.

24 This does not reflect earlier claims of the theoretical literature. See, e.g., Nagyné 2001; Nagyné 1981.

suffrage published in both Austrian and Hungarian journals was far lower than the number of pieces discussing women's work and women's labour activism. Apart from these issues, the topic of women's movements in general was the most prominent issue covered in the periodicals, which can be explained by the general profile of the associations.

Because women's work and women's labour activism were the most frequently discussed subjects, it is necessary to examine how the journals discussed these topics in greater detail. Through this analysis, three main tendencies emerged, which will be discussed in the following sections.[25] First, the intellectual, scientific, and artistic work of women living outside the borders of the Austro-Hungarian Monarchy was the most frequently discussed topic in all three journals. Their aggregated ratio was 56.5 percent among articles dealing with women's work and women's labour activism. The foregrounding of this topic can be explained by the social background of GAWA's and FA's membership. Certainly, editors wanted to inspire their readers' career development strategies by providing them with a number of positive examples, especially from more industrially developed Western countries. The second comprehensive group of articles represents the labour activism of the organizations on behalf of middle-class working women. Regarding *Woman and Society* and *The Woman: A Feminist Journal*, a considerable proportion of articles examined the working conditions and the organization of women office workers, which was due to NAWOW's contributions to the publications. Finally, articles representing the discursive strategies used by the associations and editorial offices to discuss the vulnerable situation of working lover-class women constitute the third cluster. Below, I highlight a few typical examples to illustrate the general characteristics of articles in these three categories.

Articles belonging in these clusters use a specific discourse with distinctive linguistic, stylistic, and communicative elements, demonstrating the significant overlap of the Austrian and Hungarian journals. Similarities can also be observed in terms of the articles' structure and the journalistic genres that provided frameworks for discussing each topic. One reason for this resemblance is that Rosika Schwimmer honed her journalistic skills through her work for the Austrian women's and women's movement press, i.e., largely GAWA and the

25 Articles published on women's work and women's labour activism were grouped into the following sub-categories: placement service of the association, domestic servants, health care, intellectual work, industrial work, exploitation of women labourers, work in the field of traffic, agricultural work, gender-specific labour protections, artistic work, women clerks, working women in the field of sport, women's labour activism, social work, women's labour in the service sector, scientific work, and general labour law.

editorial offices of *Documents of Women* and *New Women's Life*. She adapted the theoretical and practical knowledge she had acquired through her work in Austria to Hungarian conditions and transferred it to *Woman and Society*.

Gender-specific labour activism played a prominent role in the activism of both GAWA and FA, which is reflected on the pages of their journals. This was clearly stated in the statutes of the associations as well, which resonate with each other to a significant degree. According to the 1893 statute of GAWA, the aim of the association "is to promote [...] the economic interests of women."[26] In line with this, FA formulated its objectives in 1905 as follows: "[the aim of FA is] the emancipation of Hungarian women in all fields and the protection of women's labour interests."[27] The practical framework of this was fixed by the Legal Aid Section (Rechtsschutz-Sektion) of GAWA and by the Career and Practical Counsellor's Institution (Pályaválasztási Tanácsadó, Gyakorlati Tanácsadó) of FA. While the main profile of GAWA's Legal Aid Section was to support women in need and to provide them with legal advice free of charge, the Career and Practical Counsellor's Institution focused on career counselling, job placement, and on the organization of (re)training courses for women.[28] All the three journals regularly reported on these institutions' achievements and the challenges they faced.

3.1 *Foreign Women's Intellectual, Scientific, and Artistic work as Inspiration for Labour Activism*

More than half the articles on women's work published in *New Women's Life* dealt with the intellectual, scientific, and artistic work (57 percent) of women living outside the Monarchy. In the Hungarian journals, the proportion was almost the same (56 percent). Although I have briefly indicated the reasons editors devoted more attention to women working in these kinds of professions outside the Monarchy than those living and working within the borders, it is worth examining the issue in greater detail. In addition to the international networks of GAWA's and FA's leaders, the organizations had similar strategies for covering these issues in their journals. Both organizations purchased the periodicals of the German women's movement, the content of which

26 "Allgemeiner österr. Frauenverein" 1913.

27 A Feministák Egyesülete 1905 évi közgyűlésén elfogadott alapszabály-módosításai [Amendments to the statutes of the Feminists' Association, adopted at the 1905 Annual General Meeting], April 1905, Box 1, item a, P999, MNL OL.

28 Tájékoztatás a Feministák Egyesületének céljairól és munkatervéről [Report on the objectives and plan of work of the Feminists' Association], 1905, item a, P999, MNL OL, 3–4; Bader-Zaar 1999, 365–383.

they regularly reviewed in their periodicals. FA also subscribed to English and French journals. Articles from these periodicals were translated and often published without any alteration.[29] The other reason for sharing these kinds of articles is that the editorial offices wanted to teach their readership a new way of self-identification. Their primary tool to achieve this was to present their readers with the better working conditions and the more developed labour activism of women living in the more industrialized European countries of Western Europe (and North America).

In Anglo-Saxon countries, France, and Germany, women in the early twentieth century were able to take up (albeit not in large numbers) jobs that were closed to Austro-Hungarian women until 1914. For this reason, the editors of the journals intended to provide positive examples for progressive-minded members of GAWA and FA. Both Auguste Fickert and Rosika Schwimmer as well as other members of the respective editorial offices of FA's and GAWA's journals considered it essential to inform their readers about the career opportunities of foreign women, most often in the form of very short, two or three-line news items. They supplemented these pieces of objective news with their own commentaries, encouraging their readers to use their knowledge to obtain professional qualifications and a job that would provide a decent living.

Articles in this category can be further divided into three sub-categories. In the first category are articles about the first women employed in certain careers.[30] In the second category are articles about the longer history of women's successful integration into certain occupational fields.[31] The third category of articles features reports of honors and prizes awarded to women who had excelled in their professions.[32] Articles in all three categories are generally brief, mentioning only the bare facts, and do not include any information on these women's working conditions. All three journals mention the women by name, obviously hoping to bring them closer to readers. *New Women's Life* once reported that the most talented architect in New York City was a woman ("Frau Kellog"). The article listed her work and the buildings she had designed, but her first name was not revealed.[33] Similar articles were published in *Woman*

29 A Feministák Egyesülete idegen nyelven előfizetett lapjai [Foreign language journals of the FA], Box 55–58, P999, MNL OL; Box 1, item a, P999, MNL OL.

30 "Szemle" 1907. The newly elected women members of the Finnish Parliament are listed by names in the article. See "Rundschau. Ausland" 1910.

31 "Különféle hírek" 1908a: "Eight women now practice as lawyers in Paris," meaning that the number has doubled compared to the previous year.

32 "Különféléit [sic!]" 1911. The Grand Prize of the French Academy of Fine Arts went to the sculptor "Heuvelmanns Lucienne," a name that was Magyarized and probably misprinted.

33 "Rundschau. Ausland" 1908a.

and Society; one of them reported on a woman musician, Helene Sternsdorff, who was chosen to be the "church organist" in Solingen.[34] It was, however, not revealed that her appointment to the town synagogue took place two years before the article was published.[35] When the three journals reported on scientific and artistic organizations, the same techniques were employed: the names of institutions were shared in the original language. In 1907, *Woman and Society* reported on the Paris-based International Union of Fine Arts (Union Internationale des Beaux-Arts et Lettres) without translating its name for the Hungarian audience.[36]

Below are some typical examples of articles editorial offices used to inspire their readers. Several times, articles in the Austrian and Hungarian periodicals published the exact same news, which was either because the editors of the Hungarian journals took articles from *New Women's Life* or that all the editors subscribed to the same journals. Both *New Women's Life* and *Woman and Society* reported on the first female mayor of Europe in 1908. While the Vienna journal reported only that "in the small Buckinghamshire town of Hygh-Wycombe, a lady, Mrs. Dove, has been elected mayor," editors of *Woman and Society* considered it important to share a few details about her family life and her children as well.[37] This might have been a strategy to convince their married readers with children that a family does not necessarily preclude women from having a career.

3.2 *The Representation of Labour Activism Done by Organizations on Behalf of Middle-Class Women*

Articles in the second cluster represent the gender-specific labour activism performed by GAWA and FA on behalf of middle-class women. Articles in this category are longer than the news pieces in the first category, and they reflect the views of the editorial offices, moving away from objective reporting. Furthermore, their content is provocative, emotionally charged, and their authors' enthusiasm, anger, indignation, and even disillusionment is often perceptible. The same holds true for their titles.[38]

Between 1909 and 1911, *New Women's Life* regularly reported on one of GAWA's most important projects, namely the construction work around Heimhof,[39]

34 "Különféle hírek" 1911.

35 "Judentum im Bergischen Land" 2010.

36 "Ez is magától értetődik" 1907.

37 "Női polgármester" 1908; "Rundschau. Ausland" 1908b.

38 E.g., "Some of the hard work men do." Here, the journalist criticized men who considered child-rearing and housekeeping an easy task. "A férfiak némely súlyos munkája" 1907.

39 "Rundschau. Inland" 1908.

the so-called single-kitchen house (*Einküchenhaus*). It was a revolutionary model of urban housing development in which a large, centrally managed kitchen within a multi-apartment building replaced kitchens in individual apartments. The concept was based on the ideas of the German women's rights activist and social democrat Lily Braun (1865, Halberstadt–1916, Zehlendorf) and was adapted in Austria for the first time by Auguste Fickert. In addition to collecting donations for the building project, GAWA also made a generous contribution from its own funds. The first call for donations was published in *New Woman's Life* in 1909, and the construction took two years. Fickert did not live to see its completion: Heimhof opened in October 1911, a year after her death, and was inhabited primarily by middle-class woman office workers, doctors, and university students.[40]

The editorial office of *New Women's Life* regularly drew parallels between the working conditions of middle-class women abroad and those in Austria. In 1908, the journal reported that Finnish universities had opened their faculties of law to women, which the editors predicted would soon happen in Austria.[41] Obviously they were wrong as the Faculty of Law at the University of Vienna was opened to women only ten years later.[42] The periodical also reported on the proposals to extend old-age pension and medical insurance to women working in domestic service and agriculture, and used Anglo-Saxon countries as positive examples in connection with these developments.[43] Editors also devoted lengthy articles to the "actress question." Like several periodicals of the German women's movement, the editors of *New Women's Life* repeatedly reminded their readers of the sad financial state of actresses, "who had no wages for six months after the end of the season, between September and Pentecost."[44]

The situation of Austrian female teachers working in public schools was also a frequent subject of articles in *New Women's Life*. In addition to sharing articles about their working conditions and organizations, GAWA actively tried to advocate on their behalf by submitting petitions to the House of Representatives, and publishing them in the journal as well. In 1908, GAWA called for the employment of female language teachers in boys' secondary schools.[45] Following the death of Auguste Fickert, the new leadership of GAWA continued to promote

40 Kulka 1911; "Aufruf zur Schaffung eines Einküchenhauses" 1909.

41 "Rundschau. Ausland" 1908c.

42 Bader-Zaar 1999, 365–383.

43 "Inland" 1908.

44 "Die VI. Generalversammlung" 1911.

45 "Inland. Wien" 1908.

the rights of women teachers: in December 1912, they sent a petition to the Minister of Education demanding permission for teachers to marry. This petition was also published in *New Women's Life*.[46] They continued reporting on woman teacher's promotions, such as in the case of Mathilde Hanzel-Hübner (1884, Oberhollabrunn, Austria–1970, Vienna), a GAWA member who became first female visiting student at the Technical College in Vienna.[47]

Hungarian journals, while praising the labour activism of women living primarily in England, France, Germany, and Austria, sharply criticized Hungarian conditions, sometimes with irony, other times with anger. Concerning achievements in the social policy of other countries, readers were informed that in England and Austria, "domestic work" (work in cottage industry) was regulated by decrees that prevented the exploitation of women "engaged in the manufacturing of clothes, lingerie, and shoes."[48] It must have been rather bizarre for readers of *Woman and Society* to hear about the work of Marie Raschke (1850, Gaffert, Germany–1935, Berlin), one of the leaders of the legal committee of the Federation of German Women's Associations (Bund Deutscher Frauenvereine, 1894–1933), who was planning to establish a bank "to promote women's efforts to become self-reliant" in Berlin. An institution like this would have been unimaginable in Hungary.[49] The situation of teachers in Western countries was also given a positive spin: In 1908, it was reported that the German state had finally authorized a few teachers to marry (albeit on a case-by-case basis).[50] As mentioned above, the Hungarian journals also appreciated the labour activism of Austrian women. In 1910, they shared a statistic according to which women workers' organizing and activism in Austria surpassed that of men. This, according to the editorial office of *Woman and Society*, was "a sign that the enthusiastic agitation of their leaders was able to make progress even in such unfavorable times."[51]

Commonly discussed topics were the need to increase women's wages, the proposed ban on Sunday work and the night shift, the lack of appropriate institutions for maternity and child protection, and the issue of health insurance. In 1911, when the ban on women's night work was about to be introduced in

46 GAWA referred to the example of Swiss teachers and clerks. "Ausland" 1912.

47 "Inland" 1909b.

48 Workers were given a business license, and their working hours and wages were regulated. Ferenczi 1907.

49 "Különfélék" 1910.

50 The text of the brief news piece is the following: "Married teachers have not been tolerated in the profession, but now this injustice is being changed." "Különféle hírek" 1908a.

51 "Az osztrák munkásnők" 1911.

Hungary, Schwimmer published an extensive article on the expected reception, enforceability, and negative effects of the law.[52] Several articles tried to facilitate the expansion of the institutional framework for the pension scheme as well.

The revision of the wage scheme for civil servants was also a recurring subject in the Hungarian journals. NAWOW made several petitions to the Ministry of Commerce, asking them to remedy problems. Again, following the model of *New Women's Life*'s editorial office, the texts of these petitions were published in the journals. Board members of FA intensively worked on opening up "higher prestige" careers to women. Several polemical articles were published to legitimize women's presence in professions that heretofore were performed only by men. Well-known agricultural specialists drew readers' attention to the value of qualified women in the field of farming. An article in this subject stated, "if the devotion and contribution of women in this field was more emphasized," it would also solve several problems related to women's emancipation.[53]

Both organizations vigorously encouraged working women to "join their professional organizations [to advocate] for their own interests."[54] Furthermore, the labour activism of several of the institutions established by GAWA and FA, which was undertaken on behalf of middle-class women, was significant. While GAWA was not capable of doing much beyond its legal aid service, FA's consultancy offices were more effective. Articles in FA's journals regularly reported on the popular career counseling services and parents' meetings, which offered guidance to younger women and their parents and also publicized the discussion evenings organized by FA. A series of language or vocational training courses were organized by FA, for example, on typing, shorthand, and business correspondence.[55] Through these trainings, leaders of FA sought to overcome the shortcomings of, and therefore supplement, secondary vocational education in Hungary.[56]

3.3 *Discourse Strategies for Covering the Unprotected Situation of Lower-class Women*

Articles covering the unprotected status and exploitation of working-class women compose the third cluster of articles. Among the three categories of

52 Schwimmer and other board members of FA called for the ban or at least the restriction of men's night-shift work as well. "Mérleg" 1911.

53 Magyar 1907.

54 "Szerkesztő üzenetei" 1907.

55 E.g., "A Feministák Egyesületének évi jelentése" 1907.

56 "A Nőtisztviselők Országos Egyesülete hivatalos értesítései" 1908.

articles, the lowest number of articles were published on this issue across the three journals. The marginalization of these issues can be explained largely by the upper-middle-class social background of GAWA and FA members. Consequently, the organizations and their journals were less concerned with the exploitation of women working in, for example, factories or as domestic servants than with the acute problems of the middle-class female labour market. Articles on these themes that appeared in the Vienna- and Budapest-based journals were similar in several respects. First, they reflected on primarily the Austrian and Hungarian context, neglecting foreign examples. Second, they are largely longer analytical pieces that provide detailed analyses of the poor working conditions of lower-class women employed in industry, agriculture, and as domestic servants.

The few articles discussing the lack of working-class women's labour activism served as a tool for the FA to promote its own communication strategies and to act as if it had been actively and intensively addressing these issues. The editors' intention to encourage their readers to take collective action against the injustices lower-class women had to endure in their workplaces remained only theoretical. Although authors of the articles painted vivid pictures of the disastrous conditions of women working in tobacco factories or garbage dumps, they could do little to prevent their exploitation. And because these articles were most probably not read by lower-class women, the publicists only aim could have been educating (upper) middle-women about these issues. GAWA and FA pursued this kind of education also within the framework of lecture series and debates involving the participation of lawyers and economists. Neither the majority of GAWA and FA members nor readers of the journals had first-hand experience and information about the living and working conditions of lower-class women. Nevertheless, they made an effort to collect information on the issue: Rosika Schwimmer, for example, used to contact factory managers and trade union leaders to receive information and statistics on the situation of these women.

As a result of these factors, a serious conflict on this issue emerged among the different branches of women's organizations. Austrian and Hungarian social democratic and Christian socialist organizations accused GAWA and FA of fighting for the improvement of only (upper) middle-class women's working conditions and of fighting for women's rights only on paper and with words, i.e., in theory. In the meantime, the social democratic women's associations organized loud demonstrations, and Christian social groups tried to solve the "misery of maids" in practice, which was one of the major social problems in both Austria and Hungary at the time. Christian socialists also opened training schools for domestic servants as well as servants' homes.

At the same time, however, they (Christian socialists) condemned women's employment in the economy; thus, bourgeois-liberal and feminist, and social democratic women's associations considered the work done by Christian socialist women's associations as merely "treating the symptoms" rather than "curing the real disease."

Within the framework of women's education, *Woman and Society* reported several times on women's work in industry, for example, in the milling industry—one pillar of the Hungarian economy—in which female labourers worked thirteen hours a day.[57] The situation of female workers employed in the chemical industry was also addressed.[58] Poems criticizing "male despotism" also served editors' aims: on the one hand, they sought to evoke sympathy and pity from their readers; on the other hand, they used discursive strategies to shock and rouse their readers from their apathy.[59] Regarding female labour in industry, *New Women's Life* shared some positive news as well. In 1909, the journal enthusiastically reported that a number of vocational schools where girls could be trained as seamstresses, milliners, jewelers, and florists had been opened in Austria.[60] It was also reported that the Austrian education system encouraged girls to become hairdressers, children's dressmakers, and gold, silver, and pearl cutters.[61] However, one year later, the editorial office complained that although women could pursue industrial studies in Austria, they were rarely employed as apprentices, making it difficult for them to find employment in these fields.[62]

The only area where GAWA and FA members had direct experience was the issue of domestic servants because several members could afford to employ domestic help. Both GAWA and FA regularly addressed the issue of domestic

57 The author added that "the state is the supplier of the material for prostitution" ("Szemle" 1908).

58 In 1910, 19.3 percent of the workforce employed in the chemical industry were women. See Mucsi 1980, 333–342.

59 Charlotte Gilman Perkins (1860, Hartford, CT–1935, Pasadena, CA) was a famous American feminist. In her poem on child labour, she highlights the man's heartlessness toward his child: "Only the human father, the clever, thinking soul, Eats the wages of his child's labour with a light heart." Gilman-Perkins 1911.

60 Vocational schools for women were opened in Vienna, Graz, Klagenfurt, Prague (Praha, Prag), Brno (Brünn), and Olomouc (Olmütz). "Inland" 1909a.

61 "Inland" 1909a.

62 See the article by the artist Lili Baitz (1872, Bad Aussee, Austria–1942, Bad Aussee, Austria): "The (industrial and craft) schools are largely open to them, but they are not admitted to the workshops. Nowhere are girls accepted as apprentices. However talented they may be, it is very difficult for them to acquire more than dilettantish skill in their respective trades." Baitz 1908.

servants at the events they organized—public lectures and debates—but the subject was only sporadically discussed in the journals. Hungarian periodicals persistently reported on the corporal punishment of domestic servants and their "legal relationship with their masters."[63] In 1907, a statement by Ignác Darányi (1849, Pest–1927, Budapest), the former Minister of Agriculture, was published. According to this, "a friendly scolding and lighter punishments were as inoffensive to the servant as they were to other members of the family." This remark was, of course, mocked by the editors, who made the following comments in response: "Long live respectable families, some members of which make millions gambling at the casinos, while others cover all their living and luxuries on an income of 117 crowns a year."[64] Several references were made to the rape of domestic servants.[65] FA argued that this situation could have been prevented if women had been employed in the legislature and on the city councils. Such political presence would have given them a chance to contribute to the operations of cities, and they could have proposed measures to regulate the lives of residents.

It is worth taking a closer look at the reasons the issue of domestic servants was underrepresented in all three papers. Some sources suggest that there may have been a "division of labour" between the bourgeois-liberal feminist and the social democratic movements on this issue; that is, that while bourgeois-liberal feminist organizations agreed to report primarily on the working conditions and labour activism of middle-class women, the social democratic organizations would cover the issue of domestic servants. Following this logic, the journals may not have devoted more space to the issue of domestic servants because it was of little relevance to middle-class women's career-building strategies. Another potential interpretation is that the editorial offices were more concerned with actually solving problems rather than discussing them. As such, they were more focused on providing employment opportunities for women without qualifications and ensuring their legal protection within the framework of GAWA's legal aid service and FA's Career and Practical Counsellor Institutions.

63 On this subject matter, see Gyáni 2000; Zimmermann 1999; Gyáni 1983.
64 "Ők következetesek" 1907; Márkus 1907.
65 "Még egy sorozat" 1911. Following the contemporary practice, the article described the incident chronologically.

4 Conclusion

This chapter homes in on a distinct moment in the history of women's civil society in the Austro-Hungarian Monarchy, when women joining the newly established modern women's associations began to advocate for the protection of their (women's) interests. Comparing the work of the two most powerful bourgeois-liberal feminist associations of the Dual Monarchy and their official press organs, which chronicled these moments of activism before 1914, it demonstrates that the journals—which reveal a number of similarities between the Hungarian and Austrian associations—provided a public forum for GAWA and FA to discuss how to effectively represent the interests of working women. The chapter also shows that GAWA helped stimulate the newly established FA and its labour activism, highlighting that FA's labour activism became more strident in some respects by the eve of World War One. In connection to the knowledge transfer between GAWA and FA, I have explained the importance of the personal contacts and relationships between the leaders of the two associations and members of the Vienna and Budapest editorial offices of *New Women's Life*, *Woman and Society*, and *The Woman: A Feminist Journal*. These kinds of connections between the Austrian and the Hungarian bourgeois-liberal feminist women's movements challenge both the nationalist perspective of the existing Hungarian historical scholarship on the movement and the widespread methodological nationalism in Austria, which has resulted in an over-emphasis on the German-speaking organizations of the Monarchy.

In addition to its contributions to the history of Austrian and Hungarian women's intellectual work, this chapter offers fresh insight into the history of women's employment in industry, agriculture, and in the rapidly developing service sector. The three categories of articles discussed above were associated with the particular discursive strategies employed by the respective editorial offices of the three papers—where there was significant overlap with respect to personnel. As articles in each of the three categories reveal, there were important similarities and differences in the way GAWA and FA communicated with their followers and addressed the wider public. Relatedly, the primary aim of the editors and publicists was neither the castigation of politicians nor criticism of men in general. Rather, both Austrians and Hungarians sought to promote women's labour activism and offer solutions to those working women's problems that had not yet been resolved by social welfare policies.

In addition to the (upper)-middle classes' efforts to safeguard the interests of working women, GAWA and FA sought to defend working women from the lower classes. However, their means in this respect were limited. Despite this, the labour activism of GAWA and FA can still be considered successful overall, especially if we consider that while the social democratic and Christian-socialist women's organizations enjoyed the institutional support of political parties dominated by men, the bourgeois-liberal feminist groups performed their labour activism alone, i.e., independently from political parties. An important element of their activism was intensive communication with their followers, especially with working women from the (upper)middle classes. This communication was complemented by their educational work. Through the years, the communication strategies of FA became more direct than those of their Austrian counterparts. This was largely because FA's labour activism was framed by the Career and Practical Counsellor's Institutions. GAWA's legal aid service was not able to carry out such a wide range of activities, but the association did try to fill some of this gap through job advertisements and an information column published in *New Women's Life*.

It was the war that brought about changes to issues related to women's work and education, as the conflict made necessary women's employment in many jobs that had been historically filled exclusively by men before 1914. The war also led to GAWA and FA adopt some of the same principles as many proletarian and Christian socialist women's societies.

Bibliography

"A Feministák Egyesületének évi jelentése" [Annual report of the Feminists' Association]. 1907. *A Nő és a Társadalom* [Woman and society], 1 April 1907.

"A férfiak némely súlyos munkája" [Some of the hard work men do]. 1907. *A Nő és a Társadalom* [Woman and society], 1 September 1907.

A Nőtisztviselők Országos Egyesülete Alapszabályai [Statutes of the National Association of Female Office Workers]. 1909. Budapest: Markovits és Garai Könyvnyomdája.

"A Nőtisztviselők Országos Egyesülete hivatalos értesítései" [Official notices from the National Association of Women Office Workers]. 1908. *A Nő és a Társadalom* [Woman and society], 1 June 1908.

"Allgemeiner österr. Frauenverein" [General Austrian Women's Association]. 1913. *Neues Frauenleben* [New women's life], January 1913.

Anderson, Harriet. 1992. *Utopian Feminism: Women's Movements in "Fin-de-Siècle" Vienna*. New Haven, CT: Yale University Press.

Andor, József. 2009. "A kulcsszavakról." [About keywords]. In *A nyelv, az irodalom és a kultúra varázsa* [The magic of language, literature and culture], edited by József Sebestény and Zsuzsa Surányi, 23–28. Veszprém: Pannon Egyetemi Kiadó.

Appelt, Erna. 1985. *Von Ladenmädchen, Schreibfräulein und Gouvernanten: Die weiblichen Angestellten Wiens zwischen 1900 und 1934* [Shop girls, typists and governesses: Vienna's female employees between 1900 and 1934]. Vienna: Verlag für Gesellschaftskritik.

"Aufruf zur Schaffung eines Einküchenhauses" [Call for the creation of a single kitchen house]. 1909. *Neues Frauenleben* [New women's life], Mai 1909.

"Ausland" [Foreign countries]. 1912. *Neues Frauenleben* [New women's life], October 1912.

"Az osztrák munkásnők" [Austrian female labourers]. 1911. *A Nő és a Társadalom* [Woman and society], 1 October 1911.

Bader-Zaar, Birgitta. 1999. "Die Wiener Frauenbewegung und der Rechtsschutz für Frauen, 1895–1914" [The Viennese women's movement and legal protection for women, 1895–1914]. In *Geschichte und Recht: Festschrift für Gerald Stourzh zum 70. Geburtstag* [History and law: Commemorative volume for Gerald Stourzh on his 70th birthday], edited by Thomas Angerer and Gerald Stourzh, 365–383. Vienna: Böhlau.

Baitz, Lily. 1908. "Az iparművészet mint női hivatás." [Decorative art as a female vocation]. *A Nő és a Társadalom* [Woman and society], 1 May 1908.

Bell, Allen. 1991. *The Language of News Media*. Oxford: Blackwell.

Czeferner, Dóra. 2020. "Polgári-liberális, feminista nőszervezetek és sajtójuk az Osztrák–Magyar Monarchiában (1907–1918). Egyesületek, periodikák, tartalomelemzés" [Bourgeois-liberal, feminist women's organizations and their press activity in the Austro-Hungarian Monarchy (1907–1918): Associations, periodicals and content analysis]. PhD diss, University of Pécs.

Czeferner, Dóra. 2021. *Kultúrmisszió vagy propaganda? Feminista lapok és olvasóik Bécsben és Budapesten* [Cultural mission or propaganda? Feminist newspapers and their readers in Vienna and Budapest]. Budapest: ELKH BTK TTI.

"Die VI. Generalversammlung des Bundes österreichischer Frauenvereine" [The VI. General Assembly of the Federation of Austrian Women's Associations]. 1911. *Neues Frauenleben* [New women's life], June 1911.

Ehmer, Josef. 1996. "Zur sozialen Schichtung der Wiener Bevölkerung. 1857 bis 1910" [On the social stratification of the Viennese population. 1857 to 1910]. In: *Wien–Prag–Budapest. Urbanisierung, Kommunalpolitik, gesellschaftliche Konflikte (1867–1918)* [Vienna-Prague-Budapest. Urbanization, communal politics, social conflicts (1867–1918)], edited by Gerhard Melinz and Susan Zimmermann, 73–83. Vienna: Promedia.

"Ez is magától értetődik" [This also goes without saying]. 1907. *A Nő és a Társadalom* [Woman and society], 1 May 1907.

Feigenbaum, Rosa. 1910. "Französische Advokatinnen" [French female lawyers]. 1910. *Neues Frauenleben* [New women's life], October 1910.

Ferenczi, Imre. 1907. "Az otthonmunka" [Domestic labour]. *A Nő és a Társadalom* [Woman and society], 1 June 1907.

Gehmacher, Johanna. 2011. “Reisende in Sachen Frauenbewegung. Käthe Schirmacher zwischen Internationalismus und nationaler Identifikation” [Traveler in the matter of the women’s movement. Käthe Schirmacher between internationalism and national identification]. *Ariadne* 60, no. 2. (November): 58–64.

Gerster, Miklós. 1911. “A nő a munkásvédelemben” [Women in worker protection]. *A Nő és a Társadalom* [Woman and society], 1 March, 1911.

Gilman-Perkins, Charlotte. 1911. “A gyermekmunka” [Child labour]. *A Nő és a Társadalom* [Woman and society], 1 October 1911.

Gyáni, Gábor. 1983. *Család, háztartás és városi cselédség* [Family, household, and urban servants]. Budapest: Magvető.

Gyáni, Gábor. 2020. *A nő élete—történelmi perspektívában* [The life of a woman—in historical perspective]. Budapest: ELHK BTK TTI.

Hacker, Hanna. 2006. “Auguste Fickert (1855–1910).” In *A Biographical Dictionary of Women’s Movements and Feminism: Central, Eastern, and South Eastern Europe, 19th and 20th Centuries*, edited by Francisca de Haan, Krassimira Daskalova, and Anna Loutfi, 131–133. Budapest: CEU Press, 2006.

Hauch, Gabriella. 2006. “Arbeit, Recht und Sittlichkeit—Themen der Frauenbewegungen in der Habsburgermonarchie” [Work, law, and morality—Themes of the women’s movements in the Habsburg Monarchy]. In *Die Habsburgermonarchie 1848–1918.* Band 8, *Politische Öffentlichkeit und Zivilgesellschaft, Teilband 1: Vereine, Parteien und Interessenverbände als Träger der politischen Partizipation* [The Habsburg Monarchy 1848–1918. Vol. 8, Political public sphere and civil society, Part 1, Associations, parties and interest groups as vehicles of political participation], edited by Adam Wandruszka and Helmut Rumpler, 965–1003. Vienna: Verlag der Österreichischer Akademie der Wissenschaft.

Hanzel, Beate. 1910. “Die Not des Mittelstandes” [The plight of the middle class]. *Neues Frauenleben* [New women’s life], February 1910.

“Inland” [Inland]. 1908. *Neues Frauenleben* [New women’s life], May 1908.

“Inland. Wien” [Inland. Vienna]. 1908. *Neues Frauenleben* [New women’s life], June 1908.

“Inland” [Inland]. 1909a. *Neues Frauenleben* [New women’s life], January 1909.

“Inland” [Inland]. 1909b. *Neues Frauenleben* [New women’s life], January 1909.

“Judentum im Bergischen Land: Judentum im Bergischen Land. Chronik der jüdischen Geschichte im Bergischen Land” [Judaism in the Bergisches Land: Judaism in the Bergisches Land. Chronicle of Jewish history in the Bergisches Land]. 2010. http://www.ns-gedenkstaetten.de/nrw/wuppertal/wissenswertes/juedische-geschichte.html.

Kulka, Leopoldine. 1911. “Die Eröffnung des Heimhofes” [Opening of Heimhof]. *Neues Frauenleben* [New women’s life], November 1911.

“Különféle hírek” [Various news]. 1907. *A Nő és a Társadalom* [Woman and Society], 1 February 1907.

"Különféle hírek" [Various news]. 1908a. *A Nő és a Társadalom* [Woman and Society], 1 November 1908.

"Különféle hírek" [Various news]. 1908b. *A Nő és a Társadalom* [Woman and society], 1 November 1908.

"Különféle hírek" [Various news]. 1911. *A Nő és a Társadalom* [Woman and society], 1 November 1911.

"Különféle, hírek" [Various news]. 1908. *A Nő és a Társadalom* [Woman and society], 1 January 1908.

"Különféléit [sic!]" [Various news]. 1911. *A Nő és a Társadalom* [Woman and society], 1 October 1911.

"Különfélék. Külföld" [Various news. Foreign countries]. 1907. *A Nő és a Társadalom* [Woman and society], 1 September 1907.

"Különfélék" [Various news]. 1910. *A Nő és a Társadalom* [Woman and society], 1 May 1910.

von La Roche, Walter. 2008. *Einführung in den praktischen Journalismus: Mit genauer Beschreibung aller Ausbildungswege Deutschland Österreich Schweiz* [Introduction to practical journalism: With a detailed description of all training paths Germany Austria Switzerland]. Berlin: Econ.

Maderthaner, Wolfgang. 1986. *Arbeiterbewegung in Österreich und Ungarn bis 1914. Referate des österreich-ungarischen Historikersymposiums in Graz vom 5–9. September 1986.* [Workers' movement in Austria and Hungary to 1914. Papers presented at the Austro-Hungarian Historians' Symposium in Graz, 5–9 September 1986.] Vienna: Europaverlag.

Magyar, Kázmér. 1907. "A nő szerepköre a mező- és a kertgazdaság terén" [The role of women in agriculture and horticulture]. *A Nő és a Társadalom* [Woman and society], 1 June 1907.

Malleier, Elisabeth. 2001. *Jüdische Frauen in der Wiener bürgerlichen Frauenbewegung 1890–1893.* [Jewish women in the Viennese bourgeois women's movement 1890–1893]. Vienna: Manuskript–Forschungsbericht.

Márkus, Dezső. 1907. "Házi fegyelem gyakorlása" [Exercising home discipline]. *A Nő és a Társadalom* [Woman and society], 1 June 1907.

"Még egy sorozat" [One more series]. 1911. *A Nő és a Társadalom* [Woman and society], 1 June 1911.

"Mérleg" [Balance]. 1911. *A Nő és a Társadalom* [Woman and society], 1 March 1911.

Mucsi, Ferenc. 1980. "Weibliche Industriearbeit und sozialistische Frauen-Arbeiterbewegung in Ungarn vor dem Ersten Weltkrieg" [Female industrial labour and the socialist women's labour movement in Hungary before World War One]. In *Die Frau in der Arbeiterbewegung 1900–1939* [The woman in the labour movement 1900–1939], edited by Gerhard Botz, 333–342. Vienna: Europaverlag.

Nagyné Szegvári, Katalin. 1981. *Út a női egyenjogúsághoz* [The road to women's equality]. Budapest: Magyar Nők Országos Tanácsa, Kossuth.

Nagyné Szegvári, Katalin. 2001. *A női választójog külföldön és hazánkban* [Women's suffrage abroad and in our country]. Budapest: HVG-ORAC.

"Női polgármester" [Female mayor]. 1908. *A Nő és a Társadalom* [Woman and society], 1 November 1908.

"Ők következetesek" [They are consistent]. 1907. *A Nő és a Társadalom* [Woman and society], 1 May 1907.

Rigler, Edith. 1976. *Frauenleitbild und Frauenarbeit in Österreich. Vom ausgehenden 19. Jahrhundert bis zum Zweiten Weltkrieg* [Women's role models and women's work in Austria. From the end of the nineteenth century to World War Two]. Oldenburg: De Gruyter.

"Rundschau. Ausland" [Review. Abroad]. 1908a. *Neues Frauenleben* [New women's life], November 1908.

"Rundschau. Ausland" [Review. Abroad]. 1908b. *Neues Frauenleben* [New women's life], November 1908.

"Rundschau. Ausland" [Review. Abroad]. 1908c. *Neues Frauenleben* [New women's life], November 1908.

"Rundschau. Ausland" ["Review. Abroad"]. 1910. *Neues Frauenleben* [New women's life], February 1910.

"Rundschau. Inland" [Review. Inland]. 1908. *Neues Frauenleben* [New women's life], January 1908.

Stenographisches Protokoll über die Constituierende Versammlung des Allgemeinen Österreichischen Frauenvereines [Stenographic minutes of the Constituent Assembly of the General Austrian Women's Association]. 1893. Vienna: Allgemeiner Österreichischer Frauenverein.

Sullerot, Evelyne. 1972. *Die emanzipierte Sklavin: Geschichte und Soziologie der Frauenarbeit* [The emancipated slave: The history and sociology of women's work]. Wien: Böhlau.

"Szemle" [Review]. 1908. *A Nő és a Társadalom* [Woman and Society], 1 January 1908.

"Szemle" [Review]. 1907. *A Nő és a Társadalom* [Woman and Society], 1 May 1907.

"Szerkesztő üzenetei" [Editor's messages]. 1907. *A Nő és a Társadalom* [Woman and society], 1 February 1907.

Tájékoztatás a Feministák Egyesületének céljairól és munkatervéről [Information on the aims and work plan of the Feminists' Association]. 1905. Budapest: Márkus Samu könyvnyomdája.

van Dijk, Teun A. 2006. "Ideology and Discourse Analysis." *Journal of Political Ideologies* 11, no. 2: 115–140.

Zimmermann, Susan. 1999. *Die bessere Hälfte? Frauenbewegungen und Frauenbestrebungen im Ungarn der Habsburgermonarchie 1848 bis 1918* [The better half?

Women's movements and women's aspirations in Hungary under the Habsburg Monarchy 1848–1918]. Vienna and Budapest: Promedia Verlag and Napvilág kiadó.

Zimmermann, Susan, and Borbála Major. 2006. "Róza Schwimmer." In *A Biographical Dictionary of Women's Movements and Feminism: Central, Eastern, and South Eastern Europe, 19th and 20th Centuries*, edited by Francisca de Haan, Krassimira Daskalova, and Anna Loutfi, 484–491. Budapest: CEU Press.

CHAPTER 11

Women Workers' Protests Outside the Trade Union Framework

The Case of the Spinners in Żyrardów, Poland, 1918–1951

Jan A. Burek

Abstract

The crucial role that women played in strikes in Poland after the end of World War Two is well-established in scholarship. However, little attention has been paid to the unskilled women workers who had not been part of the organized labour movement before the war. Unskilled women workers were, in fact, seen as a new group without any relevant prewar experience that could inform their postwar behavior. Using the case of a textile factory in Żyrardów, this chapter examines continuities in forms of protest adopted by unskilled women labourers, in particular spinners. In the prewar period, spinners usually fought without the help of male-dominated unions. On the one hand, they were more likely to negotiate directly with the management and even work with the management against the interests of skilled men workers; on the other hand, they were also willing to resort to wild-cat strikes and small informal actions to achieve their goals. These experiences proved indispensable in the postwar period and allowed for, at times, effective negotiations with the state administration. Their exclusion from the structures of the labour movement resulted in a markedly increased tendency among unskilled women workers to strike in comparison with their male colleagues.

Keywords

labour protest – Poland – strike – textile industry – trade unions – unskilled workers – wild-cat strike – women workers

Scholars often consider working-class traditions a determining factor for shaping the relationship between workers and communists and workers' opposition to the introduction of Soviet-style policies on the shop floor in Central and Eastern Europe following World War Two. The evolution of these

 DOI:10.1163/9789004682481_012

traditions before the war is rarely discussed in the postwar context, however. The most apparent drawback of this approach is visible in the homogenization of the prewar labour culture and the lack of attention to women's and unskilled workers' participation in it as agents and not just subjects. So-called traditional working-class culture is frequently regarded as the culture of solely organized men workers. For example, Gareth Pritchard, in his study of the influence of German labour traditions on the introduction of Soviet-style policies in the German Democratic Republic (GDR), treats women's presence in the postwar working class as a separate issue altogether, which he does not deal with: women workers are not carriers of working-class political culture and identity, in contrast to men.[1] In the German case, the exclusion of women is particularly puzzling considering the German communist party's wide and successful outreach to women as well as the relatively large-scale unionization within the various political camps of women prior to the Nazis' ascent to power.[2] Even Mark Pittaway, who was very sensitive to both the role of workers' traditions as well as gender, invoked the "pre-socialist tradition" for the case of male skilled workers only. He explained the different behavior of semi-skilled and unskilled women, in particular their actions defending the status of the Catholic Church, by noting women's lack of experience working in urban, industrial environments and their newcomer status. They still formed a segment of the rural community and, hence, possessed conservative views.[3] Traditions and discourses of unskilled, unorganized, and predominantly women workers are treated marginally in the historiography. A partial exception is Małgorzata Fidelis, who describes older working women, i.e., women with work experience dating back to the interwar period, as deeply entrenched in the labour organizations and in Socialist discourse both before and after the war.[4]

In this chapter, I show the heterogeneity of workers' cultures in the prewar era through the case of the employees of the Żyrardów Works (Zakłady Żyrardowskie), one of the oldest and largest textile factories in Poland situated in Żyrardów, a mid-sized company town in the Warsaw region. I then uncover how the persistence of this cultural diversity impacted workers' attitudes toward the communist regime in the postwar period. I pay particular attention

1 Pritchard 2004, 5.

2 On the postwar activism of communist women in East Germany, see Harsch 2000, 156–182. On the role women played in the emergence of the German labour movement, see Canning 1992, 736–768.

3 Pittaway 2012, 100–101.

4 Fidelis 2015, 109–113.

to spinners, the group of women workers most neglected in the existing historiography, to illuminate how their experiences from the interwar era provided them with tools to contest the communist authorities. I will focus primarily on the diversity of forms of workers' protest and workers' relationship with organized labour.

I shall also underscore how women workers performed their identities in ways that labour leaders and left-wing intellectuals did not expect. Women workers drew on an array of identities that sometimes stood at odds with the view of class espoused by the organized labour movement. In the postwar reality, women workers were more likely to strike because they did so in defense of their families and local community, and they were driven by issues related to consumption and wages. Their protests were difficult to suppress by the authorities because they stood outside the framework of communist ideology. Workers who identified themselves primarily as members of the working class might have been convinced not to strike by references to past labour struggles, their organizational loyalties, and communist/socialist ideology. This, however, was not the case with many women workers who organized around less rigid, intersectional, multi-dimensional identities.

World War Two caused an undeniable rupture in the social fabric of Central and Eastern European working-class communities. The death of millions of Jewish and non-Jewish workers, the destruction of industry, and political regime change undeniably transformed the country. Furthermore, many scholars regard state socialism in Central Eastern Europe as an alien Soviet import unconnected to local developments that took place in the interwar period.[5] Indeed, the magnitude of changes caused by the war may throw into doubt the rationale for studying Central Eastern European labour history from a "transwar" perspective. There are, however, continuities that warrant this approach. Martha Lampland demonstrated that the implementation of scientific management in Central Eastern Europe was a process that strongly bound together the pre-, wartime, and postwar eras.[6]

My microhistorical research has also revealed the importance of continuities in factory-level management policies (e.g., the persistence of a Taylorist piece-rate system). This link allowed me to cross the seemingly impenetrable caesura of the war in Poland. In doing so, I also uncovered how historical agents in Żyrardów understood the history they lived through as transwar. While traumatic, the experience of war was only a part of a larger cycle of transformation

5 In Polish historiography in particular. See, e.g., Chumiński 1998.
6 Lampland 2011.

that began during World War One. These findings further confirmed that I was correct in my decision to analyze the history of Żyrardów workers from a trans-war perspective.[7]

Żyrardów is a particularly good place to study continuities in working-class culture under rapidly changing circumstances. Thanks to the stabilizing effect of the company town system, the settlement had a remarkably stable population already by the early twentieth century (in contrast to nearby Łódź).[8] Even the particularly extreme level of destitution during the Great Depression—caused by lockouts and mass redundancies in the town's only factory—did not provoke significant out-migration. It was not a place that would attract many new arrivals from the countryside after 1945 either. In comparison to Łódź or Warsaw, Żyrardów offered low pay and badly supplied stores,[9] and its main factory struggled to offer enough employment opportunities to cover the needs of its population.[10] As a result, the factory had a high proportion of workers with prewar experience who continued to be employed in the same roles, or even "at the same machines" as a communist functionary from the Żyrardów Works contended, in the postwar era.[11]

1 Unskilled Women's Strikes in the Historiography

Labour historians had long ignored or belittled non-union or non-party women's strikes and actions, treating them as eruptions of emotions and dismissing the skills workers had to possess in order to organize them, as well as their

---

7 I deal with this issue more comprehensively in Burek 2022.

8 Żarnowska 1980, 127–134.

9 "Protokół z posiedzenia komisji w sprawie niedokładnego zaopatrzenia robotników Zakładów Żyrardowskich w m-cu maju i czerwcu 1947" [Minutes of the meeting of the commission on the inaccurate supply of Żyrardów Works' workers in May and June], 12 July 1947, Folder 1, Akta Miasta Żyrardowa [Żyrardów Municipal Records], Archiwum Państwowe w Warszawie [State Archive in Warsaw, hereafter APW], Oddział w Grodzisku Mazowieckim [Grodzisk Mazowiecki Branch, hereafter OGM], Grodzisk Mazowiecki, Polska.

10 Kenney 1997, 270.

11 Protokół z zebrania Wydziału Personalnego Komitetu Fabrycznego PPR w Żyrardowie [Minutes from the meeting of the Personnel Department at the Works Committee of the PPR in Żyrardów], 2 October 1948, Komitet Miejski Polskiej Partii Robotniczej w Żyrardowie [Town Committee of the Polish Workers' Party in Żyrardów, hereafter KM PPR], Folder 16, APW, Oddział w Milanówku [Milanówek Branch, hereafter OM], Milanówek, Poland.

impact.[12] Due to the belief that the traditional institutional form of labour organization was necessary to achieve a certain level of coordination, large strikes were at times assumed to be organized by unions or political parties despite evidence to the contrary.[13] In the state-socialist historiography, such a conviction was perhaps even more pronounced than in Western Europe.

The primary goal of historians of the labour movement on the eastern side of the Iron Curtain was to trace the genealogies of the revolutionary party as the vanguard of the proletariat. While after de-Stalinization, political control over the historiographical writing decreased, studying labour history as the teleological development of the communist movement and its perceived predecessors was still expected. Within the boundaries of the Marxist-Leninist dogma, spontaneous "economic" strikes were of much less concern than were labour actions organized by political parties.[14]

A fitting example of historians' reluctance to acknowledge the abilities of non-organized women workers is the scholarship on the 1883 strike in Żyrardów, which is considered the first modern general strike in the Polish lands. The strike was, without a doubt, initiated and sustained by women winders. Various scholars, nevertheless, presented it as organized by skilled male weavers under the influence of the Social-Revolutionary Party "Proletariat," despite extremely weak evidence suggesting that party members were even present in Żyrardów at any point and, indeed, evidence that demonstrated weavers' initial reluctance to join the striking women.[15]

The seminal work of Padraic Kenney, *Rebuilding Poland*, introduced the subject of the postwar protests of women working in the textile industry into Polish labour history. Kenney also provided a broader perspective on women's labour actions in Łódź during the state-socialist era up to the formation of Solidarność (1980), demonstrating how important and effective women's strikes and demonstrations were and how they were forgotten and erased from the historiography.[16] Kenney saw the postwar textile workers' community of

12 Downs 1995, 119–120. See also Karen Hunt's more recent description of direct actions undertaken by working-class housewives during the Great War due to food shortages, which have been ignored by historians thus far. Hunt 2010, 8–26.

13 La Mare 2008, 62–80.

14 Siewierski 2012; Kolář 2012, 415. While Kolář sees 1956 as a turning point in the historiography of the labour movement, after which one could study the subject more freely, he, nevertheless, shows that writing a history that presented a fuller picture of workers' lives and struggles could have still led to problems with the party authorities.

15 This attitude is particularly pronounced in Józef Kazimierski's paper on the strike. Kazimierski 1980. See also Kazimierski 1984 and Kormanowa 1960.

16 Kenney 1999.

Łódź as divided into two groups: the prewar, egalitarian working class led by experienced men and women workers—often Socialist and/or Communist[17] organizers during the interwar period, who used class-centered discourse and struggled to preserve newly-gained control over their workplace—and the anarchic youth. Kenney did not insist on the strikes' organized character. Following the party reports, he pointed out that there was a new kind of strike that developed in the postwar era: a leaderless action. For him, leaderless strikes were the domain of younger workers and were invented in the absence of an independent organized labour movement.[18]

Transwar research on Żyrardów complicates this picture. First, the leaderless strikes were not a novelty that emerged after the end of World War Two. They were a tactic well-known to unskilled women textile workers during the interwar era. Second, labour actions in the Żyrardów Works were, without a doubt, started by women with prewar experience of work and protest but oftentimes not by former Socialists, Communists, or trade unionists. On the contrary, the shops with the largest share of members of unions and the socialist and communist parties, both before and after the war, were less likely to strike. Third, in Żyrardów, a class-centered discourse focused on control of the workplace was rarely employed in the postwar era by the striking women workers (both those with prewar and postwar work experience and those with only a postwar history of employment). As I will demonstrate, striking women were much more eager to frame their protest in terms of solidarity with the local community and motherhood, and their demands were focused on consumption and work norms rather than control of the shop floor.

2 Spinners' Protests in the Interwar Period

For the entire duration of the interwar period, the two main unions in Żyrardów, a left-wing union and a nationalist union, represented mainly the skilled male workforce, and their most prominent organizers were almost

17 The word Communist is capitalized in this chapter only in reference to the parties (or the members of these parties) which carried this word in their names. Hence, the postwar members of the Polish Workers' Party/Polish United Workers' Party (i.e., the wartime and postwar Polish communist parties) will be referred to as communists and not Communists. Since the largest Polish socialist party carried the same name before and after the war, Polish Socialist Party, no such differentiation will be made and all nouns and adjectives relating to will be capitalized.

18 Kenney 1997, 129–130.

exclusively craftsmen and weavers with the exception of a few winders working in the weaving shops.[19] Even the mass dismissals of skilled workers and the crackdown on union activity that took place in the aftermath of a large strike staged against the Taylorization of the shop floor in 1926 did not upend existing union hierarchies.

The factory management intentionally attempted to replace skilled labour with young, unskilled workers, in particular women. According to a socialist journalist, by the mid-1930s, one could hardly find any men working in production at the factory.[20] This was certainly an exaggeration, and men were employed as production workers, in particular as weavers; however, women also worked as loom operators in the weaving sections of the Żyrardów Works in the mid-1930s.[21]

Despite the changes in the gender and skill distribution of the factory labour force, the composition of the class union chapter did not seem to change significantly. Skilled workers in the weaving shops and craftsmen continued to constitute most of its membership.[22] No attempts were made to appeal to the workers of the spinning sections of the factory who were now almost exclusively young and frequently underaged women. Spinners, for example, did not

19 Until its liquidation in the 1920s, the factory school offered courses for men weavers and women winders. Thus, the profession was recognized as somewhat skilled. The winders working in the weaving shops held the highest position among women workers. The self-identification of one winder, Stanisława Miszkiewiczowa, as not simply winder but "weaver-winder" suggests that this group possibly consider themselves as distinct from not only the spinners but also from winders working in the spinning shops. "Ankieta uczestnika walki o wyzwolenie narodowe i społeczne ludu polskiego w okresie do 1939 r." [Questionnaire for a participant of the struggle for the national and social liberation of the Polish people in the period before 1939], Folder 8304, Zespół Akt Osobowych Działaczy Ruchu Robotniczego [Collection of Personal Files of the Labour Movement Activists, hereafter ZAODRR], Archiwum Akt Nowych [Archive of Modern Records, hereafter AAN], Warsaw, Poland. A Communist winder, Anna Barzenc, was a member of the presiding committee of the Marxist union chapter in Żyrardów for a better part of the interwar period. "Ankieta uczestnika walki o wyzwolenie narodowe i społeczne ludu polskiego w okresie do 1939 r." [Questionnaire for a participant for the national and social liberation of the Polish people in the period before 1939], Folder 322, ZAODRR, AAN, Warsaw, Poland. A Socialist winder turned civil servant, Agnieszka Tomaszewska, re-created and presided over the Marxist union chapter in 1929. A. K. 1939.

20 Dąbrowski 1962, 86.

21 Dąbrowski 1962, 86–87. Dąbrowski seems to claim that there were no male weavers in Żyrardów in 1934. This was not the case since Hulka-Laskowski, who lived in Żyrardów and documented the town's life, mentioned them in his book published in 1934. Hulka 1934, 246–247, 303–304.

22 Tkacz 1935.

receive a wage increase and back pay for the wages lost due to the company's failure to respect the national collective agreement. Even though management admitted that spinners should have also been paid more after striking weavers won the right to their back pay in a 1935 strike in Żyrardów, union leadership did not follow up on this issue. They left the matter in the hands of the Labour Inspectorate, which they considered powerless.[23] The disregard for unskilled women workers' struggles at the Żyrardów Works was not exceptional. For example, in 1931, the leadership of the left-wing Male and Female Textile Industry Workers Union (Związek Zawodowy Robotników i Robotnic Przemysłu Włókienniczego; also known as the class union, *związek klasowy*) in Łódź refused to recognize and support the strike of women weavers in the Geyer factory against the increase in the number of looms operated by a single weaver. It is worth noting that this was the same issue that drove union-organized male weavers to strike in the city the very same year (including a male weavers' strike at the Geyer factory only a few months later).[24]

In 1936, Maria Kirstowa, a labour inspector for the Warsaw district in the 1920s, contended that women employed in industry were disinterested in unions, and, even worse, that they undermined collective actions due to their "deeply rooted passivity." Only when pushed to the brink would they lose their emotional stability and become more "passionate" than their male colleagues. Paradoxically though, Kirstowa demonstrated that unorganized women were anything but passive or incapable of taking action. The former labour inspector cited the case of an undisclosed small-town curtain factory in which unionized weavers decided to go on strike in 1924, demanding better pay for themselves without having consulted with workers employed in the spinning section. The non-unionized women spinners not only did not join the action; they actually exhausted every avenue to break the strike. When their attempts to convince the management to hire strike-breakers—which was not possible due to the lack of willing weavers—and resume production failed, the spinners even petitioned the Labour Inspectorate to deem the strike illegal. Every day the factory machines stood still, the women were losing money they would not receive even if the strike succeeded.[25] The working women went to great lengths to stop the strike, and they were very much active but in defiance of the class solidarity promoted by Kirstowa.

---

23 "Jak 'pan pułkownik'" 1934. The leader of Żyrardów's union chapter herself claimed that the Inspectorate was not only powerless but also corrupt. "Dramat żyrardowski" 1932.

24 Kieszczyński 1969, 157–158, 186–193.

25 Kirstowa 1936, 290–297.

The unorganized women were not only capable of protesting against a strike. They were able to act on their own behalf as well. Stanisława Miszkiewiczowa, a winder at the Żyrardów Works, wrote a short memoir about one such instance in 1923. Despite only brief work experience in the Żyrardów Works and her relatively young age, Miszkiewiczowa became an informal delegate of her shop in a labour dispute with the management. There was no union involvement in the dispute whatsoever. A group of winders simply barged into the directors' offices and forced the managers present at the time to speak with them.[26] The fact that multiple workers entered the office was likely intended both as an intimidation tactic as well as a method of diffusing responsibility (there was no single leader of the action). Kirstowa's colleague Halina Krahelska describes similar tactics in her fictionalized story—which was rooted in fact—about a factory called *Szpilka*, written in the late 1930s. In Krahelska's narrative, a large group of women rather than a single delegate (the latter of which had been agreed to previously), burst into the office of a labour inspector to demand he remedy their problems with a computer, i.e., a person responsible for calculating earnings in the piece-rate system, who was cheating them out of their wages.[27]

The workers in Żyrardów demanded that they should not be required to walk up and down four flights of stairs carrying heavy skeins to warp the yarn, which became a necessity due to changes in the production process. The management caved, despite its initial refusal, and agreed to bring the machines down from the fourth floor. According to Stanisława Miszkiewiczowa, the delegation achieved its goals thanks to the strength and cleverness of her argument. When the general manager claimed that in Russia (where he had previously worked), thirteen-year-old children easily did the job and threatened that this may soon be the case in Żyrardów as well, the young organizer responded that "in a couple of years, children might be difficult to come by [*trzeba będzie szukać ze świeczką*]," suggesting that if the conditions of work persisted, women might not be able to become mothers.[28]

---

26 Stanisława Miszkiewiczowa, "Będą, będą dzieci pracować" ["The children will work, they will work"], Folder 8304, ZAODRR, AAN, Warsaw, Poland.

27 Krahelska 1937, 134–135.

28 According to Miszkiewiczowa, her retort was so humorous, one of the assistant managers had to cover his mouth with a handkerchief so as not to burst into laughter. He either had a particularly dark sense of humor or, more likely, saw comedy in a reversal of the class order: a winder cleverly talked down a director. Stanisława Miszkiewiczowa, "Będą, będą dzieci pracować" [The children will work, they will work], Folder 8304, ZAODRR, AAN, Warsaw, Poland.

Stanisława Miszkiewiczowa used her status as a potential life-giver (and as an actual mother, as she had already given birth to a son) to negotiate with the state authorities, a strategy that proved particularly effective in the newly created Republic because political elites claimed that there was a need to make up for the population losses the Polish nation suffered during the Great War. Motherhood was mobilized by Żyrardów's women workers multiple times in disputes with both factory management and the state before and after World War Two. Even seasoned communist activists in the post-World War Two era presented themselves as mothers in the party forum during disputes over wages, housing, and the availability of basic products, underscoring their responsibility for feeding their children rather than their rights as workers.[29]

Women workers resorted to the classic repertoire of union actions and staged strikes, albeit in a distinctive form: they preferred sit-down strikes over walkouts, and they avoided organizing strike committees or other, more formalized forms of representation. These tactics limited the risks involved in striking by diffusing responsibility, similar to when the group stormed the offices of the factory management. For example, in 1927, the women workers of the sewing shop in the Stradom factory in Częstochowa took part in a sit-down strike action. The striking women did not choose any representatives. Instead, a union delegate took it upon himself to negotiate with the management, which subsequently caved to the sewers' demands relating to changes in the method of measuring piece-work rates. Six years later, in the weaving and finishing shops of the nearby La Czenstochovienne factory, a similar action was staged: the women working there organized a sit-down strike without any union involvement and refused to select representatives. This time, however, the brutal intervention of the police put an end to the workers' protest.[30]

A strike action was also undertaken by the non-unionized spinners in Żyrardów. In 1938, the predominantly unskilled and unorganized women workers of the linen spinning section of the town's main factory staged a successful sit-down strike in response to the reorganization of production, which if implemented would heavily increase the workload; the action lasted a whole day and night. Information on the strike is scarce, but it seems to have followed the above pattern established by other groups of women workers.[31]

The tactics the spinners developed as a group during the interwar period, such as storming the offices of management and leaderless strikes, allowed

29 "Protokół narady przemysłowej w Żyrardowie" [Minutes from an industrial conference in Żyrardów], 24 May 1946, Folder 15, KM PPR, APW OM, Milanówek, Poland.

30 Majcher-Ociesa 2014, 165–166.

31 "Strajk odpowiedzią" 1938.

them to fight for their needs without taking on a significant amount of risk and without the financial burdens related to union membership, such as dues. These tactics became more useful in the postwar context—when it became impossible to organize strikes within a union framework—than were the traditional weapons of the prewar organized working class.

3 The First Postwar Strikes

As World War Two came to a close, in the territories of Poland, Czechoslovakia,[32] East Germany,[33] and to a lesser degree Hungary,[34] factories were taken over by their employees either right before the Red Army's arrival or shortly afterward. In eastern and central Poland, workers' councils were usually organized and manned by small groups of workers under the influence of the communist movement, usually by members of the Polish Workers' Party (i.e., the party of Polish communists that existed between 1943–1948; hereafter, PPR), or even by the PPR's special envoys. In Żyrardów, the line between the party committee and the workers' council in the Żyrardów Works was blurred, and even these bodies' members had difficulties understanding the differences between the two.[35] The first elections to the councils were called only after these organs had lost most of the power to the state administration and management in mid-1945.[36]

The attitude of the spinners toward the councils was ambiguous or even hostile, and there were two main reasons for this. First, similar to the structures of the prewar labour movement, spinners were de facto excluded from participating in the councils because they were dominated by skilled male workers.

32 Kovanda 1977, 257–259.

33 Pritchard 2004, 38–46.

34 Pittaway 2004, 462.

35 In March 1945, two months after the Soviets handed over the textile factory in Żyrardów to the Polish authorities, the communist leader of a works council in the Żyrardów Works asked about the difference between the council and the party committee in a party forum. He did not receive a clear answer. "Protokół nr 1 z posiedzenia Komitetu Partyjnego Zakładów Żyrardowskich" [Minutes no. 1 from the meeting of the Party Committee of Żyrardów Works], 30 March 1945, Folder 15, KM PPR, APW OM, Milanówek, Poland.

36 A decree regulating the functioning of the councils came into force in May 1945. It was the legal basis for calling elections; however, it also heavily restricted councils' prerogatives. For the text of the decree, see "Dekret z dnia 6 lutego 1945 r. o utworzeniu Rad Zakładowych," Dz.U. 1945 nr 8 poz. 36 (1945) [Decree of 6 February 1945, regarding the establishment of Works Councils], http://isap.sejm.gov.pl/isap.nsf/DocDetails.xsp?id=WDU19450080036.

The effect was heightened by the fact that skilled men constituted an outsized proportion of the workforce in early 1945. Production was limited by both the low demand for textiles and the lack of resources to manufacture them; for this reason, relatively few production workers were employed. At the same time, a large number of craftsmen were required to repair the damage the factory suffered at the hands of the retreating German military and the advancing Soviet army. This partially explains why the proportion of male workers was very high immediately after the war and began to fall by mid-1945 (although men worked in large numbers in the weaving section and in some other shops as well). In April 1945, male workers constituted over 63 percent of workers, and two months later, 59 percent, and their proportion of the factory workforce continued to fall.[37] Unsurprisingly, therefore, the first leader of the council of the Żyrardów Works was a metal worker, and most of his colleagues worked in maintenance.[38] The problems of spinners were not considered urgent.[39] Instead, the council and the communist party were focused on protecting the interests of craftsmen (often successfully). Second, spinners did not seem to be interested in self-managing their workplace. They were used to acting outside the structures of organized labour since the interwar period and preferred to speak with the management directly without representative institutions acting as intermediaries. Already in May 1945, the women workers from the linen spinning section went on strike after a group of spinners demanding better

---

37 Fidelis 2015, 81–82.

38 "Protokół z posiedzenia Komitetu Partyjnego" [Minutes from the meeting of the Party Committee], 18 April 1945, Folder 2, KM PPR, APW OM, Milanówek, Poland. In October 1945, metal workers were the leaders of four out of fifteen party cells in the *Zakłady*, including those in the hosiery and the finishing sections. "Spis sekretarzy komórek Partyjnych w Żyrardowie" [List of the secretaries of the party cells in Żyrardów], 11 October 1945, Folder 22, KM PPR, APW OM. The first post-war secretary of the PPR works committee was a machinist while his deputy was an ironsmith. "Protokół zebrania K[omitetu] PPR Fabrycznego w Zakładach Żyrardowskich" [Minutes from the meeting of the PPR Works Committee in Zakłady Żyrardowskie], 27 April 1945, Folder 15, KM PPR, APW OM, Milanówek, Poland. APW OM, KM PZPR, Folder 1, "Wykaz imienny delegatów obecnych na konferencji partyjnej" [List of names of the delegates present at the conference of the party], 10 February 1949, Folder 1, Komitet Miejski Polskiej Zjednoczonej Partii Robotniczej w Żyrardowie [Town Committee of the Polish United Workers' Party in Żyrardów, hereafter KM PZPR], APW OM, Milanówek, Warsaw.

39 Sadly, the minutes from the meetings of the council convened in 1945 did not survive or they were never recorded. Therefore, the priorities of the council can be assessed on the basis of the reports of the council's leader at the meetings of the party committee alone.

supplies of coal and food were barred from entering the director's office.[40] The director had learned his lesson, and in the following weeks, he negotiated with the spinners without any intermediaries.

Observing the nationwide failure of the councils and unions to represent the majority of workers, the government and communist party leadership tried to formalize negotiations between the management and workers without union intermediaries by introducing "workshop delegates" by decree in January 1947.[41] To a limited degree, delegates who were elected by small groups of workers fulfilled their intended role of relaying workers' demands to management, particularly in the early 1950s.[42] However, these individual delegates did not have the collective power held by a group of workers; thus, the tactic of storming management offices as a group continued to be employed by spinners (and also by women weavers).[43]

In case group negotiations failed, a proper strike was an option. Strikes were rare in the 1930s due to the threat of unemployment, and they became impossible in the state-owned and heavily guarded Żyrardów Works (although they still occurred in private factories elsewhere) during World War Two. After 1945, the fear subsided, and striking became almost a routine for spinners. Already in December 1945, in connection with industrial action in the Żyrardów Works, a regional PPR committee informed the national party leadership that "the attitude 'if we don't strike, we won't get anything; only those who strike get

40 "Komitet Miejski PPR w Żyrardowie do Wojewódzkiego Komitetu PPR w Warszawie" [Town Committee of the PPR in Żyrardów to the Regional Committee of the PPR in Warsaw], 5 June 1945, Folder 22, KM PPR, APW OM, Milanówek, Warsaw.

41 "Dekret z dnia 3 stycznia 1947 r. o tworzeniu przedsiębiorstw państwowych" [Decree of January 3, 1947, regarding the establishment of state-owned enterprises], Dz.U. 1947 nr 8 poz. 42, http://isap.sejm.gov.pl/isap.nsf/DocDetails.xsp?id=WDU19470080042; see also the discussion which preceded the introduction of this measure: "Protokół z posiedzenia Sekretariatu Komitetu Centralnego PPR" [Minutes from the meeting of the Secretariat of the Central Committee of the PPR], 29 July 1946 in: Kochański 2001.

42 "Kiedy będą" 1951; "Omówienie sprawy strajku jaki miał miejsce w dniu 16.08.1951 w Żyrardowie w Zakładach Włókienniczych" [Summary of the case of the strike that took place in Żyrardów in the Textile Works on 16 August 1951], 24 May 1951, Folder 352, Warszawski Komitet Wojewódzki Polskiej Zjednoczonej Partii Robotniczej [Warsaw Regional Committee of the Polish United Workers' Party, hereafter WKW PZPR], APW OM, Milanówek, Poland.

43 It is, at times, difficult to delineate between group delegations and strikes. For example, in 1951, around 200 weavers gathered in front of the director's office, meaning that the whole section effectively went on strike. "Omówienie sprawy strajku jaki miał miejsce w dniu 16.08.1951 w Żyrardowie w Zakładach Włókienniczych" [The summary of the case of the strike which took place in Żyrardów in Textile Works on 16 August 1951], 24 May 1951, Folder 352, WKW PZPR, APW OM, Milanówek, Poland.

something' began to dominate in some factories of our region."[44] The strike was often intended simply to force the works council and party committees to allow direct communication between workers' delegations and the appropriate higher authorities without intermediary representative institutions.[45]

The strike of December 1945 was a part of a long dispute over work norms that had begun in the late summer. In September, women spinners, who laboured in a piece-rate system, complained that their norms, which were based on the output of workers in Łódź factories, were impossible to fulfill due to the antiquated machines installed in the Żyrardów Works and the inadequate quality of raw materials. The norms were decreased by 5 percent twice, but the workers felt this was not enough. The strikers also asserted that it was unjust that only spinners received premiums for exceeding the norms, while workers assisting them, as fixed-rate employees, were exempt from these bonuses.[46] Seeing that the director—with whom they talked directly because they refused to negotiate with the party and works council delegates—did not have the right to fulfill their demands, they agreed to end the strike on the condition that the higher state economic and union authorities would come to a conference in Żyrardów to discuss their demands.

The problems that spinners decided to strike over were almost identical to the issues the male craftsmen and factory guards (who were generally recruited from veterans of the communist movement) raised in September. The latter were also dissatisfied with the fact that as fixed-rate employees, they were not eligible for bonuses. They did not, however, have to resort to strikes. The craftsmen successfully used the committee of the communist party in the

44 "Sprawozdanie za okres 1.11.1945–15.12.1945" [Report on the period from 1 November 1945 to 15 December 1945], Folder 295/IX/328, Komitet Centralny Polskiej Partii Robotniczej [Central Committee of the Polish Workers' Party], AAN, Warsaw, Poland. Two years later a local political police officer from Żyrardów had a similar observation. "Raport za okres sprawozdawczy 07.04.1947 r.–17.04.1947" [Report on the period from 7 April 1947 to 17 April 1947], Folder 0206/56 vol. 2, Instytut Pamięci Narodowej [Institute of National Remembrance, hereafter IPN], Warsaw, Poland.

45 In September 1945 and in April 1947, striking workers demanded that a delegation of their choosing be sent to the higher authorities. During the strike of 1947, the workers of the sewing shop won a reduction of the norms and higher wages. "Kwestionariusz o zbiorowym zatargu pracy" [Questionnaire on a collective labour dispute], 10 November 1947, Folder 1, Państwowe Zakłady Przemysłu Włókienniczego nr 1 w Żyrardowie [National Textile Works no 1 in Żyrardów], APW OGM, Grodzisk Mazowiecki, Poland.

46 "Sprawozdanie z ogólnego stanu Zakładów Żyrardowskich w okresie od dnia 10.09.45 do dnia 10.10.45" [Report on the general condition of the Żyrardów Works for the period from 10 September 1945 to 10 October 1945], Folder 8, KM PPR, APW OM, Milanówek, Poland.

Żyrardów Works to forward their demands in the form of a petition that used egalitarian communist discourse.[47] The guards, in turn, would use the conference requested by the spinners to secure wage increases.[48]

4 The Strikes of 1947

Spinners were responsible for starting the vast majority of strikes in Żyrardów during the postwar era. Weavers' strikes were rarer and usually followed strikes in the spinning shop, but the strikes of the two groups were never coordinated, and weavers and spinners always presented separate demands—and weavers' strikes were usually shorter. Conversely, craftsmen never called strikes: they had no reason to since relevant party structures and works councils were doing their best to accommodate these workers' demands. The history of a series of strikes in Żyrardów staged in the summer of 1947 and 1951 exemplify this pattern well.

By late 1947, women became a dominant part of the labour force in the Żyrardów Works. They constituted over 57 percent of factory workers (this statistic includes both production and maintenance workers).[49] Women continued to monopolize jobs operating spinning machines and also seemed to dominate loom operations as well, although we lack precise data.

On 13 August 1947 at around eight thirty in the morning, the linen spinning workers of the Żyrardów Works stopped the machines. They did not select any representatives nor did anyone seem to be the strike leader. Instead, a non-party member of the works council and a labour inspector began writing down the demands voiced by the strikers. The workers demanded the elimination of rationing, the availability of food staples (white bread, meat, *słonina*, and potatoes) in shops, coal allotments, and wage increases together with monthly backpay. The demands did not end there, though. The workers also wanted to

47 "Komitet Polskiej Partii Robotniczej w Żyrardowie do Wojewódzkiego Komitetu Polskiej Partii Robotniczej w Warszawie. Rezolucja" [Committee of the Polish Workers' Party in Żyrardów to the Regional Committee of the Polish Workers' Party in Warsaw. Resolution], 13 September 1945, Folder 8, KM PPR, APW OM, Milanówek, Poland.

48 "Sprawozdanie z ogólnego stanu Zakładów Żyrardowskich w okresie od dnia 10.09.45 do dnia 10.10.45" [Report on the general condition of the Żyrardów Works for the period from 10 September 1945 to 10 October 1945], Folder 8, KM PPR, APW OM, Milanówek, Poland.

49 "Sprawozdanie Wydziału Personalnego Kom[itetu] Fab[rycznego] PPR przy Pań[stwowych] Zak[ładach] Przem[ysłu] Włók[ienniczego] N-1" [Report of the Personnel Department of the PPR Factory Committee of the National Textile Industry Works No. 1], 2 December 1947, Folder 8, KM PPR, APW OM, Milanówek, Poland.

abolish the works council and reinstate the free market in foodstuffs.[50] When the representative of the Commission of Price Control came to speak with the spinners, he was met by workers shouting: "We don't want price control; price control bankrupts bakers and butchers; we don't have bread and meat, what do we need a government like this for?"[51] Meanwhile, workers employed in the spinning section were joined by weavers. Around one in the afternoon, just as the shifts changed, some of the spinning section workers remained in the factory, turning the strike into a sit-in, while other strikers used violence to stop strike-breakers from returning to their machines.[52]

The support for the strike in the weaving section, however, slowly crumbled. All those who were members of the communist party had resumed production much earlier, around ten thirty in the morning. They were joined by the Socialist weavers four hours later. Around five o'clock that evening, most of the weavers were back to work and formed a delegation armed with a list of demands that were similar to those of the spinners but which had been stripped of the most "political" points: the elimination of the works councils, rationing, and price controls. The spinners, who finally formed a delegation an hour later—likely because they observed that the weavers' delegates were not persecuted as strike organizers—and withdrew their demand for the abolition of the works council and instead called for changes to the council's composition.[53] They did not, however, return to their machines immediately. It was around eight o'clock at night when the strike ended. The next day, the town was well-supplied with white bread and meat, but the other workers' demands were left unaddressed.[54]

---

50 "Zestawienie meldunku nr. 104 Strajk w Zakładach Żyrardowskich" [Compilation of dispatch no. 104. Strike in the Żyrardów Works], Folder 295/VII-58, Central Committee of the Polish Workers' Party (Komitet Centralny Polskiej Partii Robotniczej, hereafter KC PPR), AAN, Warsaw, Poland.

51 "Sprawozdanie z przebiegu strajku w P[ańifstwowych] Z[akładach] P[rzemysłu] Wł[ókienniczego] 1 na oddziałach Przędzalni Lnu i Tkalni w dniu 13 sierpnia 1947" [Report on the strike in the National Textile Works no 1 in the Linen Spinning and Weaving sections on 13 August 1947], Folder 8, KM PPR, APW OM, Milanówek, Poland.

52 "Sprawozdanie z przebiegu strajku w P[ań有stwowych] Z[akładach] P[rzemysłu] Wł[ókienniczego] 1 na oddziałach Przędzalni Lnu i Tkalni w dniu 13 sierpnia 1947" [Report on the strike in National Textile Works no 1 in the Linen Spinning and Weaving sections on 13 August 1947], Folder 8, KM PPR, APW OM, Milanówek, Poland.

53 The sources are silent, however, on how exactly the composition was supposed to change and whether the workers demanded new elections.

54 "Sprawozdanie z przebiegu strajku w P[aństwowych] Z[akładach] P[rzemysłu] Wł[ókienniczego] 1 na oddziałach Przędzalni Lnu i Tkalni w dniu 13 sierpnia 1947" [Report on the strike in the National Textile Works no 1 in the Linen Spinning and Weaving sections on 13 August 1947], Folder 8, KM PPR, APW OM, Milanówek, Poland.

In my opinion, the communists were unable to accept that a strike of this magnitude was not coordinated by political actors. After it ended, local communists rushed to blame the Socialist party leadership for organizing it. The communist narrative was accepted by the PPR special delegate from the Regional Committee and passed on to the Central Committee PPR. The leader of the local socialist chapter, Agnieszka Tomaszewska, was personally singled out as the strike organizer.[55] Małgorzata Fidelis, who also analyzed these events, emphasized the fact that the (male) communists and Socialists were puzzled by the strike and attributed it to the stereotypical backwardness and irrationality of women.[56] Gender certainly played a role here, and our (my and Fidelis's) interpretations may be considered complementary: the communists alleged that the socialist organizers manipulated the women strikers easily due to their "backwardness" and lack of political consciousness.

The communist accusations against the Socialists were based on weak evidence and were, in fact, absurd. The main demand of the strikers targeted the Polish Socialist Party (Polska Partia Socjalistyczna; hereafter, PPS) directly. The workers complained about the quality of the bread baked in a Socialist-controlled cooperative and demanded a change or the elimination of a works council that had a safe Socialist majority and a Socialist president.[57] Furthermore, the sources show that PPS members neither instigated the strike nor were they the most enthusiastic participants in it.[58]

At the same time, according to one of the town's Socialist leaders, in the linen spinning section, Socialist workers did not hesitate to join the strikers. The political parties in linen spinning were generally very weak, and the workers were even hostile toward party organizers from the PPS and the PPR alike. The spinners seemed to consider belonging to the party shameful, and Socialist

55 "Protokół konferencji przedstawicieli PPS i PPR" [Minutes of the conference of the delegates of the PPS and PPR], 18 August 1947, Folder 15, KM PPR, APW OM, Milanówek, Poland; "Zestawienie meldunku nr. 104. Strajk w Zakładach Żyrardowskich" [Compilation of the dispatch no 104. Strike in the Żyrardów Works], Folder 295/VII-58; "Sprawozdanie z wyjazdu do Żyrardowa" [Report on a trip to Żyrardów], Folder 295/XI/322, KC PPR, AAN, Warsaw, Poland.

56 Fidelis 2015, 87–89.

57 APW OM, KM PPR, Folder 3, "Protokół posiedzenia Egzekutywy Komitetu Miejskiego" [Minutes from the meeting of the executive of the Town Committee], 7 August 1947, Folder 3, KM PPR, APW OM, Milanówek, Warsaw.

58 "Sprawozdanie z przebiegu strajku w P[ańmstwowych] Z[akładach] P[rzemysłu] Wł[ókienniczego] 1 na oddziałach Przędzalni Lnu i Tkalni w dniu 13 sierpnia 1947" [Report on the strike in the National Textile Works no 1 in the Linen Spinning and Weaving sections on 13 August 1947], Folder 8, KM PPR, APW OM, Milanówek, Poland.

workers hid their party pins in shame.[59] Members of the PPS in the weaving section, both men and women, were not eager to join the strike although they did so in solidarity with the whole shop. Socialist weavers, however, resumed production shortly after PPS leaders went to the shopfloor to speak with them. Similar conversations with the linen spinners did not achieve any results, and only in the combing and tow-breaking sections, which were dominated by skilled male workers, did the Socialists return to work. The situation was similar in the case of PPR workers: weavers resumed production, and spinners did not. Although the weavers might have been threatened, it is much more probable that they were simply convinced by their leaders to end the strike.[60] They had more trust in labour leaders than spinners ever did, and they were more used to maintaining party and/or union discipline. Weavers resumed production first and then formed a delegation, trusting that its demands would be heard. Spinners did so only after talks were concluded and carrying on with the strike seemed pointless: night was coming, and they were not prepared to spend it in the factory.[61]

The strike in the linen spinning section did not have the characteristics of a party- or union-organized action. Instead, it followed the tactics of the leaderless sit-down strike unskilled labourers often called during the interwar period. Furthermore, the demand to eliminate the works council was voiced only in the linen spinning shop and not in the weaving section. Unlike the weavers, the spinners did not believe, and probably rightly so, that these representative institutions would serve their interests. The works council was useless in their minds, only impeding direct communication between workers and management. Moreover, they certainly blamed the council for the failure to provide bread and coal to the workers.

Against the backdrop of the strikes in Łódź during the same period, the strike of 1947 was rather exceptional in terms of its demands. The strikes that took place in the 1940s were generally "apolitical" and focused on issues concerning

59 Socialists were not required to wear them all the time. They were given out to celebrate May Day. "Protokół z zebrania Komitetów Miejskich PPR i PPS" [Minutes from the meeting of the Town Committees of the PPR and PPS], 16 June 1947, Folder 2, KM PPR, APW OM, Milanówek, Warsaw.

60 "Protokół konferencji przedstawicieli PPS i PPR" [Minutes of the conference of the delegates of the PPS and PPR], 18 August 1947, Folder 15, KM PPR, APW OM, Milanówek, Poland.

61 "Sprawozdanie z przebiegu strajku w P[aństwowych] Z[akładach] P[rzemysłu] Wł[ókienniczego] 1 na oddziałach Przędzalni Lnu i Tkalni w dniu 13 sierpnia 1947" [Report on the strike in National Textile Works no. 1 in the Linen Spinning and Weaving sections on 13 August 1947], Folder 8, KM PPR, APW OM, Milanówek, Poland.

food supply and production norms. The most remarkable demand in this strike was the call to eliminate price controls and the Social Commissions enforcing it. In contrast to Żyrardów, the commissions in Łódź seemed to be, at least initially, very popular among workers. As Padraic Kenney noted, they were an "outlet for class anger" and produced a discourse later used against managers and the communist party outside of the institutional framework.[62] The spinners striking in Żyrardów, however, did not act as workers advocating solely for themselves. They conceived of their action as a struggle on behalf of the whole local community in which "bakers and butchers" were important members who provided valuable services. In fact, the striking spinners were more invested in the interests of bakers and butchers and the services they provided for the community than those of their fellow workers from other sections of the factory as there was no coordination between the spinners and weavers of the Żyrardów Works.

5 The Strikes of 1951

The introduction of the first fully Stalinist Six-Year Plan in 1950 effectively reduced the wages of Żyrardów workers. Moreover, the overemphasis on heavy industry and the forced collectivization campaign led to food shortages. Falling wages also limited workers' ability to procure meat on the black market. The implications of the two overlapping problems became particularly pronounced in the summer of 1951 and led to a series of short strikes in the linen spinning and weaving sections, which came to a head on 16–18 August 1951.

By that time, both the spinning and weaving sections were almost completely feminized.[63] Since 1949, the communist party began vigorously campaigning for women's equality in the workplace at the national level and enhanced its efforts to expand its female membership. In 1950, women constituted 60 percent of the party organization in the Żyrardów Works, slightly lower than the share of women among all of the factory's employees. The men, craftsmen and foremen in particular, retained their positions in the shopfloor

62 Kenney 1997, 196.

63 With the exception of the finishing shop and the highly specialized jacquard looms. There were also a couple dozen young men in the so-called Stakhanovite School working in one of the weaving shops. The assessment is based on indirect evidence since we have no statistical analysis of workers' gender. "Materiał dotyczący analizy pracy Oddziałów Produkcyjnych" [Materials regarding the analysis of work of the Production Sections], 13 September 1951, Folder 352, WKW PZPR, APW OM, Milanówek, Poland.

party structures, however. In 1951, even in the weaving section, almost all secretaries of the party cells were still male foremen.[64] Equality in the workplace was even harder to achieve. Attempts to promote women to the position of foreperson and employ them in craftsmen's jobs failed due to the resistance of factory administration and male workers. Forewomen were extremely rare: in 1951, there were 115 foremen and only 2 forewomen in Żyrardów.[65]

On 3 August 1951, shop delegates from the linen spinning section went to the party Works Committee. Their demands were not satisfied, so they subsequently headed straight to the Town Committee of the PZPR, demanding that meat be delivered to the town, as it had been missing from the shelves for a week. They were promised that it would arrive soon. The same day, a group of weavers threatened the general director with a strike if the meat did not arrive. The meat was delivered, demonstrating to the workers that putting pressure on the management and the party was a strategy that yielded tangible results. What is interesting is that the spinners and weavers acted separately from each other and were unaware of each other's actions. There was no communication between the two sections.[66] On 12 August 1951, the majority of workers employed in one of the weaving shops (around 200 of 250 employed) walked out and congregated in front of the offices of the general director, this time demanding coal. The weavers, however, quickly returned to work. They were convinced to do so after the town secretary of the PZPR and the director proposed that they elect delegates from among them to conduct further negotiations.[67]

On 16 August, around eight o'clock in the morning, multiple delegations of workers from various shops of the linen spinning section visited the office of the section director. Their main demand was related to small payments they had received two days earlier, and they also wanted to know when meat would be delivered. Not having received a satisfying answer, the delegates returned to their shops, and shortly after, a strike broke out in most of the linen spinning section, initially in wet spinning. By five o'clock that evening, the spinners

64 "Notatka o strukturze i pracy w organizacji partyjnej na Zakładach Żyrardowskich" [Memo regarding the structure and work in the party organization in Żyrardów Works], 1951, Folder 352, WKW PZPR, APW OM, Milanówek, Poland.

65 Fidelis 2015, 92–93.

66 "Omówienie sprawy strajku jaki miał miejsce w dniu 16.08.1951 w Żyrardowie w Zakładach Włókienniczych" [Report on a case of strike that took place in Żyrardów Textile Works on 16 August, 1951], 24 August 1951, Folder 352, WKW PZPR, APW OM, Milanówek, Poland.

67 "Notatka. Dotyczy: zajść w Żyrardowskich Zakł[adach] Włókienniczych na oddz[iale] tkalni bawełnianej" [Memo. Regarding: the events in the Żyrardów Textile Works in the cotton weaving section], 13 July 1951, Folder 237/X/39, KC PZPR, AAN, Warsaw, Poland.

were joined by one weaving shop situated in the adjacent building. The weavers were on strike for only three hours and did not present demands, wanting only to speak with union delegates. The linen spinning workers did not restart their machines for the whole day. The next day, the strike started in parts of the linen section and one of the weaving shops, later spreading to two other shops in the weaving section. The spinners were on strike for only an hour and a half. The strike in the weaving shops was a rolling one, so it was difficult for the reporting officers to ascertain its real scope, but it ended at six thirty that evening. In turn, however, the Żyrardów Clothing Works (Żyrardowskie Zakłady Odzieżowe), until recently the sewing section of the main factory, went on strike for the entire day. On 18 August, the workers on the first cotton spinning shift did not start their machines, although those working the second shift did.[68]

The events of 16–18 August 1951 can hardly be described as a singular strike. We should look at them as a series of limited strikes. Although the cotton spinners and the weavers were inspired by the linen spinners, their strikes took different forms and had overlapping but different demands. This was the case already in 1947, but in 1951, it became even more pronounced. Similar to 1947, the linen spinning section not only started the 1951 strikes but was on strike the longest of the sections. While spinners presented their demands before the strike, the strikers themselves did not choose any representatives.

We should differentiate between the two strikes of the weavers and between the strikes of the linen and cotton spinners. The weavers' strike on 16 August was well-organized. Unlike the actions of the linen spinning section, those of the weavers were coordinated, and around forty workers met in one of the toilets to develop a strategy before the strike broke out. The weavers' primary demand was to speak with the union bosses so that they could explain the lack of meat on the shelves. Just as in 1947, the weavers believed in the effectiveness of the trade unions even if these organs needed to be pressured to act.[69] The traditional organization seemed to hasten the strike's end. Janina Szymańska, the principal coordinator of the action and a worker with prewar experience in the Socialist party, was invited to a meeting with security and party authorities. Whether she was threatened or simply convinced that the problems of the

68 "Omówienie sprawy strajku jaki miał miejsce w dniu 16.08.1951 w Żyrardowie w Zakładach Włókienniczych" [Report on a case of strike that took place in Żyrardów Textile Works on 16 August 1951], 24 August 1951, Folder 352, WKW PZPR, APW OM, Milanówek, Poland.

69 "Omówienie sprawy strajku jaki miał miejsce w dniu 16.08.1951 w Żyrardowie w Zakładach Włókienniczych" [Report on a case of strike that took place in Żyrardów Textile Works on 16 August 1951], 24 August 1951, Folder 352, WKW PZPR, APW OM, Milanówek, Poland.

workers would be addressed, we do not know; perhaps it was both. Whatever happened, after she returned to the shop floor, the workers gathered around her, and soon the looms were running again.[70]

Gareth Pritchard, when explaining why the labour movement in Eastern Germany did not actively challenge the "Sovietizing" policies, contended that "to break with the regime would mean acknowledging that all their struggles and suffering had achieved nothing."[71] Hence, there existed a psychological mechanism that disincentivized protest and encouraged compliance. Former Socialists in Poland and Germany were certainly critical of the state-socialist reality. Nevertheless, they were more likely to conform to the position of labour institutions and end strikes after speaking with union and party functionaries. Regarding the example of strikes in the Dąbrowa Basin in 1951, Jan-Arendt de Graaf has shown that prewar members of Socialist and Communist labour organizations could have been convinced to return to work by invoking traditions of the working class and emphasizing the differences between prewar struggles with capitalists and the postwar strikes.[72] Perhaps this was the case with Janina Szymańska in Żyrardów in 1951.

The strike on August 17 was notably different. The report does not mention Szymańska at all, nor does it indicate any form of planning. Mainly young weavers, the so-called "Hanka Sawicka line" that was supposed to be an exemplary youth brigade, went on strike, and they did not present any demands. The only worker who was identified as a strike organizer by name was a member of the communist youth organization who not only instigated the action in her shop but forced those resisting to participate in it using threats and violence. The strike was a rolling one. Its form was a consequence of the lack of communication rather than careful planning. First, there was much misinformation as to whether other shops continued to strike. Second, the shortages of materials caused by a strike in one shop forced other shops to temporarily halt production. A true strike was indistinguishable from a stoppage, at least for the reporting officers.[73]

---

70 "Omówienie sprawy strajku jaki miał miejsce w dniu 16.08.1951 w Żyrardowie w Zakładach Włókienniczych" [Report on a case of strike that took place in Żyrardów Textile Works on 16 August 1951], 24 August 1951, Folder 352, WKW PZPR, APW OM, Milanówek, Poland.

71 Pritchard 2004, 187.

72 De Graaf 2020, 35.

73 "Omówienie sprawy strajku jaki miał miejsce w dniu 16.08.1951 w Żyrardowie w Zakładach Włókienniczych" [Report on a case of strike that took place in Żyrardów Textile Works on 16 August 1951], 24 August 1951, Folder 352, WKW PZPR, APW OM, Milanówek, Poland.

The second strike in the weaving shop had much in common with the strikes called in the sewing and cotton spinning sections. In these strikes, younger workers were a leading force, and threats of violence were present: an empty bottle was even thrown at strike-breakers in the cotton spinning section as they were leaving the factory.[74] Unlike the linen spinning section, the cotton spinning shops—particularly affected by the Six-Year Plan—were no longer dominated by older workers as most experienced cotton spinners transferred to other sections where the pay was better.[75] The unrestrained and violent character of the strikes in the sections where the youth dominated, in contrast with the calm and easily resolved strike in the weaving room, is not surprising. Pritchard identified a similar pattern during the Berlin Uprising; strikes organized by veterans of the labour movement were generally "disciplined" and short-lived, while those in which young workers took the lead were "unorganized, spontaneous and violent."[76] As I have shown above, at least in Żyrardów, there was a third category: a strike organized by older workers who had not belonged to prewar labour organizations. These strikes did not require using violence against strike-breakers as the bonds of solidarity were stronger than in the shops dominated by the youth, and strike-breaking was rare. They were, however, not led by a single person or a small group of workers and lasted much longer than those in sections where old labour organizers held sway.

6 Conclusion

In Żyrardów during the post-World War Two era, the labour strikes that were the most powerful and also the most difficult to suppress were not those called by long-time skilled members of the organized labour movement, as is commonly asserted in the scholarship; nor were they the actions planned by the anarchic youth. They were the labour actions staged by women spinners with prewar experience in organizing strikes and other collective actions that differed significantly from those dominated by mostly male organized workers under the capitalist regime of the interwar period. These women had not belonged to labour organizations before 1939, and they continued to treat

74 "Omówienie sprawy strajku jaki miał miejsce w dniu 16.08.1951 w Żyrardowie w Zakładach Włókienniczych" [Report on a case of strike that took place in Żyrardów Textile Works on 16 August 1951], 24 August 1951, Folder 352, WKW PZPR, APW OM, Milanówek, Poland.

75 "Uwagi dotyczące pracy Zakładów Żyrardowskich" [Remarks concerning the functioning of the Żyrardów Works] [1951], Folder 352, WKW PZPR, APW OM, Milanówek, Poland.

76 Pritchard 2004, 218.

unions and labour parties with suspicion after 1945. These women's lack of ties to organized labour made it almost impossible for the party and union activists to convince or force workers to return to work. Furthermore, spinners were more likely to use a discourse that diverged significantly from communist party ideology. They performed their intersectional, multi-dimensional identities based not only on a narrowly understood concept of class but also on the basis of their gender and their sense of belonging within the local community.

The workers who formed the core of the working-class movement before 1939, men in particular, generally remained faithful to its guidance and rarely resorted to strikes after the war. They were able to frame their demands within the accepted communist discourse and forward them through official channels. When a strike did take place, the union and party leaders were usually able to get these workers to back down. I may even go so far as to say that Socialist and communist workers alike helped maintain the stability of communist power in Żyrardów. This does not mean, however, that they accepted the policies implemented by the state.

It is difficult to expand the findings of this chapter to other Polish textile production centers. Łódź, for example, was one of the centers of Polish organized labour. Before the war, unions had greater influence there than they ever had in Żyrardów; hence, the prevalence of discourse on class struggle was likely greater there as well, as shown by Padraic Kenney. The example of Żyrardów spinners certainly proves, however, that we should pay more attention to the heterogeneity of workers' culture and recognize the ingenuity and perseverance of workers who were not able to act through, or who rejected, the structures of organized labour and study their discourses and practices both before and after World War Two.

Bibliography

A.K. 1939. "Ograniczenie pracy morderczej" [Restriction of murderous labour]. *Robotnik* [The worker], 22 January 1939.

Burek, Jan. 2022. "History Seems Different from the Shop Floor: A Micro-Historical Challenge to Established Caesurae in the History of 20th Century Poland: Transwar Continuities in Żyrardów." In *Rethinking Period Boundaries: New Approaches to Continuity and Discontinuity in Modern European History and Culture*, edited by Jade McGlynn and Lucian George, 35–58. Berlin: De Gruyter Oldenbourg.

Canning, Kathleen. 1992. "Gender and the Politics of Class Formation: Rethinking German Labor History." *The American Historical Review* 97, no. 3: 736–768.

Chumiński, Jędrzej. 1998. "Kształtowanie się form organizacyjnych i zasad programowych ruchu zawodowego i rad zakładowych w latach 1944–1945" [The development of forms of organization and programmatic rules of the union and works councils' movement in the years 1944–1945]. *Nauki Humanistyczne* [Humanities], no. 4: 165–193.

Dąbrowski, Jan. 1962. "Żyrardów w pętli" [Żyrardów in a noose]. In *Polskie drogi: wybór reportaży z lat międzywojennych* [Polish ways: A selection of reportages from the interwar years]. Warsaw: Czytelnik.

Downs, Laura Lee. 1995. *Manufacturing Inequality: Gender Division in the French and British Metalworking Industries, 1914–1939*. Ithaca, NY: Cornell University Press.

"Dramat żyrardowski przed sądem" [The tragedy of Żyrardów in court]. 1932. *Robotnik* [The worker], 1 November 1932.

Fidelis, Małgorzata. 2015. *Kobiety, komunizm i industrializacja w powojennej Polsce* [Women, communism, and industrialization in postwar Poland]. Translated by Maria Jaszczurowska. Warsaw: Wydawnictwo W.A.B.—Grupa Wydawnicza Foksal.

De Graaf, Jan. 2020. "The Occupational Strikes in the Dąbrowa Basin of April 1951: Stalinist Industrialization against the Traditions of the Polish Working Class." *International Labor and Working-Class History* 98: 22–42.

Harsch, Donna. 2000. "Approach/Avoidance: Communists and Women in East Germany, 1945–9." *Social History* 25, no. 2: 156–182.

Hulka-Laskowski, Paweł. 1934. *Mój Żyrardów: z dziejów polskiego miasta i z życia pisarza* [My Żyrardów: From the history of a Polish town and from the life of a writer]. Warsaw: Zakł. Druk. F. Wyszyński i S-ka.

Hunt, Karen. 2010. "The Politics of Food and Women's Neighborhood Activism in First World War Britain." *International Labor and Working-Class History* 77, no. 1: 8–26.

"Jak 'pan pułkownik' Koźmiński honoruje umowę" [How "Mister Colonel" Koźmiński honors the agreement]. 1934. *Włókniarz* [The textile worker], 20 September 1934.

Kazimierski, Józef. 1984. *Dzieje zakładów żyrardowskich i ich załogi w latach 1829–1885* [History of the Żyrardów Works and its staff in the years 1829–1885]. Ciechanów: Ciechanowskie Towarzystwo Naukowe.

Kazimierski, Józef. 1980. "Pierwszy powszechny strajk w Żyrardowie (23–28 IV 1883 r.)" [The first general strike in Żyrardów (23–28.05.1883)]. In *Żyrardów 1829–1945*, edited by Irena Pietrzak-Pawłowska, 145–158. Warsaw: Wydawnictwo Naukowe PWN.

Kenney, Padraic. 1999. "The Gender of Resistance in Communist Poland." *The American Historical Review* 104, no. 2: 399–425.

Kenney, Padraic. 1997. *Rebuilding Poland: Workers and Communists, 1945–1950*. Ithaca, NY: Cornell University Press.

"Kiedy będą fartuchy?" [When will the aprons arrive?]. 1951. *Głos Włókniarza* [The voice of a textile worker], March 1951.

Kieszczyński, Lucjan. 1969. *Ruch strajkowy w przemyśle włókienniczym okregu łódzkiego w latach kryzysu gospodarczego, 1929–1933* [Strikes in the textile industry of the Łódź region, 1929–1933]. Łódź: Wydawnictwo Łódzkie.

Kochański, Aleksander. 2001. "Protokoły posiedzeń Sekretariatu KC PPR 1945–1946" [Minutes from the meetings of the Secretariat of the KC PPR, 1945–1946]. *Dokumenty do dziejów PRL* [Documents on the history of the Polish People's Republic], vol. 14. Warsaw: ISP PAN.

Kolář, Pavel. 2012. "The Party as a New Utopia: Reshaping Communist Identity after Stalinism." *Social History* 37, no. 4: 402–424.

Kirstowa, Maria. 1936. "Praca kobiet" [Women's work]. In *Ze wspomnień inspektora pracy* [From the memoirs of a Labour Inspector], edited by Wiesław Sten, Halina Krahelska, and Maria Kirstowa, vol. 1. Warsaw: M. Fruchtman.

Kormanowa, Żanna. 1960. "Pierwszy strajk powszechny na ziemiach polskich" [The first general strike in the Polish lands]. In *Z walk robotników Żyrardowa 1883–1919* [From the struggles of workers in Żyrardów, 1883–1919], edited by Józef Kaźmierski, Bronisław Syzdek, and Krzysztof Zwoliński. Żyrardów: Miejski Komitet Frontu Jedności Narodu i Prezydium Miejskiej Rady Narodowej w Żyrardowie.

Kovanda, Karel. 1977. "Works Councils in Czechoslovakia, 1945–47." *Soviet Studies* 29, no. 2: 255–269.

Krahelska, Halina. 1937. *Polski strajk* [The Polish strike]. Warsaw: Towarzystwo Wydawnicze 'Rój'.

La Mare, Ursula. 2008. "Necessity and Rage: The Factory Women's Strikes in Bermondsey, 1911." *History Workshop Journal* 66, no. 1: 62–80.

Lampland, Martha. 2011. "The Technopolitical Lineage of State Planning in Hungary, 1930–1956." *In Entangled Geographies: Empire and Technopolitics in the Global Cold War*, edited by Gabrielle Hecht, 155–184. Cambridge, MA: MIT Press.

Majcher-Ociesa, Edyta. 2014. "Warunki pracy w przemyśle włókienniczym w Częstochowie w latach 1918–1939" [The conditions of work in the textile industry in Częstochowa in the years 1918–1939]. In *Praca i społeczeństwo Drugiej Rzeczypospolitej: zbiór studiów* [Work and society of the Second Republic: A collection of studies], edited by Włodzimierz Mędrzecki and Cecylia Leszczyńska. Metamorfozy Społeczne [Social Metamorphoses], vol. 9. Warsaw: Instytut Historii PAN.

Pittaway, Mark. 2012. *The Workers' State: Industrial Labor and the Making of Socialist Hungary, 1944–1958*. Pittsburgh, PA: University of Pittsburgh Press.

Pittaway, Mark. 2004. "The Politics of Legitimacy and Hungary's Postwar Transition." *Contemporary European History* 13, no. 4: 453–475.

Pritchard, Gareth. 2004. *The Making of the GDR, 1945–53*. Manchester: Manchester University Press.

Siewierski, Tomasz. 2012. "Komuniści i historycy. Polski ruch robotniczy w badaniach uczonych w PRL—wybrane aspekty." [Communists and historian. The Polish labour movement in the research of the scholars of the Polish People's Republic]. In *Partia komunistyczna w Polsce: Struktury, ludzie, dokumentacja* [The Communist Party in Poland: Structures, people, documentation], edited by Dariusz Magier, 463–479. Lublin: Archiwum Państwowe.

"Strajk odpowiedzią na przeciążenie pracą" [Strike as a response to work overload]. 1938. *Włókniarz* [The textile worker], 11 November 1938.

Tkacz. 1935. "Tkalnia wywalczyła podwyżki" [The weaving section won raises]. *Żyrardowiak. Organ rewolucyjnych robotników Zakładów Żyrardowskich* [Żyrardowiak. The publication of the revolutionary workers of the Żyrardów Works], December 1935.

Żarnowska, Anna. 1980. "Klasa robotnicza Żyrardowa" [The working class of Żyrardów]. In *Żyrardów 1829–1945*, edited by Irena Pietrzak-Pawłowska, 125–144. Warsaw: Wydawnictwo Naukowe PWN.

CHAPTER 12

Trade Union Activists, Expertise, and Gender Inequalities in the Workplace in Post-1956 Poland

A Struggle to Reveal Unequal Pay

Natalia Jarska

Abstract

This chapter focuses on women's activism around the issue of (un)equal pay in post-war Poland. In particular, it discusses two examples of activism aimed at identifying and defining the problem of gender-based wage inequalities which unfolded in the late 1950s and early 1960s. The first one is an in-depth study of working and pay conditions of women workers carried out by the Women's Commission of the Trade Unions (Komisja Kobieca Centralnej Rady Związków Zawodowych), which had been reestablished after the seven-year break during Stalinism. The second example is the research of economist and sociologist Janina Waluk, which was published in 1965. The chapter shows the ways these studies challenged the official discourse that depicted unequal pay as an exclusively capitalist phenomenon and discusses the conceptualization of (un)equal pay by Polish women activists in connection to international debates at the time. The analysis carried out by these activists reflected a multidimensional and broad understanding of the problem. This chapter shows the importance of knowledge production as labour activism under state socialism and argues that women's activism during the post-1956 period of so-called gender backlash in Poland centered on women's equality in the workplace.

Keywords

equal pay – equal pay definition – Janina Waluk – knowledge production – Poland – state socialism – women's activism – women's commission/department of the Central Council of Trade Unions (Komisja Centralna Związków Zawodowych, KCZZ)

This chapter focuses on the ways women trade union activists and women experts addressed gender inequalities in the workplace in Poland in the late 1950s and early 1960s. This period was marked by the process of de-Stalinization,

 | DOI:10.1163/9789004682481_013

the considerable liberalization of policies and public discourses, and decreasing repression. These developments, on the one hand, triggered critical debates about women's employment in Poland, which led to a reshaping of Stalinist policies that called for the intensive labour mobilization of women, the prohibition against women working in certain professions, and dismissals on the ground. On the other hand, de-Stalinization enabled a renewed discussion about working conditions as well as the reemergence of the factory-based structures of the women's movement.

This chapter discusses activism and expertise that problematized the implementation of the "equal pay for equal work" principle during this period, focusing on two examples. The first is a survey carried out by central and local activists of the Women's Commission of the Central Council of Trade Unions (Komisja Centralna Związków Zawodowych, KCZZ) between 1957 and 1960. The second case is the research conducted and published by the economist and sociologist Janina Waluk under the title "Women's Work and Pay in Poland" in 1965.[1] I focus on the ways these women challenged the official explanations and justifications of the wage gap between men and women, and how they conceptualized gender-based discrimination in Polish factories. Drawing on an inclusive definition of activism, I embrace scientific research which in the case of Waluk had an explicit feminist goal: women's equality in the workplace. I show the particular ways knowledge production relating to unequal pay developed in the state-socialist context, where the problem of gendered wage inequality was officially nonexistent and deemed to have been resolved. For this reason, knowledge production was a powerful means to challenge official claims.

The problem of equal remuneration had already emerged at the international level when the International Labour Organization was established in 1919, though activism around women's low wages in Europe dated back to the nineteenth century.[2] In the early post-World War Two period, debates about the wage gap intensified, and the premise of equal pay was accepted first in a UN resolution (1948) and then by the ILO Convention no. 100; the latter was soon ratified by many countries.[3] Between 1947 and 1948,

1 Waluk 1965. Janina Waluk (1926–2008) wrote her doctoral thesis about women's wages under the supervision of renowned economist Zofia Morecka. After completing her PhD, Waluk did research on occupational sociology and worked at Warsaw University, where she participated in strikes in 1968. This activity led to her expulsion from the university and the end of her academic career. In the late 1970s, she collaborated with the Polish democratic opposition, and starting in the summer 1980, she served as an expert for the "Solidarity" trade union.

2 Neunsinger 2018, 121.

3 Neunsinger 2018, 122.

Poland was active at the international level, advocating for equal remuneration legislation in the ILO.[4] However, as described by Eileen Boris, the equal remuneration debate was deeply embedded in early Cold War struggles, with the USSR and its satellites (Poland included) becoming increasingly hostile to the ILO and framing the equal pay issue as part of the anti-capitalist struggle.[5] This is why in Poland, the slogan of equal pay was restricted to the narrow definition of "equal work" and did not adopt the ILO's formulation of "work of equal value." Furthermore, the understanding of value, although diverse, was attached to the commodification of labour on a free market; hence, it stood in contradiction to the socialist political economy.[6] Consequently, Poland ratified the ILO Equal Remuneration Convention no. 100 only in 1954.[7]

Silke Neunsinger shows that (un)equal pay had different meanings, and the ILO Convention no. 100 opened up rather than settled the debate on the very definition of unequal pay. The Convention spoke about the "equal remuneration of men and women for the work of equal value," which was a broader definition than the UN-adopted premise of "equal pay for equal work" since it also included other compensation beyond salary. The stress on equal value also made it possible to overcome the narrow understanding of equal work as the same job, which was not useful because women mostly held different jobs than men. However, the understanding of equal value also varied, and women activists on the international and national levels struggled to measure inequality.[8] In state-socialist Poland, the most popular way to refer to the equal pay premise was "equal pay for equal work" (*równa płaca za równą pracę*).

This chapter discusses the way women activists in Poland understood (un) equal pay in the late 1950s and early 1960s and exposed the persistence of wage inequalities in a system that had officially abolished wage discrimination based on gender and adopted the "equal pay for equal work" principle. By investigating the implementation of the equal pay principle, women activists problematized the very definition of unequal pay. The chapter contextualizes these attempts in broader international discussions about (un)equal pay that unfolded after the ILO Convention no. 100 on equal remuneration was passed. Recent pioneering studies by Silke Neunsinger and Eloisa Betti have uncovered international debates on equal pay and the struggles to implement the "equal work, equal pay" premise that took place on the international and

4 Rosner 1950, 33–34.
5 Boris 2018, 107–108.
6 Lampland 2016, 165.
7 "Konwencja (nr 100) dotycząca jednakowego wynagrodzenia" 1955.
8 Neunsinger 2018, 129–130.

national levels in the postwar period.[9] As Neunsinger shows in her study, defining and measuring wage inequality stood at the core of international efforts to implement the ILO Convention no. 100 and reduce pay discrimination against women. The problem of unequal pay was recognized by women activists in state-socialist societies as well, although very little is known about particular challenges they faced. In her recent study, Susan Zimmermann has discussed Hungarian trade union women activism in the early 1970s around the realization of the equal pay principle, revealing the significance of their mobilization and struggle to improve women's wages.[10] This chapter adds to this scholarship, exploring various forms of activism advocating for equal pay in Poland. The struggle for equal pay in state socialism had a different dynamic since the problem was officially nonexistent, and activists operated in a different institutional, political, and economic setting. This chapter highlights knowledge production as a particular way to address inequalities that were officially unrecognized.

I argue that in state-socialist Poland, women activists combated unequal pay through researching and defining the phenomenon of women's lower wages. Similar to international bodies, they adopted a strategy of revealing persistent inequalities,[11] which, in the context of state socialism, also meant challenging the dominant narrative of wage equality. The research they undertook revealed that unequal pay was a multidimensional problem, while Janina Waluk's research critically engaged with definitions of equal work. These findings show that Polish women's labour activism was concerned with issues of equality during the so-called gender backlash of the post-Stalinist period. During de-Stalinization, women's equality in workplace was challenged, and gender hierarchies shifted toward greater inequality.[12] Against this backdrop, however, Waluk developed a radical approach to unequal pay. Trade union activism of the period combined attention to women's family roles and housework with the struggle to fully realize gender equality, approaches women activists did not perceive as contradictory.

The first section of the chapter sheds light on the early equal pay activism in postwar Poland and explains the framing of (un)equal pay in official discourses, constructing the background for subsequent sections. The second section focuses on the survey on women's work carried out in the late 1950s by the Women's Commission of the Trade Unions. The final part discusses Janina Waluk's findings concerning unequal pay.

9 Betti 2021.
10 Zimmermann 2020.
11 Neunsinger 2018.
12 Fidelis 2010.

1 (Un)equal Pay in State-Socialist Poland: The Early Postwar Campaign and Legislation

The women's sections of trade unions in Poland were established shortly after the war, in 1946. They existed as women's councils on the workplace level, and the central Women's Department worked closely with the Central Committee of Trade Unions (this committee was later renamed the Central Council). The early activities of the women's councils centered on working conditions and control over the enforcement of protective legislation and maternity leave. The councils also promoted the "equal pay for equal work" rule. In the late 1940s, women's councils perceived unequal pay and the lack of protective legislation—or its poor implementation—as the major problems of working women.

In the late 1940s, trade union activists campaigned in favor of "equal pay" for women and men workers, connecting their advocacy to the debate held within the World Federation of Trade Unions.[13] Within the postwar discourse on women's equality in paid employment, equal pay played an important role. In a paper entitled "Sytuacja kobiet w Polsce i nasze dążenia" ("The Situation in Poland and Our Goals") a trade union activist declared:

> Equal pay for women's and men's work needs to become practice and not only theory. Established wages in industries that employ mostly women (so-called feminine industries) are considerably lower than in industries that employ more men. [...] It is necessary to revise wages in branches such as the food industry, clothing industry, and others where the woman performs the hardest and, hierarchically, the lowest jobs for a wage to which no man would agree. [...] In mixed [sex] industries, usually the woman gets the lowest possible salary for the same work within the pay scale. This is unacceptable; the pay is for work and its results, not for gender.[14]

---

13 Plan pracy Wydziału Kobiecego Komitetu Centralnego Związków Zawodowych [Workplan of the Women's Department of the KCCZ], June 1948, V/1, Komitet Centralny Związków Zawodowych [Central Council of Trade Unions, hereafter KCZZ], Archiwum Akt Nowych [Archive of Modern Records, hereafter AAN], Warsaw, Poland, 13; Sprawozdanie Wydziału Kobiecego za czerwiec 1948 [Report of the Women's Section for June 1948], V/1, KCZZ, AAN, 71.

14 Sytuacja kobiet w Polsce i nasze dążenia [Women's situation in Poland and our goals], 1946, V/60, KCZZ, AAN, 31.

This discourse tackled two dimensions of inequality: the phenomenon of inequality between particular branches of industry depending on the sex of the majority of workers, and the problem of assigning women workers the lowest possible wage within a category. So-called light industry—traditionally feminized and increasingly so during the state-socialist period—was, in general, disadvantaged in comparison to heavy industry and extractive industries in terms of wages and welfare benefits for workers, and the light industrial sector "made the most of its output [...] by the exploitation of the cheap labor force. In this regard, pre-war traditions and communist ideological premises worked in the same direction."[15] This problem, visible to women activists in the late 1940s, would not be solved throughout the entire state-socialist period.

Sector-related inequality was not the only source of unequal pay. Between 1946 and 1949, trade unions' reports from various organizational levels—the branch-level, regional, and factory-level—frequently mentioned unequal pay and women workers' dissatisfaction with low wages.[16] The reports referred to the problem as "unequal pay for equal work." Women workers complained that they received lower wages for "the same activity/occupation" and work "equal to men," and passed resolutions at meetings demanding equal pay, which was considered a question of "social justice."[17] For example, women workers in Łódź, a city defined by its female-dominated textile industry, complained that "less experienced and qualified men occupy higher positions and wage groups."[18] Trade union activists took action against unequal pay, which was present in most of women workers' complaints.[19] Documents from the Women's Department reveal that women workers and activists understood

15 Mazurek 2011, 283–285.

16 Examples: Sprawozdanie z podróży służbowej do Krakowa [Report from a visit to Cracow], V/10, KCZZ, AAN, 2; Protokół z konferencji aktywu kobiecego odbytej w dniu 6 VI 1946 [Protocol of the women activists' meeting on 6 June 1946], V/11, KCZZ, AAN, 2; V/62, Sprawozdanie z pracy ob. Lubandy, instruktorki Wydziału Kobiecego przy OKZZ w Katowicach [Report of work of Ms. Lubanda, instructor of the Women's Department at the Regional Committee of Trade Unions in Katowice, 8–30 September 1946], V/62, KCZZ, AAN, 7.

17 Uchwała Rady Kobiet Okręgowego Komitetu Związków Zawodowych w Bydgoszczy na konferencji w dniu 16 lipca 1948 [Resolution of the Women's Council of the Regional Committee of Trade Unions in Bydgoszcz, 16 July 1948], V/56, KCZZ, AAN, 74.

18 Sprawozdanie z wyjazdu służbowego do Łodzi w czasie od 29–31 stycznia 1947 [Report from a visit to Łódź on 29–31 January 1947], V/10, KCZZ, AAN, 17.

19 Praca kierowniczki Wydziału za okres od powstania Wydziału do dnia 15 sierpnia 1947 [Report on the work of the head of the Women's Department from its onset to 15 August 1947], V/29, KCZZ, AAN, 51.

unequal pay as lower remuneration for working the same job as men, holding similar qualifications, and/or working in a feminized industry.

After the late 1940s campaign, pay discrimination was no longer discussed. Equal pay was written into the Constitution in 1952; Article 66, devoted to women's equality, stated that women in Poland had the right to equal pay for equal work. This legislation was usually mentioned as proof of the state's commitment to equal pay. Nevertheless, the constitutional principle could easily remain on paper, as it did in Italy.[20] The Women's Department was dissolved in the early 1950s, officially because it had fulfilled its role.

As scholars have convincingly shown, wages under state socialism built on traditions that existed before World War Two both in terms of continuities related to "cheap labor" and the conceptualization and measurement of labour.[21] Continuity was also present in Poland and, in particular, in the ways gender inequality was produced, as Janina Waluk revealed and discussed in her book. After the communist takeover in Poland, the wage system became an object of central planning, and wages were used to incentivize particular groups of workers and regulate consumption.[22] In the late 1940s and again from the late 1950s, wages were regulated through collective agreements.[23] Theoretically, wages were differentiated on the basis of the quantity and quality of labour, with the latter including skills, working conditions, and work intensity. As Zofia Morecka, a specialist in socialist political economy and Waluk's supervisor, explained, equal work was understood as the same work from the perspective of economic characteristics taking into account complexity, intensity, and conditions.[24] As Martha Lampland showed for the case of wages on collective farms in Hungary, socialism implemented alternative methods of defining and assessing the value of labour in the absence of free markets.[25] In socialist Poland, wages were classified through tariff schemes and pay scales, which were different depending on the particular economic sector.[26] This classification system established hierarchies and created space for gender-based discrimination.

The system in place did not eradicate gender-based pay inequality, although it was no longer visible on paper. Collective agreements did not differentiate

20 Betti 2018, 282.
21 Grama 2020; Lampland 2016.
22 Krencik 1978.
23 Szubert 1960, 53–63.
24 Morecka 1963, 8.
25 Lampland 2016.
26 Krencik 1978.

workers by sex. In the 1940s, some of them explicitly mentioned that the principle of equal pay for equal work should be respected, whereas such formulations were absent after 1956.[27] Each job position was assigned a pay group (*grupa zaszeregowania*) that depended on the level of education (skills) and experience. However, pay scales permitted the differentiation of salaries. Salaries for blue-collar workers were usually either piece-based or time-based, but in both systems, different pay groups existed. Women were often paid lower wages within the scale or were assigned to a lower pay group. The scales easily could be used to produce inequality. "Women's position is often explained in such a way that she is assigned a lower wage," and trade union activists pointed to unwritten criteria that governed the process of assigning wages.[28] In the late 1940s, women activists also noticed that sometimes collective agreements were not respected.[29] In fact, gender inequality was implicitly inscribed into the wage system. According to the law, it was legal to pay higher remuneration to skilled workers in heavy industry than those working in light industry as well as to particular skilled jobs performed by men. For the same job position, then, the differentiation of wages was still possible. However, with the absence of explicit references to gender in pay scales, it was difficult to show how this system discriminated against women.

Starting in the early 1950s, it was taken for granted that state socialism had established wage equality for men and women, while unequal pay remained a problem of capitalism that could be solved through international conventions.[30] Moreover, equal pay was one of the achievements usually listed as evidence of the socialist commitment to gender equality. As Ignacy Loga-Sowiński, the (male) leader of the Central Council of the Trade Unions explained during an internal meeting in mid-1960s:

> Our labour movement struggled for equal rights for women in bourgeois Poland, in particular foregrounding the "equal pay for equal work" premise. We know from our long history and experience of the trade union

---

27 "Układ zbiorowy pracy dla samorządowych przedsiębiorstw o charakterze użyteczności publicznej" 1947, 172.

28 Protokół ze Zjazdu Ogólnokrajowego referentek do spraw Kobiecych Zatrudnionych w Oddziałach Związku Zawodowego Pracowników Przemysłu Chemicznego [Protocol of the national meeting of the women's issues inspectors employed in branches of the Trade Union of the Chemical Industry], 31 May 1948, V/20, KCZZ, AAN, 73.

29 Protokół z Krajowej Konferencji Referentek do spraw Kobiecych przy Centralnym Związu Zawodowym Metalowców [Protocol of the National Conference of women's issues inspectors at the Trade Union of the Metal Industry], 16 October 1947, V/35, KCZZ, AAN, 64.

30 Rosner 1950, 36–53.

> that capitalists hired women as a cheaper labour force, more prone to capitalist exploitation. The problem of equalizing men's and women's salaries has been solved in the Constitution. This does not mean, however, that all problems of working women, or women in general, have been automatically solved. There are, sometimes, objective reasons that don't allow the constitutional rule to be fully implemented. For example, there are sectors of the national economy that give superiority to men in the sense of higher pay for harder work, for example in mining and in steelwork, where our law rightly prohibits women from working. This work requires enormous physical effort that can't be expected from women. This is clear and understandable for everyone. But it is also about professional skills. Women don't always have an equal starting point from where they can be promoted. We can search for different explanations such as the burden of household duties.[31]

This statement reflects an ambiguous position on pay inequality. Loga-Sowiński simultaneously acknowledged the constitutional principle of "equal pay" and its lack of "full implementation." He then undermined the principle, explaining the pay gap by claiming male physical superiority and women's lack of skills, which led to the assumption that women's work was in fact unequal to men's. Loga-Sowiński followed the established wage system that favored male workers and essentialized its justification through a gendered discourse. He referred to jobs that were well paid but which were prohibited for women.[32] While the trade union leader was convinced that women's situation in the workplace needed to be improved, he thought the activity of the trade unions should focus on how to reduce women's burdens and help them combine paid work and unpaid care work. According to this reasoning, decreasing the double burden of women would lead to greater opportunities for women to gain professional training and, therefore, to earn higher wages.

Trade unions considered unequal pay and the treatment of women as a cheap labour force as typical of capitalism.[33] A pamphlet prepared by the Central Council of the Trade Unions for the fiftieth anniversary of International

31 Wyciąg z Prezydium CRZZ [Protocol of the meeting of the Praesidium of the Central Council of the Trade Unions, hereafter CRZZ], March 1965, 102, CRZZ, Archiwum Ruchu Zawodowego [Archive of the Labour Movement, hereafter ARZ], Warsaw, Poland 62. Currently, the archival material I used and refer to in this paper is held in AAN.

32 Betti 2021.

33 This was also the case in Hungary and the transnational women's movement in state-socialist countries at the time. Zimmermann 2020, 337–338.

Women's Day in 1960 detailed how the demand for equal pay for women was raised by the labour movement in interwar Poland and then implemented shortly after World War Two. The text referred to the 1952 Constitution but not to the ILO Convention no. 100. Unequal pay was considered an issue of the past or a problem experienced only by women in the West. Differences in women's and men's salaries were believed to stem from women's lower skills:

> Normative acts and collective agreements no longer include paragraphs that allow the differentiation of wage according to gender, and wages are only dependent on the type of work. If there are differences between women's and men's salaries, they stem only from women's lower professional skills ... The full realization of the right to equal pay for equal work depends on the further systematic increase of skill levels, in particular of female blue-collar workers.[34]

Economists who published theoretical works and more practical analyses of the wage system usually did not question these assumptions. Jan Kordaszewski, the author of a book on the wage system in industry published in 1962, observed that in Poland, similar to capitalist countries, women worked in particular branches of industry because of health issues and "particular traditions" and that average wages were lower in these branches. However, in Poland, women had access to better-paid managerial positions in industry, whereas women's unemployment in capitalism "forced women to accept lower wages."[35] The logic was that socialism would help women move into better paid jobs, but it did not challenge the wage system. Overall, the solution to the problem of women's low wages was focusing on professional training and promoting women to higher positions, a strategy adopted by trade union activists starting in the late 1940s.

In the eyes of both trade union representatives and experts, differences between men's and women's wages in state-socialist Poland could not be called "unequal pay." For this reason, these disparities did not contradict the recognized premise of "equal pay for equal work," which was understood either as the same work or work that required the same effort and had the same working conditions. They considered (huge) differences in salaries to be justified on the basis of different skills or the amount of physical effort required to perform some "male" jobs. Questioning this narrative required both problematizing

34 Biuletyn Informacyjny CRZZ: 50-lecie MDK [50th Anniversary of International Women's Day], 113, CRZZ, ARZ.

35 Kordaszewski 1963, 32–34.

"equal work" as well as investigating whether women indeed earned the same wages in the same job positions and actually had fewer skills than their male colleagues. As the next sections show, women in Poland engaged in the reconceptualization of (un)equal pay.

2 The Women's Commission and the Survey about Work Conditions (1957–1960)

In the post-1956 period, the structure of the women's movement was reshaped again, and the women's commissions of trade unions reappeared in workplaces and on the branch and central level in 1957 in order to address working women's problems, which had to be rediscovered during the process of de-Stalinization. The newly reestablished Women's Commissions, led by Irena Sroczyńska, who also served as the vice president of the Textile & Clothing Industry Trade Union, addressed a wide range of issues: from working conditions and professional training, to nurseries and cooking courses for women employed in wage work. The commissions attempted to protect women from being dismissed—in the late 1950s, employment reduction policies affected women much more than men—and to contest women's unemployment. They also aimed to improve working conditions which, they believed, had been neglected during the Stalinist period.

It is important to note that the research undertaken by the women activists of the trade unions between 1957 and 1960 addressed issues of equality. The predominant discourse on women's employment in the immediate post-1956 period (de-Stalinization) was critical and often questioned ideas about gender equality in the workplace. The backlash against women's equality was especially visible in the process of reestablishing gender hierarchies in labour. Women's place in the economy would be in "female" jobs, i.e., jobs that would not endanger their maternal function in the home or society.[36] Although women's employment did not in fact decrease, dominant discourses conceptualized women's work outside home as complementary; therefore, women's right to work could be questioned when there was a job shortage (unemployment).[37] However, Women's Commissions connected the concern for protection and women's extra-professional roles, based as it was on a discourse of difference, with a quest for equality, not perceiving gender difference and equality as

36 Fidelis 2010.

37 Jarska 2019; Jarska 2014.

contradictory. The late 1950s survey shows how these two dimensions were connected in practice.

It is not clear who exactly was behind the 1957–1960 survey and whether these people were professional sociologists or economists. It was based on a detailed questionnaire activists had to complete; data gathered at local National Councils (local administration) because these councils dealt with employment and ran labour offices; and information collected at selected workplaces.[38] The survey was carried out in various cities across different regions and in seventy-eight workplaces covering a range of industrial sectors and small and large factories. The questionnaire included questions about the number of women employed at the end of 1957, 1958, and 1959 and the number of working mothers and single mothers. It also asked for a list of the most common jobs and the number of men and women employed in them; the employment plan for the period 1960–1965; and asked for detailed data about the number of men and women workers in the assigned wage group. The second part of the survey asked about salaries: the most common jobs and wages earned. Furthermore, the survey contained questions about social services for women and children, professional training (the number of men and women that do initial and higher training courses), and the reasons women resigned from training (the opinions of both women and management were to be collected). The fourth section asked about healthcare, knowledge about protective legislation, and whether this legislation was respected in practice (for example, activists were asked to check lists and cards to see if mothers of small children worked night shifts). The fifth and final section included information about absenteeism and overtime. The reports contained statistical data as well as descriptions. The questionnaire shows a complex approach to the measurement of inequalities, taking into account not only job position and wages but also training opportunities for women workers; it also tackled the question of productivity. It therefore took up similar issues raised by international bodies around the same time, when obtaining statistical data remained a key challenge.[39]

The reports lead to a couple of conclusions concerning job segregation and salaries. In most of the workplaces analyzed, women usually worked different jobs than men, although sometimes there were select jobs performed both by men and women. For instance, in a wood factory in Białystok (eastern Poland),

38 Sprawozdanie z przeprowadzonej analizy zatrudnienia kobiet (wzór) [Report of an analysis of women's employment (template)], 98, CRZZ, ARZ.

39 Neunsinger 2018.

there was nearly total job segregation.[40] There were a few women performing "male" jobs, but no man held a "female" one. In textile and clothing factories, however, some typical jobs were traditionally feminized, while others were performed by both men and women.[41]

Job segregation was crucial for establishing the gendered pay gap. In jobs performed by women, wages were much lower. For example, in a pastry factory, 230 women employed as wrappers earned 800 zlotys per month, while men employed as locksmiths earned 1,500.[42] In this case, the women might be less qualified, but other examples revealed that this explanation was not always relevant. In a clothing factory in Bydgoszcz, manual seamstresses earned around 1,000 zlotys per month, while (male) pressers earned between 1,800 and 1,940 zlotys. There were also women pressers in the same factory, but they earned less than their male colleagues—although still more than seamstresses.[43] This is an illustration of how the socialist "differentiation of wages" and pay scales worked in practice. Women performing "male" jobs could earn more than those working typically "female" jobs, but they were not so numerous, so the average pay for women in a given factory was considerably lower than that of men. The average salaries of men and women were always different, with men earning considerably more.

In factories where a greater number of men and women performed the same jobs, women earned less: usually only 80 to 90 percent of the wages earned by men, but in extreme cases only 50 percent.[44] In the leather factory "Radoskór" in Radom (central Poland), where many men and women worked as machine operators, women earned between 72 and 79 percent of men's wages. In this case, the pay gap was narrowing, but there were cases of a reverse trend. In a Cracow-based factory, employed men were given a salary increase of 25 percent, while women got only an 8 percent raise; consequently,

---

40 Sprawozdanie z przeprowadzonej kontroli zatrudnienia kobiet, Białostockie Zakłady Przemysłu Sklejek w Białymstoku [Report from an investigation of women's employment in Bialystok Plywood Industry Plant], 98, CRZZ, ARZ, 24–26.

41 For example: Bydgoskie Zakłady Przemysłu Odzieżowego, where only women worked as seamstresses but both men and women worked as pressers, 98, CRZZ, ARZ, 78.

42 Sprawozdanie z przeprowadzonej analizy zatrudnienia kobiet w Zakładach Przemysłu Cukierniczego „Bałtyk" [Report from an analysis of women's employment in Confectionary Factory "Bałtyk"], 10 August 1959, 98, CRZZ, ARZ, 165.

43 Sprawozdanie z przeprowadzonej analizy zatrudnienia kobiet w Bydgoskich Zakładach Przemysłu Odzieżowego [Report from an analysis of women's employment in Bydgoszcz Clothing Factory], 98, CRZZ, ARZ, 79.

44 Sprawozdanie z przeprowadzonej analizy zatrudnienia kobiet w Krakowskich Zakładach Szklarskich [Report from an analysis of women's employment in the Cracow Glassmaking Factory], 1959, 98, CRZZ, ARZ, 210–213.

women employees earned about 30 percent less than their male colleagues. In sum, the survey showed that equal pay for "equal work," even in the narrow sense, was not respected.

The survey revealed a complex picture of women's work, mostly in blue-collar jobs. It was clear that jobs performed most typically by women had lower wages, but it was also evident that men and women working the same jobs were not equally remunerated. This was legally possible because of the flexibility of pay scales, but the survey clearly showed how these arrangements affected women workers in particular.

The data gathered in the survey was used on different occasions. During a central meeting of women activists of trade unions held in 1960, women addressed various issues revealed by the study, commenting also on the "unequal treatment of men and women."[45] The summary of the discussion gave an example of salaries of men and women performing the same jobs in the Pharmaceutical Enterprise in Cracow, mentioned that the pay gap had been growing over the last year, and explained that "women were discriminated against when assigning jobs and pay group" and "women with high skills are employed in lower positions." The suggestion was that discrimination occurred because trade union councils were not controlling salaries well enough. According to the instructions for the survey, reports about particular workplaces were to be sent to the central and regional trade union councils and to the factory's main office. However, when the CRZZ organized a general meeting in order to discuss "work among women" in 1963, the issue of unequal pay was not discussed. Irena Janiszewska, secretary of the CRZZ, only mentioned that the salaries of lower wage groups had been increased, which slightly improved the structure of women's salaries. Increasing the lowest salaries could be indeed a strategy to combat unequal pay, as the Hungarian case shows.[46] Janiszewska also focused on the issue of skills and the promotion of women to "male" jobs.[47] Women were, according to Janiszewska, often reluctant to get additional training or take up these jobs and were therefore to blame for lower wages. In the conclusion, she once again pointed to the pay gap in capitalist countries. These examples show that while the survey provided important evidence that heightened interest in women's discrimination, simplistic arguments about women's lower wages persisted.

---

45 Podsumowanie narady aktywu kobiecego [Summary of the women activists' meeting], 1960, 103, CRZZ, ARZ.

46 Zimmermann 2020.

47 *Materiały v Plenum CRZZ* 1963, 9–10.

3 Janina Waluk in Search of Explanations for the Pay Gap

The de-Stalinization process in Poland included the reestablishment of sociology as discipline and the revival of the sociology of work, which—as argued by Małgorzata Mazurek—created an independent discourse on work that served as an alternative to the official ideological discourse of the party-state.[48] Janina Waluk's expertise on working women can also be understood as part of a broader trend of research on women's issues that developed in post-1956 Poland. Scientists and experts from diverse disciplines—sociologists, medical doctors—focused their research on women's family roles, time, housework, and paid work.[49] Many studies on women's employment addressed work, motherhood, and women's domestic roles.[50] Sociological studies of industrial work that analyzed hierarchies in different branches of industry and factories also took into account women's work, often pointing to existing stereotypes of women's work and the position of women in particular work environments. Women sociologists like Jolanta Kulpińska and Stefania Dzięcielska-Machnikowska analyzed women's work in managerial positions in the textile industry in the early 1960s, tackling the features of gender-based discrimination and the issues related to job segregation and unequal pay.[51] Other studies investigated women's absenteeism at work and women's work productivity.[52] However, Janina Waluk was the only expert who placed the issue of women's wages at the center of her research in the early 1960s.

In the introduction to her book entitled *Płaca i praca kobiet w Polsce* (*Work and Pay of Women in Poland*), published in 1965, Waluk argued that there was a lack of research on women's work conducted by experts in various social scientific disciplines. Her main question was about the reasons for the differences between men's and women's work. She thought about her research in terms of engagement, as these issues were "currently important" and had practical relevance in relation to job segregation and the gendered wage gap. In subsequent chapters, Waluk attempted to explain the disparities between the salaries of men and women, challenging existing explanations. She used official statistics and data she amassed while closely researching four Warsaw-based industrial plants, where she conducted interviews and collected quantitative data.[53]

48 Mazurek 2007, 11–31.

49 On the work of sociologists, see Klich-Kluczewska and Stańczak-Wiślicz 2020.

50 For example, Piotrowski 1963; Zarząd Główny Ligi Kobiet 1967.

51 Dzięcielska-Machnikowska and Kulpińska 1966.

52 Witkowska 1968. For the summary of various research lines, see Wrochno-Stanke 1971.

53 Waluk 1965, 7–10.

In the first chapter, Waluk analyzed the tradition of women's low wages, pointing to the fact that historically, women were employed as a cheap labour force and that women's work equated to exploitation. In interwar Poland, she argued, making references to the work of Halina Krahelska from the 1930s, women workers were treated as a separate category of labourer that was different than both skilled and unskilled workers.[54] Waluk also analyzed the criteria the wage system was based on, pointing out that there were no job descriptions nor evaluation criteria; consequently, only age and gender were taken into account. "That is how job segregation was created," she argued. In a socialist economy, equal pay was a constitutional principle, and as Waluk put it, overt discrimination was not possible. By this she meant that collective agreements and pay scales should not differentiate wages by gender, so women should earn the same pay as men for the same work.[55] Waluk, however, was well aware that this narrow understanding of equal pay was not sufficiently explanatory. Differences did exist, and it was crucial to understand their causes. Here, as Waluk pointed out, official statistics on wages and skills provided little information since sex was included as a category only starting in 1958.[56] As Silke Neunsinger explains, the construction of wage statistics and their usefulness to describe and combat unequal pay stood at the very center of international struggles against the phenomenon of the gendered pay gap in the late 1950s.[57] Janina Waluk also struggled with categories and numbers, taking the existing statistics only as a starting point to assess the pay gap.

Waluk tried to assess the differences by looking at the share of low and high salaries for both sexes and analyzing average salaries. The majority of women workers earned less than the average, whereas the majority of men earned more than the average—and among men, the share of workers with high salaries was growing. Moreover, the difference between the median of men's and women's wages was increasing. The level of education did not explain the pay gaps Waluk observed, since in groups of workers with the same level of education, the share of women in lower paid jobs was still far greater. Waluk also designed special gauges to measure pay discrepancies. In the factories she analyzed, 97 percent of women workers earned less than 2,000 zlotys per month, and 79 percent of men earned more. She then came up with two hypotheses: either there was wage discrimination (unequal pay for equal work) or the structure of jobs and the skills required were different in the case

54 Krahelska 1932.

55 Different pay scales according to gender were still used in postwar Italy. Betti 2021.

56 Waluk 1965, 19.

57 Neunsinger 2018.

of men and women. If the latter was true, questions about the causes of discrimination remained, but one should call it professional (job) discrimination, not pay discrimination. On this point, Waluk understood "equal work" as work in the same position, performed by workers with a similar level of skill. While women in industry were less likely to be skilled, according to the official statistics, Waluk's analysis considered the level of education as well as questioned the actual role skill played in the inequality experienced by women workers, which will be discussed later.

The reflection that followed these comments reveals that equality understood as "equal value" also mattered, as Waluk addressed the methodological problems of how to measure work and compare jobs. Here she took the wording of the ILO as her starting point.[58] When Waluk spoke about value, she meant the process of labour itself and argued that if we look at work from the perspective of its "social importance," then many different types of work become comparable. She explained that the wage system in Poland drew on both Soviet and Western systems, with the former concentrating on the process of work and the latter the characteristics of the worker. This combined method did not consider any description of work and, Waluk argued, left "unchanged some particular pay relations that were shaped in the interwar period." She suggested that "wage relations based on sex" had not been revised, so women's disadvantaged position persisted. Apart from this, Waluk argued that in practice, wages were based on both formal qualifications established in official wage scales *and* on the informal evaluation of the worker, in which stereotypes and assumptions played a greater role. For example, women were believed to work less effectively.[59] In one of the factories she analyzed, Waluk received three different answers to the question of why a male knitter's pay was higher than that of the female knitter (the jobs had slightly different names): men's work required more responsibility (women got distracted easily); greater physical strength was necessary to perform the man's job; and men had to support the family. Inquiring about the causes of women's lower wages, Waluk went beyond quantitative measurements and interpretations to reveal gender stereotypes that affected the perception of "work of equal value" to a great extent and independently from the formal criteria of skill.

In the second chapter of the book, Waluk looked for the relationship between the employment structure and pay differences, comparing wages in different sectors of the economy and in different industrial branches. She constructed

58 Waluk 1965, 36.
59 Waluk 1965, 40.

charts that clearly showed hierarchies: the places where many women worked also had the lowest salaries, and the gaps between the wages of men and women had even increased recently. Waluk asked a crucial question: Were salaries low because the employees were women? "We cannot exclude a positive answer to this question," she concluded. By pointing to gendered wage discrimination embedded in other inequalities that existed between industrial branches, Waluk applied a broad definition of unequal pay. Using the examples of a male technician and a female nurse (both positions that required a secondary education) and a male caretaker/housekeeper and a low-ranked female healthcare worker, she suggested that the (social) value of these jobs was similar, and differences in pay could only be the result of gender.[60]

In the third and last chapter entitled "Women's qualifications," Waluk analyzed the relationship between the level of education, skills—which she understood as both formal ("theoretical") qualifications and practical skills—and wages based on data from two factories. The combination of formal education and practical abilities was difficult to measure and compare, so Waluk only compared formal qualifications and work experience. She observed that in the case of men, salaries depended on the level of education, but this was not the case for women workers. Women with different levels of education worked in the same positions and earned very similar wages. Among white-collar workers, the greatest pay differences between men and women workers occurred within the group with the highest levels of education.[61] Within the group of workers with a secondary school education, women held lower positions than men in spite of having similar work experience and education, or women were employed in positions that did not match their skills. Among blue-collar workers, there was almost a total segregation of "male" and "female" jobs. In the few cases where women and men performed the same job (and had very similar skills), men earned more.[62] In one of the factories, even with the same level of productivity, which was measured by the fulfillment of the production norms, women earned less. Waluk concluded that in the light of these findings, the argument that women earned less because of lower skills was not true. While in general women's formal skills in paid employment were lower, skilled women workers were discriminated against and placed in lower pay categories. In the case of women, the relationship between salaries and qualifications was much weaker than for men. Skill remained a gendered category, which meant that improving women's skills could not entirely abolish unequal pay.

60 Waluk 1965, 82–83.
61 Waluk 1965, 154–155.
62 Waluk 1965, 162.

In the conclusion to the book, Waluk urged the state to "ensure compliance with the constitutional principle of equality."[63] She suggested that improving women's skills and training and adjusting professional preparation to the needs of the industry could improve women's position. Waluk thought that redirecting women's professional interests and education (for example, from general secondary education to vocational education) would improve their ability to find suitable employment and could help when assigning women particular jobs. Vocational training activities together with transferring women to "male jobs," policies pursued by women activists in Poland since the late 1940s, was a strategy recognized on the international level as a way to improve women's wages starting in the late 1950s. Further, Waluk suggested changing "pay relations based on old traditions," calling for a revision of the whole system or the establishment of a new one that would draw on "science-based job descriptions," again connecting to discussions about the same issues taking place elsewhere around the same time.[64] However, she also noticed the importance of gender stereotypes: "opinions about women's work and attitudes based on these opinions are real forces."[65] Having rejected dominant explanations of gendered pay disparities, and finding that there was no objective reason for women to be paid less, Waluk paid attention to gender hierarchies.

Janina Waluk's book problematized both the dominant argument about (un)equal pay and the very definition of equal work. In most cases, she defined the latter narrowly—as working in the same position—in order to show that the constitutional principle was not being respected. However, she went beyond this narrow understanding and considered inequality from multiple angles and levels of the employment structure. Her analysis led to the conclusion that in general, women's wages were lower because of their gender.

4 Conclusion

The survey carried out by the Women's Commission and the research done by Janina Waluk led to similar conclusions. Women and men usually worked different positions, and "female" jobs had lower salaries. If they happened to perform the same or similar jobs, men almost always earned more and were assigned to better pay groups. The trade union survey also showed that the wage gap grew wider over time because women's salaries rose more slowly

63 Waluk 1965, 169.
64 Neunsinger 2018, 138–139.
65 Waluk 1965, 173.

than men's. Waluk presented a comprehensive picture of pay disparities, and she questioned the argument that differences in skill played the biggest explanatory role. Unlike in the early 1970s in Hungary, the efforts of both the Women's Commission and Waluk never reached the policy-making level, and there was no campaign for equal pay.[66]

There is no evidence of any form of collaboration or exchange between trade union activists and Waluk on the issue of unequal pay, although in the early 1960s, sociologists and other professionals were sometimes invited by trade unions to speak to their members, and the head of the Women's Commission attended an interdisciplinary seminar on women's work at the Polish Academy of Sciences, in which Waluk also took part.[67] However, the outcomes of both the Women's Commission's survey and Waluk's research reached a broader public through the press and entered into discussions about women's work; thus, they may be considered contributions to discussions on the same issues that took place in the early 1960s. In an earlier article she published in *Życie Gospodarcze* (*Economic Life*), Waluk problematized existing definitions of equal pay, revealed the persistence of "old traditions" of women's pay discrimination, and called for a "new job classification."[68] She also discussed definitions of (un)equal pay. A journalist writing for *Rada Robotnicza* (*Workers' Council*), a trade union periodical, openly discussed multidimensional gender-based discrimination, starting with lower wages.[69]

The renewed interest in equal pay during de-Stalinization in Poland sheds new light on the so-called gender backlash that characterized the period. De-Stalinization opened up new realms of action; the Women's Commission was re-established in 1957, and experts (economists and sociologists) could develop research that addressed women's position in the workplace, revealing gender-based discrimination. For the women who designed and carried out such research, tackling unequal pay remained an important goal, and for this reason equal pay was studied independently from the protective attitude toward women workers and women's roles in the household and family. Women's Commissions took action against discrimination immediately, continuing their pre-1950 activities. It is important to note that equal pay activism

66 Zimmermann 2020.

67 Protokół obrad Komisji Kobiecej dnia 2 grudnia 1964 r. [Protocol of the meeting of the Women's Commision on 2 December 1964], 112, CRZZ, ARZ, 213–232. At this meeting, the Commission discussed time budget studies carried out by trade unions and the Institute of Work. Sokołowska 1964.

68 Waluk 1962.

69 Przybył 1962.

ceased during Stalinism, when a top-down decision abolished the Women's Commission. But while in the late 1940s, trade union activists propagated the premise of "equal pay" within a strong discourse of equality and mobilized women to stand up for their rights, in the late 1950s and 1960s, activists attempted to measure and define the phenomenon of gendered wage inequality: the survey addressed concrete pay differences, and Waluk's study sought to trace the entire system that produced these differences. What was characteristic of the post-1956 period was the emphasis on critical knowledge production. As the examples discussed here demonstrate, knowledge production was an important form of women's labour activism in state-socialist Poland, while other typical forms of activism, such as strikes or collective action, were less available to workers' organizations. In the case of wage inequality, such knowledge enabled the detection of phenomena that were typically not recognized by socialist economists and (male) trade unionists.

Women activists in Poland rarely referred to international discussions on unequal pay during the period in question, and international conventions did not have a direct impact on conditions in Poland unlike, for example, in Italy.[70] Nevertheless, equal pay activism tackled similar concerns. Discovering, describing, and defining gendered wage gaps was the aim and strategy to deal with inequality. Unequal pay, even after the passage of the ILO Convention no. 100 on equal remuneration, remained an underdeveloped concept. Similarly to the Hungarian case discussed by Susan Zimmermann, trade union activists and special women's structures within them were important for shaping the struggle for equal pay, and they embraced an inclusive framing of the concept of equal work.[71] In a socialist country, apart from political and economic differences, women's equal pay activism had to challenge what male (and not only male) leaders and experts mostly took for granted: there was no gendered wage discrimination in state socialism, and when pay scales were not differentiated by sex, unequal pay was much more difficult to identify. This feminist action, realized within the official structures of the party-state, questioned the post-1956 state-supported gender regime. As such, these efforts were an important part of the global struggle for equal pay for women workers.

70 Betti 2021.

71 Zimmermann 2020, 342–344.

Bibliography

Betti, Eloisa. 2021. "Equal Pay and Social Justice: Women's Agency, Trade Union Action and International Regulations. Italy, the ILO and the EEC in the Global Context (1951–1977)." *The International History Review* 44, no. 3: 577–594. doi: 10.1080/07075332.2020.1845778.

Betti, Eloisa. 2018. "Unexpected Alliances: Italian Women's Struggles for Equal Pay 1940s–1960s." In *Women's ILO: Transnational Networks, Global Labour Standards, and Gender Equity, 1919 to Present*, edited by Eileen Boris, Dorothea Hoehkter, and Susan Zimmermann, 276–299. Leiden: Brill.

Boris, Eileen. 2018. "Equality's Cold War: The ILO and the UN Commission on the Status of Women, 1946–1970s." In *Women's ILO: Transnational Networks, Global Labour Standards, and Gender Equity, 1919 to Present*, edited by Eileen Boris, Dorothea Hoehkter, and Susan Zimmermann, 97–120. Leiden: Brill, 2018.

Dzięcielska-Machnikowska, Stefania, and Jolanta Kulpińska. 1966. *Awans kobiety* [Women's advancement]. Łódź: Wydawnictwo Uniwersytetu Łódzkiego.

Fidelis, Malgorzata. 2010. *Women, Communism and Industrialization in Postwar Poland*, Cambridge: Cambridge University Press.

Grama, Adrian. 2020. "The Cost of Juridification: Lineages of Cheap Labor in Twentieth-Century Romania," *Labor* 17, no. 3: 30–52.

Jarska, Natalia. 2019. "Female Breadwinners in State Socialism: The Value of Women's Work for Wages in Post-Stalinist Poland." *Contemporary European History* 28, no. 4 (November): 469–483.

Jarska, Natalia. 2014. "Gender and Labour in Post-War Communist Poland. Female Unemployment 1945–70," *Acta Poloniae Historica* 110: 49–85.

Klich-Kluczewska, Barbara, and Katarzyna Stańczak-Wiślicz. 2020. "Biographical Experience and Knowledge Production: Women Sociologists and Gender Issues in Communist Poland." In *Gender, Generations, and Communism in Central and Eastern Europe and Beyond*, edited by Anna Artwińska and Agnieszka Mrozik, 146–165. New York and London: Routledge.

"Konwencja (nr 100) dotycząca jednakowego wynagrodzenia dla pracujących mężczyzn i kobiet za pracę jednakowej wartości, przyjęta w Genewie dnia 29 czerwca 1951 r." [Convention no. 100 on equal remuneration for working men and women for work of equal value, adopted in Geneva, 29 June 1951], *Dziennik Ustaw* [Journal of laws] 1955, 38 poz. 238.

Kordaszewski, Jan. 1963. *Płaca według pracy. Studium systemu płac w przemyśle* [Pay according to work. A study of the wage system in industry]. Warsaw: Książka i Wiedza.

Krahelska, Halina. 1932. *Praca kobiet w przemyśle współczesnym* [Women's work in contemporary industry]. Warsaw: Instytut Gospodarstwa Społecznego.

Krencik, Wiesław. 1978. "Kierowanie polityką płac w przemyśle polskim" [Management wage policies in Polish industry]. In *Płaca w ustroju socjalistycznym. Zagadnienia teorii i praktyki* [Pay in the socialist system. Issues of theory and practice], 158–198. Warsaw: Państwowe Wydawnictwo Ekonomiczne.

Lampland, Martha. 2016. *The Value of Labor. The Science of Commodification in Hungary, 1920–1956*. London: University of Chicago Press.

Materiały V Plenum CRZZ (18.VI.1963) i Światowego Kongresu Kobiet w Moskwie (24–29.VI.1963) [Materials from the 5th Plenum of the Central Council of the Trade Unions, 18 June 1963, and the World Congress of Women in Moscow (24–29 June 1963)]. 1963. Warsaw: Wydawnictwo Związkowe.

Mazurek, Małgorzata. 2011. "From Welfare State to Self-Welfare: Everyday Opposition among Female Textile Workers in Łódź, 1971–1981." In *Gender Politics and Mass Dictatorship*, edited by Jie-Hyun Lim and Karen Petrone, 278–300. London: Palgrave.

Mazurek, Małgorzata. 2007. "Between Sociology and Ideology. Perception of Work and Sociologists Advisors in Communist Poland, 1956–1970." *Revue d'Histoire des Sciences Humaines* [Journal of history of social science] 16 (2007): 11–31.

Morecka, Zofia. 1963. *Zjawiska różnicowania i niwelowania płac w procesie wzrostu gospodarczego* [Differentiation and leveling wages in the process of economic growth]. Warsaw: KC PZPR.

Neunsinger, Silke. 2018. "The Unobtainable Magic of Numbers: Equal Remuneration, the ILO and the International Trade Union Movement 1950s–1980s." In *Women's ILO: Transnational Networks, Global Labour Standards, and Gender Equity, 1919 to Present*, edited by Eileen Boris, Dorothea Hoehkteř, and Susan Zimmermann, 121–148. Leiden: Brill.

Piotrowski, Jerzy. 1963. *Praca zawodowa kobiety a rodzina* [Women's professional work and the family]. Warsaw: Książka i Wiedza.

Przybył, Teresa. 1962. "Trędowate" [Lepers]. *Rada Robotnicza* [Workers' council] 1, 15 November 1962.

Rosner, Jan. 1950. "Równa płaca za równą pracę mężczyzn i kobiet jako zagadnienie międzynarodowe" [Equal pay for equal work as an international issue]. *Praca i Opieka Społeczna* [Work and welfare], no. 1: 33–53.

Sokołowska, Magdalena. 1964. "Konwersatorium Pracy Kobiet w IFiS PAN [Seminar on women's work in IFiS PAN]." *Studia Socjologiczne* [Sociological studies] 1.

Szubert, Wacław. 1960. *Układy zbiorowe pracy* [Collective agreements]. Warsaw: Państwowe Wydawnictwo Naukowe.

"Układ zbiorowy pracy dla samorządowych przedsiębiorstw o charakterze użyteczności publicznej" [Collective agreement for local administration firms]. 1947. *Układy Zbiorowe Pracy* [Collective agreements].

Waluk, Janina. 1965. *Płaca i praca kobiet w Polsce* [Work and pay of women in Poland]. Warsaw: Książka i Wiedza.

Waluk, Janina. 1962. "Kobieta pracująca" [Working woman]. *Życie Gospodarcze* [Economic life], 28 October 1962.

Witkowska, Halina. 1968. *Przydatność zawodowa kobiet i mężczyzn: na przykładzie wybranych zawodów* [Women's and men's professional usefulness: On the example of selected professions]. Warsaw: Instytut Pracy.

Wrochno-Stanke, Krystyna. 1971. *Problemy pracy kobiet* [Problems of women's work]. Warsaw: Wydawnictwo Związkowe CRZZ.

Zarząd Główny Ligi Kobiet. 1967. *Kobieta—praca—dom. Problemy pracy zawodowej kobiet i rodziny współczesnej. Materiały z konferencji naukowej zorganizowanej przez Zarząd Główny Ligi Kobiet w dniach 25–27 marca 1965* [Woman—Work—Home. Problems of women's professional employment and contemporary family. Materials of a scientific session organized by the League of Women, 25–27 March 1965]. Warsaw: Wydawnictwo Związkowe CRZZ.

Zimmermann, Susan. 2020. "'It Shall Not Be a Written Gift, but a Lived Reality': Equal Pay, Women's Work, and the Politics of Labor in State-Socialist Hungary, Late 1960s to Late 1970s." In *Labor in State-Socialist Europe, 1945–1989. Contributions to a History of Work*, edited by Marsha Siefert, 337–372. Budapest: CEU Press.

CHAPTER 13

The Czechoslovak Women's Union, Labour Activism, and Expertise under Socialism, 1960s and 1970s

Marie Láníková

Abstract

In 1967, women's experts were in charge of a newly established countrywide women's organization called the Czechoslovak Women's Union (CWU). The organization promoted a sophisticated and nuanced approach to women's issues, including paid labour and (un)paid care work. Between 1967–1969, in the context of the Prague Spring, women's experts advocated women's freedom to stay at home with small children for up to 3 years or to place them in a high quality nursery and return to paid labour as soon as possible. The CWU promoted the establishment of foster care rather than institutionalized care. Local chapters concentrated on care for "abandoned" children—in children's homes. Between 1967 and 1969, the CWU promoted women's equal access to all areas of paid work. The Warsaw Pact occupation of Czechoslovakia in 1968 had strong repercussions for the CWU, as by the end of 1969, prominent leaders of the organization left it. In the 1970s, the new leadership continued to promote pro-women changes in the arena of paid work, but the discourse about what was suitable for women changed significantly. In the 1970s, the CWU approved of and subscribed to the (over)protection of the female workforce and the feminization of some kinds of work, and full equality was construed as a political goal that would be achieved only through the automation of the production process.

Keywords

bans on work – collectivized childcare – Czechoslovak Women's Union (CWU) (Československý svaz žen, ČSSŽ)– socialism – expertise – foster care – freedom of choice – labour code – maternity leave/benefits – women's employment

> So somehow it started to bother me at work that a man was doing the same job and the man was doing [the job] a lot worse, like he was less capable, yeah, but because he was the breadwinner, he got four or five

 | DOI:10.1163/9789004682481_014

> hundred crowns more [than me]. That bothered me so much, and I thought that in the Women's Union, they talked about things like that, if they were going to … manage to change something. […] Because men really were the breadwinners, and they did not have to do a good job but still earned more money. And that really bothered me.[1]

This was how one of the members of the Czechoslovak Women's Union (CWU) (Československý svaz žen, ČSSŽ)—who I spoke with in 2021—explained her motivation for joining the organization in 1975.

Working women's issues had always been one of the CWU's core interests. The women's organization defended women's right to work and their important position in the socialist economy. The CWU was established in 1967 as the only state-wide women's organization (i.e., it was not a trade union but a general women's organization) in Czechoslovakia. Between 1952 and 1967, there was no mass nation-wide women's organization, only the representative Committee of Czechoslovak Women (CCW) (Výbor československých žen), which boasted eighty members and a few rather non-functional women's committees (*výbory žen*) affiliated to local national committees (*Místní národní výbor*), i.e., municipal committees.[2]

In the edited volume *Vyvlastněný hlas: Proměny genderové kultury české společnosti 1948–1989* (*The Politics of Gender Culture under State Socialism: An Expropriated Voice*), an influential book covering women's position in the socialist society of Czechoslovakia, Hana Havelková argues that the Communist Party *expropriated* the women's agenda from the women's movement.[3] Moreover, Havelková spoke about Czechoslovak women's activism during the state-socialist period as if it barely existed; such activism aimed at the proactive advancement of women's issues and agendas was substituted by policies pursued by experts. Havelková argues that women's organizations tended to delegate the women's agenda to (women's) experts and failed to deploy feminist discourse in their activism during the Prague Spring.[4]

---

1 This research was financially supported by a research project at Masaryk University, Project Number MUNI/A/1567/2021 (Society in Times of Crisis). Unless otherwise indicated, translations are mine.

2 According to Denisa Nečasová, most of these committees existed only formally and did not organize or participate in any activities. See Nečasová 2011a; 2011b; 2014.

3 H. Havelková 2015.

4 The Prague Spring marked a boom in scientific and general intellectual development thanks to the abolition of censorship and enhanced state support for science, including the social sciences and the revival of sociology as a discipline. See Kolář and Pullmann 2016, 148.

But the authors of *The Politics of Gender Culture under State Socialism* did not look for connections between women's activists and the expert community and did not discover that women working in the academic sphere were also members of the CWU. In the historiography of Czechoslovak socialism, the existing scholarship discusses either women's activism in organizations such as the CWU or focuses on professional expertise and experts' influence, but researchers have not addressed both together. As Kateřina Lišková shows, in socialist Czechoslovakia, the expert community played an essential role in influencing gender politics and discourses; importantly, experts suggested pro-women policy changes (e.g., the legalization of abortion).[5] In this chapter, I present a new perspective on women's activism, revealing the significance of the expert qualifications of members of the CWU, especially its leaders.

Since 1967, women experts—sociologists, lawyers, or physicians—were the leaders of the newly established women's organization the CWU. I show that women's activists participating in the CWU were experts from different fields, uniting their activism with their scholarly and professional work. They took an expert approach to women's issues and cooperated closely with the broader expert community and with scholarly institutions. The organization mobilized expert knowledge, initiated and managed research, and used their findings to propose policies designed to improve the status of women. As I will show, based on an analysis of archival records, specifically the records of the Central Committee of the Czechoslovak Women's Union, Prague (Československý svaz žen—ústřední výbor, Praha, deposited in the National Archive in Prague) and the CWU's magazine *Zpravodaj Českého svazu žen* (*Newsletter of the Czech Women's Union*), expert-activist women stood at the forefront of discussions and actions related to women's work.[6] This included a focus on paid work (i.e., labour regulated through the Labour Code) and (un)paid care work, as well as motherhood (i.e., maternity benefits and child allowances).

In contrast to Hana Havelková's approach, my research shows that the CWU was highly active and critical toward the government during the period between its establishment in 1967 and 1969. For the CWU, the August 1968 occupation of Czechoslovakia by Warsaw Pact troops had major repercussions, as by the end of 1969, the main leaders of the organization—denounced as right-wing opportunists—were forced to leave the CWU.[7] In November

5 Lišková 2018.

6 Fond 360 Československý svaz žen—ústřední výbor, Praha [Central Committee of the Czechoslovak Women's Union, Prague], Národní archiv České republiky [National Archive Czech Republic] (hereafter NA), Prague, Czech Republic.

7 "ČSRŽ odsuzuje" 1970.

1969, the entire board of the CWU was dismissed. Simultaneously, the chair of the CWU Miluše Fischerová was also removed from her position in the Women's International Democratic Federation (WIDF). Her replacement as vice-president of the WIDF, Jarmila Knoblochová, was also removed in 1969.[8] Among the others removed from their positions in the CWU were, for example, sociologist Libuše Háková and lawyer and member of Parliament Gertruda Sekaninová-Čakrtová.[9]

But still, some experts continued serving on the organization's committees (i.e., Vlasta Brablcová and Jaroslava Bauerová), new women joined the organization, and the organization continued to cooperate with, among others, the State Population Commission, SPOC (Státní populační komise, SPOK), an expert organization that produced studies on population issues for the government, even during the years following the occupation.[10] Despite the fact that August 1968 halted many reforms, the reconstituted state establishment did not challenge the importance of expert knowledge for socialism; the new leadership utilized their reformist expertise, and the emphasis on scientific knowledge and productivity persisted.[11] The CWU—in cooperation with experts—continued to propose pro-women measures. But as I show in this chapter, the CWU's understanding of what was appropriate for women and how to handle women's workforce problems changed.

In what follows, I will explore the influence of the CWU on the politics of women's work in Czechoslovakia in the 1960s and 1970s. The chapter discusses changes in the general context and the dominant discourse on women's politics and changes in the composition and politics of the CWU. First, I will discuss the 1967 establishment of the CWU as an expert organization that promoted a more scholarly approach to women's issues. Then, I will focus on the concept of *freedom of choice* promoted by the CWU: the freedom to stay at home with small children for up to 3 years or to be able to place them in a high-quality nursery. I point out that members of the CWU—especially its local chapters—concentrated their attention on (un)paid care for children in children's homes (orphanages) and the shift to foster care. In the second section, I analyze the proposals and changes to the Labour Code that the CWU advanced in 1969 and 1975. Finally, I describe how the new CWU leadership in the 1970s approved of and/or subscribed to the (over)protection of women in the workforce and

8 "Usnesení Československé rady žen" 1969.

9 Although, there is no exhaustive list of women removed from their positions in the CWU, it is possible to compare the list of leaders. See "Usnesení Československé rady žen," 1969.

10 Lišková 2018; H. Havelková 2015.

11 Sommer, Spurný, and Mrňka 2019; Lišková 2018.

the feminization of some kinds of work. The archival sources I draw on for this analysis are important because they point to the influence of women's experts—which otherwise might remain invisible—on policy making; at the same time, this expertise did not mean that the CWU enjoyed unmitigated success in advancing their proposals on women's status; other actors could and were involved in discussions on women's issues.

I understand the activism of women within the official structures of the CWU as related to their ability to "manoeuvre" within the state-socialist apparatus. I draw inspiration from Jerzy Kochanowski and Claudia Kraft's concept of *rooms for manoeuvre*, and trace how members of the CWU "created rooms for manoeuvre in which, under the conditions of the given political and social order, their own interests and goals were aligned with those of the 'system.'"[12] By *rooms for manoeuvre*, then, Kraft and Kochanowski mean the "social and institutional spaces in which individuals and groups combined the logics of action of the social system with their own interests, goals and values."[13]

The *rooms for manoeuvre* concept functions as a research perspective or metaphorical space—*not* as a fixed physical space or zone—"less affected by the disciplinary power of the state."[14] Historical actors produced these *rooms for manoeuvre* constantly, through their ordinary, everyday activities within the given context. Not all historical actors had the same resources to produce the room to manoeuver. CWU members were restricted by the rules and position of the organization but simultaneously empowered by it. The CWU existed as the only official and legal social space for women's activism that women could shape or expand their realm of action. Additionally, participation in this space allowed women to claim status as an actor who should be taken seriously by other official (male) actors in discussions about women's, children's, and family issues.

The institutional context of the CWU as an official socialist organization gave women a structural advantage and expanded their ability to create more space to shape the women's agenda. The important question, then, is how women in the CWU used the established Czechoslovak state-socialist order—which they could not avoid or escape—for their own purposes. How could they—without leaving this order—"create a space for themselves to act."[15]

12 Kochanowski and Kraft 2021, 13.
13 Kochanowski and Kraft 2021, 11.
14 Kochanowski and Kraft 2021, 14.
15 Kochanowski and Kraft 2021, 12.

According to Kochanowski and Kraft, "peripherality became an advantage over the power residing at the center."[16] Thus, the CWU's local chapters—i.e., the CWU's periphery—held a particularly advantageous position. In comparison to the Central Committee, the CWU's center of power on the one hand, and, on the other hand, the most highly scrutinized organ of the CWU in Czechoslovakia, local chapters could more easily avoid the omnipresent political control of the state in their everyday activities.

Czechoslovak women activists' expertise played a key role in expanding their room to maneuver. Consequently, my research relies on the conceptual-analytical tools of the sociology of expertise as articulated by Gil Eyal.[17] In his point of view, expertise is a "network linking together agents, devices, concepts, and institutional and spatial arrangements."[18] By involving more actors and subjects that coproduce expertise, for example laymen, "a network of expertise becomes more powerful and influential by virtue of involving multiple parties [...] in shaping the aims and development of expert knowledge."[19] Experts—as a group with superior knowledge in a given area—were (in my case) certain members of the CWU, who disseminated their knowledge among other members, and using their expertise and extensive networks, they promoted changes and organized activities designed to improve the lives of women and children.[20]

16 Kochanowski and Kraft 2021, 11.

17 Eyal 2013.

18 Eyal 2013, 863.

19 Eyal 2013, 876.

20 In the Socialist Bloc, the position of technocrats was growing stronger, and state-socialist countries were generally obsessed with scientific-technological revolution and more efficient planning. See Mark and Apor 2015, 882; Pula 2018, 65–107. For example, James Mark and Péter Apor have stated that Hungarian socialism legitimacy was based mainly on economic and technocratic competence. See Mark and Apor 2015, 886. Moreover, socialist experts—capable of influencing various state policies—were embedded in transnational expert networks and institutions. They served as mediators between the socialist regime and agendas of international institutions. In this way, experts "internationalized issues, experiences, and skills acquired in their home countries; on the other, they brought in their countries debates and disciplinary priorities, which they assimilated as part of their institutional socialization abroad." See Iacob et al. 2018, 149. The United Nations Decade for Women (1975–1985) serves as great example of the global connections between women (often also experts) from the Socialist Bloc and women activists from the Global South and Western countries. See Ghodsee 2019; Bonfiglioli 2016.

1 Experts and Women's Issues in Socialist Czechoslovakia

"Highly qualified women find in their employment the meaning and purpose of their lives. Different women have different degrees of interest and self-realization in employment and family," CWU leaders wrote in the organization's new 1968 Action Program.[21] In contemporary public discourse, the 1960s are remembered as a period of political reform and liberalization in socialist Czechoslovakia. But women's experiences of the changes that took place over the course of the decade were rather ambivalent because they confronted the new, anti-emancipatory tendencies of the regime and a re-traditionalization of their roles as primarily mothers and carers.[22]

During the founding congress of the CWU, Jiří Prokopec, a demographer and secretary of the SPOC who produced studies on population issues and gender expertise on behalf of the government, warned that the position of women engaged in wage work might worsen and stressed the role of the CWU as a defender of women's rights.[23] Among the experts who opposed the employment of mothers with small children were economists as well as psychologists and pediatricians.[24] By 1963, new expertise on childcare had emerged, and according to developmental psychologists, institutionalized care and the separation of children from their mothers at too young age led to emotional deprivation and caused developmental problems.[25] Economists also started to question the goal of full employment for women and the associated collectivized childcare as expensive and inefficient and suggested reducing plans for the construction of nurseries.[26]

The CWU did not accept this traditional conceptualization of women as solely or primarily mothers lacking paid employment (as long as they had small children). As I will show, experts and highly educated women greatly assisted the organization's work toward the goal of women's emancipation and economic independence. In April 1968, the CWU itself explicitly called for support from these circles:

---

21 Akční program Čs. svazu žen 26.-27.6. 1968.

22 Lišková 2018, 157–180.

23 Prokopec 1967.

24 From the mid-1960s onward, the pages of the daily and periodical press began to discuss the necessity of high female employment ratios. According to Bauerová, the prominent figures questioning the economic effectiveness of women's full employment included economist Radoslav Selucký. Bauerová 1974, 124.

25 Lišková 2018, 164.

26 Wagnerová 2017, 86; B. Havelková 2014, 57.

> [W]e turn to you, Czechoslovak women, teachers, working women, you who work in agriculture, in offices, in the judiciary, in transport, in trade, at universities, and in research institutes; we turn to scientific workers and artists, physicians, educators, housewives, architects, to women of all ages and all careers with the call to participate with their opinions, needs, knowledge, and experiences in creating the Action Program. [...] Especially, we call for the cooperation of scientific workers from different fields, who take an interest in participating in the analysis of the current situation of women and families from different perspectives, in looking for solutions and pushing for realizable improvements, of all whose theoretical work looks at the future of the youth and the next generation.[27]

As already mentioned, during state socialism in Czechoslovakia, the expert community played an important role in influencing gender politics and discourses.[28] In the 1960s, sociological studies on women's issues were published which criticized the contemporary social reality and "openly pointed to the discrepancy between officially declared and legislated equality between women and men and the real state of things in which inequalities between the sexes persisted."[29] Sociologists, for example, Libuše Háková, paid attention to the issue of the double burden and the gender wage gap. Šprincová in *The Politics of Gender Culture under State Socialism* wrote about sociologist Háková and her expert interest in the issue of discrimination against women. Important here is the fact that Šprincová never mentioned Háková's active involvement in the CWU and, thus, neglected the important link between expertise and the women's organization. In fact, between 1967 and 1969, Háková was the vice-chair of the newly re-established women's organization and the chair of one of its expert commissions. Moreover, she contributed to the transformation of the previous, rather passive CCW into a new mass organization, the CWU. Háková had participated in the CCW since 1963, serving as chair of the Ideological Commission. In 1966, she participated in discussions about the new structure of the women's movement and urged the establishment of a more active and influential women's organization with dynamic local, district,

27 Všem československým ženám (Praha 11. dubna 1968), 8. schůze předsednictva ÚV ČSSŽ 9.4. 1968 [To All Czechoslovak Women (Prague 11 April 1968), 8. Meeting of the Central Committee of the Czechoslovak Women's Union], Box 35, Fond 360 Československý svaz žen—ústřední výbor, Praha [Central Committee of the Czechoslovak Women's Union, Prague], NA.

28 Lišková 2018, 2016; H. Havelková 2015; Wolchik 1983.

29 Šprincová 2015.

and regional chapters. Háková envisioned a new organization that would do more than provide political education:

> The Women's Committee will have more influence only when it takes the initiative to make proposals, suggestions, and comments on what to do to improve the social status of women, their working and living conditions so that they can find a place in society commensurate with their abilities. [...] The political-educational work of the Women's Committee among women will only succeed if women see at the same time that in the Women's Committee, they have an advocate and spokeswoman who is willing, able, and, I underline, has the power to forward their views, proposals and demands to the appropriate bodies and to promote solutions.[30]

Already in the first half of the 1960s, the Committee of the Czechoslovak Women discussed economists' concerns about the inefficiency of women's paid labour and the related high cost of children's facilities. One reason for economists' opposition to women's employment can be found in the economic crisis that struck Czechoslovakia at the beginning of the 1960s and economists' efforts to find ways to save money.[31]

Experts were already involved in discussions around women's issues in the 1950s. At that time, sexologists promoted an egalitarian approach to marriage. They recognized women's right to sexual pleasure and promoted women's emancipation in books on married life.[32] Low birth rates in the 1950s and 1960s also attracted experts' attention. In 1956, the state statistical office, which conducted the first research focused on women's family planning, was established,[33] followed by the SPOC in 1958. The SPOC produced studies on population issues for and lent their expertise to the government,[34] and it included specialists as well as representatives of mass organizations and, according to Wolchik, delegates of the CCW. These experts advocated for expanded access to abortion,[35] perceiving it—according to Lišková—as a path to women's

30 Výbor československých žen: Diskuze na plenárním zasedání dne 13. a 14. dubna 1966 [Committee of Czechoslovak Women: Discussion at the Plenary Session of 13 and 14 April 1966]. Box 10, Fond 360 Československý svaz žen—ústřední výbor, Praha [Central Committee of the Czechoslovak Women's Union, Prague], NA.

31 Hoppe et al. 2015.

32 Lišková 2018, 120.

33 Wolchik 1983.

34 Lišková 2018; Wolchik 1983.

35 Dudová 2012a, 2012b, 2009; Wolchik 1983. From 1 January 1958, abortion could be performed at the request of the pregnant woman, but the approval of the abortion

equality, wellbeing, and reproductive freedom. Indeed, women's right to make decisions about their bodies and maternity was at the forefront of these experts' agenda, and the legal justifications for abortion adopted in 1957 echoed, to a considerable extent, the recommendations of experts.[36]

2 "The Erudite Discussion of Experts": Expertise, Differentiated Approaches, and the Czechoslovak Women's Union's Commissions

Libuše Háková was a major defender of women's employment and professionalization. In her speech "To Promote a Marxist Conception of the Woman Question" held during the CWU's founding congress in 1967, which was later published in the *Zpravodaj Českého svazu žen*, Háková argued against a return to the idyll of the middle-class family.

> American psychologist and publicist Betty Friedan vividly described the new complications and difficulties the implementation of this model produced—including the model's negative consequences for the wife, children, and husband—in her book *The Feminine Mystique*. Although developed in the context of developed capitalism in the United States in the 1950s and 1960s, Friedan unwittingly confirmed Marx and Engels's old thesis that a woman excluded from social activity stops developing as a human being. Friedan convincingly demonstrated that even the most devoted service to the family and children could not help women achieve self-realization and could not make use of all the talents, capabilities, determination, and energy equally present in women as well as men.[37]

In her defense of the importance of women's employment, Háková creatively integrated Betty Friedan's *The Feminine Mystique* and Marx and Engel's writings, which also demonstrates the transnational influences and contacts between women from socialist and capitalist countries during the Cold War.[38]

---

commission was necessary. These commissions had three members: an elected official of the national committee, a gynecologist, and a family and youth care worker. See Jechová 2008, 120–121. Most women's requests were approved (around 90 percent). See Lišková 2018, 109–110.

36 Lišková 2018, 104–105.

37 Háková 1967.

38 Betty Friedan's book was not translated to Czech/Slovak. Háková probably acquired this book during her trip to England, where she was to meet with members of women's

According to Háková, the CWU should actively solve women's issues and not merely focus on propaganda, the latter of which reflected the core activity of the previous women's organization. Moreover, Háková stated that a wider public discussion about women's issues would not achieve the desired effect; what was needed was "the erudite discussion of experts,"[39] Háková wrote. Leaders of the CWU wanted to be the initiators and coordinators of this discussion, and from the very beginning, the CWU called for the establishment of a working group composed of demographers, economists, sociologists, philosophers, educators, and psychologists, who would—in cooperation with the CWU—develop solid proposal for solving all of women's issues.[40]

In the meeting of the delegation of the CWU with President Ludvík Svoboda (on 25 September 1968), "Dr. Libuše Háková, Vice-Chairwoman of the Central Committee of the Czechoslovak Women's Union, admitted that she had always been a bit of a feminist in that she always wanted to see all the problems of women's equality solved first."[41] As Kristen Ghodsee points out, socialist activists "fought for women's rights in their own way, using the rhetorical tools available to them within specific cultural and historical contexts."[42] Using the language of the party and citing Lenin, Marx, and Engels, women's organizations could, on the pages of their magazines and publications—or in their speeches, as in the case of Háková—invoke authors considered "bourgeois" when discussing family models. In her text about Friedan's *The Feminine Mystique*, Libuše Háková used Marx and Engels and their argument to "defend" her use of a Western, second-wave feminist text. By citing socialist classics, Háková used the opportunity to share new texts and the ideas of Western feminism and, similar to the activists Ghodsee emphasized in her work, "reminded their male Party colleagues that women's issues were a core concern of communism's ideological fathers and could not be ignored."[43]

Highlighting the importance of expertise, the chair of the CWU (between 1967 and 1969) Miluše Fischerová stated that an informed approach to all problems was crucial. Consequently, the organization itself created working groups,

organization as a delegate of the CWU. The only Western feminist text translated into Czech at the time was Simone de Beauvoir's *Second Sex* in 1967.

39 Háková 1967.

40 Háková 1967.

41 Koželková 1968.

42 Ghodsee 2019, 25. Ghodsee mentions women such as Elena Lagadinova, Maria Dinkova, Sonya Bakish, Ana Durcheva, Chibesa Kankasa, Lily Monze, and Senior Chieftainess Nkomeshya Mukamambo II, women from Bulgaria and Zambia who participated in the official state women's organizations during the Cold War.

43 Ghodsee 2019, 52.

commissions, and departments on women's issues led by expert activists. For example, the above-mentioned Dr. Libuše Háková led the Ideological Commission (Ideologická komise); Dr. Senta Radvanová chaired the Group for Social-Legal Issues (Pracovní skupina pro otázky sociálně právní). Radvanová was a lawyer who continues to be highly respected by the Czech legal community. In the 1960s, she was one of the co-authors of the new Family Law; in this capacity, she was instrumental in incorporating principles of parental empowerment into Family Law (*zákon o rodině*) No. 94/ 1963 Coll., which was valid in the Czech Republic until 2013.[44] Sociologist Dr. Jaroslava Bauerová led the Commission for Employed Women's Issues (Komise pro otázky zaměstnaných žen). Bauerová worked in the Department of Economic Sociology and Psychology (Katedra ekonomické sociologie a psychologie), which was founded in 1963 at the University of Economics (Vysoká škola ekonomická v Praze) in Prague.[45] Finally, the economist Dr. Vlasta Brablcová led the Commission for Family Issues and Children's and Youth Education (Komise pro otázky rodiny, výchovy dětí a mládeže, spolupráce rodiny a školy). The Central Committee of the CWU was instrumental in securing Brablcová's appointment as a high-ranking administrator in the Ministry of Labour and Social Affairs.[46] She remained in the office from January 1969 until January 1970, when the position was dissolved. Brablcová was then put in charge of the development of the social welfare system at the Federal Ministry of Labour and Social Affairs.[47] In November 1969, Brablcová denounced the reforms associated with the Prague spring and condemned the activities of the CWU as "right opportunism." Then, at the beginning of 1970, she became (again) the Chair of the re-established Commission for Family Issues and Children's and Youth Education of the CWU.

Each commission collected expert knowledge about its respective charge, held discussions and seminars with experts, and proposed solutions to concrete issues. The commissions also arranged for their functionaries (*funkcionářky*) to attend training, lectures, and seminars.[48] The strategy of the CWU assumed that if women activists became experts on the given topic, they would be more respected and could partner with other institutions; in this way, they would be more able to advance their agenda. According to CWU leaders, the distorted

44 Winterová and Dvořák 2009, 11.

45 Nešpor 2017.

46 Víšková 1969.

47 Kodymová and Honsů 2020, 139.

48 For example, the cycle included training about "Employed women," "Women's position in agriculture," "Contemporary family and its development," or "Upbringing of the children and youth."

political and economic development of the 1950s (a period known, above all, for blatant repression and political show trials) had relied on ideology that ignored women as a distinctive social group and, relatedly, was based on a highly simplified understanding of the social structure of Czechoslovakia.[49] For this reason, in the CWU, sociologists in particular played an important role in promoting a complex understanding of the social structure of Czechoslovak society. Additionally, the CWU's Action Program from 1968 emphasized a differentiated approach to women, notably one that considered the different life experiences, education, and family arrangements of women.

3 The Czechoslovak Women's Union, Women's Paid Work, Unpaid Work, and Care Work

"The main idea of the fight for a more equitable position for women in society is overcoming the traditional, deep-rooted role assigned to a woman from time immemorial" and "in eliminating the prejudices against women's work in people's minds, which have been passed on from generation to generation and eventually elevated to 'dogma.'"[50] This is an excerpt from the speech given by Ing. Marie Nalbaryová during the "Seminar on the Current Problems of Working Women" held by the Commission for Employed Women's Issues in 1968.

At the forefront of the CWU's agenda was women's work (including paid work, unpaid care work, and paid care work). As mentioned above, women's activist Libuše Háková creatively merged contemporaneous Western feminist writings with classics such as Marx to argue that women's employment was a necessary element of women's emancipation. The CWU asked for equal opportunities for women, suitable changes in the Labour Code, and adequate regulations related to maternity benefits. Importantly, as I will show in the following section, women's activists asked for *freedom of choice* for women to decide whether to stay at home with their child or children or to return to their paid work as quickly as possible.

49 "Z činnosti komisí ÚV ČSŽ" 1968.

50 Nalbaryová 1968.

4 "Find Ways and Create Conditions": Maternal Leave, Nurseries and Freedom of Choice

The plenary statement issued by the CWU Action Program on 11 April 1968 reads as follows:

> We consider it our task—as a case of particular urgency—to create conditions for another extension of maternity leave (to two years) [...]. We will take on this task because, in our minds, it will benefit children, families, and mothers, and it will increase and enhance the quality of the population.[51]

In 1968, the Commission for Issues of Family and Child Rearing organized a discussion with the members of SPOC, the state statistical office, and the Ministry of Finance about pro-population measures.[52] The CWU promoted extending maternity leave to two years (ideally to 2.5 to 3 years) and providing financial benefits to all mothers, not only those who engaged in paid employment. If necessary, the CWU proposed prioritizing mothers with two to four children.[53]

During the same year, maternity leave was indeed extended to 26 weeks; for single mothers and mothers of twins, leave was extended even further. As M. Fialová wrote in the CWU's newsletter: "[T]he extension of maternity leave for single mothers (*osamělé matky*) from the current 26 to 35 weeks was based on our recommendations. The original proposal concerned only mothers of twins."[54] Moreover, the CWU played an instrumental role in advocating for other benefits related to maternity and child care, such as financial support

51 Stanovisko pléna ÚV ČSSŽ k vypracování akčního programu Čs. svazu žen, Praha 11. dubna 1968 [Position of the Plenum of the Central Committee of the Czechoslovak Women's Union to the establishment of the Action Program of the CWU, Prague 11 April 1968], Box 35, Fond 360 Československý svaz žen—ústřední výbor, Praha [Central Committee of the Czechoslovak Women's Union, Prague], NA.

52 "Od akčního programu neustoupíme" 1968.

53 Stanovisko ÚV ČSSŽ k dalšímu prodlužování mateřské dovolené—ministerstvu financí (náměstku ministra financí Lérovi) [Position of the Plenum of the Central Committee of the Czechoslovak Women's Union to Another Lengthening of Maternity Leave—for the Undersecretary of the Ministry of Finance—Lér], Box 37, Fond 360 Československý svaz žen—ústřední výbor, Praha [Central Committee of the Czechoslovak Women's Union, Prague], NA.

54 Fialová 1968. In Czechoslovakia, around 10,000 children were born per year to single mothers (including singles, divorced, widows), see Manclová 1969. The situation of Vietnamese women guest workers was not discussed. About discrimination against them, see Alamgir 2020.

for motherhood (*peněžitá pomoc v mateřství*), the extended maternity benefit (*mateřský příspěvek*), a one-time subsidy for the mother after giving birth—also called a maternity grant (*podpora při narození dítěte* or *porodné*), and child allowances (*přídavky na děti*) for unemployed women.[55] Before that, women who were not employed could ask *only* for a maternity grant, which created an extremely complicated situation for recent graduates or women from areas experiencing a shortage of available employment opportunities.

Financial support for maternity (also called basic maternity leave—*základní mateřská dovolená*) was extended for the first time in 1948, from 12 to 18 weeks; in 1964, it was extended further, to 22 weeks; in 1968, to 26 weeks; and finally, in 1987, to 28 weeks. Starting in 1964, after exhausting their paid maternity leave, women could take additional unpaid maternity leave (*další mateřská dovolená*) until the child turned one year old. In 1969, a pronatalist measure called the maternity benefit (*mateřský přípěvek*)—also called extended maternity leave (*prodloužená mateřská dovolená*)—extended paid maternity leave for one year (then to two years in 1971), but only starting with the second child. Child allowances were established already in 1945, but only for working women. The socioeconomic status of parents ceased to be decisive starting in 1969. The one-time subsidy for mothers after birth worked as a universal benefit, as mothers with insured family members were entitled to it.[56] Significantly, starting in January 1969, all maternity benefits as well as childcare allowances included women who were not formerly employed but were registered as job seekers (i.e., in the case of recent graduates no later than six weeks after graduation).[57]

The CWU thus welcomed and aimed to promote the extension of maternity leave and extended financial benefits to all mothers. Still, in my view, the most important was the CWU's emphasis on women's free choice, i.e., the choice to stay home with children for a longer period of time or to return to paid work. As mentioned above, during the 1960s, a part of the expert community—especially economists and psychologists—challenged women's full employment as economically inefficient and asserted that it led to the emotional deprivation of children. The CWU openly rejected the idea that women should be forced to return to the home and constructed a careful argument that held that women's work benefited not only society but women themselves, their standard of living, and their families.

---

55 Procházka 1969.

56 Rákosník and Šustrová 2016, 49, 50, 62, 64, 65, 67.

57 Act No. 182/1968 Coll.

> Because of the high cost of nurseries, there arise objections that the social costs for nurseries are higher than the value created by an employed mother. Those who argue this way keep forgetting that a mother creates value not only for society but also for herself [...]. If a mother stops working, the cost of nurseries will be saved. However, someone has to compensate for the provision of food and clothing for mothers and their children so as to avoid decreasing families' standard of living.[58] [Furthermore], it is necessary to enable a woman who has qualifications and enjoys performing her work, as she will always want to return to it. Make this option available to women; it is advisable to continue developing nurseries so women can, without fear, entrust their child to a facility where they will be well taken care of.[59]

Moreover, the CWU referred to the research of the Institute for the Care of Mother and Child (Ústav pro péči o matku a dítě), which showed that collective child rearing could be a practical supplement to family care and the upbringing of children and that a limited time spent in nurseries was appropriate for children.[60] The CWU translated their emphasis on *freedom of choice* into demands for accessible, high-quality childcare and extended maternity leave that was sufficiently long and included a financial maternity benefit. Because many highly qualified women desired to go back to work soon after giving birth, they could freely choose this option only if they knew that qualified personnel would be available to take care of their children. Women who wished to stay at home with their smaller children (which was the mainstream view articulated in the public, political, and some expert discourse) needed to have this option—made possible through extended maternity leave and a sufficient financial "reward" (maternity benefit)—as the CWU emphasized that "care for children [was] important work for society."[61]

58 K některým problémům žen—matek malých dětí v souvislosti se společenskou funkcí jeslí, účelností a rentabilností tohoto zařízení. [About some Problems of Women—Mothers of Small Children in Connection with Social Function of Nurseries, Purposefulness, and Profitability of this Facility], Box 35, Fond 360 Československý svaz žen—ústřední výbor, Praha [Central Committee of the Czechoslovak Women's Union, Prague], NA.

59 The quote is from the same document.

60 The research was conducted in 1967 or earlier. The precise date is not, unfortunately, stated in the archival materials.

61 Knoblochová 1968.

5 "Abandoned Children": Children's Homes and Foster Care

The CWU's focus on care (work) also included care for "abandoned children" (which means children in children's homes or orphanages). The organization promoted foster care or adoption instead of institutionalized care. In May 1968, the Ministry of Justice asked one of the main leaders of the CWU—lawyer Senta Radvanová—to prepare a white paper (*věcný záměr*) for a new Law on Foster Care (*zákon o pěstounské péči*) because between 1949 and 1950, foster care vanished from the Czechoslovak legal system.[62] Among experts in the field, Radvanová was very well known for her expertise and interest in the topic in large part because in the 1960s she had played an important role in drafting the new Family Law (*zákon o rodině*)—Act No. 94/1963 on Family—which replaced the 1949 Family Law.[63] Radvanová produced and submitted a white paper to the ministry; however, due to the political situation in the second half of 1968, preparations for the new law were halted. Despite this setback, Radvanová continued to promote foster care and continuously published and lectured on the topic. "It is to Senta Radvanová's undeniable credit that she continued her efforts to pass the foster care bill and ensured that the bill did not disappear. The basic ideas and concepts of the law as she proposed them were eventually adopted in the new law (Act No 50/1973 Coll.)."[64]

Members of the CWU addressed the issue of foster care on the local level too. I can offer one example of the CWU's local response to the issue: the District Committee in Třebíč and Gottwaldov (contemporary Zlín). In the Třebíč district, which had five children's homes, women members of the CWU decided to find families for as many children as possible. Members of the CWU used the press to address the public and recruited several families who took a child with them on their (summer) holidays, on Saturdays, or for Christmas. In some cases, families decided to adopt a child.[65]

In Gottwaldov, the CWU commission paid special attention to children in institutions. Their approach was different from Třebíč. In Gottwaldov, women promoted paid foster care (*placená pěstounská péče*).

> In children's homes, there are a lot of children—so-called social orphans. Despite all efforts to return children to their parents or relatives or find them adoptive parents, a few "unwanted" children remain (surely in every

62 Rákosník and Šustrová 2016, 76.
63 Family Act No. 265/1949 Coll.—*zákon o právu rodinném.*
64 Winterová and Dvořák 2009, 11.
65 Vybíralová 1968.

> [children's] home) either because they are unattractive or dark-skinned or because they have some physical handicap. We are concerned about rescuing these children so they do not have to grow up abandoned—without family.[66]

The local branch of the CWU repeatedly negotiated with the health, education, and finance divisions of the District National Committee (Okresní národní výbor, i.e., the district municipality), and in cooperation with the court, they were able to implement paid foster care in their district for a two-year trial period.[67] The CWU in Gottwaldov was inspired by the successful efforts of women in the Olomouc district.[68] "The work of social commissions is as diverse as problems of each district. [...] The level of activities and specialization of commissions depends on their composition, their expertise, and their cooperation with other institutions in the district."[69] In other words, an expert background, especially the involvement of highly educated women (with university degrees) in the local chapters of the CWU, and their cooperation with public authorities and administration enabled women to advance their interests. Local women activists were not necessarily experts in the sense of academic credentials, but the sources show that highly educated women were very often involved in activism, especially in the various commissions of the CWU.

The local chapters of the CWU focused on the same or similar topics as the central organization. But very often, they did it in their own way, one that took the local context and conditions into account. Additionally, on the local level, CWU members were recognized as actors in charge of women's, children's, and family issues; in other words, they were considered on par with other authorities. Importantly, the local activities of the CWU and local problem solving became quite characteristic of what is called the Normalization period (*normalizace*) in Czechoslovakia, which began in 1969. During that era, women tried to solve problems at least at the village or district level, even if it was not possible to make changes at the national level.

66 OV ČSSŽ Gottwaldov 1968.
67 OV ČSSŽ Gottwaldov 1968.
68 OV ČSSŽ Gottwaldov 1968.
69 Fialová 1968.

6 The Czechoslovak Labour Code and the Recommendations of the Women's Union

In 1968, the Ministry of Labour and Social Affairs began the process of revising the Labour Code (*Zákoník práce*) and asked the CWU to identify (what it considered to be) necessary adjustments and evaluate the revisions proposed by the labour unions (Revoluční odborové hnutí).[70] The Central Committee of the CWU assigned this task to the Department for Employed Women's Issues (Úsek problematiky zaměstnaných žen), led by Ing. Marie Nalbaryová. Using the feedback of the district committees of the CWU and their expert groups, as well as specialized literature and consultations with experts on labour and social law, the department prepared eleven concrete suggestions, which were very different—more pro-women—than those submitted by the labour unions.

The CWU's proposals included: economic sanctions against organizations that violated the Labour Code; protections for pregnant women seeking employment (some organizations—this term was used as an umbrella including enterprises and other institutions that employed people—would not hire a woman if they learned she was pregnant during the initial medical exam); protections that prevented pregnant women from being dismissed. The CWU also called for an extension of the time limit for claiming wage compensation in connection with an unfair dismissal (from three months to one year); an extension of the lunch break; the imposition of an obligation on organizations to provide meals complying with the principles of good nutrition; (minor) changes in the wording related to the women's employment plan; bans on certain work; bans on night work; changes in transferring mothers of young children to other jobs and the provision of a compensatory allowance; and creating opportunities for women to work shorter hours, i.e., part-time work.[71] The CWU's newsletter informed readers that in April 1969, the board of the CWU:

> took note of the report on the incorporation of five comments of the CWU into the final text of the draft law amending the Labour Code. [The CWU] insists that the demands that were not applied—concerning women's night work, women's work in hazardous workplaces, and the protection of all pregnant women [from dismissals justified by] organizational

70 About the first Labour Code from 1965, see Vojáček 2014.

71 "Připomínky k Zákoníku práce 1.10.1968" [Comments on Labour Code 1 October 1968], Box 37, Fond 360 Československý svaz žen—ústřední výbor, Praha [Central Committee of the Czechoslovak Women's Union, Prague], NA.

> changes at the workplace—be incorporated in the next stage of the revision of the Labour Code or in the adoption of other legal provisions.[72]

The newsletter was not specific about the five changes the ministry accepted. However, in course of the reform of the Labour Code, the ministry implemented some among the proposals listed above already in 1969, while some others were implemented only in 1975, when the Labour Code was revised again.

For years, the CWU focused much of its attention on the obviously widespread violations of regulations contained in the Labour Code. The CWU emphasized issues related to hiring, changes in and the termination of employment, women's working conditions, women's health and safety at work, and then suggested imposing economic sanctions against organizations that violated regulations. The 1969 revision included severe sanctions. The District National Committee could impose fines totaling 100,000 Czechoslovak crowns (Československá koruna-CZK)against any organization that violated the Labour Code for the first time, and fines in the amount of CZK 500,000 for subsequent violations. At the time, these amounts represented heavy sanctions for violators of the Labour Code.

In my view, the most important changes included in the revised Labour Code related to the addition and/or expansion of women's workplace protections—specifically those prohibiting discrimination against pregnant women. According to the 1965 Labour Code, when an enterprise or institution sought to dismiss an employee for organizational reasons, it had to find appropriate jobs for displaced unmarried workers, workers caring for children younger than 15, and disabled workers. Otherwise, the organization could not fire these workers.[73] The 1975 Labour Code implemented the CWU's demand to include in this paragraph all pregnant women.[74] This new Labour Code also required "organizations [to] provide workers with factory meals in all shifts that comply with the principles of good nutrition and provide them with appropriate beverages at or near their workstations."[75]

Another change that the CWU proposed in 1969 concerned the prohibition of night work and certain types of hazardous work (such as working underground) for women that had been introduced in the 1965 Labour Code.[76]

72 "Předsednictvo ÚV ČSŽ v dubnu 69" 1969.

73 Act No 65/1965 Coll.

74 Act No 65/1965 Coll. Neither discussion about Labour Code included migrant workers.

75 Act No 65/1965 Coll.

76 "[W]omen were protected from different kinds of physical, biological, and chemical agents, processes and working conditions [...]. [W]here a female workforce was necessary

Czechoslovakia was part of the ILO Convention prohibiting night work for women in industry, but Czechoslovakia introduced a general ban on women's night work except for "women who hold positions of responsibility and management or who work in health, social, or cultural institutions, catering, telecommunications, postal services, railways, public transport, and livestock farming."[77] Despite this prohibition, there were many exceptions to this rule in Czechoslovakia, and the government sought to limit these exceptions. But women working the night shift opposed these "protective" measures, and exceptions to the ban were debated by the CWU, the ministry, and women workers themselves.

Already in 1967, readers of the popular women's magazine *Vlasta* (published by the CWU) sent letters to the editorial board about the bans on night work.

> I disagree with the decision that from the January 1968, women in our factory in Ervěnice will stop working night shifts. Years ago, we were matched with this job; they persuaded us to start working night shifts. Where I am from, five women stokers work shifts. We had to learn a lot, we passed many exams, and today, after gaining qualifications [and experience] we are supposed to leave the job? I like this job. I have been working here for 12 years. Why should I leave work now, when my children have already grown up (I have three sons, and I am a single mother), since this work was not bad for me when my children were small and the situation was difficult. Where should I go to work?[78]

In accord with these women's complaints, the CWU proposed passing only a general regulation on banned work instead of an exhaustive list (including many types of workplaces). Then, the enterprises and institutions could engage in concrete negotiations with women (potentially) working night shifts/ employed in banned forms of work and members of the health administration. But according to the undersecretary of the Ministry of Labour and Social Affairs Přemysl Tomášek, the ministry regarded the prohibition of women's night work as a suitable measure.[79] Moreover, as stated by Tomášek, the invalidation

---

for the smooth running of factories, sectoral exceptions were passed" (Havelková 2017, 51–52).

77 Act No 65/1965 Coll., see 152.

78 BULLETIN redakce Vlasty č. 13. Ohlas na články Vlasty za měsíc červenec—srpen 1967 [Bulletin of Editorial Department of Magazine Vlasta no. 13. Reactions to Articles in Vlasta from July-August 1967], Box 19, Fond 360 Československý svaz žen—ústřední výbor, Praha [Central Committee of the Czechoslovak Women's Union, Prague], NA.

79 "Zeptali jsme se za vás" 1969.

of this paragraph of the Labour Code (as part of the planned revisions) would mean denouncing the International Labour Organization's Convention on night work, a move that was—according to Tomášek—politically unacceptable.[80] At the same time, Tomášek admitted that the ILO Convention no. 89 (1948) "Night Work (Women) Convention (Revised)" became obsolete and led to women's discrimination, "Because a woman should freely decide, without any constraints, if she wants to work during the night, if it is acceptable for her and advantageous."[81] His position was quite ambivalent. Because the ministry refused to lift the ban, Tomášek proposed that the only workable solution was to continue recognizing the already established exceptions to the prohibition on night work. The CWU called for the ministry to "provide for an exception so that women over the age of 45 (or 50), whose children have reached the age of 12 and who have been working night shifts may, if they agree, continue to work night shifts until they become eligible for a pension."[82] The ministry did not accept this demand. And the paragraphs below show that the rhetoric of the new leadership of the CWU concerning the ban on night work changed in the 1970s.

7 Women's Workforce—Different Workforce

During the Normalization period in the 1970s, the CWU's emphasis on the freedom of choice vanished, and instead the CWU began supporting policies related to the (over)protection of women in the workplace. After changes in the CWU at the end of 1969, the Commission for Employed Women's Issues was re-established and again chaired by sociologist Dr. Jaroslava Bauerová.[83] But in harmony with the emphasis on the family and women's maternal role characteristic of era, the CWU's approach to women's work changed.[84]

80 About the Convention no. 89, see Politakis 2001. In comparison to Czechoslovakia, Hungary denounced the 1948 ILO Night Work (Women) Convention no. 89 in 1977. Widdows 1984, 1057.

81 "Zeptali jsme se za vás" 1969, 14.

82 "Připomínky k Zákoníku práce 1.10.1968" [Comments on Labour Code 1 October 1968], Box 37, Fond 360 Československý svaz žen—ústřední výbor, Praha [Central Committee of the Czechoslovak Women's Union, Prague], NA.

83 "Komise ÚV ČSŽ zahájily činnost," 1970.

84 "This retraditionalization of gender had help from an unusual ally: the economists. The same expert groups that tried to reinvigorate socialist nationalized economy also calculated tax benefits and family bonuses, and proposed policies including longer maternity leave so that mothers could stay at home and care for their children" (Lišková 2018, 19).

Whereas between 1967 and 1969, the CWU promoted lifting or at least mitigating bans concerning women's work (i.e., the ban on night work), the CWU's new leadership wanted to phase out exemptions to the ban on night work for women. This new position was voiced during the conference "What Socialism Has Given to Women, and How Women Contribute to the Development of Socialist Society," which was held in Prague in 1975 in connection with the International Women's Year.[85] Indeed, Jaroslava Bauerová declared the following in her lecture:

> Women's employment involves a challenging system of protection for women's work, as women represent a workforce that is different from men. This includes improving working and living conditions and the work environment for women, improving sanitary and social facilities, respecting legal limits on handling [heavy] loads, reducing overtime work, and eliminating exceptions to the ban on night work for women.[86]

Although the leaders of the CWU emphasized the importance of women's work, they considered women's work as different from men's and considered working women to be a distinct group that required special treatment in the world of work.[87]

At the same conference, the new chair of the CWU Marie Kabrhelová emphasized the need to improve women's working conditions and reduce the proportion of women performing heavy physical labour. Already in 1973, the CWU declared that as one its goals: "[In] the search for an optimal solution to questions concerning the status of women, the Czechoslovak women's organization will focus primarily on: adapting working conditions to

---

85 The conference was organized by the Central Committee of the Czechoslovak Women's Union. In the two-day conference, 120 experts participated, including sociologists, lawyers, economists, members of unions, and undersecretary of the Federal Ministry of Labour and Social Affairs.

86 Bauerová 1976, 104.

87 Symptomatic of this time was also the dissolution of the commission on the issues of employed women, which was replaced in 1974 by the Commission for Women and Family Care. Usnesení předsednictva ÚV Československého svazu žen ze dne 19.6.1974 k bodu: Zásady pro činnost stálých komisí ÚV ČSSŽ [Resolution of the Presidium of the Central Committee of the CWU of 19 June 1974 on the Item: Principles for the Activities of the Permanent Committees of the Central Committee of the CWU], Box 38, Fond 360 Československý svaz žen—ústřední výbor, Praha [Central Committee of the Czechoslovak Women's Union, Prague], NA.

women's natural psychological, physiological, and biological peculiarities."[88] Kabrhelová believed that changes were needed in the structure of women's employment, and she asserted that women should focus on new fields of work and gain higher qualifications; therefore, the CWU focused on educating girls about their career choices.

In 1983, Jaroslava Bauerová and Jolana Jančovičová (the latter also was a sociologist and a member of the Central Committee of the CWU and the Commission for Women and Family Care) published an article about the "Position of Women and Families in Czechoslovakia" in the *Czech Sociological Review*. Bauerová and Jančovičová emphasized the significance of paid productive work for women's emancipation. But again, they asserted need to protect women in the workplace because of women's role as mothers: "women, as bearers of new life, cannot do all the work men do, and therefore, they enjoy special protections under the law."[89]

Sociologists from the CWU did not see the feminization of work as a problem. According to Bauerová and Jančovičová, "wages are slightly lower in sectors with a high concentration of women, but women are more likely to have favorable working conditions there."[90] According to the authors, "the division of many jobs into male and female ones will take a long time and will only be eliminated by full automation."[91] Bauerová and Jančovičová did not see involving women in every area of paid work as a solution. On the contrary, in some cases, they considered the feminization of work an advantage.

During the Normalization period in the 1970s, the CWU focused on women's (un)paid work, childcare, and securing appropriate conditions for employed women. But the meaning of what was "appropriate" for women had changed. Whereas in the early days, the CWU advocated for equal opportunities for women, during Normalization, the union called for the special treatment and protection of women in the workforce in accordance with the Czechoslovak state's overall approach to women.

88 Sekretariát ČSRŽ 30.1.1973. Obsahová náplň činnosti organizace československých žen [Secretariat of the Czechoslovak Council of Women 30 January 1973. Content of the activities of the Czechoslovak Women's Organization], Box 24, Fond 360 Československý svaz žen—ústřední výbor, Praha [Central Committee of the Czechoslovak Women's Union, Prague], NA.

89 Bauerová and Jančovičová 1983, 229–230.

90 Bauerová and Jančovičová 1983, 228.

91 Bauerová and Jančovičová 1983, 230.

8 Conclusion

The focal points of the CWU's agenda were women's (un)paid work, care for children, and the establishment of appropriate conditions for employed women. The CWU also addressed the interests of women who wished to care for children exclusively. From the very beginning, the women's organization pushed for a differentiated approach, which meant considering the different experiences, needs, and interests of various groups of women and, thus, promoting the freedom of choice for women—to stay at home with their children or to return to paid employment as soon as possible. To ensure this freedom, the CWU emphasized both access to high quality childcare facilities as well as extended maternity leave and financial support for mothers.

The CWU always promoted women's right to engage in paid work. That is why in the 1960s, a period when the socialist goal of achieving gender equality through the labour mobilization of women was repeatedly challenged in Czechoslovak public and expert discourse, women activists used their expert knowledge and networks to argue against the return of women to the home. Under socialism, especially between 1967 and 1969, women sociologists, lawyers, and economists played crucial roles in the organization. The CWU's leaders conducted research, worked as experts, and used the results of their research for their activism on behalf of women. They tried to use their expert knowledge to push state organs to solve women's problems and issues related to children and the family. The question of the Labour Code and compliance was one of the CWU's main interests during the entire state-socialist period. As I have shown in this chapter, activists were instrumental in promoting changes to the Labour Code and maternity and childcare benefits.

Even during the Normalization period in the 1970s, the new leadership of the CWU continued to promote pro-women measures, but the discourse about what was best for women had fundamentally changed. At the same time, the CWU continued to stress the importance of women's work—paid and unpaid—for building a socialist society. Compared to the CWU's early years (1967 to 1969), when leaders of the organization promoted women's access to all areas of employment, during the Normalization period, the CWU highlighted the need to protect women in the workplace because they regarded women as a distinct group of workers due to their (potential) maternal role.

Overall, women played various important roles in the CWU as leaders of the Central Committee and as members of local chapters carrying out a wide array of tasks. Because of their participation in the CWU, these women enjoyed formal standing among a larger group of actors, and they were invited to add their perspective to discussions and in negotiations. At the same time, they were usually *not* decision-makers, but they could and did proactively apply pressure, and this should be (partially) considered when writing the history of women's activism during this period. One of the strategies they employed within this setting was positioning their activities within the framework of "expertise" in order to make their voices heard and to make their influence as strong as they could. Moreover, the inclusion of women who had expertise in the field/issue being addressed gave the group a distinct advantage in negotiations.

Members at the local level of the organization played different but equally important roles. On the one hand, women from local chapters could gain knowledge, access instruction, and also achieve formal status thanks to efforts made at the central level of the organization. On the other hand, women from local chapters worked to solve "their" concrete, local issues using strategies adapted to their local conditions.

Bibliography

"182/1968 Sb. Vyhláška ministerstva práce a sociálních věcí o dávkách v mateřství a o přídavcích na děti uchazečům o zaměstnání" [Decree No 182/1968 of the Ministry of Labour and Social Affairs about maternity allowance and child allowance for job seekers]. 1968. In *Sbírka zákonů Československé socialistické republiky vydána dne 29. prosince 1968* [Collection of laws of the Czechoslovak Socialist Republic published on 29 December 1968]. Prague: Ministerstvo spravedlnosti, 1968.

Akční program Čs. svazu žen 26.–27.6. 1968 [Action program of the Czechoslovak Women's Union]. 1968.

Alamgir, Alena K. 2020. "'Inappropriate Behavior': Labor Control and the Polish, Cuban and Vietnamese Workers in Czechoslovakia." In *Labor in State-Socialist Europe, 1945–1989 : Contributions to a History of Work*, edited by Marsha Siefert. Budapest: Central European University Press.

Bauerová, Jaroslava. 1976. "Informace o celostátní konferenci pořádané k Mezinárodnímu roku ženy „Co dal socialismus ženám a jak ženy přispívají k rozvoji socialistické společnosti" [Information about the nationwide conference organized for International Women's Year, "What Socialism Gave to Women and How Women Contribute to the Development of Socialist Society"]. *Sociologický Časopis* [Czech sociological review] 12: 103–111.

Bauerová, Jaroslava. 1974. *Zaměstnaná žena a rodina* [Employed woman and family]. Prague: Práce.

Bauerová, Jaroslava, and Jolana Jančovičová. 1983. "Postavení žen a rodin v ČSSR" [The position of women and families in Czechoslovakia]. *Sociologický Časopis* [Czech sociological review] 19, no. 2: 225–237.

Besnik, Pula. 2018. *Globalization Under and after Socialism: The Evolution of Transnational Capital in Central and Eastern Europe*. Stanford, CA: Stanford University Press.

Bonfiglioli, Chiara. 2016. "The First UN World Conference on Women (1975) as a Cold War Encounter: Recovering Anti-Imperialist, Non-Aligned and Socialist Genealogies." *Filozofija i Društvo* [Philosophy and society] 27, no. 3: 521–541.

"ČSRŽ odsuzuje" [Czechoslovak Council of Women denounce]. 1970. *Zpravodaj Českého svazu žen* [Newsletter of the Czech Women's Union].

Dudová, Radka. 2012a. *Interrupce v České republice: zápas o ženská těla* [*Abortion in the Czech Republic: The struggle for women's bodies*]. Prague: Sociologický ústav AV ČR.

Dudová, Radka. 2012b. "Regulation of Abortion as State-Socialist Governmentality: the Case of Czechoslovakia." *Politics and Gender* 8, no. 1: 123–144.

Dudová, Radka. 2009. "Interrupce v socialistickém Československu z foucaultovské perspektivy" [Abortion in socialist Czechoslovakia—A Foucauldian perspective]. *Gender, rovné příležitosti, výzkum* [Gender, equal opportunities, research] 10, no. 1: 25–36.

Eyal, Gil. 2013. "For a Sociology of Expertise: The Social Origins of the Autism Epidemic." *American Journal of Sociology* 118, no. 4: 863–907.

Fialová, M. 1968. "Několik poznámek k práci sociálních komisí [A few comments on the work of the Social Commissions]." *Zpravodaj Českého svazu žen* [Newsletter of the Czech Women's Union] 2, no. 12: 12.

Ghodsee, Kristen. 2019. *Second World, Second Sex: Socialist Women's Activism and Global Solidarity during the Cold War*. Durham, NC: Duke University Press.

Háková, Libuše. 1967. "Prosazovat marxistickou koncepci ženské otázky [To promote a Marxist conception of the woman question]." *Zpravodaj Českého svazu žen* [Newsletter of the Czech Women's Union] 1, no. 1: 12.

Havelková, Barbara. 2017. *Gender Equality in Law: Uncovering the Legacies of Czech State Socialism*. Oxford: Bloomsbury Publishing.

Havelková, Barbara. 2014. "The Three Stages of Gender in Law." In *The Politics of Gender Culture under State Socialism: An Expropriated Voice*, edited by Hana Havelková and Libora Oates-Indruchová, 31–56. London: Routledge.

Havelková, Hana. 2015. "(De)centralizovaná genderová politika: Role státní populační komise" [(De)centralized gender policy: The role of the State Population Commission]. In *Vyvlastněný hlas: Proměny genderové kultury české společnosti v letech 1948–1989* [The politics of gender culture under state socialism: An expropriated voice], edited by Libora Oates-Indruchová and Hana Havelková, 125–168. Prague: Sociologické nakladatelství.

Hoppe, Jiří, Markéta Škodová, Jiří Suk, and Francesco Caccamo. 2015. *O nový československý model socialismu. Čtyři interdisciplinární vědecké týmy při ČSAV a UK v 60. letech* ["Striving for a new Czechoslovak model of socialism." Four interdisciplinary scientific teams of the Czechoslovak Academy of Sciences and Charles University in the 1960s]. Prague: Ústav pro soudobé dějiny AV ČR.

Iacob, Bogdan C., Corina Doboş, Raluca Grosescu, Viviana Iacob, and Vlad Paşca. 2018. "State Socialist Experts in Transnational Perspective. East European Circulation of Knowledge during the Cold War (1950s–1980s): Introduction to the Thematic Issue." *East Central Europe* 45, no. 2–3: 145–159.

James, Mark and Péter Apor. 2015. "Socialism Goes Global: Decolonization and the Making of a New Culture of Internationalism in Socialist Hungary, 1956–1989." *The Journal of Modern History* 87, no. 4: 852–891.

Jechová, Květa. 2008. "Cesta k emancipaci. Postavení ženy v české společnosti 20. století. Pokus o vymezení problému" [The road to emancipation. The position of women in Czech society in the 20th century. An attempt to define the problem]. In *Pět studií k dějinám české společnosti po roce 1945* [Opposition and society after 1945], edited by Oldřich Tůma and Tomáš Vilímek, 69–129. Prague: Ústav pro soudobé dějiny AV ČR.

Knoblochová, Jarmila. 1968. "Jedná v zájmu žen" [Acting in the interest of women]. *Zpravodaj Českého svazu žen* [Newsletter of the Czech Women's Union] 2, no. 12: 13.

Kochanowski, Jerzy, and Claudia Kraft, eds. 2021. *Rooms for Manoeuvre: Another Look at Negotiating Processes in the Socialist Bloc*. Göttingen: Vandenhoeck & Ruprecht.

Kodymová, Pavla, and Renata Honsů. 2020. *Věra Pohlová: sociální práce a život ve 20. století* [Věra Pohlová: Social work and life in the 20th century]. Prague: Karolinum.

Kolář, Pavel, and Michal Pullmann. 2016. *Co byla normalizace? Studie o pozdním socialismu* [What was Normalization? A study of late socialism]. Prague: Lidové noviny, Ústav pro studium totalitních režimů.

"Komise ÚV ČSŽ zahájily činnost" [Commissions of the Central Committee of the Czechoslovak Women's Union have started their activities]. 1970. *Zpravodaj Českého svazu žen* [Newsletter of the Czech Women's Union].

Koželková, Soňa. 1968. "Setkání nejpřátelštější" [A meeting of the friendliest]. *Zpravodaj Českého svazu žen* [Newsletter of the Czech Women's Union] 2, no. 10: 2.

Lišková, Kateřina. 2018. *Sexual Liberation, Socialist Style: Communist Czechoslovakia and the Science of Desire, 1945–1989*. New York: Cambridge University Press.

Lišková, Kateřina. 2016. "Sex under Socialism: From Emancipation of Women to Normalized Families in Czechoslovakia." *Sexualities* 19, no. 1/2: 211–235.

Manclová, A. 1969. "Osamělé matky potřebují pomoc" [Lonely mothers need help]. *Zpravodaj Českého svazu žen* [Newsletter of the Czech Women's Union] 3, no. 3: 13.

Nalbaryová, Marie. 1968. "Dvojí role ženy" [Double role of women]. *Zpravodaj Českého svazu žen* [Newsletter of the Czech Women's Union] 2, no. 12: 10.

Nečasová, Denisa. 2014. "Women's Organizations in the Czech Lands, 1948–89: an Historical Perspective." In *The Politics of Gender Culture under State Socialism: An*

Expropriated Voice, edited by Hana Havelková and Libora Oates-Indruchová, 57–81. London: Routledge.

Nečasová, Denisa. 2011a. *Buduj vlast—posílíš mír! : ženské hnutí v českých zemích 1945–1955* [*Build your homeland—You strengthen the peace! The women's movement in the Czech lands in 1945–1955*]. Brno: Matice moravská.

Nečasová, Denisa. 2011b. "Výbory žen při místních národních výborech—pokus komunistického vedení o novou etapu 'ženského hnutí' v Československu" [Women's Committees at local National Committees—an attempt by the communist leadership to create a new stage of the "Women's Movement" in Czechoslovakia]. In *Bolševismus, komunismus a radikální socialismus v Československu. Svazek VIII* [Bolshevism, communism, and radical socialism in Czechoslovakia. Volume VIII], edited by Jiří Kocián, Jaroslav Pažout, and Jakub Rákosník, 61–91. Prague: Ústav pro soudobé dějiny AV ČR.

Nešpor, Zdeněk R. 2017. "Vysoká škola ekonomická v Praze—Sociologická encyklopedie" [University of Economics in Prague—Sociological Encyclopedia]. *Sociologická encyklopedie* [Sociological encyclopedia]. https://encyklopedie.soc.cas.cz/w/Vysok%C3%A1_%C5%A1kola_ekonomick%C3%A1_v_Praze.

"Od akčního programu neustoupíme" [We will not surrender the Action Program!]. 1968. *Zpravodaj Českého svazu žen* [Newsletter of the Czech Women's Union] 2, no. 9: 1–2.

OV ČSSŽ Gottwaldov. 1968. "V Gottwaldově se starají o děti" [In Gottwaldov, they care for children]. *Zpravodaj Českého svazu žen* [Newsletter of the Czech Women's Union] 2, no. 5: 2.

Politakis, George P. 2001. "Night Work of Women in Industry: Standards and Sensibility." *International Labour Review* 140, no. 4: 403–428.

"Předsednictvo ÚV ČSŽ v dubnu 69" [Presidium of the Central Committee of the Czechoslovak Women's Union in April '69]. 1969. *Zpravodaj Českého svazu žen* [Newsletter of the Czech Women's Union] 3, no. 5: 3.

Procházka, Karel. 1969. "Dávky v mateřství i nezaměstnaným ženám" [Maternity benefits for unemployed women]. *Zpravodaj Českého svazu žen* [Newsletter of the Czech Women's Union] 3, no. 6: 14.

Prokopec, Jiří. 1967. "Tvořit předpoklady pro spokojený život žen" [Creating the conditions for women's happy life]. *Zpravodaj Českého svazu žen* [Newsletter of the Czech Women's Union] 1, no. 1: 11.

Rákosník, Jakub, and Radka Šustrová. 2016. *Rodina v zájmu státu: Populační růst a instituce manželství v českých zemích 1918–1989* [The family in the interest of the state. Population growth and the institution of marriage in the Czech lands, 1918–1989]. Prague: Lidové noviny.

Sbírka zákonů Československé socialistické republiky 65/1965 Sb. Zákoník práce [Collection of laws of the Czechoslovak Socialist Republic Order No 65/1965 Labour Code]. 1965. Prague: Ministerstvo spravedlnosti [Ministry of Justice].

Sommer, Vítězslav, Matěj Spurný, and Jaromír Mrňka. 2019. *Řídit socialismus jako firmu: technokratické vládnutí v Československu, 1956–1989* [Running socialism like a company: Technocratic governance in Czechoslovakia, 1956–1989]. Prague: Ústav pro soudobé dějiny AV ČR, vvi.

Šprincová, Veronika. 2015. "Postavení žen v Československu v období let 1948–1989 v dobových sociologických výzkumech a datech" [The status of women in Czechoslovakia during 1948–1989 in period sociological research and data]. In *Vyvlastněný hlas: Proměny genderové kultury české společnosti v letech 1948–1989* [The politics of gender culture under state socialism: An expropriated voice], 83–124. Prague: Sociologické nakladatelství.

"Usnesení Československé rady žen" [Resolution of the Czechoslovak Council of Women]. 1969. *Zpravodaj Českého svazu žen* [Newsletter of the Czech Women's Union] 3, no. 12: 4.

Víšková, Marie. 1969. "Rozetněme řetěz minulosti" [Let's break the chain of the past]. *Zpravodaj Českého svazu žen* [Newsletter of the Czech Women's Union] 3, no. 3: 6.

Vojáček, Ladislav. 2014. "Zákoník práce z roku 1965–základ československého pracovního práva ve druhé polovině minulého století" [The Labour Code of 1965: The basis of Czechoslovak Labour Legislation in the second half of last century]. *Historický časopis* [*Journal of History*], no. 03: 501–523.

Vybíralová, Pavla. 1968. "Z činnosti a práce OV ČSSŽ v Třebíči" [From the activities and work of the District Committee of the CWU in Třebíč]. *Zpravodaj Českého svazu žen* [Newsletter of the Czech Women's Union] 2, no. 4: 14.

Wagnerová, Alena. 2017. *Žena za socialismu: Československo 1945–1974 a reflexe vývoje před rokem 1989 a po něm* [Woman under socialism. Czechoslovakia 1945–1974 and reflection of the development before and after 1989]. Prague: Sociologické nakladatelství.

Widdows, Kelvin. 1984. "The Denunciation of International Labour Conventions." *The International and Comparative Law Quarterly* 33, no. 4: 1052–1063.

Winterová, Alena, and Jan Dvořák. 2009. "Životní jubileum doc. JUDr. Senty Radvanové, CSc" [Anniversary of doc. JUDr. Senta Radvanová, CSc]. In *Pocta Sentě Radvanové k 80. narozeninám* [Tribute to Senta Radvanová on her 80th Birthday], edited by Alena Winterová and Jan Dvořák, 11–12. Prague: ASPI–Wolters Kluwer.

Wolchik, Sharon L. 1983. "The Scientific—Technological Revolution and the Role of Specialist Elites in Policy-Making in Czechoslovakia." In *Foreign and Domestic Policy in Eastern Europe in the 1980s*, edited by Michael J. Sodaro and Sharon L. Wolchik, 111–132. London: Macmillan Press.

"Z činnosti komisí ÚV ČSŽ" [From the work of the Commissions of the CWU]. 1968. *Zpravodaj Českého svazu žen* [Newsletter of the Czech Women's Union] 2, no. 2: 4.
"Zeptali jsme se za vás: odpovídá náměstek ministra práce a sociálních věcí soudruh ing. Přemysl Tomášek" [We asked for you: The Deputy Minister of Labour and Social Affairs, Comrade Ing. Přemysl Tomášek]. 1969. *Zpravodaj Českého svazu žen* [Newsletter of the Czech Women's Union] 3, no. 2: 8, 9, 14.

CHAPTER 14

Filmmaking as Activism

Documenting the "Double Burden" in Late Socialist Poland

Masha Shpolberg

Abstract

One of the great promises of state socialism was gender equality. Socialist realist films across the bloc promised women that personal and professional fulfillment would go hand-in-hand—that romance was to be found on the construction site. In the 1970s, filmmakers began to openly question this and many other myths of the socialist realist period. In Poland in particular, a series of workers' strikes drew attention to the discrepancy between official discourse and actual labour conditions, particularly the "double burden" placed on women, who were expected to put in a full shift at work and at home. Filmmakers were instrumental in making the difficult material conditions of these women's lives palpable. Unsurprisingly, many of these films were produced by a new generation of women documentarians. This chapter homes in on several short documentaries by Krystyna Gryczełowska and Irena Kamieńska, analyzing the strategies they used to illustrate the "double burden" and, ultimately, advance a critique of the socialist state predicated specifically on the way it failed its women citizens.

Keywords

Irena Kamieńska – Krystyna Gryczełowska – Poland – Solidarity (Solidarność) – documentary – labour – women's cinema – women's double burden

> Women's lives, by no means spectacular, banal in fact, say as much about politics as no end of theoretical political analysis.
>
> SLAVENKA DRAKULIĆ, *How We Survived Communism and Even Laughed*, 1991

On 10 February 1971, a strike over economic conditions broke out in the industrial city of Łódź, catching the communist authorities off-guard: it was

 | DOI:10.1163/9789004682481_015

spontaneous, fierce, and carried out largely by women.[1] Many of them were employed in the textile factories that made up half the city's industrial production. Because 77.7 percent of the city's women residents worked full-time, Łódź was frequently referred to as a "city of women" or *miasto kobiet*.[2] The 1971 strike was also unusual in one other way: its leaders had learned from the massacre that had taken place in the Baltic port cities two months earlier. They understood that workers were most vulnerable to state violence when they took to the streets. Consequently, theirs was the first strike to be carried out inside the place of work—a tactic that would lead the oppositional Solidarity (Solidarność) trade union to victory in August 1980. The Łódź workers were to emerge triumphant from this confrontation, with the state repealing the previously announced price hikes. Yet it was a strike that, film scholar Elżbieta Ostrowska argues, has been largely forgotten precisely because it was successful and did not produce any casualties.

First, Ostrowska argues, Polish collective memory is structured around traumatic events that privilege loss over achievement. Second, this cultural memory script perpetuates traditional gender divisions in that men are represented as active historical agents, whereas women are consigned to the role of passive observers and, often, mourners of male sacrifice. The Łódź strike does not fit this scenario and, consequently, has been marginalized within the memory texts of Polish culture.[3] Indeed, writing much later in the 2000s, both Polish historian Natalia Jarska and sociologist Grzegorz Matuszak termed it alternatively "the forgotten rebellion" or "the forgotten strike" (*zapomniany bunt* or *zapomniany strajk*).[4]

The Łódź women were driven by the same economic desperation as the workers who had been gunned down in the Baltic cities two months earlier. The trouble started on 12 December 1970, when the Polish government substantially raised prices on nearly all food items, creating hardship for the majority of Polish families. The cost of meat, in particular, doubled.[5] The workers'

1 It was not the first strike that saw mass participation by women, however. Historian Małgorzata Fidelis has documented a number of successful strikes carried out primarily by women textile workers in the Stalinist period (Fidelis 2010). For more on these early strikes, see also Kenney 2012.

2 Matuszak 2011. Polish film scholar Elżbieta Ostrowska analyzes the economic and political situation of Łódź women weavers in greater depth in the opening sections of her article "Vanishing Women: Łódź Textile Workers in Polish Documentary Cinema." Ostrowska 2017.

3 Ostrowska 2017, 132.

4 Jarska 2011; Matuszak 2011. Natalia Jarska is also the author of a book on women's labour in the earlier Stalinist period: Jarska 2015.

5 Goldfarb 1982, 79.

demands thus centered on a repeal of the price hikes and wage increases. Tension in the Łódź textile factories had been growing for some time, but the workers were both fearful of the violence that had put an end to the strikes in the north and hopeful that the power shift which saw Władysław Gomułka replaced by Edward Gierek on 20 December 1970 would bring about positive results.

Gierek, however, insisted on going through with the hike in food prices after entering office, and the Łódź weavers—many of whom were single mothers—were left in a financially untenable situation. Since weaving was considered a "light industry," they earned on average 20 percent less than their colleagues engaged in "heavy industry," like shipbuilding on the Baltic Sea coast.[6] Moreover, the machinery they used was extremely outdated, and health and safety measures were ineffective. Historian Krzysztof Lesiakowski estimates that 40 percent of the machines had been produced before World War Two, and 20 percent before the First. In addition to servicing obsolete equipment, Lesiakowski notes that the weavers inevitably worked in spaces characterized by extremely loud noise, poor ventilation, and high temperatures.[7] The additional burden placed on women once they reached home was even acknowledged internally by the party. The March 1971 government report on the strikes noted "the firmness and persistence" of the workers in defending their right to a raise. It estimated that 70 to 80 percent of those striking were women, adding that "the sensitivity and emotional nature of the women, aggravated by difficult living conditions—carrying the load of work, responsibility for the home, and family duties, compounded by the underdeveloped state of numerous services in the city as well as poor housing—has led to the escalation of their demands and [their] increased determination."[8]

On 10 February 1971 at noon, four hundred weavers stopped their machines at the Marchlewski Cotton Mill. Within a few hours, 180 workers at the Stomil Shoe and Rubber Factory did the same. Since there could be no strikes in a socialist state, the Polish press agency would only vaguely gesture to "interruptions of work in some factories."[9] More and more workers followed suit each day. By 15 February, a total of fifty-five thousand workers were on strike, and the government was forced to give in. That evening, the government announced

6 Jarska 2011; Lesiakowski 2002, 133.

7 Lesiakowski 2002, 133.

8 Komitet Łódzki PZPR—Wydział Organizacyjny, "Ocena wydarzeń strajkowych w miesiącu lutym 1971 r. m. Łodzi" [Assessment of the February 1971 Strike Events in the City of Łódź], (March 1971). As cited by Matuszak 2011.

9 Feron 1971.

a repeal of the December 1970 food price hikes on the radio. The strike ended officially on 17 February. In the weeks that followed, however, party authorities worked to identify and punish the leaders of the strike, seeing to it that twenty-six workers at the Marchlewski plant and eleven at the "Defenders of the Peace" factory were removed from their posts.

Nevertheless, the 1970–1971 strikes managed to instill a fear of the working class in the party leadership, and Gierek spent the rest of the decade procuring international loans to buoy the Polish economy. In their speeches, Gierek and other party officials spoke of "an economic miracle," promoted "dynamic development," and claimed that Poland was the "eighth largest economic power in the world."[10] The media were encouraged to spread this "propaganda of success."[11] As a result, popular comedies and television programs began to feature consumer goods more prominently. This was true not only in Poland but across the socialist bloc. As Susan Reid has demonstrated, the Soviet Union "staked its legitimacy at home, and its credibility abroad, on its ability to provide its population with consumer goods and a decent standard of living" starting as early as the 1950s.[12] Anikó Imre has, in turn, powerfully argued that this general "shift from production to consumption and lifestyle in the competition with the West … moved the spotlight onto women as key agents of socialist citizenship."[13]

Though cinema was initially tasked with flaunting the supposed material abundance of socialist countries, by the late socialist period, popular comedies were openly satirizing its lack. Nowhere was the critique of the state's inability to provide for its citizens more biting, however, than in documentary. This was due in part to the *cinéma vérité* aesthetic that prevailed for much of this period, and in part to the fact that documentary, seen as a lesser cinematic form, was subjected to far less rigorous censorship. Documentary shorts would occasionally be screened before fiction films in theaters, but more often, they were shown exclusively in a small handful of art cinemas (*kina studyjne*), at festivals, and at special themed screening series. Consequently, it is hard to gauge the impact of these films, which were viewed mostly by a subsection of the country's intelligentsia. It is quite likely that it was minimal at best. But this does not negate their activist charge. Many documentarians saw their films as a means of bringing different strata of society into conversation with each other, drawing attention to festering problems, advocating for those in

10 Rokicki and Stępień 2009, 86; Taras 1983, 145.

11 Mazierska 2015, 124.

12 Reid 2002, 211.

13 Imre 2017, 93.

need and encouraging them to advocate for themselves. Though the films were viewed by a narrow audience, they did, on occasion, affect government policy.[14] As this chapter will show, they also had an important diagnostic function, identifying key tensions shortly before they would erupt in strikes.

Film scholars generally concur that there were many more women to be found in documentary rather than fiction filmmaking due to entrenched gender discrimination in the industry. The job of the fiction film director was seen as requiring a distinctly masculine form of authority, and women were rarely trusted with budgets as big as those for fiction films. The roster of Polish women fiction film directors during this period was short: Agnieszka Holland, Barbara Sass, Ewa Kruk. Yet for many women, documentary was not "second best" but an affirmative choice: they saw it as a tool to investigate social realities and promote concrete change. This chapter examines work by two of these courageous figures—Krystyna Gryczełowska and Irena Kamieńska—both of whom produced searing critiques of the state's treatment of women. In *The 24 Hours of Jadwiga L.* (*24 godziny Jadwigi L.*, 1967), Gryczełowska identified the deep-seated frustration that would give birth to the 1971 strike. In *Our Friends from Łódź* (*Nasze znajome z Łodzi*, 1971), she consciously set out to analyze it. Ten years later, in *Women Workers* (*Robotnice*, 1980), Irena Kamieńska would follow in Gryczełowska's footsteps, revealing just how little had changed in terms of the Łódź women's wages and working conditions nearly a decade later. Together, their films provide a model of the ways in which film was uniquely capable of documenting the so-called "double burden" of a full shift at the factory followed by a full shift at home and communicating the fatigue it engendered to the viewer. They also demonstrate how officially sanctioned narrative tropes and discourse could be turned on their head—and against the state.

1 Reinscribing Women Documentarians into Polish Film History

Irena Kamieńska was born in 1928; Krystyna Gryczełowska in 1931. Both belong to the same generation as Kazimierz Karabasz, born in 1930 and often described as the "father" of Polish documentary film. A number of factors contributed to the cementing of Karabasz's legacy. He assumed a directorial role immediately upon joining the Documentary Film Studio in Warsaw in the mid-1950s; taught at the Łódź Film School for countless years, where he was known as a kind and

14 One specific example is Krystyna Gryczełowska's film *Wola Rafałowska* (1966), named after the village in which it was shot. This film inspired the government to legislate heirless property (Strękowski 2008).

generous mentor; and reflected on his practice in several books. It has become customary now for historians of Polish documentary to situate all other figures in relation to "the School of Karabasz," a shorthand for his non-interventionist, fly-on-the-wall approach.

Kamieńska and Gryczełowska, together with Danuta Halladin, are considered to be leading documentary filmmakers of the same period, but they toiled in relative obscurity until the Polish National Audiovisual Institute digitized some of their films and released them on a combined DVD in 2008. In a booklet accompanying the films, Mikołaj Jazdon, a leading Polish film historian, argued that "it is difficult to imagine Polish documentary cinema without their films," though he was also quick to note that "they never created films together, neither were their achievements linked through a common denominator."[15] What the three did share, however, is an interest in working women's everyday life. Now that they have died, it is hard to know the exact nature of the challenges they faced. Gender discrimination may have played a part, or it may have been the "double burden" that would become the subject of several of their films. The fact remains that the women took longer to find their way. Gryczełowska wrote commentary for others' films before directing her first documentary in 1959. Kamieńska initially studied medicine and came to filmmaking late, enrolling at the Łódź Film School from 1958 to 1964 and graduating with her diploma in film in 1967. Though Danuta Halladin also made two short documentaries about women factory workers, she did so in the late 1980s, which places the films beyond the scope of this article.[16]

Regardless of when exactly they got their start, however, all were profoundly shaped by the so-called "Black Series": a flurry of documentary films produced roughly between 1956 and 1960, when Khrushchev's denunciation of Stalin generated a period of relative cultural liberalization. These short documentaries seized the opportunity to draw attention to previously unmentionable social problems such as alcoholism, prostitution, and dissolute youth. Intentionally didactic, the films saw themselves as critical interventions in social reality capable of effecting change in the world. The "Black Series" set the tone for much of Polish documentary to follow, establishing it as a mode of filmmaking deeply invested in probing—and ultimately improving—the social reality

15 Jazdon 2008.

16 Halladin's *They Were There* (*Były tam*, 1985) and *From Where to Where* (*Skąd-dokąd*, 1988) would continue to build on Gryczełowska and Kamieńska's approaches, with the former presenting testimony by women who had contributed to the building of an ideal workers' city, Nowa Huta, and the latter presenting a series of interviews with young women leaving the countryside for the factories about their hopes and fears.

in Poland. The women documentarians in particular would become known as fierce defenders of the marginalized and overlooked, developing their own subspecialties—Gryczełowska in portraits of peasants, the elderly, and women factory workers; Kamieńska—in portraits of women as such.

In interviews, Gryczełowska credited Italian neorealism with showing her that "it was possible to make a beautiful film about people in bleak circumstances."[17] It is perhaps this willingness to embrace desolation that separates both women's work most clearly from that of Karabasz, who in his own studies of factory workers, sought out moments of dignity and uplift. His most famous film, *The Musicians* (*Muzykanci,* 1960), for example, juxtaposed tramway car builders' movements at work with their gestures once they come together to practice as a factory orchestra. Gryczełowska's and Kamieńska's films are much bleaker—and, consequently, more rebellious. Their aim is not to help the viewer find some element of redemption in the contemporary Polish reality but to revolt against it. Therefore, they are also more polemical than exploratory, and their films are structured to convey a clear message about something that needs to be urgently addressed. As Gryczełowska herself would later say, "our films paid attention to those who were in need and whose situation required intervention."[18] In 1967, she would turn her attention to working mothers worn down by the dual demands of work and home.

1.1 24 Hours in the Life of Jadwiga L. (*1968*)

Films about women's labour were nothing new in the socialist bloc. Indeed, socialist realist ideological vehicles, from the Soviet *The Radiant Path* (*Светлый путь,* 1940) to its Polish equivalent *Adventure at Mariensztadt* (*Przygoda na Mariensztacie,* 1954), found it advantageous to depict the emergence of a socialist consciousness through the experience of women. Their protagonists—women engaged in reproductive labour in the countryside—would become open to the possibility of industrial labour through a chance encounter with an attractive, already socially conscious man. They would move to the city and begin working, proving their worth through sheer effort and willpower. Eventually, their success in official worker competitions would bring them both public acclaim and the love and admiration of the men who had set them on this path. These films communicated two promises to women viewers: first, that a move from agricultural or domestic work in the village to industrial work in the city would necessarily lead to social advancement; and,

17 Gryczełowska 1975a. As quoted in Strękowski 2008.
18 Gryczełowska 1975b. As translated and quoted in Duda 2014.

second, that professional success would go hand-in-hand with personal fulfillment. They inevitably ended with the newly formed couple standing in front or on top of their accomplishments and gazing out hopefully into the future. One can't help but wonder whether the reason these films never pushed past the "happily ever after," never addressed married life, had to do with the central questions of domestic labour: who would do it when both partners came home exhausted from a full shift at work? And who would take on the additional load once children came into the picture?[19]

The "double burden," of course, was by no means unique to state socialist countries, nor did state policy adhere to a clear East-West divide. In Western Europe, concern for working mothers seems to have peaked twice in the course of the twentieth century: in the 1920s, as a result of women socialists and trade unionists' tireless campaigns for women's rights, and in the years immediately following World War Two, when freshly victorious labour governments ushered in the welfare state. Inevitably, more radical suggestions, such as Norwegian socialists' push for a "mothers' wage" in the late 1910s and 1920s, when adopted, were rebranded as policies that benefited children rather than mothers (in this particular case as "child's allowance").[20] Still, there was a growing recognition, particularly in the immediate postwar period, of the need for the state to provide at least a modicum of child care (if not relief from domestic work) so women could join or continue in the work force. This was the case in Western Europe only, of course, and not in the United States, where government policy actively sought to encourage women who had begun working as part of the war effort to return to full-time homemaking and child-rearing.

What was unique to state-socialist countries was thus not the fact of the double burden itself but rather the cognitive dissonance between the official state line on this question and the reality on the ground. When the Bolsheviks first took power, establishing the Soviet Union, they made gender equality a central tenet, granting women the right to work outside the home and promising to transform domestic duties—described by Lenin himself as "barbaric, unproductive, petty, enervating, stupefying, and depressing"—into collective remunerated labour.[21] As scholars Natalia Roudakova and Deborah

19 Film scholar Ewa Mazierska points out that children were "practically absent from Polish socialist realist films, as [was] the case with other Eastern European cinemas of the time." She suggests this might be because "the presence of children might undermine the idea that work is the most important thing in the lives of both men and women" (Mazierska 2017, 119).

20 Seip and Ibsen 1994.

21 Morvant 1995; Hannson and Lidén 1983. As quoted in Roudakova and Ballard-Reisch 1999, 21.

Ballard-Reisch explain, however, "the plans were never fully realized due to 'more urgent problems.'"[22] In particular, the demands of industrialization in the 1930s, the need to increase the birth rate, and Stalin's personal preference for traditional family structures meant that, in Brigitte Studer's words, "the regime had formalized women's 'double burden' long before the model became established in the industrialized West."[23] In the 1950s and 1960s, the Soviet government and the governments of the Central and Eastern European satellite states committed to more robust maternity leave policies as well as a network of day cares and kindergartens that would allow mothers to remain in the workforce. Through these measures, the question of gender equality was largely believed to have been resolved—despite frequent food and consumer good shortages, the lack of household appliances, and, generally, a rudimentary approach to the domestic economy that made the running of a household much more labour intensive than in more developed Western countries.[24]

The misery of working mothers, therefore, remained an open but unspoken secret, seen as both too prosaic to be worthy of public interest and too threatening since it undermined one of the regime's proudest claims. Even the documentaries that succeeded the socialist realist fairy tales of the 1960s tended to focus on the less problematic portion of the female population: young, unmarried women. These films fell largely into two groups: portraits of young women excited to be starting their professional lives (such as Danuta Halladin's *At Rosa's from 6 to 11* (*U Róży od 6-ej do 11-ej*, 1963) and Karabasz's *Krystyna M.* (1973)); and those that sought to bring attention to the largely all-women provincial textile centers where it was nearly impossible for women to meet a partner and start a family in the first place (such as Helena Amiradżibi's *Zambrów* (1962) and Irena Kamieńska's *Island of Women* (*Wyspa kobiet*, 1968)).

In this fictional and documentary film landscape, Gryczełowska's *The 24 Hours of Jadwiga L.* stood out as a film that dared to portray a long festering but unacknowledged problem. It is impossible to know whether Gryczełowska had seen Croatian director Krešimir Golik's documentary *From 3am to 10pm* (*Od 3 do 22*), produced a year and a half earlier in 1966, or whether the two

22 Roudakova and Ballard-Reisch 1999, 21.

23 Studer 2015, 133.

24 Access to appliances and labour-saving devices, of course, differed widely across the West. So, too, did women's working and living conditions within the Soviet bloc. For more on the specificities of "the double burden" across state socialist countries, see Massino 2019; Bonfiglioli 2017; Corrin 1992; Edmondson 1992; and Buckley 1989. For a fascinating comparison of women's everyday lives across the East/West divide in Central Europe, see Fodor 2003.

FIGURE 14.1 Krystyna Gryczełowska
SOURCE: PHOTOGRAPH (FILMOTEKA NARODOWA—INSTYTUT AUDIOWIZUALNY [POLISH NATIONAL FILM ARCHIVE—AUDIOVISUAL INSTITUTE], 1-P-248-6)

films' release in close succession speaks to the urgency of the issue across the region.[25] Whatever the case, Gryczełowska follows the same model, condensing a day in the life of an average woman worker into fourteen minutes. The titular Jadwiga works the night shift in a factory. The work she does there is presented as a Sisyphean task: we see her and the all-female team of workers ceaselessly performing a single, repetitive gesture: pulling and cutting what appear to be long rolls of wire. We are never informed what purpose they serve, nor is there any suggestion that the women ever get to see the finished product. Consequently, there seems to be little or no distinction between the rote gestures Jadwiga performs at the factory and those she performs at home as she cooks, irons, cleans, and cares for her husband and three children. Except for two short naps, Jadwiga is perpetually in motion, each one of her actions motivated only by the need to sustain life. While we see her husband watching television, Jadwiga does not have a moment to spare, to dedicate to play or

25 For an excellent analysis and historical contextualization of Golik's film, see Bonfiglioli 2017. I am grateful to Alexandra Ghiţ for alerting me to the existence of this film and Bonfiglioli's article.

pleasure. Worse, as the title and structure of the film suggest, she is bound to repeat the same routine day after day in an endless cycle.

Gryczełowska films her protagonist in unglamorous medium shots, much like the Belgian filmmaker Chantal Akerman would film her protagonist in the now-canonical feminist masterpiece *Jeanne Dielman, 23 quai du Commerce, 1080 Bruxelles* (1975). For the most part, she allows Jadwiga to occupy the center of the frame, filming her from the mid-thigh up. The only exception to this are the repeated close-ups of Jadwiga's legs and those of her co-workers at the factory which, in film scholar Paulina Duda's words, "emphasize how their sensual function is undermined by physical weariness."[26] Indeed, the film opens with a starkly lit close-up of Jadwiga pulling stockings over her legs while an actual *film noir* plays off-screen on the television. This shot introduces the idea of a sensual *femme fatale* that the rest of the film goes on to undercut. Where the *femme fatale* is typically active, Jadwiga seems to passively drift along, driven onward by sheer momentum; where the *femme fatale* attracts dramatic events, Jadwiga's life is an unending expanse of repetition and routine; finally, where the body of the *femme fatale* is an end in and of itself, Jadwiga's body is only ever a means—of production and (social) reproduction. In this way, that single opening shot primes us to approach Jadwiga's life critically, in terms of everything it is—and is not.

The soundtrack, too, plays an important role in emphasizing how Jadwiga has been brutalized—reduced to sheer animal life. Except for the dialogue of the off-screen *film noir*, a quick goodbye to her husband, and some words exchanged with colleagues during their break, we never get a proper verbal sequence. There is no voice-over to tell us what to think or any music, diegetic or non-diegetic, to add a moment of lightness. What the film offers instead is wall-to-wall bangs, clangs, hisses, creaks, and clinks. This auditory starkness reinforces the idea of a hostile, bleak world in which Jadwiga is but one machine among others.

Everything about the film, from Jadwiga's abbreviated name in the title to the twenty-four-hour structure drives home the idea that the film is not about this particular woman but rather about all the women she represents. This is a clever move on Gryczełowska's part. The official task of socialist realist art had been to present the "typical" person—in a highly idealized way. Here, Gryczełowska turns this officially sanctioned narrative structure into a tool of critique simply by adopting it all too earnestly—by doing exactly what the

26 Duda 2014.

form presumed but never really dared to do. She shows the life of a working woman as it is rather than as it was supposed to be.

Though Jadwiga is not a weaver and the film does not address prices, it nevertheless gives a tangible form to the frustrations that would, three years later, drive the women of Łódź into the streets. Moreover, it goes beyond merely naming the double burden: it draws on the specific affordances of cinema as a medium to make that exhaustion felt. The careful framing and the minimalist soundtrack combine to give viewers at least some sense of the indignities and hardships Jadwiga endures daily. Consequently, it draws our attention to the way submission and resistance play out not just in the public sphere but in everyday life. As historian Padraic Kenney writes, "we need to consider how women and men experienced communism and ask whether the denial of free organizations and censorship were the most painful repressions or whether the experience of communism at home or in the streets and stores was equally impelling."[27] Gryczełowska's film, in documenting the meaningless toil at the factory, the time wasted in grocery store lines, and the ceaseless work of home-making, makes a strong case for the latter.

Surprisingly, given its trenchant critique, the film was not shelved and even received a small number of reviews in the press; these were rather mixed, however. The journal *Film Magazine* (*Magazyn Filmowy*) was effusive in its praise:

> Daily responsibilities, troubles, and problems do not often make their way into the cinema, even in documentary. Filmmakers usually look for the exceptional, the impressive, the shocking. Meanwhile, everyday life can also be a touching and important topic. [...] The camera accompanies Jadwiga when she goes to work late in the evening, observes her in the factory, records conversations during break, the general weariness as the dawn approaches. And then home—sending the children off to school, shopping for groceries, cleaning, preparing lunch, a brief nap, lunch all together, [...] washing up, some rest, and again to work. Life is not easy. [...] For a long time we have not had a documentary film which, in taking up a socially just cause, would be so full of informational content.[28]

Camera (*Kamera*) magazine, in the meantime, recognized the documentary as the portrait of a "typical woman" that "very realistically portrays everyday life" but argued that presenting "truth and only the truth ... is not enough."

---

27 Kenney 1999, 400.
28 "24 godziny Jadwigi L." 1968.

The review accused the film of lacking “some kind of dramaturgy” and the filmmaker of luxuriating in “objectified observation from a distance”—of not expressing a clear take on the material. As a result of this, the review noted, the film “lacked focus” and failed to “pull the viewer into the orbit of the issues and problems” presented.[29] Janusz Skwara, in a 1978 article synthesizing different portrayals of labour on screen, would similarly miss the point. While he praised the film as being “highly unusual for its time,” he shifted the blame onto the protagonist, “a woman unable to sensibly fit together her official work and her housework,” and the “overly primitive conditions in the industrial plant of the sixties as well as obvious defects in the economy at large.” That reviewers could interpret the film in so many different ways paradoxically speaks to one of its key strengths: in refusing any kind of narration, Gryczełowska moved away from the authoritarian subordination of the image to a predetermined message. This allowed those who were receptive to the film’s critique to hear it, and those who were not (censors and regime-friendly reviewers) to allow it to slip by unhindered.

1.2 Our Friends from Łódź (*1971*)

Gryczełowska’s subsequent film, *Our Friends From Łódź,* was shot immediately in the aftermath of the 1971 strikes and would make clear that the women’s misery was not their fault but that of a state that underpaid and exploited them, as well as a patriarchal culture that insisted on viewing housework as “women’s work.” This time around, the director sought to address not just a particular stage in a woman’s life—which, after all, one could argue might get easier once the children are grown—but the way in which the overall arc of her life, from youth to late middle age, was predetermined. The film consists of three mini-portraits: of a young woman just starting out in professional life, a single mother with three young children, and a middle-aged woman with grown daughters. Each one is identified by a title card bearing her first name only: Urszula, Helena, Genowefa. Gryczełowska again stays away from voice-of-God narration that tells the viewer what to think, using the medium instead to foreground the women’s voices. One cannot help but wonder if Jadwiga’s silence, meant to convey how beaten down and hopeless she feels, has given way to a somewhat greater sense of agency in the wake of the strikes—or at least a tangible need to help the women speak, and to listen. Indeed, Ostrowska, in her study of the filmic representation of Łódz textile workers, singles the film out as the only one “in which the female protagonists openly articulate

29 “Dzień—jak co dzień” 1969.

FIGURE 14.2 Irena Kamieńska
SOURCE: PHOTOGRAPH (FILMOTEKA NARODOWA—INSTYTUT AUDIOWIZUALNY [POLISH NATIONAL FILM ARCHIVE—AUDIOVISUAL INSTITUTE], 1-F-3103-33)

themselves expressing their dissatisfaction with their work and the quality of their lives."[30]

As one might expect, the nineteen-year-old Urszula is full of hope and desires "a concrete" profession far from the factory, "a good husband, a beautiful apartment with nice furniture," and "two children, twins: two boys." The older women are increasingly tired and bitter. Helena speaks of her exhaustion and her inability to give her children a decent standard of living; Genowefa—about the debilitating physical effects of her many years at the factory, her frustration with the lack of help from her husband, and her hope that if they go to university, her daughters might escape her fate. Though the personalities of the three women are quite different, it is clear that they are meant to be read simultaneously as three separate individuals and three stages in a composite individual's life. Though Urszula, the youngest, may be full of optimism, the film implies that it won't last long—she is bound to move through the same stages as Helena and Genowefa; the factory labour that she now sees as a temporary way to earn a livelihood while looking for romance will soon become

30 Ostrowska 2017, 17.

a permanent yoke. Film scholar Justyna Jaworska also points out the ironic parallel between the Ancient Greek Moirai—the Three Fates who spun, dispensed, and cut the thread of life, and Gryczełowska's three weavers who have no agency over their own fate.[31]

Where socialist realism had promised women empowerment and self-determination, *Our Friends From Łódź* demonstrates just how few options are available to them in reality. In the weaving capital of Poland, employment is largely limited to the main industry in town; in a patriarchal society with double standards, romantic choices are limited to living with men who refuse to help, like Genowefa, or, like Helena, living without them. What is worse, the film argues that the system takes away not only the women's hopes and sense of agency but also their physical health and their most rudimentary sense of self. Each of the three portraits sketches out a stage in the arc of the women's progressive alienation from their own bodies. Gryczełowska interviews Urszula as she gets ready to go out: she shares her dreams for the future as she brushes her hair and applies make-up, drawing attention to the body as an object. In addition to seeing Urszula at work, we also follow her to a dance class in the park. As Ostrowska notes, this scene is "less about the objectification of the female body" than "about the reclamation of her body from the (communist) regime of work."[32] Indeed, Urszula seems at her happiest and least self-conscious in this scene.

If Urszula's body is a sexualized body still capable of pleasure, Ostrowska argues, then Helena's body is "almost exclusively … a maternal body" defined by her relationship to her children, and Genowefa's is a "sick body," defined by her various medical conditions.[33] The film's suggestion is clear: the sense of autonomy Urszula feels over her body, her ability to "shake off" the stultifying postures of factory labour, is temporary: as time goes on, her body will be increasingly instrumentalized until, like Jadwiga L.'s, it is only a means and not an end in and of itself. Polish film scholar Justyna Jaworska also notes that the women's hair in the three segments becomes an important symbol of their aspirations and priorities. While Urszula spends a long time styling hers, Helena and Genowefa wear theirs short: a concession to their lack of time and interest in romance.[34]

The soundtrack again works in concert with the image to affirm the filmmaker's message. As Jaworska writes:

31 Jaworska 2017.
32 Ostrowska 2017, 9.
33 Ostrowska 2017, 11.
34 Jaworska 2017.

> Here is the twenty-year-old talking in the first person about herself ... The thirty-year-old, silent at the looms, but in the scene in which she feeds her children shifts from the first person to the third ("mummy will give you more bread"), as if motherhood, this sphere of intimacy and freedom after hours of alienating work, cut her off from herself. Finally, Genowefa speaks again in the first person, but always from a distance while we see her work, which she has been doing silently for years. This is, to parody Guy Debord, "complete alienation"—the separation of the voice from the suffering body, understood now only as an appendage of the machine.[35]

These shifts endow Gryczełowska's decision to use a different documentary mode in each segment of the film with additional meaning. Urzula's ability to speak directly into the camera suggests that her body and sense of self are still indivisible. Helena has begun losing ownership of her body, as work and children lay claim to it. Genowefa, finally, seems to float above her deteriorating and seemingly doomed body. She has given up on it and now dispassionately observes herself going through the motions from above.

Gryczełowska was explicit that it was the first set of strikes on the Baltic Sea Coast that drew her to this subject. In an interview in *Film* magazine, she explained: "At the beginning of that year, I resolved to make a film about the life conditions of women textile workers; this was right after the 'December events'—it seemed a singularly relevant subject."[36] It is surprising then, that none of the women nor the film itself ever mention the subsequent strike in Łódź. Ostrowska writes that this was likely done intentionally to avoid censorship.[37] One piece of evidence supporting this argument is that Gryczełowska made another film that year, a recording of a visit by a representative of the new Gierek government to disgruntled peasants. Reflecting on this film and the simultaneously very political and bland title she gave it, *In February 1971 ...* Gryczełowska explained:

> The title could, and even should, say: "Five Weeks after December," but it's almost certain that the government censors wouldn't have liked that because after those few weeks, things were just beginning to feel 'OK' in the PRL [Polish People's Republic]. [...] The very word 'December' became something unseemly, along the same principle that in a house where someone has hung himself, you shouldn't speak of rope. And that

35 Jaworska. Unless otherwise noted, all translations are my own.

36 Gryczełowska 1971. As quoted in Strękowski 2008.

37 Ostrowska 2017, 11.

> was the beginning of the new, 'post-December' era. I was overcome with the desire to show even just a fragment of this new reality, but without stalling, [sought] to do it quickly, while everything was still fresh in the memory, while it was still right 'after the battle.'[38]

Doubtless, she felt the same way about the women's strike in Łódź. Addressing the issues that led to the strike rather than the strike itself proved a wise move as it allowed the film to be screened at the 1972 Krakow Film Festival, where it went on to win the Bronze Lajkonik, or third place, "for its unmediated presentation of the important social problem of working women."[39]

1.3 Women Workers (Robotnice, *1980*)

Urszula Tes, author of a monograph on Irena Kamieńska, argues that an interest in women and how they live permeates the filmmaker's whole oeuvre. Within that body of work, however, Tes identifies two distinct sub-streams: one featuring women who are "active and enthusiastic," who take control of their lives and try to improve the world around them, often despite great resistance; and a second, featuring women who are completely "resigned and joyless," who see no way out of their situation.[40] She places Kamieńska's breakthrough *Women Workers* (*Robotnice,* 1980) squarely in the latter category. The film is one of three in which Kamieńska examined the lives of women engaged in manual labour. The aforementioned *Island of Women* (*Wyspa kobiet,* 1968) sounded the alarm about young women's inability to get married and start families when confined to largely all-female industrial towns. *Day After Day* (*Dzień za dniem,* 1988), in turn, presented a bitter portrait of two women, twin sisters, at the other end of their professional careers as bricklayers and transporters. On the brink of retirement, the twins reflect on a lifetime of hard labour and the gap between official propaganda and daily reality.

Working Women, produced in between these two documentaries, features women of all different ages, though many of the ones who speak identify as mothers and appear to be in their thirties and forties. The film first shows the women at work and, later, on their break, presenting their complaints to the crew. In the observational scenes, Tes notes, everything is structured around dramatic juxtapositions.[41] Visually, cinematographer Krzysztof Pakulski chose to use high-contrast black-and-white film and to alternate extreme wide shots

38 Krystyna Gryczełowska, in Janicka and Kołodyński 2000. As quoted in Strękowski 2008.
39 "Nasze Znajome z Łodzi" 2022.
40 Tes 2019, 39.
41 Tes 2019, 41.

that give us a sense of the damp and dust-filled factory spaces, with close-ups of the women's swollen feet and bandaged hands. The result are images deeply reminiscent of Lewis Hine's photography, suggesting that not much has changed—not only since the 1970–1971 strikes but also since the turn of the century. Aurally, too, the din of the machines counters the women's stern silence as they work.

In the break scenes, however, the women do not hesitate to voice their complaints. They explain that they had asked the factory management for very basic material improvements: lighter protective gear to replace their heavy aprons, comfortable shoes to replace their wooden clogs, efficient masks that would allow them to breathe, soap and warm water for showers, as well as buses on Saturdays to make it possible for them to get to work without having to walk for miles. The management, however, had dismissed all these demands. As Kamieńska herself would later put it, "they felt humiliated, not so much by the conditions in which they were forced to work—the dust, the moisture, the noise, the stench, the terribly primitive conditions—than by the attitude adopted toward them, their needs, and their assertions by the local establishment, the management of the plant, and the Party bosses."[42]

Women Workers is more preoccupied with working conditions and the authorities' unwillingness to listen to workers in what is ostensibly a workers' state than the "double burden" as such. Unlike in Gryczełowska's films, we never get to follow the women home. The concerns they voice, however, are very much defined by it: how to feed their children on their tiny salaries, and how to manage taking care of them while still getting to work on time given deficiencies in transportation. Yet the film is worth considering here because, like Gryczełowska's films, it was produced in close proximity to another massive wave of strikes. Kamieńska shot *Women Workers* in the small town of Krosno, near the Ukrainian border, in February 1980. In August of that same year, the Gdańsk Shipyards would be up in arms again over a new set of price hikes, initiating a nationwide revolt. In this strike, too, women would play a key role only to be erased before the first accounts of the events were even written. It was the dismissal of a woman—the hero of labour turned opposition activist Anna Walentynowicz—from her post that sparked this second wave of strikes.[43] And it was Walentynowicz and other women like her who closed

42 "Świadomy wybór" [A conscious decision] 1981, 12. As quoted in Tes 2019, 40.

43 Interestingly, Walentynowicz explained in an interview with the nonfiction writer Hanna Krall that she was first motivated to speak out against injustice when she saw that the Women's League (with which she was involved) was perennially being cheated of funds by the shipyard leadership. The interview was set to appear in *Polityka* magazine in

the shipyard gates at the end of the first day, urging the workers to stay on and continue the strike as well as to transform it from a strike about "bread" into something bigger.[44] But despite women's contributions—recently excavated and documented in Kristi Long's, Shana Penn's, and Marta Dzido's accounts—they would be kept out of the leadership of the newly-formed Solidarity trade union.[45]

Gryczełowska and Kamieńska intentionally chose to concentrate on the conditions that necessitated activism rather than women's activism itself. Their films, however, captured not only the conditions but also the emotions—frustration, indignation, anger—that moved women workers in 1971 and 1980 to turn off their machines and go on strike. The record of women's labour activism was, thus, arguably better preserved in their films than in the historical accounts that would follow. And if the first two films were not widely viewed, *Women Workers* was eventually able to enjoy a glorious reception. The film was produced in February 1980, the same time as Marcel Łoziński's daring *Microphone Test* (*Próba mikrofonu*). For that film, Łoziński recruited the DJ of the internal radio station at the Pollena-Uroda make-up factory, which also employed primarily women. The DJ, Michał, spent several days interviewing his colleagues about whether they felt like co-managers of the factory, in accordance with state doctrine. He then presented the factory leadership with a tape of the workers' disgruntled answers. If Kamieńska's film had taken the first step toward confrontation in presenting the women's unabashed complaints, Łoziński went a step further, filming the authorities' reactions to this log of irreverent griping. Where the earlier documentaries had operated within what scholar Bill Nichols has termed the "observational" mode of documentary, Kamieńska and Łoziński, sensing the political situation shifting, were intuitively driven to experiment with the "participatory" mode.[46] Their films not only acknowledged the presence of the camera—they used it as a catalyst to provoke situations and initiate conversations that otherwise would not take place. In this way, their films become exercises in democracy and free speech. For both Kamieńska and Łoziński, the task of the filmmaker was no longer to present a thoughtful, delicate, and uplifting portrait, as in Karabasz's work, or even a carefully constructed *j'accuse!*, as in Gryczełowska's. It was to use the

October 1980 but was censored. *Polityka* placed a digital copy of it online in February 2017. Krall 2017.

44 Walentynowicz 1985.

45 See Dzido 2014; Penn 2006 and Long 1996.

46 Nichols 2017.

film as both a megaphone to amplify workers' voices and an arena for direct confrontation with the state.[47]

2 Conclusion

It is not surprising that both *Women Workers* and *Microphone Test* were immediately shelved upon completion. Solidarity's victory in August 1980, however, initiated a miraculous period of eighteen months when previously censored works could finally be shown and circulated. Both films were taken off the shelves and screened at the Gdańsk film festival already at the end of that month, and then again on television on 28 September 1980.[48] Nine months later, *Women Workers* was awarded the Grand Prix at the 1981 Krakow Film Festival, beating out, as the newspapers noted, 101 films from twenty-nine countries.[49] Picking up on a term very much in vogue in the West, critic Alicja Iskierko praised the film as a rare "look from below" at the world of labour.[50] "Where reality cries out, the artist chooses restraint," she wrote. "The only commentary accompanying these images of women's daily hell are their own words, slippery and saturated with more of a sense of hopelessness than anger, words uttered between a bite of bread with jam and a sip of tea from a jar," adding that what we see on screen "is not work; it is hard labour."[51]

The film provided Solidarity and its supporters with incontrovertible evidence of the inhumane conditions in which many Polish workers toiled before August 1980. As critic Maria Malatyńska wrote at the time, "A face, hands, feet thrown directly at the viewer say more about how a person is treated than even the most ardent speeches at a rally."[52] One cannot help but wonder if the film would have been as effective in this evidentiary capacity had the workers on screen been male. Focusing on women allowed Gryczełowska and Kamieńska to advocate for some of the most silenced and heavily oppressed members of society; this focus also served as a unique tool for pushing back against the state. Like the striking women of Łódź, the filmmakers sensed that, on the

47 Łoziński's film is set in a largely female make-up factory, so his film can also be said to engage in elevating women's voices, though the issues they raise are not as gender-specific as in Gryczełowska and Kamieńska's films.

48 "Próba demokracji"1980.

49 "'Robotnice' zdobyły 'Złotego Smoka'" 1981; "Grand Prix dla polskiego filmu 'Robotnice'" 1981; "Grand Prix dla filmu 'Robotnice'" 1981.

50 Iskierko 1980.

51 Iskierko 1980.

52 Strękowski 2003.

one hand, the authorities would not take a film about women workers and their complaints as seriously as those of men, perhaps allowing the film to pass through uncensored, while on the other hand, the authorities knew they would look like monsters if they tried to publicly deny the women's claims. Emphasizing women's dual role as workers and mothers turned the patriarchal nature of Polish society to the women's advantage, as they were seen to be petitioning not only for themselves but on behalf of their children. In this way, the films contributed to activists' search for the rhetorical means that would be most effective in the context of state socialism.

By then, the "double burden" was a fact acknowledged by all social actors: the party, the opposition, and women themselves. In 1977, even a figure as iconic as the labour hero Wanda Gościmińska would feel free to publicly state: "When one got home after a day of drudgery beside machines and an afternoon meeting, one still had to take care of the cooking and cleaning ... One thought only about how to endure and not fall asleep, and how Sunday could not come sooner."[53] In 1981, Solidarity leaders, too, would openly acknowledge that "the acquisition of food has become for women [workers] a second shift."[54] The drivers of this transformation were doubtless the strikes themselves and the political actions that accompanied them. The films produced in and around the strikes by Gryczełowska and Kamieńska, however, helped identify everyday life—not industrial production, the space race, or some other part of the public sphere—as the site where the communist project had failed.

Bibliography

"24 godziny Jadwigi L" [The 24 hours of Jadwiga L.]. 1968. *Magazyn Filmowy* [Film magazine] 1.

Będkowski, Leszek. 1981. "Dlaczego do protestu doszło w Łodzi: Drugi dzień akcji 'Solidarności'" [How it came to the protest in Łódź: Second day of Solidarity's actions]. *Życie Warszawy* [Warsaw Life], 29 July 1981.

Bonfiglioli, Chiara. 2017. "A Working Day That Has No End: The Double Burden in Socialist Yugoslavia." *Themenportal Europäische Geschichte* [Thematic portal of European history]. https://www.europa.clio-online.de/essay/id/fdae-1705.

Buckley, Mary E. A. 1989. *Women and Ideology in the Soviet Union*. Ann Arbor: University of Michigan Press.

53 Gościmińska 1977.

54 Będkowski 1981.

Corrin, Chris, ed. 1992. *Superwomen and the Double Burden: Women's Experience of Change in Central and Eastern Europe and the Former Soviet Union.* Toronto: Second Story Press.

Duda, Paulina. 2014. "A Conceptual Documentarian of the Needy: Krystyna Gryczełowska's Documentaries." *East European Film Bulletin* 48, December. https://eefb.org/retrospectives/krystyna-gryczelowskas-documentaries/.

Dzido, Marta. 2014. *Solidarność według kobiet* [Solidarity according to women]. Documentary film.

"Dzień—jak codzień" [Day after day]. 1969. *Kamera* [Camera] 4.

Edmondson, Linda, ed. 1992. *Women and Society in Russia and the Soviet Union.* Cambridge: Cambridge University Press.

Feron, James. 1971. "Polish Leaders Act to End Strike." *New York Times,* 15 February 1971. https://www.nytimes.com/1971/02/15/archives/polish-leaders-act-to-end-strike-lodz-textile-workers-told-by.html.

Fidelis, Małgorzata. 2010. *Women, Communism, and Industrialization in Postwar Poland.* Cambridge: Cambridge University Press.

Fodor, Éva. 2003. *Working Difference: Women's Working Lives in Hungary and Austria 1945–1995.* Durham, NC: Duke University Press.

Goldfarb, Jeffrey C. 1982. *On Cultural Freedom: An Exploration of Public Life in Poland and America.* Chicago, IL: University of Chicago Press.

Gościmińska, Wanda. 1977. "Nie byliśmy z pomników" [We weren't like the monuments]. *Trybuna Ludu* [People's tribune] 121, 24 May 1977.

"Grand Prix dla polskiego filmu 'Robotnice'" [Grand Prix for the Polish film *Women Workers*]. 1981. *Życie Warszawy* [Warsaw life] 132, 8 June 8, 1981.

"Grand Prix dla filmu 'Robotnice'" [Grand Prix for the film *Women Workers*]. 1981. *Trybuna Ludu* [People's tribune] 133, 8 June 1981.

Gryczełowska, Krystyna. 1975a. *Film* 16.

Gryczełowska, Krystyna. 1975b. "Wywiad z Krystyną Gryczełowską" [Interview with Krystyna Gryczełowska]. *Film* 22.

Gryczełowska, Krystyna. 1971. *Film* 36.

Hannson, Carola, and Karin Lidén. 1983. *Moscow Women: Thirteen Interviews.* New York: Parthenon Books.

Imre, Anikó. 2017. "Gender Socialism, and European Film Cultures." In *The Routledge Companion to Cinema and Gender*, edited by Kristin Lené Hole, Dijana Jelača, E. Ann Kaplan, and Patrice Petro, 88–98. London: Routledge.

Iskierko, Alicja. 1980. "Widok z dołu" [View from below]. *Ekran* [Screen] 30, 21 September 1980.

Janicka, Bożena, and Andrzej Kołodyński. 2000. *Chełmska 21: 50 lat Wytwórni Filmów Dokumentalnych i Fabularnych w Warszawie.* [Chełmska 21: 50 years of the documentary and feature film studio in Warsaw]. Warsaw: Documentary and Feature Film Studio.

Jarska, Natalia. 2015. *Kobiety z marmuru: Robotnice w Polsce w latach 1945–1960* [Women of marble: Women workers in Poland, 1945–1960]. Warsaw: Institute of National Remembrance.

Jarska, Natalia. 2011. "Zapomniany bunt: kobiety wygrały z Gierkiem" [The forgotten rebellion: The women won against Gierek]. *Tygodnik Powszechny* [Universal weekly], 17 April 2011. https://www.tygodnikpowszechny.pl/zapomniany-bunt-kobiety-wygraly-z-gierkiem-140706.

Jaworska, Justyna. 2017. "Urszula, Helena, Genowefa. Tryby narracji w *Naszych znajomych z Łodzi*" [Urszula, Helena, Genowefa: Modes of narration in *Our Friends from Łódź*]. *Pleograf. Kwartalnik Akademii Polskiego Filmu* [Pleograf: The quarterly magazine of the Polish Film Academy] 3. https://akademiapolskiegofilmu.pl/pl/historia-polskiego-filmu/artykuly/urszula-helena-genowefa-tryby-narracji-w-naszych-znajomych-z-lodzi/610.

Jazdon, Mikołaj. 2008. Booklet accompanying "Polska Szkoła Dokumentu. Gryczełowska / Kamieńska / Halladin" [The Polish school of documentary: Gryczełowska / Kamieńska / Halladin], DVD. Warsaw: Polskie Wydawnictwo Audiowizualne.

Kenney, Padraic. 2012 [1997]. *Rebuilding Poland: Workers and Communists, 1945–1950.* Ithaca, NY: Cornell University Press.

Kenney, Padraic. 1999. "The Gender of Resistance in Communist Poland." *American Historical Review* 104, no. 1 (April): 399–425.

Krall, Hanna. 2017. "Ludzie może i nie są źli" [People maybe aren't evil]. *Polityka* [Politics], February 2017. https://www.polityka.pl/tygodnikpolityka/60/1694782,1,prezentujemy-archiwalny-reportaz-hanny-krall.read.

Lesiakowski, Krzysztof. 2002. "Strajk robotników łódzkich w lutym 1971 roku" [Łódź workers' strike in February 1971]. *Pamięć i sprawiedliwość* [Memory and justice] 1: 133–142.

Lewis, Jane. 1994. "Models of Equality for Women: The Case of State Support for Children in Twentieth-century Britain." In *Maternity and the Rise of the European Welfare States, 1880s-1950s,* edited by Gisela Bock and Pat Thane, 73–93. London: Routledge.

Long, Kristi S. 1996. *We All Fought for Freedom: Women in Poland's Solidarity Movement.* Boulder, CO: Westview Press.

Massino, Jill. 2019. *Ambiguous Transitions: Gender, the State, and Everyday Life in Socialist and Postsocialist Romania.* New York and Oxford: Berghahn Books.

Matuszak, Grzegorz. 2011. "Zapomniane strajki" [Forgotten strikes]. *Historie Łódzkie—historia Łodzki* [*Łódź Stories—History of Łódź*]. 20 November 2011. http://www.historialodzi.obraz.com.pl/zapomniane-strajki/.

Mazierska, Ewa. 2017. *Poland Daily: Economy, Work, Consumption and Social Class in Polish Cinema.* New York and Oxford: Berghahn Books.

Mazierska, Ewa. 2015. *From Self-Fulfilment to Survival of the Fittest: Work in European Cinema from the 1960s to the Present.* New York and Oxford: Berghahn Books.

Morvant, P. 1995. "Bearing the 'Double Burden' in Russia." *Transition* 9, no. 8: 4–9.

"Nasze Znajome z Łodzi" [Our friends from Łódź]. Accessed 17 May 2022. www.filmpolski.pl.

Nichols, Bill. 2017 [2001]. *Introduction to Documentary.* Bloomington: Indiana University Press.

Ostrowska, Elżbieta. 2017. "Vanishing Women: Łódź Textile Workers in Polish Documentary Cinema." *Studies in Documentary Film* 11, no. 2: 121–140.

Penn, Shana. 2006. *Solidarity's Secret: the Women Who Defeated Communism in Poland.* Ann Arbor: University of Michigan.

"Próba demokracji" [An attempt at democracy]. 1980. *Kobieta i Życie* [Woman and life] 45, 9 November 1980.

Reid, Susan E. 2002. "Cold War in the Kitchen: Gender and the de-Stalinization of the Soviet Union under Khrushchev." *Slavic Review* 61, no. 2: 211–252.

"'Robotnice' zdobyły 'Złotego Smoka'" [*Women Workers* wins a "Golden Smok"]. 1981. *Kurier Polski* [Polish courier] 111, 8 June 1981.

Rokicki, Konrad, and Sławomir Stępień. 2009. *W objęciach Wielkiego brata: Sowieci w Polsce 1944–1993* [In the arms of big brother: The Soviets in Poland 1944–1993]. Warsaw: Institute of National Remembrance.

Roudakova, Natalia, and Deborah S. Ballard-Reisch. 1999. "Femininity and the Double Burden: Dialogues on the Socialization of Russian Daughters into Womanhood." *Anthropology of East Europe Review* 17, no. 1: 21–34.

Seip, Anne-Lise, and Hilde Ibsen. 1994. "Family Welfare, Which Policy? Norway's Road to Child Allowances." In *Maternity and the Rise of the European Welfare States, 1880s–1950s,* edited by Gisela Bock and Pat Thane, 40–60. London: Routledge.

Strękowski, Jan. 2003. "Irena Kamieńska." *www.culture.pl,* July 2003. https://culture.pl/pl/tworca/irena-kamienska.

Strękowski, Jan. 2008. "Krystyna Gryczełowska." *Culture.pl,* September 2008, https://culture.pl/en/artist/krystyna-gryczelowska.

Studer, Brigitte. 2015. "Communism and Feminism." Translated by Regan Kramer. *Clio. Women, Gender, History,* no. 41: 126–139.

"Świadomy wybór. Rozmowa z reż. Ireną Kamieńską" [A conscious choice: A conversation with Irena Kamieńska]. 1981. *Zwierciadło* [Mirror] 29.

Taras, Ray. 1983. *Ideology in a Socialist State: Poland 1956–1983.* Cambridge, MA: Harvard University Press.

Tes, Urszula. 2019. "Dokumentalne portrety kobiet w filmach Ireny Kamieńskiej" [Documentary portraits of women in Irena Kamieńska's films]. *Dziennikarstwo i Media* [Journalism and media] 10: 37–43.

Thane, Pat. 1994. "Visions of Gender in the Making of the British Welfare State: The Case of Women in the British Labour Party and Social Policy, 1906–1945." In *Maternity and the Rise of the European Welfare States, 1880s–1950s*, edited by Gisela Bock and Pat Thane, 93–119. London: Routledge.

Walentynowicz, Anna. 1985. "Don't Wait for Instructions: An Interview with Anna Walentynowicz." Translated by Teresa Hanicka and Kina Krzeczunowicz. *Polish Underground Extracts* 11, July 1985. http://storage.osaarchivum.org/low/b0/1e/b01e11f4-6474-4981-8630-39a3423d502e_l.pdf.

PART 3

Activist Travels through Changing Political Landscapes: The Uses of Life Histories

CHAPTER 15

Just Around the Corner

Women's Self-Organized Care for the Elderly before and after 1989 in East Germany, Poland, and the Czech Republic

Maren Hachmeister

Abstract

There is a long-term absence of attention to care work in the history of women's labour activism. This chapter places women caregivers center stage, highlighting their participation in the field of care. Using examples of elderly care in East Germany, Poland, and Czechoslovakia, it provides a comparison of care arrangements from the state-socialist period to the postsocialist transformation after 1989/1990. Findings from qualitative interviews provide more detailed insight into the East German case. Because women's care work was not accompanied by mainstream forms of protest—in contrast to women's labour in general—care activism has so far remained under-researched and under-conceptualized in gender and labour history. This chapter introduces the term "care activism," tracing different forms of small-scale or even the silent activism of women care workers, and thereby contributes to a more nuanced understanding of activism in general, and women's labour activism in particular.

Keywords

care activism – care work – Czech Republic – Czechoslovakia – elderly care – German Democratic Republic (GDR) – Poland – political transformation – post-socialism – self-organization – volunteerism

This chapter, as an experiment, discusses the work and commitment of women elder caregivers in three (post)socialist societies—or certain elements of this work and commitment—as activism. It is an experiment in so far as care for older people can take various forms, thus offering women different opportunities to "be an activist" or take action for some reason. First of all, paid nursing and institutional care comes to mind. Like other people who engage in paid work, employed caregivers, i.e., people engaged in paid nursing

 | DOI:10.1163/9789004682481_016

and institutional care, may participate in trade unions, become members of workplace-related groups, or submit complaints to their superiors. If necessary, they have several instruments at hand to express their dissatisfaction or to address problems before taking to the streets. More informal forms of care, such as care provided by families or voluntary helpers, however, lack such formalized frameworks to assert interests or engage in activism. In this chapter, I argue that care provided by voluntary helpers may also involve an activist dimension by exploring the ways in which women's labour activism appeared in the field of care work beyond paid employment.

Self-organized neighborhood and home-based care services were an extremely common way of providing care for older people in the state-socialist societies of East Central Europe.[1] Those who committed to such self-organized forms of caregiving have not yet received much attention in a history of women's labour, much less women's labour activism. Research on women's labour activism so far (and by no means less importantly) has devoted much attention to formal work and workplace relations, making visible, for instance, the tireless efforts of women trade unionists fighting for the needs of pregnant workers, mothers, and retirees within the structures of their workplaces.[2] In an attempt to capture cases and concerns of self-organized caregivers, I will more broadly address "care activism" in this chapter. By care activism, I mean patterns of thought and behavior closely related to care work.

In the transformation of socialist societies into postsocialist ones, care work involved mostly unpaid services performed by women, often on a part-time basis or during their "free" time. This included care for older people, which was provided informally by family members or, for example, in the form of home-based care services.[3] A number of studies in the fields of social anthropology and sociology have already addressed this topic.[4] An important finding has been that one can certainly speak of care *work* even if such work was not performed professionally and/or for money.[5] In a European history of work, as historian Marsha Siefert phrased it, diverse forms of work "have been shown to coexist with wage labour in different regional and temporal contexts, bringing their own underlying costs and demands."[6] Formal and informal arrangements of care work, I think, can be added to that list.

1 Dudová 2018, 43.
2 See Laczkó 2017.
3 Dudová 2018, 43.
4 See Robbins 2021; Kaźmierska and Waniek 2020; Kramer 2020; Janiak-Jasińska 2016.
5 Kohlen 2016, 192.
6 Siefert 2020, 2.

But those who took care of older people were (and still are) rarely visible as a distinctive group of "activists," not least because of their mixed forms of work and often atomized working conditions. Yet, instead of concluding that persons engaged in such work were not relevant to labour-related activism, I suggest that if we look at these actors and their activities from a different perspective, specific forms of activism become visible. The communist parties in East Central Europe and East Germany propagated social care as a task for society as a whole. Against this distinctive ideological background, I assume that the majority of people did indeed perform some form of unpaid care work either at their own home or at someone else's. State-socialist ideology declared social welfare a public issue, at least rhetorically; but care work took place in the private sphere. Furthermore, care for older people in particular manifested as a private, even non-political issue that, for a variety of reasons, mainly involved the family and took place within home.[7] This fact is often obscured in the archival sources of the time. In this chapter, I am interested in showing how we can trace the history of care activism, its forms, aims, and agents, primarily using the example of unpaid care workers and the structures in which they assembled. After all, caregivers were most actively involved in various forms of informal care that developed during the 1960s and 1970s which, to some extent, presaged the significantly more visible shift toward self-care brought about by the political changes in 1989.

During the post-1989 transformation, when political and social change occurred simultaneously in East Central Europe and East Germany, many caregivers continued working. In the sense of a "supportive tissue,"[8] they ensured that care was provided to older people in need. A comparison of East Germany, Poland, and the Czech Republic is particularly revealing because similar conditions in all three countries shaped the transformation processes. While thousands of people took to the streets to advocate for sociopolitical change during the peaceful revolutions, care workers in all three countries remained remarkably invisible in these events. In the course of the 1990s, all three countries then experienced a radical transformation of their welfare systems, shifting from overarching caring states to care economies that placed a greater emphasis on self-care.[9] Both paid and unpaid care was drastically reorganized in multiple—institutional, legal, practical, and financial—ways. A comparison of these three (post)socialist societies allows us to examine this shared transformation experience in more detail and to assess its long-lasting consequences.

7 See Dudová 2018; Wagnerová 2017; Šustrová and Rákosník 2016; Chaloupková 2013.
8 Conradi 2011, 128.
9 See Haug 2013; Madörin 2010.

An additional focus on care activism can help us evaluate women caregivers' diverse responses to this transformation.

I assume that women caregivers were faced with a highly gendered division of care work during this period. Spending more time on caregiving, i.e., on activities securing the well-being and ultimately the survival of other human beings, meant having less time to engage in classical forms of activism.[10] Susan Zimmermann has pointed out that unpaid care work was, in fact, as much a part of the state-socialist "catching-up development" as was the inclusion of women in paid work.[11] I would add that this unpaid care work, of course, continued to be needed throughout the postsocialist transformations. How, then, could women caregivers shape their working conditions when they formed such a heterogeneous group in which only very few received labour contracts and, thus, labour protections? Did they seek material remuneration or symbolic recognition from the public or the state?

To address these issues, I think it may be helpful to pay closer attention to (what I call) care activism. The character of this activism was connected to two important features of (post)socialist societies. First, as stated above, classical forms of labour activism were not available to caregivers (even if only from their own perspective) who engaged in less formalized forms of care. As I will demonstrate, this prompted the invention of alternative means of activism such as, for example, self-organization. Second, women who cared for elderly persons aspired to create a world with care at its center. This mindset led them to identify strongly with their individual contributions to everyday care practices (and how to improve them) rather than to question political or state authorities. This approach seems to have helped women develop self-esteem, coping strategies, resilience, and agency. Care activism in this sense was an attitude; it was not comparable to mainstream labour activism, but it was still an important motivation for women caregivers. While the use of the term activism here may be debatable, I will use it (for the time being, i.e., experimentally) to describe the actions of women caregivers that were intended to establish, uphold, and deepen the shared values of good care and, in this sense, to implement an ethics of care under the difficult political conditions of the period.

It will not go unmentioned that these women's activities coincided with academic and feminist debates on the ethics of care, which were introduced in the work of scholars like Carol Gilligan, Joan Tronto, and Nel Noddings. These

10 See Kohlen 2016.

11 Zimmermann 2010, 16.

debates later resulted in the idea that care practices hold a great deal of potential in terms of provoking societal transformation.[12] Recognizing what forms of care were needed and being able to take the necessary steps to provide it gave the women I interviewed a strong sense of agency, which in turn increased their cohesion around the common values motivating their work. The fact that their work constantly identified deficiencies in the existing social welfare systems further strengthened their drive to self-organize.

Speaking more broadly, the question who takes care of the elderly also provides insight into the broader social organization of a society.[13] Thus, I regard care as a topic relevant for understanding contemporary history, the history of everyday life, and gender studies. In the past decade or so, care has been intensely researched in terms of cultural and gender history and anthropology.[14] Proceeding from this research, I will address the roles of women in (post) socialist societies, and care work as the domain of women in particular, as topics embedded within the research on postsocialist transformations and as innovative ways of conceptualizing women's labour activism.

Based on materials from German, Czech, and Polish archives, I will first introduce three organizations in which women engaged in elderly care were involved before and after 1989: the Polish Committee for Social Help (Polski Komitet Pomocy Społecznej), the Pensioners' Clubs (Kluby důchodců) of the Czechoslovak municipal national committees (Městské národní výbory), and the East German People's Solidarity (Volkssolidarität). I will then discuss the East German case in more detail, presenting findings from oral history interviews with women members of People's Solidarity that shed light on the experiences of women working at the intersections of paid and unpaid care since the 1980s. I will conclude with some reflections on the long-term absence of care activism that continues to reverberate in the current nursing crisis exacerbated by the global COVID-19 pandemic. In this way, I demonstrate how significant self-organized activities outside of more formal labour relations were in the transformation process and how arrangements for care located "just around the corner" (i.e., community-based care) can be integrated into a contemporary history of women's labour activism.

12 See Conradi 2015; Thelen 2015; Noddings 2013; Tronto 1993; Gilligan 1982.

13 See Thelen 2015; Firth 1955.

14 See Read 2019; Havelková 2014; Bonfiglioli 2013.

1 Three Models of Elderly Care before 1989

In every society there are expectations related to the process of aging. They are shaped by collective memory, state propaganda, and individual experiences. Social anthropologists Tatjana Thelen and Cati Coe demonstrate that aging is indeed a highly political concern, explaining that "many states emphasize the welfare of older persons in their policies and planning, because of a perceived care crisis due to societal aging."[15]

In the People's Republic of Poland, Czechoslovakia, and the German Democratic Republic (GDR), the ideal conception of old age encouraged older people to participate in society, to actively engage with other generations, and to keep themselves "mentally and physically fit [...] so as not to burden the progress of socialism."[16] In brief: old age was a topic important enough that it shaped the state-socialist welfare agenda. In everyday life, though, voluntary—not state directed—care practices appear to have been critical for providing for the elderly. Because state institutions were often overburdened, voluntary helpers took over numerous tasks, supposedly in the spirit of the socialist common good, for which the state honored them.[17] However, sociologist Radka Dudová observed that at the time, elderly care was also deeply gendered both in terms of who received care and who provided it.[18] Women in the household continued to be the main providers of care despite the fact that their participation in the work force was heavily promoted. My hypothesis is that this gender regime was extended to the activities of socialist mass organizations, through which women voluntarily—and without pay—cared for elderly persons far beyond their own families.

In Poland, the Polish Committee for Social Help (Polski Komitet Pomocy Społecznej, PKPS), which was established in 1958, was the organization that stands out for its provision of care for the elderly. Although the PKPS was one of the largest social organizations nationwide, it has remained rather unknown to this day. In 1968, alongside voluntary fire fighters and the Polish Red Cross, it was recognized as an organization of so-called higher utility (*stowarzyszenie wyższej użyteczności*[19]) in a decree of the Council of Ministers (Rada

15 Thelen and Coe 2019, 280.
16 See Hachmeister 2022, 181.
17 See Kodymová 2015, 42.
18 Dudová 2018, 42.
19 See Apel [Call] (20 September 1976), sg. 3215, inv. no. 397, Afisze, plakaty i druki ulotne z terenu Przemyśla w zasobie Archiwum Państwowege w Przemyślu. Archiwum Państwowe [State Archive], Przemyśl, Poland.

Ministrów).[20] The government awarded this label only mass organizations that performed exceptional charitable work in Polish society. By 1980, the PKPS assembled nearly two million voluntary helpers under its umbrella; these helpers were then confronted with the needs of well over two million people over the age of seventy, representing more than 6.5 percent of the total population.[21]

At the time the PKPS was founded, mainly regional and unpaid social guardians (*terenowi opiekuni społeczni*) were caring for the elderly in their local communities. They were part of a network that had been created after the "Khrushchev Thaw" in the mid-1950s and had been charged with coordinating social care in cooperation with the state administration. These social guardians were nominated by local social organizations or the National Councils (Rady Narodowe) and performed their duties without financial remuneration.[22] It was not until the mid-1960s that the profession of social worker (*pracownik socjalny*) emerged in Poland.[23] PKPS home helpers were, thus, a common phenomenon of the era. In contrast to the earlier social guardians, PKPS home helpers operated within an organizational structure but they remained volunteers, unlike the social workers employed later. Local groups of PKPS home helpers provided home care which included "various household chores performed by home helpers who do the house cleaning and shopping, prepare meals, feed disabled persons, do the laundry, provide the dependent with heating coal and water and take care of the various day-to-day matters."[24] It is precisely such housekeeping tasks, not only medical duties, that count as care for the elderly. As defined by political scientist Joan Tronto, care is "everything that we do to maintain, continue, and repair our 'world' so that we can live in it as well as possible."[25] The "world" in which PKPS home helpers were active usually encompassed the proximate neighborhood "just around the corner." Like the social guardians, the idea behind this arrangement was that help could be provided instantly and on the spot.

In contrast to this type of care work, which took place in individual homes, the Pensioners' Clubs of the Czechoslovak municipal national committees

20 Rozporządzenie Rady Ministrów w sprawie uznania Polskiego Komitetu Pomocy Społecznej za stowarzyszenie wyższej użyteczności [Decree of the Council of Ministers on the recognition of the Polish Committee for Social Help as a higher utility association]. https://isap.sejm.gov.pl/isap.nsf/DocDetails.xsp?id=WDU19680430310.

21 Brenk 2018, 76.

22 Brenk 2012, 139.

23 Brenk 2012, 140.

24 Synak 1989, 111–112.

25 Tronto 1993, 103.

aimed to provide care for the elderly outside the home. The aim of this initiative was to include pensioners as "fellow citizens"[26] (*spoluobčany*) in society, i.e., to encourage them to get out of the home and into the public sphere. Numerous local clubs were founded for this purpose starting in the early 1960s. In contrast to the home care of the PKPS in Poland, which remained rather hidden and may even have been stigmatized as a sign of poverty in the public's perception, the activities of the Pensioners' Clubs in Czechoslovakia were often publicly promoted and celebrated. The establishment of new clubs was also advertised locally as social events.[27] In these clubs, older people could pursue a variety of interests: they could participate in group afternoons, watch TV, listen to the radio, play board games, or just enjoy sitting in a heated room.[28] The organizers were especially concerned with the social needs of the elderly. As some organizers of the club in Benešov u Semil (a village in the Liberec region) put it in a 1969 letter: "We believe that our pensioners will like it there, and that they will be happy to go there."[29]

Sociologist Pavla Kodymová explained that in the 1960s and 1970s, the national district and municipal committees (Okresní a městské národní výbory) started to systematically target certain groups for social work, one of which was senior citizens.[30] Sociologist of gender Hana Maříková also stresses that after the "failed transformation" of 1968, the Czechoslovak communist party was under immense pressure to develop solutions to the problem of elderly care. One of the main problems was the lack of capacity in residential care facilities. This is why, especially during the Normalization period, care for the elderly often (re)turned to the family and informal care services.[31] The Pensioners' Clubs were an attempt to counteract this problem with an institutional approach.

The establishment of the clubs, therefore, coincided with a time when it was politically desirable to invest in efforts to provide good care to the elderly. In the case of Most, a city in the Ústí nad Labem region in Northern Bohemia,

26 "Péče o starší spoluobčany" [Care for the elderly fellow citizens] (2 August 1984), Průboj, Ústí nad Labem, IV/B 24, kart. 1. Státní Okresní Archiv Most [State District Archive]. Most, Czech Republic.

27 Letter (10 September 1969), inv. č. 102/17, Místní národní výbor Benešov u Semil. Státní Okresní Archiv Semily [State District Archive]. Semily, Czech Republic.

28 Letter (23 July 1969), inv. č. 102/17, Okresní národní výbor Semily. Státní Okresní Archiv Semily [State District Archive]. Semily, Czech Republic.

29 Letter (10 September 1969), inv. č. 102/17, Místní národní výbor Benešov u Semil. Státní Okresní Archiv Semily [State District Archive]. Semily, Czech Republic.

30 Kodymová 2015, 41.

31 Maříková and Plasová 2012, 4.

even as late as 1982, it was acknowledged that "in this way, the national committees realize the humanitarian objectives of our social policy."[32] These so-called humanitarian objectives (*humánní cíle*) indicated that the issue was not simply about providing care but also about the social integration of the elderly. According to Kodymová, however, there was a significant shortage of trained social workers.[33] Therefore, it is not surprising that the Pensioners' Clubs were ultimately run by volunteers. In some places, the clubs were also linked closely to the Senior Citizens' Association (Svaz důchodců)[34] or local voluntary nurses (*dobrovolné pečovatelky*).[35] All the caregivers involved here were unpaid. In Semily (a town in the Liberec region), the national committee of the district actively supported such arrangements; at the same time, it ruled out the professional development of voluntary nurses. In 1970, the responsible head of department wrote the following flimsy excuse for this position: "The lack of nursing home capacity has been addressed by building an extensive network of volunteer caregivers who cannot be replaced by professional caregivers in the mountainous terrain of our district."[36]

The third example is the People's Solidarity (Volkssolidarität, VS) in the GDR. Founded in 1945, this organization specialized in care for the elderly in the GDR, with the explicit aim "to leave no one alone and to give everyone the opportunity to participate in social life until old age."[37] Again, this is a large organization that until the 1980s had over two million registered members.[38] Its women home helpers (*Hauswirtschaftspflegerinnen*) offered household assistance very similar to the PKPS, focusing on housekeeping tasks, meal provision, and the daily needs of the older people. However, as with the voluntary nurses in Czechoslovakia, VS home help was not intended to provide an entry point for women into the nursing profession. Home helpers were to be

32 "Nikdo nezůstane osamocen aneb zabezpečení ve stáří" [No one is left alone or insecure in old age] (3 June 1982), Průboj, Ústí nad Labem, IV/B 24, kart. 1. Státní Okresní Archiv Most [State District Archive]. Most, Czech Republic.

33 Kodymová 2015, 41.

34 "Aby člověk nikdy nebyl sám" [So that one is never alone] (2 November 1994), Severočeský regionální deník SD, Ústí nad Labem IV/B 24, kart. 1. Státní Okresní Archiv Most [State District Archive]. Most, Czech Republic.

35 "Nikdo nezůstane osamocen aneb zabezpečení ve stáří" [No one is left alone or insecure in old age] (3 June 1982), Průboj, Ústí nad Labem, IV/B 24, kart. 1. Státní Okresní Archiv Most [State District Archive]. Most, Czech Republic.

36 Komentář [Comment] (2 February 1977), kart. 1977, Okresní národní výbor Semily. Státní Okresní Archiv Semily [State District Archive]. Semily, Czech Republic.

37 Sekretariat des Zentralausschusses der Volkssolidarität 1981, 6.

38 Angerhausen 2003, 128.

recruited, if possible, from "non-working circles"[39] and were, therefore, either housewives or women who performed duties for the VS in addition to their regular full-time employment. Regarding their qualifications, it was merely stated that "they must be versed in household maintenance and have a good knowledge of first aid, if possible, or declare a willingness to acquire it."[40] There was no further vocational training provided for them. Ultimately, this meant that they were considered to be in an employment relationship with the VS, had a modest working income, but were not actually perceived as working women.[41]

Home helpers were indeed subsidized by the state, and similar to other countries in East Central Europe, "the work of women outside the home was supported by a heavily subsidized network of services offering alternatives to home chores."[42] Yet, as one former VS coordinator told me, many home helpers were transferred to the VS from their original workplaces as a punishment after applying for an exit permit to West Germany. He said they were "pushed aside [and shunted] to the VS to work in places where they could do no harm."[43]

In addition to home help, the VS operated so-called veterans' clubs (*Veteranenklubs*), where the elderly—then called veterans of work (*Veteranen der Arbeit*)—could get a hot meal or participate in a daily recreational program. In a brochure from 1960, the VS promoted its club in Berlin with the following quote from a woman visitor: "I was so alone and felt weak and sick. I'm sure I'd be dead already if you hadn't created this beautiful club."[44] Similar to the Czechoslovak Pensioners' Clubs, the focus here was on the social needs of the elderly.

As the three examples show, there were alternative, resourceful forms of care for the elderly that complemented institutional care arrangements and might, for that reason alone, be considered forms of care activism. All three examples merged into their countries' respective social care policies, which all relied on a combination of public authorities, nursing homes, mass organizations, neighborhood help, and informal care provided by relatives. In one way or another, their structures, but rarely their activists, were co-financed by the socialist state. In all three countries, national Red Cross societies were also involved, managing the medical care of elderly people in their homes. If further help was needed, it was usually relatives who were responsible for

39 Reichert 1967, 264.
40 Reichert 1967, 264.
41 Reichert 1967, 264.
42 Ferge 1997, 161.
43 Male member of the Volkssolidarität in Saxony, interviewed 2 August 2021.
44 Zentralsekretariat der Volkssolidarität 1960, 1.

arranging it. Places in nursing homes were available only for the most dependent elderly persons, if at all. Sociologist Brunon Synak found out in 1989 that the majority in Polish society strongly disapproved of nursing homes. Since the family had been defined as the most natural resource for care, "according to the conviction of the majority of the older generation, receiving formal care (especially institutional care) reflects a lack of loyalty to traditional family patterns and values."[45] This gendered division of care and domestic work within the family apparently continued to shape women's paid and unpaid labour throughout the post-socialist transformation.[46] For this reason, organizations and the women caregivers who helped the elderly during this period deserve special attention.

I would like to emphasize that it was mainly women who engaged in "eye to eye"[47] care for the elderly, even though the process of enabling care involved both women and men. Organizations such as the PKPS or the VS, which had hundreds of thousands of members, could by no means recruit caregivers from only one gender. But the women among them often did the shopping, cooking, washing, and feeding. These tasks bring me back to the core of care work and the main purpose of care activism: meeting the needs an individual cannot achieve alone or, in the case of the elderly, may no longer be able to achieve on his or her own. In this respect, voluntary care and activism as discussed in the introduction are remarkably similar: both point to deficits of the existing system or even to state failures, especially in the field of social welfare. Paradoxically, communist parties did not interpret voluntary involvement in elder care as criticism of the regime. Instead of intervening to make their own claims concerning care provision more explicit, they welcomed unpaid care work and reframed it as a contribution to the socialist common good.

This position makes sense since caregivers oftentimes did not turn to state authorities for assistance but rather turned to their neighbors and friends for help when it came to doing something for the elderly. This kind of purposeful joint initiative is what I would call self-organization. Sociologist Jeff Shantz and lawyer Dean Spade would probably speak of "mutual aid." They have used this related analytical term to describe everyday relationships of reciprocal aid, which they, interestingly, define as explicitly "anti-authoritarian."[48] Likewise, sociologist Shana Cohen concludes that local social activism "often explicitly

45 Synak 1989, 125.
46 See Dudová 2014; Ferge 1997.
47 Watemberg Izraeli 2020, 191.
48 See Shantz 2020, 48; Spade 2020, 138.

opposes the state's policies."[49] In the field of care work, however, such intentions are difficult to prove. For this reason, I argue that the cases of the PKPS, the Pensioners' Clubs, and the VS contain elements of self-organization which, in particular, ensured local care for the elderly. It is true that these organizations were embedded in state-socialist structures, but instead of demanding solutions from the state, "activists" in all three tried to solve problems themselves through collaborative action. While today we call this unpaid work,[50] so-called "socially necessary work" was taken for granted at the time. This is likely a systemic explanation for the absence of care activism that would otherwise have been directed against the communist governments. Under these circumstances, women were already coping with the double or even triple burden of unpaid housework, paid work, and political engagement; thus, there was little space left for care activism.[51]

But what changed for caregivers after the socialist ideology undergirding the existing system of elder care in the region disappeared? Why did they continue to perform such work instead of, for example, protesting in the streets for paid care work, or doing something else entirely? Moreover, did their involvement in paid and unpaid care work have anything to do with gender? I will explore these questions using the example of the VS in the following section. Interviews with representatives of the VS illustrate the motivations and perceptions of women care workers in the (post)socialist societies of East Germany and East Central Europe in an exemplary manner. The interviews were conducted between 2020 and 2022, during the high point of the COVID-19 pandemic restrictions. Travel restrictions and contact restraints complicated my interactions with this group of elderly women. My initial plan to conduct similar interviews in Poland and the Czech Republic, therefore, unfortunately had to be abandoned. Nevertheless, the experiences of VS representatives in East Germany characterize the experiences of those involved in elderly care across the entire region from the postwar period to the postsocialist transformation. They reveal different forms of women's care work; allow us to question whether such activities can be regarded as care *activism*; and help us better understand what this activism actually looked like at the time.

49 Cohen 2019, 52.

50 See Read 2019; Thelen 2014.

51 See Bonfiglioli 2020, 208.

2 Care and the "Great Change" after 1989

With the regime changes in 1989, multiple transformation processes were set in motion, and within a few years, "citizens dared to set out toward democratic societies and capitalist private economies based on the Western model."[52] Did women's self-organized care for the elderly also experience such a "great change,"[53] a rupture or a new beginning? According to historians Ana Kladnik and Thomas Lindenberger, some of the structures and practices formerly "maintained from below, partly demanded and promoted from above […] survived the far-reaching transformation and even helped shape it."[54] This also applies to the field of care. However, the reasons no mainstream care activism existed before the regime changes in 1989 did not change after the transformation.

Care work performed on behalf of the elderly was always systemically relevant: people in need of care continued to need care regardless of the political upheaval. Likewise, of course, those who cared for the elderly continued to be needed. Moving from one system to another while maintaining standards of care presented an enormous challenge for both those providing and those receiving it. In the Czech case, this happened in a particularly dramatic way as "the availability of residential care facilities decreased. […] And as the economy was liberalized in the course of the 1990s and 2000s, the state gave priority to family-based elder care."[55] In addition to care provided by families, services sold on the market of the newly emerging care economies became increasingly important. No matter what form it took, economist Mascha Madörin points out, care work comprises "life-sustaining and vital activities, without which societies would not be able to exist and economic growth would be impossible."[56] To sum up: care work was disrupted by the processes of privatization and marketization after 1989, but at the same time, continuity in care was required. It is therefore useful to understand transformation also as "a social change stretched in time and space."[57] With these considerations in mind, I spoke with women in East Germany who volunteered to care for the elderly starting in 1980 until 2000.

---

52 Kladnik and Lindenberger 2019, 251.
53 See Kaźmierska and Waniek 2020.
54 Kladnik and Lindenberger 2019, 251.
55 Dudová 2018, 43.
56 Madörin 2006, 283.
57 Kaźmierska and Waniek 2020, 589.

A now 87-year-old former electrical engineer, wife, and mother of two children, who had been a VS member for many years, decided to take an active role in the organization in 1991. Regarding her motivations, she told me the following: "You had to do something yourself so that something would happen. It has always been like that. If you didn't take care of it, you got run over."[58] My interlocutor made it very clear here that, in her opinion, there were always problems that needed to be solved. In her narrative, the boundaries between the past and the present almost faded, as she spoke in general terms about how things have "always been." Her experience as a caregiver apparently taught her that no problems would ever be solved unless she addressed them herself; what is more, if she did nothing herself, she too would "get run over." This attitude resulted in an immediate readiness to act—perhaps even a need to act—which motivated her to perform voluntary care work for years. For this woman, caring went beyond defining herself simply as a provider of care for a recipient of care. She explained her strong commitment to care work by expressing her desire to change something in her own life and not only in the lives of those for whom she cared. After all, she wanted to ensure that "something would happen." So, why should she have to rely on others, for example, the state?

We must keep in mind that this is a retrospective narrative in which the interviewee may be ascribing agency to herself in hindsight. Still, her statement reflects typical transformation experiences (i.e., the long-lasting remaking of life-worlds) and the fundamental changes that affected peoples' lives and life chances.[59] Certainly, this quote could be attributed to an activist who promoted better care for the elderly with the intention of achieving political and social change. In another setting, this attitude would probably have led her to overt forms of activism. Yet, in the midst of a period already defined by change, she concluded that she must continue her work as before.

A similar narrative is apparent in the following quote from a now 94-year-old woman, then a single mother and teacher, who had volunteered for the VS since the postwar period:

> I took care of elderly people when they needed help [...] I did everything that came up; we built local groups, took care of elderly people, went to the doctor with them. Then you would call them every now and then, the people are happy [...] It was a bad time when the "Wende" [transition/turn] came. People were afraid, you had to comfort them. We were an

---

58 Woman member of the Volkssolidarität in Saxony, interviewed 16 February 2021.

59 See Brückweh 2020.

> organization that worked through [the changes]. That was when people needed us most! You just had to push through.[60]

This woman emphasized that her responsibilities could vary a lot. Unlike a professional nurse, she was literally there for "everything that came up." She was a domestic helper, a cook, a companion, and also a representative for the elderly, all wrapped into one person. She was around when "people needed us most." As she describes her ongoing and determined action, she explains her activities as reactions: She fulfilled her care work, whatever the situation, because whatever happened, she was flexible enough to react to it. I interpret this attitude as a form of activism (albeit a silent form).

Although this interviewee described herself as a care volunteer rather than a care worker, as someone who assists rather than an activist, I chose this specific quote to illustrate care activism because I believe that this term represents my interviewees' convictions. In their opinion, there was always something they could do, and there were a lot of things they could change. For them, change referred no to the great political transformations of the time but to the changes—improvements—their daily actions brought to the lives of "their" elderly care recipients. In their neighborhoods, these women were the ones who made things happen, who improvised and invented—on a low budget or with no budget at all—both before and after 1989. The 94-year-old recalled her involvement as a caregiver with "action-rich verbs" to emphasize that in desperate situations, she was the one who retained agency.[61] As she herself put it: "You just had to push through."

In my view, such "bottom-up-voices"[62] make it very clear that care for the elderly pre- and post-1989 took place at the margins of the existing system: in situations for which there was no institutional solution, in moments when care provided by relatives was not possible. They were filling gaps. Furthermore, both women acted on their own initiative. After 1989 at the latest, there was no longer a regime that would have demanded this kind of commitment from them nor one that would reward it ideologically. The VS was the organization that served as the backdrop of their work, as a coordination point and a contact that undergirded their commitment and made it a little more effective. Among members of this organization, a common narrative is that everyone carried on and that this was how they survived the fall of communism. If we understand self-organization as an activity that is not directed by the state or

60 Woman member of the Volkssolidarität in Saxony, interviewed 12 February 2021.

61 Meyer 2018, 60.

62 Kaźmierska and Waniek 2020, 590.

any other authority, an activity that takes place on one's own initiative, then these women's involvement in the VS was self-organized. Moreover, I suggest that we think of this work as a kind of women's care activism that remained rather unseen and silent, but it nevertheless contributed to the development of new local structures of caring and, in the process, led to the formation of close interpersonal relationships. After all, pointing out existing deficiencies, initiating solutions, and working together with others to solve problems are central dimensions of activism.

But is it possible to interpret these two quotes as perpetuating previously established practices? Or did carrying on (or caring on) "just around the corner" contribute to social change? Political scientist Elisabeth Conradi argues, yes, as "care practice does not only alter social interaction; it contributes to the transformation of society. […] by trying to improve listening, support, assistance or help, the structural, political and organizational barriers to good care […] become visible, and as such can be addressed in public discourse or by way of careful counteraction."[63] I agree with her, but I would add that women's care activism did not reach a large public sphere in the postsocialist transformation period.

The nature of women's care activism is particularly well illustrated in the following quote from my interview with a 92-year-old woman who took over a local VS group from her husband in 1983 and has organized activities for older people in her town ever since:

> Everything that had to be done walking, I did. […] So, I was always on the move […] when I did something, I enjoyed doing it, and I did it well. I really didn't let things slide; I made an effort to do something nice so people were happy to come. […] The best thing was the excursions; those attracted the most people. What kind of excursions did you have in GDR times? There was nothing. The bus was always full, we saw many, many beautiful things. All the things you couldn't do in the GDR.[64]

There are two examples of her very individual activism in this quote. First, she performed tasks on foot. As I learned through this interview, this could involve her delivering letters personally instead of asking for funds or donations for stamps. Additionally, since many elderly people had limited mobility, she took many walks to visit people in their homes. However, she organized bus trips to

63 Conradi 2015, 125.

64 Woman member of the Volkssolidarität in Saxony, interviewed 19 October 2020.

restore some mobility to elderly people and to take them to places they had not been permitted to visit prior to the fall of the Berlin Wall. What at first glance appears to be a simple recreational activity required a great deal of time and personal commitment on the part of the interviewee. Her underlying ambition was not to improve her own situation but to give people the good care and attention she felt they deserved in their old age. As sociologist Till Hilmar has already shown through a comparison of East German and Czech transformation experiences after 1989, there is indeed a moral tension between what is perceived as deserved or undeserved as there is "some connection between who one is or what one does and what one can legitimately expect in return."[65] From this point of view, we can rethink individual activism. My interviewees' individual activism actually was aimed at societal change much more than I had previously assumed—maybe more than they realized themselves.

This quote also clearly demonstrates that for this woman and the other interviewees, the meaning of care work was not limited to nursing activities or provisioning. From my discussion with this interviewee, it was obvious that caring for the elderly also meant taking care of their social and cultural needs, bringing joy to the elderly, including them in activities, and treating them as valued members of society. Here again, we see that self-organized care of the elderly filled gaps. It went beyond predictable necessities and addressed aspects of human togetherness, community, and, in general, sought to ensure the dignity of people in their old age.

Before 1989, this conception of care corresponded to official rhetoric, but the reality on the ground was much different than this ideal, which is why this VS interviewee was practically working on the margins of the socialist care system. After 1989, such care arrangements were dismissed as socialist and supposedly outdated. For this interviewee, performing her care activities in both systems meant challenging prevailing narratives and, at the same time, maintaining the bonds between a group of like-minded caregivers and care recipients. It is hardly surprising, then, that in terms of language, this 92-year-old woman describes herself as a "mover" who "did" something. Moreover, this interviewee revealed a clearly moral understanding of her care work, as for her it was unimaginable to "let things slide."

In the course of my research, I met a number of women who were "moving" something forward through their personal commitment to care work. When in the mid-1980s the VS compensated for some of the severe economic difficulties in the GDR, the above-mentioned care activism abandoned the level of silent

65 Hilmar 2019, 1.

protest for more public advocacy. A now 73-year-old woman who coordinated home helpers for the VS in a major city in Saxony confirmed this:

> In my first winter [in that position in the VS], it was a really tough winter. The food supply was delivered by hand, by bike, and old baby carriages and so on; there was nothing motorized. And we got there through the heavy snow. [...] And there were some old mothers [grannies] sitting in their houses without any coal in the cellar. We took care of that. [...] We really went from pillar to post, we went to the city district administration and said we wouldn't leave unless they somehow produced a ration card for coal. [...] I was proud that no one in my district froze to death that winter.[66]

In contrast to other situations where the caregiver's responsibilities prevented mainstream forms of labour activism, this quote shows how the very responsibility for human lives could provoke care activism. Members of the VS were responsible for distributing food and coal to households, and they also got involved when there was no food or coal available at all. In the case of my interviewee, this went so far as to put pressure on political decision-makers. Care activism manifested itself here in the joint advocacy for freezing "old mothers," with the aim of improving their situation and meeting their existential needs. To clarify, in this specific case, there was only a rather small number of people in danger of freezing. Yet, the determination with which they were supported by the interviewee and her VS colleagues is astonishing. In my opinion, this case illustrates very well the shared values of caregivers in the VS and the local dedication of my interviewee. Even though she was as concerned about elderly men as she was about "old mothers" in her neighborhood, I think it is significant that she told me so explicitly about how women were able to help each other during the harsh winter. Care activism, in her case, apparently also included a profound solidarity among women.

It could be argued that only those persons directly involved learned about the courageous intervention of the interviewee. Again, activism remained more or less invisible. However, this quotation contains some features of women's care activism that were already hinted at in the other interviews analyzed: Those involved in care literally had to move, and often moved on behalf of others, be it on foot or by other means. This actually collates well with historians Barbara Molony and Jennifer Nelson's suggestion that women's activism be defined in

66 Woman member of the Volkssolidarität in Saxony, interviewed 24 January 2022.

a broader sense as "women in movement" rather than just "women's movements."[67] Moreover, there were always human lives, or at least quality of life, at stake, and this is what care workers aimed to sustain. The last interviewee stated explicitly how proud she was "that no one in [her] district froze to death that winter." On the one hand, this statement refers to values and obligations she faced when caring for the elderly. On the other hand, she (retrospectively) identified pride as a reward for her efforts. In the following quote, she spoke in more detail about the kinds of personalities she observed among those helping the elderly at the time:

> No one ever gave up their work [in the residential groups]. That actually continued beyond the "Wende" [transition/turn] as far as the work in the residential communities is concerned. Until I left, there were still group leaders there who had been there during the socialist times. [...] They somehow stubbornly continued doing it.[68]

As with the first interviewee discussed in this chapter, the notion of continuity is very pronounced here. During the postsocialist transformation, i.e., a time of rapid and dramatic change, caregivers apparently concluded that they must continue their work as before. The attribution of "stubbornness" conceals numerous individual steps and decisions that I suspect could be captured in my definition of care activism. Here, the interviewee referred to stubbornness as the quality of *not* surrendering to the difficult circumstances, of wanting to achieve something more or different, to preserve functioning care arrangements, and to stick together. Her choice of words suggests a high level of emotional and moral identification with care work, which she observed in herself and in other "group leaders." Accordingly, "no one ever gave up their work." At this point, it becomes very clear once again that caregivers understood their predominantly unpaid care as work. This fixation on work as the defining characteristic of their actions is a rather typical postsocialist legacy that can also be observed in other groups of people and in other countries in the region. According to the interviewee, there were basically two ways in which this work could turn into activism: either it could be interrupted in order to bring precarious conditions to the attention of decision-makers, or it could be "stubbornly" continued without making such difficulties known. Both approaches required experienced and determined people, as the following quote highlights:

67 Molony and Nelson 2017, 4.

68 Woman member of the Volkssolidarität in Saxony, interviewed 24 January 2022.

> You had to cope with the economy of scarcity. You had to come up with something, that's what we used to say. […] You had to make something out of nothing. And the old people were much more shaped by this than I was. […] There were many who did this who had never been in the SED [Socialist Unity Party of Germany]. That was another factor. There were many who were not party members […] and in any case, had never been in the SED. […] And I think that it always also depends on the people involved.[69]

In this quote, members of the VS, the care activists so to speak, are portrayed as resourceful, accustomed to scarcity, and, above all, independent from the then ruling communist party. Did these features render care activism obsolete? Would these people always "come up with something," even (or especially) when the "great change" occurred in 1989? In the interviewee's opinion, that "depends on the people involved." For three of the interviewees mentioned in this chapter, indeed a very personal "great change" happened after 1989, when they themselves entered retirement. On the one hand, this meant that they had more time for their voluntary activities in the VS. On the other hand, workplaces where they had previously been "active" were now inaccessible to them. They leaned more on typical women's strategies, or, as historian Susan Zimmermann put it, "a culture of mutual self-help among women in neighborhoods, firms, and the family"[70] that had been developed and refined during the socialist period.

Feminist debates in recent decades have been concerned with making care, i.e., an activity traditionally performed by women, "a public issue of equity and demanding the recognition of 'care' as a necessary social task."[71] However, an analysis of the interviews I conducted with former VS care workers suggests that we need to completely rethink our notions of care activism in order to understand it as a form of resilience and lived solidarity that manifests in silent practices of (women's) care-giving. During the postsocialist transformation period, my East German interviewees had first-hand experience of this model of care work and activism.

69 Woman member of the Volkssolidarität in Saxony, interviewed 24 January 2022.

70 Zimmermann 2010, 14.

71 Brückner 2010, 43.

3 Concluding Thoughts

By comparing select cases of elder care, this chapter reveals how care work took similar forms in three socialist societies, all of which involved both women's paid and unpaid labour. Forms of self-organized elder care presented in this chapter occurred "just around the corner," where local groups, mostly organized by women, offered help to older people in need. Such arrangements of care developed in East Central Europe as well as in East Germany, typically in the 1960s and 1970s, alongside reassessments of national social welfare policies. Many local caregivers remained involved in care work during the transformation period after 1989, during which they faced simultaneously the dissipation of socialist care ideals and the creation of new care economies. The example of the GDR's People's Solidarity helps illuminate the individual motivations of women who provided care, such as the ability to act, solidarity, or conceptualizations of good care.

The idea that where there is women's labour, there is also women's labour activism obviously does not apply without some caveats. Activism in the field of elder care looked quite different from mainstream labour activism, which is why I have suggested capturing it under the term "care activism" instead. Following on the work of historians Barbara Molony and Jennifer Nelson, who argue that "women's activism existed in practice, and thus historians can create a narrative of activism; […] but activism is not itself an analytic category,"[72] I am fully aware of the contested nature of this term and the need for further conceptual elaboration.

In this chapter I have argued that women caregivers appropriated certain patterns of understanding of and action directed toward (post)socialist care provisions that led not to mainstream activism but rather to attitudes that enabled individuals to retain their agency in times of crisis and, most importantly, to implement their shared values of good care. I, thus, present unpaid caregivers as agents of care activism who have notably changed their social environments: They were the persons who knew what the elderly needed, who were in contact with their families, the local authorities, and other caregivers. Consequently, they were the ones who changed the lives of many people. It was they who, from first-hand experience, knew how elder care could still be improved and where the qualifications—or maybe the professional profiles—of caregivers could be enhanced. The crucial difference from more classical forms of women's labour activism was that caregivers did not draw attention

72 Molony and Nelson 2017, 1.

to these shortcomings by advocating for better working conditions. On the contrary, they achieved change by advocating and acting for others, i.e., care recipients and their needs. Interviews with four women members of the VS have confirmed that such supposedly silent forms of care activism differed significantly from silence.

In many countries in Central and East Central Europe today there continues to be a lack of more mainstream activism by care workers—i.e., activism aimed first at the improvement of their own working conditions, with the wider implication that on this basis, they would be able to supply better care. Caregivers, whether in formal or informal settings, only recently returned to the top of countries' political agendas when the global COVID-19 pandemic made us aware of how much we all depend on the help of others. To a certain extent, the COVID-19 crisis mirrored the transformation experiences of care workers in the GDR, Czechoslovakia (Czechia), and Poland after 1989, demonstrating that those in need of care as well as their caregivers are particularly vulnerable in times of crisis and require widespread societal support. In the words of a journalist writing for the German newspaper *Süddeutsche Zeitung* (*Southern German Newspaper*) in May 2020: "Alongside all the expressions of respect, a genuine and lasting solidarity is needed with those who, out of solidarity with the sick and those in need of care, the elderly, and children, continue to work [...], for better or for worse."[73]

But what exactly are the working conditions that caregivers should endure under these circumstances? Talking to women from the VS helped me understand that they did not lack an awareness of their precarious working conditions. They also shared many concerns, a fact that might have led to a more open form of activism on their part. Following on the conclusions of care and gender researcher Hanne Marlene Dahl, one would expect conflict to arise when "[n]early everywhere the 'elder burden' and the 'demographic challenges' are at the top of the national political agenda. [...] Hence, we observe struggles within states [...], and between the elderly in need of care, their family members and the care worker."[74] Instead of looking for such visible struggles, in this chapter I have suggested that it is more important to focus on self-empowering and coping strategies and the resilience and agency of caregivers. This approach worked well for interpreting the narratives of the four women I interviewed, who identified individual commitment and a certain "stubbornness" as key features of local care arrangements.

73 Seiderer-Nack 2020.

74 Dahl 2017, 3.

Historian Małgorzata Karpińska reminds us that frameworks for (care) activism were socially and culturally narrow during the postsocialist transformation since society assigns women and men different tasks and roles, which likewise define cultural, economic, and social boundaries. She found a "discrepancy between the declared and actual attitudes of societies towards the elderly. [...] [T]he cultural image of the old person and the official standard of treating the elderly very frequently fail to match social reality."[75] Additionally, moral values and "prevalent ideas of social needs" often define which care is provided by the individual, and which kind is offered by the state.[76] The four women interviewed for this chapter considered it a moral duty to undertake care work as their individual responsibility.

By comparing elderly care arrangements in three (post)socialist societies, I have shown that there were quite similar coping strategies for filling deficits or gaps. These included organized approaches through groups and associations in the immediate neighborhood of the elderly, providing meeting places, and offering age-specific activities. Care activism in the above cases consisted of "caring on" and "pushing through" while social welfare was being politically renegotiated. Learning about these forms of care work means becoming aware of the boundaries and the shortcomings of the existing system. With such a view, perhaps we can contribute to overcoming the conceptual and empirical deficits when it comes to studying care work and its position within the history of women's labour activism.

Bibliography

Angerhausen, Susanne. 2003. *Radikaler Organisationswandel. Wie die "Volkssolidarität" die deutsche Vereinigung überlebte* [Radical organizational change. How the "Volkssolidarität" survived German Reunification]. Opladen: Leske Budrich.

Artwińska, Anna. 2020. *Gender, Generations, and Communism in Central and Eastern Europe and Beyond.* New York: Taylor & Francis.

Benoit, Cecilia. 2011. *Valuing Care Work: Comparative Perspectives.* Toronto: University of Toronto Press.

Betti, Eloisa. 2020. "Generations of Italian Communist Women and the Making of a Women's Rights Agenda in the Cold War (1945–68). Historiography, Memory, and New Archival Evidence." In *Gender, Generations, and Communism in Central and*

75 Karpińska and Szwarz 2016, 23.

76 Šustrová 2020, 108.

Eastern Europe and Beyond, edited by Anna Artwińska, 82–101. New York: Taylor & Francis.

Bonfiglioli, Chiara. 2013. "Gendering Post-Socialist Transition. Studies of Changing Gender Perspectives." *Debatte: Journal of Contemporary Central and Eastern Europe* 21, no. 1: 120–122.

Bonfiglioli, Chiara. 2020. "Discussing Women's Double and Triple Burden in Socialist Yugoslavia: Women Working in the Garment Industry." In *Labor in State-Socialist Europe, 1945–1989. Contributions to a History of Work*, edited by Marsha Siefert, 195–215. Budapest: Central European University Press.

Brenk, Mikołaj. 2018. *Organizacja pomocy społecznej w Polsce 1918–2018: podręcznik akademicki* [The organization of social welfare in Poland 1918–2018: An academic textbook]. Warsaw: Wydawnictwo Naukowe SCHOLAR.

Brenk, Mikołaj. 2012. "Od społecznika do profesjonalisty—ewolucja zawodu pracownika socjalnego w Polsce" [From social worker to professional: The evolution of social work as a profession in Poland]. *Kultura-Społeczeństwo-Edukacja* [Culture–Society–Education], no. 2: 135–149.

Brückner, Margit. 2010. "Entwicklungen der Care-Debatte—Wurzeln und Begrifflichkeiten" [Developments of the debate on care—roots and concepts]. In *Die Ent-Sorgung menschlicher Reproduktionsarbeit entlang von Geschlechter- und Armutsgrenzen* [The disposal of human reproductive work along gender and poverty lines], edited by Ursula Apitzsch and Marianne Schmidbauer, 43–58. Opladen: Verlag Barbara Budrich.

Brückweh, Kerstin. 2020. *Die lange Geschichte der "Wende": Geschichtswissenschaft im Dialog* [The long history of the "*Wende*": Historical science in dialogue]. Berlin: Christoph Links Verlag.

Chaloupková, Jana. 2013. "Neformální péče v rodině: sociodemográcké charakteristiky pečujících osob" [Informal care in the family: Socio-demographic characteristics of caregivers]. *Data and Research—SDA Info* 127, no. 2: 107–123.

Cohen, Shana. 2019. "Solidarity and the Future of Global Social Policy: Looking for Direction in Local Social Activism." *Global Social Policy* 19, no. 1–2: 46–64.

Conradi, Elisabeth. 2011. *Kosmopolitische Zivilgesellschaft/Inklusion durch gelingendes Handeln* [Cosmopolitan civil society / Inclusion through successful action]. Frankfurt am Main: Campus-Verlag.

Conradi, Elisabeth. 2015. "Redoing Care: Societal Transformation through Critical Practice." *Ethics and Social Welfare* 9, no. 2: 113–129.

Dahl, Hanne Marlene. 2017. *Struggles in (Elderly) Care: A Feminist View*. London: Palgrave Macmillan.

Dudová, Radka. 2018. "Doing Gender and Age: The Case of Informal Elderly Care in the Czech Republic." *International Journal of Ageing and Later Life* 12, no. 1: 41–73.

Dudová, Radka. 2014. "Proč ženy pečují? Gender a neformální péče o seniory" [Why do women care? Gender and informal care for the elderly]. *Gender, rovné příležitosti, výzkum* 15, no. 1: 41–54.

Ferge, Zsuzsa. 1997. "Women and Social Transformation in Central-Eastern Europe." *Czech Sociological Review* 5, no. 2: 159–178.

Firth, Raymond. 1955. "Some Principles of Social Organization." *The Journal of the Royal Anthropological Institute of Great Britain and Ireland* 85, no. 1/2: 1–18.

Ghodsee, Kristen. 2018. *Second World, Second Sex: Socialist Women's Activism and Global Solidarity During the Cold War.* Durham, NC: Duke University Press.

Gilligan, Carol. 1982. *In a Different Voice.* Cambridge, MA: Harvard University Press.

Hachmeister, Maren. 2022. "Care at Home—Voluntary Care in the Lives of Those who Provide and Need Help in Three Socialist States." *Studia historica Brunensia* 69, no. 1: 175–194.

Haug, Frigga. 2013. "Das Care-Syndrom: ohne Geschichte hat die Frauenbewegung keine Perspektive" [The care syndrome: Without history, the women's movement has no perspective]. *Widerspruch: Beiträge zu sozialistischer Politik* [Contradiction: Contributions to socialist politics] 32, no. 62: 81–92.

Havelková, Hana, and Oates-Indruchová, Libora. 2014. *The Politics of Gender Culture under State Socialism. An expropriated voice.* New York: Routledge.

Hilmar, Till. 2019. "The Temporal Logic of Deservingness: Inequality Beliefs in Two Postsocialist Societies." *Socius: Sociological Research for a Dynamic World* 5: 1–16.

Janiak-Jasińska, Agnieszka. 2016. *Ludzie starzy i starość na ziemiach polskich od XVIII do XXI wieku* [Old people and old age in Poland from the 18th to the 21st century]. Warsaw: Wydawnictwo "DiG," 2016.

Karpińska, Małgorzata, and Andrzej Szwarz. 2016. "Introduction. a Few Remarks on the Socio-cultural Aspects of Old Age in Historical Research." In *Ludzie starzy i starość na ziemiach polskich od XVIII do XXI wieku (na tle porównawczym) Tom I* [Old people and old age in the Polish lands from the 18th to the 21st century (in a comparative context)], edited by Agniezska Janiak-Jasińska, 19–27. Warsaw: Wydawnictwo "DiG."

Kaźmierska, Kaja and Katarzyna Waniek. 2020. *Telling the Great Change: The Process of the Systemic Transformation in Poland in Biographical Perspective.* Łódż: Wydawnictwo Uniwersytetu Łódzkiego.

Kladnik, Ana, and Thomas Lindenberger. 2019. "Traditionen der Freiwilligkeit im Transformationsregime. Das Beispiel der Freiwilligen Feuerwehr" [Traditions of volunteering in the transformation regime: The example of the Voluntary Fire Brigade]. *Historische Zeitschrift* Beiheft [Historical magazine supplement] 76: 249–273.

Kodymová, Pavla. 2015. "Terénní sociální práce v péči o seniory v době normalizace" [The field social work in elderly care in the normalization period]. *Fórum Socialni Prace* [Social work forum] 2: 41–49.

Kohlen, Helen. 2016. "Sorge als Arbeit ohne ethische Reflexion? Entwicklungslinien der deutschen Debatte um Sorge als Arbeit und der internationale Care-Ethik" [Care as work without ethical reflection? Lines of development of the German debate on care as work and international care ethics]. In *Dimensionen der Sorge: Soziologische, philosophische und theologische Perspektiven* [Dimensions of concern: Sociological, philosophical, and theological perspectives], edited by Anna Henkel, 189–208. Baden-Baden: Nomos Verlagsgesellschaft mbH & Co. KG.

Korolczuk, Elżbieta. 2020. *Bunt kobiet. Czarne Protesty i Strajki Kobiet* [Women's revolt: The black protests and women's strikes]. Gdańsk: Europejskie Centrum Solidarności. https://depot.ceon.pl/handle/123456789/18107.

Kramer, Nicole. 2020. "Prekäre Geschäfte. Privatisierung und Vermarktlichung der Altenpflege im deutsch-englischen Vergleich" [Precarious business. Privatization and marketization of care for the elderly in German-English comparison]. *ZZF—Centre for Contemporary History: Zeithistorische Forschungen* [ZZF—Center for Contemporary History: Contemporary historical research] 17/2, no. 2: 234–260.

Laczkó, Éva. 2017. "Interview with Éva Laczkó (by Susan Zimmermann)," 1 September and 23 November, 2017. *Abstract of Transcript*. ZARAH Project, N/A. ZARAH DB database. https://public.zarahdb.eu/document/175.

Madörin, Mascha. 2010. "Care Ökonomie – eine Herausforderung für die Wirtschaftswissenschaften" [Care economy - A challenge for the economic sciences]. In *Gender and Economics: Feministische Kritik der politischen Ökonomie* [Gender and economics: Feminist critique of political economy], edited by Christine Bauhardt and Gülay Çağlar, 81–104.

Madörin, Mascha. 2006. "Plädoyer für eine eigenständige Theorie der Care-Ökonomie" [A plea for an independent theory of the care economy]. In *Geschlechterverhältnisse in der Ökonomie* [Gender relations in the economy], edited by Torsten Niechoj and Marco Tullney, 277–297. Magdeburg: Metropolis-Verlag.

Maříková, Hana, and Blanka Plasová. 2012. "Kontinuita anebo změna v systému zajištění péče o seniory v České republice od roku 1948 vzhledem k genderovanosti politik péče" [Continuity or change in the system of care provisions for the elderly in the Czech Republic since 1948 in relation to gendered care policies]. *Fórum sociální politiky* [Social work forum] 3: 2–6.

Meyer, Silke. 2018. "Narrative Ethics and Cultural Analysis: Insolvency Stories and Moral Debt Relief." *Fabula* 59, no. 1–2: 50–69.

Molony, Barbara and Jennifer Nelson. 2017. *Women's Activism and 'Second Wave' Feminism: Transnational Histories*. London: Bloomsbury Academic.

Nečasová, Denisa. 2011. "Buduj vlast—posílíš mír! Ženské hnutí v českých zemích 1945–1955" [Build the homeland—You will strengthen peace! The women's movement in the Czech Lands, 1945–1955]. *Bohemia* 53, no. 1: 50–52.

Noddings, Nel. 2013. *Caring: A Relational Approach to Ethics and Moral Education.* Berkeley: University of California Press.

Oxford Learners' Dictionaries: "Activism." https://www.oxfordlearnersdictionaries.com.

Read, Rosie. 2019. "Caring Values and the Values of Care: Women, Maternalism and Caring Work in the Czech Republic." *Contemporary European History* 28: 500–511.

Reichert, Heinz. 1967. *Sozialfürsorge in der Deutschen Demokratischen Republik* [Social welfare in the German Democratic Republic]. Berlin: Staatsverlag der Deutschen Demokratischen Republik.

Robbins, Jessica. 2021. *Aging Nationally in Contemporary Poland: Memory, Kinship, and Personhood*, New Brunswick, NJ: Rutgers University Press.

Seiderer-Nack, Julia. 2020. "Die Pflege-Berufe brauchen mehr als Respekt" [The nursing professions need more than respect]. *Süddeutsche Zeitung*, 3 May 2020. https://www.sueddeutsche.de/politik/gastbeitrag-corona-pflegeberufe-reform-1.4894211.

Shantz, Jeff. 2020. *Commonist Tendencies: Mutual Aid beyond Communism.* Brooklyn, New York: Punctum Books.

Siefert, Marsha. 2020. *Labor in State-Socialist Europe, 1945–1989. Contributions to a History of Work.* Budapest: Central European University Press, 2020.

Spade, Dean. 2020. "Solidarity not Charity." *Social Text* 38, no. 1/142: 131–151.

Šustrová, Radka. 2020. "The Struggle for Respect: the State, World War One Veterans, and Social Welfare Policy in Interwar Czechoslovakia." *Zeitgeschichte* [Contemporary history] 47, no. 1: 107–135.

Šustrová, Radka, and Jakub Rákosník. 2016. *Rodina v zájmu státu. Populační růst a instituce manželství v českých zemích 1918–1989* [Family in the interest of the state: Population growth and the institution of marriage in the Czech Lands 1918–1989]. Prague: Nakladatelství Lidové noviny.

Synak, Brunon. 1989. "Formal Care for Elderly People in Poland." *Journal of Cross-Cultural Gerontology* 4: 107–127.

Thelen, Tatjana, Cati Coe. 2019. "Political Belonging through Elderly Care: Temporalities, Representations and Mutuality." *Anthropological Theory* 19, no. 2: 279–299.

Thelen, Tatjana. 2015. "Care as Social Organization: Creating, Maintaining and Dissolving Significant Relations." *Anthropological Theory* 15, no. 4: 497–515.

Thelen, Tatjana. 2014. *Care/Sorge, Konstruktion, Reproduktion und Auflösung bedeutsamer Bindungen* [Care, construction, reproduction and dissolution of significant relations]. Bielefeld: Transcript Verlag.

Tronto, Joan. 1993. *Moral Boundaries. A Political Argument for an Ethic of Care.* New York: Routledge.

Volkssolidarität. 1981. *Volkshelfer—Vertrauter der Veteranen* [People's helper—Veterans' confidante]. Berlin: Sekretariat des Zentralausschusses der Volkssolidarität.

Volkssolidarität. 1960. *Einsam? Die Veteranenklubs der Volkssolidarität bieten Geselligkeit, Wissen, Freude und Frohsinn!* [Lonely? The veterans' clubs of People's Solidarity offers conviviality, knowledge, joy, and cheerfulness!]. Berlin: Zentralsekretariat der Volkssolidarität.

Wagnerová, Alena. 2017. *Žena za socialismu: Československo 1945–1974 a reflexe vývoje před rokem 1989 a po něm* [Woman under socialism: Czechoslovakia 1945–1974 and reflections on developments before and after 1989]. Prague: Sociologické nakladatelství (SLON).

Watemberg Izraeli, Sagy. 2020. "A Reflection on the Reflective Ethics of Charity." *Approaching Religion* 10, no. 2: 187–192.

Zimmermann, Susan. 2010. "Gender Regime and Gender Struggle in Hungarian State Socialism." *Aspasia. International Yearbook for Women's and Gender History of Central, Eastern and Southeastern Europe* 4: 1–24.

CHAPTER 16

"The Most Important Thing Is That a New Society Can Come Into Being"

Anna Kéthly (1889–1976), a Stubborn and Stalwart Fighter in the Struggle for Democratic Socialism, Women's Rights, and Trade Union Rights

Jean-Pierre Liotard-Vogt

Abstract

This chapter focuses on the life and fate of the Hungarian politician Anna Kéthly (1889–1976), who was also known as a feminist and labour activist. Covering almost sixty years of history, from the late 1910s to the mid-1970s, it focuses on Kéthly's contributions to the struggle for social democracy, women's rights, and workers' rights in Hungary, relying on Kéthly's published correspondence, as well as some unpublished writings analyzed here for the first time. Kéthly's militant vocabulary and her biblical metaphors are striking in their longevity—from her opposition to the authoritarian Horthy regime as a member of the Hungarian Parliament during the interwar period, to the opposition to the communist regime she pursued in exile after 1956. Kéthly self-identified as a social democrat as well a trade unionist. Indeed, the chapter concludes that her labour activism during the time she lived abroad was quite original and went far beyond her political activism in Hungary, which has often been the focus of scholarly attention. Kéthly continuously focused on the rights and life circumstances of the Hungarian working class under communism. She was also concerned with feminism and feminist activism, albeit more discreetly, and persistently advocated for concrete solutions to the unequal relations between men and women.

Keywords

Anna Kéthly – Hungarian Association of Private Clerks (Magyarországi Magántisztviselők Országos Szövetsége, HAPC) – Hungarian feminism – Hungarians in exile – Hungary – International Confederation of Trade Unions (ICFTU) – opposition to communism – social democratic women – woman activist

 | DOI:10.1163/9789004682481_017

Anna Kéthly was a twentieth-century Hungarian politician and trade unionist. Although she was a well-known figure in Hungary for almost sixty years, she seems to have disappeared almost entirely from national memory, save for a statue erected in her honor in 2015. Despite her relative obscurity in the popular imagination, the historiography of Anna Kéthly's life and work is quite large and has been produced mainly by independent researchers.[1] However, while there are many works that cover select parts of her life or discuss her in passing,[2] there is no up-to-date biography of her life and work. Moreover, there is very little published material on her role as a union activist before and after World War Two. Fortunately, archival sources exist which allow for an exploration of Kéthly's links with the International Confederation of Free Trade Unions (ICFTU), an anticommunist international trade union founded on 7 December 1949 that supported her through a solidarity fund until her death in 1976.[3] Within the ICFTU, the American Federation of Labor-Congress of Industrial Organizations (AFL-CIO) was very powerful. Kéthly was in particularly close contact with the chief of its department of international affairs, Jay Lovestone.[4]

Born in 1889, Kéthly was a member of Hungarian parliament in 1922 and held a prominent position in the lower tier of Hungarian politics during the interwar period, moving into the upper echelons between 1945 and 1948, before she was imprisoned from 1950 to 1954. She then went into exile after 1956 as a result of her important role during the 1956 Hungarian Revolution.[5] She settled in Belgium, where she died in 1976 at the age of eighty-seven. During her

1 I will mention the work of the archivist and historian Erzsébet Strassenreiter, who devoted her life to collecting documents on Kéthly, beginning in the communist period and continuing thereafter. This "singular couple" could be the subject of their own paper. The works of the independent scholars Zsuzsanna Kádár, mainly about Kéthly's years in prison (1950–1954), and Csaba Loppert's work concerning her involvement in the uprising of 1956 are also noteworthy. Librarian Rita Klem focused on the eve of Kéthly's political career; historian Claudia Papp on the relationships between Kéthly and non-socialist movements; and professor of gender studies Andrea Pető has written about the role of Kéthly within the women's movement. Last, but not least, archivist and historian Mihály Zichy wrote about Kéthly's years in parliament and also collected and published part of her correspondence. Kádár 2017; Loppert 2017; Strassenreiter 2011; Klem 2004; Papp 2004; Zichy 2004; Pető 2003.

2 There is no separate entry for Anna Kéthly in the standard reference volume on Central European feminism: De Haan, Daskalova, and Loutfi 2006.

3 The ICFTU, founded in 1945 and separated from the WFTU in 1949, is a transnational trade union organization that brought together many non-communist unions around the world during the Cold War.

4 Morgan 1999.

5 On Anna Kéthly and the social democrats during the entire post-1956 period, see Loppert 2017.

twenty years in exile, she was the most prominent figure of the Hungarian radical democratic opposition to the communist regime up until her death, and she was known for her staunch refusal to compromise and her open distrust of the government's actions, which she regarded as manipulations.

This chapter focuses on three dimensions that defined her public life: first, her unwavering loyalty to social democracy (with Marxist foundations, moreover); second, her commitment to women's struggles for equality and her close and friendly relationships with the feminist movement; and third, her trade unionism as the (co)-leader of the Hungarian Association of Private Clerks (Magyarországi Magántisztviselők Országos Szövetsége, HAPC)[6] before World War Two and as a beneficiary of the ICFTU Solidarity Fund after 1956.[7] However, her political trajectory was far from straight, marked as it was by reversals and divergences.[8] Yet, as historian Françoise Thébaud points out with regard to historical writing on feminist activists:

> In studying the personal life, the biographer of course is looking for a coherence of life between the ideas that are put forward and practical actions, but he tries also to understand the changing configurations of identities and multifaceted commitments. For these women, there is always the question what the most important struggle is at a given time.[9]

This insight is particularly useful when discussing Kéthly, whose life was ruptured by the establishment of a communist regime in Hungary after 1948. I will also show that upheavals in her political life were closely connected to those of Hungary as a whole and led her to alter to her political agenda. Kéthly's activism evolved from a struggle for the rights of women's activists within the Social Democratic Party of Hungary (Magyarországi Szociáldemokrata Párt, SDPH) and for working women in the relatively conservative society of the Horthy era (1920–1944) to a universal commitment to anticommunism between 1948 and 1976.[10] At the same time, she continued to socialize with women of the Socialist International and other non-governmental organizations.

---

6 See Bódy 2001, 108 on the composition of the social group of private employees (mostly commercial assistants, industrial assistants, nurses, hotel employees, and janitors).

7 Boxer 2007.

8 Dosse 2005.

9 Thébaud 2010, 40. Unless otherwise indicated, translations are mine.

10 Admiral Miklós Horthy became the Regent of Hungary following the collapse of the Habsburg Monarchy and the creation of an independent Hungarian state. The period between 1920 and 1944 is generally referred to as the Horthy era in Hungary.

Nevertheless, in spite of her exceptional career and the work she had to do to constitute herself as a political subject in a world dominated by men, this chapter critically analyzes her activist trajectory and political thinking. For example, it will demonstrate that she was motivated by ideology when she openly opposed the educational policy of Count Kuno Klebelsberg, the Minister of Education and Religious Affairs of the Bethlen government from 1922 to 1926. Notable is also her lack of serious analysis of the political regimes she fought. It is quite astonishing for a Marxist to equate the Kádár regime with the Egyptian dynasties of antiquity and to speak of "pharaohs" ruling over "slaves."[11] I will therefore point out blind spots in her thinking.

1 Kéthly as a Committed Social Democrat

1.1 *Childhood, Youth, and Initial Contact with Politics*

Anna Kéthly was born into a working-class family in a suburb of Budapest. Her father was an itinerant labourer, who worked on train or tramway construction sites and moved around the Habsburg Empire looking for work. Her mother was a housewife born in Somogy county in southwestern Hungary, one of the poorest regions in the country at the time. She birthed fourteen children, of whom five died young. Kéthly's early political education is a bit mysterious, although her father was a member of the SDPH. She herself gave several complementary, but not contradictory, versions of her first contact with socialism. In a speech in Zurich at the Socialist International's commemoration of her eightieth birthday, she emphasized her curiosity as a child, which eventually drew her to a funny character living in a shanty in front of her suburban house. She recounted that every evening, small groups of workers visited him to listen to speeches about socialism.[12] One evening, her curiosity drove her toward the socialist's shack, where she heard the following statement: "A socialist is a living torch, blessed are those who, at the end of their lives, can say that they brought light to many people." She did not actually understand what he was saying at first, but she thought of this prophet over and over again when she encountered injustice and impoverished children.[13] The moral/ethical part of the socialism of her childhood probably also affected this girl, who was also imbued with Christian imagery.

11 Kéthly 1961b, 1.

12 "Kéthly Anna felszólalása a születésnapjára rendezett ünnepen" [Speech of Anna Kéthly at her birthday party], Zürich, 15 November 1969, in Kéthly 2007, 51.

13 Kéthly 2007, 51.

In an article published in the emigrant newspaper she edited from 1957 to 1963—the *Népszava London* (*Voice of the People London*), addressed more fully below—she told a different story. She recalled standing on the pavement of Budapest in 1896 with her grandmother, watching two collective demonstrations: the Millennium[14] parade with aristocrats in beautiful costumes (*díszmagyar*) that she admired, and then a May Day parade organized by the SDPH, in which a wide range of craftsmen including tailors, carpenters, printers, and industrials workers participated. In her mind, this working-class memory complemented—even completed—the national memory she had also witnessed in the Millennium celebrations.[15] In a third recollection, she took part in a political meeting with Dezső Bokányi, one of the party's best speakers, in May 1903, and this made a strong impression on her.[16]

Her initial commitment to social democracy was based on impressions, emotions, and meetings, and only thereafter expanded through reading and her participation in activities organized by the HAPC[17] and women's associations around 1919. Although she is thought to have officially entered the local section of the Budapest social democratic party in 1917, at the age of twenty-eight,[18] the scant evidence related to her earliest public activities[19] do not indicate any "purely political activities" before 1921. From 1919 to 1921, she was a social activist committed to democracy and pacifism. She feared the type of political violence perpetrated by the red activists during the short-lived the Hungarian Soviet Republic (1919) and supported by Béla Kun's councils, which led her away from communism for good, even if she seems to have been sensitive to the patriotism undergirding the commitment of some of her comrades in the Hungarian Red Army.[20]

14 Expression used to define the millennial anniversary of the settlement of so-called Magyar tribes along the Danubian basin.

15 Kéthly 1958a.

16 Mentioned in the interview with her friend Zseni Várnai. Kéthly 1946a, 18. About political life in Hungary from the Austrian Empire to the Second World War, see Janos 1982.

17 Note that Hungarian social democracy, similar to the German or Austrian model, was based on the symbiosis of party and trade unions so that, at least until the First World War, unionization was the main (and tolerated by the authorities) form of party membership. See Lux 2008.

18 Strassenreiter 2011, 12.

19 Müller 1964, 368.

20 Letter from Anna Kéthly to Béla Király, 23 March 1960, in Kéthly 2007, 272–273.

1.2 *On the Public Stage*

Anna Kéthly officially came onto the public stage in 1921, during the SDPH's traditional May Day meeting, which preceded the annual parade. She was actually nominated to be the party registrar by Mrs. Müller, the head of the women's association of the party, who wanted Kéthly's appointment to demonstrate the party's commitment to equality between men and women. Kéthly was immediately noticed by both those social democrats who remained in the country and those who had gone into exile because of political repression, and she soon became a public figure. Her charisma helped party functionaries explain her accelerated rise within the party to the point of becoming a candidate in the third position on the list of the first electoral district of Budapest (Buda) during the national elections of 1922. Two candidates were elected, but the second was also elected in a provincial district and chose to represent it instead. Kéthly took her place, becoming the youngest member of Parliament and the second woman elected to serve in the body.[21] During her long parliamentary career, she spoke out on concrete social issues (workers' rights, public education policy, the rights of widows and orphans) mostly without explicitly connecting these issues to the general political demands of the Social Democratic Party; she relegated these discussions to her articles in the partisan press, both the mass-market daily *Népszava* (*Voice of the People*) or more theoretical periodicals such as *Szocializmus* (*Socialism*).

She sometimes followed a very narrow ideological line in her discussion of issues. Concerning public education, Kéthly, as a member of the education committee, addressed Parliament when bills concerned this field, such as in a speech given on February 10, 1926 about the plan to construct rural schools presented by the Minister of Education and Religious Affairs, Count Kuno Klebelsberg. This particularly ambitious project envisaged a complex system of financing school construction through revenue collected from landowners and taxpayers. City councils were to collect these various contributions and pass them on to contractors. In this case, Kéthly had some difficulty arguing against the project, which required rural elites to contribute and aimed to eliminate rural illiteracy. In the opening of her parliamentary speech, she recognized that the project was a "grand design" but then denounced the methods of its implementation with unconvincing arguments: on the one hand, local financing risked placing the future schools under the control of local notables; on the other hand, there was a question concerning the lingering religious orientation or schools that contradicted what the French would call *laicité*. "We

21 The first was a nun, Margit Schlachta, elected in 1920.

socialists know only state and public schools, and we are enemies of denominational education." In short, under the pretext of unreachable goals, she and her party refused to vote in favor of quite progressive law.[22]

Kéthly never changed her *credo*, her fundamental political orientation, during her long political life. She was and remained a Social Democrat, whose main ideas were directly rooted in the experience of World War One and its chaotic and bloody aftermath in Hungary. She always maintained the hope of a socialist society achieved through democracy. This was true during the Horthy period, the early postwar years (1944–1948), the years of repression and imprisonment (1948–1956), her "emergence from nothingness"[23] in 1956, and her two decades in exile (1956–1976). Along with many of those she corresponded with during her exile, she looked back on history at the end of her life, articulating her own definition of socialism and the consistency of her Marxist convictions: "Without ideology, an effective workers' movement is not possible, people must follow concrete and precise ideas, we must think within the framework of a system of clear ideas, and not from vague generalities such as 'humanism,' 'democracy.' For my part, I reject the view that Marxism is no longer relevant."[24]

From a Marxist perspective, she condemned the emerging economic relations between West and East through *detente*. For example, in 1965, in a letter to her secretary Ágnes Martony, she described as shameful the economic agreement signed between the (Fried.) Krupp AG and the Hungarian government related to the latter supplying industrial buildings and a labour force, considering it an exploitation of Hungarian productive forces organized by the communist dictatorship in the service of German capitalists.[25] Nevertheless, Kéthly acknowledged the difficulty of pursuing the socialist ideal in so far as man is not omnipotent, but she highlighted the need to try: "We poor people on earth cannot create in such a way that we do not come into contact with the dirt of everyday life, [we can] only rebuke those who look down from the ivory tower at the bustling crowd below."[26] Between 1971 and 1973, when she was more than eighty years old, she became the prime mover behind a project known as the Alternative.

22 See *Országgyűlés Képviselőházának naplója* 1927, passim, sitting of 10 February 1926.

23 Kéthly 1956.

24 Letter from Anna Kéthly to Vilmos Vass, 31 July 1972, in Kéthly 2011, 202.

25 Letter from Anna Kéthly to Ágnes Martony, 18 March 1965, in Kéthly 2007, 301.

26 Letter from Anna Kéthly to István Szabó, 18 May 1959, in Kéthly 2007, 36.

1.3 *The Alternative*

The Alternative refers to a set of proposals the Hungarian Social Democratic Party-in-exile developed under Kéthly's leadership in the early 1970s. These proposals were summarized in a thirty-page document presented at a meeting of the Hungarian Social Democrats-in-exile held in Vienna in June 1973 in the presence of delegates from the Socialist International. These proposals included a reaffirmation of the Marxist identity of the party, the desire to establish a neutral Hungary and to experiment with new forms of democracy based on the experiences of the workers' councils that emerged during the Revolution of 1956, and, finally, it called for the reconciliation of social progress and the market economy.[27]

The famous Hungarian-born French historian and sociologist Pierre Kende—a former communist who joined the 1956 Revolution, was later exiled to France, and then became a member of the left-wing intellectual opposition to Kádár's regime—told me about the many trips Kéthly made to Paris, when she was already over eighty years old, to meet him in a little café not far from Saint-Germain-des-Prés. He recalled she spoke like a student during the many hours they spent together, working to elaborate a socialism of the possible.[28] Above all, she hoped for "intelligent and humane" changes in a future Hungary liberated from communism.[29]

2 Kéthly as a Socialist Feminist

2.1 *Facing Horthy's Counter-Revolutionary Power and Changes in Women's Rights*

The changes she likely had in mind when speaking to Pierre Kende necessarily involved women, as the question of their rights was always a major dimension of Kéthly's political thinking. To understand her positions, it is necessary to understand the history of women's suffrage in Hungary. A franchise reform law was passed on 22 November 1918, granting the right to vote to all women aged twenty-four and older (for men, it was twenty-one), who could read and write (a regulation applying only to women), and who had been Hungarian citizens for more than six years. Béla Kun's Soviet Republic lowered the age of political majority to eighteen, but only for working women (and men). After its fall in August 1919, Hungary experienced a particularly intense counterrevolutionary

27 "Szociáldemokrata Alternatíva-1973" 1991.
28 Interview with Pierre Kende, Malakoff [France], 22 June 2020.
29 Letter from Anna Kéthly to Pierre Kende, 31 October 1973, in Kéthly 2011, 223.

reaction, during which women activists were among the victims of political reprisals and violence.[30] Women's (and men's) right to vote reverted to the age of twenty-four, and women alone had to have completed four years of elementary studies. It was at this time that Kéthly became an activist in the women's branch of the socialist party, which essentially focused on caring for imprisoned women and their children.

The counterrevolutionary regime had its own women's organization, the National Federation of Hungarian Women (Magyar Asszonyok Nemzeti Szövetsége, NFHW), founded in January 1919 by the writer Cécile Tormay. This organization aimed to promote a conservative and Christian model of women's roles in society and to fight, in its own sphere, against progressive feminism, which it blamed (along with other things) for Hungary's military defeat and territorial losses.[31] First, the NFHW attacked the Feminists' Association (Feministák Egyesülete, FA), which was created in 1903 by the accountant Rosika Bédy-Schwimmer, who struggled for women's suffrage and ran the journal *A Nő és a Társadalom* (*Woman and Society*), which was concerned with and reported on the everyday lives of women workers. During World War One, Schwimmer was an unwavering pacifist activist, before becoming among the world's first female ambassador (to Switzerland) during the short-lived republican government led by Count Mihály Károlyi between November 1918 and February 1919.[32]

Second, the NFHW targeted the Association of Social Democratic Women, whose leading figure was the young social democratic clerk Mariska Gárdos. In 1905, Gárdos, at the age of barely twenty, gathered crowds of working-class women in one of Budapest's most prestigious places (the Vigadó) to announce the launch of a newspaper for socialist women workers entitled *Nőmunkás* (*Woman Worker*).[33] Gárdos also constantly battled with the male party leadership over the recognition of social democratic women's identity and claims. After a time, she was sidelined because of her strident woman's activism, although she made a big comeback during the Hungarian Soviet Republic of Béla Kun (21 March 1919–1 August 1919). After its collapse, she fled to Austria, paving the way for a more moderate personality like Anna Kéthly to take the lead on working women's issues.

---

30 Selected testimonies on the repression of women activists in 1919–1920 in Csillag 1981. About the women's movement in Hungary between 1918 and 1923, see Szapor 2017.

31 On the rejection of the values of the FA by the NFHW, see Acsády 2011.

32 On the period before the First World War, see Zimmermann 1999.

33 For more on the political destiny of Bédy Schwimmer and Gárdos, see Zimmermann 1996.

2.2 *Early Discussions on Feminist Issues*

In October 1920,[34] a young, and virtually unknown social democratic woman named Anna Kéthly sent an open letter to the Social Democratic Party, which was then published in *Woman Worker*. The letter accused the party's almost all-male leadership of what today would be called *machismo*. She mentioned qualities such as "modesty" and "humility" that party leaders ascribed to women as grounds for a purely theoretical equality, which was certainly written into the party's programs but which in reality amounted to a recognition of women as having a purely decorative role in the party. The letter ended with a call for the mobilization of socialist women that had an undeniably feminist accent: "We women comrades! Let's go ahead and show them that we are not a negligible quantity."[35] The editor-in-chief at the time supported Kéthly's campaign. The editorial from 15 October 1921 demanded the education of women,[36] and the one from 1 December 1921, also signed by Kéthly,[37] sarcastically called on women to maintain their ignorance of public affairs and confine themselves to the kitchen and the education of children in an effort to lampoon attitudes toward women. Kéthly's approach meets Karen Offen's definition of a feminist, providing "women's own formulation of needs, the awareness of the institutionalized, gender-specific discrimination against women group as well as the demand for a change of such ideological concepts or institutions to correct male dominance in culture and society."[38]

Kéthly also knew that in order to have a real impact among her comrades, she needed to justify her demands using socialist ideology. She therefore referred to the Marxist thinker August Bebel to make a case for improving the position of women in public and private life.[39] In 1928, she also wrote a preface to his famous book *Women and Socialism*, which explained the origins men's domination over women in the capitalist system and the domestic sphere.[40] She, finally, convinced Hungarian social democrats, with the help of other activists, to increase the proportion of women engaged in street politics. As a

34 Kéthly 1920, 2.

35 Kéthly was one among many other social democratic women in Europe fighting for the equality of women in labour parties during interwar period. For more on the gender gap in European social democracy during this time, see Gruber and Graves 1998.

36 Kéthly 1921a, 1.

37 Kéthly 1921b, 1.

38 Offen 1988, 152. Concerning socialist feminism, see the seminal paper of Barbara Ehreinreich. Ehrenreich 2005.

39 See Klem 2004, 225. The author speaks about Kéthly opening a political meeting advocating Bebel.

40 Kéthly 1928a.

result of her work, social democrat women managed to hold fifty public meetings separate from male party members during the Budapest electoral campaign of 1930.[41]

Anna Kéthly's electoral campaign—which occurred following the implementation of a new electoral law that further limited women's right to vote by excluding women (but not men) younger than thirty from franchise—provoked comments about her appearance and the female body. A newspaper in Szeged, one of the largest cities of southern Hungary with a rather liberal tradition, made the following remarks about Kéthly: "the creole face, the dark look of her eyes, [...] her calm speech gives her a lot of masculinity."[42] Her political credibility was linked to her physical appearance, and her unemotional elocution was attributed to a "virile" character. During the campaign, she spoke at many women's meetings and became very popular.[43] Her election to Parliament was certainly noticed, but it did not provoke excessive commentary. Her connection with Margit Slachta, a leading figure of the devotional Catholic women's movement associated with the government party who had been elected the previous term, was nevertheless emphasized, perhaps especially because both women were single and childless. In her public image and in interviews and official declarations, Kéthly minimized her feminist identity and asserted herself as a member of the party. This was the case, for example, in an interview she gave to the most famous liberal newspaper, *Pesti Napló* (*Pest Daily*), during which she declared that she was not a feminist, arguing that feminism would only cure the symptoms of a sick society; rather, she asserted herself as a socialist who wanted to cure society as a whole. For this reason, she declared, "we don't need a special women's policy."[44]

2.3 *Kéthly's Activities in the Hungarian Parliament and the Labour and Socialist International*

A member of Parliament from 1922 to 1948, Kéthly was a tireless defender of working women, widows, and orphans. Throughout this time, she remained dedicated to the protection of the weakest, which explains why she could, in certain cases, ask for the differential treatment of women. In one case, she argued in favor of special labour protections for women workers, asking for a complete prohibition on woman's night work which, if not abolished, could compromise the future of the country. Actually, the question of women's night

41 Papp 2004, 174.
42 *Szeged*, 1922, 2.
43 Klem 2004, 226.
44 Interview with Anna Kéthly in "Beszélgetés Budapest női képviselőjelöltjeivel" 1922, 4.

work and, more broadly, women-specific labour regulations, had triggered a major European-wide debate in the interwar period. While the International Labour Organization (ILO) and International Federation of Trade Unions (IFTU) supported women-specific restrictions on night work, feminists supporting the full legal equality of women, like those involved in the Open Door International (ODI), opposed such measures.[45]

Kéthly also addressed practical considerations related to women's work, which was often harder (and even more poorly paid) than men's. This is the case in her speech from 17 November 1927, in which she characterized women as "slave[s]" who laboured as workers, wives, and mothers. She gave concrete examples of workers in glass and lamp factories, who worked at temperatures between 40 and 45°C (104–113°F) for more than twelve hours a day. She also referred to women workers' health problems and the challenges of childbirth, drawing attention to the ruling classes' prejudices about working-class women's so-called lack of sense of collective responsibility and lack of culture. According to these prejudices "the working woman does not have enough culture to understand" that the period before and after giving birth to a child "doesn't only belong to herself but also to the community [and] that she owes it to the community to take special care of herself during this period." Kéthly rejected such views, arguing that "this is not a question of the culture of the woman worker" but "a severe economic problem" since the woman worker simply was "forced to work" during the pre- and postpartum period.[46]

Finally, she recognized how issues related to the woman question magnified the broader inequalities of capitalist society. During a speech in Parliament on 4 April 1930, Kéthly insisted on respect for the principle of "equal work, equal pay," especially in industries where women workers were the most exploited.[47] She rarely spoke about women's rights in a strictly political sense. Of her more than 300 interventions in Parliament, only one speech from 20 March 1929 took such a stance, defending as it did the right of women to vote in local elections, which at the time was called into question by a bill. She stated that women's right to vote in local elections existed in most European countries.[48]

This allusion to other European countries is typical of Kéthly. Indeed, she had a particularly broad view of political, social, and economic issues and never hesitated to use foreign examples to defend her arguments. She had many regular contacts, in particular women, thanks to the transnational dimensions of

45 Zimmermann 2019, 205.
46 *Országgyűlés Képviselőházának naplója,* 1927 passim, sitting of 17 November 1927.
47 *Országgyűlés Képviselőházának naplója* 1927 passim, sitting of 4 April 1930.
48 *Országgyűlés Képviselőházának naplója* 1927 passim, sitting of 20 March 1929.

her activism.[49] She participated in three Women's Conferences of the Labour and Socialist International between 1925 and 1931 (in Marseilles in 1925, Brussels in 1928, and Vienna in 1931), where she cultivated robust networks, deep bonds of comradeship, and strong friendships, in particular with the Austrian delegate Gabriele Proft and Marion Philips from England. Absolute pacifism, the link between war, fascism, and women's inequality was among the dominant themes of her interventions at these conferences, which were always received with great respect by the audience. On her return to Hungary, she reported on the major themes of the conferences in publications like the *Voice of the People*, *Woman Worker*, or *Socialism*.

2.4 *Kéthly's Relationship with the Feminists' Association* (FA)

Kéthly's activities raise the question: Was she a representative of only her party concerning women's rights, or did she also support the FA? Within the broader European context, this question reveals the supposed cleavages between so-called bourgeois suffragists and revolutionary or left-wing women activists, which has received nuanced treatment by Marylin Boxer.[50] "Bourgeois" was used pejoratively by Marxist-socialist women like the German activist and politician Clara Zetkin at the beginning of the twentieth century, and this became the orthodox position of the international socialists (and even more so, communists) after the World War One. In Hungary, members of the FA, most of whom were working women such as schoolteachers, post office employees, or clerks themselves, were actively engaged in efforts to secure working women's rights.

Claudia Papp, who has studied the archives of the FA during the interwar period,[51] discovered a close relationship between Kéthly and the FA: her name appears on a register of individual members of the association, on an invitation to a dinner (which attests to her socializing with FA activists),[52] and on invitations to the association's annual congress.[53] Papp also refers to Kéthly's cooperation with the FA on actions related to women's rights[54] both in Hungary and abroad. It is also worth noting that she was scheduled to speak at the tenth

49 On the transnational activism of socialist women in the interwar period, see Ghit 2021.

50 Boxer 2007.

51 Papp 2004.

52 Letter from the Feminists' Association to Anna Kéthly, 10 December 1926, Domestic Correspondence Number 8, Feministák Egyesülete [Feminists' Association], P999, Magyar Nemzeti Levéltár Országos Levéltára [National Archives of Hungary, MNL OL], Budapest, Hungary.

53 Letter from the Feminists' Association to Kéthly, 15 April 1926, Domestic Correspondence Number 8, P999, MNL OL.

54 Papp 2004, 452–453.

Congress of the International Alliance of Women (IAW) held at the Sorbonne in Paris in June 1926, but withdrew at the last minute. Eugenie Meller-Miskolczy, the Corresponding Secretary of the FA attending the congress, paid tribute to Kéthly at the congress, describing her as one of their (FA's) own:

> Infinite gratitude and warm admiration for the wonderful work of our member, Miss Anna Kéthly, in our National Assembly. Being a member of the Social Democratic Party, it is quite admirable how she has succeeded in winning the deep respect of all members of the National Assembly. She never fails to make use of every available occasion to speak on behalf of the economically and socially weak and of women and children. Her proposals and beautiful speeches on this subject are so numerous that it is absolutely impossible to quote or enumerate them.[55]

2.5 *Total Pacifism*

One of the main struggles shared by Kéthly and the FA was the fight for peace and the refusal to use belligerent methods to challenge the Treaty of Trianon. This militant commitment to peace was very badly received in postwar Hungarian society, where territorial revisionism enjoyed near-total consensus. Kéthly's parliamentary immunity made it possible for her to contribute to and publicize the pacifist cause. For example, together with the FA, she regularly participated in the international summer school for peace (once serving as a lecturer in Lepence, Hungary in 1929) as a member of the transnational network of the Women's International League for Peace and Freedom (WILPF). She also expressed her distaste for war in International Socialist Women's forums, in particular at the International Women's Conference in Brussels in 1928, where she expressed absolute opposition to the mobilization of women in times of war. She held that women must refuse to serve even in civil defense structures and campaign for the closure of arms factories. In this vein, she also published a theoretical article in *Socialism* the same year.[56]

As a journalist for the *Woman Worker* starting in 1921, and later as its editor-in-chief between 1926 to 1938, Kéthly could also publish and promote radical propaganda in favor of world peace. As late as 1937, an editorial in the *Woman Worker* reported on the International Women's Peace Conference held in Lucahovice, Czechoslovakia. The general theme was the total opposition to

55 Rapport sur le 10e congrès de l'Alliance Internationale pour le suffrage des femmes [Report on the 10th Congress of the International Alliance for Women's Suffrage], Paris 30 May–6 June 1926, 236.

56 Kéthly 1928b.

war—regardless of whether it takes place in Europe or in Asia and involves "white, black or yellow" soldiers—as well as the refusal to distinguish between defensive and offensive warfare; therefore, no particular characterization of the Franco camp (in the Spanish Civil War, 1936–1939) was given, and the only mention of it related to the fact that Moroccan soldiers were associated with it.[57]

The social democratic press reported rather benevolently on the pacifist agenda of the feminist movements. Nevertheless, an affirmation of political orthodoxy explains the ideological rejection of "feminists" in some articles published in the *Woman Worker*. (Bourgeois) "feminists" were accused of being idealists, offering nothing more than biological justifications for the so-called aggression of men and the so-called pacifism of women. Feminists were also accused of using only congresses and petitions to elevate women's place in the existing society, whereas socialist women fought alongside men to destroy capitalism and imperialism, which constituted the real reasons for the inferior position of women in society.[58]

After World War Two, Kéthly remained a pacifist activist. She did not pursue women's politics in the SDPH to the same extent, but she published writings that took stock of the history of the women's movement. For example, in 1946, she wrote an introduction to a short essay by the Austrian socialist Marianne Pollack in which she placed the women's movements in a broader political framework from which only the Social Democratic Party emerged as fully legitimate because it fought for a new social order. In contrast, feminist organizations were accused of being only "female-orientated" and advocating for depoliticization.[59] In 1948, she published another essay in the yearbook of the *Voice of the People* in which she again insisted on the link between capitalism, war, and the status of women.[60]

2.6 *Kéthly on Women and her Own Public Persona*

Anna Kéthly's thinking was shaped by number of opinions about women and their roles in society. They must be able to choose who to marry and enjoy an egalitarian relationship afterward; however, they must also be a (good) mother and wife as well as a good housewife; hence, her objection to women who live in luxury and pay employees to educate their children and clean their house.[61]

57 [Unsigned, most probably Anna Kéthly] 1937, front page.
58 Papp 2004, 455.
59 Kéthly 1946b, 3–6.
60 Kéthly 1948, 26.
61 [Unsigned, most probably Anna Kéthly], 1934, front page.

Kéthly clearly criticized certain new patterns of behavior among married women that spread throughout Hungary in the 1920s and 1930s, inspired by the American "flapper" or the French "*garçonne*." Hungarian historian Balázs Sipos published seminal study on this phenomenon, which revises interpretations that insisted on the purely reactionary character of the interwar period with regard to gender relations. According to Sipos, even in the Christian national atmosphere of the time, some women belonging to the Budapest bourgeoisie (Sipos speaks mainly of women from this milieu) abandoned their homes to go shopping or dancing and entrusted the education of their children to domestic servants.[62]

Kéthly also took up the idea of women's gender-specific skills, in particular in social policy: "There are things that women understand better, for example social policy."[63] Finally, she tackled the prejudices of her time. For example, in an article advocating the vocational career, Kéthly argued that professions intended essentially for boys were suitable for girls too. For example, she considered the job of (auto) driver (*gépkocsi vezető*) as legitimate as that of an actor, painter, or artist in general.

The public persona of Kéthly herself was complex. She remained single and childless her entire life, and she exhibited no fear when speaking to entire assemblies of working-class men, as for example, on 8 January 1930, when she greeted construction workers as a delegate of the social democratic parliamentary faction. She was stern and sometimes rude, which is why she gained the respect of her conservative male political opponents. Public opinion said that "there is only one man in the parliament, and it's a woman."[64]

However, Kéthly abandoned her somewhat austere appearance when she attended concerts or the theater with friends she met in the social democratic movement. These friendships, some of them lifelong, played a major role in her life.

2.7 *The Women's Agenda after 1948*

After 1948, Kéthly adopted an anticommunist stance, first in Hungary and then in the West after the occupation of her country by the Soviet army in 1956. However, I did not find evidence that she took a special interest in the condition of women in communist Hungary, either in her correspondence or in articles she published in newspapers during her years in exile. The anticommunist struggle overwhelmed all other struggles until her death, even if those

62 Sipos 2019.

63 Kéthly 1930, 7.

64 In the original: "*Egyetlen férfi van a parlamentben, és az is nő.*"

struggles related to women. In the 1960s and 1970s, Kéthly continued to attend the international conferences of socialist women regularly, but there is no mention of women's liberation movements in the various exile publications for which Kéthly was editor-in-chief or in which she played an important role. She never quoted from the writings of feminist activists either. In terms of her social life, however, she tended to socialize with groups of women, as in 1969, when she celebrated her eightieth birthday among the members of Future-oriented Socialist Women (Femmes Prévoyantes Socialistes), a mutualist feminist organization; in a photo from the time, we can see her sharing a modest meal with her Belgian comrades.

Despite this shift in focus, she never stopped thinking about the condition of women. As a unique testimony of her ideas, she wrote a long-form article in 1975, on the occasion of the first International Women's Year, for a literary journal published for exiles in Paris entitled *Irodalmi Újság* (*Literary Newspaper*). In it, she discussed the struggles of social democratic women who fought for the "transformation of society" and the women of the Hungarian feminist movement whose "admirable" figures were more concerned with equality within the existing framework. She ended the article with a call for the equality of women's work and the abolition of the central role of money in conjugal relations.[65]

3 A Politician as Labour Activist

Her defense of women's rights was intimately linked to Kéthly's union experience,[66] which preceded it chronologically. She initially joined a union of private employees around 1909, before joining the union of public employees of Kassa (today Košice in Slovakia) in 1916.[67] She was a shorthand typist, probably working as an office clerk in the public sector, and became a permanent trade union official in charge of secretarial work. She was supposed to be "very modest," a quality typically associated with women.[68] She was first mentioned as an official of the private-sector clerks' movement in June 1919, when she traveled

65 Kéthly, "1975-A nők éve" [1975: Women's Year] in Kéthly 1994, 413–414.

66 Strassenreiter 2011, 12.

67 It should be noted here that the beginning of young Kéthly's professional and trade union career remains somewhat obscure. The most detailed source—her "confession" written during her years of imprisonment during the Rákosi regime—remains, at the very least, questionable. This is why in order to give an account of her career, I rely on articles in the press that appeared just after her election to parliament.

68 Szakasits 1922, 94.

to Kassa to assist in the victory of Red Army.[69] Her qualities as a stenographer certainly contributed to her political ascent. After her entrance into politics, she became—once again, rather quickly—one of the most important personalities in the social democratic HAPC.[70]

3.1 *Delegate of* HAPC *in Parliament*

In Parliament, faithful to the directives of the social democratic movement, she behaved as a trade unionist, defending the interests of employees, among others, when the situation arose. She intervened on 3 and 4 November 1923 to protest the prohibition of a congress of the HAPC by police authorities.[71] During her speech on 11 June 1927, she criticized a plan for compulsory governmental health insurance by arguing that the organizations resulting from it would be dependent on the state. Nevertheless, she admitted the legitimacy of a specific fund for employees, which she believed was the result of the union's struggles.[72] On 1 February 1928, she reported on a visit to the town of Gyöngyös, northwest of Budapest, which had suffered a catastrophic fire in 1917. In the Hungarian tradition of working-class sociography,[73] she accurately described the housing market situation in the medium-sized city, which saw the construction of luxury housing but very little social housing after the tragedy. Because of the lack of new and affordable housing, rents were too high for working-class families, and seven or eight individuals were crammed into a small space. Moreover, between fifty and sixty families were evicted, according to Kéthly.[74] She also identified the issues of low wages and increased working hours of employees as subjects of concern.[75] Parliament was a platform to defend the rights of the workers without explicitly connecting demands to socialist ideology. This restrained speech was clearly the result of the Peyer-Bethlen pact, signed in December 1921, which permitted the existence of the social democratic movement in the authoritarian Horthy regime while at the same time limiting its realm of action; in particular, the pact prohibited

---

69 Molnár 2020, 168.

70 *Magántisztviselő* in Hungarian. This professional category was formed at the end of the nineteenth century as a result of the mobilization of various guilds that did not wish to be assimilated into the emerging working class. Paradoxically, it was social democracy, ideologically opposed to anything that interposed itself between the proletariat and the bourgeoisie, that contributed to giving this body an identity. See Bódy 2001.

71 Zichy 2004.

72 *Országgyűlés Képviselőházának naplója* 1927 passim, sitting of 11 June 1927.

73 See Litván 1974.

74 *Országgyűlés Képviselőházának naplója* 1927 passim, sitting of 1 February 1928.

75 *Országgyűlés Képviselőházának naplója* 1927 passim, sitting of 6 February 1929.

the *politicization* of the trade unions dependent on the SDPH.[76] This created a situation in which activists, who generally occupied multiple positions in the movement (e.g., party leader, newspaper editor, trade unionist), had to carefully balance their speeches in order to avoid sanctions that could go as far as imprisonment.

3.2 *A Cold War Trade Unionist*

Trade unionism does not appear to have been a major element of Kéthly's public life between 1945 and 1948. She was arrested as a so-called rightist social democrat in 1950; was accused of being an English spy due to her transnational contacts in the interwar period; and was imprisoned for four years during the Stalinist era in Hungary. After her release in 1954, she was mainly focused on trying to reconnect with members of the SDPH. Her labour identity returned strategically to the forefront of her politics from the very first days of her exile in the West, insofar as the American branch of the ICFTU, through its representative Jay Lovestone, became her patron, ensuring her passage from Vienna to New York in 1956.[77] Lovestone's letters to Kéthly contain constant coaching, which is further confirmed by Kéthly's calendar between 1956 and 1958, which shows regular appointments with him—up to three times a week.[78] In a letter from 20 May 1959, Lovestone almost demanded she come to a conference of the ILO: "As you know the annual convention of the international labour organization will be meeting very soon at Geneva […] we are very anxious that you should come to Geneva." A hotel room was even reserved for Kéthly.

During her years in exile in Brussels from 1958 to 1976, she received an annual pension from the ICFTU, whose European branch was based in Brussels, in the amount of 120,000 Belgian Francs in 1971 (around 25,000 Euros in 2022). The ICFTU also financed the émigré newspaper *Voice of the People* (*London*), published from 1957 to 1963, which was supposed to be the newspaper of the free Hungarian trade unions, the existence of which was actually denied by some emigrants.[79] It must be noted that the *Voice of the People* printed in Hungary

76 Károly Peyer was the chief of the social democrats; István Bethlen was the prime minister of Hungary in 1921. Their agreement was initially secret.

77 She was in Vienna attending a convention of the Socialist International when Soviet troops invaded Hungary.

78 See Morgan 1999 and Anna Kéthly's Diary, Andor Bölcsföldi papers, Anna Kéthly 469/1747 Manuscripts collections, Országos Széchényi Könyvtár [National Széchényi Library], Budapest, Hungary.

79 Letter from an unknown Hungarian emigrant to Anna Kéthly: "Egy levél amelyre a Minagyasszonyunk és Gyámolitóanyánk Kéthly AnnaMária 'elfelejtett' válaszolni" [A letter to which AnnaMária, our Lady and guardian mother "has forgotten" to answer], Folder

had become the official newspaper of the trade unions when the Communist Party took control in 1948. Kéthly was the editor-in-chief of the London-based *Voice of the People* and made it a high-quality anti-totalitarian paper—i.e., the main goal of which was the end of the communist regime in Hungary—in which many intellectuals, some social democrats, some not, published. She herself wrote the editorials and many articles. It differed substantially from the traditional trade union newspapers of the Horthy era—such as the newspaper of private employees, the *Journal of Private Clerks* (*Magántisztviselők Lapja*), which were essentially confined to the internal workings of the union—in that it had a strong focus on international affairs. Although she continued her commitment to trade unionism and workers' rights, Kéthly was vigorously attacked by the Kádár regime's press organs, which depicted her as a renegade fighting for capitalism.

The condition of the workers in Hungary was nevertheless a regular element in *Voice of the People* (*London*), as illustrated in an article of 1 June 1958 about the comparison between "The Brussels exhibition and Hungarian reality."[80] From 1956 to 1959, Kéthly also campaigned to exclude Kádár's Hungary from the ILO and, of course, lost.[81] On 1 May 1961, in an article with an evocative title, she presented Hungarian workers as "real slaves"—comparable to those of the pharaohs in ancient Egypt[82]—of the colonized states of Eastern Europe whose "official unions" were led by civil servants who exploit workers.

She had no illusions about the Western ruling classes' commitment to anti-communism: she thought that big industry would push governments toward moderation and peaceful coexistence, particularly the government of the United States.[83] Until the end of her life, Kéthly received information about the experiences and conditions of Hungarian workers. She maintained that the tragedy of communism was that it was unable to raise living standards and labour conditions of the workers; for example, in the large workers' district of Csepel in the Hungarian capital city Budapest. The state-socialist regime presented Csepel as a model development, but according to Kéthly, "[t]housands

---

13, Strassenreiter Erzsébet [Erzsébet Strassenreiter papers] 307, Személyi gyűjtemények, visszaemlékezések [Private collections, Memoirs], Institute of Political History, Budapest, Hungary.

80 Kéthly 1958b, 1.

81 Letter from Anna Kéthly to the Sekers family, 2 September 1959, Kéthly 2007, 158.

82 Kéthly 1961b, 1.

83 See Letter from Anna Kéthly to József Schöller, 23 May 1963, Andor Bölcsföldi papers, Anna Kéthly 469/590, Manuscripts collections, Országos Széchényi Könyvtár [National Széchényi Library], Budapest, Hungary.

of flats are missing, thousands of workers are living in barracks, many machines in the factories are more than fifty years old."[84]

This type of analysis was quite common in the circles of the democratic left during the Cold War. The main problem was that proponents of this view remained silent on (at least a segment of) the population's obedience to or, at minimum, non-confrontational stance toward the Kádár regime, which was facilitated by the recognition of a minimal sphere of freedom in the private domain and the economic sphere. Kéthly was not able to produce a proper analysis of the totalitarian phenomenon—defined as a distinctive modernist political phenomenon defined by the absolute control over civil society by the state or a single party—and the dangers even the slightest signs of an open society posed to it. Strikingly, she applied the same language to describe Horthy's regime and communist totalitarianism. She was trapped in patterns of thought based on a mixture of a somewhat unnuanced Marxism (e.g., the Horthy regime as "fascist or semi-fascist") and left-wing patriotism/nationalism, as we can see, for example, in an article in *Voice of the People* (*London*).[85] Here, she lamented the Hungarian people's historical oppression and entitled her article after a famous verse from the *National Song* (*Nemzeti Dal*) written by the poet Sándor Petőfi during the Hungarian Revolution of 1848.

4 Conclusion

Anna Kéthly's life path was truly unusual for a female politician in Hungary and, more generally, in Central Europe. Born in the Habsburg Empire in the last quarter of the twentieth century, Kéthly was member of the leadership of a socialist feminist organization at the age of thirty, a member of Parliament at thirty-three, and a trade union leader at around the same age. If she failed to reach the highest echelons of power (except briefly after World War One), this had nothing to do with her gender but everything to do with the perpetual minority position of the noncommunist left in twentieth-century Hungary. Her ideological trajectory, despite turns and diversions, remained deeply rooted in her intellectual apprenticeships and youthful experiences, which explain both her limits and her greatness.

---

84 Letter from József Schöller to Anna Kéthly, 4 June 1974, Andor Bölcsföldi papers, Anna Kéthly 469/590, Manuscripts collections, Országos Széchényi Könyvtár [National Széchényi Library], Budapest, Hungary.

85 Kéthly 1961a, 1.

Regarding her limits, Kéthly never really engaged in an in-depth critical analysis of the regimes she fought. Informed by Marxist ideas at the very end of World War One, she was part of a mental universe in which an authoritarian regime like that of Regent Miklós Horthy could only be understood as a "reaction" or "(semi)fascism," that is, a more violent and brutal form of the Bach regime imposed by Austria after the failure of the Hungarian Revolution of 1848.[86] In turn, communism in Hungary, of which she had had a glimpse in 1919, was merely a form of "colonial oppression."[87] Indeed, she saw the Kádár regime as a puppet regime based on Hungarian workers' exploitation for the benefit of the Russian Empire, now renamed the Soviet Union. In Kéthly's writings and speeches, she invariably reverted back to images and metaphors based on parables from Egyptian antiquity or the Bible whenever she criticized the authoritarian or totalitarian political system. She sketched elaborate scenarios for the aftermath the regime but never thought about *how* these regimes might collapse.

As to her greatness, her stubborn fidelity to the ideals of her youth *a contrario* explains her constant stance throughout her long life of militancy: She remained an *observer*, directly or indirectly, confronted with many infringements on workers' rights. Her notes on the condition of workers under the Kádár regime, which were based on information sent to her by correspondents and friends who remained in the country, were perhaps still the most vivid and dynamic part of her existence and her memory. She remained exemplary as a woman *labour activist* until the end of her life, an identity that moved beyond her unwavering commitment to freedom and democracy in her country.

Summing up Kéthly's activism as it pertained to women workers, it should be remembered that from 1919 on, it was rooted in a singular awareness—both theoretical and practical and nourished by the writings of Rosa Luxemburg—of the exclusively male-dominated power structure within her party. The struggles she waged in the *Voice of the People* and through her cooperation with the FA were aimed at "denaturalizing" male domination and introducing the theme of equality between men and women in Parliament, of which she was a member starting in 1922. After the establishment of the communist regime in 1948, she decided to choose "the most important struggle" of the moment, namely the struggle for freedom. Nevertheless, she remained conscious of gender inequality, and in an article published in 1975, which can be considered her intellectual treatise on gender relations, she advocated for financial

86 Alexander Bach was a brutal Austrian Minister of the Interior, who repressed Hungary from 1849 to 1859.

87 *Gyarmati elnyomatás* in Hungarian; a term used by Kéthly. Kéthly 1961b, 1.

compensation for women's domestic work, which echoed similar activist efforts by leftist women associated with the women's liberation movement. According to Kéthly, women's struggles are always aimed at improving their condition in the most concrete and effective way possible. In this sense, she undoubtedly can be considered a life-long feminist activist.

Bibliography

Acsády, Judit. 2011. "Diverse Constructions: Feminist and Conservative Women's Movements and their Contribution to the Reconstruction of Gender Relations in Hungary after the First World War 1918–1923." In *Aftermaths of War: Women's Movements and Female Activists*, edited by Ingrid Sharp and Matthew Stibbe, 309–333. Leiden: Brill Academic Publishers.

Az 1927. évi január hó 25-ére hirdetett Országgyűlés Képviselőházának naplója [Chronicle of the House of Parliamentary Representatives announced 25 January 1927], vol. 5. 1927. https://library.hungaricana.hu/en/view/OGYK_KN-1927_05/.

Az 1927. évi január hó 25-ére hirdetett Országgyűlés Képviselőházának naplója [Chronicle of the House of Parliamentary Representatives, announced 25 January 1927], vol. 6. 1927. https://library.hungaricana.hu/en/view/OGYK_KN-1927_06/.

Az 1927. évi január hó 25-ére hirdetett Országgyűlés Képviselőházának naplója [Chronicle of the House of Parliamentary Representatives announced 25 January 1927], vol. 8. 1927. https://library.hungaricana.hu/en/view/OGYK_KN-1927_08/.

Az 1927. évi január hó 25-ére hirdetett Országgyűlés Képviselőházának naplója [Chronicle of the House of Parliamentary Representatives announced 25 January 1927], vol. 17. 1927. https://library.hungaricana.hu/en/view/OGYK_KN-1927_17/.

Az 1927. évi január hó 25-ére hirdetett Országgyűlés Képviselőházának naplója [Chronicle of the House of Parliamentary Representatives announced 25 January 1927], vol. 18. 1927. https://library.hungaricana.hu/en/view/OGYK_KN-1927_18/.

Az 1927. évi január hó 25-ére hirdetett Országgyűlés Képviselőházának naplója [Chronicle of the House of Parliamentary Representatives announced 25 January 1927], vol. 26. 1927. https://library.hungaricana.hu/en/view/OGYK_KN-1927_26/.

"Beszélgetés Budapest női képviselőjelöltjeivel" [Conversation with women candidates from Budapest]. 1922. *Pesti Napló* [Pest daily], 28 May 1922, 4.

Bódy, Zsombor. 2001. "La formation du groupe social des 'Magantiszviselö' en Hongrie 1890–1930" [The Formation of the Social Group Known as *Magántisztviselö* in Hungary, 1890–1930]. *Genèses* 42 (March): 106–120.

Boxer, Marilyn J. 2007. "Rethinking the Socialist Construction and International Career of the Concept 'Bourgeois Feminism.'" *American Historical Review* 112, no. 1 (February): 131–158.

Csillag, Rózsi. 1981. "A Gellért Szálló Pincéjében" [In the cellar of the Gellert Hotel]. In *Tanúságtevők 4.a.: Visszaemlékezések a magyarországi munkásmozgalom történetéből 1919–1933* [Testimonies 4.a: Memories of the history of the workers' movement in Hungary, 1919–1933], edited by Katalin Petrák, 35–50. Budapest, Kossuth Könyvkiadó.

Dosse, François. 2005. *Le pari biographique. Ecrire une vie* [The biographical challenge: Writing a life]. Paris: La Découverte.

Ehrenreich, Barbara. 2005. "What Is Socialist Feminism?" *Monthly Review* 57: 70–77.

Fonó, Zsuzsa. 1978. *A magyar munkásnők helyzete és szervettsége a két világháború között* [The condition and organization of Hungarian women workers between the two world wars]. Budapest: Szakszervezetek Elméleti Kutató Intézete.

Ghit, Alexandra. 2021. "Solidarity and Inequality: European Socialist Women's International Organizing in the Interwar Period." *ZARAH blog*, 21 June 2021. https://zarah-ceu.org/solidarity-and-inequality-european-socialist-womens-international-organizing-in-the-interwar-period/.

Gruber, Helmut, and Pamela Graves. 1998. *Women and Socialism, Socialism and Women: Europe between the Two World Wars*. New York: Bergahn.

De Haan, Francisca, Krassimira Daskalova, and Anna Loutfi. 2006. *A Biographical Dictionary of Women's Movements and Feminisms: Central, Eastern, and South Eastern Europe, 19th and 20th Centuries*. Budapest: Central European University Press.

Janos, Andrew C. 1982. *The Politics of Backwardness in Hungary, 1825–1945*. Princeton, NJ: Princeton University Press.

Kádár Zsuzsanna. B. 2017. "Kéthly Anna börtönben és emigrációban" [Anna Kéthly in prison and emigration]. In *Kéthly Annát a kormányba!—Magyar szociáldemokraták az 1956-os forradalomban* [Anna Kéthly into the government! Hungarian Social Democrats in the Revolution of 1956], edited by Csaba Loppert, 47–64. Budapest: Kéthly Anna Kulturális Egyesület.

Kéthly, Anna. 1920. "Egyenlők vagyunk? " [Are we equals?]. *Nőmunkás* [Woman worker], 1 October 1920.

Kéthly, Anna. 1921a. "A nők és a politika" [Women and politics]. *Nőmunkás* [Woman worker], 15 October 1921.

Kéthly, Anna. 1921b. "Ne politizáljunk!" [Let's not politicize!]. *Nőmunkás* [Woman worker], 1 December 1921.

Kéthly, Anna. 1928a [1895]. "Introduction." In *A nő és a szocializmus* [Woman and socialism], by August Bebel. Budapest: Népszava editions. First translation in 1895.

Kéthly, Anna. 1928b. "A Nők a Szocialista Munkás-Internacionáléban" [Women in the Labour and Socialist International]. *Szocializmus* [Socialism] 18, no. 9 (September): 326–331.

Kéthly, Anna. 1930. "Az Alföld dolgozó népe hitvallást tett a szociáldemokrata eszmék mellett" [Workers of Alföld have pledged their faith to social democratic ideas]. *Népszava* [Voice of the people], 28 January 1930.

Kéthly, Anna. 1934. "A polgári házasság ellen" [Against civil marriage or against bourgeois households]. *Nőmunkás* [Woman worker], 28 October 1934.

Kéthly, Anna. 1937. "'Örülök, hogy nincs gyermekem'" [I am happy that I do not have children]. *Nőmunkás* [Woman worker], September 1937.

Kéthly, Anna. 1946a. "A Kéthly: Várnai Zseni beszélgetése Kéthly Annával" [Kéthly: Zseni Várnai's conversation with Anna Kéthly]. *Szívárvany* [Rainbow], 29 July 1946.

Kéthly, Anna. 1946b. "Preface." In *Egy nő megtanulja: mi a szocializmus* [A woman learns: what is socialism], edited by Marianne Pollak. Budapest: Népszava Könyvkiadó.

Kéthly, Anna. 1948. "Szociáldemokrata Nők a békéért" [Social Democratic women for peace]. *Népszava Náptara* [Agenda of the Voice of the people].

Kéthly, Anna. 1956. "Szocialdemokraták vagyunk!" [We Are Social Democrats!]. *Népszava* [Voice of the people], no. 1, 1 November 1956.

Kéthly, Anna 1958a. "Május" [May]. *Népszava* (London) [Voice of the people (London)], no. 5, May 1958.

Kéthly, Anna. 1958b. "Brüsszeli kirakat és magyar valóság" [The Brussels shop-window and Hungarian reality]. *Népszava (London)* [Voice of the people (London)], no. 6, 1 June 1958.

Kéthly, Anna. 1961a. "Rabok legyünk, vagy szabadok?" [Shall we be slaves or free?]. *Népszava (London)* [Voice of the people (London)], no.4, 1 April 1961.

Kéthly, Anna. 1961b. "A fáraók élnek" [Pharaohs do live]. *Népszava (London)* [Voice of the people (London)], no. 5, 1 May 1961.

Kéthly, Anna. 1994. *Szabadságot Magyarországnak: Irások, beszédek, tanúságtétel a magyar szabadságért a száműzetésben 1956–1976* [Freedom for Hungary: Writings, speeches, testimony for Hungarian freedom in exile 1956–1976]. Budapest: Kéthly Anna Alapítvány.

Kéthly, Anna. 2007. *Száműzve, de le nem győzve: Kéthly Anna emigrációs levelezése* [Exiled but not defeated: Emigration correspondence of Anna Kéthly], edited by Mihály Zichy. Budapest: Országos Széchenyi Könyvtár, Széphalom Könyvműhely.

Kéthly, Anna. 2011. *Kéthly Anna válogatott levelei* [Selected Letters of Anna Kéthly]. Edited by Erzsébet Strassenreiter. Budapest: Napvilág Kiadó.

Klem, Rita. 2004. "Kéthly Anna 1922-es választási kampánya" [Anna Kéthly and the electoral campaign of 1922]. *A Móra Ferenc Múzeum Évkönyvei: Studia Historica* [The yearbook of the Ferenc Móra Museum: Historical studies] 7: 207–228. https://library.hungaricana.hu/hu/view/MEGY_CSON_EK_SHST_07/?pg=0&layout=s.

Litván, György, ed. 1974. *Magyar munkásszociográfiák* [Hungarian workers sociography]. Budapest: Kossuth Kiadó.

Loppert, Csaba. 2017. *Kéthly Annát a kormányba!*—Magyar szociáldemokraták az 1956-os forradalomban [Anna Kéthly to the government! Hungarian Social Democrats in the 1956 Revolution]. Budapest: Kéthly Anna Kulturális Egyesület.

Lux, Judit. 2008. *A magyarországi szakszervezetek történetéből* [From the history of Hungarian trade unions]. Budapest: Friedrich Ebert Alapítvany. http://polhist.hu/wp-content/uploads/2017/11/lux2008.pdf.

Molnár, Miklós. 2020. *Kassától Košicéig: Molnár Miklós-emlékkönyv 5. kötet* [From Kassa to Košicé: Miklós Molnár memoirs, vol. 5]. Edited by László Bukovszky, Attila Simon, and Veronika Szeghy-Gayer. Budapest: Fórum Kisebbségkutató Intézet.

Morgan, Ted. 1999. *A Covert Life: Jay Lovestone, Communist, Anti-communist and Spy-Master*. New York: Random House.

Müller, Ernőné. 1964. *Eszmélés: Emlékezések magyarországi munkásmozgalmi élményeimre* [Awakening: memories of my experiences in the labour movement in Hungary]. Budapest: Kossuth Könyvkiadó.

Offen, Karen. 1988. "Defining Feminism: A Comparative Historical Approach." *Signs* 14, no. 1: 119–157.

Papp, Claudia. 2004. *"Die Kraft der weiblichen Seele": Feminismus in Ungarn, 1918–1941* ["The power of the female soul": Feminism in Hungary, 1918–1941]. Münster: Lit-Verlag.

Pető, Andrea. 2003. *Women in Hungarian Politics, 1945–1951*. Boulder, CO: East European Monographs.

"Schlachta Margit riválisa Szegeden" [Margit Schlachta's rival in Szeged]. 1922. *Szeged*, 2 May 1922.

Sipos, Balázs. 2019. *Women and Politics. Nationalism and Femininity in Interwar Hungary*. Trondheim: Trondheim Studies on Eastern Europe.

Strassenreiter, Erzsébet. 2011. "Kéthly Anna politikai pályaképe" [Tableau of the political career of Anna Kéthly]. In *Kéthly Anna válogatott levelei* [Selected letters of Anna Kéthly], edited by Erzsébet Strassenreiter, 11–83. Budapest: Napvilág Kiadó.

Szakasits, Árpád. 1922. *Szociáldemokraták a parlamentben* [Social democrats in parliament]. Budapest: Népszava.

Szapor, Judith. 2017. *Hungarian Women's Activism in the Wake of the First World War: From Rights to Revanche*. New York: Bloomsbury Academic.

"Szociáldemokrata Alternatíva-1973" [The social democratic Alternative-1973]. 1991. *Múltunk, politikatörténeti folyóirat* [Our past: Political history review] 36, no. 2–3: 228.

Thébaud, Françoise. 2010. *Socialisme, femmes et féminisme* [Socialism, women, and feminism]. Paris: Fondation Jean-Jaurès. https://www.jean-jaures.org/publication/socialisme-femmes-et-feminisme/?post_id=14830&export_pdf=1.

Zichy, Mihály. 2004. "Kéthly Anna a Parlamentben 1922–1943 1. rész" [Anna Kéthly in Parliament, 1922–1943. First part]. *Magyar Szemle* 13, nos. 11–12 (August): 42–63.

https://magyarszemle.hu/data/Lapszamok/2005/2004/MagyarSzemle_2004_Resz6.pdf.

Zimmermann, Susan. 1999. *Die bessere Hälfte? Frauenbewegungen und Frauenbestrebungen im Ungarn der Habsburgermonarchie 1848 bis 1918* [The better half? Women's movements and women's aspirations in Hungary of the Habsburg Monarchy, 1848 to 1918]. Budapest and Vienna: Promedia Verlag and Napvilág Kiadó.

Zimmermann, Susan. 2019. "Equality of Women's Economic Status? A Major Bone of Contention in the International Gender Politics Emerging During the Interwar Period." *The International History Review* 41, no. 1: 200–227. doi: 10.1080/07075332.2017.1395761.

Zimmermann, Susan. 1996. "Hogyan lettek feministák? Gárdos Mariska és Schwimmer Rózsika a századforduló Magyarországán" [How they became feminists: The origins of the women's movement in Central Europe at the turn of the century]. Translated by Zsuzsa Glavina. *Eszmélet* 7, no. 32: 57–92. http://eszmelet.hu/susan_zimmermann-hogyan-lettek-feministak/.

CHAPTER 17

A Croatian American Woman's Path to Labour-Left Racial Egalitarianism in the Industrial City, 1922–1944

Eric Fure-Slocum

Abstract

Nada Oristo Hudson, born in Croatia in 1922, arrived in the United States just as the Great Depression began. She and her sister Zlata grew up in a working-class neighborhood of Milwaukee, Wisconsin that was mixed ethnically and even modestly diverse racially, unlike many other areas in the deeply segregated city. This setting, along with ongoing exposure to South Slavic organizations that frequently aligned themselves with labour-left groups, led Hudson to become increasingly involved with popular front causes in which she became an advocate for racial egalitarianism. Discussing the history of the life and activism of a Croatian American woman in the industrial city and exploring family and migration as well as neighborhood and organizational influences, this chapter seeks to explain Hudson's role in a 1944 dispute over race and housing, when she confronted segregationists and helped defend the right of a Black family to live in a newly renovated apartment just a few blocks from where she lived. Hudson's labour-left Americanization set her on a path toward racial egalitarianism, not only as an abstract ideal but as an objective to be achieved through concrete local action.

Keywords

communism – Croatian American – Great Depression – labour-left organizations – Milwaukee – Wisconsin – racial egalitarianism – World War Two – women and activism

In early May of 1944, the *Milwaukee Journal* (*MJ*) recounted the scene at a westside Milwaukee meeting convened by neighborhood segregationists. Led by realtor Fred Barthel, this group aimed to force out a Black family of defense workers who had recently moved into a renovated building in the

 | DOI:10.1163/9789004682481_018

city's Sixteenth Ward. Counter-protesters also showed up, arguing that Edward and Eola Morris, along with their daughter, had the right to stay in their home. Among the counter-protesters were James Dorsey, leader of the local NAACP (National Association for the Advancement of Colored People), and Nada Hudson, a Croatian immigrant. By publicly condemning this attempt to deny access to housing for Black residents, Hudson drew the ire of segregationists who disparaged her as a renter and as a woman.[1]

Nada Hudson grew up in this industrial, working-class neighborhood, becoming involved in antifascist and civil rights initiatives closely tied to a militant labour movement in the 1930s and 1940s, before the Cold War undercut labour-left politics. Although the historical record for Hudson is limited and fragmentary, this essay uses the tools of social history and microhistory to excavate her life in working-class Milwaukee, situating her in the social and political contexts of Croatian migration, Depression-era life in a working-class neighborhood, emerging antifascist politics, and Civil Rights unionism during and shortly after World War Two. By paying close attention to this twenty-one-year-old Croatian American and writing the backstory of her involvement in the 1944 dispute, this essay contributes to histories of Eastern European women by exploring the dynamics of migration, class, gender, and race in a twentieth-century U.S. industrial city.

Hudson's early activism, and an effort to place her both historically and spatially, raises three questions. How did her family history—migrating from Eastern Europe and growing up as a Croatian American in a family that embraced "diaspora leftism"—shape her activism? How did growing up in this ethnically and racially mixed neighborhood, one in which Eastern European migrants lived adjacent to one of the city's few outlying Black working-class neighborhoods, affect her activism? How does this account of a labour-left Croatian American woman contribute to our understanding of interwar and wartime egalitarianism, providing not a correction but a counterexample to histories of Eastern European immigrants' path toward exclusionary whiteness? In the spirit of microhistory, this investigation makes no claims about Nada Hudson's life as typical or representative. Instead, these questions, spurred by a close examination of Hudson's early life, leading up to the 1944 dispute, illuminate a moment in the culture of labour-left activism, influenced by migration and Eastern European immigrants' everyday lives. Nada Hudson threw herself into this wartime clash over housing and race, carrying a commitment

1 "Want Negroes to Stay Away" 1944. See a 16 May 1944 *MJ* photograph in which labour-left allies of the Morris family presented a 468-signature petition; Hudson and Eola Morris sat at the center of the group, with Edward Morris to the side.

to antiracism spawned by her experience as a Croatian American growing up in this ethnically and racially mixed neighborhood and by her political formation within a vibrant ethnic and labour-left community that thrived during the 1930s and early 1940s in the industrial city.[2]

1 Family Background and Migration

Nada Goldner was born in 1922 in Sušak, a coastal urban industrial area in Croatia that is now part of Rijeka (Fiume). Her sister Zlata was born there a year earlier. Their mother, Paulina Tomljanović, came from Lič in the nearby mountainous Gorski Kotar region, and their father, Rudolfo Goldner, had been born farther east in the Slavonian region of Croatia. The surname Goldner apparently came from Rudolfo's mother, who was Jewish; she and his Catholic father never married. Both Rudolfo and Paulina, growing up in the Croatian areas of Austria-Hungary and marrying in 1920, witnessed war, the dissolution of an empire, and the post-Great War founding of the Kingdom of Serbs, Croats, and Slovenes (or Yugoslavia).[3]

Rudolfo Goldner came to the United States in the fall of 1923, just a year after Nada's birth and shortly before the restrictive U.S. Immigration Act of 1924. Like most South Slavic migrants, he was drawn by the promise of industrial work. Goldner's socialist politics likely also played a role.[4] Goldner soon made his way to Duluth, Minnesota, where relatives had settled and where four years earlier Paulina's brother was killed by a boom crane in a steel mill, leaving a widow and five children.[5] Goldner lived in a neighborhood that housed many of Duluth's South Slavic residents who worked at U.S Steel's sprawling Minnesota Steel Company. Croatian, Serbian, and Slovenian businesses and

2 On diaspora leftism, see Dyakonova 2019, 19. On 1940s egalitarianism, see Korstad 2018; Cobble 2004; Lipsitz 1994; Korstad and Lichtenstein 1988. On working-class immigrants and racial egalitarianism, see Enyeart 2019; Guglielmo 2010; cf., Roediger 2005; Cohen 1990. On political agency and feminism, see McNay 2010. On microhistory versus biography, see Lepore 2001, 133.

3 In the early 1920s, Sušak was part of Yugoslavia; Italy controlled the rest of Rijeka/Fiume. Momirski 2021; Kralj 2012, 259–261; Megan Hudson, Polly Hudson, and Ingrid Buxton, interview by Eric Fure-Slocum, 27 May 2021, (recording and transcript in author's possession) [hereafter Hudson and Buxton interview].

4 On Croatian and Austro-Hungarian migration, see Larson 2020; Steidl, Fischer-Nebmaier, and Oberly 2017; Zahra 2016; Brunnbauer 2012; Miletić 2012. On immigration restriction, see Ngai 2004.

5 "Steel Plant Laborer Killed by Large Crane" 1919.

social organizations also lined the streets of this neighborhood.[6] Along with dangerous working conditions, immigrants in 1920s industrial cities encountered both reactionary politics, driven by xenophobic movements, and radical working-class politics. Goldner likely found political compatriots in Duluth's immigrant neighborhoods, including socialists, communists, Wobblies, and other radicals rooted in the contentious labour politics of Duluth and the Iron Range. These radical labour and ethnic groups provided space for what the historian James Barrett defines as "Americanization from the bottom up," often counteracting employers' and nativists' assimilation schemes.[7]

Sometime between 1926 and 1928, Rudolfo Goldner left Duluth and made his way to Milwaukee. He likely was attracted to the city by jobs in Milwaukee's diverse, albeit troubled, industrial economy, by the presence of a sizeable Croatian and South Slavic community, and perhaps by Milwaukee's socialism—a politics that made an imprint on working-class life and access to public amenities. Goldner soon became a naturalized U.S. citizen, taking his oath on 11 April 1929. This newly acquired citizenship and his move to Milwaukee suggest Goldner's intent to remain in the United States.[8]

Later in 1929, Paulina Goldner and her two daughters Zlata and Nada boarded a passenger ship in Trieste (Trst/Triest), before it steamed to the U.S. with 1,300 South Slavic, Greek, and Italian passengers. According to the Vulcania's manifest, the three Goldners, who declared their nationality as "Jugoslavia" and language as Croatian, had lived most recently in Paulina's hometown. Although changes in U.S. immigration policy in the 1920s, building on earlier restrictions from Asian countries, now also limited migration from Southern and Eastern Europe, the Goldners managed to obtain visas in Zagreb as "non-quota" admittees due to Rudolfo's citizenship. Paulina, Zlata, and Nada landed in New York on 3 December 1929. With forty dollars and tickets to Milwaukee, the three Goldners made their way west to join Rudolfo. Soon after arriving in Milwaukee and settling into the working-class Sixteenth Ward, Paulina also became a naturalized U.S. citizen, as did her daughters,

---

6 Alanen 2007; Hudelson and Ross 2006; Holmquist et al. 1981.

7 Pinta 2021; Hudelson and Ross 2006; Barrett 1992.

8 "Rudolph Goldner Naturalization Card," Naturalization Petitions for the United States District and Circuit Courts, Northern District of Illinois and Naturalization Service District 9, Microfilm Serial 1285, Roll 66, National Archives and Records Administration, College Park, Maryland [hereafter NARA], *Ancestry.com Library Edition* [hereafter *Ancestry*], *Wright's Milwaukee* 1929. The earliest evidence of Goldner in Milwaukee is "Officers Are Named by Esperanto Club" 1928. On Milwaukee South Slavic communities, see Gurda 1999, 175, 178, 180, 226, 258; Ward 1976; Sebanc 1972. Milwaukee's socialist mayors were Emil Seidel (1910–1912), Daniel Hoan (1916–1940), and Frank Zeidler (1948–1960). McGuinness 2009.

establishing themselves in the United States just as the emerging economic depression added to the many difficulties immigrants faced.[9]

A new surname followed on the heels of the family's recently attained citizenship status. Rudolfo "translated" the family name from the German-Jewish surname Goldner, meaning goldsmith, to Oristo. This change indicated, in part, his enthusiasm for Esperanto, a language embracing a spirit of universalism, which he learned while in Europe, along with his seven other languages. In the U.S., he taught Esperanto, even offering lessons later in the 1930s under the auspices of the New Deal Works Progress Administration (WPA). But other factors apparently contributed to this name change. According to a puzzling *Milwaukee Journal* account, Goldner "changed his name because he believes it has a Jewish connotation and he belongs to a benefit order that excludes Jews." This group was likely the First Croatian Benefit Association, which soon would be upended by internal turmoil.[10] As the economy spiraled downward in the early Depression years, many working-class immigrant families turned to ethnic mutual benefit societies to survive. The secular Goldner family might have shed this marker of their Jewish identity out of economic need, having confronted the perils of interwar antisemitism in Europe and the U.S. that also targeted immigrants with radical leanings. Rudolfo continued, however, using Goldner as a middle name. The choice of this Esperanto name, an atypical step toward Americanization that was riddled with ambiguity, suggests a strategic universalism and secular pluralism that animated the family's radical politics and foreshadowed the later-1930s labour-left political culture.[11]

9 New York, Passenger and Crew Lists, 1820–1957, 1929 arrival, microfilm serial T715, 1897–1957, role 4637, line 19, page 177, *Ancestry*; "Paulina Goldner (Oristo) Naturalization Card," Naturalization Petitions for the United States District and Circuit Courts, Northern District of Illinois and Naturalization Service District 9, Microfilm Serial 1285, Roll 134, NARA, *Ancestry*; New York, Passenger and Crew Lists, mf T715, 1897–1957, role 4637, line 19, *Ancestry*. On immigration laws and naturalization, see Marinari 2020, 43–70; Schneider 2011, 214–222; Bader-Zaar 2004; Ngai 2004, 21–53.

10 "Rudolph Oristo Is Name" 1931; "Exit Rudolf Goldner, Enter Mr. Oristo" 1931; "Row Among the City's Croatians" 1931. Goldner's language facility proved useful as a chauffeur in Europe. Hudson and Buxton interview. On the Croatian Esperanto League and Universal Esperanto Association, which he represented, see Hamann 1928, 545–552; "Officers Are Named by Esperanto Club" 1928. On Oristo's classes, see "Esperanto Study Will Be Offered as WPA Project" 1936; "Courses in Esperanto" 1937; "New School Here to Teach the ABCs of Marxism" 1934. On Esperanto's universalism and roots, see Schor 2016, 59–108.

11 Cohen 1990. On Jewish immigrants' interwar name changes, see Fermaglich 2015. On interwar antisemitism in the United States, Milwaukee, and Croatia, see Valbousquet 2021; Goldstein 2003; August 2001; Sekelj 1988; Swichkow 1973.

So, as the 1930s began, the family had reunited, claimed U.S. citizenship, changed their name, joined Milwaukee's Croatian and South Slavic communities, and settled into an ethnically and racially mixed neighborhood. For Nada and Zlata Oristo, still in their pre-teens, this was indeed a period of rapid change, made even more challenging by Great Depression hardships. The economic and political turmoil of these years destabilized working-class families while also opening avenues for political and social affiliations that would prove formative.[12]

2 Sixteenth Ward Neighborhoods

The Goldner/Oristo family lived first in the southern-most part of the Sixteenth Ward's Merrill Park neighborhood. During the 1930s and early 1940s they moved from apartment to apartment, occupying at least half-a-dozen different rental units, mostly in the southern half of Merrill Park and later near the eastern boundary of Pigsville. These two neighborhoods clung to the edge of the Menomonee River Valley, an area that divided the city's North and South Sides and was filled with factories, stockyards, and railroad yards (see Map 17.1).[13]

Four features of the westside working-class neighborhood in which Nada and Zlata Oristo grew up are salient for this history. First, Merrill Park and portions of Pigsville were diverse ethnically and modestly diverse racially. The neighborhood housed many immigrants and first-generation residents from Southern, Eastern, and Central Europe. While overwhelmingly white, Merrill Park was also home to African Americans. A second and related feature of the neighborhood was the informal boundary line that segregated Merrill Park's Black residents into the Ward's southeastern corner. The 1944 conflicts over race and housing that engaged Nada Hudson stemmed from an initiative by segregationists to fortify this boundary in a neighborhood that was diverse but

12 U.S. Bureau of the Census, *1930 United States Federal Census* [hereafter *1930 U.S. Census*], Milwaukee, Wisconsin, page 19A, Enumeration District 0197, FHL microfilm 2342325, *Ancestry*; Hudson and Buxton interview. On Depression-era childhood in Milwaukee, see Webb 2006.

13 The family's Merrill Park addresses included: 46 N. 32nd St.; 30 N. 32nd St.; 100-A N. 32nd St.; 3712 Stevenson St.; 3224 W. Mt. Vernon Ave.; 218 N. 30th St; and 3756 W. Stevenson Street. Upon arrival, Rudolfo lived in an older Croatian neighborhood: 459 Walker St. "Rudolfo Goldner Naturalization Card"; Goldner/Oristo in *1930 U.S. Census*; U.S. Bureau of the Census, *1940 United States Federal Census* [hereafter *1940 U.S. Census*], Milwaukee, Wisconsin, roll T627_4556, pages 6A, 6B, Enumeration District 72–360, *Ancestry*; *Wright's Milwaukee* 1940, 511; *Wright's Milwaukee* 1944–45, 533.

not integrated. Third, the portions of the Sixteenth Ward discussed in this episode comprised a relatively small area. Its diverse residents likely encountered one another regularly, crossing racial boundaries as they walked, rode streetcars, or hopped on buses traveling to work, school, shopping, and meetings. Fourth, immigrants and Black workers had been drawn to this neighborhood by industrial and railroad jobs in the adjoining Menomonee Valley and other nearby factories. As a result, this neighborhood was filled with union members, many involved directly or indirectly in the rapidly growing Congress of Industrial Organizations (CIO).[14]

German Lutherans and then Irish immigrants were early residents of Merrill Park. By the early twentieth century, immigrants from Eastern and Southern Europe—especially Croatians, Slovenians, and Italians—settled into this working-class neighborhood. Along with apartments on the northern edge of the district, Merrill Park featured wood-frame, single-family houses and duplexes built during the decades around the turn of the century, many divided into rental units. This district recorded a higher percentage of renters than the citywide rate, with three-quarters of the units in the neighborhood filled by renters versus about two-thirds for Milwaukee as a whole. A prominent local landmark was St. Rose of Lima parish and school, where Irish Catholic residents worshipped and socialized. The parish adapted as newer residents moved in, making space for a Ukrainian service or for Italian parishioners, as religiously observant immigrants sought out services conducted in a familiar language. Croatian Catholics attended Croatian-language services at Sacred Heart Catholic Church just north of downtown or at St. Augustine Catholic Church in West Allis.[15]

---

14 Portraits of these Sixteenth Ward neighborhoods are drawn from: Buenker 2016, 132–139; Gurda 2015, 75–93; Gurda 1980, 44–45; Quinn 1979; Tien 1962, 198–202; Social Explorer Census 1950; Research Clearinghouse of Milwaukee 1950; Milwaukee County Community Fund 1945; Social Explorer Census 1940; 1940 U.S. Census, 52; 1930 U.S. Census. Merrill Park corresponds roughly to census tract 73 and Pigsville to tract 74 on the 1940 and 1950 census maps (see Map 17.1).

15 Gurda 1980, 21–58. Two 1940s-era Milwaukee mayors, brothers Carl and Frank Zeidler, grew up in Merrill Park. On St. Rose of Lima Catholic Church, see Gurda 1991, 5–8, 24–26; Schimpf 1987; St. Rose of Lima 1938; Grace M. Falbo, Oral History Transcript, conducted by Lawrence Balassaro and Diane Vecchio, River Hills, Wisconsin, 5 April 1991, 14, in "An Oral History of the Italians in Milwaukee," Milwaukee County Historical Society, Mss. 1770 [hereafter Falbo Oral History]. The parish boundaries covered Merrill Park and Pigsville. Sacred Heart Catholic Church moved out of the near-northside in the 1950s; both churches retain Croatian connections. Sacred Heart Parish; St. Augustine Church; Hostutler 2009; Ward 1991, 493–498; Sebanc 1972, 135.

To the west of Merrill Park, the Pigsville neighborhood was more insular and divided, both ethnically and religiously. Located where the Menomonee River curves, its hilly river-valley topography separated ethnic groups from one another, also distancing the neighborhood from the rest of the city. At the end of the 1930s, 16.2 percent of Pigsville's residents were immigrants, topping both the city's average and that of Merrill Park. Earlier German settlers affiliated with the theologically conservative Wisconsin Synod established Apostles Lutheran Church, a location that also served as a meeting place for the local segregation campaign.[16] Southeastern and Eastern Europeans—including Slovaks, Czechs, Poles, Croatians, Serbians, and Russians—settled next in Pigsville. Homeownership rates were higher here than in Merrill Park, placing the district a point above the city-wide rate of 32 percent.

Many neighborhood residents were industrial and service economy workers. About two-thirds of Merrill Park's residents and three-fourths of Pigsville's residents in 1940 were craftsmen, domestics, service workers, or labourers, including a high proportion of operatives, the core of the industrial economy. Neighborhood residents worked in the factories, rail yards, and shops in the valley, as well as other jobs just a streetcar or bus ride away, including the sprawling Allis-Chalmers plant in West Allis. Rudolfo Oristo found work as a machinist at the nearby Falk Corp., until he was fired possibly because of union activity and a workers compensation dispute. Paulina Oristo, who had been trained as a needleworker, mostly cleaned houses and cooked for families. Median annual incomes at the end of the 1940s ranged from $3,170 in Merrill Park to $3,275 in Pigsville, both well below the city rate of $3,747 or county rate of $3,900. The Depression hit these already struggling neighborhoods hard. Many families, including the Oristos, faced under- and unemployment throughout the 1930s. Public jobs programs such as the WPA offered some relief. In addition to his WPA Esperanto stint, Rudolfo Oristo was hired to transcribe Braille. Like many others, the Oristos turned to ethnic organizations and public agencies for food and other aid.[17]

16 Apostles Lutheran Church was located between N. 38th and N. 39th Streets on W. Michigan Avenue.

17 Home Owners' Loan Corporation, "Area Description—Security Map of Milwaukee," Areas D7, D7A, 1 October 1937, in Nelson, *Mapping Inequality*. The Area D7 description notes that the Merrill Park areas in which the Oristos lived, "between 27th and 35th, south of Claybourn," as home to factory workers, with Mt. Vernon Avenue containing some of the poorest housing. On the Oristos' employment, see "Falk Earnings Data Checked" 1937; "Rudolfo G. Oristo Obituary" 1951; Hudson and Buxton interview; Falbo Oral History, 12; "Esperanto Study Will Be Offered as WPA Project" 1936; Oristo in *1940 U.S. Census*; "World War II Drafts Cards (Fourth Registration) for the State of Wisconsin," Records of the

While Merrill Park was mostly white, African Americans and other people of color (including a small number of residents from Mexico) lived in the neighborhood's southeast section, making it the second largest concentration of African American residents in this highly segregated city. Almost ninety percent of Milwaukee's Black residents lived in the Sixth and Tenth Wards, areas just north of downtown. Black families began moving to Merrill Park in the 1920s, drawn by jobs in the railroad yards. Almost all were renters. Although the area's Black population declined during the Great Depression, likely due to economic hardship and hostility from white property owners, local Black institutions such as the Mount Vernon Gospel Church and the West Side Church of God in Christ took root. During the war and after, the neighborhood's Black population grew as the industrial workforce expanded, housing almost one hundred Black residents in 1940, equivalent to the city's modest percentage of Black residents. By 1950, Merrill Park's Black population increased almost fivefold, more than double the city's growth rate.[18]

In a 1937 analysis and 1938 mapping of Milwaukee real estate by the Home Owners' Loan Corporation (HOLC), these neighborhoods had been "redlined," rated as high-risk investment areas. Their "D," or red, rating was due in part to the industrial areas bordering these neighborhoods. The reports also noted a concentration of "lower income industrial workers" in Merrill Park and Pigsville, the presence of "many" families on relief, and the poor condition of an aging housing stock. Racial diversity, surprisingly, was not highlighted in the area's rating. The HOLC documented instead the mixed population of "Germans & Yugoslavians." In any case, the low rating meant that federal assistance in the form of publicly insured, long-term mortgages was channeled away from these neighborhoods. While private lenders' disinvestment in these

Selective Service System, 1940–, record group 147, box 231, microfilm series M2126, roll 77, NARA *Ancestry*. See also Buenker 2016, 133–139; Quinn et al. 1995.

18 As in other industrial cities, Black residents were confined largely to segregated neighborhoods. On outlying Black neighborhoods, see Michney 2017. In 1945, Black residents accounted for about two percent of Milwaukee's population. Fure-Slocum 2013; Trotter 2007; Citizens' Governmental Research Bureau 1946. On the neighborhood's racial composition, see Gurda 1980, 21– 88; Tien 1962, 198– 202; U.S. Bureau of the Census 1950; 1940 U.S. Census, manuscript sheets for Milwaukee's Sixteenth Ward, blocks 26, 28, 29, 31, *Ancestry*; Milwaukee County Community Fund 1945, census tracts 73 and 74. The Mount Vernon Gospel Church was at 320 N. 33rd Street; the West Side Church of God in Christ was on the valley's edge at 119 N. 32nd Street, near where the Oristo family first lived. Shadd 1950, 30, 55. On Latinx and Asian American Milwaukeeans, see González 2017, 13–28; Rodriguez and Shelley 2009, 162–191.

neighborhoods likely pre-dated the HOLC's judgement, the "security maps" reinforced these patterns, leaving prospective homeowners and landlords with insufficient financing options and forcing lower-income buyers to turn to risky arrangements such as contracts for deed.[19]

These obstacles likely heightened residents' anxieties about economic security and home values, playing into the fears and racialized discourses about housing values that segregationists stirred up during the 1944 conflicts. Local realtors' arguments built, of course, on the foundation laid earlier racially restrictive covenants and by the National Association of Real Estate Boards' (NAREB) Code of Ethics (adopted in 1913, revised in 1924), warning against transactions that would allow into a neighborhood a "member of any race or nationality, or any individual whose presence will clearly be detrimental to property values."[20] A 1943 NAREB manual spelled out this prohibition, equating upwardly mobile African-Americans with bootleggers, prostitutes, and gangsters—naming all as sources of "blight" that realtors had an obligation to exclude.[21]

During World War Two, as African Americans moved to northern cities seeking jobs in defense industries, conflicts broke out in neighborhoods as some white residents fought to reinforce racial boundaries and defend white privilege. As scholars and activists have recounted, these incidents—whether violent or noisy—were integral to a history of racism that enforced strictures of a Jim Crow society in all regions of the country. At midcentury, these disputes over race and housing pitted segregationist white residents, backed especially by real estate interests, against Black residents, backed by a labour-left coalition of civil rights activists, union members, and popular front activists.[22]

---

19 HOLC, "Area Description—Security Map of Milwaukee," Areas D7, D7A, in Nelson, *Mapping Inequality*. Concordia, an area just north of these neighborhoods, had been more well-to-do until the 1920s but now was labelled as declining (yellow). On the impact of redlining and related policies, see Michney and Winling 2020; Light 2010; Satter 2009; Gordon 2008, 83–98.

20 Quoted in Glotzer 2015, 488. See also Gordon 2008; Quinn 1979.

21 The 1943 language as quoted in: Avila 2004, 8–9; Hirsch 1993, 75. On the NAREB's influence over government agencies, including the Federal Housing Administration, see Freund 2007. For Milwaukee and Wisconsin, see Metropolitan Milwaukee Fair Housing Council 2005, 71–74.

22 See Meyer 2000; Sugrue 1996; Hirsch 1983. On labour-left coalitions, see Kimble 2015.

3 Neighborhood and Organizational Life

While available sources say little about Nada's and Zlata's childhoods, the ethnic and racial contours of their working-class neighborhood during a time of economic hardship suggest formative aspects of their everyday experience. As they learned English, attended school, and traveled more widely in their neighborhood, they would have encountered other Croatian Americans, as well as other immigrants and their children. The Oristo family's apartments in the southeastern portion of Merrill Park and later near the Mount Vernon Gospel Church put them into regular contact with their Black neighbors. Unlike many other white children in racially segregated Milwaukee, Nada and Zlata probably grew accustomed to navigating their neighborhood with periodic or even daily encounters between Black and white residents.[23]

As the sisters traversed their neighborhood, their parents' values and organizational ties also likely affected how they understood their surroundings. Grace Falbo, an Italian immigrant who grew up in Merrill Park and lived just a few blocks away from the Oristo family, recalls a neighborhood with Italian, German, Irish, Croatian, Jewish, and Black children, playing and attending school together. In her oral history, she speaks fondly about her friendships across racial, ethnic, and religious lines, including with the Croatian sisters "Nada and Slada [sic]." For Falbo, the Oristo girls were notable as "Yugoslavian" friends who "knew communism." Their father also had a reputation for radical political activities.[24]

The Oristos, who continued to speak Croatian in the home, participated in both Croatian cultural associations and labour-left organizations during the 1930s and 1940s. A brief exploration illustrates the rich organizational life and interconnections between these groups. Especially important was the emergence of antifascist and antiracist politics in these South Slavic associations, with ties to popular front labour-left groups in the lead-up to World

23 Upon arrival, both daughters spoke and wrote Croatian. By 1930, Zlata spoke English, while Nada was still learning the language. New York, Passenger and Crew Lists, mf T715, 1897–1957, role 4637, line 19, *Ancestry*; Galdner (Goldner) in *1930 U.S. Census*.

24 Falbo Oral History, 7–18. This oral history reflects racial views formed in the wake of the Civil Rights movement. Falbo's family lived first near N. 27th St. and W. Clybourn and then N. 35th St. and W. Clybourn. She went to Mary Hill School and then to the Wisconsin Avenue School. Falbo recalls Rudolfo Oristo being "arrested for writing a letter to the king of Yugoslavia" (12). While this might not be a reliable childhood account, it suggests his continued engagement with the politics of Yugoslavia. On Milwaukee's CP, see Mukherji 2017, 127–132.

War Two.[25] While evidence of the impact that their parents' community and organizational life had on the Oristo daughters' political trajectory is largely circumstantial, the choices that Nada and Zlata made during their high school years and beyond suggest that Croatian radical politics had a significant pull, guiding them on a path toward racial egalitarianism and civil rights activism.

Paulina Oristo was involved in Croatian social organizations and regularly read the Croatian Fraternal Union's (CFU) weekly *Fraternalist* (*Zajedničar*), a Croatian-language newspaper published in Allegheny, Pennsylvania that included an English-language section during the 1930s. She and her family also likely listened to the Croatian Radio Hour that began airing on wemp in early 1937 and featured Croatian-language programming and tamburitza music. Soon after arriving in Milwaukee, Paulina demonstrated Croatian cooking at the International Institute of the YWCA (the Young Women's Christian Association). While little is documented about her political or social views, Paulina Oristo made clear to family members that she rejected the Catholic Church into which she had been born and sympathized with socialist principles. Importantly, her ethnic commitments did not lead to insularity but instead complemented her open-mindedness. For her husband, commitments to Esperanto and left-wing politics, were accompanied by regular involvement in Croatian and South Slavic associational life and cultural activities, including directing plays for the Three Slobodas Croatian-American cultural club. These activities and the media the family consumed (in both Croatian and English) contributed to their cultural and political identity, connected to interwar Croatia but increasingly rooted in the industrial city's Croatian and South Slavic communities, providing avenues for the socialist politics they carried with them from Europe.[26]

---

25 For capacious interpretations of the "popular front," see Jones 2005, 125–150; Denning 1996. While the official Popular Front period of the Communist International ran from 1935 to 1939, a broad-based and longer-running grassroots popular front supported industrial unions, social democratic policies, and racial equality.

26 Hudson and Buxton interview; "Lesson in Cooking Real Croatian Meal" 1931; "Program for the First Anniversary of the Croatian Radio Hour," WEMP, 23 January 1938, Box 2, CFU Collection, University of Wisconsin-Milwaukee Archives, Milwaukee, WI [hereafter UWM Archives]; "Play to Be Given" 1940. See also "10th Anniversary Celebration Program," CFU Branch No. 392 (West Allis), 5 October 1941, Milwaukee Hall; and Souvenir Program, 25th Anniversary Celebration, Croatian Women, Branch No. 3 (Milwaukee), 5 May 1957, Croatian Center Hall, Milwaukee; both in folder "Ethnic-Croatian," Local Pamphlets Collection, Milwaukee Public Library. Kralj 2012, 114–158; Greene 2009.

The Oristo's active role in the CFU's Nada Lodge No. 255 might have been especially influential for Nada's and Zlata's ethnic and political formation.[27] This lodge was one of about six CFU-affiliated lodges in the Milwaukee and West Allis areas, joining a lengthy list of other South Slavic benefit, recreation, and cultural organizations. As a mutual aid society, the CFU offered a cushion during emergencies, especially significant during the Depression. With the motto "One for All—All for One," the CFU brought Croatian immigrants and their children together. By the mid-1930s, it featured an ethnic pluralism that rallied support for New Deal relief and progressive social movements, fostering an outward-looking working-class Americanization. Although stymied periodically by internecine battles between leftists and nationalists, the CFU became an ally and resource for labour organizing, especially the CIO, and for interwar antifascist causes. Connections such as this were essential to the CIO's "culture of unity" during these years, when these industrial unions began to reach across the ethnic and racial barriers that employers had used to keep workers divided. This was evident, for instance, during the 1939 Croatian American Day picnic, spearheaded by CFU lodges and other groups in the Croatian Central Committee of Milwaukee. Among the keynote speakers to this crowd of five thousand was Harold Christoffel, president of United Auto Workers (UAW) Local 248 (CIO) at Allis Chalmers. A militant and effective union leader who later would be the target of red-baiting, Christoffel praised the "fraternalism displayed by Croatian groups," underscoring the reciprocal relationship between the CIO and the CFU. While we have no direct evidence placing Nada Oristo at this picnic, she and her family may well have attended or at least heard about this large Croatian gathering.[28]

---

27 The Nada lodge was reportedly the oldest and largest Croatian organization in Wisconsin. "Oldest Croatian Lodge to Observe Anniversary" 1953, 26. "Rudolfo G. Oristo Obituary" 1951. Zlata later took out her own CFU membership: "Month of April 1955 Membership" 1955.

28 "Articles of Incorporation of Croatian Fraternal Union Center, Inc., filed 3 April 1952," folder "Croatian Fraternal Union," Box 7, Croatian Fraternal Union Records, UWM Archives. The Lodges listed are: #261, #807, and #255 in Milwaukee: #391, #392, and #731 in West Allis; "Croatian Union Votes Aid to the Indigent" 1935; "Milwaukee's Fifth 'Croatian Day' Will Be Held Next Saturday, July 23" 1939; "Croats Meet; Factions Row" 1935; "Croats Mass 5,000 Strong at Their Picnic" 1939; Steidl et al. 2017, 96–98. On the CFU and labour-left activism, see March 2017; Rachleff 1998; Kraljic 2009; Rachleff 1989; Nelson et al. 1981, 44–45. On the importance of ethnic resources for the CIO, see Cohen 1990. CFU lodges hosted sports teams (e.g., bowling, softball, basketball) that played other ethnic and labour teams in industrial leagues. "Stanzers Win in Allis Loop" 1938; "Wrecker Nine Plans Entry in Triple A Loop" 1940. Research is needed on early CFU policies, especially its turn from limiting membership to "the white race" to advocacy of pluralism and racial egalitarianism. "Articles of Organization, 1925," Croatian Independent Sick Benefit Society of West Allis, Wis., Box 7, CFU Collection, UWM Archives. On Christoffel, see Meyer 1992.

The CFU's labour-left politics fed into other initiatives, converging with a broader antifascist politics of the later 1930s and the war years. Representing the CFU, Rudolfo Oristo joined a committee, organized by Josephine Nordstrand of the popular-front Milwaukee County Conference on Social Legislation, which sought to defeat a set of "anti-alien bills." Bringing together representatives from ethnic and labour groups, this group proposed to smooth immigrants' path to citizenship and support resident noncitizens who were on relief during these tough economic times.[29] The Milwaukee area CFUs also contributed regularly to the war effort, announcing pledges to buy defense bonds or donate to the Red Cross and backing allies in the Balkans who fought the Axis. They frequently joined with other ethnic and benefit societies to publicize these commitments. And the CFU educated members and the public about the war, especially the conflicts in Yugoslavia.[30]

While these CFU efforts linked U.S. migration and egalitarian social policy to the fate of Croatia and Yugoslavia, transnational and pan-Slavic concerns were central to the American Slav Congress (ASC) and United Committee of South-Slavic Americans (UCSSA), formed after the Nazi-Soviet non-aggression pact collapsed. Both groups were active in the Milwaukee area, with the CFU and its members participating. The ASC, rooted in industrial unionism and the International Workers Order, drew together Slavic Americans who constituted a sizable proportion of the city's industrial workforce. With labour leader Leo Krzycki at the helm (a Milwaukee-born Polish American socialist who rose in the ranks of the Amalgamated Clothing Workers and helped to organize the CIO), the ASC drew considerable attention in Milwaukee. Edmund Bobrowicz, an organizer for the CIO's International Fur and Leather Workers Union (IFLWU) and future congressional candidate who was red baited, was also active in the ASC. The Milwaukee County ASC claimed to represent "100,000 Americans of Slavic descent … [embracing] 67 Polish, 22 Croatian, 14 Slovak, and 13 Czech organizations." An early rally of the Milwaukee branch turned out 5,000 people, hearing from leaders of the CIO and the American Federation of Labor (AFL).[31]

---

29 "Group Turns Guns on Antialien Bills" 1939; "Conference Held Here on Antialien Bills in Congress" 1939; "Starnes Bill Opposed" 1940; Buff 2017, 27–52. On fascist and antifascist politics, see Enyeart 2019; and Fronczak 2018.

30 "Lodges Aid Red Cross, Pledge Defense Bonds" 1942; "Groups Join Those Giving to the Red Cross" 1942; "$7,862 Raised in Slav Drive" 1944.

31 The Milwaukee branch used the name American Slav Council. "Milwaukee American Slav Council Activity," 25 August 1942, American Slav Congress 1942–1943, U.S. Office of Strategic Services, Foreign Nationalities Branch Files, 1942–1945, NARA, ProQuest History Vault; "Banachowicz Named to Attend Congress" 1942, 12; "Slavs to Perfect Permanent

The UCSSA, a national organization headed by the Slovenian writer and activist Louis Adamic, brought together South Slavs who supported antifascist forces in Yugoslavia against the Axis and monarchists. Milwaukee's chapter of the UCSSA consisted of twenty-six Yugoslav lodges and societies. Adamic and the Croatian violinist Zlatko Baloković visited the city regularly as featured speakers. The group emphasized Yugoslav unity in the United States and the Balkans, as well as Allied allegiance.[32] Along with educational forums and meetings that drew upwards of one thousand attendees, the UCSSA joined with the wartime labour-left to protest against fascist sympathizers and Bund gatherings in the Milwaukee area. For instance, the UCSSA, UAW District Council No. 1, UAW Local 75, and the African American Independent Order of St. Luke joined together to publicly oppose the use of a municipal hall by the right-wing America First Party leader Gerald L. K. Smith.[33]

Importantly, the ASC and UCSSA made civil rights and egalitarianism a part of their agenda, tying fights against fascism to battles against racial prejudice and inequality in American society, echoing the Double V campaigns of Black civil rights groups. Anticommunists attacked the UCSSA for its support of Tito and, together with the ASC, for their reluctance to criticize the Soviet Union during the war. Foreshadowing Cold War anticommunism, these attacks underscored connections between the UCSSA, the ASC, and labour-left groups, especially the CIO.[34]

Arriving in Milwaukee as a socialist, Rudolfo Oristo apparently soon became involved in the Communist Party of the United States of America (CPUSA), likely drawn by the sizeable South Slavic unit in the local CPUSA. While the local CPUSA bore the marks of its ties to the Soviet Union, taking dogmatic positions on international issues, the local CPUSA activists focused especially

---

Unit Here Next Sunday" 1942; "Postwar Task Big One, Slav Council Told" 1942; U.S. House Un-American Activities Committee 1950; Ubriaco 1999. On Leo Krzycki, see Miller 1976. On communist/anticommunist rifts: "County Slav Council Quits National Body" 1943; "Ukrainians Rap Slav Group Rift" 1943; "Roosevelt War Aims Endorsed by Slavs" 1944. See also Zecker 2018.

32 Larson 2020, 307–364; Enyeart 2019, 74, 84; Lees 2007, 133–135; Sebanc 1972, 141. The CFU contributed to the UCSSA's formation. Reports of the group's activities appeared regularly in the local press: "Plan for Meeting of South Slav Group" 1943; "Slavs to Eye Unity Setup" 1944; "Adamic Slaps Ruth Mitchell: Aiding Fascists, Slav Author Declares" 1944; "Milanov, Violinist and Slavic Groups to Appear Today" 1944. See the UCSSA's newsletter "The Bulletin," edited by Adamic, including a plea against divisiveness: Kosanovich 1944.

33 "Soviet Hailed by South Slavs" 1944, 13; Protest Notice 1944; "Fight Renting Hall to Smith" 1944. On the Bund, Berninger 1987–1988.

34 Enyeart 2019, 95; "The Ill Wind from Moscow" 1944. Double V stood for victory abroad and at home, fighting fascism and racism.

on local and national concerns, including unemployment organizing, support for labour, and antiracist campaigns. Oristo also was active in organized labour, first in the AFL while working at Falk and then declaring his allegiance to the rapidly growing CIO during the second half of the decade. So, the alignment of the CFU and other South Slavic organizations with the CIO, popular front groups, and sometimes the CPUSA fit neatly with his politics. He kept on this path, engaging in labour-left politics during and after the war, running on the People's Progressive Party slate as ward committeeman aligned with Henry Wallace's insurgent run for president in 1948.[35]

Given their social and political alignments, the Oristos likely took part in meetings, rallies, or picnics organized by these many groups, hearing strains of labour-left antifascism and egalitarianism throughout these years. As young girls and high-school students, Nada and Zlata Oristo probably accompanied their parents to CFU and other Croatian community events, maybe participating in musical or other cultural activities that involved children and families. They undoubtedly learned about the CFU, the CPUSA, and organized labour at home, immersing them in the radical egalitarian politics and antifascism that united these groups during the 1930s. Given the notable labour and South Slavic presence in their neighborhood, such experiences shaped them politically.

Zlata and Nada Oristo were strong students during their secondary school years at Milwaukee's West Division High School. Nada was member of the honor society and was elected class officer (secretary) in her senior year. Both sisters belonged to the Latin Club, perhaps inspired by their father's interest in languages. Encouraged by their parents to take up music, Zlata played the violin, and Nada played the cello, performing with high school ensembles and the Milwaukee Youth Orchestra. Zlata graduated at the end of the school year in 1939. Nada's commencement was held mid-year in January 1940. For a while after graduating, they continued to live with their parents in a small Sixteenth Ward apartment. With their father working a WPA job, the daughters presumably looked for work to help support the family, encountering an economy that was slowly picking up due to early demands for wartime production.[36]

---

35 "Falk earning Data Checked" 1937; Mukherji 2017; "Rudolfo G. Oristo Obituary" 1951; "Reds Seeking Election Posts as Wallaceites 1948." After the war, Rudolfo and Paulina moved south of the Menomonee valley to the Fifth Ward, near where Rudolfo first lived in Milwaukee. Also running on the Progressive party 1948 ticket were Werner Buchel (Fifteenth Ward), a Morris family supporter in 1944, and Mildred Ostovich (Sixteenth Ward), married to a UAW Local 248 activist.

36 West Division High School 1936, 71, 104; West Division High School 1937, 65, 87, 95; West Division High School 1938, 76, 82, 84, 85, 93; West Division High School 1940, 19, 36;

Sometime during the later 1930s, Nada and Zlata Oristo joined the Young Communist League (YCL). Given their parents' politics and the popular front politics evident in the interwar Croatian American community, the YCL was not a large leap. The radical, antifascist, and pro-labour politics of the YCL were indeed familiar. Nada Oristo also found acceptance in the YCL that she had not experienced at school. With English as her second language, which she began to learn after arriving in Milwaukee, she apparently was self-conscious about her speaking and writing despite her achievements as a student in high school. Her family's poverty also weighed on her. The YCL might have given her tools to come to terms with the family's economic hardships, comprehending how their position was shaped by both immigrant and class experiences in the industrial city. Likewise, the prominence of South Slavs in Milwaukee's CPUSA may have contributed to both social acceptance and greater understanding, turning what had been marks of shame in other arenas of her life into badges of honor. She also met her future husband in the YCL, a Republican banker's son from Madison, James Hudson. In these ways, then, Nada Oristo Hudson's path to Americanization as well as to future labour-left activism and family life passed through this small but influential radical organization—a group that drew her initially because of a heightened awareness of class, ethnic, and racial divisions in her everyday life and beyond. While direct evidence about her YCL days is scant, involvement in the group during the later 1930s would have reinforced the politics she encountered in Croatian and South Slavic organizations, bringing the problems of fascism and racism to the fore, along with a close identification with the growing industrial union movement in Milwaukee and elsewhere.[37]

Nada Oristo's engagement with the YCL deepened when she later shouldered both citywide and national leadership roles in the YCL's successor

---

Hudson and Buxton interview; "298 Diplomas at West High" 1939; "Honor Students to Give Address" 1940; Oristo in *1940 U.S. Census*.

37 Nada Hudson's daughters discussed her self-doubts in Hudson and Buxton interview. On the YCL and CP, see Pettengill 2020; Dyakonova 2019; Maraniss 2019; Mukherji 2017, 117, 118, 130; Storch 2007; Isserman 1982. Nada Oristo and James Hudson married in 1941. He enlisted in the army, serving in Europe. His radical politics likely consigned him to behind-the-lines jobs. Before the army, he completed three years of college. Zlata Oristo and James Buxton, who also apparently met in the YCL, married in 1944. Buxton served in the Pacific. "James Hudson," *U.S. World War II Army Enlistment Records, 1938–1946*, NARA, Electronic Army Serial Number Merged File, Record Group 64, *Ancestry*; *U.S. Department of Veterans Affairs* BIRLS *Death File, 1850–2010*, *Ancestry*; U.S. Bureau of the Census, *1940 United States Federal Census*, Madison, Dane, Wisconsin, roll m-t0627-04469, page 4B, Enumeration District 13–41A, *Ancestry*.

organization, American Youth for Democracy (AYD). In 1943, she was elected to the national council of the AYD during its inaugural convention in New York City, also becoming the secretary for the AYD in Milwaukee. She held this position during the 1944 housing dispute and continued in this role after the war. While her earlier experience in the YCL and other South Slavic organizations may have reflected conventional gender roles, given the submerged status of gender egalitarianism in interwar labour-left organizing, Nada Oristo had nevertheless gained important organizational experience. During the war, she and other women moved into leadership roles in popular front groups, some labour organizations, and civil rights organizing. For instance, women held over two-thirds of the positions on the AYD's inaugural national council. So, while Nada Hudson was labeled a soldier's wife during the following year's Sixteenth Ward conflict, her AYD activism embodied what historian Dorothy Sue Cobble calls "the other women's movement," a midcentury working-class feminism.[38]

During the war, with their husbands away in the military, Nada and Zlata rented a flat together at 3756 W. Stevenson Street—in Merrill Park, near the eastern edge of Pigsville. Both sisters worked, likely involved in defense production. Zlata's daughter recalls that she sewed parachutes and uniforms. Nada's daughters think that she was employed in a tannery, producing leather for boots, belts, rifle slings, and other military supplies. Work in a tannery would have put Nada in contact with leaders from the CIO's IFLWU, the left-wing union led by organizers George Bradow and Edmund Bobrowicz, as well as the Black labour and housing activist Joe Ellis. Whether they connected through the workplace or in labour-left organizations, these radical activists and Hudson would work together in wartime and postwar civil rights initiatives including the Civil Rights Congress (CRC).[39]

38 "Proceedings of the First Constitutional Convention of the American Youth for Democracy," New York City, 16–17 October 1943, folder 8, box 252, American Youth for Democracy Records, Tamiment Library, New York University, New York; Cronin 1945, 116–117; "Want Negroes to Stay Away 1944"; "Front Groups Widely Used in Red Strategy" 1946. On the complexities of women's roles in radical and labour organizations during the 1930s and 1940s, see Schreiber 2022; Dumenil 2020; Faue 2017; Guglielmo 2010; Cobble 2004.

39 On wartime employment: Fehring 2020; Pifer, 2003; Gurda 1994, 33. See also an oral history with a Serbian American woman who made parachutes and paratroopers' jump suits. Dorothy Petrovich, Oral history Interview, 26 March 1993, "Wisconsin Women during World War II," Wisconsin Historical Society, Madison, WI. On the CRC (formerly the National Negro Congress): "Civil Rights Parley Opens" 1947; Gellman 2012.

4 1944 and Beyond

By the time of the Sixteenth Ward housing controversies, Nada Oristo Hudson lived less than four blocks away from a newly renovated house in which the Morris family rented an apartment.[40] Hudson publicly opposed the segregationists who sought not only to oust the Morris family but also to draw a line at 35th Street to contain Merrill Park's Black residents in a section east of that boundary.

During the controversy, segregationists belittled Nada Hudson. An audience member interrupted her defense of the Morris family, calling out "Are you a property owner?" Her answer of "no" provoked a "blast of boos" from the crowd. By trying to shame Hudson as a renter, the anti-Morris agitators cast doubt on her legitimacy as a participant in neighborhood decisions. Could somebody who did not own property be a full participant—a full citizen—in this neighborhood? Even though rental units far outnumbered owner-occupied housing in Merrill Park, and Hudson had lived here for almost fifteen years, these segregationist homeowners tried to claim exclusive authority to determine the neighborhood's future, including (or maybe especially) the area's racial landscape. They fueled fears about property values in mixed-race neighborhoods—anxieties reinforced by racially restrictive covenants, redlining, and other real estate practices.[41]

The NAACP's James Dorsey defended Hudson against these charges, questioning not only the "homeowner entitlement" voiced at the meeting but the patriotism and masculinity of the men who jeered Hudson, a serviceman's wife. "You men who just booed down that lady, booed down the wife of a man who is fighting to make your homes safe for you." Dorsey's defense upheld Hudson's right as a resident to be heard. But by focusing attention on men's wartime roles—contrasting the neighborhood segregationists who enjoyed the safety of stateside life with Hudson's husband who fought fascism overseas—Dorsey played into wartime gender constraints that tied Hudson's rights and public voice to her status as a soldier's wife. Or as the historian Robert Westbrook argues, she gained standing as an object of men's wartime sacrifice, far from any ideal of gender egalitarianism or working-class feminism. Lost in this exchange about renters' status, women's dependence, and men's wartime sacrifice was any recognition of Nada Hudson's Croatian American radicalism, solidly rooted in her experience growing up as an immigrant in 1930s Merrill

40 *Wright's Milwaukee City Directory, 1944–45*, 533.

41 "Want Negroes to Stay Away" 1944; Gordon 2008.

Park, surrounded by labour-left and antifascist politics, all of which enabled her to act on these ideals of racial egalitarianism.[42]

The segregationists' drive toward exclusion and separation was not an isolated case, of course. Wartime hate-filled campaigns peaked in 1943—notably in wartime production and military centers such as Detroit and Los Angeles—but were evident throughout the war years and throughout the United States. At the same time, racist surges clashed with local and national campaigns for wartime racial and ethnic unity, improved "interracial relations," racial pluralism, and civil rights. Another important wing of wartime racial egalitarianism that shaped Hudson stemmed from a radical labour-left, antifascist, and antiracist movement that included industrial labour unions, communist party activists, and other popular front organizations in the 1930s and 1940s.[43]

After the war, Nada Hudson continued her involvement with the AYD and worked briefly for the Milwaukee CIO. She was also active in a multiracial, labour-left cohort that launched the CRC in Milwaukee. As Cold War anticommunist investigations intensified, Hudson came under scrutiny. Early postwar Red Scare targets included militant CIO leaders, the CRC, and the CPUSA's Wisconsin leadership. In the early 1950s, Nada and James Hudson were suspected of fomenting Black revolution, allegedly handing a manual to an activist who then informed on them to the Federal Bureau of Investigation (FBI). The family went underground, relocating to Chicago; Nada and James assumed new names. In the mid-1950s, the Hudsons returned to Milwaukee, settling just down the hill from Zlata and her family in a nearby suburb. Although the Hudsons eventually left the CPUSA, visits from FBI agents continued. Nevertheless, Nada and Zlata sustained their commitment to the civil rights and peace movements, maintaining lifelong friendships with fellow labour-left activists such as Harold Christoffel. Years later, during the 1960s open housing battles against segregation in Milwaukee, the police interrogated a young activist. He discovered that the police intended to prove that the protesters were "communist dupes," basing this flimsy charge on evidence that his mother had grown up in the Sixteenth Ward with Nada Oristo Hudson.[44]

42 "Want Negroes to Stay Away" 1944. On wartime sacrifice and gender, see Basso 2013; Westbrook 2004, 39–91.

43 Sugrue 2012, 87–102.

44 Cronin 1945, 117; "Civil Rights Parley Opens" 1947; "Red Fascist Groups Named" 1948; U.S. House Un-American Activities Committee 1955, 803; "Red Planned Revolt, Claim" 1952; Hudson and Buxton interview; Hagedorn 2017, 4; Jones 2009.

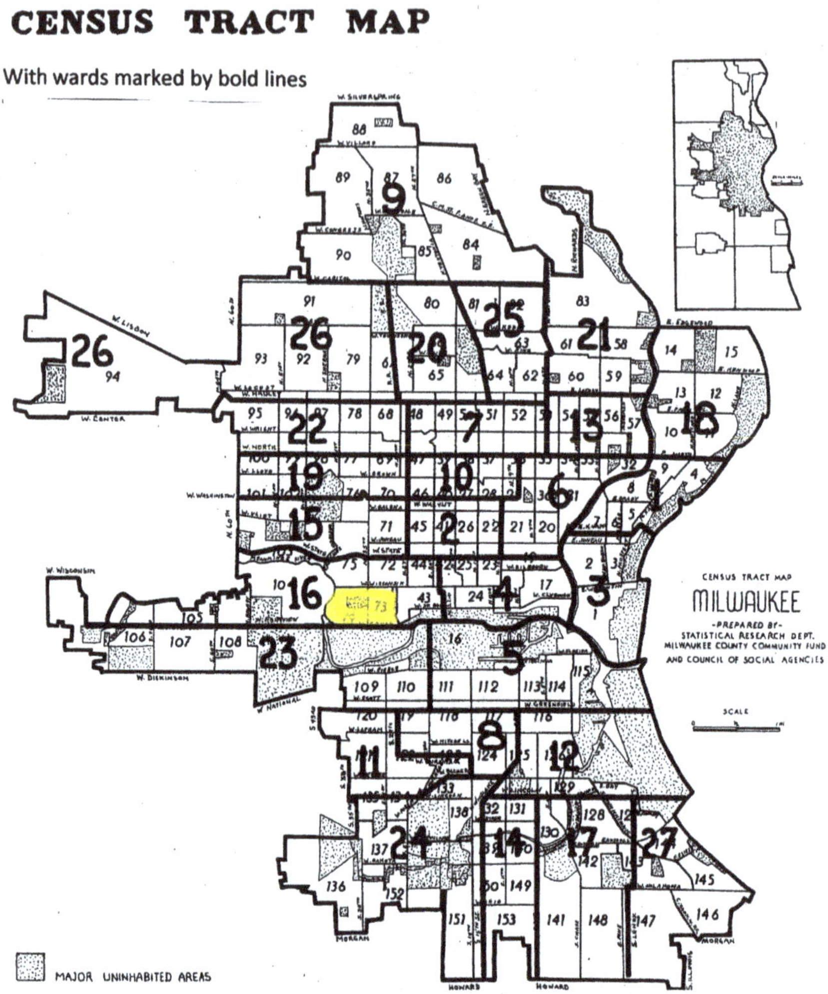

MAP 17.1 Milwaukee census tract map with city wards, 1945
SOURCE: MAP. MILWAUKEE COUNTY COMMUNITY FUND AND COUNCIL OF SOCIAL AGENCIES, *CENSUS TRACT FACTS: A HANDBOOK OF BASIC SOCIAL DATA OF MILWAUKEE COUNTY, WISCONSIN* (MILWAUKEE: STATISTICAL RESEARCH DEPARTMENT, 1945)

5 Conclusion

As the historian David Roediger argues, many Southern and Eastern European immigrants and their children during the first half of the twentieth century traveled a route to Americanization by differentiating themselves from African Americans, that is "working toward whiteness." In short, immigrants' inclusion in mainstream society and their material gains accrued by claiming white privilege at the expense and exclusion of Black citizens. Roediger's work underscores convincingly how white racism and processes of immigrants' racial formation undergird American society.

While a reconstruction of Nada Oristo Hudson's path to labour-left racial egalitarianism does not contradict Roediger's important argument, this "exceptional" case complicates the larger narrative. An excavation of the Goldner-Oristo-Hudson journey from post-World War One Eastern Europe to World War Two-era Milwaukee offers insight into historical contingencies that fostered a young Croatian America woman's attachment to racial egalitarianism rather than propelling her along the heavily traveled road toward racial exclusion and separation. This family's socialist alignments, transported from Europe, took root in an ethnically and racially mixed, industrial, working-class neighborhood during the Great Depression. In this setting, their political commitments and education about American society were nurtured by a vibrant South Slavic and labour-left organizational life, constituting an alternative path toward midcentury Americanization. While no doubt benefiting from white privilege in a society structured by racial hierarchies, Nada Hudson fought for racial egalitarianism not only as an abstract ideal but as a concrete aim in her neighborhood and city.[45]

Bibliography

"298 Diplomas at West High." 1939. *Milwaukee Journal*, 4 June 1939, 43.

"$7,862 Raised in Slav Drive." 1944. *Milwaukee Journal*, 6 November 1944, 12.

"Adamic Slaps Ruth Mitchell: Aiding Fascists, Slav Author Declares." 1944. *Milwaukee Sentinel Extra*, 10 January 1944, 11.

Alanen, Arnold R. 2007. *Morgan Park: Duluth, U.S. Steel, and the Forging of a Company Town*. Minneapolis: University of Minnesota Press.

August, Tom. 2001. "'In the Midst of Many People': A History of Jewish-Gentile Community Relations in Milwaukee." *Milwaukee History* 24, nos. 3 & 4 (Fall-Winter): 3–42.

Avila, Eric. 2004. "Popular Culture in the Age of White Flight: Film Noir, Disneyland, and the Cold War (Sub)Urban Imaginary." *Journal of Urban History* 31, no. 1 (November): 3–22.

45 Roediger 2005. See also Zecker 2021; Guglielmo 2010; Cobble 2004. Microhistorians use the term "exceptional" to denote atypical cases requiring examination. See De Vries 2019.

Bader-Zaar, Birgitta. 2004. "Grundrechte in der Historischen Immigrationsforschung: Das Beispiel chinesischer und japanischer Einwanderer in den Vereinigten Staaten im 'langen' 19. Jahrhundert" [Fundamental rights in historical immigration research: The example of Chinese and Japanese immigrants in the United States in the "long" nineteenth century]. *Wiener Zeitschrift zur Geschichte der Neuzeit* [Vienna Journal of Modern History] 4, no. 1: 119–125.

"Banachowicz Named to Attend Congress." 1942. *Milwaukee Journal*, 22 April 1942, 12.

Barrett, James R. 1992. "Americanization from the Bottom Up: Immigration and the Remaking of the Working Class in the United States, 1880–1930." *Journal of American History* 79, no. 3 (December): 996–1020.

Basso, Matthew L. 2013. *Meet Joe Copper: Masculinity and Race on Montana's World War II Home Front*. Chicago: University of Chicago Press.

Berninger, Dieter. 1987–1988. "Milwaukee's German-American Community and the Nazi Challenge of the 1930s." *Wisconsin Magazine of History* 71 (Winter): 118–142.

Brunnbauer, Ulf. 2012. "Emigration Policies and Nation-building in Interwar Yugoslavia." *European History Quarterly* 42, no. 4: 602–627.

Buenker, John D., Beverly J.K. Buenker, eds. 2016. *Milwaukee in the 1930s: A Federal Writers Project City Guide*. Madison: Wisconsin Historical Society Press.

Buff, Rachel Ida. 2017. *Against the Deportation Terror: Organizing for Immigrant Rights in the Twentieth Century*. Philadelphia: Temple University Press.

Citizens' Governmental Research Bureau. 1946. *Milwaukee's Negro Community*. Milwaukee: Council of Social Agencies.

"Civil Rights Parley Opens." 1947. *Milwaukee Journal*, 24 March 1947.

Cobble, Dorothy Sue. 2004. *The Other Women's Movement: Workplace Justice and Social Rights in Modern America*. Princeton: Princeton University Press.

Cohen, Lizabeth. 1990. *Making a New Deal: Industrial Workers in Chicago, 1919–1939*. New York: Cambridge University Press.

"Conference Held Here on Antialien Bills in Congress." 1939. *Milwaukee Journal*, 1 June 1939.

"County Slav Council Quits National Body." 1943. *Milwaukee Sentinel Extra*, 22 December 1943, 17.

"Courses in Esperanto." 1937. *Milwaukee Journal*, 12 March 1937, 59.

"Croatian Union Votes Aid to the Indigent." 1935. *Milwaukee Journal*, 14 June 1935, 34.

"Croats Meet; Factions Row." 1935. *Milwaukee Journal*, 10 June 1935, 13.

"Croats Mass 5,000 Strong at Their Picnic." 1939. *Milwaukee Sentinel Extra*, 24 July 1939, 9.

Cronin, Rev. John F. 1945. "The Problem of American Communism in 1945: Facts and Recommendations." 29 October 1945. http://mdhistory.msa.maryland.gov/hiss/cronin-report.pdf.

Denning, Michael. 1996. *The Cultural Front: The Laboring of American Culture in the Twentieth Century*. New York: Verso.

De Vries, Jan. 2019. "Playing with Scales: The Global and the Micro, the Macro and the Nano." *Past and Present*, Supplement 14: 23–36.

Dumenil, Lynn. 2020. *American Working Women in World War II*. Boston: Bedford/St. Martins.

Dyakonova, Daria Pankratova. 2019. "Canadian Reds: The Young Communist League of Canada, International Communism, and the Soviet Experience, 1917–1939." PhD Diss., University of Montreal.

Enyeart, John P. 2019. *Death to Fascism: Louis Adamic's Fight for Democracy*. Urbana: University of Illinois Press.

"Esperanto Study Will Be Offered as WPA Project." 1936. *Milwaukee Sentinel Extra*, 9 October 1936, 13.

"Exit Rudolf Goldner, Enter Mr. Oristo." 1931. *Milwaukee Journal*, 20 March 1931, 21.

"Falk Earnings Data Checked." 1937. *Milwaukee Journal*, 19 August 1937, 13.

Faue, Elizabeth. 2017. *Rethinking the American Labor Movement*. New York: Routledge, 2017.

Fehring, Thomas H. 2020. *When Milwaukee Went to War: On the Homefront during WWII*. Milwaukee: Milwaukee War Memorial Center, 2020.

Fermaglich, Kirsten. 2015. "'Too Long, Too Foreign ... Too Jewish': Jews, Name Changing, and Family Mobility in New York City, 1917–1942." *Journal of American Ethnic History* 34, no. 3 (Spring): 34–57.

"Fight Renting Hall to Smith." 1944. *Milwaukee Sentinel*, 15 April 1944, 4.

Freund, David M. P. 2007. *Colored Property: State Policy and White Racial Politics in Suburban America*. Chicago: University of Chicago Press.

Fronczak, Joseph. 2018. "The Fascist Game: Transnational Political Transmission and the Genesis of the U.S. Modern Right." *Journal of American History* 105, no. 3 (December): 563–588.

"Front Groups Widely Used in Red Strategy." 1946. *Milwaukee Journal*, 24 September 1946.

Fure-Slocum, Eric. 2013. *Contesting the Postwar City: Working-Class and Growth Politics in 1940s Milwaukee*. New York: Cambridge University Press.

Gellman, Erik S. 2012. *Death Blow to Jim Crow: The National Negro Congress and the Rise of Militant Civil Rights*. Chapel Hill: University of North Carolina Press.

Glotzer, Paige. 2015. "Exclusion in Arcadia: How Suburban Developers Circulated Ideas about Discrimination, 1890–1950." *Journal of Urban History* 41, no. 3: 479–494.

Goldstein, Ivo. 2003. "The Catholic Church in Croatia and the 'Jewish Problem,' 1918–1941." *East European Jewish Affairs* 33, no. 2 (Winter): 121–134.

González, Sergio M. 2017. *Mexicans in Wisconsin*. Madison: Wisconsin Historical Society Press.

Gordon, Colin. 2008. *Mapping Decline: St. Louis and the Fate of the American City*. Philadelphia: University of Pennsylvania Press.

Greene, Victor. 2009. "Dealing with Diversity: Milwaukee's Multiethnic Festivals and Urban Identity, 1840–1940." In *Perspectives on Milwaukee's Past*, edited by Margo Anderson and Victor Greene, 285–315. Urbana: University of Illinois Press.

"Group Turns Guns on Antialien Bills." 1939. *Milwaukee Journal*, 1 June 1939.

"Groups Join Those Giving to the Red Cross." 1942. *Milwaukee Sentinel*, 23 January 1942, 12.

Guglielmo, Jennifer. 2010. *Living the Revolution: Italian Women's Resistance and Radicalism in New York City, 1880–1945*. Chapel Hill: University of North Carolina Press.

Gurda, John. 2015. *Milwaukee: City of Neighborhoods*. Milwaukee: Historic Milwaukee Inc.

Gurda, John. 1999. *The Making of Milwaukee: City of Neighborhoods*. Milwaukee: Milwaukee County Historical Society.

Gurda, John. 1994. "Profits and Patriotism: Milwaukee Industry in World War II." *Wisconsin Magazine of History* 78, no. 1 (Autumn): 24–34.

Gurda, John. 1991. "The Church and the Neighborhood." In *Milwaukee Catholicism: Essays on Church and Community*, edited by Steven M. Avella, 1–34. Milwaukee: Knights of Columbus, 1991.

Gurda, John. 1980. *The West End: Merrill Park, Pigsville, Concordia*. Milwaukee: Milwaukee Humanities Program.

Hagedorn, John M. 2017. "My Turning Point." 4, http://gangresearch.net/Archives/hagedorn/articles/Groppi.pdf.

Hamann, F.A. 1928. "The Progress of Esperanto since the World War." *Modern Language Journal* 12, no. 7 (April): 545–552.

Hirsch, Arnold R. 1993. "With or Without Jim Crow: Black Residential Segregation in the United States." In *Urban Policy in Twentieth-Century America*, edited by Arnold R. Hirsch and Raymond A. Mohl, 65–99. New Brunswick, NJ: Rutgers University Press.

Hirsch, Arnold R. 1983. *Making the Second Ghetto: Race and Housing in Chicago, 1940–1960*. New York: Cambridge University Press.

Holmquist, June D., Joseph Stipanovich, and Kenneth B. Moss. 1981. "The South Slavs: Bulgarians, Croatians, Montenegrins, Serbs, and Slovenes." In *They Chose Minnesota: a Survey of the State's Ethnic Groups*, edited by June D. Holmquist, 381–404. St. Paul: Minnesota Historical Press.

"Honor Students to Give Address." 1940. *Milwaukee Sentinel Extra*, 23 January 1940.

Hostutler, Jason. 2009. "Smokestacks and Steeples: A Case Study of the Reciprocal Relationship between the Catholic Church and Industrial Milwaukee, 1870–1929." PhD diss., Marquette University.

Hudelson, Richard, and Carl Ross. 2006. *By the Ore Docks: A Working People's History of Duluth*. Minneapolis: University of Minnesota Press.

Isserman, Maurice. 1982. *Which Side Were You On? the American Communist Party during the Second World War*. Urbana: University of Illinois Press.

Jones, Patrick D. 2009. *The Selma of the North: Civil Rights Insurgency in Milwaukee*. Cambridge: Harvard University Press.

Jones, William P. 2005. *The Tribe of Black Ulysses: African American Lumber Workers in the Jim Crow South*. Urbana: University of Illinois Press.

Kimble, Lionel. 2015. *A New Deal for Bronzeville: Housing, Employment, and Civil Rights in Black Chicago, 1935–1955*. Carbondale: Southern Illinois Press.

Korstad, Robert. 2018. "Civil Rights Unionism and the Black Freedom Struggle." *American Communist History* 7, no. 2 (December): 255–258.

Korstad, Robert, and Nelson Lichtenstein. 1988. "Opportunities Found and Lost: Labor, Radicals, and the Early Civil Rights Movement." *Journal of American History* 75, no. 3 (December): 786–811.

Kosanovich, Sava. 1944. "A Serbian Speaks Out." *The Bulletin* 11, no. 2 (15 January): 1–2.

Kralj, Dejan. 2012. "Balkan Minds: Transnationals Nationalism and the Transformation of South Slavic Immigrant Identity in Chicago, 1890–1941." PhD diss., Loyola University Chicago.

Kraljic, John. 2009. "The Croatian Section of the Communist Party of the United States and the 'United Front': 1934–1939." *Review of Croatian History* 5, no. 1: 137–167.

Larson, Ethan. 2020. "The New 'Old Country': The Kingdom of Yugoslavia and the Creation of a Yugoslav Diaspora, 1914–1951." PhD diss, University of Illinois at Urbana-Champaign.

Lees, Lorraine M. 2007. *Yugoslav-American and National Security during World War II*. Urbana: University of Illinois Press.

Lepore, Jill. 2001. "Historians Who Love Too Much: Reflections on Microhistory and Biography." *Journal of American History* 88, no. 1 (June): 129–144.

"Lesson in Cooking Real Croatian Meal." 1931. *Milwaukee Journal*, 11 February 1931, 14.

Light, Jennifer S. 2010. "Nationality and Neighborhood Risk at the Origins of FHA Underwriting." *Journal of Urban History* 36, no. 5: 634–671.

Lipsitz, George. 1994. *Rainbow at Midnight: Labor and Culture in the 1940s*. Urbana: University of Illinois Press.

"Lodges Aid Red Cross, Pledge Defense Bonds." 1942. *Milwaukee Journal*, 4 January 1942, 20.

Maraniss, David. 2019. *A Good American Family: The Red Scare and My Father*. New York: Simon and Schuster.

March, Richard. 2017. *A Great Vision: A Militant Family's Journey through the Twentieth Century*. New York: Hard Ball Press.

Marinari, Maddalena. 2020. *Unwanted: Italian and Jewish Mobilization against Restrictive Immigration Laws, 1882–1965*. Chapel Hill: University of North Carolina Press.

McGuinness, Aims. 2009. "The Revolution Begins Here: Milwaukee and the History of Socialism." In *Perspectives on Milwaukee's Past*, edited by Margo Anderson and Victor Greene, 79–106. Urbana: University of Illinois Press.

McNay, Lois. 2010. "Feminism and Post-Agency Politics: The Problem of Agency." *Constellations* 17, no. 4: 512–525.

Metropolitan Milwaukee Fair Housing Council. 2005. "City of Milwaukee Analysis of Impediments to Fair Housing." August 2005.

Meyer, Stephen. 1992. *"Stalin Over Wisconsin": The Making and Unmaking of Militant Unionism, 1900–1950*. New Brunswick, NJ: Rutgers University Press.

Meyer, Stephen Grant. 2000. *As Long as They Don't Move Next Door: Segregation and Racial Conflict in American Neighborhoods*. Lanham, MD: Rowman and Littlefield.

Michney, Todd M. 2017. *Surrogate Suburbs: Black Upward Mobility and Neighborhood Change in Cleveland, 1900–1980*. Chapel Hill: University of North Carolina Press.

Michney, Todd M., and LaDale Winling. 2020. "New Perspectives on New Deal Housing Policy: Explicating and Mapping HOLC Loans to African American." *Journal of Urban History* 46, no. 1: 150–180.

"Milanov, Violinist and Slavic Groups to Appear Today." 1944. *Milwaukee Journal*, 30 April 1944, 53.

Miletić, Aleksandar R. 2012. *Journey Under Surveillance: The Overseas Emigration Policy of the Kingdom of Serbs, Croats and Slovenes in Global Context, 1918–1928*. Zürich: LIT Verlag.

Miller, Eugene. 1976. "Leo Krzycki—Polish American Labor Leader." *Polish American Studies* 33, no. 2 (Autumn): 52–64.

Milwaukee County Community Fund and Council of Social Agencies. 1945. *Census Tract Facts: A Handbook of Basic Social Data of Milwaukee County, Wisconsin*. Milwaukee, WI: Statistical Research Department.

"Milwaukee's Fifth 'Croatian Day' Will Be Held Next Saturday, July 23." 1939. *Zajedničar* [Fraternalist], 19 July 1939, 9.

Momirski, Lucija Ažman. 2021. "The Resilience of the Port Cities of Trieste, Rijeka, and Koper." *Journal of Urban History* 47, no. 2: 293–316.

"Month of April 1955 Membership." 1955. *Zajedničar*, 25 May 1955, 10.

Mukherji, S. Ani. 2017. "Reds among the Sewer Socialists and McCarthyites: The Communist Party in Milwaukee." *American Communist History* 16, no. 3–4: 112–142.

Nelson, Robert K., LaDale Winling, Richard Marciano, Nathan Connolly, et al. n.d. *Mapping Inequality: Redlining in New Deal America*. Richmond, VA: University of Richmond. https://dsl.richmond.edu/panorama/redlining/#loc=10/43.03/88.279&city=milwaukee-co.-wi.

Nelson, Steve, James R. Barrett, and Rob Ruck. 1981. *Steve Nelson: American Radical*. Pittsburgh: University of Pittsburgh Press.

"New School Here to Teach the ABCs of Marxism." 1934. *Milwaukee Sentinel*, 10 December 1934, 5.

Ngai, Mae M. 2004. *Impossible Subjects: Illegal Aliens and the Making of Modern America*. Princeton: Princeton University Press.

"Officers are Named by Esperanto Club." 1928. *Milwaukee Journal*, 15 May 1928.

"Oldest Croatian Lodge to Observe Anniversary." 1953. *Milwaukee Journal*, 23 October 1953, 26.

Pettengill, Ryan S. 2020. *Communists and Community: Activism in Detroit's Labor Movement, 1941–1956*. Philadelphia: Temple University Press.

Photograph of the Morris family and supporters. 1944. *Milwaukee Journal*, 16 May 1944, 21.

Pifer, Richard L. 2003. *A City at War: Milwaukee Labor during World War II*. Madison: Wisconsin Historical Society.

Pinta, Saku. 2021. "Educate, Organize, Emancipate: The Work People's College and the Industrial Workers of the World." In *Anarchist Pedagogies: Collective Actions, Theories, and Critical Reflections on Education*, edited by Robert H. Haworth, 47–68. Oakland, CA: PM Press.

"Plan for Meeting of South Slav Group." 1943. *Milwaukee Journal*, 3 December 1943, 29.

"Play to Be Given." 1940. *Milwaukee Journal*, 16 November 1940, 14.

"Postwar Task Big One, Slav Council Told." 1942. *Milwaukee Sentinel*, 19 October 1942, 13.

Protest Notice. 1944. *Milwaukee Journal*, 15 April 1944, 3.

Quinn, Lois M. 1979. *Racially Restrictive Covenants: The Making of All-White Suburbs in Milwaukee County*. Milwaukee: Metropolitan Integration Research Center.

Quinn, Lois M., John Pawasarat, and Laura Serebin. 1995. *Jobs for Workers on Relief in Milwaukee County, 1930–1994*. Milwaukee, WI: Employment and Training Institute.

Rachleff, Peter. 1998. "The Dynamics of 'Americanization': The Croatian Fraternal Union between the Wars, 1920s–30s." In *Labor Histories: Class, Politics, and the Working-Class Experience*, edited by Eric Arnesen, Julie Greene, and Bruce Laurie, 340–362. Urbana: University of Illinois Press.

Rachleff, Peter. 1989. "Class, Ethnicity, and the New Deal: The Croatian Fraternal Union in the 1930s." In *The Ethnic Enigma: The Salience of Ethnicity for European-Origin Groups*, edited by Peter Kivisto, 89–113. Philadelphia: The Balch Institute.

"Red Fascist Groups Named." 1948. *Milwaukee Journal*, 26 September 1948, 19.

"Red Planned Revolt, Claim." 1952. *Milwaukee Journal*, 8 May 1952, 10.

"Reds Seeking Election Posts as Wallaceites." 1948. *Milwaukee Journal*, 8 August 1948.

Research Clearinghouse of Milwaukee. 1950. *Milwaukee County, City, Suburbs, Today and Yesterday: A Statistical History of the Community*. Milwaukee.

Rodriguez, Joseph A., and Mark Shelley. 2009. "Latinos and Asians in Milwaukee." In *Perspectives on Milwaukee's Past*, edited by Margo Anderson and Victor Greene, 162–191. Urbana: University of Illinois Press.

Roediger, David R. 2005. *Working Toward Whiteness: How America's Immigrants Became White*. New York: Basic Books.

"Roosevelt War Aims Endorsed by Slavs." 1944. *Milwaukee Journal*, 24 January 1944, 2.

"Row Among the City's Croatians Results in Court's Order." 1931. *Milwaukee Journal*, 4 November 1931, 2.

"Rudolfo G. Oristo Obituary." 1951. *Milwaukee Journal*, 16 December 1951, 59.

"Rudolph Oristo Is Name." 1931. *Milwaukee Journal*, 22 March 1931, 7.

Sacred Heart Parish. n.d. "A History of Sacred Heart Croatian Parish in Milwaukee." https://www.sacredheartmilwaukee.org/parish-history-outline.

Satter, Beryl. 2009. *Family Properties: How the Struggle over Race and Real Estate Transformed Chicago and Urban America*. New York: Metropolitan Books.

Schimpf, David. 1987. *St. Rose of Lima Parish, 1888–1988*. Brookfield, WI: Burton & Mayer, Inc.

Schneider, Dorothee. 2011. *Crossing Borders: Migration and Citizenship in the Twentieth-Century United States*. Cambridge: Harvard University Press.

Schor, Esther. 2016. *The Bridge of Words: Esperanto and the Dream of a Universal Language*. New York: Metropolitan Books.

Schreiber, Rachel. 2022. *Elaine Black Yoneda: Jewish Immigration, Labor Activism, and Japanese American Exclusion and Incarceration*. Philadelphia: Temple University Press.

Sebanc, James. 1972. "Immigration and the Emergence of Yugoslav Social Communities in Wisconsin, 1900–1971." MA thesis, University of Wisconsin-Milwaukee.

Sekelj, Laslo. 1988. "Anti-Semitism in Yugoslavia, 1918–1945." *Eastern European Quarterly* 22, no. 2 (June): 159–172.

Sentinel, John. 1946. "Communist Prober Reads CIO News." *Milwaukee Sentinel*, 1 October 1946, 1.

Shadd, Mary Ellen. 1950. *Negro Business Directory of the State of Wisconsin, 1950–1951*. Milwaukee.

"Slavs to Eye Unity Setup." 1944. *Milwaukee Sentinel Extra*, 2 January 1944, 19.

"Slavs to Perfect Permanent Unit Here Next Sunday." 1942. *Milwaukee Sentinel Extra*, 15 October 1942, 15.

Social Explorer Tables (SE). n.d. *Census 1950 Census Tract Only*. Digitally transcribed by Inter-university Consortium for Political and Social Research, edited and verified by Michael Haines, compiled, edited, verified and additional data entered by Social Explorer.

Social Explorer Tables (SE). n.d. *Census 1940 Census Tract Only*. Digitally transcribed by Inter-university Consortium for Political and Social Research, edited and verified by Michael Haines, compiled, edited, verified and additional data entered by Social Explorer.

"Soviet Hailed by South Slavs." 1944. *Milwaukee Journal*, 10 January 1944, 13.

St. Augustine Church. n.d. "West Allis Catholic Church Chronicles: West Allis Church History."

St. Rose of Lima. 1938. *Golden Jubilee, Church of St. Rose of Lima, 1888–1938, Milwaukee, Wisconsin*. Milwaukee: St. Rose of Lima.

"Stanzers Win in Allis Loop." 1938. *Milwaukee Sentinel Extra*, 1 August 1938, 13.

"Starnes Bill Opposed." 1940. *Milwaukee Sentinel Extra*, 19 January 1940, 13.

"Steel Plant Laborer Killed by Large Crane." 1919. *Duluth Herald*, 27 May 1919.

Steidl, Annemarie, Wladimir Fischer-Nebmaier, and James Oberly. 2017. *From a Multiethnic Empire to a Nation of Nations: Austro-Hungarian Migrants in the U.S., 1870–1940*. Innsbruck: StudienVerlag.

Storch, Randi. 2007. *Red Chicago: American Communism and Its Grassroots, 1928–35*. Urbana: University of Illinois Press.

Sugrue, Thomas J. 1996. *The Origins of the Urban Crisis: Race and Inequality in Postwar Detroit*. Princeton: Princeton University Press.

Sugrue, Thomas. 2012. "Hillburn, Hattiesburg, and Hitler: Wartime Activists Think Globally and Act Locally." In *Fog of War: The Second World War and the Civil Rights Movement*, edited by Kevin M. Kruse and Stephen Tuck, 87–102. New York: Oxford University Press.

Swichkow, Louis J. 1973. "A Dual Heritage: The Jewish Community of Milwaukee, 1900–1970." PhD diss., Marquette University.

"The Ill Wind from Moscow." 1944. *Milwaukee Sentinel Extra*, 11 September 1944, 8.

Tien, H. Yuan, ed. 1962. *Milwaukee Metropolitan Area Fact Book: 1940, 1950, and 1960*. Madison: University of Wisconsin Press.

Trotter, Joe William, Jr. 2007. *Black Milwaukee: The Making of an Industrial Proletariat, 1915–1945*. 2nd ed. Urbana: University of Illinois Press.

Ubriaco, Robert D., Jr. 1999. "Choosing Sides: Restructuring the Political Landscape in Milwaukee's Polish Community, 1945–1948." *Milwaukee History* 22, no. 2 (Summer): 78–98.

"Ukrainians Rap Slav Group Rift." 1943. *Milwaukee Sentinel Extra*, 31 December 1943, 6.

United States Department of Commerce, Bureau of the Census. 1952. *1950 United States Census of Population, Census Tract Statistics: Milwaukee, Wisconsin and Adjacent Area.* Washington, DC: U.S. Government Printing Office.

United States House of Representatives, Un-American Activities Committee. 1955. *Investigation of Communist Activities in the Milwaukee, Wis., Area*, 84th Cong., 1st Sess., 28–29 March 1955. Washington, DC: U.S. Government Printing Office.

United States House of Representatives, Un-American Activities Committee. 1950. *Report on the American Slav Congress and Associated Organizations*, 81st Congress, 2nd Session, 26 June 1949. Washington, DC: U.S. Government Printing Office.

Vabousquet, Nina. 2021. "'Un-American' Antisemitism? the American Jewish Committee's Response to Global Antisemitism in the Interwar Period." *American Jewish History* 105, no. 1/2 (January/April): 77–102.

"Want Negroes to Stay Away: Protests Heard as Rally in the 16th Ward Argues the Housing Issue." 1944. *Milwaukee Journal*, 2 May 1944.

Ward, Charles A. 1991. "Croatian and Serbian Church Communities in Milwaukee." In *Languages in Contact and Contrast: Essays in Contact Linguistics*, eds. Vladimir Ivir and Damir Kalogjera, 493–498. Berlin: Mouton de Gruyer.

Ward, Charles A. 1976. "The Serbian and Croatian Communities in Milwaukee." *General Linguistics* 16, no. 2/3: 151–165.

Webb, Daryl. 2006. "'A Great Promise and a Great Threat': Milwaukee Children and the Great Depression." PhD diss., Marquette University.

West Division High School. 1940. *Comet* Yearbook, Milwaukee, WI. U.S. School Yearbooks, *1880–2012*. Accessed on *Ancestry.com Library Edition*.

West Division High School. 1938. *Comet* Yearbook, Milwaukee, WI. U.S. School Yearbooks, *1880–2012*. Accessed on *Ancestry.com Library Edition*.

West Division High School. 1937. *Comet* Yearbook, Milwaukee, WI. U.S. School Yearbooks, *1880–2012*. Accessed on *Ancestry.com Library Edition*.

West Division High School. 1936. *Comet* Yearbook, Milwaukee, WI. U.S. School Yearbooks, *1880–2012*. Accessed on *Ancestry.com Library Edition*.

Westbrook, Robert B. 2004. *Why We Fought: Forging American Obligations in World War II*. Washington, DC: Smithsonian Books.

"Wrecker Nine Plans Entry in Triple A Loop." 1940. *Milwaukee Journal*, 16 April 1940.

Wright's Milwaukee City Directory, 1944–45. 1945. Kansas City, MO: Wright Directory Co.

Wright's Milwaukee City Directory, 1940. 1940. Kansas City, MO: Wright Directory Co.

Wright's Milwaukee City Directory, 1929. 1929. Kansas City, MO: Wright Directory Co.

Zahra, Tara. 2016. *The Great Departure: Mass Migration from Eastern Europe and the Making of the Free World*. New York: w.w. Norton.

Zajedničar [Fraternalist]. Microfilm Reel 11 (1939–1940), Allegheny, PA. Immigration History and Research Center, University of Minnesota, Minneapolis, MN.

Zecker, Robert M. 2021. "'Nothing Less than Full Freedom': Radical Immigrant Newspapers Champion Civil Rights." *American Communist History* 20, no. 3–4: 165–188.

Zecker, Robert M. 2018. *"A Road to Peace and Freedom": The International Workers Order and the Struggle for Economic Justice and Civil Rights, 1930–1954*. Philadelphia: Temple University Press.

CHAPTER 18

Hilde Krones and the "Generation of Fulfillment"

Georg Spitaler

Abstract

The Austrian socialist Hilde Krones (1910–1948) grew up in Red Vienna and joined the proscribed Revolutionary Socialists in 1934. After Austria's liberation from Nazism in 1945, she was an elected a member of parliament for the Socialist Party of Austria (Sozialistische Partei Österreichs, SPÖ), a leading member of the Party's Women's Organization and was one of the few female members of the Party Executive Committee until her suicide in 1948. As a political activist, life and love were closely tied to Krones's political work. Focusing on this conceptualization of work, her "ways of relating" (*Beziehungsweisen*), and the idea of "fulfillment" once promised to her generation of young activists, this chapter investigates the "haunting" texts, concepts, and objects of her personal archive. Embodying *Jetztzeit* moments of the present, Krones's archive is put into dialogue with current political concepts and feelings such as *left melancholy* and the urgent matter of envisioning emancipatory futures in the face of political depression and "capitalist realism" in the twenty-first century. In a theoretical *séance*, the chapter aims to make use of "hauntology" and the "imaginative archive"—methodologies that engage with traces, phantoms, gaps, and fissures in order to find resources for political hope in the present.

Keywords

activism – Austria – hauntology – Hilde Krones – imaginative archive – *Jetztzeit* – political feelings – revolutionary socialists – Socialist Party of Austria (Sozialistische Partei Österreichs, SPÖ) – ways of relating

In August 1944, Hilde Krones (1910–1948), an employee of the Vienna branch of Bayer IG Farben, wrote to her superior Director Paulmann in Germany:

> Dear Doctor Paulmann, I know that the "men's society" in which I live has its own norms in many respects, and that the *égalité* proclaimed in 1789, even though more than 150 years have passed in the meantime, has still

 | DOI:10.1163/9789004682481_019

> not been implemented in reality. As an old adherent to *realpolitik*, I have also come to terms with this. Nevertheless, there must be a possibility of finding a middle way here. For example, it would largely correspond to the facts if my official job title were to be changed to "Authorized Signatory Managing Director" or the like.[1]

Krones, who had been with the company since 1930, had become the de facto head of her department due to her competence and the war-related absence of her male colleagues—a role she now formally asserted. But she also had another identity: having grown up in Red Vienna, the Austrian capital of municipal socialism between 1918/19 and 1934, she had been an activist with the proscribed Revolutionary Socialists (Revolutionäre Sozialisten) during the years of Austro-fascism and Nazism. The fact that a socialist opponent of the Nazis invoked the unredeemed values of the French Revolution in her struggle for professional recognition—reminiscent of a contemporary feminist—from her superior, a manager in a key Nazi firm, astonished me as a reader. The letter from Hilde Krones's archive incorporated, it seemed to me, the *Jetztzeit*, or "now-time," that Walter Benjamin writes about in his famous formulation about temporality and leftist history.[2] Krones's reference to the Enlightenment in the midst of the madness of National Socialism resembles the "tiger's leap into the past"[3] described by Benjamin: it was a bold argument she courageously advanced in order to advocate for her interests. In her letter, Krones associated herself with the realm of *realpolitik*, but she would not become a full-time politician until after the liberation in 1945, when she was one of the leading functionaries of the Socialist Party of Austria (Sozialistische Partei Österreichs, SPÖ) in the brief period before her suicide in 1948. Yet she never became a pragmatic advocate of *realpolitik*; instead, in the context of the budding Cold War and the Allied occupation, she was marginalized as an uncompromising representative of the left wing by her power-conscious opponents within the party.

1 Her current job title was "secretary" (*Korrespondentin*). Hilde Krones to Richard Paulmann, 23 August 1944, Folder 6, Box 1, Nachlass (hereafter: NL) Hilde Krones [Hilde Krones Papers], Verein für Geschichte der ArbeiterInnenbewegung (VGA) [Austrian Labour History Society] (hereafter VGA), Vienna, Austria. This article is part of a larger book project on the Hilde Krones archive that the author is currently working on. Translation into English by Jason Heilman.

2 Benjamin 2007 [1942], 261.

3 Benjamin, 2007, 261.

Specific conceptualizations of *work* shaped her political biography on a number of levels. First, as a revolutionary socialist, she was among a generation of activists who committed their lives to "revolution as work" or the work of revolution, as Brigitte Studer framed it with regard to the Communist International.[4] In a similar vein, Krones was a committed activist for equality of the sexes in the private, political, and economic spheres, and although not a trade unionist, she can be ranked among those "socialist-feminists" whose life was centered on improving the position of working-class women.[5] Second, the equal participation of women in the sphere of *paid labour* was at the center of her socialist conception of women's liberation, a fact that had consequences for various aspects of her personal and political life. In the following chapter, I will demonstrate the relevance of the case of Hilde Krones for this volume by linking her notions of *work* and *activism* to my broader agenda of entering into a dialogue with the private and public emotions present in her archive, such as hope, melancholy, fear, and depression. The chapter begins with some theoretical and methodological comments and a discussion of Krones's place in scholarship and party (SPÖ) memory. It then engages with her personal archive, which spans from Red Vienna, to Nazism and the liberation after World War Two, to her death in 1948.

1 Melancholy, Hauntology, and the Imaginative Archive

Drawing on the theoretical and methodological concepts of *hauntology* and the *imaginative archive*, my chapter deals with some of the "haunting" materials from the archive of Hilde Krones,[6] not least her death. In so doing, I am entering into a dialogue with the political feelings, terms, and concepts articulated in these materials—conducting a theoretical *séance* that addresses questions to these texts and searches for the buried hopes and lost futures of the emancipatory politics entombed in the rubble of twentieth-century history.

In this respect, the death of Hilde Krones can be placed in a long line of "necromancies": in his account of the artistic and theoretical memory work concerning the left-wing history of revolution in the twentieth century, Enzo Traverso emphasizes the importance that funereal images have played in

4 Studer 2020, 26–33.

5 Zimmermann 2021, 660–661. Similar to many of the international trade unionists portrayed by Susan Zimmermann, Krones never used the term *feminist* to describe herself, thus distancing herself from the bourgeois women's movement.

6 NL Hilde Krones [Hilde Krones Papers], VGA.

left-wing iconography as a "symbiotic relationship between revolution and death."[7] He points out that after 1989 at the latest, this memory of a past future transformed into mourning. The lost utopias of the left would have become a *U-topia* (Paul Celan), "a no-longer-existing place, a destroyed utopia that is the object of melancholy art." In this sense, archives of workers' history today are also places "to remember hopes turned into no-places, something that no longer exists."[8]

It is no coincidence that Traverso focuses on the feeling of *melancholy* in his book. In so doing, he connects to a debate that has been wrestling with the legacies of leftist theory and practice and the political feelings associated with them since at least the 1990s. In an influential essay, Wendy Brown diagnosed what she saw as a backward-looking and unproductive left melancholy, caught in a ghostly spirit,[9] a condition in which the "attachment to the object of one's sorrowful loss supersedes any desire to recover from this loss, to live free in the present."[10] With reference to Walter Benjamin, she described this melancholy as a tendency of the Left to have settled into its own theoretical certainties and historical defeat—and in the process, to have lost its capacity for a critical analysis of the present directed toward the future, for a dialectical grasp of the *Jetztzeit*.[11] This view did not go unchallenged; Jodi Dean, for example, describes the causes and manifestations of left melancholy in almost the opposite way. According to her, Benjamin criticized the Left not for its Marxist traditionalism but for "the sublimation of left ideals in market-oriented writing and publishing,"[12] a Left that had "already conceded to the inevitably of capitalism."[13] Dean published her text some fifteen years after Wendy Brown, in the context of the global protest movements of the 2000s, from the Arab Spring to Occupy Wall Street. In this temporal context, emancipatory hopes seemed to grow. Today, in the face of the global success of authoritarian populist parties and leaders whose rhetorical strategies resemble those of early fascism in many ways; the restoration of global capitalism after the 2008 crisis; and against the backdrop of the climate crisis, these hopes seem dampened to me.

One such—what I would call—"dampened" theory, which nevertheless tried to find traces of hope in a depressive mood, was formulated by the British

7 Traverso 2016, 106.
8 Traverso 2016, 119.
9 Brown 1999, 26.
10 Brown 1999, 20.
11 Brown 1999, 20.
12 Dean 2012, 163.
13 Dean 2012, 174.

cultural theorist Mark Fisher. In *Ghosts of My Life: Writings on Depression, Hauntology and Lost Futures*,[14] he described the difficulty of developing an emancipatory vision of the future in the face of the traumatic present of "capitalist realism."[15] What prevails is "the widespread sense that not only is capitalism the only viable political and economic system, but also that it is now impossible even to imagine a coherent alternative to it."[16] Fisher simultaneously identified the phenomena of *specters* that haunt our present, referring to Jacques Derrida's concept of hauntology (*hantologie*), coined by the latter in his book *Specters of Marx*.[17] Capitalist realism has driven out and banished socialism as if it had never existed; it has made mourning for the lost object impossible and is therefore haunted by it.[18] On the other hand, Fisher argued, there exists a specific melancholic attachment to the "popular modernism" of the 1950s to the 1980s and the unfulfilled emancipatory promises of the future associated with it. Fisher argued, however, that hauntology should not involve a backward-looking nostalgia for Fordism or the real-existing social democracy of the 1970s. "What should haunt us is not the *no longer* of actually existing social democracy, but the *not yet* of the futures that popular modernism trained us to expect, but which never materialised."[19] As an evocation of a past "that never was,"[20] hauntology, in Fisher's sense, is simultaneously an expression being haunted by a repressed past and a future that never happened, but also a refusal to give up the desire for this possible future.

In this context, another approach to the haunted legacies of the twentieth century seems applicable. In her exploration of the anarchist icon Emma Goldman, Clare Hemmings devised a theoretically advanced methodology of the *imaginative archive* as a site in which she establishes a relationship with the historical figure and their political sentiments based on her own political passions and the political questions of the present. Drawing on experiences from queer theory and postcolonial literary studies, she reconstructs sources that have not been preserved for historical reasons; she even writes them as part of an imaginary dialogue with Goldman herself, creating a new archive, "one that has yet to be written or read."[21] The imaginative archive illuminates "the gaps and fissures in the existing archives;" it includes:

14 Fisher 2014.
15 Fisher 2009.
16 Fisher 2009, 2.
17 Derrida 1994, 10.
18 Derrida 1994, 99.
19 Fisher 2014, 27.
20 Fisher 2014, 137.
21 Hemmings 2018, 8.

> the straining to hear the voices that have never been heard, the attachments that cannot be given meaning, and the utopian desire for another future grounded in a different past. [...] It grapples with the relationship between the dead and the living in order to enact the future one wants to bring about in the present.[22]

In a case like the death of Hilde Krones, the reasons for which cannot be completely clarified, working with her personal archive invites us to reflect on the tension between historical sources and our own projections and affective reactions, especially in relation to the *uncanny*—"that which the historian knows but must deny" (Joan Scott)—the contradictions, blind spots, and traumas of historical memory as well as contemporary political theory.[23]

2 Buried Archives

The reception of Hilde Krones's life and work includes phases of empty time and *Jetztzeit*—of the deep burial and careful exhumation of the dead. Within the party, after her death at the age of thirty-eight—portrayed by the party press as the tragic end of a talented young politician—and funeral, efforts were made to quickly stifle the memory of the dissident Hilde Krones. Commemorative articles in the journal of the Socialist Freedom Fighters Association (Bund Sozialistischer Freiheitskämpfer) led to harsh internal criticism from party leader Adolf Schärf and other top SPÖ politicians.[24] Krones's local party organization in the Ottakring district of Vienna held memorials at her grave in at least 1949 and 1968. In the years immediately after her death, Krones was vigorously commemorated in the publication *The New Forward* (*Der Neue Vorwärts*) by her comrade-in-arms Erwin Scharf, and the case of Krones was also used in polemics against the SPÖ published in the communist *People's Voice* (*Volksstimme*). Her "rediscovery" by scholars took place only in the context of the emergence of the New Left in the 1970s. In Fritz Weber's assessment of the SPÖ during the Cold War and his critique of the political orientation of social democracy after 1945, Krones's character—along with Erwin Scharf, who stood center stage—plays an important supporting role.[25]

---

22 Hemmings 2018, 8.

23 Hemmings 2018, 26–28.

24 Felix Slavik to Rosa Jochmann, Otto Probst to Rosa Jochmann, 11 January 1951, PN6/258, Neues Parteiarchiv [New Party Archive], VGA; Rosa Jochmann to Felix Slavik, 15 January 1950 [sic, 1951], PN6/249, Neues Parteiarchiv, VGA; Duma 2019, 361.

25 Weber 2011 [1977].

The only feminist examination of Krones's life to date was published in 1989 by Doris Ingrisch, who wrote an excellent biographical essay that drew on Hilde Krones's papers.[26]

After the boom in workers' history and history from below—including the gendered and feminist variants thereof—in the 1970s and 1980s, however, Krones's archive was rarely touched. Only in last fifteen years or so has there been a new increase in interest in the (often forgotten) women protagonists of the workers' movement in Austria. This applies both to the early period up to the democratic upheaval of 1918–1919, for example the social democratic icon Adelheid Popp or the participation of women in the council movement,[27] but also to the traumatic ruptures of 1934 and 1938, and the democratic revival in 1945, for example with women politicians or activists such as Rosa Jochmann[28] and Tilly Spiegel.[29] Family constellations as well as private and political partnerships also garnered attention, as in the recent double biography of Marianne and Oscar Pollak,[30] as well as in Gabriella Hauch's group-biographical research on members of the socialist and communist Strasser family.[31] The counter-history of a left-wing family, marginalized by Austrian historiography but reconstructed by Hauch from buried sources, shares, in my opinion, a "hauntological" interest with the search for traces of Hilde Krones presented here. Some scholarship published around the centennial of Red Vienna explicitly referred to Mark Fisher or Walter Benjamin and read concepts and debates from the awakening of communal socialism in Vienna as "space[s] of possibility" for the *Jetztzeit* of the present.[32]

2.1 *Ways of Relating*

Born Hilde Handl in 1910, Hilde Krones would become a child of Red Vienna, shaped politically and culturally by the legacy of the period that lasted from 1918 to 1934. After the early death of her father, a baker's assistant, her mother took a job as a social worker so she could graduate from the *Handelsakademie*, the commercial high school,[33] which was a prerequisite for her later career

26 Ingrisch 1989.
27 Helfert 2021; Popp 2019; Trausmuth 2019; Hauch 2009.
28 Mayerhofer 2020; Duma 2019.
29 Markova 2019.
30 Konrad 2021.
31 See, for example, Hauch 2020, 2018, 2015, 2014.
32 See Heindl 2020, 60–86; McFarland, Spitaler, and Zechner, 2020, 8–9; Schwarz, Spitaler, and Wikidal 2019, 14; Spitaler 2018.
33 Hilde Krones, "Biografische Skizze" [Biographical sketch], Folder 10, Box 1, NL Hilde Krones, VGA.

advancement. From her childhood on, Hilde grew up in the cultural and political organizations of the Social Democratic Workers' Party (Sozialdemokratische Arbeiterpartei, SDAP), including the Children's Friends (Kinderfreunde), the Socialist Workers' Youth (Sozialistische Arbeiterjugend), the Young Front (Jungfront), and a workers' gymnastics club.[34] She wrote her *Matura* in 1928 on "Youth Psychology and the Youth Movement";[35] she was familiar with the concepts of individual psychology, and as her correspondence reveals, she continued to practice leisure activities associated with working-class culture such as steam bathing, fold boating, gymnastics, and nudism during the war years.

Her longer-term romantic relationships were exclusively with her socialist comrades, and there is a striking parallelism in the political and private ruptures—between endings and new beginnings—she experienced in these facets of her life. A few months after the Austrian workers' uprising in 1934, she began a relationship with Franz Krones, an engineer and municipal official eight years her senior. But both of them had to end their existing relationships in order to be together, and in Hilde Krones's case, she was involved with Paul Schärf, a nephew of Adolf Schärf, who later became party chairman. Despite her reservations about patriarchal marriage law in Austria, Hilde Handl and Franz Krones would ultimately marry mere weeks after the outbreak of the war in 1939, when the German law permitting civil divorce was already in place in Catholic Austria.[36] After her marriage to Franz, Hilde continued to work at the Bayer office. Given her commitment to the idea that equality of the sexes centered explicitly on women's participation in the sphere of paid labour, a professional job offered her financial independence. This focus on women's labour and women's autonomy also informed her views on birth control and care work. Albeit with some regret, she decided not to bring children into a world that forced mothers to be dependent on men.[37] Furthermore, due to her belief in "modern marriage," she did not cook for her husband, instead relying on both her and Franz's mothers to feed them.[38] She also paid a cleaning woman and her sister-in-law for domestic labour. In the summer of 1945, shortly after the liberation, Hilde began a love affair with Erwin Scharf, four years her junior,

34 Krones, "Biografische Skizze" [Biographical sketch].

35 Hilde Handl, "Jugendpsychologie und Jugendbewegung," Maturaarbeit [high school thesis, draft], 1928, Folder 37, Box 3, NL Hilde Krones, VGA.

36 Mesner 1997, 187–188.

37 Hilde Handl to Franz Krones [draft], n.d. [1934], Folder 28, Box 3.

38 Hilde Krones to Franz Krones, 23 March 1944, field letter, Folder 46, Box 6, NL Hilde Krones, VGA.

who had just returned from the Yugoslavian Partisans and had been appointed party secretary of the Socialist Party.

The documents and materials preserved in Hilde Krones's archive—diaries, letters, photographs, drafts of political essays, and speeches—include both private and public texts, and the sentiments articulated in them connect these two levels, not least in light of the political ruptures of 1934 (the crushed Austrian workers' uprising), 1938 (the *Anschluss* with Nazi Germany), and 1945 (the liberation). As a revolutionary socialist, the period from 1917 to 1919 (with the Russian Revolution serving as a model and example as compared to the democratic socialism of Red Vienna of 1919–1934) as well as the *future*—as a space of realized emancipation, played central roles in Hilde Krones's papers. A concept that retrospectively brings together these private and public feelings is *Beziehungsweisen* or "ways of relating." Coining this concept, Bini Adamczak examined the political gender models developed during the Russian Revolution of 1917, the Stalinist era of the 1930s, and the events of 1968[39] in order to pose the question—as a means of developing a central aspect of future emancipative revolutions—how "emotionality and rationality, intimacy and instrumentality [should be] related to each other, how relations of the private and the public, the intimate and the anonymous are mediated to each other."[40] Adamczak argues that before 1968, a "desire for solidary ways of relating" was historically "not intelligible," "because it lacked a political language to articulate itself."[41] However the generation of activists who had spent their youth in Red Vienna was trained in the socialist youth movement with a pedagogy and vocabulary of affect, influenced by Freudo-Marxism and individual psychology.

Red Vienna was retrospectively described as a space of possibility, as an "era of great hope," as the sociologist Marie Jahoda, who was involved in it, described it.[42] Krones was one of those young activists whom party theorist Otto Bauer had once called the "generation of fulfillment," i.e. those who would see the end of capitalism.[43] In the era of fascism, this future seemed a long way off. Bauer's promise continued to exist in their imagination, but Krones's political circle of friends now spoke of themselves as the "generation of experimentation" whose fate was open.[44] Along with hope came other feelings: melancholy and sadness—about what was lost with the end of Red Vienna—fear

39 Adamczak 2017.

40 Adamczak 2017, 107.

41 Adamczak 2017, 286.

42 Franz, Kiczka, Misik, Spitaler, Vana, and Werner 2019, 418.

43 Bauer 1976 [1924], 872.

44 Hilde Handl to Franz Krones, 31 December 1938, Folder 38, Box 4, NL Hilde Krones, VGA.

and doubt, and an unyielding commitment to the goal of socialism, even if it was unclear whether they would ever experience it for themselves. "[W]here will we end up? Maybe on the dung heap," Hilde wrote to Franz Krones at the turn of 1938–1939. "We have gone too far to feel sufficiently comfortable [as a happy couple in private life]—and we are too deeply mired in today—at least I am—to be completely happy with just a blank check [of a better future, without living in the present, GS]."[45] As a political couple that stood together against the world, Hilde and Franz explicitly linked private and political "ways of relating" as a path from "I and You" to the collective "We." "Does being happy mean living in bourgeois peace and comfort? Or haven't I always felt deep inside, in the moments of greatest pain, the greatest anguish, in the moments when life made the most difficult demands on me, a burning feeling of happiness about being allowed to experience the world with you—even if that means suffering."[46]

In her reflections, metaphors of work and activism played an important role: the hopes of *building* a better future, of (re-)constructing what was lost and what was yet to come. In 1942, in another letter to Franz Krones, she wrote:

> How difficult it is when what we create is only a brick for the house of the future—only those who can see it completed have the final conviction, the happiness of the creator—to us, apparently only suffering prevails. [...] Yes, to be fertilizer, too, [...] is an extremely important function—a beautiful one it is not.[47]

When Franz Krones was called up in 1942 as an engineer for the military construction unit *Organisation Todt*,[48] Hilde implemented a rigid program to structure her everyday life—and maintain hope for a shared private and political future. The day after her husband's departure, she started attending a Russian language course in Vienna. The two of them had studied Russian in private, but now she continued her studies publicly as an act of hope for a revolutionary future and for a time when her skills of Russian would be of use. Hilde and Franz wrote each other a letter every day almost until the end of the war. Hilde also maintained her clandestine political work, including

---

45 Hilde Handl to Franz Krones, 31 December 1938.

46 Hilde Krones to Franz Krones, 31 December 1938.

47 Hilde Krones to Franz Krones, 22 October 1942, Folder 40, Box 4, NL Hilde Krones, VGA.

48 *Organisation Todt* (OT), named after its head Fritz Todt, carried out military construction work in occupied Europe, using forced labour. Since 1943, the organization was also involved in the construction of concentration camps.

regular meetings with comrades and support for families whose relatives were in prison or concentration camps. In the *Feldpost* letters, which were subject to censorship, information about this aspect of her life can be read between the lines. Explicitly, however, Hilde's letters tell of everyday wartime life in Vienna and of her feelings. Again, a motto she often used was "work and don't despair." "Turn all pain into energy! That is the deepest secret of life," she wrote after liberation.[49] Her favorite poem describes "days of pain" as black marble steps—"'But today I know, as I look behind: the train of steps has led me upward!' [...] [H]ow difficult it is to come to this realization in the middle of the path. There, you usually only feel the exhaustion; there, the tears do not extinguish everything."[50]

While transcribing the 650 or so preserved field letters Hilde Krones wrote to Franz Krones between 1942 and 1945, this long wait for change, the draining years of silence and stillness seemed almost tangible to me. They were heading toward a euphoric moment that Hilde Krones described as—almost— revolutionary. About the self-liberation of her neighborhood in Ottakring by local communists and socialists—including Krones—in April 1945, when this part of Vienna was handed over to the Red Army more or less without a fight, Hilde wrote: "It was a joy to watch. A mess, a screaming match—but it had a primal revolutionary élan and much, much individual willingness to sacrifice."[51]

Just a few days later, Hilde Krones took part in the reconstitution of the Social Democratic Party (as the Socialist Party of Austria, SPÖ) at Vienna's city hall as a representative of the Revolutionary Socialists, and she became a member of the party's executive committee.[52] There she met Erwin Scharf, with whom she began an affair in the summer of 1945, while her husband Franz was still on his way home from a brief period in U.S. captivity. The new political beginning for Austria was thus also accompanied by a private one for Hilde—and this may come as a surprise given how prominent the theme of her and Franz's future was in her correspondence. Was Hilde Krones an unreliable narrator in her letters? Franz Krones must also have been surprised; he reproached his wife strongly in his letters and fought for their relationship. In a note to Hilde, he

49 Hilde Krones to Erwin Scharf, 18 July 1945, draft, Folder 35, Box 3, NL Hilde Krones, VGA.
50 Hilde Krones to Erwin Scharf, 18 July 1945.
51 Hilde Krones, "Tagebuch der Ereignisse" [Diary of events], 12 to 29 April 1945, Folder 49, Box 6, NL Hilde Krones, VGA.
52 It seems that during the liberation, her basic Russian language skills were indeed helpful in negotiating with Red Army soldiers and the Soviet administration. Hilde Krones, "Tagebuch der Ereignisse" [Diary of events]; Schärf 1948, 91.

tried to explain the contradiction between her wartime letters and her new feelings to himself:

> Once upon a time? In a fairy-tale? Yes, since life was a fairy tale in the past years of death. For *Kasperle* and doe [pet names they gave themselves], life looked for its last refuge and found it. *Kasperle* and doe were the living rear guard of death. Strong and growing life overcomes death, fairy-tale becomes reality. [...] It is a crying shame, but one must not be afraid of life, since in fact it *is* itself the fairy-tale.[53]

As close as the contact between Hilde and Franz was during the war years, in the decisive months after March 1945, Hilde went without any news of him, and he was not by her side, unlike Erwin Scharf. In her letter-diary, she noted at this time:

> And in spite of all preoccupations—in spite of the fact that I am plunged into the maelstrom—I am miserable. In some way, I suspected that at the moment when life in general would become more bearable, our personal, individual lives would go to pot. But you see, at that time we still thought that at least the great general [sentiment after the war] would be such that momentum and enthusiasm would take hold of us and offer us a replacement for another piece of personal happiness. And in the meantime, the doorway, the famous one into which we can and must place our foot, has scarcely been opened. I am in an incessant struggle—in the party—in business—everywhere—I am so tense every minute—and am so tired and so despondent inside. You need to come very soon, for I don't know how long I'll be able to endure this alone.[54]

In the years that followed, a complicated spatial and relational arrangement developed out of the joint political work, life, and love Hilde shared with Erwin Scharf and, to an extent, with Franz Krones, who remained a close political confidant and advisor.

Politically, in 1945 the revolutionary dream soon turned into a nightmare for Hilde Krones. Scharf, Krones, and some comrades-in-arms from the circle of Revolutionary Socialists clung to their hope, which had kept alive despite repression, of a revolutionary upheaval in Austria, i.e., the time of fulfillment.

53 Franz Krones to Hilde Krones, 17 September 1945, Folder 49, Box 6, NL Hilde Krones, VGA.

54 Tagebuch [Diary] Hilde Krones 26 May to 27 June 1945, Folder 49, Box 6, NL Hilde Krones, VGA.

Referring to Otto Bauer's concept of "integral socialism,"[55] which had been developed in exile, they advocated within the SPÖ for a cooperative policy of "unity of action" with the Communist Party of Austria (Kommunistische Partei Österreichs, KPÖ) and hoped the Soviet Union would be an ally; this was a plan that had little chance of realization under the political constellation of the postwar years, not least because of the unpopularity of the Russian occupying force among the general population. Hilde Krones also realized very quickly that this was a "desperate struggle":[56]

> I can't even say that I imagined it much differently—I remember that during [your] previous home leaves, we always kept in mind that, with the world constellation, the approaching politics will by no means be straightforward, by no means revolutionary in our sense—but now that it is there, I still suffer, nevertheless. We fervently hoped that the coming of the Russians would help us in this respect—but this did not happen either—on the contrary, the pressure on Russia to enter into treaties with the bourgeois world has only made it even more of a mess.[57]

Nevertheless, the summer of 1945 was initially also a euphoric new beginning for Hilde Krones. She plunged into a relationship with Ewin Scharf, with whom she quickly formed a close political and private partnership. Hilde and Erwin, however, could not carry on their relationship in public as both were still married: Erwin Scharf had a wife and children in faraway Carinthia. Draft letters from 1945 to 1947 suggest that Hilde repeatedly struggled with the fact that Scharf apparently did not profess his love with the same consistency as she did.

2.2 *Egalité*

Returning to the events described at the start of this chapter, Hilde Krones herself was aware that she had ventured far in her 1944 letter to Bayer Director Paulmann quoted in the introduction. The same evening she wrote the letter, she was overcome by "inhibitions about my own courage," as she wrote to Franz Krones.[58] She did not quite prevail in the matter; as of February 1945, her final job title was "Deputy Department Head with Signature Authority."[59] But

55 Bauer 1936, 312–336.

56 Mesner 1990, 479.

57 Hilde Krones to Franz Krones, draft, 20 May 1945, Folder 49, Box 6, NL Hilde Krones, VGA.

58 Hilde Krones to Franz Krones, 23 August 1944, field letter, Folder 49, Box 6, NL Krones, VGA.

59 Deutsches Reich, Arbeitsbuch [Employee's record book] Hilde Krones, geb. [nee] Handl, Folder 9, Box 1, NL Krones, VGA.

by this time, the days of the "Third Reich" were already numbered. After the liberation of Vienna, Hilde Krones also initially took advantage of the situation professionally: together with other senior employees of Bayer's Vienna branch, she set up her own business, and in June 1945, she became co-managing director of the Austrochem company.

At first glance, the specter of the French Revolution haunting the 1944 letter gives us a sense of proximity to the present day: Krones's argument seems to be in line with contemporary feminist texts that refer to the French Revolution's promise of equality, which was still not fulfilled. If you question the "object" more closely, it becomes apparent that her own reference to the bourgeois revolution of 1789 contained the specific perspective of a revolutionary socialist: The French Revolution appears in several places in Krones's papers, not least in several speech drafts from 1945 to 1948. In a radio speech on "The Woman in Parliament" (1946), Krones sketched a historical outline of women's struggle for political equality from the era of primitive communism to the present. It was left to the French Revolution, she said, "to raise the revolutionary cry: 'If a woman has the right to mount the scaffold, she must also have the right to mount the tribune.'[60] This call has not faded away; as a conscious political demand, it has been taken up and carried forward by the workers' movements of the socialist parties."[61]

Through her reference to the French Revolution, Krones drew on discursive frameworks that had been established by prominent Austrian social democratic women's activists in the first decades of the twentieth century. In several articles and speeches, Adelheid Popp, Therese Schlesinger, Marianne Pollak, and Emmy Freundlich had pointed to the revolutions of 1789, 1848, and the Paris *Commune* of 1871 to highlight the existence of women revolutionaries throughout history.[62] At the same time, they portrayed the French Revolution as an unfinished legacy in a dual sense: in the Austrian context, the bourgeois revolution had only been fully realized by the constitutional revolution of 1918 that established the new (German) Austrian republic. But the "political democracy" that had been achieved in 1918 still lacked the features of social equality and social democracy for which socialism strived.[63]

60 A famous quote by Olympe de Gouges; for a detailed account of the French Revolution as a point of reference for German and Austrian Social Democracy until 1934 (such as Adler 1906), see Ducange 2019.

61 Hilde Krones, "Die Frau im Parlament" [The woman in parliament], radio speech, 17 July 1946, PN18/211, Neues Parteiarchiv, VGA.

62 See Helfert 2021, 218–221, 267, 304; Popp 1918.

63 Freundlich 1928, 3.

This critical position, which had emerged during the years of Red Vienna, was also taken up by Hilde Krones in her radio speech: Complete equality is only possible "in a classless society freed from the mania of private property and profit—in socialism," she argued.[64] Now, after the traumatic backlash of Austro-fascism and Nazism, the ideals of bourgeois enlightenment seemed to be even more discredited than in the 1920s and early 1930s. In a draft speech to professional women, Krones distanced herself from the French Revolution by linking it to the political program of the bourgeoisie as an "old and weak" politics whose demands of "liberty, equality, fraternity" had "long since proved to be an illusion."[65] In this light, her reference to *egalité* in the letter to the IG Farben director appears as a brave but also a strategic argument, directed toward a bourgeois decision-maker who might be convinced by an appeal to his own—potential—bourgeois ideals.[66] It is, therefore, no coincidence that Krones elaborated on gender relations and working conditions under National Socialism in the same draft speech:

> And what did the stinking militaristic air of brutal Hitlerism, with its contempt for everything spiritual, feminine, and human have to offer us? Besides boundless misery and miserable death by bombing, at most an unedifying participation in an economy that served the most insane mass murder of all times. […] On an equal footing with men, we [women] have had to take upon ourselves all the sufferings of fascism. In the armaments factories—in wartime work, we were equal. *Now we demand full equality in the opportunity for advancement!* (emphasis in the original).[67]

As an executive employee of the Bayer Group, Hilde Krones had also been personally involved in the war economy until 1945. Even if the area of crop protection in which she worked was not directly linked to the war industry—or to IG Farben's technical involvement in the Shoah—"participation in the mass murder" of the war must have been problematic for Krones herself. Indeed, in the theory of fascism and the analysis of the war motives she shared with her husband Franz Krones and with Marxist theorists of the time, "monopoly

64 Hilde Krones, "Die Frau im Parlament" [The woman in parliament].

65 Hilde Krones, "Haben wir wirklich die Wahl?" [Do we really have the choice?], typoscript [n.d.], Folder 20, Box 2, NL Hilde Krones, VGA.

66 In other letters, Dr. Paulmann was portrayed by her as a paternalistic but supportive boss. Despite his prominent position, she does not explicitly characterize him as an ardent National Socialist.

67 H. Krones, "Haben wir wirklich die Wahl?" [Do we really have the choice?].

capital"—and explicitly also IG Farben—was considered the driving force behind the political and military devastation of the continent.[68] An obituary for Hilde Krones, presumably written by her husband Franz Krones, tried to solve this contradiction by stating that her job at IG Farben gave her "insight into the German capitalist monopoly economy, which she exploit[ed] for her socialist political activity."[69] Still, the absence of explicit reflection on the horrors of the Shoah in Hilde Krones's papers is a haunting aspect of her archive, pointing to traumatic blind spots.

3 Liberation from Fear

In December 1947, the expanded Women's Central Committee of the SPÖ discussed the motto for Women's Day, 1948. Various slogans were discussed which sought to appeal to women beyond already convinced party functionaries. The proposal of "the right to work"—together with "equal pay for equal work," a demand made by the Central Women's Conference in October 1947[70]—led to a debate in which Hilde Krones also took part.[71] Marianne Pollak, a journalist and editor-in-chief of the socialist women's magazine *Die Frau*, advanced the counterproposal: "a happy world for our children; women, join the fight" as a "future-oriented" motto that would also appeal to the broader public. Rosa Jochmann, a prominent member of the former socialist antifascist resistance, also opposed the "right to work" motto: "we want to bring all women to our Women's Day [festivities], but women themselves resent each other for working." Significant in light of the postwar backlash against women's employment[72] was the statement made by trade unionist Wilhelmine Moik:

68 See F. Krones 1946, 12; F. Krones, "Die Neue Demokratie" [The new democracy], 1 September 1945, speech at the Sozialistischer Klub, PN2/2813, Neues Parteiarchiv [New Party Archive], VGA. On the contemporary debate, see Wippermann 1981.

69 Aufzeichnungen zu Hilde Krones [Notes on Hilde Krones], Folder 30, Box 3, NL Hilde Krones, VGA.

70 Frauenzentralkomitee 1947, 62. For interwar debates on the "right to work" on the level of international trade unions, see Zimmermann 2021, 427–464; for the equal pay debate in the contemporary context of the nascent Cold War, see Johanna Wolf's contribution to this volume.

71 "Protokolle des Frauenzentral-Komitees der Sozialischen Partei Österreichs" [Protocols of the Women's Central Committee, Socialist Party of Austria], 8 December 1947, 163, PN18/753, Neues Parteiarchiv, VGA.

72 See Duchen and Bandhauer-Schöffmann 2000, 3; Thurner 1992.

> [W]e cannot make women's right to work a slogan at a time when so many women must be laid off from the post office and the railroad because otherwise, they will come to us for help, which we cannot afford to give them. The wives of those [war] returnees who cannot go back to their old jobs because of women's work would also turn against us.[73]

Her comrade Ferdinanda Flossmann added that she hoped "that the motto would express that women want to fight for their independence and not against men. Perhaps a motto will be found that also speaks of peace."[74] This reference to peace was typical of the time. As early as 1945, women were addressed by the SPÖ as "representatives of a better and more peaceful future [...] and therefore, in a special way, serve as advocates of peace."[75] The motto of Women's Day 1946 was "For World Peace," and this would prevail again in 1948, when the motto finally chosen was "Women of two world wars fight for world peace."[76] In this meeting, however, Hilde Krones formulated a different proposal: she was against the motif of children proposed by Marianne Pollak, hoping that "a motto would be found that offers something to everyone, such as 'The Liberation from Fear' or the 'Right to Work, Right to Life, Right to Peace.'"[77]

Her reference to the "right to work" seems obvious given her own conception of women's emancipation, and the mention of "life" was in line with her hope for life overcoming death after the devastating years of war. Her approval of the "peace" motto, though, might also be linked to her attempted politics of cooperation with the KPÖ. In two reports most likely addressed to her confidants in the Communist Party, she suggested "world peace"—soon to become also a central tenet of Communist political campaigning in Cold War Europe[78]—as a common signifier that might help the two rival parties organize joint public events.[79] Striking in relation to the haunting terms and political feelings held within her archive was her emphasis on liberation from *fear*: Krones repeatedly addressed the concept of fear in her letters and public appearances, for example, in her speech at the SPÖ party congress in 1946 in which she warned

73 "Protokolle des Frauenzentral-Komitees" [Protocols of the Women's Central Committee], 163.

74 "Protokolle des Frauenzentral-Komitees" [Protocols of the Women's Central Committee], 163.

75 Niederkofler 2009, 121–122.

76 Frauenzentralkomitee 1948.

77 "Protokolle des Frauenzentral-Komitees" [Protocols of the Women's Central Committee], 163.

78 For Austria, see Mugrauer 2020, 705–716.

79 "Wiedererrichtung der Frauenorganisation" [Re-establishment of the Women's Organization], n.d. [1946]; [Report on the Women's Organization], n.d. [1947], both Folder 54, Box 7, NL Hildes Krones, VGA.

against the party being "filled with fear" and therefore shying away from substantive disputes. Specifically, she spoke of the fear of becoming the setting for "world power struggles" between the United States and the Soviet Union, which could lead to the creation of an Iron Curtain in Austria as in Germany, and "of the creeping systematic increase in the influence of reaction in the government, administrative apparatus, and the executive."[80]

In her wartime letters to Franz Krones, she also repeatedly wrote of her "fear and anxiety" for her loved ones, and it was presumably Franz Krones who, in an obituary in *The Socialist Fighter* (*Der Sozialistische Kämpfer*), also described her fear of Nazi terror, a feeling she tried to counter with bravery: "In her beloved mountains, when we ridiculed her for her hesitation at a tricky crossing, she once coined the formulation: 'Courage is simple and easy; bravery is an achievement. Courage does *without* hesitation; bravery does *in spite of* hesitation.' In that sense, she was very brave."[81]

From the perspective of our current political moment, which in many countries is characterized by an authoritarian-populist politics of fear[82] that intentionally minimizes hope—Hilde Krones's motto also appears to be filled with *Jetztzeit*. Bini Adamczak reminds us that Theodor Adorno once described "the goal of the revolution" as "the abolition of fear"[83]—an idea that resonates with the formulation of the revolutionary socialist Krones and which concretely references the traumatic experiences of National Socialism, which haunted the victims much more than the perpetrators.[84]

4 On the Threshold of Hope and Death

In their political struggle, which was directed primarily against the SPÖ's governmental coalition with the conservative Austrian People's Party (Österreichische Volkspartei, ÖVP) after the 1945 elections, the left-wing socialists around Scharf and Krones very quickly fell apart.[85] After the party congress in 1947, Scharf lost his position as party secretary, and the left-wing opposition within the party gradually lost its ability to publish in party press organs. Scharf

80 Hilde Krones, "Zur politischen Debatte" [On the political debate], draft, Folder 12, Box 1, NL Hildes Krones, VGA.
81 "Hilde Krones" 1949, 2. See Ingrisch 1989, 301.
82 See, for example, Wodak 2015.
83 Adamczak 2017, 78.
84 Adamczak 2017, 80.
85 For more detail, see Weber 2011.

was banned from speaking in public in June 1948 due to his publication of the magazine *The Fighter* (*Der Kämpfer*), and he defied this ban by circulating the pamphlet *I Must Not Keep Silent*.[86] This led to an open break between him and party leadership and culminated in his expulsion from the party. Even analyzing her personal papers, it is difficult to determine whether Hilde Krones supported this move; Erwin Scharf, however, later claimed that Hilde had been well aware of his plans.[87] At the party congress in the autumn of 1948, Krones gave a forlorn speech in defense of her partner, but she lost her position on the Party Control Committee and the Women's Central Committee, respectively, and by December 1948, her future in the party was an open question.

In several speeches from 1945, Hilde Krones described the mood in destroyed Vienna: "numbness, paralysis, hopelessness, aimlessness, no belief in a way out, work fatigue, political exhaustion."[88] People were standing at the threshold of death, the threshold of the future:

> But we are still alive. And if we want to go on living, then we have to clear away the rubble that hinders us; then we have to look for a way out. There is no choice for us: we must go up and out with all our strength and abilities or we must perish.[89]

Hilde Krones threw herself into the project of reconstruction, of *working* for a different future, with enormous personal commitment and in numerous political capacities: as a member of parliament, a speaker and author, in the Women's Central Committee, in political training, in her district (Ottakring), in the Vienna state party organization, and on trips throughout Austria. In 1945, the photojournalist Franz Blaha produced a series of images showing Hilde and Franz Krones, together with Erwin Scharf, pushing a cart during cleanup work in Vienna.

These photos stressed optimism, served as a visual metaphor for Hilde Krones's notion of activist life—the work of building the future—and probably also represented "being able to pull the wagon of history together," a wish

86 Scharf 1948.

87 Erwin Scharf, "Für Susanne [Sohn] zum Aufsatz von Doris Ingrisch" [For Susanne, regarding Doris Ingrisch's article], n.d. [1989], NL Erwin Scharf [Erwin Scharf Papers], Alfred-Klahr-Gesellschaft [Alfred Klahr Society], Vienna, Austria.

88 "Disposition für eine Wahlrede" [Disposition for an election speech], n.d. [1945], Folder 20, Box 2, NL Hilde Krones, VGA.

89 "Schwelle des Todes, Schwelle der Zukunft" [Threshold of death, threshold of the future], draft, Folder 20, Box 2, NL Hilde Krones, VGA.

FIGURE 18.1 Hilde and Franz Krones, together with Erwin Scharf and a female comrade yet to be identified (from right to left), pushing a cart during cleanup work in Vienna, Austria, 1945
SOURCE: PHOTOGRAPH. FRANZ BLAHA (VEREIN FÜR GESCHICHTE DER ARBEITERINNENBEWEGUNG [AUSTRIAN LABOR HISTORY SOCIETY], HILDE CRONES PAPERS)

for the future that Hilde had expressed in a June 1944 letter to Franz Krones.[90] However, the extensive day-to-day political work that kept her busy from dawn to dusk, in addition to her full-time job at Austrochem, and the atmosphere of mistrust within the party during the emerging Cold War sapped her strength. In the summer of 1948, she described her depressive mood of "passivity and self-withdrawal" to her political confidant Otto Leichter.[91] In October 1948, Hilde Krones wrote a last will and testament that began: "Strangely—without any external cause, I have the feeling that I am a clock that is running down—ceaselessly running down. There, one comes up with quite strange ideas."[92] She had attempted suicide as a young woman; in her letters and diary entries,

---

90 Hilde Krones to Franz Krones, 13 June 1944, field letter, Folder 48, Box 6, NL Hilde Krones, VGA.

91 Otto Leichter to Hilde Krones, 5 September 1948, Folder 22, Box 2, NL Hilde Krones, VGA.

92 Hilde Krones, "Wien im Oktober 1948" [Vienna, October 1948], transcript, Folder 10, Box 1, NL Hilde Krones, VGA.

FIGURE 18.2 Hilde Krones (2nd from right) during cleanup work in the district of Ottakring, Vienna, Austria, 1945
SOURCE: PHOTOGRAPH. FRANZ BLAHA (VEREIN FÜR GESCHICHTE DER ARBEITERINNENBEWEGUNG [AUSTRIAN LABOR HISTORY SOCIETY], HILDE CRONES PAPERS)

she discussed the subject of suicide and depression at several points. In 1942, she wrote to Franz Krones that the thought of suicide during murderous times of suffering was a "great consolation […] when the bundle of wood becomes all too heavy." But her political "duties and tasks" denied her this option.[93] In 1934, quoting Otto Bauer, she wrote to Franz Krones in political and private distress:

> "Perhaps it will come to fulfillment once again" read the last sentence of your letter. I replied to you […] that I live for this "perhaps." If today I am certain that this "perhaps" is blocked and buried for me, then I don't know what I would do. Perhaps I would then throw off the fulfillment of duty. But still, I have a glimmer—Whoever carries the spark of the holy fire—knows nothing of the end and knows only the eternal becoming. I will get the spark—perhaps—and if not—even the darkness is beautiful.[94]

93 Hilde Krones to Franz Krones, 9 November 1942, field letter, Folder 40, Box 4, NL Hilde Krones, VGA.

94 Hilde Krones, Diary, 23 October 1934, Folder 37, Box 3, NL Hilde Krones, VGA.

On 13 December 1948, Hilde Krones took an overdose of sleeping pills; when she was found, it was too late. Her "silent scream"[95] suggests that she had lost hope in the "perhaps." Nevertheless, there are still gaps in her will that the archive cannot fill. The political context seems evident: "Hilde's death [was] a lone protest against the party executive, a kind of 'self-immolation,'" wrote Erwin Scharf many decades later.[96] In the context of the nascent Cold War, her agency as an activist,[97] her capacity to "turn all pain into energy," to "work and not despair," was waning, and her concept of work and life were falling apart.

But what was the role played by "ways of relating," that is, the relationships in her life in which the political and the private were linked and intertwined—particularly her relationships to her closest confidants like Erwin Scharf? The archive contains only a few letters from the last year of her life, but Rosa Jochmann, remembering a conversation shortly before her death, pointed to these relationships (highlighting a "private" motive for her suicide): "[S]he was very unhappy because she was expecting a letter from the comrade she loved (the letter came on the day Hilde had already been found unconscious)."[98]

Those who conjure spirits must know they will not bring back only friendly ghosts but also repressed horror. One of the gaps in Hilde Krones's archive is any explicit concern about or reference to Stalinist terror, which was unfolding at the time in neighboring Central European countries as well as in postwar Vienna. This blind spot was used by the centrist party majority and by other left-wing socialists[99] against the group gathered around Scharf and Krones. As mentioned earlier, the archive contains confidential reports by Hilde Krones about the Women's Central Committee and the party executive, which, given their content, were possibly intended for her friends in the KPÖ or for others who supported "unity of action."[100] Krones was accused of divulging internal party information to the Soviet Union by her political opponents in the SPÖ.[101]

Through her grief for the "lost" and the "absent"—who, as revolutionaries, became victims of the communist project during Stalinism,[102] Bini Adamczak meditates on how their "absence comes painfully into the consciousness of

95 Ingrisch 1989, 331.
96 Erwin Scharf, "Für Susanne [Sohn]."
97 For a discussion of agency and women's labour activism, see Zimmermann 2021, 660–687.
98 Rosa Jochmann to Karl Mark, 24 August 1987, Folder 17, Box 2, NL Rosa Jochmann [Rosa Jochmann papers], VGA.
99 See, for example, Hindels 1948, 267.
100 See, for instance, "Wiedererrichtung der Frauenorganisation" [Re-establishment of the Women's Organization], n.d. [1946]; [Report on the Women's Organization], n.d. [1947].
101 See Scharf 1988, 168.
102 Adamczak 2021, 108.

those who [...] dare to add to the discomfort of the present by asking which inheritance we could have accepted, [and] what our departure point might have been had these communists survived just a bit longer, just a bit more successfully."[103] Hilde Krones was not a communist but a socialist with unfulfilled hopes in the Soviet Union, and she was not a victim of Stalinism—but still, Adamczak's proposed method of "[f]eeling our way haltingly toward the moments of hope, which can only be salvaged truthfully through history, not by dispensing with it,"[104] resembles my own position of *feeling backward*.[105] The archive of Hilde Krones and its haunting terms and concepts, which I interrogate through an imaginative *séance*, offers an exemplary opportunity to confront this challenge.

Bibliography

Adamczak, Bini. 2021. *Yesterday's Tomorrow: On the Loneliness of Communist Specters and the Reconstruction of the Future*. Translated by Adrian Nathan West, with an Introduction by Raymond Geuss. Cambridge, MA: MIT Press.

Adamczak, Bini. 2017. *Beziehungsweise Revolution. 1917, 1968 und kommende* [Relational revolutions. 1917, 1968, and revolutions to come]. Berlin: Suhrkamp.

Adler, Emma. 1906. *Die berühmten Frauen der französischen Revolution* [Famous women of the French Revolution]. Vienna: C.W. Stern.

Bauer, Otto. 1976 [1924]. "Die Arbeiterjugend und die Weltlage des Sozialismus" [The workers' youth and the world position of socialism]. In *Otto Bauer Werkausgabe* [Edited works of Otto Bauer], vol. 2, 867–83. Vienna: Europa Verlag.

Bauer, Otto. 1936. *Zwischen zwei Weltkriegen? Die Krise der Weltwirtschaft, der Demokratie und des Sozialismus* [Between two world wars? The crisis of the world economy, democracy and socialism]. Bratislava: Eugen Prager.

Benjamin, Walter. 2007 [1942]. "Theses on the Philosophy of History." In *Illuminations. Essays and Reflections*, edited and with an introduction by Hannah Arendt, 253–264. New York: Schonen.

Brown, Wendy. 1999. "Resisting Left Melancholy." *boundary 2* 26, no 3: 19–27.

Dean, Jodi. 2012. *The Communist Horizon*. London: Verso.

Derrida, Jacques. 1994. *Specters of Marx. the State of the Debt, the Work of Mourning, and the New International*. New York: Routledge.

103 Adamczak 2021, 109.

104 Adamczak 2021, 115.

105 To borrow a term coined by Love 2007.

Ducange, Jean-Numa. 2019. *The French Revolution and Social Democracy. the Transmission of History and Its Political Uses in Germany and Austria 1889–1934*. Chicago: Haymarket Books.

Duchen, Claire, and Irene Bandhauer-Schöffmann. 2000. "Introduction." In *When the War Was Over: Women, War and Peace in Europe, 1940–1956*, edited by Claire Duchen and Irene Bandhauer-Schöffmann, 1–9. London: Leicester University Press.

Duma, Veronika. 2019. *Rosa Jochmann. Politische Akteurin und Zeitzeugin* [Rosa Jochmann. political actor and witness]. Vienna: ÖGB Verlag.

Fisher, Mark. 2014. *Ghosts of My Life. Writings on Depression, Hauntology and Lost Futures*. Winchester: Zero Books.

Fisher, Mark. 2009. *Capitalist Realism. Is There No Alternative?* Winchester: Zero Books.

Franz, Yvonne, Raphael Kiczka, Robert Misik, Georg Spitaler, Irina Vana, and Paul Werner. 2019. "Debatte: Hoffnung auf die Egalitäre Stadt" [Debate: Hoping for the egalitarian city]. In *Das Rote Wien 1919–1934. Ideen, Debatten, Praxis* [Red Vienna 1919–1934: Ideas, debates, practice], edited by Werner Michael Schwarz, Georg Spitaler, and Elke Wikidal, 412–419. Basel: Birkhäuser.

Frauenzentralkomitee der Sozialischen Partei Österreichs [Women's Central Committee of the SPÖ]. 1947. *Frauenzentralkonferenz 22. und 23. Oktober 1947* [Central Women's Conference, October 22–23, 1947]. Vienna.

Frauenzentralkomitee der Sozialistischen Partei Österreichs [Women's Central Committee of the SPÖ]. 1948. *Frauen zweier Weltkriege kämpft für den Weltfrieden! Internationaler Sozialistischer Frauentag 1948* [Women of two world wars fight for world peace! International Socialist Women's Day 1948]. Vienna.

Freundlich, Emmy. 1928. *Wege zur Gemeinwirtschaft* [Toward a co-operative economy]. Jena: Karl Zwing.

Hauch, Gabriella. 2020. "Isa Strasser: 'Land ohne Schlaf' (1970). Ein autobiografischer Roman über das Leben in Moskau in den 1920er-Jahren" [Isa Strasser: *Land without Sleep* (1970), an autobiographical novel on life in Moscow in the 1920s]. In *Ausgeschlossen einflussreich. Handlungsspielräume an den Rändern etablierter Machtstrukturen* [Excluded, influential. The scope of agency on the fringes of established power structures], edited by Lisia Bürgi and Eva Keller, 105–210. Basel: Schwabe.

Hauch, Gabriella. 2018. "'Es ist notwendig, dass klar und offen gesprochen wird.' Josef Strasser (1870–1935), ein demokratischer Kommunist in Österreich" ["It is necessary to talk clearly and frankly." Josef Strasser (1870–1935), a democratic communist in Austria], *Jahrbuch für Historische Kommunismusforschung* [Yearbook for historical research on communism]: 61–78.

Hauch, Gabriella. 2015. "'Welcher Weg ist einzuschlagen …?' Spurensuche nach Isa Strasser, geb. von Schwartzkoppen (1891–1970)" ["Which path to follow …?" Searching for Isa Strasser, nee von Schwartzkoppen (1891–1970)]. In *Bananen, Cola,*

Zeitgeschichte: Oliver Rathkolb und das lange 20. Jahrhundert [Bananas, Coke, contemporary history. Oliver Rathkolb and the Long 20th century], vol. 1, edited by Lucile Dreidemy et al., 137–149. Vienna: Böhlau.

Hauch, Gabriella. 2014. "'Besiegt ist, wer nie den Kampf aufgenommen, wer ihn nie gewollt.' Nadja Strasser, geb. Neoma Ramm (1871–1955)" ["Defeated are those who never took on the struggle, who never wished to fight it." Nadja Strasser, nee Neoma Ramm (1871–1955)]. In *Die helle und die dunkle Seite der Moderne. Festschrift für Siegfried Mattl zum 60. Geburtstag* [The bright and the dark side of modernity. Festschrift for Siegfried Mattl on his 60th Birthday], edited by Werner Michael Schwarz and Ingo Zechner, 162–71. Vienna: Turia + Kant.

Hauch, Gabriella. 2009. *Frauen bewegen Politik. Österreich 1848–1938* [Women moving politics. Austria 1848–1938]. Innsbruck: StudienVerlag.

Heindl, Gabu. 2020. *Stadtkonflikte. Radikale Demokratie in Architektur und Stadtplanung.* [City conflicts: Radical democracy in architecture and city planning]. Vienna: Mandelbaum.

Helfert, Veronika. 2021. *Frauen wacht auf! Eine Frauen- und Geschlechtergeschichte von Revolution und Rätebewegung in Österreich, 1916–1924* [Women, wake up! A women's and gender history of revolution and the council's movement in Austria, 1916–1924]. Göttingen: V&R Unipress.

Hemmings, Clare. 2018. *Considering Emma Goldman. Feminist Political Ambivalence and the Imaginative Archive*. Durham: Duke University Press.

"Hilde Krones." 1949. *Der Sozialistische Kämpfer* [The socialist fighter] 1, no. 8 (December): 2–3.

Hindels, Josef. 1948. "Reformisten und Linkssozialisten" [Reformists and left socialists]. *Die Zukunft* [The future] 3, no. 9 (mid-September): 263–268.

Ingrisch, Doris. 1989. "Ohne Kompromiß. Das Leben von Hilde Krones" [Without compromise: The life of Hilde Krones]. In *"Die Partei hat mich nie enttäuscht" Österreichische Sozialdemokratinnen* ["The party never let me down" Austrian social democratic women], edited by Edith Prost, 289–338. Vienna: Verlag für Gesellschaftskritik.

Konrad, Helmut. 2021. *Das Private ist Politisch. Marianne und Oscar Pollak* [The private is political: Marianne and Oscar Pollak]. Vienna: Picus.

Krones, Franz. 1946. "Gleichgewicht der Klassenkräfte" [Balance of class forces]. *Die Zukunft* [The future] 1, no 7 (mid-September): 10–14.

Love, Heather. 2007. *Feeling Backward: Loss and the Politics of Queer History*. Cambridge, MA: Harvard University Press.

Markova, Ina. 2019. *Tilly Spiegel. Eine politische Biografie* [Tilly Spiegel: A political biography]. Vienna: nap.

Mayerhofer, Rainer. 2020. *Doch die Menschen liebe ich über alles. Rosa Jochmann—eine Biografie in Briefen.* [But the people I love the most: Rosa Jochmann—a biography in letters]. Vienna: ÖGB Verlag.

McFarland, Rob, Georg Spitaler, and Ingo Zechner. 2020. "Introduction." In *The Red Vienna Sourcebook*, edited by Rob McFarland, Georg Spitaler, and Ingo Zechner, 1–11. Rochester, NY: Camden House.

Mesner, Maria. 1997. "Die Neugestaltung des Ehe- und Familienrechts. Re-Definitionspotentiale und Geschlechterverhältnisse der Aufbau-Zeit" [Redesigning marriage- and family law. Potentials for redefining gender relations in the Reconstruction Era], *Zeitgeschichte* [Contemporary history] 24, no 5/6 (May/June): 186–203.

Mesner, Maria. 1990. "'Weil ein anfänglich sehr kleiner Kreis von Freunden unbeirrt zusammen gehalten' hat … Die Umorientierung der SPÖ unter Renner und Schärf" ["Because an initially very small circle of friends stuck together, undeterred" … The reorientation of the SPÖ under Renner and Schärf]. In *Die Bewegung. Hundert Jahre Sozialdemokratie in Österreich* [The movement: A hundred years of social democracy in Austria], edited by Erich Fröschl, Maria Mesner, and Helge Zoitl, 476–486. Vienna: Passagen.

Mugrauer, Manfred. 2020. *Die Politik der KPÖ 1945–1955. Von der Regierungsbank in die innenpolitische Isolation* [The politics of the KPÖ 1945–1955. From government bench to domestic political isolation]. Vienna: V&R Unipress.

Niederkofler, Heidi. 2009. *Mehrheit verpflichtet. Frauenorganisationen der politischen Parteien in Österreich in der Nachkriegszeit* [The responsibility of the majority. Women's organizations of Austrian political parties in the postwar era]. Vienna: Löcker.

Popp, Adelheid. 2019. *Jugend einer Arbeiterin. Mit Essays von Katharina Prager und Sibylle Hamann* [Youth of a woman worker: With essays by Katharina Prager and Sibylle Hamann], edited by Sibylle Hamann. Vienna: Picus.

Popp, Adelheid. 1918. "Die Frau im neuen Staat" [The woman in the new state]. *Der Kampf. Sozialdemokratische Monatsschrift* [The struggle: Social democratic monthly] 11, no. 11 (November): 729–732.

Schärf, Adolf. 1948. *April 1945 in Wien* [April 1945 in Vienna]. Vienna: Verlag der Wiener Volksbuchhandlung.

Scharf, Erwin. 1988. *Ich hab's gewagt mit Sinnen … Entscheidungen im antifaschistischen Widerstand—Erlebnisse in der politischen Konfrontation* [Daring while staying sane … Decisive moments in the antifascist resistance—Experiences in political confrontation]. Vienna: Globus Verlag.

Scharf, Erwin. 1948. *Ich darf nicht schweigen. Drei Jahre Politik des Parteivorstandes der SPÖ—von innen gesehen* [I must not keep silent. Three years of the SPÖ's Executive Party Committee, as seen from the inside]. Vienna.

Schwarz, Werner Michael, Georg Spitaler, and Elke Wikidal. 2019. "Einleitung" [Introduction]. In *Das Rote Wien 1919–1934. Ideen, Debatten, Praxis* [Red Vienna 1919–1934: Ideas, debates, practice], edited by Werner Michael Schwarz, Georg Spitaler, and Elke Wikidal, 12–15. Basel: Birkhäuser.

Spitaler, Georg. 2018. "Ein Spuk-Bild des linken Sports: 'Nie schiesst der Fascismus im roten Wien ein Goal!'" [A haunting image of left-wing sports. "Fascism never scores a goal in Red Vienna!"]. In *Images des Sports in Österreich. Innensichten und Außenwahrnehmungen* [Images of sports in Austria. Internal views and external perceptions], edited by Matthias Marschik, Agnes Meisinger, Rudolf Müllner, Johann Skocek, and Georg Spitaler, 189–200. Vienna: V&R Unipress.

Studer, Brigitte. 2020. *Reisende der Weltrevolution. Eine Globalgeschichte der Kommunistischen Internationale* [Travelers of the world revolution. A global history of the Communist International]. Berlin: Suhrkamp.

Thurner, Erika. 1992. "Frauen-Nachkriegsleben in Österreich—im Zentrum und in der Provinz" [Women's life in postwar Austria—Center and periphery]. In *Wiederaufbau Weiblich. Dokumentation der Tagung "Frauen in der österreichischen und deutschen Nachkriegszeit"* [Reconstruction female. Documenting the conference "Women in Postwar Austria and Germany"], edited by Irene Bandhauer-Schöffmann and Ela Hornung, 3–14. Salzburg: Geyer-Edition.

Trausmuth, Gernot. 2019. *Ich fürchte niemanden. Adelheid Popp und der Kampf für das Frauenwahlrecht* [I am not afraid of anyone. Adelheid Popp and the struggle for women's suffrage]. Vienna: Mandelbaum.

Traverso, Enzo. 2016. *Left-Wing Melancholia: Marxism, History, and Memory*. New York: Columbia University Press.

Weber, Fritz. 2011 [1977]. *Der kalte Krieg in der SPÖ* [The Cold War in the SPÖ], 2nd. rev. ed., Münster: LIT.

Wippermann, Wolfgang. 1981. *Zur Analyse des Faschismus. Die sozialistischen und kommunistischen Faschismustheorien 1921–1945* [Analyzing fascism. Socialist and communist theories of fascism 1921–1945]. Frankfurt am Main: Diesterweg.

Wodak, Ruth. 2015. *The Politics of Fear: What Right-wing Populist Discourses Mean*. Los Angeles: Sage.

Zimmermann, Susan. 2021. *Frauenpolitik und Männergewerkschaft. Internationale Geschlechterpolitik, IGB-Gewerkschafterinnen und die Arbeiter- und Frauenbewegungen der Zwischenkriegszeit.* [Women's politics and men's trade unionism. International gender politics, women IFTU trade unionists and the workers' and women's movements of the interwar period]. Vienna: Löcker.

Index

Note: In the case of frequently used terms, selected references are listed in the index (and numerous references from chapters in which a particular term plays a central role are omitted). If organizations are specified in the list of abbreviations with their full name in the respective original language as well as the English translation, these organizations are listed in the index under their original name followed by the supplementary information. All other organizations are indicated under their original name as well as the English translation.

www.ingramcontent.com/pod-product-compliance
Lightning Source LLC
LaVergne TN
LVHW010622300926
849162LV00001B/31
9789004682467